CODING TECHNIQUES FOR MICROSOFT® VISUAL BASIC® .NET

John Connell

PUBLISHED BY
Microsoft Press
A Division of Microsoft Corporation
One Microsoft Way
Redmond, Washington 98052-6399

Library of Congress Cataloging-in-Publication Data
Connell, John.
Coding Techniques for Microsoft Visual Basic .NET / John Connell.
p. cm.
ISBN 0-7356-1254-4
1. Microsoft Visual BASIC. 2. BASIC (Computer program language) I. Title.

QA76.73.B3 C659 2001
005.2'762--dc21 2001051181

Printed and bound in the United States of America.

2 3 4 5 6 7 8 9 QWE 6 5 4 3 2

Distributed in Canada by Penguin Books Canada Limited.

A CIP catalogue record for this book is available from the British Library.

Microsoft Press books are available through booksellers and distributors worldwide. For further information about international editions, contact your local Microsoft Corporation office or contact Microsoft Press International directly at fax (425) 936-7329. Visit our Web site at www.microsoft.com/mspress. Send comments to *mspinput@microsoft.com*.

Acquisitions Editor: Danielle Bird
Project Editor: John Pierce
Technical Editor: Jim Fuchs

Body Part No. X08-05019

This book is dedicated to my mom and dad, Mercedes and John W. Connell. They provided me with unwavering support during this project, as they have in all my pursuits. My two sons, Garrett and Grady, of whom I am immeasurably proud, as well as my baby sister, Patricia, were also there to provide moral support and humor during the long hours. Thanks, guys, I couldn't have done it without you.

Table of Contents

Acknowledgments xv

Introduction xvii

1 Visual Basic .NET from the Ground Up 1

What a Long, Strange Trip It's Been 2

From COM to .NET 4

The .NET World 6

Why You Need to Learn Visual Basic .NET 8

What Are the Pieces and How Do They Fit Together? A .NET Framework Overview 9

Web Services 11

User Interface 11

Data and XML 12

Base Class Library 12

Common Language Runtime 13

Where Do We Start to Access Functionality from Visual Basic .NET Source Code? 15

Visual Basic .NET Is Object Oriented 16

A Brief Look at How the Visual Basic .NET Language Works 18

How Is a Visual Basic .NET Program Put Together? 20

Metadata—Data About Data 20

The Just-In-Time Compiler 21

Execution of Visual Basic .NET Code 22

Assemble the Troops 23

Configuring the Interactive Development Environment 23

A First Look at the Visual Basic .NET IDE 25

Some Visual Basic .NET Code 27

Files Created by the IDE for Our First .NET Program 33

Another Word on Assemblies 38

A Closer Look at the Code 41

You Mean I Get an Inheritance? 41

Starting Up Our *Form1* Class 42

Warning! Don't Fiddle with the Designer's Code 46

The Big Event 47
Nothing but .NET 48

2 Object-Oriented Programming in Visual Basic .NET 49

An Object Lesson 49
Starting Out with Objects 50
A Class Is Really Only a Blueprint 50
Let's Talk Objects 51
Our Form as an Object 52
Reading, Writing, Invoking 54
Inheritance 56
Understanding Namespaces 58
Inheriting from *System.Windows.Forms.Form*: Forms and Controls 62
A Word About Visual Basic .NET Controls 63
Check Out the Code 65
The Code Added for the Button 67
Enough Talk: Press F5 and Run Your Program 69
The Doppelganger Program: Creating Clones of the *Form1* Class 70
Important Object Concepts from the Doppelganger Program 71
Using the Class View to Spy on Structure and Access Modifiers 76
More About Access Types 78
Overloading Methods 79
Some of the Overloaded *Show* Methods 81
Polymorphism 83
What's Controlling Our Form When We Run It? 84
Try This Out 84
Your First Real Visual Basic .NET Program 86
Telling the Application Object Which Form to Run 88
Let's Add Some Controls 90
Examining the Handiwork of the IDE-Generated Code 94
How Do We Hardwire the Controls? 98
Can You Name That Namespace? 98
Date and Time Arithmetic 99
Formatting the Date and Time 101
Let's Run This Baby! 103
Conclusion 105

3 **Writing Your First Class** **109**

Creating the *Employee* Class 110

Examining the Class Code 113

Our Class's Namespace 118

Declaring Our Class 118

Using Shared Variables 120

Class Constructors 120

Overloading Constructors 121

MyBase.New 122

Assigning Values to Our Private Data Fields 123

Overriding 124

#Region 126

The *Employee* Class Properties 127

More About Inheritance 130

Virtual Methods 134

Synchronizing the Class View 134

Creating Instances of the *Employee* Class 136

Conclusion 140

4 **Visual Basic .NET Data Types and Features** **143**

Getting to Know Data Types 143

Visual Basic .NET Data Types 144

Value Types 145

Reference Types 147

Data Type Features 148

The *System.Object* Class 149

Strong Typing 152

Type Safety 152

Data Widening 157

Garbage Collection: Getting Rid of Our Objects 160

The Stack and the Managed Heap 160

Conclusion 161

5 **Examining the .NET Class Framework Using Files and Strings** **163**

What Exactly Is the .NET Framework? 164

Tapping into the .NET Framework 165

It All Starts with the *System* Namespace 165

Learning to Find and Use What You Need 169
Searching in Windows Class Viewer 170
Using the Namespaces 171
Examining the *File* Class 171
Streams 173
What's the Difference Between a File and a Stream? 174
Reading and Writing Binary, Numeric, or Text Data 174
Using the *File* and *StreamWriter* Classes in the .NET Framework 175
Reading Our File 176
The *FileInfo* Class 177
Creating a New File 179
Enumerating Directory Entries Using the Framework 180
Let's Talk Strings 183
What's New in Strings? 184
Uninitialized Strings 184
Working with Strings 185
Copying and Cloning a String 187
Conclusion 190

6 Arrays and Collections in Visual Basic .NET 191

Building Your First Visual Basic .NET Array 192
Array Boundaries 194
Why Arrays Are Based on the *System.Array* Class 198
What If I Don't Know How Many Elements I Need Ahead of Time? 202
Arrays Start at Zero in Visual Basic .NET 204
Initializing the Array During Declaration 204
Arrays Are Reference Types 205
Arrays in Action: A Roman Numeral Calculator 207
Writing the Code 208
Examining the Code 209
Caching Our Variables 210
Visual Basic .NET Collections 212
The *ArrayList* Collection 213
Queues 216
Stacks 218
Eliza and the Beginning of Artificial Intelligence 219
Eliza in Action 220
Coding Eliza 222

Topology of Our Dialog.vb Code Module 224
Writing the Dialog.vb Code Module 226
Examining Our Code 234
Arrays vs. Collections 235
The Entry Point for Eliza 236
Is the Patient Discussing the Good Doctor? 240
Can Eliza Return a Quick Response? 241
Can Eliza Translate the Patient's Response to Make It a Question? 243
Return a Previous Patient Phrase 247
When All Else Fails 250
Calling the Module from the Form 251
Conclusion 253

7 Handling Errors and Debugging Programs 255

What Can Possibly Go Wrong? 255
Types of Visual Basic .NET Errors 258
The Classic Visual Basic *Err* Object Is Gone in Visual Basic .NET 259
Try, *Catch*, and *Finally* 259
Adding Structured Error Handling 261
The *Try...Catch* Block 262
Making Our Simple Program Even More Bullet Proof 264
The *Finally* Block 266
Setting a Breakpoint in Your Code 267
Running the Program Using the Debugger 268
Stepping Through Our Code 270
Helpful Debugging Windows 271
The Call Stack 276
The *Debug* and *Trace* Classes 278
Debug.WriteLine 278
Debug.Assert 279
Tracing 281
Adding a Tracing Class to Our Code 282
Examining the *ErrorTrace.vb* Code 284
Setting the Trace Level 288
Adding the *Errors.vb* Class to a Program 289
Adding Event Logging to Your Programs 293
The Philosophy of Logging Events to the Event Viewer 295

Adding Event Logging to the *ErrorTrace.vb* Class 296
Using Our New Event Logging Capability 300
Conclusion 301

8 Assemblies in Detail 303

The Right to Assemble 303
Private Assemblies 304
Shared Assemblies 305
The Other Parts of an Assembly 308
Reflection: How to Go About Examining Assemblies 309
The Assembly Spy Program 310
Building the Assembly Spy Program 313
Let's Write Some Code 315
Examining the Code 320
Self-Examination: Contemplating Our Own Assembly 329
Code Signing 330
Creating a Strongly Named Assembly 330
The Global Assembly Cache Revisited 333
Assembly Versioning 335
New Variable Scoping in Visual Basic .NET 338
Namespace Scope 340
Determining the Scope of a Variable 340
Conclusion 341

9 File System Monitoring 343

The File Sentinel Program 344
How the File Sentinel Program Works 345
Starting to Write the File Sentinel Program 346
Adding the *Sentinel* Class to Our Program 349
Delegates 356
Handling the *Changed*, *Created*, and *Deleted* Events 358
Handling the *Renamed* and *Error* Events 360
Writing to Our Log File 361
Wiring Up the User Interface 362
Possible Enhancements to the File Sentinel 370
Introduction to Windows Services 372
The Life and Death of a Service 372
Building Our File Sentinel into a Windows Service 373
Adding Our *Sentinel* Class to Our Service 374

Updating the Service1.vb File 375
How Our Service Works 377
Looking at vbMonitorService in the Services Window 387
Debugging a Windows Service 389
Conclusion 392

10 Data Access with ADO.NET 393

From ADO to ADO.NET 393
ADO.NET from 50,000 Feet 394
Individual Tables, Not the Join, Are in a *DataSet* 395
Comparing Classic ADO and ADO.NET 397
A Closer Look at the Foundation of ADO.NET: The *DataSet* Object 399
The *DataTable* Object 400
The *DataSet* Object and XML 401
DataView Objects 402
Managed Providers in ADO.NET 402
A Common Provider Model 404
Enough Talk, Let's Look at Some Code 405
Connecting to Our Data Source 406
Commands to Manipulate Data from the Data Source 406
Creating the *DataReader* Object 407
Putting the Pieces of Our *DataReader* Together 408
Writing a Simple *SQLClient* Class *DataSet* Program 410
Getting Started 410
Adding a *DataAdapter* Object to Our Program 414
Finishing the User Interface 418
A Sneak Preview of Our Data from the *DataAdapter* 419
XML Schema for the Customers Table 421
Just Add Code 422
Running Our Program 423
Editing Our Data 424
How the Code Works 424
Updating the Data Source 426
Conclusion 429

11 Data Sets in Detail 431

Looking Again at the ADO.NET Object Model 431
Data Sets and XML 434

Building the Data Set and XML Viewer Project 436
Adding the *Connection*, *Data Adapter*, and *DataSet* Objects 438
Adding Code to Our Program 439
How It Works 440
Generating XML from Our Data Set 441
Updating the Data Source 441
ADO.NET and XML 443
Examining Our Program's XML Output 443
The XML Schema Output 444
Persisting Our XML Information 446
Testing Our Persistence Code 447
Examining the *DiffGram* 449
Leveraging Our XML File for New Classes 452
The Xsd.exe Program 452
Adding a Relationship to Our Program 455
The Data Sets and XML Program 456
Creating the Parent/Child Relationship 457
Adding a Relationship to Our Tables 458
Examining *DataSet* Properties 461
Populating a Data Grid from a Persisted XML File 462
Run the Program 463
How the Program Works 464
Hand Coding a Simple Program 465
Data Binding 467
Creating the Program 467
Adding the Code That Wires the Controls to the Data Set 469
Run the Program 470
How It Works 471
Updating Our Data Grid 476
Conclusion 476

12 ADO.NET Data Binding 477

The *BindingContext* Object 477
The *CurrencyManager* Object 479
Record Navigation 479
A Simple Example 479
Add the Code 481
How the Code Works 484

The *DataTable*, *DataRow*, and *DataColumn* Objects 488

Examining the *DataTable* Schema 488

Building a Table Programmatically 490

How the Code Works 491

Finding Specific Records 493

Conclusion 495

13 ASP.NET and Web Services 497

A Look Back at ASP 497

Why ASP.NET? 498

Our First Web Form 500

New Server Controls 503

The HTML Presentation Template 505

Viewing the Code-Behind File 508

Setting the Properties on Our Web Page 509

Adding the Calendar Control Code 510

Running the Web Form 511

Examining the HTML Sent to the Browser 512

Building a Loan Payment Calculator 514

Building Our Loan Application Project 517

Adding Code to the Code-Behind Form 519

The Life of a Web Form 520

How Our Program Works 521

Taking a Closer Look at Our Drop-Down List 523

Adding the Payment Schedule Page 524

Adding Our Class Code 526

How the Calculator Works 529

Tracing Our Program 532

Web Services: The New Marketplace 533

What Are Web Services? 533

OK, Now How Do We Communicate? 534

Finding Out Who Is Offering What in the Global Marketplace 535

Where Are Web Services Going? 537

Building a Web Service 538

Run the Program 540

Consuming the MagicEightBall Web Service 543

Building Our Web Services Client Program 545

Adding a Proxy Class to Our Program 546
Adding Code to get Our Magic Eight Ball Answers 547
Conclusion 548

14 Visual Inheritance and Custom Controls 549

Visual Inheritance 549
Building a Base Form 550
Adding the Inherited Form 552
Creating a Custom Control 555
Changing the Background Color of a Text Box 555
Building Our Control 556
Adding Code to Our Control 556
Adding Our Custom Control to the Host Form 558
How it Works 559
Putting it Together: What We've Learned So Far 561
How Do We Save the Notes? XML, Of Course 562
Building the Sticky Notes Progam 564
Constructing a Sticky Note 570
Adding Code to the Sticky Note 571
How Does it Work? 574
Adding Even Handler Delegates 575
The *serialize* Class in More Detail 577
When the User Quits the Sticky Notes Program 582
How the *BaseNote* Sticky Yellow Form Works 585
Deploying Our Sticky Notes Program 588
Installing Our Program on a Client Machine 592
Install the Sticky Notes Program 593
Conclusion 594

Appendix: Some Helpful ADO.NET Wizards 595

Using the Data Form Wizard 595
Run the Program 600
Under the Hood 601
Generating a Crystal Report from a Data Source 603
Building a Crystal Report 603
Getting Ready to View Our Report 609

Index 613

Acknowledgements

Special thanks to Keith D. Adams, childhood friend and Renaissance man; Mr. Morgan Gasior and his computer-scientist wife, Darlene, who provided an endless supply of visionary ideas and showed me the sky; John Dilenschneider, gentleman and computer scientist extraordinaire, for his guidance and friendship; my long-time mentors—Dean Helmut Epp, Ph.D., Dr. Martin Kalin, and Dr. David Miller—for their wit, intelligence, and vision; and Jeff Optholt for seeing things as they really are.

Extra special thanks to John Pierce and Jim Fuchs of Microsoft Press. These two gentlemen worked tirelessly and with impeccable professionalism to make this book into something special. Thanks, John and Jim. In spite of the hard work, you both made this project fun and never lost patience.

Introduction

Over the years, I've been fortunate to design and write production programs with Microsoft Visual Basic that are currently in use at several Fortune 500 companies in the United States. I also teach, hire, and manage technical professionals, which has given me insight into the minds of many Visual Basic programmers. In my university classes, I have seen over and over those aspects of programming with Visual Basic that make sense to programmers, as well as areas such as object-oriented programming that some programmers find a bit confusing. *Coding Techniques for Microsoft Visual Basic .NET* will take you to the next level of programming, lifting the veils from the areas of programming you're unsure of while enhancing your knowledge of the areas that you already work with every day.

Who This Book Is For

This book was written *for* Visual Basic programmers *by* a Visual Basic programmer. In my description of how to work with Visual Basic .NET, I first build a foundation, providing background about the changes in computing and software development that make knowing about the Microsoft .NET Framework of vital interest to programmers as well as a practical necessity. I cover the essentials of object-oriented programming in Visual Basic .NET and explain how to build your own classes and work with the .NET Framework classes, how to work with arrays and collections, and how to debug and handle errors in your programs. From our foundation, we climb to the next level. I cover the details of how to work with .NET assemblies, how to work with files and data streams, and how to monitor files over a network, including how to build a Windows service application that runs on a server. In three full chapters I cover how programming for data access has changed with Visual Basic .NET and ADO.NET. Then we move to the world of Web services—programs and components designed to run on the Internet. In the last chapter, I bring together what's been covered throughout the earlier chapters. Along the way, you'll see plenty of useful and interesting sample code.

Learning Visual Basic .NET by Writing Working Programs

In most computer books I've read, regardless of the programming language they cover, the author provides academic snippets of code to illustrate a point or construct. This approach is helpful, but it leaves readers wondering how one piece of code fits into the larger scheme of a full working program. I've found that the best way to learn a new computer language such as Visual Basic .NET is to write full working programs in that language. Having a goal in mind—and writing a program to solve a problem—engages many dimensions of a programming language and also solidifies how the pieces fit and work together. I take this approach in this book, walking you through several sample applications that illustrate important points about Visual Basic .NET.

If you're coming to Visual Basic .NET from another programming language—such as C, C++, Java, or even COBOL—it won't take long until you feel right at home. The Microsoft .NET Framework is the wave of the future, and Visual Basic programmers are the best prepared to take advantage of this new technology. *Coding Techniques for Microsoft Visual Basic .NET* will make you proficient in the fundamentals of .NET technology, and I'm confident that you'll quickly see the power and ease of what can be accomplished with .NET and will start to look at programming in an exciting new way. Last but not least, you'll have fun in the process.

What's in *Coding Techniques for Microsoft Visual Basic .NET*?

In the list that follows, I describe the highlights of each chapter, summarizing what you'll learn as you progress through the book.

- **Chapter 1, Visual Basic from the Ground Up.** I start off by examining and explaining .NET and why it's a revolutionary (instead of an evolutionary) approach to programming for the twenty-first century. One of the major benefits of the .NET Framework is its capability to write a program once that can automatically target any hardware or operating system. This flexibility is crucial at a time when programmers need to create applications for desktop PCs as well as applications for the Internet. I review the evolution of Visual Basic from the computer language that skyrocketed Windows programming into the mainstream all the way to Visual Basic .NET. I explain at a high level some of the key features of the .NET Framework, such as the class framework, the common language runtime, Web services, assemblies, and the new Visual Studio .NET interactive development environment (IDE)—the cockpit that you'll use when working with these new capabilities. You'll get your first look at some Visual Basic .NET code to give you a sense of what's required to write a Visual Basic .NET program. After reading Chapter 1, you'll have a good understanding of where we're going and what's important.

- **Chapter 2, Object-Oriented Programming in Visual Basic .NET.** Visual Basic .NET is now a fully object-oriented language, so it finally joins the ranks of the so-called sophisticated languages, such as C++ and Java. If you are new to object-oriented programming, you'll find this chapter an easy way to get up to speed. To illustrate how objects are spawned from classes, I use a simple Visual Basic .NET form and illustrate properties and methods, inheritance, and namespaces. I also cover shared variables, overloading, polymorphism, and encapsulation. Because a large part of the power of .NET comes from the base classes supplied by the .NET Framework, I show how to use the various namespaces and how to access this built-in functionality.

- **Chapter 3, Writing Your First Class.** Following up on Chapter 2, in Chapter 3 I explain how to write your own class and then how to create a second class that inherits from the base class. You'll also learn about the *imports* directive, how to add an assembly to a project, how to work with shared member variables, and why and when to use the *Option Strict* and *Option Explicit* directives. While building a class, you'll use overloaded constructors that permit you to initialize an object upon instantiation. At the conclusion of Chapter 3, object-oriented programming will be demystified, and you'll be pleasantly surprised at how compelling it really is.

- **Chapter 4, Visual Basic .NET Data Types and Features.** While understanding reference and value (primitive) data types in earlier versions of Visual Basic was helpful, understanding these concepts in Visual Basic .NET is crucial because of the way objects—and everything is an object in .NET—are compared and initialized. Data types in .NET are strongly typed (each variable must have a specific data type) and are also type safe (you can only access a variable through its data type). When a variable is no longer needed, it is flagged for deletion by a nondeterministic finalization algorithm, euphemistically known as garbage collection. If you have always set your reference variables to *Nothing*, you'll be interested in the way in which Visual Basic .NET handles freeing up resources and memory. Upon completing Chapter 4, you'll have a good grasp of how variables are brought to life, initialized, and disposed of in Visual Basic .NET.

- **Chapter 5, Examining the .NET Class Framework Using Files and Strings.** The .NET class framework's object-oriented, hierarchical class library is the powerhouse behind .NET. Starting with namespaces, I cover the framework from the ground up, explaining how the framework is organized and using some concrete examples to examine exactly how to work with it. For those of you new to object-oriented programming, this chapter will show precisely how to find what you need in the framework and exactly how to use it. Using a built-in tool, the Windows Class Viewer, you'll master the depth and breadth of the framework and learn techniques to quickly zero in on what you need. In the process, I describe the C# class notation used to designate parameters, overloaded constructors and methods, and return types. In the chapter's main example, I show how the file and stream classes are accessed from the framework and used to read and write to disk. I also examine strings and their new, immutable nature. The techniques for copying, cloning, and formatting strings are illustrated and explained.

- **Chapter 6, Arrays and Collections in Visual Basic .NET.** As you might expect, arrays are handled differently in Visual Basic .NET than in earlier versions of Visual Basic. The .NET Framework class *System.Array* is the base class for all array types. Because arrays are objects (what isn't?), each array you create will have its own knowledge of how many elements it contains, how many dimensions it has included, its boundaries, and so forth. Best of all, by using the *System.Array Sort* method, Visual Basic arrays can now be sorted and reversed automatically. Not only that, .NET arrays can be searched using various approaches such as the built-in binary search. I'll create a calculator program that translates numbers to Roman numerals to illustrate arrays. While an array is really a simple collection, a collection is a group of objects. A collection can be inherited from the *System.Collection* namespace of the .NET Framework. The *Collection* namespace contains interfaces and classes to create new objects such as array lists, hash tables, queues, stacks, and dictionaries. Some of these data structures might be new to Visual Basic programmers. I wrap up Chapter 6 by writing a program that mimics a nondeterministic Rogerian psychologist. I use some advanced features of .NET arrays to accomplish this. Users can run this fun project to examine the psychology of human/machine interaction with Visual Basic .NET.

- **Chapter 7, Handling Errors and Debugging Programs.** Errors don't crash programs, but unhandled errors do. Errors (syntax, run-time, or logic) can occur at any time, and when they do an exception is thrown. Visual Basic .NET uses a structured *Try...Catch...Finally* construct to replace the unstructured *Goto ErrorHandler* used in previous versions of Visual Basic. Structured error handling is built into the core of the .NET Framework, so its power is immediately available to us. In this chapter, I use the calculator program from Chapter 6 and show everything that can go wrong in the program and how to use structured error handling to deal with each potential error. I also examine the debugger. The Visual Studio .NET IDE provides programmers with several debugging windows that give them a clear view on everything from variable values to assembly code in a running program. We'll write a generic error handling class, ErrorTrace.vb, that provides trace logs and can be added to any Visual Basic .NET program. I finish this chapter by showing how to write to the Windows NT or Windows 2000 event log from a Visual Basic .NET program.
- **Chapter 8, Assemblies in Detail.** Assemblies are the building blocks of Visual Basic .NET programs. They are the fundamental unit for deployment, version control, reuse, and security. In this chapter, I build a program, named AssemblySpy, that examines the internals of any .NET assembly written in a .NET-compliant language. This program uses new graphical .NET controls for its user interface and provides information on static and instance fields, properties, events, methods, and constructors. I describe the benefits of private and shared assemblies as well as the reasons for creating "strongly named" assemblies for versioning and sharing. Strongly named assemblies allow for side-by-side execution so that two assemblies with the same name can run in the same directory. Microsoft .NET programs compiled against an assembly with a strong name know which assembly to use, thus eliminating DLL conflicts that have plagued Windows programming.
- **Chapter 9, File System Monitoring.** Built into the .NET Framework, in the *System.IO* namespace, is the *FileSystemWatcher* class. This class fires events when files or directories are changed, created, deleted, or renamed. I'll examine this class in detail by adding it to a class we'll build, named *SystemObserver*, that inherits from *FileSystemWatcher*. I'll also explain the new notion of delegates, which permit

programmers to define and react to their own events. I'll add delegates to the *SystemObserver* class that respond to events of *FileSystemWatcher*. We'll also build a Windows program named File Sentinel and import the *SystemObserver* class. This program provides a user interface that permits a user to select files or directories. File Sentinel can monitor any file or directory (such as a cookies file) and notify you when something important happens. At the end of this chapter, I show you how to develop a Windows Service application (formerly known as an NT service). We'll turn the *SystemObserver* class into a Windows service to illustrate the reusability of our code.

- **Chapter 10, Data Access with ADO.NET.** ADO.NET components have been redesigned to provide a more consistent object model while also providing increased scalability for Internet programming. This is accomplished by using the new disconnected *DataSet* object, which provides a common way to represent and manipulate data on a client. Where traditional data access programming held a connection to the data store, ADO.NET is completely disconnected. This approach uses what are known as *managed providers*, which include a connection object, a command object, a *DataReader* object, and various *DataAdapter* objects. The most compelling aspect of ADO.NET is that the in-memory data set now represents its contents in text-based XML, which can be passed back and forth through any HTTP port 80 firewall, making data sharing between heterogeneous and non-Windows systems a reality.

- **Chapter 11, Data Sets in Detail.** In this chapter, I delve deeper into the ADO.NET object model. I start by writing a program that illustrates how data sets represent their contents in XML, examining both the schema and the XML representation of the data. I show how data is manipulated locally and how changes are then written back to the source. I also demonstrate how to use a tool supplied with Visual Studio .NET, Xsd.exe, that can take an XML file (say from a new vendor) and generate an XML schema definition (XSD) file from it. The XSD file can then be used to create a Visual Basic .NET class that knows how to add, delete, and modify the previously unknown XML file. Next we programmatically build a *DataTable* object in a data set and dynamically add a relationship between fields to build a parent/child relationship. The data from the data set is persisted to disk in XML, and then a data grid control is used to reconstitute the data from the XML file. The data grid does not know or care whether the information comes from a database or an XML file—in either case it has all the information it needs to build itself. A look at the new *DataView* object illustrates how you can create two separate views of a single data table.

- **Chapter 12, ADO.NET Data Binding.** This chapter completes our examination of ADO.NET by reviewing the *BindingContext* object. Because an ADO.NET disconnected recordset does not have an explicit implementation of a cursor, I describe how to navigate among records with the *BindingContext* object and its related *CurrencyManager* objects. I walk through a program that navigates among records in a single table to show how this is done. I wrap up the chapter by building a table programmatically and adding records to it. We search for specific records in the table and manipulate them.

- **Chapter 13, ASP.NET and Web Services.** In Visual Basic .NET, you can build a Web Form with the same ease as a Windows Form. The same, consistent object model is used. I'll examine how ASP.NET provides a simplified development experience while also providing improved scalability. I look at the new server-side graphical controls as well as the new "code behind" concept, which lets you separate code for business logic from code for the user interface. We build a working ASP.NET loan calculator program to fully review Web Forms, object state, server-side controls, postbacks, field validators, variable caching, data binding to a dynamically built data table, and more. Moving on to Web Services, you'll see how SOAP (Simple Object Access Protocol) breaks down protocol-specific barriers by sending plain text that triggers API methods on remote servers. Web services can advertise their APIs and data types by utilizing the Web Services Description Language (WSDL). I illustrate these concepts with a sample program that uses a Magic 8 ball and a Windows program that consumes the Magic 8 ball Web service. Creating and consuming Web services are my favorite parts of Visual Basic .NET.

- **Chapter 14, Visual Inheritance and Custom Controls.** As you found out early on, everything in Visual Basic .NET is an object, including Windows forms. Because we can inherit from an existing object, in this chapter we'll build a standard form that provides a consistent look and feel and then inherit from the base form to build identical child forms. We will also build a custom Visual Basic .NET control. I wrap up the book with a fun project that takes just about everything you've learned in the book and puts it to use—a program that places electronic yellow sticky notes on your computer screen. The program automatically saves a note's contents, size, and location and reconstitutes any existing sticky notes when the program is run the next time. I describe how to deploy Visual Basic .NET programs and create a setup project that will deploy our sticky notes project on any Windows 2000, Windows ME, or Windows XP machine, even if the .NET common language runtime is not yet installed.

About the Companion CD

All the sample code is on the companion CD that accompanies this book. The code has been tested using post beta 2 builds of Microsoft Visual Studio .NET and running on Microsoft Windows 2000 Server with Service Pack 2 installed. To use the Web Forms samples, Internet Information Services (IIS) must be installed. You should install IIS before you install Visual Studio .NET. If you install Visual Studio .NET first, you might see the following error message:

```
Error while trying to run project: Unable to start debugging on the Web
server. The server does not support debugging of ASP.NET or ATL Server
applications. Run setup to install the Visual Studio .NET server compo-
nents. If setup has been run verify that a valid URL has been speci-
fied.
You may also want to refer to the ASP.NET and ATL Server debugging
topic in the online documentation. Would you like to disable future
attempts to debug ASP.NET pages for this project?
```

To fix this problem try the following steps (see the Visual Studio .NET online help for more information):

1. Make sure IIS and the Microsoft FrontPage 2000 Server Extensions are installed using Add/Remove Windows Components in Add/Remove Programs.
2. Uninstall the .NET Framework in Add/Remove Programs.
3. Rerun Visual Studio .NET setup, and reinstall the .NET Framework.

The sample programs developed in Chapters 10, 11, and 12, about ADO.NET, also require Microsoft SQL Server 2000, and one sample program requires Microsoft Access 2000 or Microsoft Access 2002. You must have sufficient rights to install and run these applications.

Note that the final version of Visual Studio .NET was not available when this book went to press. The programs were tested against Visual Studio .NET release candidate 2, but changes in the final version might require small modifications to the sample programs.

System Requirements

You'll need the following software to run the samples included on the companion CD:

- Microsoft Visual Studio .NET
- Microsoft Windows 2000 or Microsoft Windows XP
- IIS 5 or later
- Microsoft SQL Server 2000
- Microsoft Access 2000 or Microsoft Access 2002

Do You Have Any Questions?

Every effort has been made to ensure the accuracy of this book and the contents of the companion CD. Should you run into any problems or issues, refer to the following resources:

Microsoft Press provides corrections for books through the World Wide Web at:

http://www.microsoft.com/mspress/support/

If you have comments, questions, or ideas regarding this book or the companion CD, please send them to Microsoft Press using either of the following methods:

E-mail:

mspinput@microsoft.com

Postal Mail:

Microsoft Press

Attn: Coding Techniques for Microsoft Visual Basic .NET Editor

One Microsoft Way

Redmond, WA 98052-6399

Please note that product support is not offered through the above addresses.

1

Visual Basic .NET from the Ground Up

Welcome to the brave new world of Microsoft Visual Basic .NET. You might be reading this book because you are one of the almost 3.5 million Visual Basic programmers around the world who have made Visual Basic the most popular Windows programming language in history. Or you might be experienced in other computer programming languages, such as C, C++, or Java, and want to understand the new Microsoft .NET (pronounced "dot net") technology. Or you might just be curious. In any case, this book is for you.

Before we jump head first into Visual Basic .NET, it's instructive to understand how we've arrived at this important juncture, where the .NET technology is rapidly going to become a prerequisite for every serious production programmer. It's mind numbing to think that the IBM PC was introduced in 1981 with a floppy drive, no hard drive, a green phosphorous monitor, and 128 KB of RAM. The PC has even been heralded as *Time* magazine's "Man of the Year," with a photograph of the machine featured on the cover. This notoriety was extraordinary because this annual special issue of the magazine had always featured the photograph of a prominent world leader or another influential individual. This time—ouch! no pun intended—the magazine cover featured a machine. In retrospect, those were simpler days.

A short 20 years later, PCs have grown up to be muscular machines using the Internet to communicate with every other PC or wireless device on the planet. And most exciting of all, no end to this evolution is in sight. In less than a generation, computer technology has mushroomed to the point where if you can imagine an application, you can probably build it. We literally are limited only by our imagination.

What a Long, Strange Trip It's Been

In the dim, dark past of the early 1980s, shrouded in the mists of time, systems-applications developers used the C language to program the various single-tasking, small computer operating systems that populated the landscape. MS-DOS emerged as the premier operating system. It was fast and lightweight because it was written in assembler to take advantage of the limited memory and speed these small systems had. The application programming interface (API) for DOS was really a small set of software interrupts. Some of you might fondly remember building interrupt handlers for communications. If you wanted to run a communications program, you would interrogate the communications port to see whether a byte arrived down the wire. Because DOS programs are single threaded, DOS kept command of the computer at all times. A communications program would sit in a loop and constantly peek in the communication buffer to check on the arrival of a new byte. This sort of program would be considered less than optimal with today's software development challenges.

The Windows operating system API was designed in the early 1980s, and programmers still used C to program it. This API was cryptic, to be generous. It contained hundreds of functions, each with a long and sometimes counterintuitive name. Moving to Windows was a sea change—a monumentally different way of approaching computer programming. Programmers now had to deal with features like a graphical user interface and multitasking. This move was initially resisted by many developers, who said that Windows programs were slow and difficult to write. Windows would never catch on.

> **Note** For you purists, multiple programs were not really run simultaneously. However, with early cooperative multitasking and, later, preemptive multitasking, the user was given the impression that many programs were running at the same time. The Windows operating system simply rotated CPU time slices so fast—faster than humans could discern—that several programs appeared to run simultaneously. But because the standard desktop computer has only one CPU, it can, of course, run only one program at any one time. Essentially Windows provided a good implementation of smoke and mirrors.

As more and more programs had to cohabit on the same machine, a mechanism was needed that let the system respond to the correct program. For example, I might be writing a document in Word and want to add a number in Excel. How in the world would the operating system handle this? The ingenious way was through *events*. In the event-driven model, the operating system sends messages to specific programs when the user does something. The individual program intercepts the message and fires an event. It is the program that is responsible for responding to an event fired within the program.

If I click on Excel after working in Word to enter a number, the operating system gives Excel the focus. Excel now becomes the active program. When I enter a number from the keyboard, Windows sends the number (bundled up in a message) to Excel. An event in Excel fires, and any code within the event handler is responsible for doing something with the number.

Windows changed the way to program in fundamental ways. Instead of a program sitting in a loop to check and see whether something happened, Windows would notify us by sending our program an event such as a keystroke or a click of the mouse. In the meantime, our program could go about its business and perform other tasks instead of mindlessly waiting for a specific thing to occur. A good analogy is if I want to call you on the phone and the line is busy. I could stand by the phone and keep dialing every five minutes to see whether you've hung up, but that's not a good use of my time. Conversely, I could subscribe to a service that will call me the moment you hang up. Now I can do something useful, like cut the grass while waiting for you to finish chatting, and be notified when I can finally get through.

Even with all of these changes, user productivity soared and Windows was soon running on the vast majority of all desktop computers. However, in the mid-1980s, most computers were still running on only Intel 286, 16-bit chips. The influential book by Dr. Bjarne Stroustrup, *The C++ Programming Language*, was published in 1986 and officially kicked off the object-oriented programming (OOP) movement. At about the same time, the 32-bit 386 chip was introduced and started gaining popularity. C++ gained a foothold among developers in corporate America, and class libraries were built to help speed development with interacting objects.

While C++ is a superset of C, the language is a completely different animal because it is object oriented. Making the move to C++ from any non–object-oriented, procedural language required a large jump in thinking about the way programs are written. Programmers were now faced with thinking about programs in terms of self-contained objects and events instead of linearly executed code. They were forced to learn strange and terrifying new concepts with intimidating names, such as *polymorphism*, *inheritance*, *encapsulation*, and *overloading*. C++ was abstract, and most programmers found the learning curve steep. An average programmer required about 6 months just to become familiar with the new language. Because Visual Basic was relatively less complex, most programmers who could not make the conceptual leap to C++, or who simply wanted an easier and more productive language for Windows 3.0 development, successfully moved to Visual Basic when version 1 was introduced in 1991.

Visual Basic has a long and productive history. The Visual Basic language has not stood still as technological challenges have grown and changed. As the needs of corporate end users evolved, Visual Basic has kept pace nicely, becoming faster and providing better functionality with each new version. Visual Basic 3.0 added DAO (Data Access Objects) capability to seamlessly access databases and other data sources. Visual Basic 4.0 offered two separate and distinct compilers, one for 16-bit and the other for 32-bit development. Version 4.0 also let developers build programs based on the Component Object Model (COM) by providing the capability to create dynamic-link libraries (DLLs). Class-based programming also made its debut in this version. In Visual Basic 5.0, the language added the capability to build and distribute ActiveX controls. And Visual Basic 6.0, introduced in late 1998, was rewritten entirely and provided new Web controls and interface inheritance for classes.

Why am I telling you all of this? Because the programming world is changing once again, and this time the Internet has taken center stage. Andy Grove, CEO of Intel Corporation and, ironically, *Time* magazine's "Man of the Year" for 1997, would probably call this juncture in software development an "inflection point." In his excellent book, *Only the Paranoid Survive*, he describes an inflection point as a crossroads where the right path to take might not be clear at the time. If you make the correct choice at the inflection point you not only survive, you thrive. Make the wrong choice, and you join the ranks of those who said DOS would live forever.

The movement from traditional programming languages such as Visual Basic to Visual Basic .NET is considered by many, including Bill Gates, to be more dramatic than the shift from DOS to Windows. What was that Chinese curse? "May you live in interesting times"? More appropriate to programmers might be the French proverb, "The only constant is change."

Visual Basic .NET is not only the next version of the language, it is the next *revolution* of the language, and the language has fundamentally changed for the better.

From COM to .NET

As you probably know, Visual Basic and Visual C++ have separate run times, each with its own distinct behaviors. C++ revolutionized software development by making object-oriented programming widely used. However, C++ objects could only be used by C++ code, which didn't benefit most programmers; the majority don't use C++ as a result of the steep learning curve required to understand it. In order to solve the problem of interlanguage communication, Microsoft developed COM.

COM is really a contract, a set of laws that determine how to build a COM component. If your component follows the COM rules, it can work with other COM components no matter which language they are written in. When you added a new tool to the Visual Basic 6.0 toolbox, that .ocx file was probably written in C++, but you didn't need to know or care. You just wanted the functionality the control provided.

COM deals primarily with interfaces. Not graphical user interfaces, but application programming interfaces. In fact, a COM object is primarily composed of interfaces. If a component adhered to the COM blueprint for how to lay itself out in memory and provided a set of standard interfaces, other COM-compliant software could reuse the component.

COM acts as a binary object–interoperability standard. A COM software component is a piece of reusable software in binary form—a self-contained block of functionality such as a grid control or a text box. COM components register themselves in the Windows registry, and any program that knows how to find them can use them. While this approach has, for the most part, worked well, inadvertent version or interface changes by an unwary programmer have caused occasional problems. And when you wanted to spawn a process on a remote machine across the Internet, things rapidly became tricky.

Distributed COM, or DCOM, attempted to solve this problem. Unfortunately, DCOM is difficult to configure and set up and works only on Windows machines. In order to accept marshaled DCOM data, a port in the firewall had to be opened and therefore exposed to hackers. This requirement made more than one corporate IT manager raise an eyebrow. CORBA was developed as a competing but incompatible approach to interoperability in the UNIX world.

As the corporate world becomes more comfortable with the Internet and relies on it for mission-critical system needs, a better solution than DCOM is needed. Businesses all over the globe are setting up shop on the Internet at a breakneck pace. Electronic Data Interchange (EDI), the scheme born in 1985 that's used for ordering, invoicing, payments, and updating back-office systems, is experiencing a renaissance of sorts with the Internet. If business-to-business e-commerce is going to reach its full potential, a platform-independent and language-independent standard is needed. The .NET Framework provides the pieces to make this level of interoperability a reality.

The .NET World

The *raison d'etre* of .NET is to provide users with access to their information, files, or programs anywhere, anytime, and on any platform or device. Users should not have to know where the information is located or the details about how to retrieve it. For example, over the next several years Microsoft and other companies will phase out delivering software on CDs. Instead they will deliver the functionality that users get today from software installed on their desktops via Web Services delivered over the Internet. Consumers of those services will no longer buy software, install it on a machine, and then maintain it. Instead they will license the functionality as an on-demand service. The software bits will be downloaded, installed, and maintained by a Web Service. Updates and patches will happen automatically via the Internet. If you need to use a particular piece of software for a project, such as an expensive CAD/CAM program, but don't want to purchase it, you'll be able to use it via a Web Service and be charged by use.

As you can see, this is a large vision that considers the technology and business horizon in the not too distant future. Learning Visual Basic .NET not only puts you on the forefront of this exciting and revolutionary vision, but it also permits you to be more productive with today's applications. Bill Gates summed up things nicely when he told a group of developers recently, "Today, we have a world of applications and Web sites. In the .NET world, everything that was an application becomes a Web Service." Web Services means the sum is greater than the parts.

A .NET Example

I always find understanding a new concept easier with a concrete example. Let's say you're charged with developing a program that moves funds across different currencies for a financial institution. Designing this program requires that currency conversion rates be calculated in real time, which allows a customer to send a dollar-denominated wire transfer and have it converted to deutsche marks (DM) for payment to your branch in Berlin. The customer of your service would have to know, in real time, how many dollars are required to pay the bill of DM10,000 the moment the wire was sent. You could try to figure out how to create a real-time currency conversion program, but where would you start? How do you get the rates? What is the risk of getting it wrong? How timely is the information? And on and on.

Programmers might spend months or more just writing the specifications and the code for a program like this. Then there is testing and debugging, which will take another few months. My company, however, offers a Web Service that provides real-time currency conversion rates. My Web site provides a service, and your Web site consumes it. When a customer logs into your secure Web site, behind the scenes Visual Basic .NET code makes a request for conversion rates from my site using a protocol called *SOAP* (for Simple Object Access Protocol; more on SOAP later—for now, trust me). You don't have to know or care whether my site runs on Windows 2000, Solaris, UNIX, or whatever.

The .NET strategy permits us to do away with DCOM to get information from another computer platform anywhere on the globe in a secure and efficient manner. Your Web Service consumes my Web Service in a method that is completely secure and transparent to your customer. You might also sign up with another Web Service provider that offers the best arbitrage rates on currency and yet another provider that validates and stores customer security information. When your Web Service consumes several other Web Services to provide a customized product or service, that is known as a *federation* of Web Services. Your customer does not know that you are using a federation of Web Services, built and maintained by others, to provide your end product. By using various Web Services (secure, transparent, functionality providers), you not only outsource the development by using their code but also outsource the risk because the service providers have domain experts on staff and have the various government certifications and insurance. You simply consume their secure Web Services and add the results to your own service. This scenario is the ultimate in code reusability because it's on a global scale. Your development team is free to spend precious time and resources on developing applications to meet the needs of your customers by consuming Web Services from experts in various domains and assembling them in customized ways.

But let me stress that if you write any Windows software, Visual Basic .NET will continue to provide current and additional functionality. Your software will also be able to run on non-Windows platforms, very much like Java.

Note Most people know the Java language mantra "write once, run everywhere" from a few years back, referring to the Java Virtual Machine. After working with early renditions of Java, some developers used to joke that the phrase should really be "write once, debug everywhere." The designers of the .NET Framework certainly got the "write once, run everywhere" concept right.

Why You Need to Learn Visual Basic .NET

While classic Visual Basic is a powerful and relatively simple programming language, it has reached a "glass ceiling" in addressing the requirements of current technology. For example, classic Visual Basic provides no direct access to underlying APIs, nor does it provide inheritance—the ability to incorporate functionality from another class. Classic Visual Basic programs are also difficult to fine-tune because they are far removed from the underlying mechanics of what's going on.

In addition, classic Visual Basic works fine for developing software for the Windows platforms because Windows 95, Windows 98, Windows Me, Windows NT 4.0, and Windows 2000 all rely on the Intel x86 architecture. But today's developers simply need more horse power, for more horses.

Visual Basic .NET is an entirely new way of developing software. It will let Visual Basic programmers address the advances in hardware, communications technology, miniaturization, and the Internet, which are all converging at a breakneck pace. I for one don't want to go through again the sort of development issues encountered when PCs moved from 16-bit to 32-bit architecture and two separate executables had to be tracked and managed depending on the platform a customer was using. In the next year or so, this management nuisance will seem like good times by comparison to the array of different platforms we will have to program for. The new 64-bit Windows is right around the corner, and more and more companies are relying on the Internet to distribute information and services. These companies want to distribute information to cell phones and wireless hand-held devices. Newer smart devices and appliances are also being developed daily. These wireless devices, as well as Windows CE, which is used in Pocket PCs, all run on a non-Intel x86 CPU—and let's not forget about the Palm OS based on the Dragonball chip. The obvious problem is how can a Visual Basic developer build software and distribute it to all of these disparate devices. With classic Visual Basic, that's impossible.

Instead of having to learn new techniques to optimize programs for specific hardware and operating systems, use separate architecture-specific compilers for each new (or yet devised) platform, and then track each and every version, developers can use .NET. At the center of this new approach is the *common language runtime* (CLR). The CLR (which I'll describe in more detail later in this chapter) provides many benefits to Visual Basic programmers, not the least of which is the means to program in any .NET language—Visual Basic, C++, C#, or one of 17 others that target the CLR. Components written in Visual Basic .NET can be called and used by those written in COBOL .NET, for example.

> **Note** Don't get the idea that Visual Basic .NET is designed exclusively for developing applications for the Internet. To the contrary, while Internet services and code reuse are now available to us, Visual Basic .NET makes developing stand-alone Windows programs easier than ever as well. Microsoft has devoted lots of resources to ensure that you can continue to build robust and fast Windows-based applications. We don't lose our classic Visual Basic expertise. Instead we gain functionality and power.

When you program with Visual Basic .NET, most applications can be deployed with zero-impact installations; in other words, installing an application is guaranteed not to affect applications already installed on a system. One of the immediate benefits you will reap is the ability to simply use XCOPY to install your entire application. You no longer have to write complicated and error-prone registry entries. You don't have to use regedit32 to register components. And, one of my personal favorites, you don't have to contend anymore with conflicting or out-of-date DLLs. How many times have you installed a new program only to find that programs that were working now don't? Often this error was caused by an older or incompatible version of a DLL being installed over the current file by the new program. This problem alone caused countless hours of sleuthing, at least in my experience. The Microsoft .NET Framework puts an end to DLL Hell once and for all.

In most cases you simply install your Visual Basic .NET application and all the files associated with it in a directory, and you're done. At first blush, this approach might sound unbeatable, but there is more. Consider when you have to uninstall a classic Visual Basic program. The results are often unpredictable. Many times the client machine is left with orphaned files and registry entries. With Visual Basic .NET you simply delete the contents of a directory (or directory tree) and the application is completely removed from the machine. Help Desks everywhere will love this.

What Are the Pieces and How Do They Fit Together? A .NET Framework Overview

Where do we start? The reason this chapter is titled "Visual Basic .NET from the Ground Up" is that we really do start at the bottom. Conceptually, the Visual Basic .NET compiler sits atop the .NET Framework. The Visual Basic .NET compiler simply exposes various parts of the .NET Framework that are specific to the Visual Basic language. The Visual Basic compiler enforces syntax, but all of the real action occurs at the level of the .NET Framework.

At the heart of the .NET Framework is the common language runtime. The CLR manages execution of .NET code and provides services that make the development process easier. Compilers and tools make the runtime's functionality available. Code that you write that targets the runtime is known as *managed code*. The CLR manages the code for, among other operations, cross-language integration and exception handling, starting and killing threads, security, versioning, and deployment support.

The CLR makes it easy for Visual Basic .NET developers to design and build applications whose objects can interact with objects written in other languages. This interaction is possible because the various language compilers and development tools that target the CLR use a common data type system defined by the runtime. Visual Basic .NET includes new data types, and older Visual Basic 6 types, such as the variant, are no longer supported. These changes were to accommodate the CLR specifications. (I'll start discussing the new data types and implications for developers in Chapters 2 and 3.) How you experience the runtime depends on which language compiler you use—each one exposes a slightly different subset of runtime functionality. But what the compiler does expose is identical across languages. This brings to mind one word—interoperability.

Let's take a look at all the moving parts of the .NET Framework. As shown in Figure 1-1, at the top level is the Visual Basic compiler (as well as compilers for many other languages). Below the compiler is the common language specification (CLS). This specification is a set of rules that govern the minimum language features that must be supported to ensure that a language will interoperate with other CLS-compliant components and tools. As long as a language conforms to the CLS, it is guaranteed to work with the CLR. In this way, when third-party compilers target the .NET Framework, as long as they conform to the CLS, the code is guaranteed to run.

As you can see from the illustration, Visual Basic is now a peer of C++, C#, and any other language targeting .NET. Visual Basic .NET now has the same variable types, arrays, user-defined types, classes, graphical forms, visual controls, and interfaces as these other languages. This common structure makes calling a class in one .NET language from another .NET language effortless.

Figure 1-1 also indicates that you can use the Visual Studio .NET integrated development environment (IDE) to program with Visual Basic and target the .NET platform. Because the new IDE is similar to the Visual Basic 6 IDE (although more streamlined), Visual Basic programmers will immediately feel at home.

Data and XML

Both Web Services and the User Interface sit on top of the Data and XML block. As you progress through this book, you will learn just how important eXtensible Markup Language (XML) is to passing data over the Internet. If you are familiar with HTML, you will note a similarity. While both HTML and XML use markup tags, HTML markup is used for instructions about how to display data, while XML markup is used to describe and represent data. Both work hand-in-hand with the SOAP protocol, which permits instructions and data to be encapsulated in XML and wrapped in an HTML file that can be sent through corporate firewalls. All firewalls permit text to be sent through Port 80, the port for browsing Web sites. SOAP is text based, so no rogue ports that could be compromised by hackers need to be opened to accommodate the SOAP format.

> **Note** XML is rapidly becoming the *lingua franca* of the Web. You have probably read that XML has taken center stage for moving data across the Internet, so it is central to the .NET strategy. In a simple program we create later in this chapter, you'll see what the format of XML looks like. I don't cover XML basics in this book. You should become familiar with XML to work effectively with Visual Studio .NET.

Base Class Library

The base class library (BCL) is underneath the Data and XML block. This area is the origin for the base class of all .NET programs. Everything in Visual Basic .NET is an object, and all objects originate from a class named *System*. The BCL also provides collections, localization, text objects, interoperability with non-.NET code and ActiveX controls, and a variety of other services.

Most classic Visual Basic programmers are familiar with APIs. But C++ programmers use the Microsoft Foundation Classes (MFC), while developers using Java to create Windows applications rely on yet a different framework. The unified programming classes in the BCL ensure that all languages use this same object-oriented, hierarchical, and extensible set of class libraries.

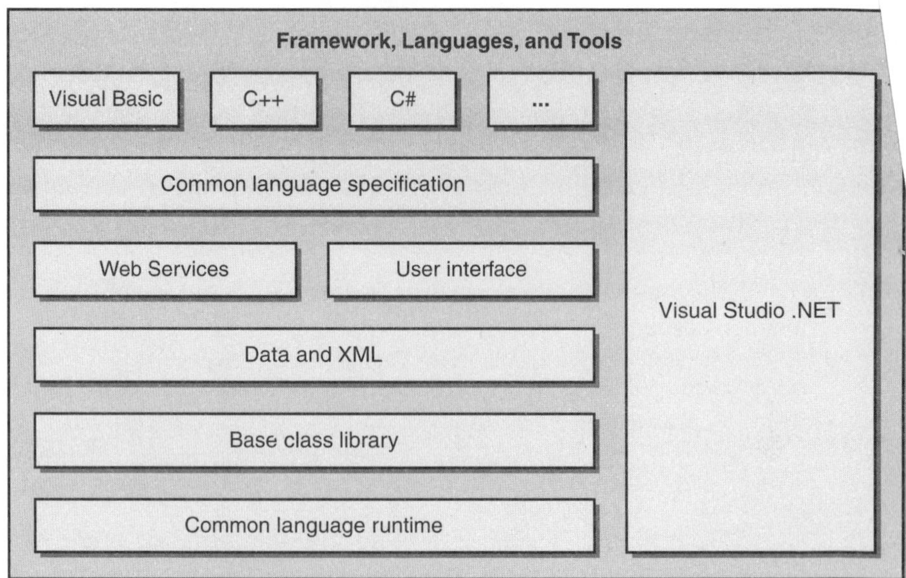

Figure 1-1 An overview of the .NET Framework.

Web Services

Web Services provide a Web-enabled user interface with tools that include various Hypertext Markup Language (HTML) controls and Web controls. Web Services also handle various Web protocols, security, and session state. The beauty is that the Web Services idiom is the same as that for Windows Forms, which are part of the User Interface component next to Web Services. You can build a Web form just as easily as a Windows form, which reduces the learning curve for .NET development. Web Forms applications generate standard HTML 3.2, permitting the form to be rendered on any browser on any platform without you having to do a thing. If you have ever struggled to write code to detect the brand of client browser and the particular version of the browser that's running and then substitute the correct scripting code, you will really appreciate this.

User Interface

At the same level as Web Services is the User Interface. This block represents the design information for Windows (or PC-based) forms. The User Interface is where Windows forms live. It also provides code for drawing to the screen, printing, rendering text, and displaying images. A sophisticated two-dimensional drawing capability is also built-in that will permit advanced users to do things like create gradient color buttons, once the province only of C++ programmers.

Common Language Runtime

Holding up the framework is the common language runtime, which I described briefly earlier. The CLR does the heavy lifting for .NET Framework programs. Of course, run times are nothing new for programming languages. To run a classic Visual Basic program, the VBRUN run time has to be installed on the client machine. Likewise, Visual C++ must have MSVCRT installed, Java must have its own run time installed, and so on. Only the CLR is needed to make .NET code run on any machine.

The CLR is a set of standard resources that any .NET program can take advantage of, from any .NET-supported language. All languages will be more equal in capability than they have ever been before—.NET is the great equalizer. But not all .NET languages will support all .NET services. You can perform some operations in Visual Basic .NET that you can't do in C#, and vice versa. The capabilities of each language are dictated by the language's compiler.

The CLR includes support for the BCL, where the architecture for our controls and forms actually live. It is also responsible for managing threads and exceptions (what were errors held in the *Err* object in classic Visual Basic). Garbage collection—or releasing objects that are no longer in use—is also done by the CLR. (I'll touch on garbage collection again later in this chapter and describe it in more detail in Chapter 4, "Visual Basic .NET Data Types and Features.")

As I mentioned, the CLR takes the code generated by the Visual Basic .NET compiler (or any other compiler that targets .NET, for that matter) and converts it to the native language of the current platform architecture. Through this conversion, the magic of interplatform execution is achieved. Visual Basic programmers write code in the Visual Basic syntax, and the CLR is responsible for converting it to any platform that can run the CLR. Programmers are abstracted several levels from the hardware and really don't need to know or care what platform their code will be run on. As long as we use proper Visual Basic syntax and the application can be built without the compiler barking at us, .NET takes care of the rest.

As you can see in Figures 1-1 and 1-2, the CLR provides support for everything above it, as well as the conversion of Visual Basic .NET code to the specific architecture an application is running on. It also automatically provides *type-safe code*, which means that the code can do only what we want it to do.

You have all heard stories about rogue code that either through sloppiness or maliciousness overran buffers and trashed a machine, killing all other programs on board. By design, this situation can't happen with Visual Basic .NET code.

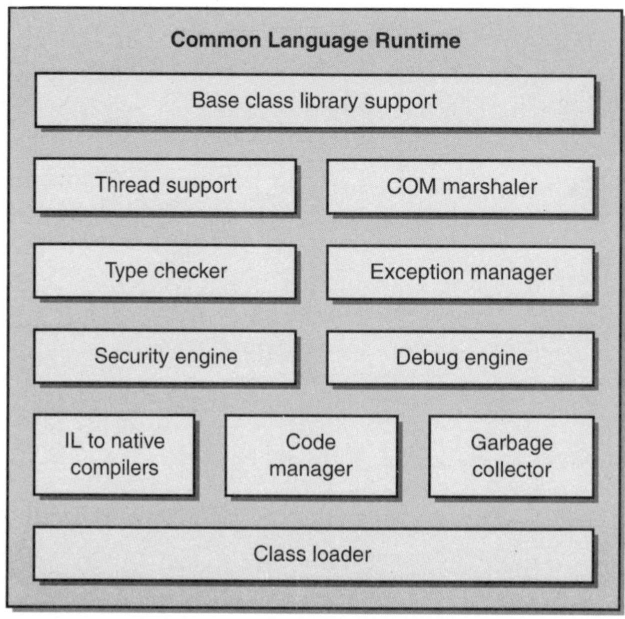

Figure 1-2 The common language runtime provides a number of powerful services.

When code is targeted for .NET, it is called *managed code,* which means that the code automatically runs under a "contract of cooperation" with the CLR. Managed code supplies the information necessary for the runtime to provide services such as memory management, cross-language integration, code access security, and the automatic lifetime control of all of our objects.

Don't worry if trying to digest all this information seems like trying to drink water from a fire hose. As you start building your first Visual Basic .NET programs, you'll rapidly see how the pieces fit together.

Abstraction Layers

The idea of an abstraction layer is not new. The concept is an extension of the Hardware Abstraction Layer (HAL) in the Windows operating system. Before Windows 3.0, if you wrote a program for a PC, you had to know the answer to all sorts of questions. For example, how do I print a document? Because each printer has its own driver and printer control language, you had to write software that accommodated and spoke to all sorts of printers. What monitor was used? Did the PC have expanded or extended memory? Sheesh! This code was incredibly difficult to write. When the Windows operating system came on the scene, it became the great equalizer. All you had to do was program to Windows, and it took care of the messy details. You could just say "print" and Windows figured out how to do it. Windows handled monitor resolution, memory management, and all the other nagging details that had to be handled by programmers in the DOS world. With .NET, the CLR is also the great equalizer but on a grander scale. Instead of just handling individual printers and monitors, it handles the differences in the underlying hardware architecture. This capability is nothing short of amazing and will provide an incredible boost in productivity immediately.

Where Do We Start to Access Functionality from Visual Basic .NET Source Code?

What you might notice first when looking over this architecture is that all related logical functionality is grouped in the .NET Framework's components for easy management. You can access this functionality in your programs by referring to what's called a *namespace*. Namespaces are a hierarchical naming scheme for grouping types into logical categories of related functionality in .NET. For example, when you create your first form, the IDE will add *Imports System.Windows.Forms* to the code. The new *Imports* directive is similar to adding references in Visual Basic 6.0. Importing a namespace is all you need to do to inherit the functionality from the User Interface block in order to build and draw forms. I suspect that you are starting to see the elegance and power of this approach.

What I hope is also starting to become clear is that .NET provides a host of services that are there for the taking, finally making the Holy Grail of code reuse a reality. These services, along with other benefits, are designed to increase our productivity over the course of development—from design and coding to deployment and security. You can continue to develop stand-alone applications for PCs with Visual Basic .NET, but you can also handle any task on any platform that the job demands or might demand in the future.

Visual Basic .NET Is Object Oriented

As a Visual Basic programmer, you might be thinking that up till now you didn't need to learn object-oriented programming. Classic Visual Basic served your needs nicely. You could do most anything you needed to with some advanced knowledge of the language. However, many programming luminaries feel that the shift from the current programming paradigm to .NET will be at least if not more monumental than the shift from DOS to Windows. A new, energized object-oriented Visual Basic is the tool that is needed.

If you are new to object-oriented programming, don't let this worry you. As I cover the new facets of the language, I'll also explain and illustrate object-oriented techniques. The concepts presented in this chapter (and described in more detail in Chapter 2, "Object-Oriented Programming in Visual Basic .NET") will be amplified throughout the book. If concepts aren't completely clear after you finish this chapter, they soon will be.

Remember that with power comes responsibility. Classes and objects were first introduced in Visual Basic 4.0 and enhanced in versions 5.0 and 6.0. Unfortunately, studies show that over 50 percent of all Visual Basic programmers chose to disregard them. While we could safely turn our backs on classes and objects in previous versions of Visual Basic, we can no longer ignore them with Visual Basic .NET.

As in Java, everything in Visual Basic .NET is an object. But what exactly does that mean? Well, something like an *integer* object now has its own methods that can format the value the object has or change itself into a string. Object-orientation is part and parcel of Visual Basic .NET, so you don't want to avoid it any longer.

To be honest with you from the start, Visual Basic .NET will require a steeper learning curve than classic Visual Basic. I will cover all aspects of Visual

Basic .NET programming, including concepts such as events and classes, which some programmers find difficult. Each part will be covered in detail. And once you learn Visual Basic .NET, you can very easily move to C# or even Visual C++ .NET. A welcome by-product of learning Visual Basic .NET now is that this knowledge will also expand your understanding and use of other languages, which will make you much more marketable.

Unlike programming in previous versions of Visual Basic, programming in Visual Basic .NET requires an understanding of not only the framework I just covered, but the language itself and the infrastructure of how .NET programs are assembled. When teaching Visual Basic 6 to my graduate students, I hold off covering classes and objects until later in the semester. We pace ourselves because there is so much you can do without objects in classic Visual Basic. Because we don't have that luxury in this book, the first few chapters will be front loaded with new concepts such as the .NET Framework, how Visual Basic .NET programs are built, and the fundamentals of object-oriented programming. The remainder of the book will provide programs to hammer home these concepts.

Of course, classic Visual Basic was designed for simplicity, and while simplicity accounted for Visual Basic's phenomenal success, it also meant the language evolved along a different path from C++. With Visual Basic, creating applications with various buttons, text boxes, and other graphical gizmos was relatively straightforward. However, object-oriented capabilities such as inheritance just weren't part of the language. Visual Basic .NET has lost some of this simplicity in favor of more power, flexibility, and robustness. Visual Basic has grown up and joined the ranks of other pure object-oriented languages to handle the programming tasks of the twenty-first century.

As classic Visual Basic evolved, it became more complex. Programmers could build DLLs, ActiveX controls and servers, and classes. Along with this power came a level of difficulty. Advanced Visual Basic programmers had to know about the Windows API, COM, DCOM, ADO, classes, objects, and the rest. Likewise, classic Visual C++ evolved by getting easier. Various graphical tools, frameworks, wizards, code generators, and templates were added to assist in handling the lower-level tasks of Windows programming. As Visual Basic grew in complexity and C++ got easier, we reached an intersection of language complexity and language power. At that intersection is .NET. Both languages have evolved to a point at which they are now relatively equal in power and complexity. As I said earlier, .NET is the great equalizer.

The Visual Basic .NET Web Forms and the Windows Form designers permit a developer to easily create standardized interfaces. Both of these technologies rely heavily on classes. For example, in Visual Basic 6, when a form was added to a project, all of the complexity of construction was hidden. All of the public interfaces were hidden from the programmer. However, they were always there, and the form was still a class under the hood. In Visual Basic .NET, a Windows Forms module contains all of the code to *instantiate* (create an instance of) itself as well as any controls placed on the form. Programmers are responsible for adding code for handling events. In Visual Basic .NET, you can't even create a form without understanding the concept of a class.

A Brief Look at How the Visual Basic .NET Language Works

If you're like me, you want to see code. Now! For a short preview of how the Visual Basic language has evolved, take a look at Figure 1-3. If you are already a Visual Basic programmer, you will immediately notice a difference in the Visual Basic .NET syntax. You use a *Dim* statement to create an integer variable (*iInteger*) as you normally would, but you can now initialize the variable in the same statement, as you can in advanced languages. Very clean and efficient.

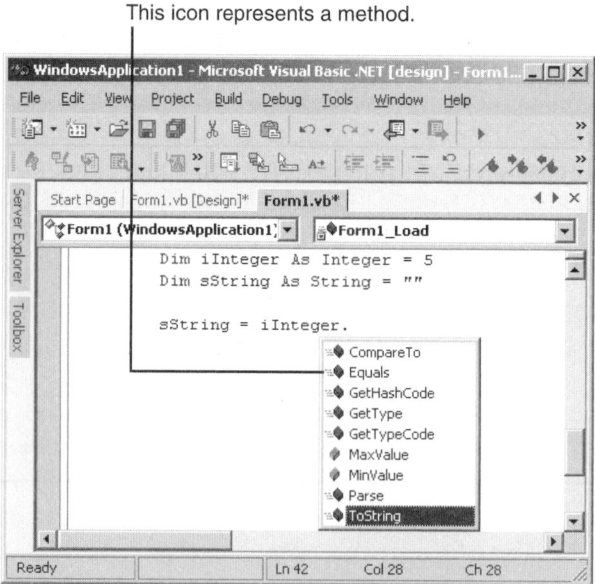

Figure 1-3 You can now create and initialize a variable in one statement in Visual Basic .NET.

Because *iInteger* is an object in Visual Basic .NET, it has its own properties and methods. Adding a period (or scope resolution modifier) after the variable name displays the properties and methods that the object owns with the IntelliSense feature of the code editor.

> **Note** You are probably familiar with the IntelliSense feature in previous versions of the Visual Basic code editor. The Visual Basic .NET source code editor offers automatic completion of various keywords as you type. IntelliSense provides an array of options that make language references easily accessible. When coding, you do not need to leave the text editor to perform searches on language elements. You can keep your context, find the information you need, insert language elements directly into your code, and even have IntelliSense complete your typing for you. Classic Visual Basic used type libraries for IntelliSense. If something was late bound, or a type library wasn't available, you didn't have any IntelliSense help. With .NET, all the data types are available all the time when you use early binding.

In this example, we are going to use the *ToString* method of the *iInteger* object shown in Figure 1-3 to make a string copy of the contents and assign it to the string object named *sString*. When the operation is complete, *sString* will contain the value *5*. The contents of *iInteger* remain unchanged. The *iInteger* variable object has a *Format* method that you can use to change the look of the contents to currency, percent, and so forth for display purposes.

Because we are talking about integers, another change to be aware of is that the underlying data representation of integers has been upgraded in Visual Basic .NET. In Visual Basic 6, the *Integer* keyword is defined as a 16-bit integer, and the *Long* keyword is defined as a 32-bit integer. To make Visual Basic .NET more compliant with common C syntax and adhere to the general standard in all .NET languages, *Integer* is now a 32-bit integer and a *Long* is a 64-bit integer. If you still need a 16-bit integer, Visual Basic .NET has added the new *Short* data type. However, because a *Short* is 16 bits and processors have 32-bit registers, using a *Short* is actually slower than using a 32-bit integer. In practice, you will rarely use a *Short*. But you can see that with .NET, it's important to understand data types.

So an *Integer* is now a *Short*, and a *Long* is now an *Integer*. While most Visual Basic programmers wrote tight code and usually knew exactly what data type was being used, some were a bit cavalier and used buckets of variants. You now have to know all about the data type you are using. And, by the way, Visual Basic .NET no longer supports variants. The .NET analog is an *Object*.

To give you a flavor of some other general changes, Visual Basic .NET no longer uses fixed-length strings, control arrays, or COM objects, just to name a few differences. Other changes include variable scope, error handling, and the way you call functions. The *Set* command, used for setting a reference to an object, is gone because now everything is an object, making that keyword redundant. All of the graphical user interface controls, such as the command button, text box, and option button, have been reengineered. As you can see, the changes are fairly wide ranging, making Visual Basic .NET more of a new language than an incremental upgrade from Visual Basic 6. But again, most old-world programming concepts apply, so what you already know will be used as a foundation when stepping up to Visual Basic .NET.

How Is a Visual Basic .NET Program Put Together?

The first step in building a Visual Basic .NET program is to compile Visual Basic .NET source code as managed code. The compiler translates the source code into *Microsoft Intermediate Language* (MSIL). MSIL is a CPU-independent set of instructions that can be efficiently converted to native code. MSIL is rich in various instructions that define loading, storing, initializing, calling, arithmetic and logic operations, control flow, memory access, exception handling, and more. All code based on MSIL executes as managed code.

MSIL can't be executed by itself, however; it's an intermediate language not too dissimilar in concept from classic Visual Basic P-code. Every .NET language emits MSIL code when compiled. The MSIL does not know or care what language it was generated from, so the second step in building a program is to run the MSIL through the *just-in-time* (JIT) *compiler* to make it platform specific. (The JIT compiler is described in more detail shortly.) Because the CLR provides one or more JIT compilers for each computer architecture, the same MSIL can be JIT-compiled and executed on any architecture supported by the runtime.

Metadata—Data About Data

When the Visual Basic compiler (or any .NET language compiler) produces MSIL from the source code, it also produces what is called *metadata*. Metadata (data about data) describes the types used in your source code. Metadata is stored in a file called a *manifest*, which includes the definition of each type, the signatures of each type's members, the members that your code references, and all the other data that the runtime needs at execution.

Metadata is completely self-describing. The type libraries Visual Basic 6 programmers have come to know and love are no longer necessary. Metadata also obviates the need to add complicated and error-prone references to the system registry, as you had to do in Visual Basic 6.

Metadata is generated by the compiler from Visual Basic source code and is stored in the executable in binary format. Metadata is a requirement of .NET. It specifies what types are exported and what types are referenced. It includes

Assemble the Troops

In .NET software development, a module is an executable file. A module can be either a library or an executable. Modules usually have either a .dll or an .exe file extension. An assembly is a logical set of one or more modules. I say *logical* because an assembly will consist of one or more files (such as DLLs, EXEs, HTMLs) that are required to run your application. The assembly has to know exactly what is included in this group.

If you think of a UPS driver who delivers many packages to many customers around town, the driver needs to know what packages are on the truck and who receives them. Typically, drivers rely on a paper manifest to list the contents of the truck and possibly the location of specific packages on the truck. The .NET Framework uses this same logic. Included in the assembly is the manifest, which contains the metadata. The manifest contains a listing of what files are in the assembly as well as where to locate each item. When the runtime loads a program, it locates the assembly and attempts to resolve an assembly reference. The term *probing* is often used when discussing how the runtime locates assemblies. The runtime refers to the set of heuristics used to locate the assembly on the basis of its name and culture (country format).

It's important to note than an assembly is the smallest unit of executable code that can be deployed (or versioned for that matter). When we deploy code, only assemblies have version numbers. Shortly I'll show you a manifest and an assembly to give you a flavor of how they work. But enough theory for the moment. Let's set up the IDE, build a small Visual Basic .NET program, and look at the files that are created.

Configuring the Interactive Development Environment

The IDE contains all the tools you need to build Visual Basic .NET applications. Because the IDE includes many options to accommodate programming in several languages, you'll first want to optimize the IDE layout for Visual Basic. The Visual Studio start page lets you create a profile that's the most convenient for Visual Basic programming. If you haven't done so already, load Visual Studio .NET and then follow these steps:

1. Click the My Profile link at the bottom of the column on the left of the home page.
2. Using the drop-down list at the top, set the Profile to Visual Basic Developer, and then choose Visual Basic 6 from the Window Layout drop-down list, as shown in Figure 1-5.

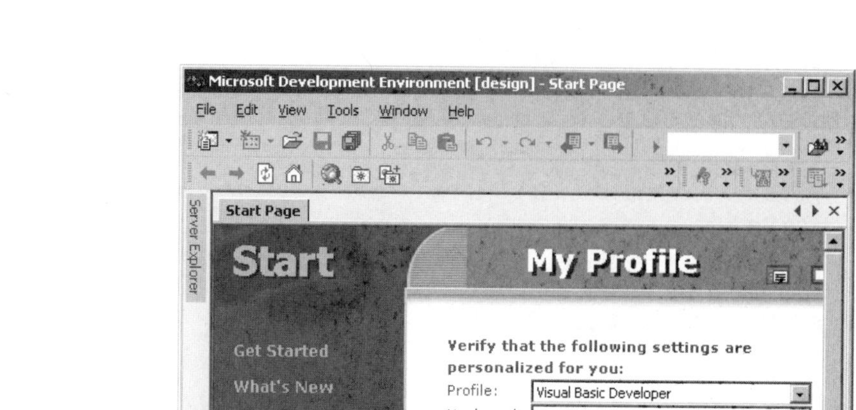

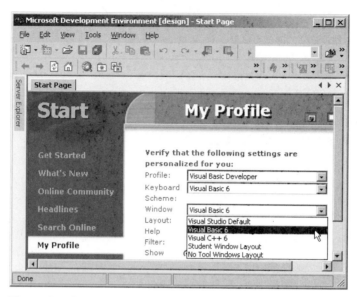

Figure 1-5 Setting up a profile.

3. Click the Get Started link at the top of the column at the left of the start page. This option configures the IDE, and all the tools required for developing Visual Basic .NET applications will be displayed, as shown in Figure 1-6. The folks in Redmond did an excellent job of making the Toolbox, Solution Explorer, Class View, and Properties windows available in the limited real estate of the screen. In addition, many of these windows use tabs in order to make the maximum amount of information available while using the minimum amount of screen space.

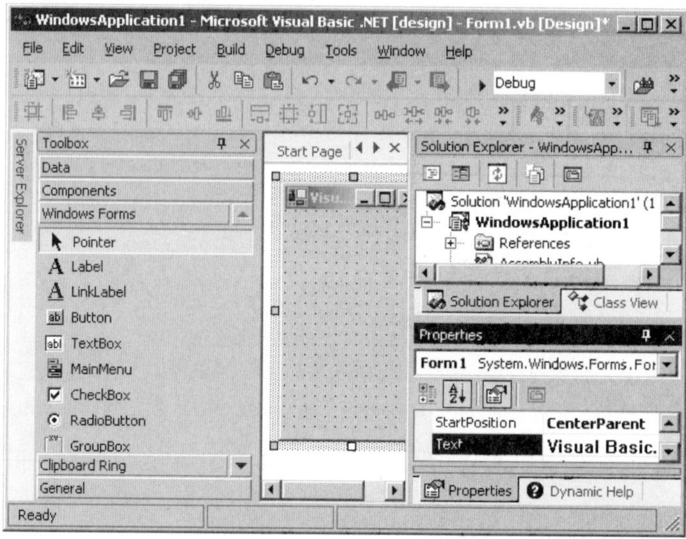

Figure 1-6 The IDE configured for Visual Basic .NET development.

Of course, you can and will change this view as you become more familiar with the IDE. Additional views can be displayed at any time by selecting options from the View menu. Any of the current windows can be dismissed and displayed again by selecting them from the View menu.

A First Look at the Visual Basic .NET IDE

We'll now start looking at how a very simple Visual Basic .NET program is written. This example is contrived on purpose, the intent being to provide an overview of the .NET environment and to preview some of the tools available to you—in other words, to let you get your mind around writing a program in this new way. Follow these steps to get started:

1. Select File | New | Project to display the New Project dialog box. Your options might vary, but for this example select the Visual Basic Projects folder on the left. On the right, notice that several types of Visual Basic .NET project types are available—very much like previous versions of Visual Basic.

2. Leave the default project name of WindowsApplication1 and select a new subdirectory to build and save the code, as shown in Figure 1-7. As you'll see, the IDE creates subdirectories below the directory in which you save WindowsApplication1. Click OK to create the project.

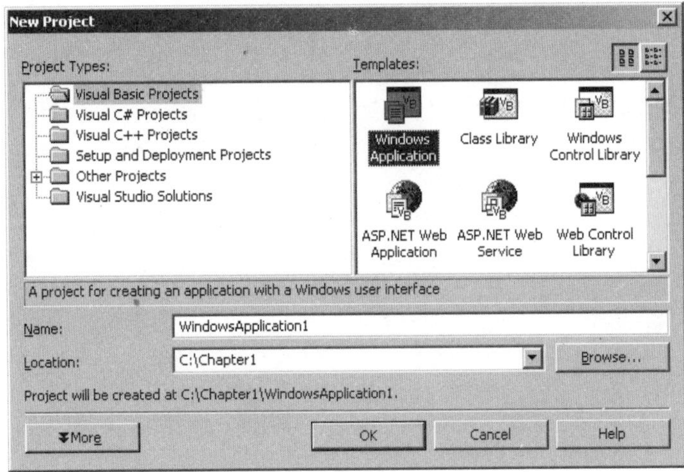

Figure 1-7 The New Project dialog box.

After a few seconds of disk whirring, the basic project will be set up in the IDE. The various windows will be populated with items for your project. Notice that a Form1.vb [Design] tab is added to the main tabbed window, as shown in Figure 1-8. The tabbed window is where you'll do most of your work. This window displays both the graphical interface of your program as well as the code.

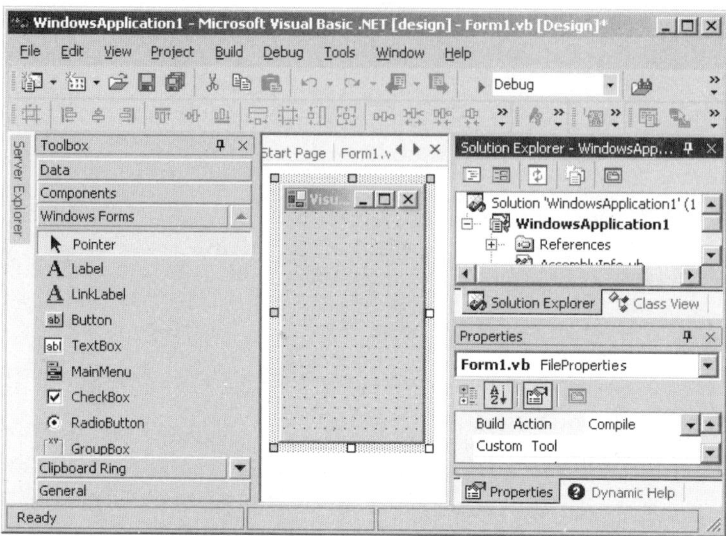

Figure 1-8 The new project in the Visual Basic .NET IDE.

To classic Visual Basic programmers, the Visual Studio .NET IDE looks streamlined and modern. It includes the graphical controls, Forms Designer, Properties, and Solution Explorer windows. If you have ever built a program in classic Visual Basic, you know that projects are the building blocks of applications. In the past, you used the Project Explorer to manage projects, and while you could add projects to the Project Explorer to create a "group," a group quickly became difficult to manage. Recognizing this, Microsoft added the Solution Explorer to the Visual Studio .NET IDE to take the place of the Project Explorer. The Solution Explorer handles the details of file management. It provides you with an organized view of your projects and their files. In addition, right-clicking on any item in the Solution Explorer provides ready access to the commands that pertain to it.

If a project is a building block for an application, you can think of a solution as the foundation. Keep in mind that a single solution can contain multiple projects. The Solution Explorer can easily manage the complexity of juggling multiple projects and the solution to which they belong. The Solution Explorer displays a hierarchical structure of your projects and depicts relationships between them. Of course, you can still manage your projects individually; however, the notion of a solution using the Solution Explorer facilitates managing the complexity of numerous tasks, especially for developers of a multiproject solution.

When you create an application that consists of multiple projects, you should create a local solution directory to contain your local (non-Web) projects, solution files (.sln and .suo), and any shared solution items. Such a directory-based structure mirrors the organization of your solution in Solution Explorer and so maintains the logical relationships of the components on disk. Depending on whether your application will be entirely local or potentially contain some Web-based projects, you can create a solution directory in one of two ways.

- When you create a blank solution and later add projects and files to it.
- When you create the first project in a solution with the New Project dialog box and select the Create Directory For Solution option.

Because the Solution Explorer is the IDE element through which you centrally organize and manage all the projects and files needed to design, develop, and deploy a .NET application, a solution is also used to manage the miscellaneous files—files external to your solution—that are opened outside the context of a solution or project. These files are not included in builds and cannot be included with a solution under source control. Miscellaneous files are, however, associated with a solution by reference. When you open a solution, all the miscellaneous files that were opened when the solution was last closed will be reopened. When we start building solutions later in the book, you will see just how handy this innovative touch can be.

Some Visual Basic .NET Code

Now let's take a look at the code underlying the form created by Visual Basic .NET. Double-click the form to bring up the Code window. Here you can start to see the real differences in how Visual Basic .NET forms and applications are built.

In classic Visual Basic, when you double-click a form to display the Code window, you are presented with an empty *Form_Load* event template that looks like this:

```
Private Sub Form_Load()
End Sub
```

You started to write code in the prebuilt event procedures such as *Form_Load*. And, of course, events were handed down from the mountain top, never to be expanded on. You had to use what you were given and like it.

In a Visual Basic .NET project, however, you get the following template. All of the code and the comments are generated by the .NET Forms Designer. Each program you write that targets the desktop will start like this if you use the Forms Designer. Of course, you can write the code yourself when you get more familiar with the syntax.

```
Public Class Form1
    Inherits System.Windows.Forms.Form

#Region " Windows Form Designer generated code "

    Public Sub New()
        MyBase.New()

        'This call is required by the Windows Form Designer.
        InitializeComponent()

        'Add any initialization after the
        ' InitializeComponent() call

    End Sub

    'Form overrides dispose to clean up the component list.
    Protected Overloads Overrides _
    Sub Dispose(ByVal disposing As Boolean)

        If disposing Then
            If Not (components Is Nothing) Then
                components.Dispose()
            End If
        End If
        MyBase.Dispose(disposing)
    End Sub

    'Required by the Windows Form Designer
    Private components As System.ComponentModel.IContainer

    'NOTE: The following procedure is required by the
    ' Windows Form Designer
    'It can be modified using the Windows Form Designer.
    'Do not modify it using the code editor.
    <System.Diagnostics.DebuggerStepThrough()> _
    Private Sub InitializeComponent()
        '
        'Form1
        '
        Me.AutoScaleBaseSize = New System.Drawing.Size(5, 13)
        Me.ClientSize = New System.Drawing.Size(292, 266)
        Me.Name = "Form1"
        Me.Text = "Form1"

    End Sub

#End Region
```

```
    Private Sub Form1_Load(ByVal sender As System.Object, _
        ByVal e As System.EventArgs) Handles MyBase.Load

    End Sub
End Class
```

Don't be alarmed by all of this new code; it will become clear shortly. I'll review each line and discuss what it does and why.

In classic Visual Basic, all of the public global interfaces were hidden from developers. Much of what you are seeing in the code created by Visual Basic .NET was there one way or another in classic Visual Basic, but it was hidden from the programmer's view. While hiding much of what went on under the hood accounted for the simplicity of the language, it was also the limiting factor of the language. Although some of you might be saying to yourself about now, "But I liked it simple."

Notice that the tabbed window in the IDE now has a tab for both the design environment as well as the .vb code. Click on the designer tab and check that the form has the focus. The familiar Properties window is populated with the various properties you can set within it. Select the *Start Position* property, as shown in Figure 1-9, and then choose Center Parent. Change the *Text* property from Form1 to **Visual Basic .NET—Our First Form**.

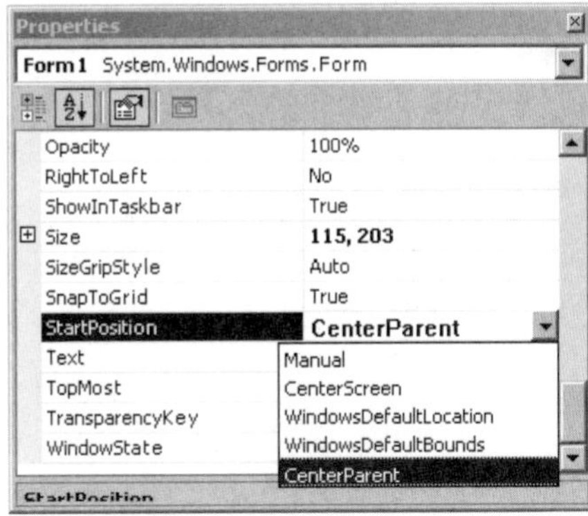

Figure 1-9 Changing form properties.

Unlike with classic Visual Basic, you'll notice in Visual Basic .NET that the value of a property doesn't change until you either press Enter or move to another property. The timing of this change occurs because the IDE is actually writing the new property value to your source code. Rather than waste CPU cycles updating at every keystroke—having to handle backspaces, and so on—waiting until a property is completely changed is more efficient.

> **Note** Look at the top drop-down box in the Properties window. It reads *Form1 System.Windows.Forms.Form.* I stated earlier that everything in .NET is an object and that all objects originate from the mother of all objects, the *System* object. A form is no different. It is also created from the *System* object.

Now you're ready to run your program. Of course, nothing will happen except you'll see a form with a custom caption displayed in the middle of the screen. Follow these steps:

1. Select Debug | Start or simply press F5. (OK, I admit that it's not very important, but the new default icon is pretty cool.) The new form appears on your screen, as shown in Figure 1-10.

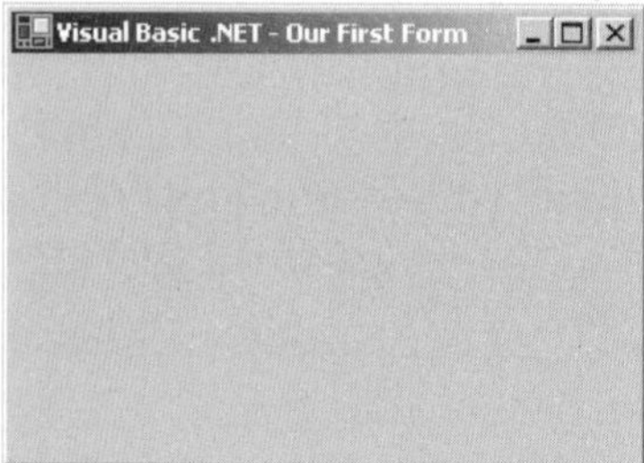

Figure 1-10 The form we just created.

2. Dismiss the form to return to design mode. If the output window is not displayed, select View | Other Windows | Output.

   You can see in Figure 1-11 all of the files used and loaded into memory that are required to run the program. The symbols loaded refer to namespaces, functions, and classes used in our program. We will be discussing these in detail starting in Chapter 2. Mscorlib.dll is the common language runtime.

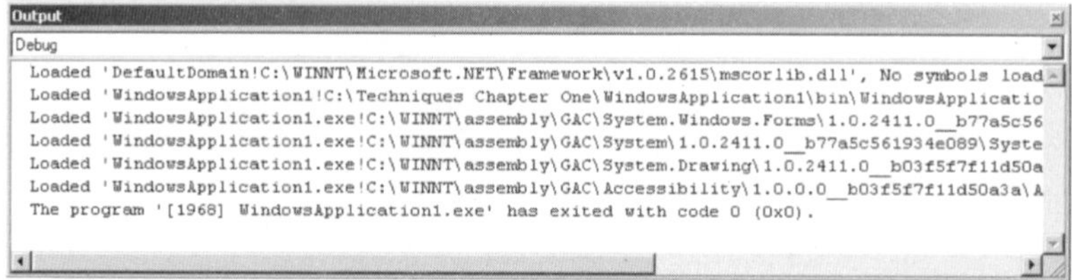

Figure 1-11 The files created by our program.

3. Click the Design tab to display the form, and then double-click it to view the code. You'll see that the designer modified the source code for you.

Notice the expand buttons along the left side of the code window. These result from a handy new keyword named *#Region*, which lets you specify a block of code that you can expand or collapse when using the outlining feature of the Visual Studio code editor. The Procedure View | Full Module View options for viewing source code in classic Visual Basic have been eliminated, so if you depended on these options, you should use *#Region Name* with a corresponding *#End Region* statement to bracket logical segments of code in Visual Basic .NET. You can then expand or contract these blocks of code for easy viewing.

The region in this view is collapsed, as shown in Figure 1-12. You can provide a descriptive name for your own regions to manage your own code. In this case, the IDE used the descriptive name *Windows Form Designer generated code* to let you know exactly what's in the region.

```
Public Class Form1
    Inherits System.Windows.Forms.Form

[Windows Form Designer generated code]

End Class
```

Figure 1-12 Regions defined in the Code window.

Look at the code that was modified by the IDE when the properties in the Properties window were changed. Notice how the designer changed the *Text* property and added the *FormStartPosition* property to the source code. Actually, if you didn't change *FormStartPosition*, it would still be used but with a default value. Because you changed the default value, the property is shown because the default behavior was modified.

```
#Region " Windows Form Designer generated code "

    Public Sub New()
        MyBase.New()

        'This call is required by the Windows Form Designer.
        InitializeComponent()

        'Add any initialization after the
        ' InitializeComponent() call

    End Sub
```

(continued)

```
    'Form overrides dispose to clean up the component list.
    Protected Overloads Overrides _
    Sub Dispose(ByVal disposing As Boolean)

        If disposing Then
            If Not (components Is Nothing) Then
                components.Dispose()
            End If
        End If
        MyBase.Dispose(disposing)
    End Sub

    'Required by the Windows Form Designer
    Private components As System.ComponentModel.IContainer

    'NOTE: The following procedure is required by the
    ' Windows Form Designer.
    'It can be modified using the Windows Form Designer.
    'Do not modify it using the code editor.
    <System.Diagnostics.DebuggerStepThrough()> _
    Private Sub InitializeComponent()
        '
        'Form1
        '
        Me.AutoScaleBaseSize = New System.Drawing.Size(5, 13)
        Me.ClientSize = New System.Drawing.Size(292, 266)
        Me.Name = "Form1"
        Me.StartPosition = _
            System.Windows.Forms.FormStartPosition.CenterParent
        Me.Text = "Visual Basic .NET - Our First form"

    End Sub

#End Region
```

If you have used any of the wizards in Visual Basic before, you are no stranger to the commented code automatically added to your form. Pay heed to the warning about not modifying any code in the *InitializeComponent* procedure. Each and every entry there can and should be modified in the Properties window as you did when changing the form's text and starting position.

Now let's build the program into an executable and see what files are created. To do this, select Release from the drop-down box on the main menu, and then select Build from the Build menu. The program should build successfully, as shown in Figure 1-13.

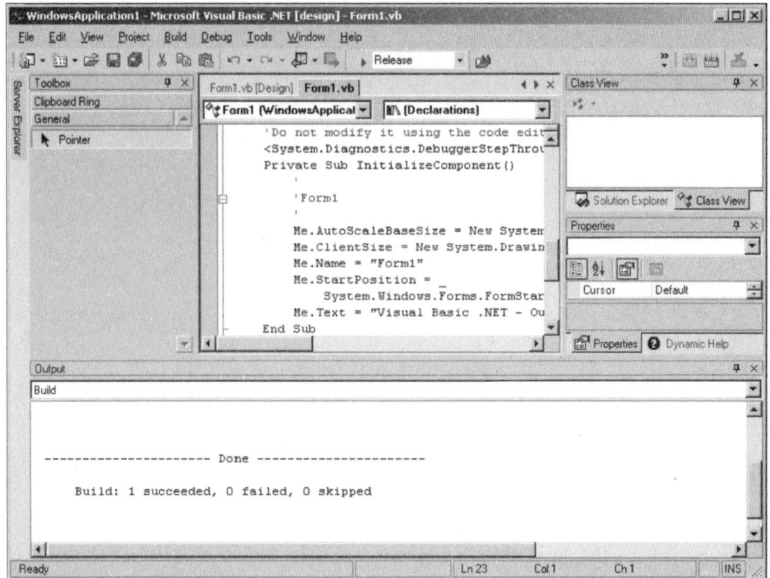

Figure 1-13 Visual Basic .NET tells us that our program has been built successfully.

Notice the output from the Solution Builder. It is very much like a Visual C++ program showing the progress of the build. Not much could go wrong with this program, of course, because we changed only two properties on the form. The output tells you that the build succeeded.

Files Created by the IDE for Our First .NET Program

Open the Explorer in Windows and take a look at the directory in which you created this program. The Visual Basic .NET compiler automatically created several subdirectories and populated them with project files. As you can see in Figure 1-14, a project folder with the application name *WindowsApplication1* was created in the directory where Visual Basic saved the project.

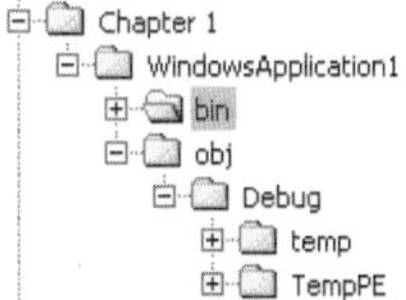

Figure 1-14 The folders our program created.

A Visual Basic .NET application uses a lot of new files. It's important to know what the IDE is doing with these files and why it's doing what it does. Our project directory, WindowsApplication1, contains the files required by the IDE to load the project. These are shown in Figure 1-15.

Name	Size	Type	Modified
Form1.resx	2 KB	Assembly Resource file	5/28/2001 6:26 PM
WindowsApplication1.vbproj.user	2 KB	USER File	5/28/2001 6:24 PM
WindowsApplication1.vbproj	4 KB	Visual Basic.Net Project file	5/28/2001 6:24 PM
Form1.vb	2 KB	Visual Basic Source file	5/28/2001 6:24 PM
WindowsApplication1.suo	7 KB	Solution User Options	5/28/2001 6:09 PM
WindowsApplication1.sln	1 KB	Visual Studio Solution	5/28/2001 6:09 PM
AssemblyInfo.vb	1 KB	Visual Basic Source file	5/28/2001 6:09 PM
obj		File Folder	5/28/2001 6:09 PM
bin		File Folder	5/28/2001 6:09 PM

Figure 1-15 Inside the WindowsApplication1 folder are the files required by the IDE to load the project.

The *Form1.vb* file is the source code for our form. If you open it with WordPad, you can see the code. *WindowsApplication1.sln* is the Visual Studio Solution file. It stores information about the project that is used to both uniquely identify the project and provide general information about the project. This file contains entries such as the following:

```
Microsoft Visual Studio Solution File, Format Version 7.00
Project("{F184B08F-C81C-45F6-A57F-5ABD9991F28F}") =
    "WindowsApplication1", "WindowsApplication1.vbproj",
    "{4046615B-BE03-4966-B975-F539A394E7AD}"
EndProject
Global
    GlobalSection(SolutionConfiguration) = preSolution
        ConfigName.0 = Debug
        ConfigName.1 = Release
    EndGlobalSection
    GlobalSection(ProjectDependencies) = postSolution
    EndGlobalSection
    GlobalSection(ProjectConfiguration) = postSolution
        {4046615B-BE03-4966-B975-F539A394E7AD}.Debug.ActiveCfg =
            Debug|.NET
        {4046615B-BE03-4966-B975-F539A394E7AD}.Debug.Build.0 =
            Debug|.NET
        {4046615B-BE03-4966-B975-F539A394E7AD}.Release.ActiveCfg
            = Release|.NET
        {4046615B-BE03-4966-B975-F539A394E7AD}.Release.Build.0
            = Release|.NET
    EndGlobalSection
    GlobalSection(ExtensibilityGlobals) = postSolution
    EndGlobalSection
    GlobalSection(ExtensibilityAddIns) = postSolution
    EndGlobalSection
EndGlobal
```

Another file in the directory, the .suo file, is a binary file and is used in part to store IDE solution configuration information.

WindowsApplication1.vbproj is the Visual Basic .Net Project file. The data in this file is stored in XML. For those of you familiar with HTML, XML probably almost makes sense. Earlier I mentioned that HTML is a markup language used for formatting and displaying information, and XML is a self-describing language that describes data. As you can see, the Visual Basic .NET Project file is conceptually like an .ini file in Windows 3.1 or registry entries in later versions of Windows. It contains headings such as Settings, Reference, Imports, and Files, with information elements that, prior to .NET, would have been stored in the registry. Here's what the data in the file looks like:

```
<VisualStudioProject>
    <VisualBasic
        ProjectType = "Local"
        ProductVersion = "7.0.9254"
        SchemaVersion = "1.0"
        ProjectGuid = "{74315F66-BB05-499D-AEB3-F786953A49CB}"
    >
        <Build>
            <Settings
                ApplicationIcon = ""
                AssemblyKeyContainerName = ""
                AssemblyName = "WindowsApplication1"
                AssemblyOriginatorKeyFile = ""
                AssemblyOriginatorKeyMode = "None"
                DefaultClientScript = "JScript"
                DefaultHTMLPageLayout = "Grid"
                DefaultTargetSchema = "IE50"
                DelaySign = "false"
                OutputType = "WinExe"
                OptionCompare = "Binary"
                OptionExplicit = "On"
                OptionStrict = "Off"
                RootNamespace = "WindowsApplication1"
                StartupObject = "WindowsApplication1.Form1"
            >
                <Config
                    Name = "Debug"
                    BaseAddress = "285212672"
                    ConfigurationOverrideFile = ""
                    DefineConstants = ""
                    DefineDebug = "true"
                    DefineTrace = "true"
                    DebugSymbols = "true"
                    IncrementalBuild = "true"
```

(continued)

```
                Optimize = "false"
                OutputPath = "bin\"
                RegisterForComInterop = "false"
                RemoveIntegerChecks = "false"
                TreatWarningsAsErrors = "false"
                WarningLevel = "1"
            />
            <Config
                Name = "Release"
                BaseAddress = "285212672"
                ConfigurationOverrideFile = ""
                DefineConstants = ""
                DefineDebug = "false"
                DefineTrace = "true"
                DebugSymbols = "false"
                IncrementalBuild = "false"
                Optimize = "false"
                OutputPath = "bin\"
                RegisterForComInterop = "false"
                RemoveIntegerChecks = "false"
                TreatWarningsAsErrors = "false"
                WarningLevel = "1"
            />
        </Settings>
        <References>
            <Reference
                Name = "System"
                AssemblyName = "System"
            />
            <Reference
                Name = "System.Data"
                AssemblyName = "System.Data"
            />
            <Reference
                Name = "System.Drawing"
                AssemblyName = "System.Drawing"
            />
            <Reference
                Name = "System.Windows.Forms"
                AssemblyName = "System.Windows.Forms"
            />
            <Reference
                Name = "System.XML"
```

```
                AssemblyName = "System.Xml"
            />
        </References>
        <Imports>
            <Import Namespace = "Microsoft.VisualBasic" />
            <Import Namespace = "System" />
            <Import Namespace = "System.Collections" />
            <Import Namespace = "System.Data" />
            <Import Namespace = "System.Drawing" />
            <Import Namespace = "System.Diagnostics" />
            <Import Namespace = "System.Windows.Forms" />
        </Imports>
    </Build>
    <Files>
        <Include>
            <File
                RelPath = "AssemblyInfo.vb"
                SubType = "Code"
                BuildAction = "Compile"
            />
            <File
                RelPath = "Form1.vb"
                SubType = "Form"
                BuildAction = "Compile"
            />
            <File
                RelPath = "Form1.resx"
                DependentUpon = "Form1.vb"
                BuildAction = "EmbeddedResource"
            />
        </Include>
    </Files>
  </VisualBasic>
</VisualStudioProject>
```

The executable file that Visual Basic .NET builds, WindowsApplication1.exe, can be found in the Obj\Release (or Obj\Debug) folder. Right-click on the file, and then select Properties. You'll see the properties dialog box for the program, shown in Figure 1-16. When you learn how to deploy production code, custom icons and a description will be added to the executable. For now, you're looking at a stock, no frills, bare bones .NET executable.

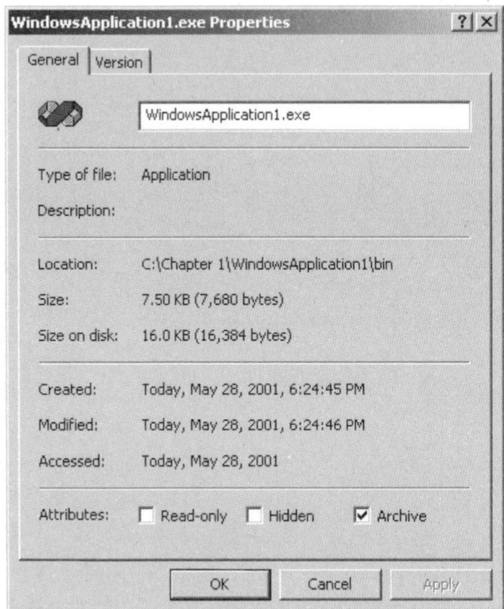

Figure 1-16 The properties dialog box for WindowsApplication1.exe.

Another Word on Assemblies

I mentioned earlier that .NET programs contain everything needed by the system to fully describe the application. Our assembly is the simplest example possible, as all the files that make up the assembly (namely WindowsApplication1.exe) are deployed in the application folder and are not shared by other applications. Our assembly can't be referenced by other assemblies outside the application directory. Also, our simple program does not undergo version checking. To uninstall our application, made up of a single-file assembly, we only need to delete the directory that contains it. Fortunately, for many software applications, an assembly with these options is all that is needed for deploying the program.

In Chapter 8, "Assemblies in Detail," I'll describe how you can create an assembly that can be shared by multiple applications. This type of assembly has a shared name and is deployed in the global assembly cache. In addition, you can determine what load-optimization setting best fits an application. But more on that later. Let's use the divide and conquer approach by taking these new concepts in pieces and building on them as we progress in .NET proficiency.

If you want to examine the assembly for WindowsApplication1.exe, you can use a utility provided with Visual Studio .NET. The IL disassembler, Ildasm.exe, allows you to peek into the intermediate language (IL) that was created by the Visual Basic .NET compiler.

> **Tip** As you work through the examples in the rest of the book, I'd encourage you to poke around with the disassembler to get a feel for how things go together. This will be extremely helpful for learning about the underpinnings of your programs.

Recall that the IL is the intermediate file (namely WindowsApplication1.exe) that is sent to the CLR and that the JIT compiler compiles on demand. Don't worry if the IL looks like Klingon at this point. The terminology will become second nature by the time you finish reading this book. The disassembly of WindowsApplication1.exe is shown in Figure 1-17.

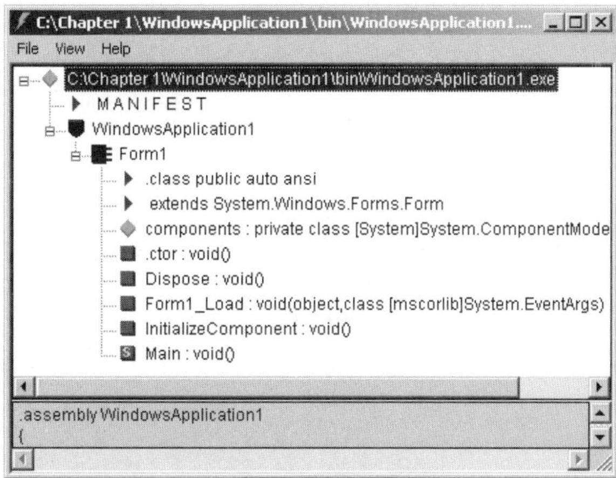

Figure 1-17 A peek inside the assembly.

At a glance you can see everything that is used in this assembly. You will soon be dreaming of these little symbols as you become more proficient with .NET development.

Symbol	Description
	Manifest of the assembly. It lists everything contained in the assembly.
	Namespace. In our simple program, the namespace is the name of our program.
	Class. We have the hidden project and *Form1* classes in our assembly.
	Static method. A method shared among objects.
	Field. A data element.
	Method. Something the object can do.
	Property. Something the object is.

Double-clicking Manifest in the assembly displays the manifest's contents. Figure 1-18 shows a small portion of the manifest of our assembly.

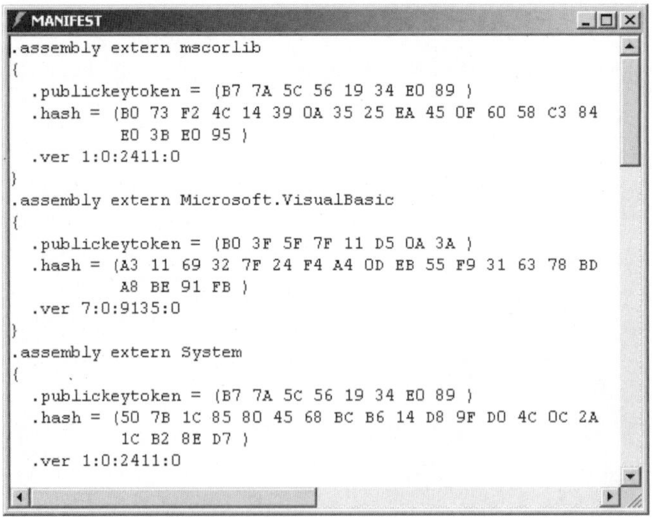

MANIFEST

```
.assembly extern mscorlib
{
  .publickeytoken = (B7 7A 5C 56 19 34 E0 89 )
  .hash = (B0 73 F2 4C 14 39 0A 35 25 EA 45 0F 60 58 C3 84
          E0 3B E0 95 )
  .ver 1:0:2411:0
}
.assembly extern Microsoft.VisualBasic
{
  .publickeytoken = (B0 3F 5F 7F 11 D5 0A 3A )
  .hash = (A3 11 69 32 7F 24 F4 A4 0D EB 55 F9 31 63 78 BD
          A8 BE 91 FB )
  .ver 7:0:9135:0
}
.assembly extern System
{
  .publickeytoken = (B7 7A 5C 56 19 34 E0 89 )
  .hash = (50 7B 1C 85 80 45 68 BC B6 14 D8 9F D0 4C 0C 2A
          1C B2 8E D7 )
  .ver 1:0:2411:0
```

Figure 1-18 Inside the manifest.

Keeping in mind that a module is a physical file on disk, take a look at the last several lines of the manifest file. Our assembly has a single module, namely WindowsApplication1.exe. Complex assemblies might have many more modules. Although this example is extremely simple, with it we have covered all of the parts that .NET uses to take source code and convert it to a working application.

A Closer Look at the Code

Forms are really classes that describe the user interface for your application. When a form is displayed, an instance of the form's class is created that can be used like any other object. You can add custom methods and properties to a form to have it do whatever it needs to. While object-oriented programming provides an array of benefits, from easy maintenance to protecting data, the real benefit is honest-to-goodness code reuse. As programs become more and more complex in order to deal with the wide variety of hardware platforms and mediums—the Internet and wireless devices, for example—the only way programmers can move ahead is to become familiar with objects. There simply is no other way.

Let's review the code for our simple application in more detail. This review will introduce object-oriented techniques and a few new keywords. I realize that these concepts might be new and possibly a bit daunting to some classic Visual Basic programmers. Just read and digest as much as you can for the remainder of the chapter. I'll amplify these concepts as we progress through the book.

You Mean I Get an Inheritance?

When discussing his discoveries, Isaac Newton once said, "If I have seen further, it is because I've stood on the shoulders of giants." The same concept applies to object-oriented programming—we reap the benefits of what was written before us. To add prebuilt functionality to your programs, you have to import the functionality into your code. Not surprisingly, doing that is a snap with Visual Basic .NET. The new *Imports* keyword makes it easy.

A module can contain any number of *Imports* statements. Think of this keyword as a free ticket to import the functionality of other .NET Framework classes into your programs. *Imports* statements must occur in a module before any references to the other classes' built-in functionality is made within the module. By importing the namespaces that define these framework classes, you can then refer to an included type—such as *Form*—without having to fully qualify the type name, as in *System.Windows.Forms.Form*.

```
Imports System.ComponentModel
Imports System.Drawing
Imports System.Windows.Forms.Form
```

With one statement, *Imports System.Windows.Forms.Form*, you specify that the client class, *Form1*, inherits the functionality of the *Form* class in the Windows Forms library. The *System.Windows.Forms* namespace contains classes for creating Windows-based applications. In this namespace, you'll find not only the *Form* class but many other controls that can be added to forms to create user interfaces.

```
Public Class Form1
    Inherits System.Windows.Forms.Form
```

As I mentioned, language independence is an important aspect of the CLR's inheritance model. Not only can you inherit functionality from the run time, but you can inherit it from classes written in any language compatible with .NET. The previous line of code states that *Form1* inherits the functionality of the *System.Windows.Forms.Form* namespace.

The *Inherits* directive specifies the class (also known as the *base class*—in this case *Windows.Forms.Form*) from which the current class inherits. The *Inherits* keyword is allowed only in class declarations.

Think about what happens when a new form is added to your project. The form is born knowing how to do all sorts of things. It has its own menu, it knows how to resize itself, respond to events, and host controls, just to name a few. Imagine if you had to write the code to perform all those behaviors. Instead, you simply inherit the functionality of a form base class and modify your form so that it suits your needs. It's pretty obvious that inheriting prebuilt functionality permits your programs not only to be smaller, but also to do more real work.

> **Note** Creating a new Windows form by inheriting from a base form is a handy way to duplicate your best efforts without going through the hassle of entirely re-creating a form every time you require one. You might have a specific look and feel for forms in your company. Simply create the model form once and inherit from it each time it's needed. However, keep in mind that in order for you to inherit from a form, the file or namespace containing that form must have already been built into an executable file or DLL. Of course, a reference to the namespace must be added to the class inheriting the form using the *Imports* keyword.

Starting Up Our *Form1* Class

A class, such as our *Form1* class, needs a constructor, a procedure that controls initialization of new objects. In previous versions of Visual Basic, the constructor was hidden from programmers, but it was there all along. Visual Basic .NET provides the *Public Sub New* constructor event. The *Sub New* method will run only once—when the class is created. Furthermore, the code in the *Sub New* method will always run before any other code in a class.

Because we have a constructor that builds the object, having a destructor to tear down the object when its usefulness is finished only seems right. In fact, a *Sub Destruct* method does exist, but you don't see it in the code. The *Destruct* method is called automatically by the system when an object is destroyed. In fact, you could not call the method explicitly even if you tried.

The .NET Framework destroys an object when the system determines that the object is no longer needed. When the object is set to *Nothing* or goes out of scope, *Sub Destruct* will be called by the system. However, unlike the *Sub New* method, you cannot determine exactly when the .NET Framework will execute the *Sub Destruct* method. You can only be sure that eventually the system will call *Sub Destruct* some time after the .NET Framework determines that the object is no longer needed. Our program will execute the *Dispose* method, which tells the CLR that the object is no longer needed. However, the object will not be released from memory until the garbage collector makes its rounds, which could be several minutes after the object is flagged for extinction. I'll cover garbage collection in more detail later on. I'll discuss what is called *deterministic finalization* and *garbage collection* (taking out used-up objects) in detail in Chapter 4.

```
Protected Overloads Overrides _
Sub Dispose(ByVal disposing As Boolean)

    If disposing Then
        If Not (components Is Nothing) Then
            components.Dispose()
        End If
    End If
    MyBase.Dispose(disposing)
End Sub
```

In previous versions of Visual Basic, you set any references to objects to *Nothing*—for example, *Set MyObject = Nothing*—and the underlying COM plumbing would free up all memory and release any resources being used. In Visual Basic .NET, you can still use the *Nothing* keyword, but the object probably won't be freed at exactly that time. *Nothing* in Visual Basic .NET serves as an indicator that an object can be freed up when the garbage collector makes its rounds.

In classic Visual Basic, you placed initialization code for a form in the *Form_Initialize* or *Form_Load* event procedures. In Visual Basic .NET, the constructor, *Sub New,* replaces both of these events. When the constructor begins executing, you can be sure that all of the controls have been sited on the form and initialized right after *InitializeComponent* is called.

In classic Visual Basic, beginners would often run into trouble trying to set a visible property (such as the text in a text box) on a control before it was completely sited and initialized on a form. For example, programmers sometimes would set a visible property of a control, such as *txtTextBox.Text = "Hello World"*, in the *Form_Load* event. Because the form was still initializing and the *txtTextBox* control was still being built, the programmer would get the extremely descriptive "Object Not Set" error. The programmer would be left with some head scratching to do because the error didn't provide a clue about what was wrong. With Visual Basic .NET, you can now safely place any initialization code directly after the call to *InitializeComponent* and be sure that it won't cause problems. Notice that the IDE adds a comment to let you know where you can initialize controls.

```
Public Sub New()
    MyBase.New()

    'This call is required by the Windows Form Designer.
    InitializeComponent()

    'Add any initialization after the
    'InitializeComponent() call
End Sub
```

As soon as the form's class constructor starts to execute, the following line actually creates the form object:

```
MyBase.New()
```

The *MyBase* keyword refers to the immediate base class and its inherited members—in this case, the events and properties of the form. It's important to note that the call to the constructor, *MyBase.New*, must be the first statement in the *New* class constructor. Of course, this order makes sense because the form would not exist until we created it with the call to *MyBase.New*.

```
Public Class Form1
```

The *MyBase.New* command is in the *Sub New* constructor of the *Form1* class, which means that the constructor of the class calls the *New* method of *MyBase* to create a new object, in this case a form. From now on you can use *MyBase* from within the class to access public members defined in the base class. *MyBase* can't be used to access private members in the base class. (I'll describe public and private members shortly.) For our simple program, we really don't need to access the base class, so we won't have to work with *MyBase* now. *MyBase* cannot be assigned to a variable, passed to procedures, or used in *Is* comparisons. Why? *MyBase* is not a real object; it just acts like one. I'll discuss this type of behavior in detail in Chapter 2, when I describe Visual Basic .NET object-oriented programming.

> **Note** When I saw the keyword *MyBase*, I started scratching my head. Who named that? Why wasn't it some geek-sounding term like *ObjectBase*? That would make me feel more technical. But *MyBase*? All I could figure out is that Microsoft has a propensity to name everything with the prefix *My*. Take a look at Windows. Right there is My Computer, My Documents, My Network Places, My Files, and so on. I suppose the theme was carried through to My Visual Basic .NET.

Next we have some code that looks like it gets rid of the object but includes the *Overrides* modifier.

```
Protected Overloads Overrides _
Sub Dispose(ByVal disposing As Boolean)
```

Remember that derived classes inherit the methods defined in their base class. *Form1* inherited all of the behavior (resizing, responding to clicks, a menu) from the base form class. Usually, most of the standard methods in the base class will be fine for your purposes. Using the *Overrides* keyword in a derived class lets you define a new implementation of an inherited method. In other words, overriding permits you to modify the inherited behavior of the base class. In this case, when the *Dispose* method is called, it alerts the system garbage collector that the object is fair game to be eliminated.

```
Protected Overloads Overrides _
Sub Dispose(ByVal disposing As Boolean)

    If disposing Then
        If Not (components Is Nothing) Then
            components.Dispose()
        End If
    End If
    MyBase.Dispose(disposing)
End Sub
```

The IDE included the overridden *Dispose* method so that we could dispose of additional items instead of just the default form. The *Dispose* method is called on *MyBase,* and the *Dispose* method is also called on the *components* object. In our simple program, the *Dispose* method is called (if necessary) when the form is dismissed. Essentially, when this method is called, the form frees all system resources it may have allocated, releases references to any other objects, and renders itself unusable. It's now officially an ex-form.

Warning! Don't Fiddle with the Designer's Code

Yes, this sounds ominous, but it's really self-defense for the Windows Form designer to ensure that it can read what it wrote without some pesky programmer mucking things up. This area should be *hands off* for programmers. However, if you have ever used any of the wizards in classic Visual Basic, you have already seen how they put a hands off notice on code they write and will need to read again. This code gets parsed by the wizard and must be left in the way it was written.

Earlier I described the region of code that was added automatically for the Windows Form designer. You should not fiddle with this code because anything you need to change can be accessed from the Properties window. The IDE will write your changes in this region itself.

```
'Required by the Windows Form Designer
Private components As System.ComponentModel.Container

    'NOTE: The following procedure is required by the
    ' Windows Form Designer.
    'It can be modified using the Windows Form Designer.
    'Do not modify it using the code editor.
    <System.Diagnostics.DebuggerStepThrough()> _
    Private Sub InitializeComponent()
        '
        'Form1
        '
        Me.AutoScaleBaseSize = New System.Drawing.Size(5, 13)
        Me.ClientSize = New System.Drawing.Size(292, 266)
        Me.Name = "Form1"
        Me.StartPosition = _
            System.Windows.Forms.FormStartPosition.CenterParent
        Me.Text = "Visual Basic .NET - Our First Form"

    End Sub
```

The first line of code creates the variable *components* and declares it to be of type *System.ComponentModel.Container*. The *components* object will store all of the changes that you make to the form, such as the title change, and permits the changes to persist. The *InitializeComponent* procedure that follows contains the code you should not modify with the code editor.

In a real program, you would change various properties of the form, such as the text (the caption), size, its position on the screen, color, and so forth. Anything you need to modify in the *InitializeComponent* subroutine can be changed directly in the Properties window for the form. In fact, when you change a property such as the *Text* or *Backcolor* property in the Property window, you'll notice that the form in design mode does not change until you either hit Enter or move off the text entry box. The designer wants to be sure that you've finished typing. When it is sure you've finished, it revisits this segment of code and updates it appropriately.

Of course, you want your form to remember these changes when you run it again. In classic Visual Basic, these changes were stored in the form's .frm file, which was plain ASCII. You could open the form's .frm file with Notepad and see all of these settings. When the form was run, the simple text .frm file was read and the form was created. Each form was stored in a separate .frm file. If images or other non-ASCII data had to be stored on the form, this data was saved in a .frx file with the same name as the form. Various offsets were stored in the .frm file to let the form know where to place the binary data stored in the .frx files. So this same information was always there, it was just hidden from us. Instead of hiding these properties, Visual Basic .NET uses the *Me* keyword to expose the properties directly in your code.

```
'NOTE: The following procedure is required by the
' Windows Form Designer.
'It can be modified using the Windows Form Designer.
'Do not modify it using the code editor.
<System.Diagnostics.DebuggerStepThrough()> _
Private Sub InitializeComponent()
    '
    'Form1
    '
    Me.AutoScaleBaseSize = New System.Drawing.Size(5, 13)
    Me.ClientSize = New System.Drawing.Size(292, 266)
    Me.Name = "Form1"
    Me.StartPosition = _
        System.Windows.Forms.FormStartPosition.CenterParent
    Me.Text = "Visual Basic .NET - Our First Form"

End Sub
```

If you are new to object-oriented programming, the *Me* keyword might look a bit weird. Actually, the keyword *Me* represents a read-only variable referring to the current object. In other words, *Me* refers to the *current instance* of an object—the one in which your code is currently running. Use the *Me* keyword to refer to this current instance. All procedures associated with this particular instance of an object have access to the object referred to as *Me*. Using *Me* is particularly useful for passing information about the current instance to a procedure in another module. If you come from C++, you use the *this* pointer to accomplish the same thing.

The Big Event

Remember that an event is an action to which you can respond. You want to "handle" the event in your code. Event-driven applications execute code in response to an event. Each form and control exposes a predefined set of events that you can program against. If one of these events occurs and the associated event handler contains code, that code is invoked. The types of events *raised* by an object vary, but many types are common to most controls. For example, every form has a *Load* event handler that is executed when the form loads. The Forms Designer added the *Load* event handler for our form. As with any event, we can choose to handle it or not.

```
Private Sub Form1_Load(ByVal sender As System.Object, _
    ByVal e As System.EventArgs) Handles MyBase.Load

End Sub
```

Event handlers were upgraded in Visual Basic .NET. Now we can determine the sender of the event and receive data that is passed in via the *System.EventArgs* parameter. For example, we might interrogate the sender parameter and find that an event was fired by a mouse click. Then, by looking at *EventArgs*, we can retrieve additional information such as the X and Y position of the mouse when it was clicked. We will examine events in detail in later chapters. But as you can see, to our object an event handler is just another subroutine.

Nothing but .NET

Well, that was intense. Let's review what we learned in this chapter. First, from our stroll down memory lane, you now know the business and technological reasons why .NET is here to stay. You also were introduced to the components of the .NET technology. I covered key terms such as the *assembly*, *metadata*, *Microsoft Intermediate Language*, *just-in-time compiler*, and *common language runtime*. You saw how to write a simple Visual Basic .NET program and examined the code and files that were created. We also checked out the IL disassembler and even peeked into the assembly manifest. And finally, we looked from on high at the pieces of our first Visual Basic .NET program and examined what was happening and why. And through all of that, we didn't write a single line of code!

Before pressing on, I'd suggest spending a few minutes reviewing the diagrams in this chapter. When you feel comfortable with the structure of the .NET Framework and how Visual Basic .NET fits into the picture, you'll be ready to start learning more about object-oriented programming in Chapter 2.

2

Object-Oriented Programming in Visual Basic .NET

As you read in Chapter 1, "Visual Basic .NET from the Ground Up," you really can't do anything in Visual Basic .NET without coming face to face with objects. When you create a standard form in a new project, you have access to the code for the form's class. While this code was present in classic Visual Basic, it was hidden from a programmer's view. Now it is presented to you in the integrated development environment (IDE). A solid understanding of object-oriented programming is a prerequisite for getting the most from Visual Basic .NET. If you are new to object-oriented programming (sometimes abbreviated OOP) or up till now have tried to avoid using it directly, this chapter will make you a believer, and you'll see that it's pretty straightforward, which wasn't the case at first for me.

An Object Lesson

When I started to learn object-oriented programming about 10 years ago, I found its concepts somewhat difficult. I read every book I could get my hands on and thought about all that I'd read, but it still didn't make sense. I performed due diligence and put in the time, but for some reason OOP didn't click. "What's this business about creating a class and calling methods? After all, didn't I do the same thing with C math libraries for years?"

Then one day I had a revelation! All at once I realized how simple the concepts of object-oriented programming really are, and I became a believer. I spent time reflecting on why I took so long to understand a concept that turned out to be so simple and realized that the reason was twofold. First, the authors of the books I read seemed to obfuscate OOP by using terms such as overloading, encapsulation, inheritance, and polymorphism all over the place before they were clearly defined (at least for me). While I might have muddled my way through this terminological maze, the knockout punch was the examples the authors provided, which were contrived and never about anything that could be used by a programmer to solve real problems. Although I tried to match alien concepts with contrived and overly difficult examples (again, at least to me), OOP didn't sink in. I had pictures of cookie cutters, stars, and rectangles dancing in my head. These images were the hands-down favorites of every author discussing object-oriented programming. To me, they hadn't made any sense.

To save you the time I spent scratching my head and thinking about objects until my brain hurt, I'll use prefabricated objects such as a Windows form and a few control objects to illustrate object-oriented concepts. By working with something that you already use in your programming, the jump to thinking about objects is much, much easier. Over time, I've found this approach to be the clearest way to illustrate the principles of OOP.

I'll cover objects and classes, properties, methods, inheritance, overloading, polymorphism, and sharing, all within the context of what you know. In Chapter 3, "Writing Your First Class" when you start to write your own classes, you'll fully understand the concepts and you'll be able to concentrate on the code.

Starting Out with Objects

Let's start out by describing our terms. Many beginners have a difficult time sorting out the difference between a class and an object. I hear them using the terms interchangeably. As I wrote in Chapter 1, a class contains the instructions for how to construct an object in the computer's memory. Here's an analogy.

A Class Is Really Only a Blueprint

Think of a class as a blueprint for building a house. A blueprint isn't a house; it's a sheaf of papers with drawings and dimensions that tell a contractor how to build a house. When the contractor follows the blueprints and builds the house, you have an object. An object is a physical manifestation of a class, just like a house is a physical manifestation of a blueprint.

A blueprint might indicate the location for each window and the type of window to use. A class can include the types of controls and their positions on a form, as well as various data types to use. A house is built with the appropriate windows in the right location. A form object is created with the controls displayed as the form class directed. Of course, contractors use the same blueprints to build several houses, as shown in Figure 2-1. Likewise, you can create several objects from the same class. Because the objects follow the same class blueprint, each of the objects will look and function in the same way.

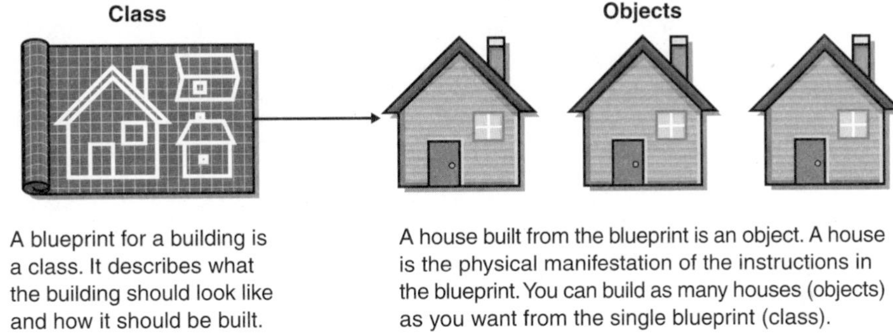

A blueprint for a building is a class. It describes what the building should look like and how it should be built.

A house built from the blueprint is an object. A house is the physical manifestation of the instructions in the blueprint. You can build as many houses (objects) as you want from the single blueprint (class).

Figure 2-1 A blueprint is like a class; houses built from the blueprints are like objects.

Let's Talk Objects

The best way to introduce a few of the key object-oriented concepts is with an example. Start up Visual Studio .NET and follow these steps:

1. Create a new Windows Application project. You'll have a blank form.
2. Drag a button control from the tool palette to the form. If you've worked with Visual Basic 6, this is old hat to you. Keep the default names of the form and the button control.

> **Note** There are three ways to add a control to a form. You can double-click the control, you can click once on the control and then once on the form, or you can click the control and then drag it to the form.

3. Double-click the button control. Double-clicking the control automatically adds the *Click* event handler to the form's class.
4. Click the Form1.vb tab and modify the *Text* property of both the button and the form objects. For the form, change the *Text* property to "Mirror Image". For the button, change the value to "&Clone Me!" You can tell the form and the button are both objects because you can set their properties and see that both have inherited the know-how to do things such as resize themselves.

Note The ampersand (&) used in the button's *Text* property automatically provides an *accelerator* key combination for power users. Visual Basic .NET adds an underscore to the character that immediately follows the ampersand when the text is displayed on the control. A user can press Alt plus the accelerator key to simulate clicking the button.

5. Size the form and button so that they look something like what's shown in Figure 2-2.

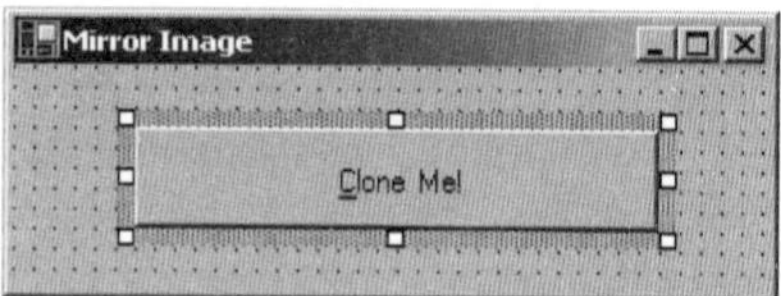

Figure 2-2 Your form should look like this.

Our Form as an Object

All objects are created as identical copies of their class; they are mirror images. Your form is a perfect example of an object. Once you instantiate an object from your class, however, the object is separate from any other object you instantiate from the class. After your form is created in your project, you can resize it in the Designer, for example. The form itself is responsible for handling the implementation of how it is resized and redrawn. It is born knowing how to do that and everything else a form does, such as displaying its own default menu and dismissing itself when you click its Close button.

A key point you should understand about objects is that they are a combination of data and code. The fundamental advantage of OOP is that the data and the operations that manipulate the data are both contained in the object. An object can be treated as a self-contained unit.

Objects are the building blocks of an object-oriented program, and an object-oriented program is essentially a collection of objects. In the simple program we just created, we have a button object on a form object. When the form appears, it has a color, size, and position on the screen. These characteristics are among what are called its *properties*. Properties define the state of an object.

The form also knows how to minimize and maximize itself and how to resize itself when you drag its edges with a mouse. In other words, the form has a set of built-in behaviors, and these behaviors are implemented by what are called *methods*. Methods tell an object how to do things.

Seeing Properties and Methods in the IDE

The IntelliSense feature in the IDE puts everything the form is or can do at your fingertips. For example, when you enter "Form1" in the code editor, Visual Basic .NET knows that this refers to an object because you've defined *Form1* as such—an object that inherits from the *Windows.Forms.Form* class. The IDE displays each legitimate property or method when you enter a dot (.) after *Form1*. The dot, or *scope resolution modifier*, separates the object from its methods or properties. The general form is *Object.Method* or *Object.Property*. Properties are marked by an icon of a hand holding a card, while methods are indicated by purple flying bricks.

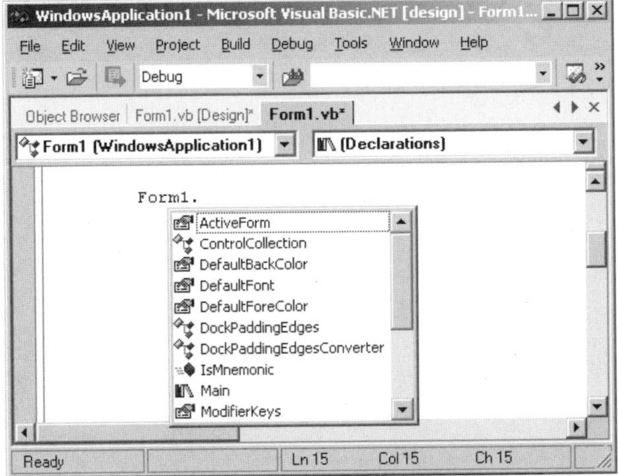

Notice that *Form1* was declared with an uppercase "F," but you could have entered *form1* with a lowercase "f." Unlike C, C++, or C#, Visual Basic is not case sensitive, but the IDE will automatically correct your typing and make the spelling consistent.

You could create five forms, each of a different size and with different captions, so that each has its own *Size* and *Text* properties set to a different value. Each object contains its own properties. Each is a self-contained black box of functionality that contains data (its size and color) and code for how it does things (resizing or redrawing itself, for example).

If you've programmed before in classic Visual Basic, these concepts might be familiar. For example, any time you placed a list box control on a form and changed its name or size, you were modifying its properties. Whenever you added an item to the list box with *AddItem*, you were calling one of the list box's methods.

So, just to summarize, the key elements of an object are

- **Properties.** A characteristic of a form (or other object), such as its size, color, and position or the font used for displaying text. Properties contain values that are unique to each object. Most visual controls, such as our form, expose properties to define their appearance.
- **Methods.** Something an object knows how to do. A form object, for example, can resize itself, display a menu, or hide itself.

Reading, Writing, Invoking

You communicate with an object programmatically by reading and writing its properties and invoking its methods. If you wanted to read the current *Height* property of a form and display it in a message box, you would write the following line in the *Load* event of the form:

```
Private Sub Form1_Load(ByVal sender As System.Object,
    ByVal e As System.EventArgs) Handles MyBase.Load
    MessageBox.Show("Form1's height is " & _
        Me.Height, Me.Text)
End Sub
```

> **Note** The keyword *Me,* which we first saw in Chapter 1, might look strange to those of you new to OOP. *Me* is the equivalent of the *this* pointer in C++. *Me* is used to reference the current object, which happens to be a form. The *Me* keyword is one of the first elements you will have to become familiar with in Visual Basic .NET.

The first call in this code fragment is to the *Show* method of the *MessageBox* class, new to Visual Basic .NET. The *Show* method knows how to display a message box. The first parameter is what will be displayed as the message. Because we want to display the height of the form, we read its *Height* property as the second parameter of the *Show* method. The code *Me.Height* reads the form's *Height* property. The final parameter of the *Show* method is the title to show in the message box's caption. The code *Me.Text* reads the form's *Text* property. Now when you run the program, the dialog box shown in Figure 2-3 appears.

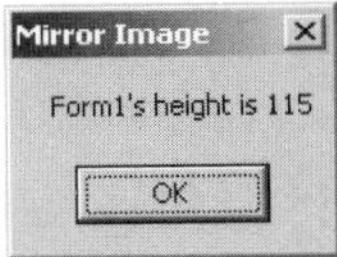

Figure 2-3 This message box displays the form's height.

If you wanted to change the form's *Height* property—write to it instead of read it—you simply assign a new value to the property. To change the form's height from 115 pixels to 203 pixels when the user clicks the button, you would write this code:

```
Protected Sub Button1_Click(ByVal sender As Object, _
    ByVal e As System.EventArgs)

    Me.Height = 203
    MessageBox.Show("Form1's height is " & _
        Me.Height, Me.Text)
End Sub
```

When the user clicks the button, the first line of code assigns the value 203 to the form's *Height* property, invoking the form's *Size* method. The form immediately adjusts to the new size. The message box displays the height, confirming that the form resized itself, as shown in Figure 2-4. All you did was assign a new property value; the form object already knew how to resize itself through its *Size* method.

Figure 2-4 The resized form.

The form object automatically knows whether you are reading or writing a value by the position of the object reference relative to the equal sign (=). To assign a value to a property, you use code like the following:

```
Me.Height = 203
```

With the object reference on the left side of the equal sign, the object knows you are assigning a value to the property.

To read the value of a property, you use code like the following:

```
MyVariable = Me.Height
```

Here the object reference is on the right side of the equal sign, which means you're reading the property's value. As I stressed before, you don't know how the property is stored inside the object. It might be stored in Portuguese, pig Latin, or any language at all. All you know is that you can read an integer from the property or write an integer to set the property. How the object performs these operations is its business. An object can seem very much like the Wizard of Oz when he says, "Pay no attention to the man behind the curtain."

This kind of implementation is one of the productive aspects of working with objects. To use an object you simply read or write its properties and call the methods that it exposes. The object is responsible for doing the real work. An object might be prepackaged like a form, or it might be one you write yourself.

Inheritance

As you can see, a form is a pretty smart object. It has all sorts of properties and methods that you can use immediately because they are part of the *base class* (also known as the *parent class*) that the form object inherits from. As I've said, inheritance is one of the fundamental tenets of object-oriented programming. Through inheritance, you can derive classes from other classes that have already been written. In our example, the base class is *System.Windows.Forms.Form*.

```
Public Class Form1
    Inherits System.Windows.Forms.Form
```

When a class inherits from a base class, it inherits the properties and methods of that class. Properties and methods are often referred to as the *members* of a class. You can then use or add to these members in your own class in whatever way you need.

The Buffed Up Message Box

The message box we're using in this example is a tried and true friend of the Visual Basic programmer, but a few changes have been made to the message box that classic Visual Basic programmers should note. In Visual Basic 6, the *MsgBox* function supported optional arguments to specify a Help topic that would be displayed when the user pressed F1. Because the underlying mechanism for displaying Help topics has changed significantly in Visual Basic .NET, the *HelpFile* and *Context* arguments have been eliminated.

The older *MsgBox* syntax is still available in Visual Basic .NET. The *Microsoft.VisualBasic.Interaction* class exposes a *MsgBox* method that approximates the functionality of the Visual Basic 6 *MsgBox* function. However, I suggest you move to the new *MessageBox* class. It's entirely possible that in later versions of Visual Basic .NET, legacy Visual Basic syntax will be eliminated. By using the *Show* method of the *MessageBox* class, *System.Windows.Forms.MessageBox* provides fairly extensive support for informing and instructing the user.

Sometimes a user must dismiss a message box before continuing. Forms and dialog boxes can be displayed as either *modal* or *modeless* (the default). A modal form or dialog box must be closed (hidden or unloaded) before you can continue working with the application. Most forms, however, are displayed as modeless forms, which means that you can switch from one form to another by simply clicking the form you want to be active. Dialog boxes or message boxes that display important messages should always be modal. The user should always be required to close the dialog box or respond to its message before proceeding.

At times you might want to show a form modally, such as a form you've customized for entering a password or logging in. You want the user to address this form before moving on. Simply call the form's *ShowDialog* method to accomplish this.

```
mydialog = New Dialog1()
mydialog.ShowDialog()
```

Understanding Namespaces

A large part of the power of Visual Basic .NET comes from the base classes supplied by the Microsoft .NET Framework. Microsoft has provided a vast array of ready-built classes for your use. The .NET Framework includes a variety of base classes that encapsulate data structures, perform I/O, give you access to information about a loaded class, and provide ways for you to perform rich GUI generation and data access and develop server controls. These built-in types are designed to be the foundation on which all .NET applications, components, and controls are built.

These base classes are simple to use, and you can easily derive from them to include their functionality in your own specialized classes. To bring some order to this power, the .NET base classes are grouped into what are called *namespaces*. As I mentioned earlier, our form is an instance of the *System.Windows.Forms.Form* class. In other words, the form lives in the .NET Framework namespace dedicated to Windows client user interface programming.

Think of a namespace as a container for related classes in the same way that a folder on your hard drive contains related files. In a .NET program you'll make use of many of the base classes, and any significant Visual Basic .NET program that you develop will have many more of your own namespaces. (I'll describe how to create your own namespaces in Chapter 3.) Having a firm understanding of the concept of namespaces is required before you do just about anything in Visual Basic .NET.

Because we need a way to identify and find the built-in items required for a program, the .NET Framework types are named using a dot-syntax naming scheme that connotes a naming hierarchy. You can see this syntax in the familiar class *System.Windows.Forms.Form*.

```
Public Class Form1
    Inherits System.Windows.Forms.Form
```

This syntax tells us that the *Form* class is related to other classes that use the *System.Windows.Forms* namespace. These classes, representing objects such as graphical controls, are all part of the namespace. The part of the name up to the last dot (*System.Windows.Forms*) is referred to as the *namespace* name, and the last part (*Form*) as the *class* name. These naming patterns group related classes into namespaces and are used to build and document class libraries. This naming syntax has no effect on a class's visibility, how you access its members, how your classes inherit from the class, or how the linker binds your code.

As you've seen, the root namespace for the types in the .NET Framework is the *System* namespace. This namespace includes classes that represent the base data types used by all applications. These include *Object* (the root of the inheritance hierarchy), *Byte, Char, Array, Int32, String,* and so on. I'll review Visual Basic .NET data types in more detail in Chapter 4, "Visual Basic Data Types and Features."

Along with the base data types, the *System* namespace itself includes almost 100 classes. These classes range from those for handling exceptions (errors) and events to those dealing with core run-time concepts such as application domains and the automatic memory manager. Since it's impossible to cover everything about .NET in a single book, my goal is for you to work with these built-in classes enough that you'll be able to find what you need on your own.

In addition to the base data types touched on above, the *System* namespace contains 24 second-level namespaces. Table 2-1 lists the categories of functionality that are built in and the namespaces in each category.

Table 2-1 Second-Level Namespaces in the *System* Namespace

Category	Namespace
Data	*System.Data*
	System.Xml
	System.Xml.Serialization
Component model	*System.CodeDom*
	System.ComponentModel
Configuration	*System.Configuration*
Framework services	*System.Diagnostics*
	System.DirectoryServices
	System.Management
	System.ServiceProcess
	System.Messaging
	System.Timers
Globalization	*System.Globalization*
	System.Resources
Network programming	*System.NET*
Programming basics	*System.Collections*
	System.IO
	System.Text
	System.Text.RegularExpressions
	System.Threading

(continued)

Table 2-1 Second-Level Namespaces in the *System* Namespace *(continued)*

Category	Namespace
Reflection	*System.Reflection*
Rich, client-side GUI	*System.Drawing*
	System.Windows.Forms
Run-time infrastructure services	*System.Runtime.CompilerServices*
	System.Runtime.InteropServices
	System.Runtime.Remoting
	System.Runtime.Serialization
Security services	*System.Security*
Web services	*System.Web*
	System.Web.Services

Revisiting the Solution Explorer

Open the Solution Explorer by selecting View | Solution Explorer in the IDE. Click the References entry to expand it, and you'll see the items shown in the following illustration. The list contains the default references for a project. Even though namespaces live in assemblies (i.e., files), the Solution Explorer displays the namespaces, and it's more helpful to us to know the namespace than it is to know the particular assembly.

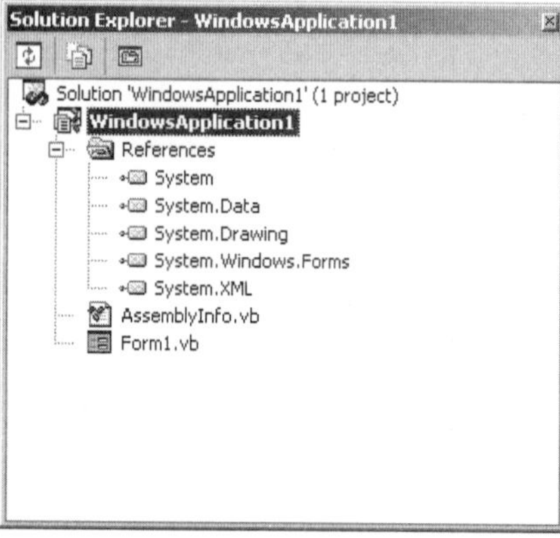

Revisiting the Solution Explorer *(continued)*

Of course, if you use any of the base classes that are defined in libraries, you need to ensure that the Visual Basic .NET compiler knows where to look for them—you need to understand how the compiler finds the namespaces you import. In more sophisticated projects later in the book, you'll import namespaces that are not among the defaults. You'll have to add references to these namespaces so that the compiler can probe the assemblies and find them. To add a reference, right-click References in the Solution Explorer and select Add Reference to open the Add Reference dialog box, shown here.

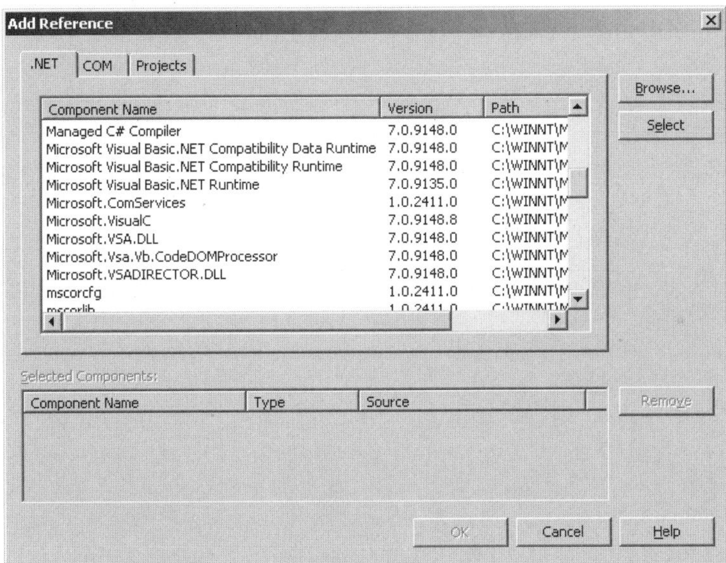

The namespaces are listed in the Component Name column. You can also see the version and the path that provides the fully qualified reference to the assembly file where the namespace items are housed. Don't select anything now. This glimpse is just to round out our exploration of the IDE for a project.

Inheriting from *System.Windows.Forms.Form*: Forms and Controls

The *Windows.Forms* namespace contains more than 300 entries, so it has quite a bit of functionality already built for you. This functionality enables a Visual Basic .NET programmer to be more productive than ever.

The *Form* class is the template used to create the form object at run time. When a form is displayed, an instance of the *System.Windows.Forms* class is created and can then be used like any other object. Class inheritance occurred in classic Visual Basic, except that it was hidden from you.

An important first step in developing any Windows Forms application is to implement the user interface. Because a .NET Windows program is typically a rich client application, the user interface is made up entirely of various Windows Forms controls. The *Forms* class as well as user interface controls classes such as *Button* and *TextBox* also live in the *System.Windows.Forms* namespace. Because forms and controls inherit properties and methods, using form and control objects permits an application to handle the low-level details; for example, when a user clicks a button.

Essentially, the Windows Forms framework encapsulates (hides the details of) native Win32 application programming interfaces (APIs). The framework then exposes secure, managed classes to the programmer for creating Win32 client-side applications. The Windows Forms framework also provides many controls—buttons, check boxes, drop-down lists, combo boxes, data grid, and other graphical and nongraphical gizmos—that encapsulate all sorts of functionality.

Like any other object, a control is a black box of functionality. For example, when you draw a button on a form, the button is born knowing how to respond to events such as a mouse click, a mouse hover, or even moves of the mouse wheel. The implementation of how the control intercepts operating system messages and converts them to events is hidden from you. You simply respond to any of the events that are important to you. You reuse OPC (other people's code).

A cool thing about the Visual Basic .NET IDE is that when you drop a control from the toolbox onto the surface of a form, all the boilerplate code that a programmer needs to use the control is automatically generated for you by the Visual Studio .NET Windows Forms Designer. This way, you can focus on writing the code that is specific to your application.

Each form created from the *Forms* class has the same initial property values for each instance. Table 2-2 lists the default values.

Table 2-2 Default Values for *Form* Class Properties

Property	Value
BorderStyle	*FormBorderStyle.Sizable*
ControlBox	True
MaximizeBox	True
MinimizeBox	True
StartPosition	*FormStartPosition.WindowsDefaultLocation*
WinForms.Form.ShowInTaskBar	True
WindowsState	*Form.WindowsState.Normal*
AutoScale	True

Using the form's Properties box, you can change these properties or any others that are displayed. The Designer takes care of updating the form's class code to reflect the changes. As you saw earlier in the chapter, you can also modify the form's properties programmatically during run time.

A Word About Visual Basic .NET Controls

Keep in mind that a control such as a button can't exist in a vacuum. It must be hosted by a form. The control is sited on the form and initialized. You can see in the previous code examples that the button control is declared and some of its properties are set within the form's class. A form object and its control objects form a symbiotic relationship. Later in the book, you'll create your own Visual Basic .NET controls that can be used in your project or any other .NET project written in any .NET language. However, you can see from the toolbox, shown in Figure 2-5, that enough built-in (intrinsic) controls come with Visual Basic .NET to keep us happy for a while.

> **Tip** Select View | Toolbox from the IDE main menu and dock the toolbox on the left side of the IDE, if necessary. Right-click the caption bar and select Auto Hide. This command keeps the toolbox hidden on the left side of the IDE. When you need a tool, simply move the mouse over the box that says Toolbox and it will slide out. This setting keeps the toolbox handy, and you don't always have to explicitly request it from the View menu of the IDE.

Figure 2-5 The Visual Basic .NET toolbox.

Note As I touched on in Chapter 1, COM is no longer the preferred method of binary compatibility, but you can import COM and ActiveX controls created in classic Visual Basic to a .NET form. However, a Visual Basic .NET form can only host the new Windows Forms controls, and an ActiveX control can be hosted only in an ActiveX control container, such as a classic Visual Basic form. The Windows Forms ActiveX Control Importer (Aximp.exe) program can help you. It can convert the type definitions found inside a COM type library of an ActiveX control into a Windows Forms control. Aximp.exe generates a "wrapper" control, derived from *System.Windows.Forms.RichControl*. On the outside the control looks like a .NET control, while on the inside it's still an ActiveX control. If you have a bit of time, energy, and money invested in COM controls, you can still leverage them in Visual Basic .NET.

To add a reference to a COM control, click the COM tab in the Solution Explorer. The items on the tab are displayed after a few moments, as the registry is searched for all COM items. You can then select the item or items you want and add the reference to your project. If at all possible, however, try to refrain from adding non-.NET components. They are considered unmanaged code because the common language runtime can't handle security or memory management for them. However, you have the option to include them if you need to.

A control object doesn't exist until you actually draw it on a form. When you drop a control from the toolbox onto a form, you are creating an instance of the control class. That particular instance of the control class is the control object you refer to in your application, *Button1* in our example. Visual Basic .NET can host only the controls found on the toolbox palette in the IDE. The controls in Visual Basic .NET have been rewritten from the ground up.

Check Out the Code

If you added the code shown earlier that resizes the form and the message box, please delete it now, resize the form to its original size, and then open the code window. It's time to take a closer look at the code generated for us by the Designer.

Double-click the form to bring up the code editor. Much of the code you see will be familiar from Chapter 1. However, take time to let the structure sink in.

Note that the code is sandwiched between the *Public Class Form1* and *End Class* statements. All the code between these statements defines our class. The *Form1* class has its constructor, *Sub New*, so it knows how to create itself. *Sub Dispose* tells our class how to tear itself down, and *Sub InitializeComponent* is used by the development environment to persist the property values you set in the Windows Forms Designer. So, when you set a button's *Size* and *Text* properties, these values will persist with the form when you quit the project and will be the current values when you start it up again. Our class contains the mechanisms to perform these operations internally, hidden from the prying eyes of the outside world. The subroutine also sets several properties.

```
Public Class Form1
    Inherits System.Windows.Forms.Form

#Region " Windows Form Designer generated code "

    Public Sub New()
        MyBase.New()

        'This call is required by the Windows Form Designer
        InitializeComponent()

        'Add any initialization after the
        ' InitializeComponent() call
```

(continued)

```
    End Sub

    'Form overrides dispose to clean up the component list
    Protected Overloads Overrides _
    Sub Dispose(ByVal disposing As Boolean)

        If disposing Then
            If Not (components Is Nothing) Then
                components.Dispose()
            End If
        End If
        MyBase.Dispose(disposing)
    End Sub
    Friend WithEvents Button1 As System.Windows.Forms.Button

    'Required by the Windows Form Designer
    Private components As System.ComponentModel.Container

    'NOTE: The following procedure is required by the
    ' Windows Form Designer.
    'It can be modified using the Windows Form Designer.
    'Do not modify it using the code editor.
    <System.Diagnostics.DebuggerStepThrough()> _
    Private Sub InitializeComponent()
        Me.Button1 = New System.Windows.Forms.Button()
        Me.SuspendLayout()
        '
        'Button1
        '
        Me.Button1.Location = New System.Drawing.Point(48, 24)
        Me.Button1.Name = "Button1"
        Me.Button1.Size = New System.Drawing.Size(184, 48)
        Me.Button1.TabIndex = 0
        Me.Button1.Text = "&Clone Me!"
        '
        'Form1
        '
        Me.AutoScaleBaseSize = New System.Drawing.Size(5, 13)
        Me.ClientSize = New System.Drawing.Size(292, 94)
        Me.Controls.AddRange(New _
            System.Windows.Forms.Control() {Me.Button1})
        Me.Name = "Form1"
        Me.Text = "Mirror Image"
        Me.ResumeLayout(False)

    End Sub

#End Region
```

```
    Private Sub Button1_Click(ByVal sender As System.Object, _
        ByVal e As System.EventArgs) Handles Button1.Click

    End Sub

    Private Sub Form1_Load(ByVal sender As System.Object, _
        ByVal e As System.EventArgs) Handles MyBase.Load

        MessageBox.Show("Form1's height is " & _
            Me.Height, Me.Text)
    End Sub
End Class
```

The Code Added for the Button

Take a few moments and review the new code. The first item automatically declared for us is a button named *Button1*.

```
Friend WithEvents Button1 As System.Windows.Forms.Button
```

The *Button1* object variable will become an instance of the inherited class *System.Windows.Forms.Button*. When you need to refer to the button object, *Button1* is the name you will use.

The keyword *Friend* is the *access modifier*. I'll describe access modifiers in more detail later in the chapter. You use various modifiers to manage access to the methods and properties of the objects in your programs. The *Friend* access modifier makes an element visible to other objects in your component, but not to external objects.

The second keyword, *WithEvents*, specifies that *Button1* is an object variable that can respond to events such as the *Click* event. Using *WithEvents* means that your program can include event handler code that responds to events that the button knows about. If you developed your own ActiveX controls or objects in classic Visual Basic, you're no stranger to the *WithEvents* keyword. It's important to note that the *New* keyword can't be used to declare object variables that use *WithEvents*.

To see how smart a button really is, select *Button1* in the top left drop-down box in the code editor, which displays all of the objects in the current form. Next click the right drop-down box to display all the events the button knows how to respond to, as shown in Figure 2-6. If you want to have your control respond to any of the built-in events, simply select the event and the IDE will write the event template (or skeleton) for you. It's then up to you to place code in the event procedure to instruct the button how to react when that event occurs.

Locating a Button and a Form

When you move a button control on a form, behind the scenes the IDE keeps track of where you place it. The *Location* property tells the form where the upper right corner of the button is placed, and the *Size* property defines how big the button will be.

```
Me.Button1.Location = New System.Drawing.Point(48, 24)
Me.Button1.Name = "Button1"
Me.Button1.Size = New System.Drawing.Size(184, 48)
Me.Button1.TabIndex = 0
Me.Button1.Text = "&Clone Me!"
```

The point on the form for the upper left corner of the button, the *x* and *y* coordinates of (48, 24), is measured in pixels. Of course, your mileage may vary; in your project these numbers might be different depending on where your button is located on your form.

For every visual component, screen size and resolution can vary depending on your users' systems. Because some operating systems permit you to have multiple monitors attached to a PC, another user's screen or screens might have trouble recognizing the boundaries of the display area, and this confusion can cause your form's location to change unpredictably for the user, in spite of the *Location* property setting. To manage this situation, the default setting for the *StartPosition* property for a form is "WindowsDefaultLocation". This setting tells the operating system of the user to compute the best location for the form at startup based on the current hardware. Of course, you could set the *StartPosition* property to "Center". If you needed the form to be displayed elsewhere, you could modify its location programmatically just after it's displayed.

If you think that your users will have all sorts of Windows configurations, you can use the form's *DesktopLocation* property to set the location of your form. This property sets the location relative to the taskbar. You might use this property if the user's taskbar has been docked to the top or to the left of the user's screen. Although not very many people do this, docking the taskbar in this way covers the desktop coordinates (0,0) with the toolbar. So if you set your form to appear with a *DesktopLocation* of (0, 0), it always appears in the upper left corner of the primary monitor. This property will compensate for the taskbar if it is docked at the top. While the *DesktopLocation* property is set like any other property, it does not show up in the properties box. You can set it only in code. You might write something like the following:

```
Me.DesktopLocation = new Point (100,100)
```

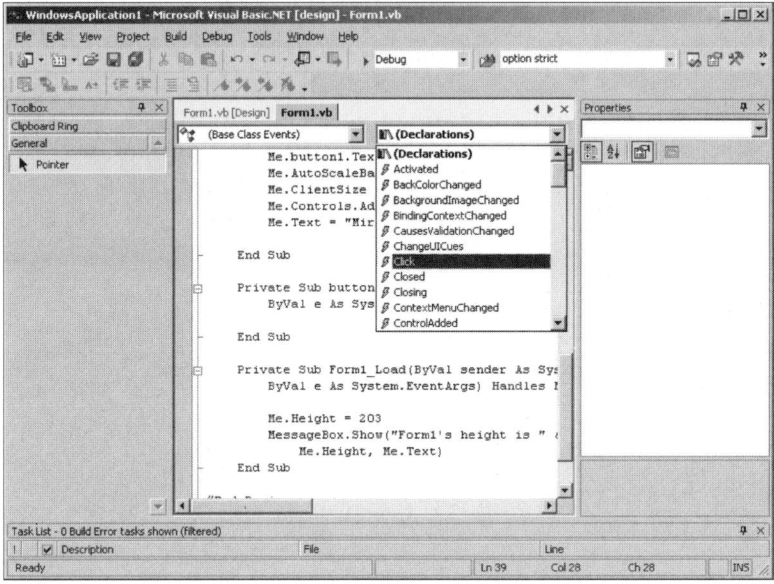

Figure 2-6 The list of button events as seen from the IDE.

Enough Talk: Press F5 and Run Your Program

Just as I said, press F5 and run your program. The Visual Basic .NET compiler builds your project, and the form is displayed. While we have a button on the form, we didn't program any of the button's events (assuming you deleted the code inside the *Button1_Click* event handler). Because we don't have any code in the *Click* event handler, when you click the button, there's nothing for it to do; the event handler is immediately exited without a trace. You could press the button shown in Figure 2-7 until the sun turns cold and nothing would happen.

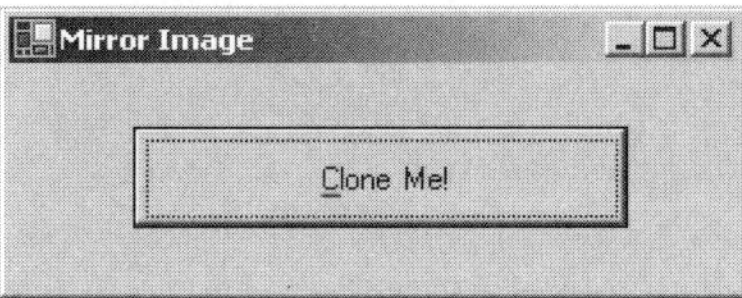

Figure 2-7 An uneventful button.

Even though not much is going on at this point, we did set the *Text* property of the form to "Mirror Image" for a reason. As you've learned, each Visual Basic .NET object inherits a common set of characteristics and capabilities (properties, methods, and events) that are defined by the base class. However, each instance of an object you create with *Sub New* is an individual object with its own name. Each object can be separately enabled and disabled, placed in a different location on the form, and so on. Click the form's Close button to dismiss the form, and let's have some fun with our simple program while at the same time looking at the principles of object-oriented programming in action.

The Doppelganger Program: Creating Clones of the *Form1* Class

Let's put this theory of object inheritance into practice. Let's create several identical objects from the same class.

1. Double-click the form in the Designer to bring up the code window. Between the *Class* declaration and *Sub New*, add the two lines of code highlighted below.

```
Public Class Form1
    Inherits System.Windows.Forms.Form

#Region " Windows Form Designer generated code "
    Dim myform As Form1
    Shared iFormCounter As Integer = 0
    Public Sub New()
        MyBase.New()

        'This call is required by the Windows Form Designer
        InitializeComponent()

        'Add any initialization after the
        ' InitializeComponent() call
    End Sub
```

2. Add the following code to the *Click* event handler of *Button1*. With it, you are going to create a new object from the *Form1* class each time you click the button. And, to tell each new form apart, you'll add a number to the form's *Text* property.

```
Private Sub Button1_Click(ByVal sender As Object,_
    ByVal e As System.EventArgs)

    myform = New Form1()
    iFormCounter += 1
    myform.Text = "Doppelganger - Number " & _
        iFormCounter.ToString
    myform.Show()
End Sub
```

With this code we change the *Text* caption to "Doppelganger" and assign a number to the instance. Notice how to use the *ToString* method of the *iFormCounter* object variable. Because everything in .NET is an object, including integers, each object has built-in methods and properties. And since the *Text* property requires a string, we simply create a string from an integer, leaving the underlying value unchanged. In this example, we are creating new instances of our original class, all within the class itself.

3. Press F5 again to run the program. The first form will be displayed with the caption "Mirror Image". Click the Clone Me! button several times to create additional forms from the *Form1* class, as shown in Figure 2-8. With the exception of the *Text* property, each new form is an identical copy of the original *Form1* class.

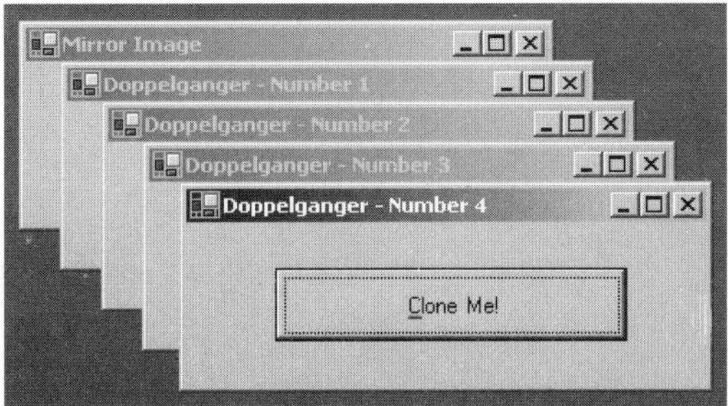

Figure 2-8 Clicking Clone Me! instantiates identical copies of the *Form1* class.

If you glance at the taskbar, you will see that each form has its own icon. Each form is a self-contained unit with the same capabilities as the original. We simply instantiated multiple copies of the *Form1* class, each with its own identity. Select one of the clones and try its Control menu and Minimize button. You'll see that they work as advertised on each form. Each copy knows how to do everything the base class knows how to do. Reusability, the Holy Grail of modern programming, is a reality with Visual Basic .NET objects.

Important Object Concepts from the Doppelganger Program

We wanted to create several copies of our object, so the first variable we put into scope with a *Dim* statement was that of type *Form1*. We also used a counter to display which form is which, using the variable *iFormCounter* to keep track for us.

Another new Visual Basic .NET keyword you'll become familiar with is *Shared*.

```
Dim myform As Form1
Shared iFormCounter As Integer = 0
```

You'll want to understand the use of *Shared* right away. Shared members are properties, procedures, or fields (such as *iFormCounter*) that are available to all instances of a class. (If you are familiar with other object-oriented languages, shared items are sometimes called *static* or *class* members.) The *Shared* keyword is useful in Visual Basic applications that use inheritance. Shared data members such as *iFormCounter* exist independently of any particular instance of a class, so shared items are not implicitly passed to instances of the class. For this reason, no unqualified references are permitted in your code. In upcoming chapters, I'll cover various uses of shared data members and inheritance in more detail.

Take a look at the *Click* event of *Button1*. Each time the user clicks the button, a new *Form1* object is created.

```
Private Sub Button1_Click(ByVal sender As Object, _
    ByVal e As System.EventArgs)

    myform = New Form1()
    iFormCounter += 1
    myform.Text = "Doppelganger - Number " & _
        iFormCounter.ToString
    myform.Show()
End Sub
```

The *New* keyword calls the constructor *Sub New* of *Form1* and creates a new object. That object is assigned to the object variable *myform*. You can access the newly minted *Form1* object by referring to its object variable. If our simple sample were a production program, you would have either created an array or a collection of new forms or given each a unique name. But for now, we want to focus on classes. We'll get to everything else in due time.

Recall that our form inherits from *Windows.Forms.Form*. When you create a new form, the form's constructor is called immediately and this creates a new form. *Sub New* is always called first and is called only once.

```
Public Sub New()
    MyBase.New()
```

Notice, however, that the first line of *Sub New* is a call to the inherited class, which calls its constructor. Before any work is performed, the parent class's constructor is called. If a parent class is derived from yet another class, that class's constructor is called first, and so on up the chain. Constructor code gets called from the top of the inheritance chain down, with your derived class's constructor code called last. This sequence makes perfect sense because the base class has to be instantiated first so that the rest of the inherited classes can be derived from it. Deriving a new form from the base class form permits you to immediately access all the functionality of that parent form. You can simply build on what is already provided.

> **Note** One of the ways in which C++ programmers would often shoot themselves in the foot was inheriting from multiple classes incorrectly. In all .NET-compliant languages, you can inherit only from one base class. This "best of breed" approach will go a long way toward making programs more understandable and bug free.

After the new *Form1* object is created, we want to count how many new forms are floating around. We increment the shared variable *iFormCounter* by 1 each time the button is clicked. Because a shared variable is just that—a variable shared by each instance of the class—we know our variable will provide an accurate count.

```
iFormCounter += 1
```

The incrementing syntax might look strange to a classic Visual Basic programmer. You would usually have to write something like

```
iFormCounter = iFormCounter + 1.
```

You can still use this syntax if you want, but in Visual Basic .NET, you can use the new method I've shown, and it has its advantages. One of the elegant and clean features of the C language that I always missed when working with Visual Basic was this way of incrementing or decrementing values. Since I'm lazy, I like the new method because it requires less typing and has less potential for typos. (I'm getting better at typing; I'm down to one mistake per word.) However, this notation is also more streamlined and intuitive. Visual Basic .NET provides a streamlined operator set, shown in Table 2-3. If you come from C or C++, these operators will be familiar to you.

I suggest that you use these operators instead of the longhand assignment from classic Visual Basic. These operators are not only more streamlined, but using them will permit you to move to other .NET languages down the road.

> **Tip** Recall that we explicitly initialized *iFormCounter* to 0 in the class. If we had left out *= 0*, our program would still have worked because the default behavior of the language initializes numeric variables to 0. However, professional programmers should never rely on the default behavior of the language. Initializing a value to 0 makes the code more readable and leaves no room for ambiguity, which makes your programs easier to debug. Also, the underlying default behavior of the language could change in later versions of Visual Basic .NET. Being explicit shows a precise thought process; you are telling the language exactly what you want, leaving no room for errors.

The last two lines of code are pretty straightforward. We are assigning some verbiage to the *Text* property of the new form and then calling its *Show* method to display it. Because our variable *iFormCounter* is now an object (what isn't?), it knows how to convert itself to a string. When we call the built-in *ToString* method of our object variable *iFormCounter*, a string of the value is returned and displayed as part of the text string.

```
myform.Text = "Doppelganger - Number " & _
    iFormCounter.ToString
myform.Show()
```

Table 2-3 New Operators You Can Use in Visual Basic .NET

Operator	Example	Description
+=	Variable += Expression	Adds the value of an expression to the value of a variable and assigns the result to the variable.
−=	Variable −= Expression	Subtracts the value of an expression from the value of a variable and assigns the result to the variable.
&=	Variable &= Expression	Concatenates a string expression to a string variable and assigns the result to the variable.
*=	Variable *= Expression	Multiplies the value of a variable by the value of an expression and assigns the result to the variable.

(continued)

Table 2-3 New Operators You Can Use in Visual Basic .NET *(continued)*

Operator	Example	Description
/=	Variable /= Expression	Divides the value of a variable by the floating point value of an expression and assigns the result to the variable.
\=	Variable \= Expression	Divides the value of a variable by the value of an expression and assigns the integer result to the variable.
^=	Variable ^= Expression	Raises the value of a variable to the power of an exponent and assigns the result back to the variable.

If you have any lingering doubt that each new form is its own object, add the following message box code right after the *myform.Show* statement. This code will display a unique number (a handle) that Windows uses to track each visible object. It will be different for each form and different each time you run the program. Handles are referred to as "magic cookies" by grizzled programmers because they are unique and there is no way to know in advance what they will be. The only guarantee is that they will be unique. (They're magic.) Again, this code is for illustration only.

```
myform = New Form1()
iFormCounter += 1
myform.Text = "Doppelganger - Number " & _
    iFormCounter.ToString
myform.Show()
MessageBox.Show(myform.Text & " has a handle of " & _
    myform.Handle.ToString, "Doppelganger", _
    MessageBoxButtons.OK, MessageBoxIcon.Information)
```

Whenever you click the button to display a new form, you will see the sort of magic cookie that Windows uses to track this and other visible components, as shown in Figure 2-9.

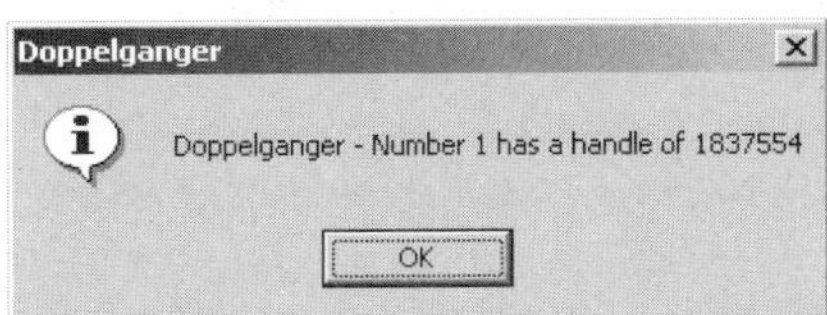

Figure 2-9 One of our form objects showing off its Windows handle.

More About Handles

While beginners usually think of a form as a window, to the Windows operating system everything is a window: forms, buttons, option boxes, text boxes, and so on. Windows has an internal table that tracks each of these visible items. In Visual Basic .NET, several controls, such as the line control, were removed. In classic Visual Basic, line controls and labels were known as *lightweight* controls because they didn't have a handle. This means that they couldn't receive focus. Line controls were removed and the label control was buffed up in Visual Basic .NET so that it would have its own handle.

Never use a handle for tracking items because Windows changes them often as it automatically compacts memory internally and shifts things around for optimization. As such, a handle for the same object can and will change as the program runs. Advanced classic Visual Basic programmers passed form and control handles as parameters for API functions. Another beauty of Visual Basic .NET is that you never have to do this. In short, you don't need to be concerned with handles anymore.

Using the Class View to Spy on Structure and Access Modifiers

Choose Class View from the View menu in the IDE. This view will become your best friend as you begin writing your own classes. It shows the classes in the current solution and displays the hierarchy that starts with classes at the highest level of the solution, all the way down to individual elements of the class.

At the top level of the tree is the current project, the one I named WindowsApplication1. Under the Classes hierarchy, you can see a single class, namely *Form1*. If you expand the Bases And Interfaces node, you'll see the properties and methods that *Form1* inherits from the base class. This view also shows the five defined methods of *Form1* (*Button1_Click*, *Dispose*, *Form1_Load*, *InitializeComponent*, and *New*).

Recall that within a class, methods are implemented by using subroutines and functions, but to the outside world they are methods. Notice that the *New* method doesn't have a key icon next to it. The absence of a key means that the method is defined with the *Public* access modifier. Public access means that the method can be used by code from the world outside the class. Having public members makes sense if our class is used in another program. For example, the *New* method needs to be exposed to the outside world so that an object of the class can be instantiated.

A key icon indicates that the item uses the *Protected* access modifier. A protected class member is accessible to entities contained in a derived class, provided that the access takes place through the derived class. If you built another class that inherited from a class with a protected member, the derived class would have access to the member.

As I mentioned earlier, an entity using the *Friend* access modifier is accessible only within the assembly that contains the entity declaration. The *Protected Friend* modifier unites protected and friend accessibility; in other words, variables of this type are accessible from all code within the same assembly and are also accessible from all derived classes.

Notice that the three fields of the *Form1* class—*components*, *iFormCounter*, and *myform*—are declared with the *Private* access modifier. Private variables or objects are available only to the class, module, or structure in which they are declared. This level of access means that no code outside the *Form1* class can access properties or events of the *Button1* object. If someone inherits from our form, they cannot get at the code implementing the button. Using the access modifier *Private* on objects within a class allows you to exercise an object-oriented methodology called *encapsulation*, which simply means that you hide your objects from the outside world and expose only the methods you want. I'll discuss encapsulation (sometimes referred to as data hiding) again in Chapter 3 when we build our own classes.

For a programmer to add the *WindowsApplication1* namespace to a new class and inherit a form of type *Form1*, our program would have to be compiled and turned into an executable. During this process, the assembly and manifest are built. The programmer using our class would add a reference to the executable file in the Solution Explorer and then simply import the namespace. By doing that, the programmer could instantly create *WindowsApplication1* forms. However, because the fields use the *Private* access modifier, the programmer could not get at those. He or she could access only the public method, *New*, as indicated by the icons next to the methods in Figure 2-10.

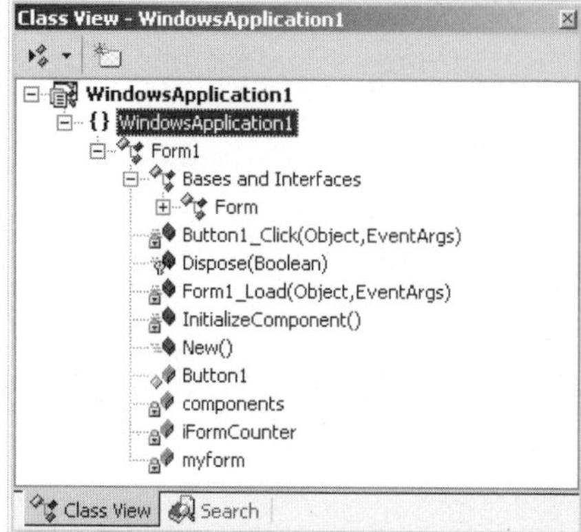

Figure 2-10 The WindowsApplication1 program in Class view.

More About Access Types

The access modifiers, *Public*, *Protected*, *Friend*, *Protected Friend*, and *Private*, specify the accessibility of the entity, but accessibility does not change the scope of an entity's name. An object might be seen but not be accessible. If no access modifier is specified, a default access type is used depending on the context. But remember what I said earlier about not relying on the default behavior of the language. It's good practice to add the access modifier that you want and not rely on the one the language gives you. Being consistent in this practice helps reduce bugs. A summary of access modifiers is provided in Table 2-4.

Now that you know about access modifiers, let's see how we would add them to the code in our example. If we make our form private, that reference variable can be seen only in our class. It cannot be accessed from the outside. Data encapsulation such as this ensures that the variable can't be modified by unexpected sources.

```
Public Class Form1
    Inherits System.Windows.Forms.Form

    Private myform As Form
    Shared iFormCounter As Integer = 0
```

You aren't restricted in the kind of access you can specify in a declaration that's made in context with a different kind of access. For example, a type declared with private access might contain a type member with public access. You have incredible flexibility in what you can permit the outside world to see.

Table 2-4 Access Modifiers

Modifier	Description
Public	Entities declared with the *Public* modifier have public access. There are no restrictions on the use of public entities.
Protected	Protected access can be specified only on members of classes. A protected member is accessible to a derived class provided that either the member is not an instance member or the access takes place through an instance of the derived class. Protected access is not a superset of friend access.
Friend	An entity with friend access is accessible only within the program that contains the entity declaration.
Protected Friend	Entities declared with the *Protected Friend* modifiers have the union of protected and friend access.
Private	A private entity is accessible only within its declaration context, including any nested entities.

Overloading Methods

Another important concept in object-oriented programming is *overloading* methods. You've been overloading methods all along in your work in classic Visual Basic, but you might not have realized it. Overloading permits a programmer to use the same method name, such as *MessageBox.Show*, but pass in different parameters at different times. Overloading changes the signature of the method, which consists of the method name and a parameter list.

Let's say you added the following line of code to a button's *Click* event handler.

```
MessageBox.Show("To be or not to be...")
```

The signature here is the method name and a single string parameter. You should see something like what's shown in Figure 2-11. (I know you're cringing and wondering why I'm having you work with something as elementary as messages in a message box. Well, let's just press on and you'll see the method in my madness in a moment.)

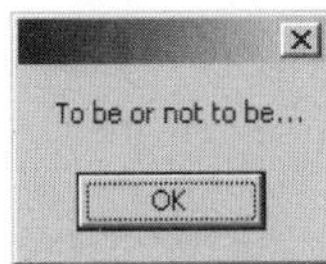

Figure 2-11 To be or not to be a form, that is the question.

If you want to display a caption in the message box, you could use the *Show* method but change the signature to pass two strings, as you can see in the following code and in Figure 2-12.

```
MessageBox.Show("To be or not to be...", "The Bard")
```

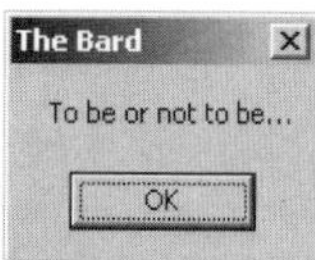

Figure 2-12 Another method signature; this one includes a caption.

After examining this masterpiece, do you feel there's still room for improvement? Let's add an icon for a visual clue that this text is indeed a question. By modifying the signature of the *Show* method, you can pass in three parameters: two strings and a constant for the icon. The *MessageBox* class has several built-in constants that determine the icon the message box displays.

```
MessageBox.Show("To be or not to be...", "The Bard", _
    MessageBoxButtons.OK, MessageBoxIcon.Question)
```

> **Note** The underscore (_) in the code fragment above is a line continuation character that permits you to continue a code statement on the next line. The Visual Basic .NET compiler treats this as a single line of code.

You can now see the question mark, as shown in Figure 2-13.

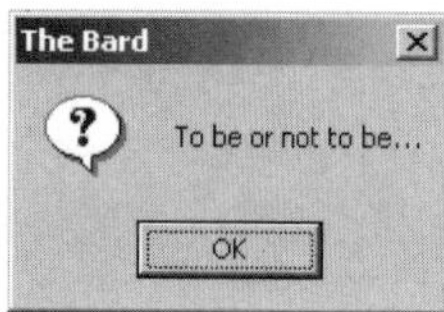

Figure 2-13 In the form of a question.

Finally, in case the user isn't in a philosophical mood when the message box is displayed, you decide to give him an option and add the following code:

```
MessageBox.Show("To be or not to be...", "The Bard", _
    MessageBoxButtons.AbortRetryIgnore, _
    MessageBoxIcon.Question)
```

After you make these changes, the message box looks like Figure 2-14.

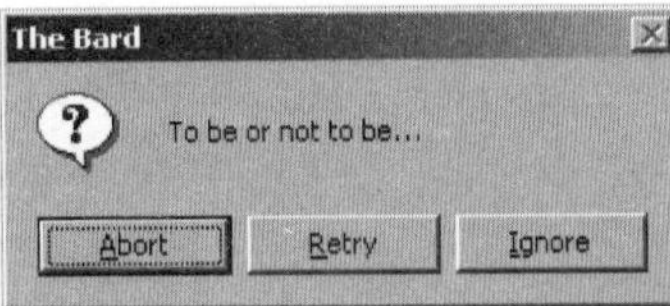

Figure 2-14 Providing options for the unphilosophical user.

You get the idea. By overloading the *Show* method of the *MessageBox* class, the message box takes the appropriate action and invokes the appropriate internal methods to do the right thing. How does it do that?

> ### Seeing the *MessageBox* Class
>
> Because a message box is really a window, as everything that's visible is to Windows, its class is found in the *System.Windows.Forms* namespace. Using IntelliSense, you can see that *MessageBox* is a real class because it has the tri-brick icon. In case you were wondering, the two overlapping rectangles used for some of the other choices is the icon used to designate a constant. Under the hood of a constant is a number. If you've used the Object Browser in classic Visual Basic, you will be no stranger to these icons.

Some of the Overloaded *Show* Methods

If you were to peek inside the *MessageBox* class, you would find not one, but several *Show* methods. Each of them takes a different set of parameters, so each has a different signature. We'll look at the *Show* method versions illustrated in the preceding section in some more detail here, but the *MessageBox* class includes additional versions as well. The class contains several function declarations with different parameter lists, but each has the same function name. Each function, however, includes the *Overloads* keyword.

```
Overloads Public Shared Function Show(ByVal text As String) _
    As DialogResult

Overloads Public Shared Function Show(ByVal text As String, _
    ByVal caption As String) As DialogResult

Overloads Public Shared Function Show(ByVal text As String, _
    ByVal caption As String, ByVal style As Integer) _
    As DialogResult
```

The various icons and buttons displayed in a message box are properties of the *MessageBox* class, as you can see from Figure 2-15. Each of these properties is a constant with an integer value. Notice the IntelliSense display, which provides help on each parameter to the method.

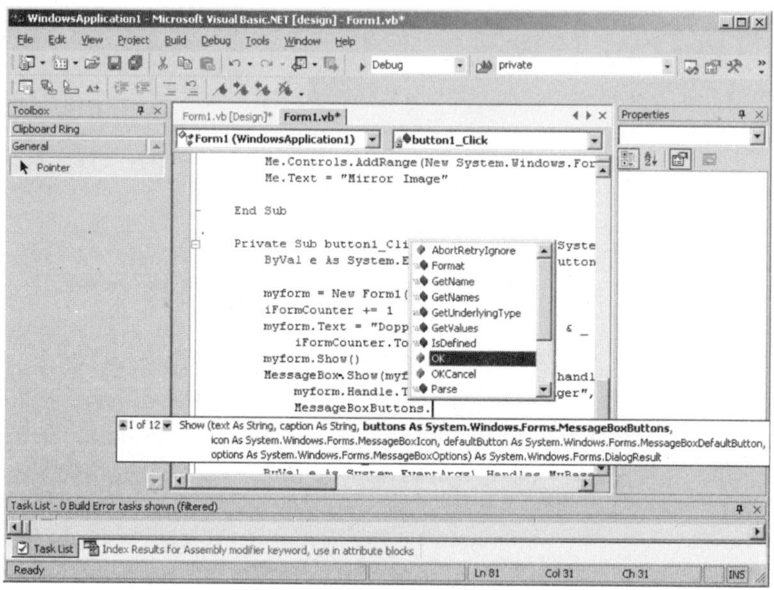

Figure 2-15 A list of the *MessageBox* class properties and IntelliSense help.

Note You cannot instantiate a new instance of the *MessageBox* class. To display a message box, you call the class's shared method *Show*. Because this method is shared, you know that no matter how many message boxes you use, only one *Show* method is used for each grouping of parameters. The title, message, buttons, and icons displayed in the message box are determined by the parameters that you pass to this method. A very talented lead programmer/architect who works in my department has the first name Joe. About a year ago, we hired another very talented programmer to report to Joe. Unfortunately for us, his name is also Joe. While struggling to differentiate them, I realized that we had overloaded Joes. After several cups of coffee, we resolved the issue by giving the second Joe the nickname Joe++.

Polymorphism

The term *polymorphism* comes from the Greek language and literally means "many forms." In the context of object-oriented programming, it means "do the right thing." For example, many classes can provide the same property or method, and a caller doesn't have to know what class an object belongs to before calling the property or method. A programmer might call *Form1.Size* or *Text1.Size* and know that the object will do what's right to resize itself.

Most object-oriented programming systems provide polymorphism through inheritance. For example, you might have two forms that inherit from the *Windows.Forms.Form* class. Each form could override the class's *Close* method. When the *Close* method is invoked for *Form1*, it might ensure that all database connections are closed. The *Close* method of *Form2* might display a message box. The user simply closes each form, and then each form does the right thing. Not too terribly difficult, eh?

While you can implement polymorphism through inheritance, you can also use it through a programming interface that you can write. With polymorphism you can create hierarchies of classes and then treat the objects in the hierarchy as either similar or different depending on your needs. As we delve more deeply into classes later in the book, I'll examine this concept in more detail. The endgame, however, is the same. A program calls the same method on a different object and the right thing happens. Polymorphism is another large word for a straightforward concept.

The Three Pillars of Object-Oriented Programming: As Easy as PIE

Object-oriented programming is as easy as *PIE*. That's Polymorphism, Inheritance, and Encapsulation. We just covered the three cornerstones of all object-oriented programming.

- **Polymorphism.** Overriding methods of the same name for different objects to perform different actions.
- **Inheritance.** Deriving an object from a base class to inherit its properties and methods.
- **Encapsulation.** Hiding data within a class so that it can be manipulated only by subroutines or functions within the class itself.

What's Controlling Our Form When We Run It?

Before we leave the topic of forms, I'd like to cover one more important concept, that of the *Application* object. Hidden from view in our form is a procedure named *Sub Main*. This procedure is the real controller of our application.

In an application designed for the desktop, a controller that handles the application is required. In classic Visual Basic, we did have the global *App* object, but we didn't do much with it except grab the value of *App.Name* or some other property for display purposes. Still, the *App* object was responsible for running our application. Now, in Visual Basic .NET, we have to become friends with it.

When you run your project, *Sub Main* runs first. *Sub Main* calls the *Application* object's *Run* method and passes in as a parameter the form you want to display.

```
System.Windows.Forms.Application.Run(New Form1)
```

When this code runs, the *New* keyword causes *Form1*'s constructor, *Sub New*, to be called, and a new form is created. In our example, the first form is automatically used as our startup form. The *Application* object uses this form to run. Let's check this out by taking a closer look.

Try This Out

Run your program again. Click the Clone Me! button four times to create four copies of the original form. Now close the original form, the one whose caption reads "Mirror Image". Phoof! All of the other forms disappear. When you dismiss the main form for the application, *Form1* in our example, its destructor, *Sub Dispose*, is called. Because all copies of our class are based on this class and this class no longer exists, each of their destructors is called in turn.

The .NET *Application* object is a traffic cop. It is initialized with the form you want to show at startup. It is responsible for keeping the form object in scope and dispatching messages to the form or control that currently has the focus. Each form class has a shared *Sub Main* procedure that looks like the following:

```
Shared Sub Main()
    System.Windows.Forms.Application.Run(New Form1)
End Sub
```

If a form didn't use the *Application.Run* method, when you ran your program, the form would be displayed and then disappear instantaneously because it goes out of scope. In other words, the code executes in the correct order, but because nothing is there to keep it active, the form self-destructs.

The *Application.Run* method creates a message loop that keeps our form displayed and looks for messages from the operating system, such as mouse clicks or data entry, that are targeted at our program. Any messages for our form are routed to *Application.Run*. From there the messages are routed to the appropriate message handlers in the form, which may involve forwarding the message to contained objects such as our button or other contained controls. The loop will continue to run until the form is terminated.

If you want to change the startup form, you could add the code above and place the name of the form to run in the *Run* method of the *Application* object. Remember that because the *Run* method is shared, only a single copy runs for all forms.

Because the default behavior of an *Application* object is to have its *Run* method start the first form created, the designers of Visual Basic .NET elected to hide the method from us. But to get at it and use its power, simply create a new statement by typing *application* and a dot (.). IntelliSense will show you the *Application* object's properties and methods. You can see from Figure 2-16 that you can use the *Application* object to grab the product name or product version among other information. If you want to get and display the current product name or version, just interrogate (read) those properties.

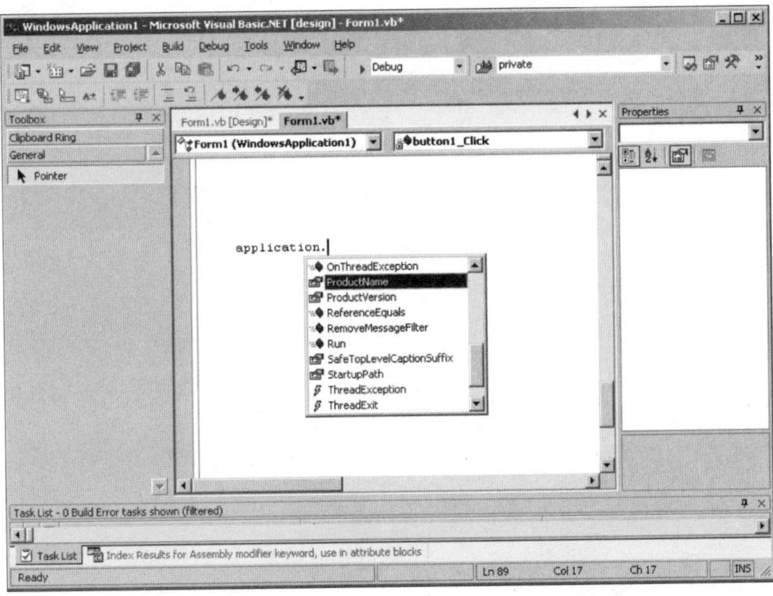

Figure 2-16 Looking at the *Application* object's methods.

As in classic Visual Basic, the *Application* object runs our application in the background. In Visual Basic .NET, however, its use has been expanded and we can get at what we need. I'll cover more about the *Application* object as topics arise.

Your First Real Visual Basic .NET Program

I know you want to write some code. In this section, we'll write a simple program that displays the time of day. While a straightforward and humble goal, writing this program will teach you how the new event paradigm works, let you work with some of the new .NET controls, and build your knowledge of the .NET object model. Of course, this program will also beef up your knowledge of object-oriented programming and the use of namespaces as well as introduce you to some new date arithmetic. One of the great new enhancements to the IDE is the Menu Editor. This is a world-class editor that makes adding menu items a cinch. The running program will look like Figure 2-17.

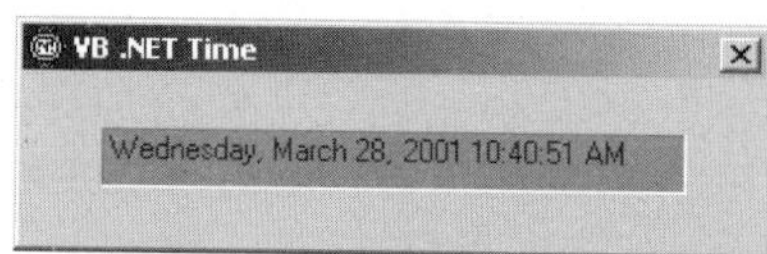

Figure 2-17 Our program.

1. Start a new Visual Basic project and select the Windows Application template. Name the project VB .NET Clock, as shown in Figure 2-18.

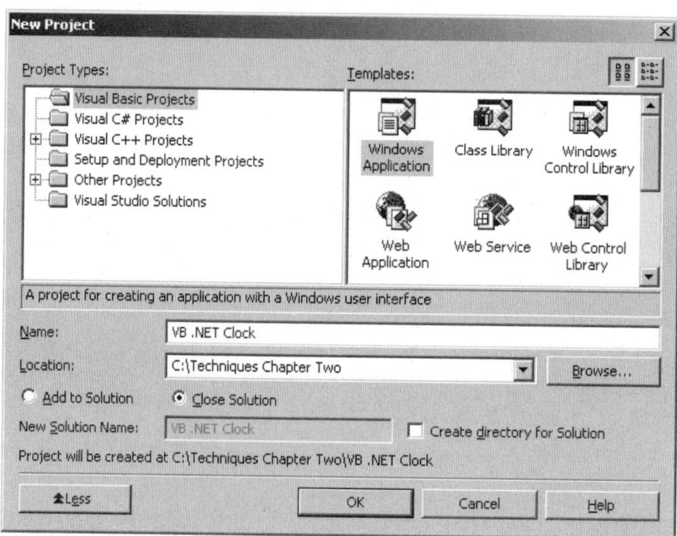

Figure 2-18 The new VB .NET Clock project.

> **Tip** As a rule of thumb, always create a new subdirectory for each new project. It's easy to accept the default settings and just click through. But unlike classic Visual Basic, the Visual Basic .NET IDE will actually create a new subdirectory for you with the name of the project. Many novices to Visual Basic would unknowingly create many projects in the same directory, and things got messy fast. Default forms and files were overwritten, and programmers worked on one form only to find that the original had been destroyed. The Visual Basic .NET IDE protects us from ourselves in this respect. If you consciously create a new directory for each new project, the IDE will automatically build the respective subdirectories for you. Keeping your projects separate is not only good programming practice, but when you start working in teams it is critical. Click the Create Directory For Solution check box if a folder does not exist.

As any professional programmer would do, the first thing you want to do is rename any form and control before writing code for it. Defining a clear, standardized naming convention is always the first step when developing a new program. Gone are the days when you would name a variable *HB86* or use your girlfriend's name. In the same vein, *Form1* is not very descriptive of what our form does.

Not only does a consistent naming style enhance the readability of source code and make maintenance of it easier, it also shows how well a developer comprehends a software system. While guidelines you can follow do exist, you should choose a convention that works for you and your team. Most of all, after you choose a style, stick with it in all cases. The saying "A stubborn consistency is the hobgoblin of small minds" does not apply to Visual Basic .NET coding convention practice.

As I discuss the components of programs such as variables, routines, tables, and the like, I'll suggest some naming conventions and illustrate and explain them. Because we are starting this example with a form, let's call it *frmTime* instead of the default *Form1*. This name tells us the object is a form and something about what the object does.

2. The default form is displayed and the boilerplate code generated. If the Solution Explorer is not visible, click View | Solution Explorer. Right-click *Form1.vb*, and then select Properties. Change the *FileName* property from *Form1.vb* to *frmTime.vb,* as shown in Figure 2-19.

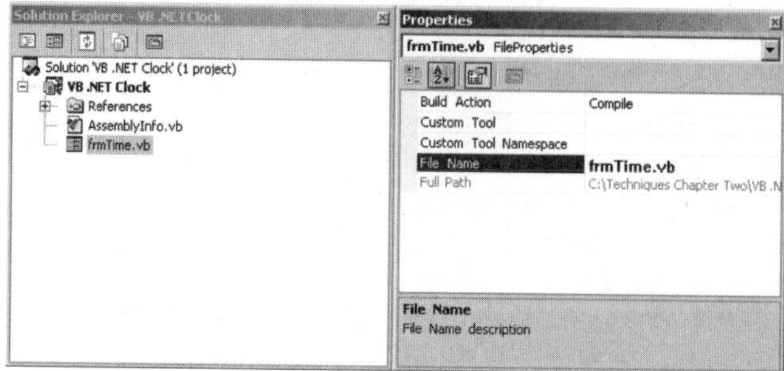

Figure 2-19 Change the form's *FileName* property to *frmTime.vb.*

3. We now want to change the name of the class that creates the time display form. We have to change the default name of *Form1* to *frmTimeClass*. First change the name of the class to *frmTimeClass*.

```
Public Class frmTimeClass
    Inherits System.Windows.Forms.Form
```

4. Now move down to the region marked *#Region Windows Form Designer generated code*. This region is where the form's controls are declared. The next name change is to the form's name. Change the name from *Form1* to *frmTimeClass*, as shown here:

```
Me.Name = "frmTime"
```

Telling the Application Object Which Form to Run

The next step in our program is to tell the *Application* object to run *frmTimeClass* and not the default, defunct, and extinct *Form1*. That's easy. Bring up the Solution Explorer again. Right-click the name of the project VB .NET Clock, select Properties, as shown in Figure 2-20, and you'll see the Properties box for the project.

Remember that a project usually consists of separate components that are stored as individual files in a solution. Our simple project consists of a form and a project file. More complex projects might consist of these items plus database scripts, modules, HTML files, stored procedures, and even a reference to an existing Web service.

A project functions as a container from which you can assemble components and deploy a finished application. The output of our project will be an executable program (VB .NET Clock.exe). Later in the book we will create a dynamic-link library (DLL) file and other types of projects. It's important to keep in mind that all projects are contained within a solution. Each project in that solution contains a unique project file. This project file lists the files contained in the project and is used to both store and track other information about those files. Each time you save a project, the project file is updated.

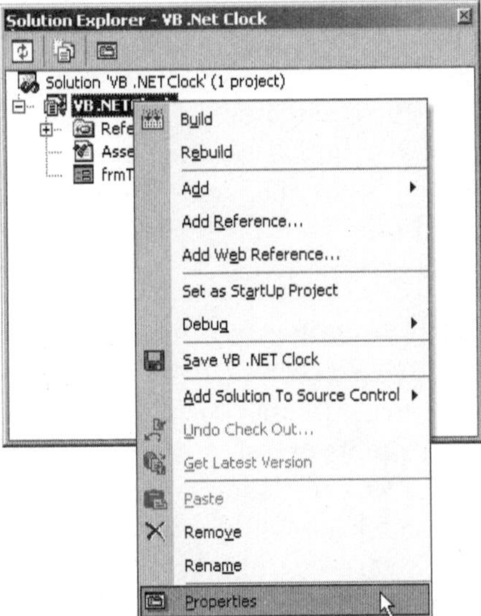

Figure 2-20 The Properties box.

Project property pages are a slick new way of consolidating the information about a project that a programmer can modify. You can see that the default assembly name is the name of the project. The project name is also the root namespace. If you want to include the functionality of this project in another project, you simply need the directive *Imports VB .NET Clock*. Remember that for a developer, a namespace provides a grouping of related types. Click the Startup Object drop-down box and select the new *frmTimeClass* form, as shown in Figure 2-21. Click OK.

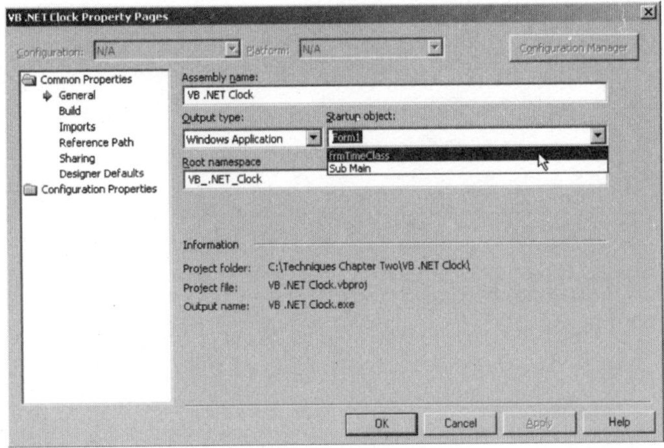

Figure 2-21 Changing the startup form to *frmTimeClass*.

Let's Add Some Controls

If you don't see the Toolbox, select View|Toolbox. As I mentioned, all of the controls in Visual Basic .NET have been reengineered and upgraded from the classic .OCX controls. The controls have similar but not identical behaviors to those you might be used to. One of the best enhancements in Visual Basic .NET is that these new controls are not required to be registered. You can forget about RegSvr32 in Visual Basic .NET.

1. Add a label to the form, and then scroll down in the Toolbox and add a Timer control and a NotifyIcon control from the Toolbox, as shown in Figure 2-22. You'll notice that the IDE places all controls that are either not visible at run time or not part of the form in a region directly below the form. This arrangement is a nice design touch because the form's real estate is not cluttered with controls that are not directly manipulated by the user. Unlike classic Visual Basic, you can now see exactly how the form will look when it is run because these controls will be invisible at run time.

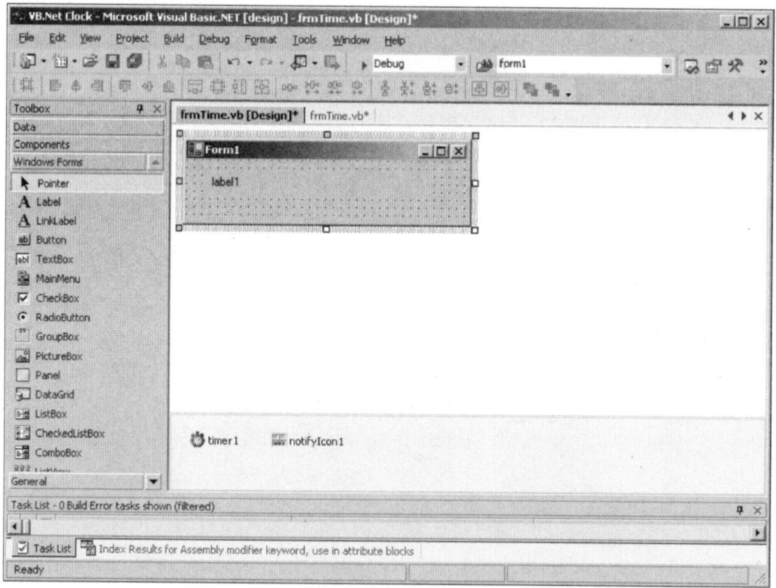

Figure 2-22 Add these controls to your form.

> **Tip** To be sure you understand how Visual Basic .NET names items, take a look at the caption of the IDE. On the left it indicates that you are working in the project VB .NET Clock. On the right, you can see that you are displaying the file frm-Time.vb, which contains our class. The current tab confirms that you are editing the file frmTime.vb in the Forms Designer.

Because this program will display a clock, we want to eliminate the minimize and maximize buttons on the title bar, as well as the form's built-in Control menu. We make these changes because we don't want users to change the size of our form, which would do nothing except ruin its look. Adding a custom icon might also provide a nice professional touch.

> **Note** Purists might say, "Wait! You have to let users decide everything! Users should be able to decide how they want to size the form. Every option that can be given to a user should be." In the real world, however, you should provide users with only sensible choices. In the case of our clock, permitting them to maximize the form to take up the entire screen serves no purpose except to confuse and possibly anger the user. In user interface design, a little bit of programming discipline goes a long way toward a user friendly application. Ironically, everyone thinks they are experts at UI design because it's so easy to make one. Quite the contrary. You will find that creating an elegant human-machine interface is one of the biggest challenges in visual programming.

2. Go to the Forms Designer and click the form to give it focus. Right-click, and then select Properties. Change the properties of the form as shown in Table 2-5, and then modify the properties on the label, timer, and notify icon as shown. Be sure to change the names of the label, timer, and notify icon controls as shown in the table.

Table 2-5 Properties for Our Form and Controls

Object	Property	Value
frmTimeClass	*FormBorderStyle*	FixedDialog
	Icon	LOCATED: [Drive] Program Files\Microsoft Visual Studio .NET\Common7\Graphics\Icons\Misc\Watch01.ico
	MaximizeBox	False
	MinimizeBox	False
	StartPosition	CenterScreen
	Text	VB .NET Time
Label1	*Name*	lblTime
	BackColor	Green (choose the color from the Web tab of the drop-down list; it will say Lime)
	BorderStyle	Fixed3D
	ForeColor	Blue (choose the color from the Web tab of the drop-down list)
	Text	""
Timer1	*Name*	tiTimer
	Enabled	True
	Interval	500
NotifyIcon1	*Name*	tIcon
	Icon	LOCATED: [Drive] Program Files\Microsoft Visual Studio .NET\Common7\Graphics\Icons\Misc\Watch01.ico
	Text	VB .NET Time
	Visible	True

After you've changed the properties, the finished product in the design environment should look like Figure 2-23. Even though you've changed only some properties on the form and three controls, you were programming. In classic Visual Basic, changes like these were not always apparent because the code was hidden from you. In Visual Basic .NET, you can see the code generated by the changes you made.

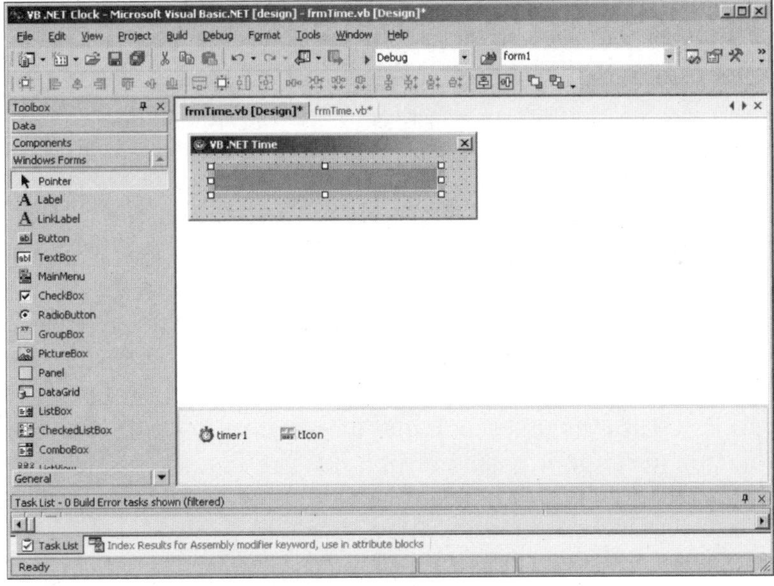

Figure 2-23 The completed form.

A user can only dismiss the form using the Close button. Maximizing the form to the size of the screen is impossible. Users can still use the form's drop-down Control menu, but because we removed the ability to resize the form, the menu permits the user only to move or exit the form.

> **Note** Click the green label to give it focus. Select Format | Center In Form | Horizontally to space the label from side to side. Next select Format | Center In Form | Vertically to space the label from top to bottom. Before you deploy any application with a user interface, use the Format options to ensure a balanced, symmetrical look. Controls that are impeccably aligned are the mark of a pro. With the Format options in Visual Basic .NET, there is no excuse.

Thinking About the User Interface

Shortly after the Big Bang, programmers started slinging code. Only when the code was complete did a programmer start to think about a user interface. The UI was almost always an afterthought. Now that the earth has cooled and the world has moved to visual programming languages such as Visual Basic .NET, the first step in programming is to design and draw the user interface. After all, the interface *is* the program to your users. The user has absolutely no idea about events, classes, inheritance, properties, and so on. You might have the most elegant code running inside your program, but the user will angrily point out that a button isn't centered on the form. Or you might commit the worst faux pas—a misspelled word on a menu! While good visual design can't rescue a program that crashes or runs like a drunk snail, it can give a professional first impression.

Examining the Handiwork of the IDE-Generated Code

The code required to wire up the controls we added to the form is taken care of by the IDE. Spend a few minutes reviewing the code highlighted below, which was added to the code generated for our form program in Chapter 1. Notice that all the new code was added in the *Windows Form Designer generated code* region. So, while you can see it, you don't have to be concerned with the code there. However, reviewing what this code does is instructive for when you want to write your own controls code. In the highlighted code, you will also start to see how objects are created and their properties set. Double-click the form to bring up the code.

```
Public Class frmTimeClass
    Inherits System.Windows.Forms.Form

#Region " Windows Form Designer generated code "

    Public Sub New()
        MyBase.New()

        'This call is required by the
        ' Windows Form Designer
        InitializeComponent()

        'Add any initialization after the
        ' InitializeComponent() call

    End Sub
```

```
'Form overrides dispose to clean up the component list
Protected Overloads Overrides _
Sub Dispose(ByVal disposing As Boolean)
    If disposing Then
        If Not (components Is Nothing) Then
            components.Dispose()
        End If
    End If
    MyBase.Dispose(disposing)
End Sub
Friend WithEvents lblTime As System.Windows.Forms.Label
Friend WithEvents tiTimer As System.Windows.Forms.Timer
Friend WithEvents tIcon As System.Windows.Forms.NotifyIcon
Private components As System.ComponentModel.IContainer

'Required by the Windows Form Designer

'NOTE: The following procedure is required by the
' Windows Form Designer.
'It can be modified using the Windows Form Designer.
'Do not modify it using the code editor.
<System.Diagnostics.DebuggerStepThrough()> _
Private Sub InitializeComponent()
    Me.components = New System.ComponentModel.Container()
    Dim resources As System.resources.ResourceManager = _
        New System.resources.ResourceManager( _
        GetType(frmTimeClass))
    Me.lblTime = New System.Windows.Forms.Label()
    Me.tiTimer = New System.Windows.Forms.Timer(Me.components)
    Me.tIcon = _
        New System.Windows.Forms.NotifyIcon(Me.components)
    Me.SuspendLayout()
    '
    'lblTime
    '
    Me.lblTime.BackColor = System.Drawing.Color.Lime
    Me.lblTime.BorderStyle = _
        System.Windows.Forms.BorderStyle.Fixed3D
    Me.lblTime.ForeColor = System.Drawing.Color.Blue
    Me.lblTime.Location = New System.Drawing.Point(47, 21)
    Me.lblTime.Name = "lblTime"
    Me.lblTime.Size = New System.Drawing.Size(200, 23)
    Me.lblTime.TabIndex = 0
    '
    'tiTimer
    '
    Me.tiTimer.Enabled = True
    Me.tiTimer.Interval = 500
```

(continued)

```
        '
        'tIcon
        '
        Me.tIcon.Icon = CType(resources.GetObject("tIcon.Icon"), _
            System.Drawing.Icon)
        Me.tIcon.Text = "VB .NET Time"
        Me.tIcon.Visible = True
        '
        'frmTimeClass
        '
        Me.AutoScaleBaseSize = New System.Drawing.Size(5, 13)
        Me.ClientSize = New System.Drawing.Size(294, 64)
        Me.Controls.AddRange(New System.Windows.Forms.Control() _
            {Me.lblTime})
        Me.FormBorderStyle = _
            System.Windows.Forms.FormBorderStyle.FixedDialog
        Me.Icon = CType(resources.GetObject("$this.Icon"), _
            System.Drawing.Icon)
        Me.MaximizeBox = False
        Me.MinimizeBox = False
        Me.Name = "frmTimeClass"
        Me.StartPosition = _
            System.Windows.Forms.FormStartPosition.CenterScreen
        Me.Text = "VB .NET Time"
        Me.ResumeLayout(False)

    End Sub

#End Region

End Class
```

To a classic Visual Basic programmer, this looks like an incredible amount of code for a program that doesn't do anything useful yet. But keep a couple of things in mind. First, you didn't write a single character in the editor yet, except to change the default name of the form class. Everything else has been provided for you by the IDE. Second, in classic Visual Basic programs, code like this was always present, but it was hidden from view. Visual Basic .NET simply provides access to code that was always there.

Examining the code the IDE inserted, you can see that our three controls were added. As I mentioned earlier, the controls live in the *System.Windows.Forms* namespace. If you've ever built objects in Visual Basic 6 that raised events, the *WithEvents* keyword is not new to you. It tells our class that the controls will be raising various events, such as the timer tick. The *WithEvents* keyword gives us access to any event in a control declared this way.

```
Friend WithEvents lblTime As System.Windows.Forms.Label
Friend WithEvents tiTimer As System.Windows.Forms.Timer
Friend WithEvents tIcon As System.Windows.Forms.NotifyIcon
```

Switch to the Forms Designer, display the Properties box, and click the drop-down list at the top of the box. As you can see in Figure 2-24, the fully qualified location of each of the controls is shown in the list. These locations match the namespaces in which the controls live. Not surprisingly, they are all found in the *System.Windows.Forms* namespace.

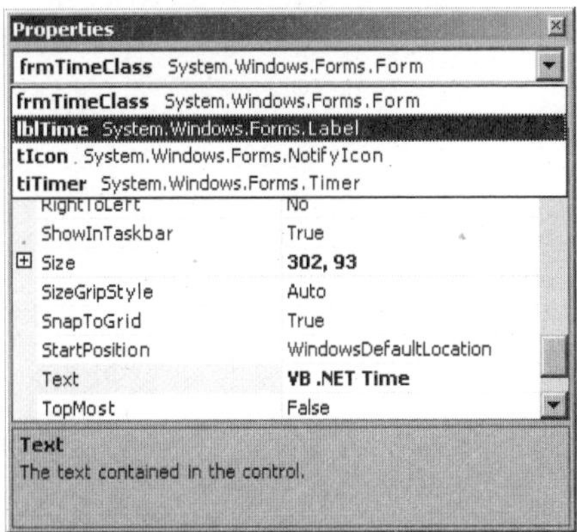

Figure 2-24 The controls on the form are part of the *System.Windows.Forms* namespace.

The next line that bears examination dimensions the Resource Manager. The *ResourceManager* class looks up culture-specific resources, provides resource fallback when a localized resource does not exist, and also supports resource serialization such as saving information to disk.

```
Dim resources As System.Resources.ResourceManager = _
    New System.Resources.ResourceManager( _
    GetType(frmTimeClass))
```

Almost every production-quality application needs to make use of resources. A resource is any nonexecutable data that is logically deployed with your application. The icons we added to the form and the notify icon are examples of resources. This data can be string literals, images, and persisted objects, among other items. As you know, the icon we used is stored as a binary file. Visual Basic .NET takes resource data and persists it in a separate resource file or sometimes in a designated section of a portable executable (PE) file. We used resource files in classic Visual Basic to store locale-dependent icons and strings. Likewise, you can create your own resource files in Visual Basic .NET. A resource file is a perfect vehicle for storing literal strings for menu choices in various languages, for example. You could have a resource file with menu strings in English and Spanish, and your program could then detect the current regional setting and use the correct strings. For now we are just storing an icon. The best part is that Visual Basic .NET takes on the responsibility of storing this information for you.

The rest of the new code is for setting control properties and storing icons. We changed the properties in the Properties box of the control, and the IDE wrote the changes to our code.

How Do We Hardwire the Controls?

You'll notice that neither the timer nor the notify icon have any code yet. Go back to the Designer and double-click each of the controls. The default events will then be added to your code.

```
Protected Sub tiTimer_Tick(ByVal sender As Object, _
    ByVal e As System.EventArgs)

End Sub

Private Sub tIcon_Disposed(ByVal sender As System.Object, _
    ByVal e As System.EventArgs) Handles tIcon.Disposed

End Sub
```

Now you're ready to add some code to have the clock display the current date and time.

Can You Name That Namespace?

Remember that to use the prebuilt classes in the .NET common language runtime, you have to import their functionality. With classic Visual Basic, you would use built-in date methods to perform date manipulation and arithmetic. We will do much the same thing here, but because of the breadth of functionality, we will import only what we want.

The .NET Framework is built to be truly international. The framework's designers provided different formats for the way numbers, dates, and currency are rendered from country to country and culture to culture. They grouped this functionality in the *System.Globalization* namespace. This namespace contains information such as the language, the writing system, and the calendar used by various cultures. It also includes methods for common operations such as printing dates and sorting strings. In fact, to give you a sense of how specialized your programs can become, the *Globalization* namespace is where you would find the particulars of the Thai Buddhist Calendar Class.

Go ahead and add the *Imports System.Globalization* statement to your program as shown here:

```
Imports System.Globalization
```

Now that the date format information is visible to our module, we can take advantage of it. Add the following highlighted code to the *tiTimer_Tick* event handler.

```
Protected Sub tiTimer_Tick(ByVal sender As Object, _
    ByVal e As System.EventArgs)

    Dim dtDateTime As DateTime = Now()
    Dim sMsgDate As String

        sMsgDate = dtDateTime.ToString("F")
    lblTime.Text = sMsgDate
End Sub
```

That's all the code you need. Let's take a look at what it does.

Date and Time Arithmetic

First, the timer is set to 500 milliseconds. This setting means that the *Tick* event of the *tiTimer* control will fire every one-half second. Each time it fires, the code in the event handler will execute. The code will grab the current system time and store it in the *dtDateTime* variable of the data type *DateTime*. You can see that we've used the new Visual Basic .NET feature that permits us to dimension and initialize a variable on the same line.

```
Dim dtDateTime As DateTime = Now()
```

In classic Visual Basic 6, a *Date* type is stored in a *Double* format using 4 bytes. In Visual Basic .NET, a *Date* uses the .NET Framework and common language runtime *DateTime* data type, which is an 8-byte integer value. The new *DateTime* object has a property named *Ticks* that stores the date and time as the number of 100-nanosecond intervals since 12:00 A.M. January 1, 1 A.D. (year) in the Gregorian calendar. The new *DateTime* object also has several helpful methods that permit you to determine whether one *DateTime* object is before, after, or equal to another *DateTime* object.

> **Tip** Because of the different representations of dates in Visual Basic .NET, there is no implicit conversion between the *Date* and *Double* data types as in Visual Basic 6. If you have to convert between a *Double* and the Visual Basic 6 representation of *Date*, you can use the *ToOADate* and *FromOADate* methods of the *DateTime* class. However, if you are not converting older classic Visual Basic programs to Visual Basic .NET, you don't have to worry about this.

The *Strings* class is born knowing how to do all sorts of things related to dates. As you enter the code, IntelliSense will show all of the operations the code knows how to perform, as shown in Figure 2-25. We want to select the *FormatDateTime* method of the *Strings* class to format the date and time for presentation in our label control. We want the formatting to be applied every one-half second.

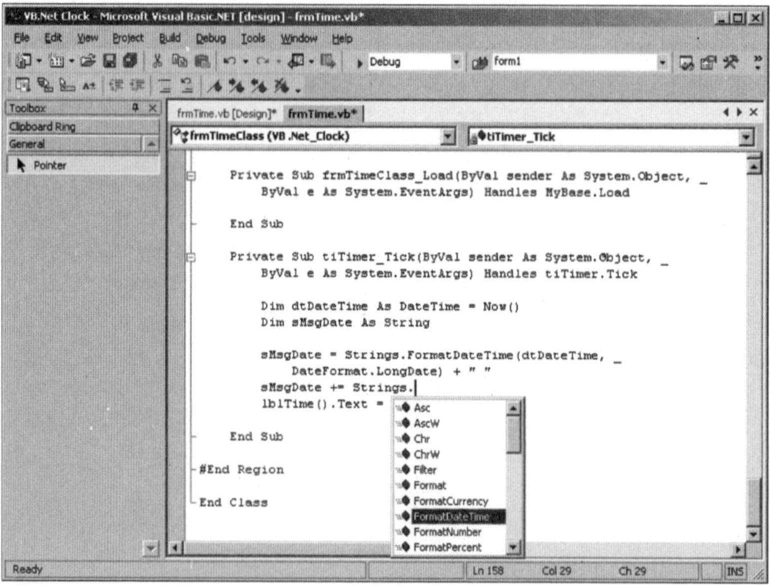

Figure 2-25 The *Strings* class has several formatting methods.

> **Note** IntelliSense shows methods of objects with purple flying bricks. Properties are represented by a hand holding a card, presumably the value of the property is written on the card.

I'm aware that many of you are thinking that even with this trivial program, Visual Basic .NET appears to have an overwhelming number of cryptic options compared to classic Visual Basic. You might be thinking, "How would I know where to start looking for the .NET classes and their properties?"

After we work through more examples in the next few chapters, you'll begin to see how the options fit together. You'll understand exactly where to look for something and how to use it. But this familiarity comes only with practice. There is simply no other way. For now, I want you to become familiar with the power of our new environment. As you progress, you'll find that new vistas are open to you in your programming experience. As you learn your way around the functionality built into the .NET Framework, you'll find your productivity skyrocketing.

Formatting the Date and Time

We passed in the character *F* as the first parameter of the *Format* method. Listed in Table 2-6 are the format strings that you can choose from when displaying either the date, time, or date and time from a *DateTime* object. This table shows the characters to use in the first parameter to display the various built-in date patterns. Remember that we did all this with a single line of code.

```
sMsgDate = dtDateTime.ToString("F")
```

Sometimes, you might run into a situation in which you want to display the date or time in a custom format. Using a custom format poses no problem for Visual Basic .NET. You can use one of the characters or combination of characters listed in Table 2-7 to create a format that fits your requirements. Be sure to enclose the character or characters in quotation marks ("").

Table 2-6 The Built-In Date and Time Formats Available in Visual Basic .NET

Format Character	Resulting Format Pattern
D	MM/dd/yyyy
D	dddd, MMMM dd, yyyy
F	dddd, MMMM dd, yyyy HH:mm
F (the one we used)	dddd, MMMM dd, yyyy HH:mm:ss
G	MM/dd/yyyy HH:mm
G	MM/dd/yyyy HH:mm:ss
m, M	MMMM dd
r, R	ddd, dd MMM yyyy HH':'mm':'ss 'GMT'
S	yyyy-MM-dd HH:mm:ss
T	HH:mm
T	HH:mm:ss
U	yyyy-MM-dd HH:mm:ss
U	dddd, MMMM dd, yyyy HH:mm:ss
y, Y	MMMM, yyyy

Table 2-7 Characters to Use to Create a Custom Date and Time Format

Format Pattern	Description
d	The day of the month. Single-digit days will not have a leading zero.
dd	The day of the month. Single-digit days will have a leading zero.
ddd	The abbreviated name of the day of the week.
dddd	The full name of the day of the week.
M	The numeric month. Single-digit months will not have a leading zero.
MM	The numeric month. Single-digit months will have a leading zero.
MMM	The abbreviated name of the month.
MMMM	The full name of the month.
y	The year without the century. If the year without the century is less than 10, the year is displayed with no leading zero.
yy	The year without the century. If the year without the century is less than 10, the year is displayed with a leading zero.

Table 2-7 Characters to Use to Create a Custom Date and Time Format

Format Pattern	Description
yyyy	The year including the century in four digits.
h	The hour in a 12-hour clock. Single-digit hours will not have a leading zero.
hh	The hour in a 12-hour clock. Single-digit hours will have a leading zero.
H	The hour in a 24-hour clock. Single-digit hours will not have a leading zero.
HH	The hour in a 24-hour clock. Single-digit hours will have a leading zero.
m	The minute. Single-digit minutes will not have a leading zero.
mm	The minute. Single-digit minutes will have a leading zero.
S	The second. Single-digit seconds will not have a leading zero.
ss	The second. Single-digit seconds will have a leading zero.
T	The first character in the A.M./P.M. designator.
tt	The A.M./P.M. designator.
z	The time zone offset (hour only). Single-digit hours will not have a leading zero.
zz	The time zone offset (hour only). Single-digit hours will have a leading zero.
zzz	The full time zone offset (hour and minutes). Single-digit hours and minutes will have leading zeros.
:	The default time separator.
/	The default date separator.
% *c*	Where *c* is a standard format character. Displays the standard format pattern associated with the format character.
\ *c*	Where *c* is any character. Displays the character literally.

Let's Run This Baby!

Choose Debug | Start, or simply press F5. You'll see the Solution Builder telling you it's building the program. The build should succeed, as shown in Figure 2-26. Because we are not deploying our program yet, all indicators are 0. We're ready for liftoff.

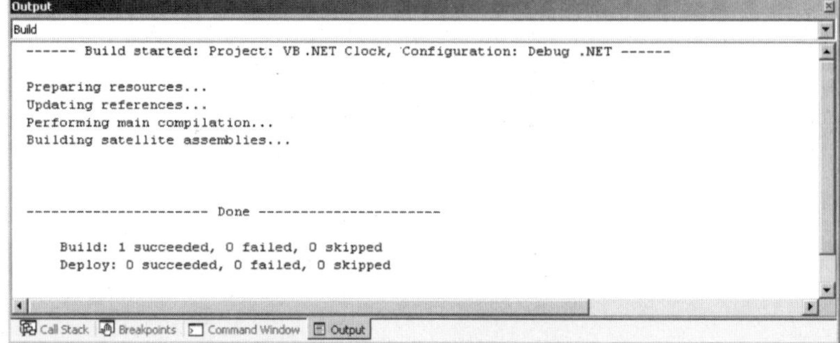

Figure 2-26 A successful build.

You should see the loading sequence of the assemblies used in our program displayed in the Output window, shown in Figure 2-27. The .NET runtime library, Mscorlib.dll, is loaded, then the executable, and finally the respective assemblies needed to run our code.

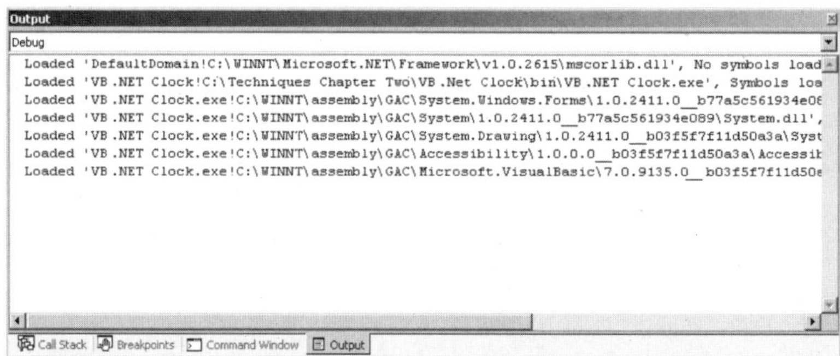

Figure 2-27 The assemblies needed to run VB .NET Clock.

If everything goes according to plan, you'll see the clock in the center of the screen, as shown in Figure 2-28. The user can't resize it but can only dismiss it by using the Close button. The time is updated twice a second.

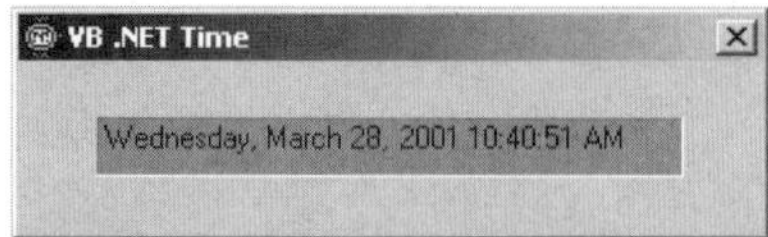

Figure 2-28 The VB .NET Time program in action.

Also notice the notify icon at the far right side of the taskbar, shown in Figure 2-29. If you let your mouse hover over it for a second, the tooltip will pop up telling you that an instance of the VB .NET Time program is running. Not too shabby for setting a few properties and writing a few lines of code.

Figure 2-29 VB .NET Time's notify icon in the taskbar.

Since you've gone through this explanation about what's happening, why not spend a few minutes experimenting with the methods that display various custom date and time formats. Personally, I prefer a 12-hour clock with an A.M./P.M. designator. Simple enough. Modify the format method of the *dtDateTime* object as follows and rerun the program.

```
sMsgDate = dtDateTime.ToString("hh:mm:ss tt")
```

This format will provide the current system time in 12-hour format, as shown in Figure 2-30.

Figure 2-30 VB .NET Time showing the time in 12-hour format.

Except for the single *Import* statement, all the functionality is sandwiched between *Class* and *End Class* statements. Visual Basic .NET is all about classes.

```
Public Class frmTimeClass
:
End Class
```

Conclusion

We've covered quite a bit in this chapter. Let's recap. First you learned that a class is a blueprint for an object; the actual object is a manifestation (or instance) of that class. A class can inherit capabilities from a parent, or base, class. A class has properties that contain information about its state, such as its size or color. The internal variables that hold the properties are called *fields* when they are referred to inside the class. A class also has code that instructs it to do things. From outside the class, these actions are known as *methods*. Inside the class, subroutines and functions implement a class's methods.

A class has a constructor, *Sub New*, that builds an object of the class, as well as a destructor, *Sub Dispose*, that tears down the class. When you want a new instance of a class, the *New* keyword usually will call a function named *Sub Main*, which in turn calls *Sub New*. If the class inherits from a parent class, the first line in the constructor calls the constructor of the parent class. All of the base classes are instantiated from top to bottom, with our class being last.

Within *Sub Main* is the line *System.Windows.Forms.Application.Run(New Form1)*. The *Application* class's *Run* method calls *Form1*'s constructor to build the class. Then the *Run* method executes an internal message loop that looks for Windows messages directed at *Form1*. When the *Run* method receives a message such as a button click, it directs the message to the form, which further directs the message to the button.

Each form or visible object has its own numbered handle. A handle is used by Windows to keep an internal list of which object (form, button, label, and so on) is which. The operating system uses handles to direct specific messages to specific programs to be intercepted by the *Run* method.

We also touched on events. Anyone who has programmed in a Windows environment is familiar with them. An event notifies our program that something interesting has happened. Our program finds out about events from the *Application.Run* method.

When we need to hide data within our class, such as we did with the *iFormCounter* integer variable that held the number of Doppelganger forms, the *Private* access modifier is used. There are also the *Public*, *Protected*, and *Friend* modifiers. Because we wanted only one counter to hold a value for all the forms, we used the *Shared* keyword. Using *Shared* makes sure that all the instances of the *Form1* class use the same variable. When we initialized *iFormCounter*, we used the new capability of Visual Basic .NET to initialize the variable on the same line as we declared it. Because we were incrementing *iFormCounter*, we examined the new notation that permits us to do things such as *iFormCounter += 1*.

I explained and illustrated method overloading using the *MessageBox* class. By modifying the number of parameters, the *MessageBox* class has several functions with the name *Show*, but each version has a different signature. The *Show* function whose signature matches the parameters passed in is the one that's called. While looking at the *MessageBox* class, we covered the various constants that permit us to customize a message box for the task at hand.

Next we touched on polymorphism, which means "many forms." In object-oriented programming, polymorphism means "do the right thing." Calling *Form1.Size* and *Text1.Size* ensures that each object knows how to resize itself. While there is more to polymorphism, the endgame is that each object will "do the right thing."

We also covered namespaces, or the hierarchical notion of grouping logical classes. We examined a table that shows how the major functionality in the .NET Framework is grouped. In the *frmTime* class we created, we imported a namespace, *System.Globalization*, and used one of its classes so that we could use the local culture format. Then we examined various date and time formats and customized our class to modify the way it displays the output.

As your programs grow in sophistication, you'll need to add references to the namespaces where additional functionality lives. We illustrated how to bring up the Add Reference dialog box in the Solution Explorer and add the required reference. In the *frmTime* form, we imported our own namespace and used some date-formatting capabilities. Everything we did in this chapter was inside a class. I think you will agree that we covered quite a bit of ground here. I strongly recommend that if anything in this conclusion is unclear or fuzzy, go back to the text and read the specific section again. Understanding these concepts is necessary to fully understand Visual Basic .NET or any other object-oriented language.

3

Writing Your First Class

In Chapter 2, "Object-Oriented Programming in Visual Basic .NET," I described the object-oriented approach to programming by using existing .NET Framework classes. I've found that using existing classes is a good way to get your mind around what you need to know about objects. But if you're like me, the best way to understand a programming concept is to write code that uses it.

In this chapter, we're going to write a pure class *sans* graphical interface. Even though we saw that Windows forms almost write themselves in Visual Studio .NET, it's important to strip away whatever might detract from understanding the fundamentals of classes when beginning to learn what they're all about. By writing a bare-bones class, we can cover every aspect of building a class and prepare ourselves for the chapters to come.

Following this approach, you'll also get a sense of the way in which many classes are constructed for production applications in businesses. We will write a class, named *Employee*, that holds information about employees. The class will be streamlined, but it will hit all the highlights of object-oriented programming (OOP), such as encapsulation, overloading, overriding, creating properties, creating a read-only property, private member fields, and using a shared data field. While we're at it, we'll add a *#Region* to demonstrate how you can create your own module view, making your code easy to work with by hiding and exposing various parts of the code. In this short example, we'll also create our own namespace. This simple class will cover all of the concepts needed to write sophisticated, robust Visual Basic .NET programs. Once you understand these important concepts, constructing more meaningful and robust classes will be straightforward.

> **Note** While I stated that this class does not inherit from any predefined class, it does inherit from the *System.Object* class. It's impossible to do anything in Visual Basic .NET without implicitly inheriting from *System.Object*.

Creating the *Employee* Class

To get started, open Visual Studio .NET and follow along with these steps:

1. Create a new project in Visual Basic .NET. Select Visual Basic Projects as the project type and then, because we're going to build our own class, select the Empty Project template, as shown in Figure 3-1. Add the name Employee and the location as C:\VB .NET Coding Techniques\Chap03. Now that we have an empty project, we have to add the features that we want rather than have the integrated development environment (IDE) provide us with a default form.

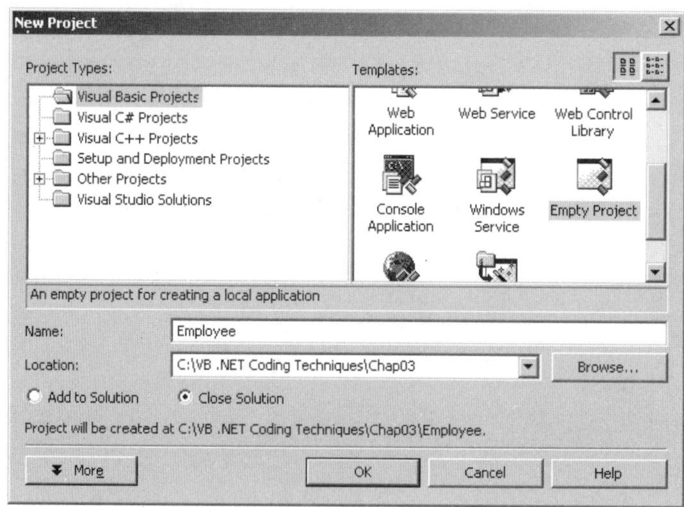

Figure 3-1 Create an empty project.

It might appear that nothing has happened because the project is empty. Take a look at the menu bar of the IDE, however, and you can see that it says Employee.

2. Select Project | Add Class to add a class module to the project. Give the new class the name Employee.vb, shown in Figure 3-2, and then click Open to add the empty class declaration to the project.

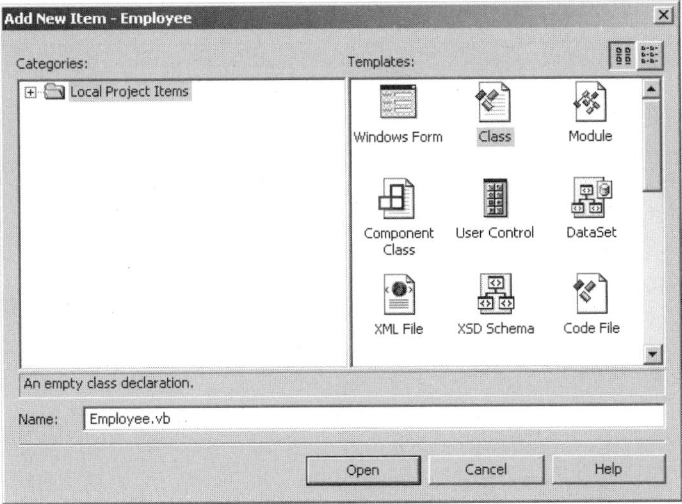

Figure 3-2 Add a class to the project.

Now we have a single tab in our project, the new *Employee.vb* class. The *Public Class Employee* template is added for us, as you can see in Figure 3-3. Delete the contents of the class because we want to add the code ourselves.

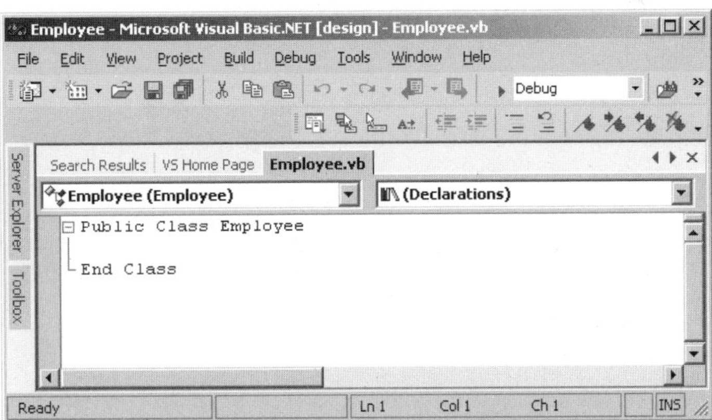

Figure 3-3 The new class is created from a template.

3. Replace the existing code in the *Employee.vb* class module with the following code. This code defines the class, establishing the template for objects created from the class in memory.

```
Option Strict On

Imports System

Namespace employees

    Public Class Employee

        Private m_sFirstName As String = ""
        Private m_sLastName As String = ""
        Private m_bVBNETTrained As Boolean = False
        Private m_iEmpNumber As Integer = 0

        Private Shared iTotEmployees As Integer = 0

        Sub new()
            MyBase.New()
            iTotEmployees += 1
            m_iEmpNumber = iTotEmployees
        End Sub

        Sub new(ByVal fName As String, ByVal lName As String)
            MyBase.New()
            m_sFirstName = fName
            m_sLastName = lName
            iTotEmployees += 1
            m_iEmpNumber = iTotEmployees
        End Sub

        Overridable Function Serialize() As Boolean
            If ((m_sFirstName <> "") And (m_sLastName <> "")) _
            Then
                Return True
            Else
                Return False
            End If
        End Function

#Region "Employee Properties"

        Public ReadOnly Property EmployeeNumber() As Integer
            Get
                Return m_iEmpNumber
            End Get
        End Property

        Property FirstName() As String
            Get
                FirstName = m_sFirstName
            End Get
```

```
            Set
                m_sFirstName = Value
            End Set
        End Property

        Property LastName() As String
            Get
                LastName = m_sLastName
            End Get
            Set
                m_sLastName = Value
            End Set
        End Property


        Property VBNet() As Boolean
            Get
                VBNet = m_bVBNETTrained
            End Get
            Set
                m_bVBNETTrained = Value
            End Set
        End Property

#End Region

    End Class

End Namespace
```

Examining the Class Code

This class won't run until we implement it in a program that creates a new instance of the class, but let's examine how the class is constructed so that we understand each of its components. A bit later in the chapter, we'll build a test harness to demonstrate how to actually create and use an instance of the class.

The first step we take is to import the *System* namespace. As you know, every class is derived from the root namespace, *System*, which is where *System.Object* lives. Our class module, like other modules, can contain any number of *Imports* statements. Remember that *Imports* statements must occur in a module before any references to identifiers within the module, so you always want to place these statements at the beginning of a module. The only code that would go before an *Imports* statement is the *Option Strict* or *Option Explicit* directive. I'll cover these statements in more detail in Chapter 4, "Visual Basic .NET Data Types and Features."

Adding a Reference to Our Project

Because we didn't create this project as a Windows application but as an empty project, Visual Basic .NET has no idea what we are going to import. We don't need to clutter an empty project with default references that might not be used, so no references are added when we start. Take a look at the Solution Explorer, shown in Figure 3-4. You'll see that the references structure is empty. (If the Solution Explorer is not visible, click View | Solution Explorer.)

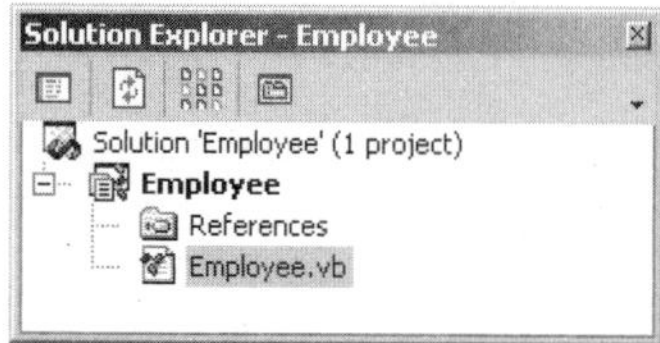

Figure 3-4 The project contains no references.

Just putting an *Imports* statement at the start of the code is not enough. We have to add the Visual Basic .NET Framework references that the project will use. We also have to add a reference to the project's assembly so that Visual Basic .NET can find it. Adding a reference to a Visual Basic .NET project is similar to adding one to a project in classic Visual Basic. For example, if you wanted to create a reference to an Excel workbook to do some Office Automation in classic Visual Basic, you would create the Excel object. However, classic Visual Basic had no idea what you were talking about until a reference to the Microsoft Excel Workbook Type Library was added.

The designers of Visual Basic 6 had to make some difficult decisions about what to include in the language and what could be added later on when needed. For example, if you've ever used Win32 API calls in Visual Basic or even imported a reference to the Excel Type Library, you know that these capabilities basically extend the base language. You can perform operations with API calls that are not possible with only Visual Basic. However, the designers of Visual Basic didn't need to include all the functionality contained in the hundreds of API calls, or even those used when referencing an Excel spreadsheet. All of this functionality could easily be accessed by including API function definitions or adding a reference to the Excel Type Library to our code. The designers of Visual Basic .NET faced the same design issues. Importing all namespaces in all assemblies into our .NET programs isn't necessary. We need to import (or reference) only those namespaces that contain classes useful for the problem at hand.

1. Right-click References to display the Add Reference menu option, shown in Figure 3-5.

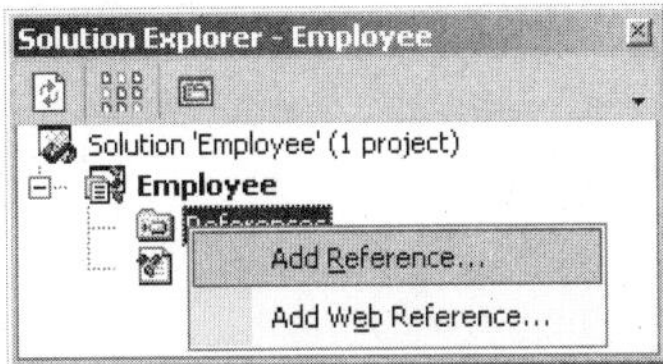

Figure 3-5 Adding a reference in the Solution Explorer.

Selecting Add Reference displays a tabbed dialog box that lists each of the .NET Framework namespaces, shown in Figure 3-6. Each reference we add is a reference to an assembly. As you know, each assembly lives in its own dynamic-link library (DLL) in a physical file on disk. The *System* namespace assembly, for example, is really System.dll.

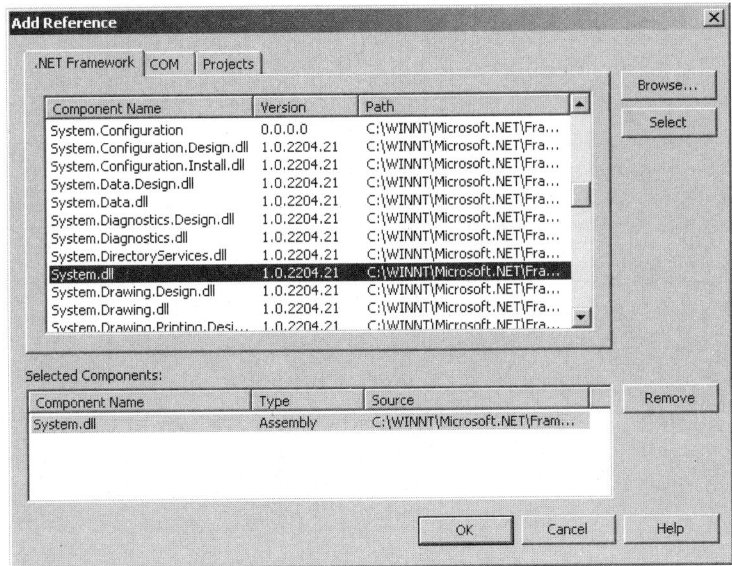

Figure 3-6 Each reference is a DLL file on disk.

2. Double-click System.dll in the Component Name column to add it to the Selected Components list. Click OK to add this reference to the project.

> **Tip** Many times you'll want to use the *Imports* statement for an assembly. You write the code, but the IDE tells you that the particular reference is not defined because the reference to the assembly you wanted to import was not added to the Solution Explorer. Default references usually do the job, but not always. Be sure to peek at the references in the Solution Explorer to ensure that your program knows how to find the particular assembly that contains the classes you want to import and use.

The Solution Explorer should now look like Figure 3-7. It shows the *Employee* class and a reference to a .NET namespace.

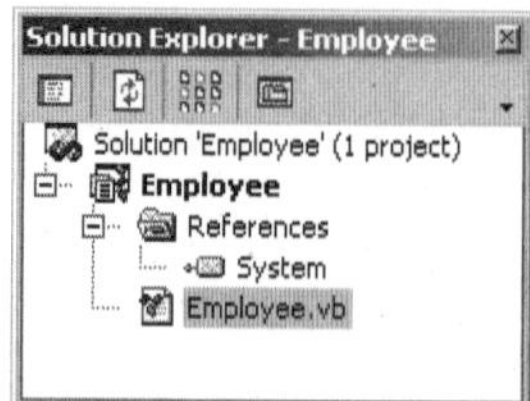

Figure 3-7 The reference to *Employee.vb.*

DLLs in .NET

For those classic Visual Basic programmers among you, the concept of a DLL can be illustrated by thinking of a graphical control. For example, you might have added a Bound DataGrid or a calendar control to your tool palette. All classic Visual Basic controls had the extension *.ocx*, but they were really DLLs with a different name. Once you had a calendar control on the toolbox, you could create as many calendars as you needed from the single control on the palette. You might have had a form that had six separate calendars on it. While each calendar object had its own name and could be programmed independently, only a single instance of the calendar was stored in an OCX file. Each time you placed another calendar control on a form, a new instance was created from the single calendar class that lived in the OCX.

DLLs in .NET *(continued)*

The .NET Framework operates in the same way. For example, if you right-click the toolbox and select Customize Toolbox, the dialog box shown below pops up. Selecting the .NET Framework Components tab reveals that all the graphical controls still live in DLLs. If you add a reference to a check box control, you can see that it lives in *System.Windows.Forms.DLL*. You can draw as many check boxes on your form as you need, but they all come from a single class that lives in a single DLL. Under the hood, you are simply creating multiple instances from the same class.

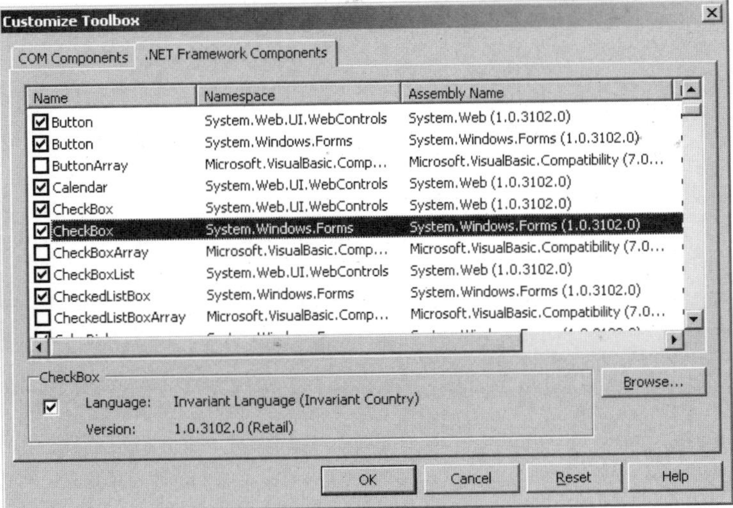

That's the beauty of object-oriented programming. The Holy Grail of modern programming can be summed up in a single word: reusability. Because we can modularize our program into classes, each becomes a self-contained unit. This segregation makes each unit much easier to debug. Once you have a fully functioning and debugged class, you can put it aside knowing that that part of your program works fine. By generalizing our code, we can reuse the classes we build ourselves, dramatically speeding up development of subsequent programs. When your program references a DLL, the functionality that lives in the file is available to another program. This expands the language tremendously. Using DLLs is like getting a cornucopia of functionality free of charge, and the functions operate just as fast as if they were native to the program calling them.

Our Class's Namespace

Notice that our code uses a namespace named *employees*. Remember that a namespace declaration enables you to group related types into a hierarchical categorization. The entire *Employee* class is contained in the *employees* namespace. While our simple program has only a single class in the namespace, you will usually include much larger programs within a namespace.

The purpose of using a unique namespace construct is to prevent what is known as a *namespace collision*. For example, let's say that both you and I create a class named *Employee*. Having two classes with the same name could be very confusing to a program attempting to use a specific *Employee* class. However, when we add a namespace, we change the name of our class to *namespace.classname*, and this naming scheme makes the names of our classes unique. When we want to use our *Employee* class, we reference it by calling *employees.Employee*.

Microsoft recommends using the names of your company and products as nested namespaces. For example, if I worked for Litware, Inc., and our *Employee* class was used in a human resource software program named *EmpTracker*, I would create a namespace such as *Namespace Litware.EmpTracker*.

Someone needing to use this class would have to reference it by using a statement such as the following:

```
Dim newEmp1 As New Litware.EmpTracker.Employee
```

Although not foolproof, in most cases this naming convention will fully qualify the specific *Employee* class I want to use. Unless someone duplicates the name of my company, the name of my product, *and* the name of my class, we can be pretty sure the right class will be called. When you are writing production code, always use this namespace naming scheme.

Declaring Our Class

Next the class itself is declared, sandwiched between the *Namespace* and *End Namespace* statements. Our class is declared using the *Public* access modifier so that it is available to all procedures in all classes, modules, and structures in all applications that might need to use it.

```
Public Class Employee
```

When we want to store information about a new employee, we simply create a new object for that employee. Of course, when we create an instance of our *Employee* class by using the keyword *New*, the instance is created in memory and at that point becomes an object.

Each individual instance of our *Employee* class will hold specific information about an individual employee, such as the employee's first name and last name, whether the employee is trained in Visual Basic .NET, and the employee's unique identification number. (Our company might have ten John Smith's working for it, and because each John Smith is different, using just the name won't be enough. In a real application, we might use an employee's Social Security number to fully qualify each employee.)

```
Private m_sFirstName As String = ""
Private m_sLastName As String = ""
Private m_bVBNETTrained As Boolean = False
Private m_iEmpNumber As Integer = 0
```

The variables used to hold this information—*m_sFirstName*, *m_sLastName*, *m_bVBNETTrained*, and *m_iEmpNumber*—are declared as *Private*. These variables are known as a class's *member fields*, or *data elements*. These variables are declared as private, so they are available only to the class, module, or structure in which they are declared. You'll recall from Chapter 2 that this level of access means that they can't be read or written to from outside the class unless we provide a property with which to do so.

Properties allow us to control the values that are entered into or read from the classes' fields from the outside world. For example, we might want to check data to ensure that it's numeric before assigning that data to a numeric class data field. We also probably want to edit or perform reasonability checks on all incoming values. Properties are just the place to do this.

> **Note** Notice that the private variables are prefixed with *m_*. By convention, this prefix designates that the variables are class (m)ember data fields. Each variable also has a descriptive name so that readers of the code know exactly what the members are used for. I like to preface each name with a single character that tells the reader the data type of the variable. When I see *m_sFirstName* in the code, it's immediately apparent that this is a member variable, so it's private and a member of the class. The *s* tells me it's a string, and, of course, the descriptive name of the variable is self-documenting.

By keeping the member variables private to the class, we make use of *data encapsulation*, or *data hiding*, one of the important object-oriented programming concepts introduced in Chapter 2. The ability to hide data ensures the integrity of the class's data elements.

> **Tip** I'd like to point out once more the capability of Visual Basic .NET to initialize variables on the same line as they are declared. The language will provide a default value of *0* for integers and a default value of " " for strings. However, in keeping with our professional programming approach, we are never going to rely on the default behavior of the language. Making the default value explicit is good programming practice because it enhances code readability, ensures the programmer knows precisely what the value will be, and does not leave the initial value to chance.

Using Shared Variables

The next line of code in our class is an example of a shared variable. Remember that when the *Shared* keyword is used, a single copy of the variable is shared between all objects of type *Employee*.

```
Private Shared iTotEmployees As Integer = 0
```

You can think of a shared variable in the same way you think of global variables. The only difference is that a shared variable is seen and shared only by members of the same class. Because each employee will have a unique *iEmpNumber*, we will use the shared variable *iTotEmployees* to keep track of how many employees are currently assigned. Our code will increment the shared *iTotEmployees* variable each time a new employee object is created. That number will be assigned to the new employee object's *iEmpNumber*. The shared variable *iTotEmployees* can be seen by all instances of the *Employee* class, while an individual instance of the class can only see the individual employee's *m_iEmpNumber*.

Class Constructors

When another programmer wants to create a new *Employee* object from our *Employee* class, he or she uses the *New* keyword. To create a new *Employee* object, you would use the *New* keyword like this:

```
Dim newEmp1 As New employees.Employee()
```

When the compiler encounters this *Dim* statement, it creates a new instance of the *Employee* class and uses the reference variable *newEmp1* to communicate with the object. The programmer can now work with the newly created object by using *newEmp1*.

In classic Visual Basic, this way of using *New* in the dimensioning statement was misleading. The class was not actually instantiated; the statement simply reserved space for the object variable at compile time. Even though you used *New*, the object variable was still initialized to *Nothing*. The object wasn't actually created in memory until you touched the object for the first time with an operation such as setting a property. Visual Basic .NET works the way Visual Basic 6 should have. When you use the *New* keyword, an object is created at that time. This mechanism is much more intuitive and is similar to object creation in other OOP languages.

When the *New* keyword is encountered by the compiler, the class is instantiated as an object by calling its constructor, *New*. Class constructors initialize instances of a class and are run by the common language runtime environment when an instance is created.

```
Sub New()
    MyBase.New()
    iTotEmployees += 1
    iEmpNumber = iTotEmployees
End Sub
```

The *New* and *Destruct* procedures in Visual Basic .NET replace the *Class_Initialize* and *Class_Terminate* methods used in classic Visual Basic to initialize and destroy objects. However, unlike *Class_Initialize*, the *New* constructor will run only once when a class is created. It cannot be called explicitly anywhere other than in the first line of code in another constructor from either the same class or from a derived class. The code in the *New* method will always run before any other code in a class. And, unlike classic Visual Basic, Visual Basic .NET permits you to pass parameters into a constructor. Not only that, the constructor can also be overloaded in .NET.

Overloading Constructors

Instead of simply creating a *New* constructor in the way we just did, it might be helpful to create additional overloaded constructors to illustrate the concept of passing parameters to a constructor. Notice that we do not have to use the access modifier *Overloads* for our constructors. The compiler is smart enough to recognize that when it sees two *New* procedures in a class, overloaded constructors are around. However, each *New* must have a signature (the name of the procedure and the parameter list) that is different in the number or type of arguments. Simply making one parameter *ByVal* and an identical parameter *ByRef* does not work. Because our first constructor's signature does not take any parameters (the pair of parentheses indicate it's empty), none of the private member variables, such as name or age, can be given values other than the default initialization.

The following constructor signatures allow you to create a new *Employee* class object by calling the constructor using either no parameters or with the parameters for first and last names. The compiler will select the correct overloaded constructor with which to create an *Employee* object on the basis of the signature you use.

```
Sub New()
Sub New(ByVal fName As String, ByVal lName As String)
```

In practice, overloading is useful when your object class dictates that you use similar names for procedures that operate on different data types. For example, in the *Employee* class we are passing in strings. You can see how we could overload a constructor to pass in either an employee's name or Social Security number. Visual Basic .NET knows how to call the correct constructor by examining the parameters and matching them with the correct constructor.

Overloading is also useful in procedures in which you would previously use the *Optional* keyword or a parameter array to pass in a variable number of parameters. In those cases, extra code had to be written to determine whether any optional parameters were indeed passed. If a param array was used, more code had to be written to determine the number and type of parameters passed in. Overloading makes passing in a variable number and type of parameters much cleaner and simpler.

MyBase.New

MyBase.New must be the first line of code in the constructor. This statement calls the base-class constructor of the class from which our class is derived, initializing the base class that our class inherits from. It also performs implicit variable initializations. (The keyword *MyBase* refers to a class's immediate base class and allows a class to call methods in its base class.) Because we are not explicitly inheriting from a class in this example, we implicitly inherit from the *Object* class, the ultimate base class for all .NET objects.

If our class is derived from another class, using *MyBase* would call the parent class's constructor. If that class was derived from another class, its constructor would be called by our parent class's constructor and so on up the chain to ensure that the topmost class was initialized first. The code would then return down the sequence and initialize all the parent classes in turn before it got to ours. This sequence ensures that any classes that our class inherits from are fully initialized before our class tries to use them.

While the Windows form we used in Chapter 2 had inherited members, our *Employee* class will have only methods we define (for example, *New*), as well as the methods inherited from the *System.Object* class. *MyBase* is generally used to access public members defined in the base class. *MyBase* cannot, however, be used to access any private members in the base class. *MyBase* cannot be assigned to a variable or passed to procedures because *MyBase* is not a real object. Finally, *MyBase* can't be used in modules, only in classes.

Assigning Values to Our Private Data Fields

We want to hide the implementation of how the employee number, *m_iEmpNumber*, is assigned from the outside world. Because the assignment of the new employee number should be automatic, it can be completed in the constructor. Upon creation of an *Employee* object, the *iTotEmployees* shared variable is incremented by 1 using the new streamlined += syntax. Of course, *iTotEmployees* is visible to all instances of the *Employee* class because it is shared.

The new value of *iTotEmployees* is then immediately assigned to the specific class's private variable, *m_iEmpNumber*.

```
Sub New()
    MyBase.New()
    iTotEmployees += 1
    m_iEmpNumber = iTotEmployees
End Sub
```

In the overloaded constructor in which we pass in values, these values are immediately assigned to the *Employee* class member data fields for the employee name.

```
Sub New(ByVal fName As String, ByVal lName As String)
    m_sFirstName = fName
    m_sLastName = lName
    iTotEmployees += 1
    m_iEmpNumber = iTotEmployees
End Sub
```

Notice that the two parameters in the overloaded constructor are passed in *ByVal*(ue) instead of *ByRef*(erence). When a parameter is passed in *ByVal*, a copy of the original is passed in, not the original itself. The procedure can modify the value passed in, but the original value remains intact. On the other hand, if the parameter is passed in *ByRef*, a reference to the memory location is passed in, which means that any change made to the parameter within the procedure changes the original value. While *ByRef* is typically faster, it can cause unintended side effects and can make tracking down bugs difficult. I'll describe

ByVal and *ByRef* in more detail in Chapter 4. I'll also highlight situations in which you want to use *ByRef* later in the book; it's usually desirable to use *ByVal*.

> **Note** In Visual Basic 6, if you do not specify *ByVal* or *ByRef* for a procedure parameter, the passing mechanism defaults to *ByRef*, which means that if the variable is modified by the called procedure it is also modified in the calling program. In Visual Basic .NET, the passing mechanism defaults to *ByVal* for every parameter when you declare a procedure. This protects parameters against modification.

Overriding

As you've learned, derived classes inherit the methods defined in their base class. All methods carry the *NotOverridable* keyword by default. If a method in a base class is marked with the *Overridable* keyword, however, you can use the *Overrides* keyword in a derived class to override the base class's method with your own.

Here's another instance of when to make explicit what Visual Basic .NET does by default. If you don't want any classes that inherit our *Employee* class to ever override a method, you would use the *NotOverridable* keyword to qualify the method. In practice this keyword is rarely used because it's redundant. However, when you don't want a method to be overridden, follow good programming form and use the *NotOverridable* keyword. Not only does this keyword protect you from how the default behavior of a method might change down the road, but it also makes your intention crystal clear.

Let's see how overriding is used in our *Employee* class example. If we create 10 employee objects and add data to their member variables, our labor will do us little good if we can't then save the information to a physical storage medium such as a disk file. We want to persist the objects by saving them so that we can read them back into memory later. Serializing the objects to disk in a binary format will save all the data we entered in our objects.

The great news is that Visual Basic .NET handles serialization for us through built-in framework classes. However, we don't want to save *Employee* objects that don't have critical information such as an employee's first or last name. By adding a simple function, named *Serialize*, we can return a *Boolean* True or False after we determine whether the name fields are populated.

We also might want to create another more specialized class sometime in the future that inherits from *Employee*. For example, we might want to create a *Division* class that inherits from the *Employee* class and has member data fields that need to be interrogated to ensure that they contain data before saving the object.

Because Visual Basic .NET methods are not overridable by default, you must explicitly use the keyword *Overridable* for those methods you want derived classes to be able to override. This designation permits us to either use the method as-is in this class or override it in a child class. Overridden methods are often used to implement polymorphism, which, you'll remember, means *many forms*. In object-oriented programming, the behavior of a polymorphic method depends on the object being called.

```
Overridable Function Serialize() As Boolean
    If ((m_sFirstName <> "") And (m_sLastName <> "")) Then
        Return True
    Else
        Return False
    End If
End Function
```

Several aspects of this function are worth noting. First, while we implement *Serialize* as a function, to the outside world it's a method. Within our class, we implement methods by using either subroutines or functions. The difference between a subroutine and a function is, of course, that a function returns a value whereas a subroutine does not.

Code that created an instance of our *Employee* class could now do a quick check by including the following statements:

```
If (MyEmployee.Serialize = True) then
    'Do something important
End If
```

When a value is returned to the caller, the new Visual Basic .NET keyword *Return* is used. You can still use the Visual Basic 6 syntax for assigning the return value to the name of the function: *Serialize* = *True*. Both return syntaxes work fine.

The final item to note is the use of parentheses. While parentheses are not required to make the program run, the use of them is a habit I developed way back in grad school. Spending a second or two to type them in is a good idea for a few reasons.

First, with parentheses, the comparisons being made aren't ambiguous, which enhances readability by orders of magnitude, especially for complex comparisons. When you are performing numeric comparisons, you use parentheses to order the comparisons, of course. In our example, a purist might say that using parentheses is marginally expensive in processing time. However, the time lost is negligible when compared to the absolute readability the parentheses provide. A quick glance at this line leaves no doubt about exactly what is being examined. Using parentheses is a professional touch that ensures you are comparing what you think you are comparing.

```
If ((m_sFirstName <> "") And (m_sLastName <> "")) Then
⋮
```

#Region

Remember that when we added the class properties, we sandwiched them between the *#Region* / *#End Region* statements. *#Region* takes a single string parameter that is used to describe what code is hidden.

```
#Region "Employee Properties"
⋮
#End Region
```

Regions are another great feature of the .NET IDE. When programming in classic Visual Basic, I used the procedure view all the time to isolate just the code I was working on. The *#Region* feature provides the same functionality—any code placed within a region can be collapsed or expanded so that the workspace isn't cluttered. In Figure 3-8, you can see that the *Employee Properties* region is currently collapsed. Clicking the plus sign expands the code for the properties. The ability to place custom text such as *Employee Properties* in a region to let us know what's included makes working with huge chunks of code a breeze.

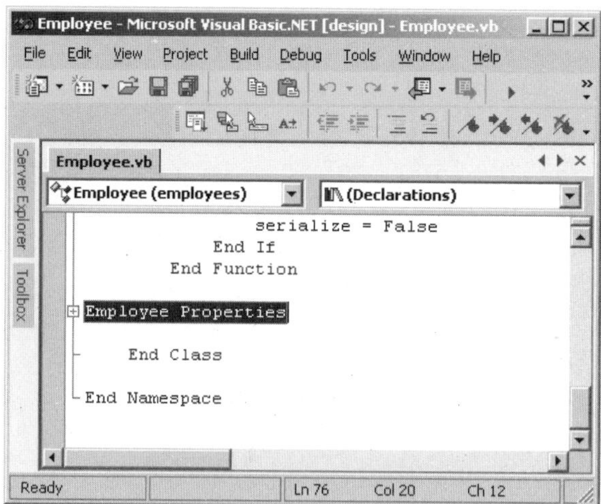

Figure 3-8 The *Employee Properties* region is collapsed.

The *Employee* Class Properties

Properties are the gatekeepers for our private data fields, such as *m_iEmpNumber*. I mentioned earlier that these variables are instance variables. Each instance of the object has its own *m_iEmpNumber*.

Let's say that you draw two buttons on a form and you set the *Text* property of the first to *Hola* and the second to *Adios*. While both buttons are instances of the same button class and live in the same DLL, each button is a unique object instantiated in memory. Each has its own individual *Text* property and *Location* property set to something different. Likewise, each instance of our *Employee* class has its own value for the private data field *iEmpNumber*.

```
Private m_iEmpNumber As Integer = 0
```

If this *Employee* class data field is private, how can it be read from or written to? That's where properties come in. We provide access to our private variables only through properties. By doing this, the class instance variables can't be changed accidentally or maliciously.

Think of your house as a class. Even though you have windows in the house, you permit access only through the door. Someone could crawl into the house through a window, of course, but you can lock it so that such access is not allowed. By forcing all access to the house through the door, you can do things such as put a doormat on the floor so that visitors can wipe their feet, or you can lock the door when you're not at home. You control access to the house.

Properties control access to your classes' private data fields, which permits you to validate or edit any data that's passed in. You can place business rules in the property to ensure that data falls within your predefined rules.

A data field usually has a *Get* property that returns a value to the world outside the class and a *Set* property that's used to take a value in from the outside and assign it to a private variable. Properties that can be accessed from outside your class must use the *Public* access modifier.

The control that properties provide gives a programmer flexibility. As I mentioned, you might want to edit or validate data within a property before you assign it to the data field. Or, in the case of the *Employee* class's *m_iEmpNumber* variable, you want users to be able to read the number but not change it. That restriction is easily accomplished by using the *ReadOnly* access modifier. If you want a property to be write-only, you use the *WriteOnly* access modifier. Notice that in our example, the return value is an integer, as defined by the property's signature.

```
Public ReadOnly Property EmployeeNumber() As Integer
    Get
        Return m_iEmpNumber
    End Get
End Property
```

Most properties permit private data instance variables to be either read from or written to from outside the class. For example, we can either get (read) the string *FirstName* or set (write) a new value from the outside and assign it to the *m_sFirstName* private data field. Unlike Visual Basic 6, in which the value to be written is explicitly passed into the property, Visual Basic .NET uses the new *Value* keyword. The type of the keyword is defined in the signature of the property. In our example, only a string data type can be passed into the property as a value.

```
Property FirstName() As String
    Get
        FirstName = m_sFirstName
    End Get
    Set
        m_sFirstName = Value
    End Set
End Property
```

If a program wanted to use our *Employee* class, the code might look something like this.

```
Dim newEmp1 As New employees.Employee()

With newEmp1
    .FirstName = "Garrett"
    .LastName = "Connell"
    .VBNet = True
End With
```

The class is created with the *New* keyword, and a reference to the newly minted object is given to the reference variable *newEmp1*. We can then set the *FirstName*, *LastName*, and *VBNet* properties by simply assigning values to them.

From the outside, nothing reveals that the *FirstName* property really sets a private variable, *m_sFirstName*. That's another benefit of using properties: the outside world does not need to know or care how the property is implemented within the class. For example, when you set a button's *Text* property, you have no idea how this is done, but who cares? How it's done is not important to us. We want to use the black box functionality of the button class. Likewise, a user of our *Employee* class doesn't care how we implement the property; it's only important that it can be set and read.

Note We could have written the preceding property assignment code by fully qualifying each property using *Object.Property = Value*.

```
newEmp1.FirstName = "Garrett"
newEmp1.LastName = "Connell"
newEmp1.VBNet = True
```

Whenever you have two or more properties you are reading or writing, your code will execute more quickly if you use the *With Object / End With* syntax. When Visual Basic .NET sees a dot ("."), it must take time to resolve it. The *With* statement allows you to perform a series of statements on a specified object without requalifying the name of the object. Once a *With* block is entered, the object can't be changed. As a result, you can't use a single *With* statement to affect a number of different objects.

Another benefit of using properties and methods is that if we don't change the interface contract (i.e., the signature of the property or method), we can update and modify the implementation of the property or method and the outside world will never know. You might later want to add additional business rules or stricter validation based on what users enter. Simply add the new code and recompile the assembly, and the calling program will be none the wiser because we changed the implementation and not the interface to the outside world. The objective is to not break any programs that call and use our object.

Building a class is like a legal contract. You set out certain conditions (properties and methods) that the class user abides by. Once set, these conditions can't be changed. A contract like this was a fundamental rule of COM for Visual Basic 6 and still applies in Visual Basic .NET. You can add procedures, methods, or properties in newer renditions of a class. However, you can never change any methods or properties that have already been published—these interfaces to our class are sacrosanct. Any legacy programs that might use your object will continue to work without being affected, and newer programs can take advantage of the functionality you added in later releases of your class.

Take a look at the assignment of the *FirstName* property in our object. Because the property is on the left side of the equal sign, the compiler recognizes that it should invoke the *Set* portion of the property. If we wrote a statement like *sString = newEmp1.FirstName,* the compiler recognizes a read operation and invokes the *Get* portion of the property. All we do is provide *Get* and *Set* code. The compiler does the heavy lifting in determining which one to use.

More About Inheritance

Unlike some other object-oriented languages, Visual Basic .NET only provides for single inheritance—a class can inherit only from a single parent class. Of course, that parent class can inherit from another class and so on. As I mentioned in Chapter 2, languages such as C++ permit you to inherit from multiple classes simultaneously. Problems from multiple inheritance are one of the largest sources of bugs in C++.

To fully understand objects, let's create another small class, *Division*, that inherits the functionality of our *Employee* class. As you can see by now, inherited classes are like an upside-down pyramid. A parent class is general—wide like the overturned base of a pyramid. As child classes inherit from parent classes, they become more and more specialized, or narrow. An inherited class enjoys the functionality of the parent class plus any specialized functionality it might implement.

Our *Division* class will be a bit more specialized and permit us to assign an employee to a division and indicate how long the employee has been in that division. Follow these steps to create the *Division* class:

1. Click Project | Add Class. Add another class module to the project as you did for the *Employee* class. Name the class *Division.vb*, and then click Open to add the empty class declaration to the project.
2. Replace the existing *Division.vb* class code with the following code.

```
Imports System
Imports Employee.employees.Employee
Imports Microsoft.VisualBasic.ControlChars
Imports System.Windows.Forms


Namespace CompanyDivision

    Public Class Division
        Inherits employees.Employee

        Private m_sDivision As String = ""
        Private m_iMonthsInDivision As Integer = 0

        Sub New()
            MyBase.New()
        End Sub

        Sub New(ByVal fName As String, ByVal lName As String)
            MyBase.New((fName), (lName))
        End Sub
```

```
        Overrides Function Serialize() As Boolean
            If ((m_sDivision <> "") And _
                (m_iMonthsInDivision <> 0)) Then

                If MyBase.Serialize = True Then
                    Return True
                Else
                    Return False
                End If
            Else
                Return False
            End If
        End Function


#Region "Division Properties"
        Property Division() As String
            Get
                Division = m_sDivision
            End Get
            Set
                m_sDivision = Value
            End Set
        End Property

        Property MonthsInDivision() As Integer
            Get
                MonthsInDivision = m_iMonthsInDivision
            End Get
            Set
                m_iMonthsInDivision = Value
            End Set
        End Property

#End Region

    End Class
End Namespace
```

3. Our project already includes the *System* reference, but we now have to add the *System.Windows.Forms.dll* reference. Click View | Solution Explorer to display the Solution Explorer, if necessary. Right-click References, and select Add Reference. You'll see the Add Reference dialog box again, shown in Figure 3-9. Select the assembly mentioned earlier, and then click OK.

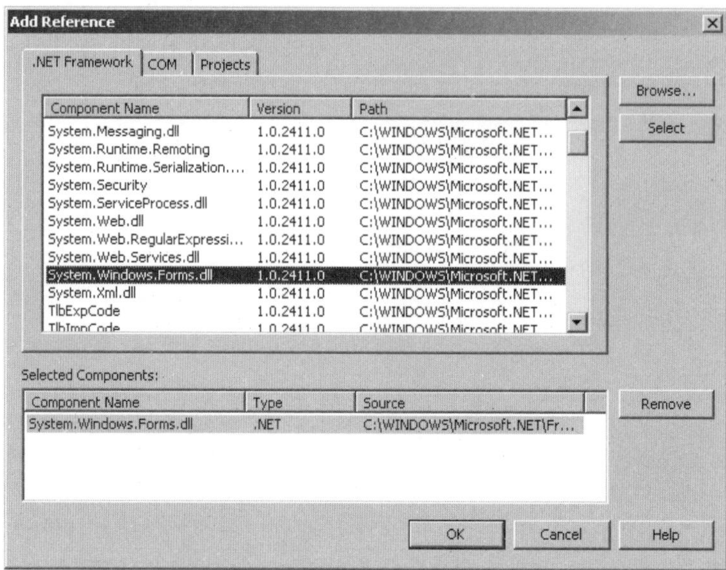

Figure 3-9 Add a reference to *System.Windows.Forms.dll.*

The Solution Explorer should now look like Figure 3-10. You can see that the three references are included, along with the new *Division.vb* class module.

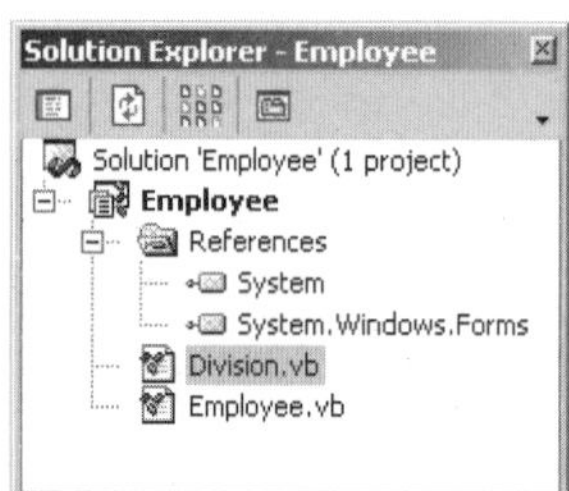

Figure 3-10 The Solution Explorer should look like this.

Most of what you learned about the *Employee* class applies to the *Division* class, so I won't review those concepts. We sandwiched the *Division* class within the *CompanyDivision* namespace. The *Division* class inherits all the functionality of the *employees.Employee* class.

```
Namespace CompanyDivision

    Public Class Division
        Inherits employees.Employee
```

The *Division* class's constructors are overloaded to provide multiple implementations of *New*. Remember that the first line in a constructor must be a call to the constructor of its parent class, in this case *Employee*. We call the *Employee* constructor with the *MyBase* keyword to ensure that the *Employee* class is fully initialized before we try to use any of its members within the *Division* class. Both overloaded constructors provide signatures for *MyBase* that match the constructors in the parent class.

```
Sub New()
    MyBase.New()
End Sub
```

Notice in the following code the double parentheses around the parameters of the call to *MyBase.New* in the constructor that takes two strings as its arguments. It so happens that we are passing in both parameters by value. However, I've used this syntax to show how you can force an argument to be passed by value no matter how it is declared. While the parentheses are not needed here, this syntax is how you would force parameters to be passed by value even if the parent expected parameters passed by reference.

```
Sub New(ByVal fName As String, ByVal lName As String)
    MyBase.New((fName), (lName))
End Sub
```

The *Serialize* function in *Division* overrides the implementation in the parent *Employee* class. However, as I indicated earlier, we don't want to save an instance of a *Division* class if important fields have been accidentally omitted. The overridden *Serialize* method checks the *Division* class's private data fields. If those fields have been populated, the first and last name member fields in the parent *Employee* class need to be checked. We can check these fields by calling the parent class's *Serialize* method. This overridden method first checks to see whether the *Division* class's private variables have been set. If they have, *MyBase.Serialize* is called to ensure the names have been entered in the *Employee* class. If and only if both checks return True, the overridden method returns True to the caller.

```
Overrides Function Serialize() As Boolean
    If ((m_sDivision <> "") And _
        (m_iMonthsInDivision <> 0)) Then

        If MyBase.Serialize = True Then
            Return True
        Else
            Return False
        End If
    Else
        Return False
    End If
End Function
```

Virtual Methods

All Visual Basic .NET methods are virtual methods, which means that if both the parent class and the child class include methods with the same name, the child class's implementation of the method is always called first when the method is invoked from the outside world. The method that is called is always the one that's included in the class used to create the object. If we create a type *Employee* class, its *Serialize* method is invoked. If we create a child class, *Division*, that inherits from the parent *Employee* class, it's the *Serialize* method implemented in the *Division* class that's called.

On the other hand, we might inherit a class and implement a method only in the parent class. When the method is invoked, Visual Basic .NET does not find it in the child class, so it searches up the inheritance chain until it finds the method in the parent class. But, because all methods are virtual, searching always starts in the child class at the bottom of the hierarchy and moves upward.

In the same way that you can prevent a method from being overridden by using the *NotOverridable* keyword, if you don't want another class to inherit our entire *Division* class, adding the keyword *NotInheritable* ensures inheritance will not happen.

```
Public NotInheritable Class Division
    Inherits employees.Employee
```

Synchronizing the Class View

Now that we have both classes defined, let's examine the class hierarchy to be sure that everything is as we expect it to be. Visual Basic .NET has a handy tool that allows you to view a class hierarchically. Go to the code window in the IDE, right-click, and then select Synchronize Class View. This command displays the Class View window. At the top level is the assembly name *Employee*. Within the assembly is the namespace *CompanyDivision* designated by a pair of curly brackets ({}). Inside the namespace is our child class, *Division*, and within *Division* is the Bases And Interfaces group, which contains a representation of our *Employee* class we inherited from.

The constructors, methods, and properties of the *Employee* class are also displayed, as you can see in Figure 3-11. Next the private member variables of *Employee* are shown with a lock icon. After the private member variables of *Employee* are the methods, properties, and private data members of the *Division* class. Below that is the namespace *employees* that, if expanded, shows the items in the *Employee* class.

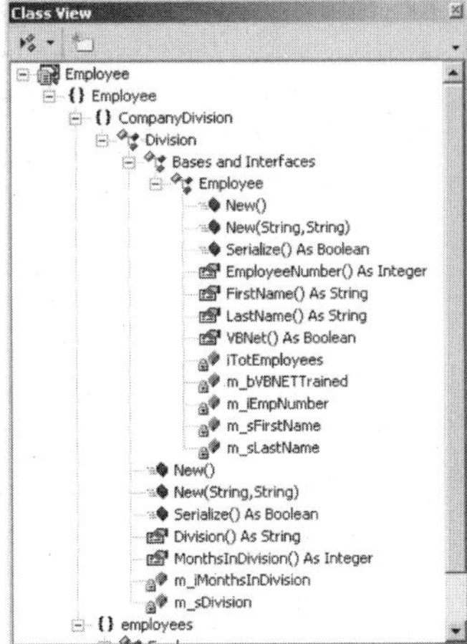

Figure 3-11 The Class View window allows you to view a class hierarchically.

Another helpful tool is the Object Browser. The Object Browser leads you to just about anything you might want to know about a class. To display the Object Browser, select View | Other Windows | Object Browser, or simply press F2. On the left are the objects available. Our *employees* namespace is also listed. On the right, the members of the *Division* class are displayed. Clicking one of the items shows its signature in the bottom panel. At the bottom of Figure 3-12, you can see that *Division* inherits *Employee.employees.Employee*.

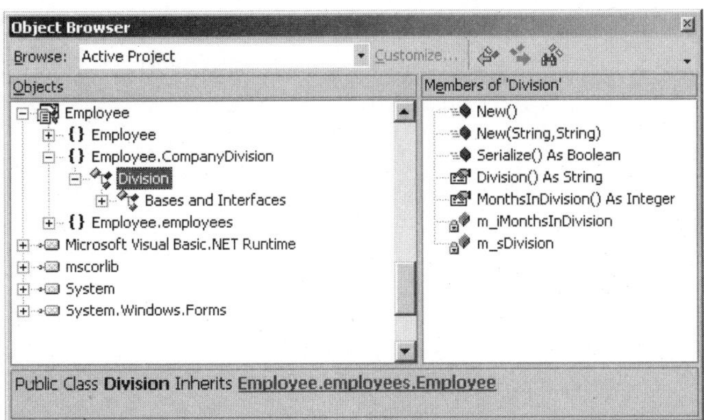

Figure 3-12 The Object Browser displays the classes available in projects and libraries.

> **Tip** I remember when Microsoft Internet Explorer version 4 came out. I wanted to program its object model (its hierarchy of classes) using Visual Basic. Unfortunately, the documentation about how to do this was as scarce as hen's teeth. By using the Object Browser in classic Visual Basic I could see which methods were available, and I was able to access the Internet Explorer. I strongly suggest that you use the Object Browser to poke around and look at the assemblies listed to get a sense of what's prebuilt and available for you to use in Visual Basic .NET.

Creating Instances of the *Employee* Class

So far we've built a class and examined it with X-ray glasses, but we haven't run it yet. Let's run our program now.

1. In the Division.vb tab in your code editor, add the following code right after the *End Namespace* line that encapsulates the class. The next section of code, *Sub Main* and the *showEmployee* subroutine, will be encapsulated within a module, a code file that contains functions. This module will provide a harness in which to test our simple class within the same code window. We will create two instances of the *Division* class. Each instance will use a different overloaded constructor. Then we will set properties for each instance and pass the objects to the *showEmployee* subroutine to be displayed.

```
Public Module modmain

    '"Main" is application's entry point
    Sub Main()
        Dim newEmp1 As New CompanyDivision.Division()
        Dim newEmp2 As New _
            CompanyDivision.Division("Marea", "Castaneda")

        With newEmp1
            .FirstName = "Garrett"
            .LastName = "Connell"
            .Division = "MIS"
            .MonthsInDivision = 18
        End With
```

```
        showEmployee(newEmp1)

        newEmp2.Division = "Administration"
        newEmp2.MonthsInDivision = 7

        If TypeOf newEmp2 Is _
            CompanyDivision.Division Then

            If newEmp2.Serialize = True Then
                showEmployee(newEmp2)
            End If
        End If

    End Sub

    'This private subroutine will be passed a Division
    'class and print the contents. Note that the
    'signature shows it will take a
    'CompanyDivision.Division data type as a parameter.

    Private Sub showEmployee(ByRef currentEmployee As _
        CompanyDivision.Division)
        Dim sDisplayString As String

        sDisplayString = "Employee Name: " & _
            currentEmployee.FirstName & _
            " " & currentEmployee.LastName & crlf
        sDisplayString += "Employee Division: " &  _
            currentEmployee.Division & crlf
        sDisplayString += "Employee Months: " &  _
            currentEmployee.MonthsInDivision & crlf
        sDisplaystring += "Employee Number: " &  _
            currentEmployee.EmployeeNumber & crlf

        MessageBox.Show(sDisplayString, "Employee Scanner", _
            MessageBoxButtons.OK, MessageBoxIcon.Information)

    End Sub

End Module
```

2. We have to instruct the compiler to start the program by using our new *Sub Main*. Select View | Solution Explorer, right-click the *Employee* assembly, and then select Properties from the menu. The Assembly name and the Root namespace should say *Employee*.

3. Select Sub Main in the Startup object drop-down list. Your selection in this list tells the compiler to use *Sub Main* when the program

starts. Click OK to close the dialog box, and then select Debug | Start to run our program. You'll see output like that shown in Figure 3-13.

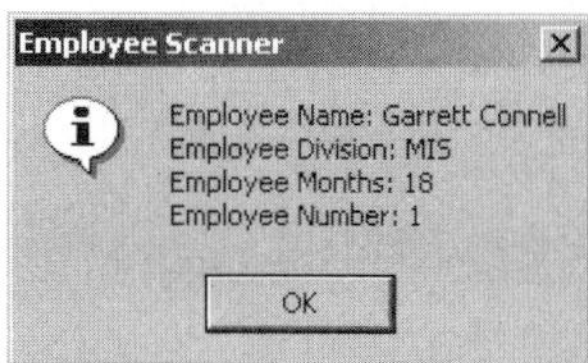

Figure 3-13 The first employee's information.

The two instances of the *Division* class that we created are assigned to reference variables *newEmp1* and *newEmp2*. The first instance calls the empty constructor, but the second passes in parameters for the first and last name. Because we inherited from *Employee*, *MyBase* is called to initialize the base class *Employee*.

```
Public Module modmain

    '"Main" is application's entry point
    Sub Main()
        Dim newEmp1 As New CompanyDivision.Division()
        Dim newEmp2 As New _
            CompanyDivision.Division("Marea", "Castaneda")
```

Next we set the properties of our class. The first two name properties are called in the parent class because we don't have implementations of *FirstName* or *LastName* in the *Division* class. The next two properties are implemented in the child class. After these properties are set, the *showEmployee* procedure is called. This procedure prints out the contents of the object. You can see that by setting properties we have communicated with both the child and parent classes.

```
With newEmp1
    .FirstName = "Garrett"
    .LastName = "Connell"
    .Division = "MIS"
    .MonthsInDivision = 18
End With

showEmployee(newEmp1)
```

We now set the two *Division* properties in *newEmp2*. Because we instantiated this object by passing in the first and last name to the constructor, we only need to set *Division* and *MonthsInDivision*.

```
newEmp2.Division = "Administration"
newEmp2.MonthsInDivision = 7
```

You'll often need to determine exactly which type of object you are dealing with. You can use the built-in *TypeOf* operator to check whether the run-time type of a value is compatible with a given type. In other words, the first operand (*newEmp2*) must be a reference type, and the second operand (*CompanyDivision.Division*) must be a type name. The *TypeOf* operator returns True if a conversion from the run-time type of the operand to the type exists.

If *newEmp2* is of data type *CompanyDivision.Division*, the *Serialize* method is called. Because all methods in Visual Basic .NET are virtual, the child implementation is called. However, it so happens that our child implementation then calls the parent implementation of *Serialize* via *MyBase*. If all of these checks return True, we print the contents of this object.

```
If TypeOf newEmp2 Is CompanyDivision.Division Then
    If newEmp2.Serialize = True Then
        showEmployee(newEmp2)
    End If
End If
```

Of course, everything is as it should be, so the contents of *newEmp2* are displayed successfully, as you can see in Figure 3-14.

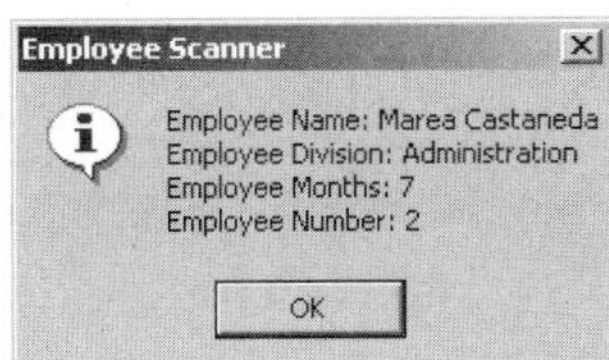

Figure 3-14 The second employee's information.

This example shows that even though we instantiated two separate objects from the *Division* class, each object is an individual with its own values for its private data members. Under the hood, Visual Basic .NET uses only a single instance of the methods and properties of our classes, but it maintains separate member data variables.

The subroutine *showEmployee* takes in an object of type *CompanyDivision.Division* as a parameter. You can see that the subroutine is strongly typed—it will accept a parameter only of type *CompanyDivision.Division*. We dimension a local string variable and concatenate the various values of the object passed in as a parameter and display them.

```
Private Sub showEmployee(ByRef currentEmployee As _
    CompanyDivision.Division)
    Dim sDisplayString As String

    sDisplayString = "Employee Name: " & _
        currentEmployee.FirstName & _
        " " & currentEmployee.LastName & crlf
```

(continued)

```
sDisplayString += "Employee Division: " & _
    currentEmployee.Division & crlf
sDisplayString += "Employee Months: " & _
    currentEmployee.MonthsInDivision & crlf
sDisplaystring += "Employee Number: " & _
    currentEmployee.EmployeeNumber & crlf

MessageBox.Show(sDisplayString, "Employee Scanner", _
    MessageBoxButtons.OK, MessageBoxIcon.Information)

End Sub
```

Notice the *crlf* (carriage return/line feed) characters at the end of each line. These characters are not provided by the .NET Framework but by the *Microsoft.VisualBasic* assembly. Whenever you create a new Visual Basic .NET program that uses features of the language, import the *Microsoft.VisualBasic* namespace.

Conclusion: Object-Oriented Programming Demystified

Except for some nuances I will touch on later, you should now have an idea of what object-oriented programming is all about. Base classes are always the most general, and as child classes inherit from a parent, they become more specialized. This concept will be illustrated throughout the remaining chapters as we tackle the .NET Framework classes.

As you can see, the idea in Visual Basic .NET is to build a program that uses and manages objects. The objects are reusable and extensible in that you can derive other objects from them for any specialized needs. Once the classes you write are debugged, they truly become black boxes of functionality. You place them in your programmer's toolbox and use them when you need to.

Let's do a quick recap of everything we covered in building our classes. If anything is unclear, go back and reread the sections about the topics that are still fuzzy. A solid understanding of these concepts is required to get the most out of Visual Basic .NET. In our *Employee / Division* class example, we covered the following:

- **Constructors.** Using the *New* keyword, when a class is instantiated, the constructor is invoked. If the class inherits a parent class, the *MyBase.New* statement must be the first line of code within the constructor. This statement instantiates the parent class by calling its constructor. If that class is inherited from another class, the first line in the parent's constructor invokes its parent class and so on up the inheritance chain. You can overload constructors, but you don't need to use the *Overloads* keyword. The compiler is smart enough to figure out which constructor to use as long as the signatures are different.

- **Encapsulation.** Hiding class data members by using the *Private* keyword. Encapsulation ensures that these members can be accessed only within the class itself or by way of properties from the outside world.
- **Inheritance.** Inheriting all the functionality of another class and adding to it specialized methods, properties, and data members.
- **Overloading.** Permits multiple variations of a method using the same name but embodying a different signature.
- **Overriding.** Permits overriding the implementation of a parent class method with that of a child method with the same name.
- **Private data members.** Variables that contain information specific to a particular instance of an object. In our *Employee* class, each instance contained the name of a specific person.
- **Properties.** (including *ReadOnly* and *WriteOnly*). Permits the outside world to read or write values to private data members in a class. Within properties, a programmer can add edit checks, business rules, and error checking.
- **Virtual methods.** The child implementation of a method is always called before the parent implementation.

I know this is quite a bit to digest for those of you new to object-oriented programming. Once you grok objects, however, easing into the .NET Framework will be a breeze.

> **Note** The term *grok* is from Robert A. Heinlein's science-fiction novel *Stranger in a Strange Land.* The main character, Valentine Michael Smith, was the only survivor of the first manned mission to Mars. Martians raised him, so when he returns to Earth, he is a true innocent. Valentine uses the term *grok* to mean understand, as in "I grok Visual Basic .NET classes" or "Do you grok objects?" Programmers are notorious sci-fi fans, so you might already know the term. A wag once remarked that if you use the term *grok* in a job interview, you can write your own ticket.

4

Visual Basic .NET Data Types and Features

So far we've used a few easy examples to understand how programs are created in Visual Basic .NET. As you've learned, you need to understand concepts such as object-oriented programming up front to work with the code that's generated in Visual Basic .NET—even to display and use a simple form.

Another concept you need to be sure you understand is data types. A data type is a blueprint for the layout of a section of memory. This blueprint determines the range of values the memory can store and the operations you can perform on the memory. Of course, every variable, array, constant, property, procedure argument, and procedure return value has a data type. You'll see shortly that understanding data types goes far beyond simple numeric types—it extends to every object.

Getting to Know Data Types

As you know, a variable is really the name of a memory location that is used to store data. When you dimension a variable, you give it a name and a data type. The variable's data type determines how the data is stored in the computer's memory.

Many classic Visual Basic programmers have had limited exposure to data types. These programmers occasionally use variables that are not dimensioned, and other times they use *Variant* variables to hold string, integer, or *Boolean* values. Earlier versions of Visual Basic allowed you to play fast and loose with data types in this manner. If you didn't dimension a variable, Visual Basic would give the variable the default data type—a 16-byte *Variant*.

Although the *Variant* type has valid uses such as holding a reference to an Excel spreadsheet object, the *Variant* type is usually the last refuge of a sloppy programmer. I have seen some mighty sloppy Visual Basic code in which every variable is a *Variant*. This lack of precision not only wastes memory, it also is dangerous. For example, you can assign a *Double* value to a *Variant* and then inadvertently assign a string to the same variable. Previous Visual Basic compilers won't even blink at this blatant mismatch of data types.

Visual Basic .NET is far stricter about how you use variables. The value you assign to a variable must be *assignment compatible* with the variable's type. If you declare a variable to be an *Integer*, you can't automatically assign a *Short* value to it. Visual Basic .NET also disallows type coercion. Those of you who like to write code similar to *myString = "The number is " + 10* will really need to pay attention.

Visual Basic .NET Data Types

Visual Basic .NET uses two types of variables: *value types* and *reference types*. Understanding the differences between value and reference data types is important for several reasons:

- They are handled differently by the memory management system.
- They test for equality differently.
- They are initialized differently by the common language runtime (CLR).
- They are treated differently in assignment statements.

A variable is a value type if it holds its data within its own memory location. A reference type, on the other hand, contains a reference (or *pointer*) to another memory location that contains the actual data. Value types include all numeric and binary data types, such as the *Integer* type, the *Char* type, and the *Date* type. Reference types include strings, arrays, and all classes. Consider the following code fragment:

```
Dim newEmp1 As New myClass()
Dim newEmp2 As New myClass()
Dim iInteger1 As Integer = 12
Dim iInteger2 As Integer = 12

MessageBox.Show(iInteger1.Equals(iInteger2).ToString)  'True

MessageBox.Show(newEmp1.Equals(newEmp2).ToString)      'False
newEmp2 = newEmp1
MessageBox.Show(newEmp1.Equals(newEmp2).ToString)      'True
```

This example has two value variables (*iInteger1* and *iInteger2*) and two reference variables (*newEmp1* and *newEmp2*). Both *iInteger1* and *iInteger2* are assigned the value 12. Obviously, these variables are equal because their data is equal, and the message box will display True. However, the two variables are separate and distinct because they occupy different memory locations. If we assigned 42 to *iInteger1*, the value of *iInteger2* would remain 12.

Now examine the statements concerning the reference variables *newEmp1* and *newEmp2*. These variables are initially dimensioned to point to different instances of *myClass*, and the first message box will print False. Next, *newEmp1* is assigned to *newEmp2*. Because these variables are reference variables, they now point to the same object in the same memory location, as shown in Figure 4-1. If any data fields in *newEmp1* are changed or modified, they are also modified in *newEmp2* because both variables reference the same memory location.

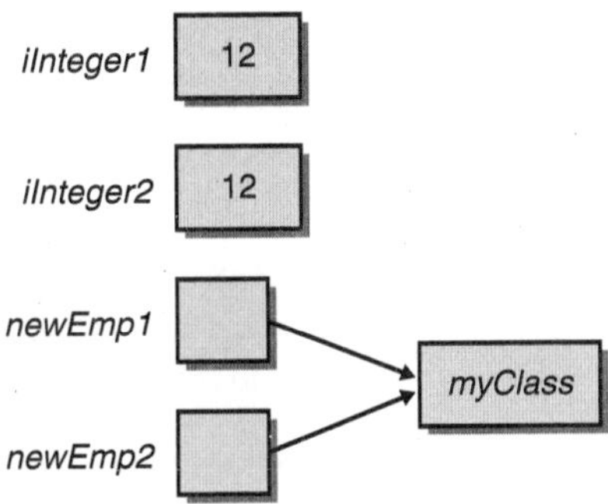

Figure 4-1 Reference variables point to memory locations.

When two reference variables are checked for equality, the check is really to see whether both variables reference the same memory location. If they do, as shown in Figure 4-1, they are considered equal. However, if each points to a different object of the same type—even if both objects have the same byte-for-byte values—the variables compare as unequal.

Value Types

A value type is also considered a *primitive type* in the .NET Framework. (A primitive type is a data type that is natively supported by the compiler. All primitive types are value types.) Value types are always accessed directly. In fact, you can't create a reference to a value type. And unlike reference types, setting a value type to Null is not possible. Value types always hold a value, even if you haven't yet assigned one. When a value type variable is dimensioned, it's initialized to a value representative of its type. If you dimension an *Integer* variable and don't assign a value to it, the Visual Basic .NET compiler automatically initializes the variable to 0.

The Visual Basic primitive types are identified through keywords, which are really aliases for predefined structure types in the *System* namespace. This fact means that a primitive type and the structure type for which it's an alias are completely indistinguishable. The Visual Basic keyword *Byte* is exactly the same as *System.Byte*.

Value types are *sealed*, meaning that no other type can be derived from them. Each value type is allocated a specific, fixed-size block of memory and—as I mentioned previously—is automatically initialized to a specific value by the compiler. Table 4-1 lists the Visual Basic .NET value types.

Table 4-1 Visual Basic .NET Value Types

Visual Basic Type	.NET Runtime Type Structure	Memory Storage Size	Default Value	Value Range
Boolean	*System.Boolean*	4 bytes	False	True or False
Byte	*System.Byte*	1 byte	0	0 through 255 (unsigned)
Char	*System.Char*	2 bytes	Chr(0)	0 through 65,535 (unsigned)
Date	*System.DateTime*	8 bytes	# 01/01/0001 12:00:00AM #	January 1, 1 CE through December 31, 9999
Decimal	*System.Decimal*	12 bytes	0D	+/−79,228,162,514,264,337,593,543, 950,335 with no decimal point; +/−7.9228162514264337593543950 335 with 28 places to the right of the decimal; smallest nonzero number is +/−0.0000000000000000000000000001
Double (double-precision floating-point)	*System.Double*	8 bytes	0.0	−1.79769313486231E308 through −4.94065645841247E-324 for negative values; 4.94065645841247E-324 through 1.79769313486232E308 for positive values
Integer	*System.Int32*	4 bytes	0	−2,147,483,648 through 2,147,483,647
Long (long integer)	*System.Int64*	8 bytes	0	−9,223,372,036,854,775,808 through 9,223,372,036,854,775,807
Short	*System.Int16*	2 bytes	0	−32,768 through 32,767
Single (single-precision floating-point)	*System.Single*	4 bytes	0.0	−3.402823E38 through −1.401298E-45 for negative values; 1.401298E-45 through 3.402823E38 for positive values
Structure	*System.ValueType*			Even though some members might be reference types, the *Structure* is a value type.

> **Note** The *Currency* data type in classic Visual Basic is obsolete in the .NET Framework. When dealing with monetary transactions, be sure to use the *Decimal* data type with two decimal places in order to prevent rounding errors.

The *Structure* data type is a legacy data type; it's the Visual Basic .NET name for the user-defined type (UDT) in previous versions of Visual Basic. A *Structure* is a concatenation of one or more members of data types, as shown here:

```
Structure DriveInfo
    DriveNumber() As Short
    DriveType As String
    DriveSpace as Long
    AvailableSpace as Long
End Structure
```

A *Structure* is treated as a single unit, although its members can be accessed individually. *Structures* have two limitations: they cannot explicitly inherit from another type (although they implicitly inherit the methods of the *System.Object* class), and a class cannot inherit from a *Structure*.

Structures are frowned upon in object-oriented programming. A class can do everything that a *Structure* can do—and more—so you should use classes instead of *Structures*.

Reference Types

As I mentioned earlier, a reference variable points to the memory location of the variable's data. This arrangement allows the garbage collector to track an object flagged for deletion and free the object's memory when it's no longer needed.

A reference variable always contains a reference to an object of its type, or null (*Nothing*) if you haven't explicitly initialized the variable. (A null reference points to nothing. It's illegal to do anything with a null reference except assign it a legitimate value.) Table 4-2 lists the Visual Basic .NET reference types.

Table 4-2 Visual Basic .NET Reference Types

Visual Basic Type	.NET Runtime Type Structure	Memory Storage Size	Value Range
Object	*System.Object* (class)	4 bytes	Varies
String (variable-length)	*System.String* (class)	10 + (2 × string length) bytes	0 through approximately 2 billion Unicode characters

As you learned in Chapter 2, "Object-Oriented Programming in Visual Basic .NET," an object is an instantiation of a class, and an *Object* variable is a reference variable that holds a pointer to the actual object. The *Object* variable itself always consumes exactly 4 bytes because it's simply a pointer to the memory location where the object it points to is located.

Recall that when a reference variable is created, it's initialized to null. Because of this arrangement, you must be sure to assign an actual object to the variable before you try to use it. Consider the following example:

```
Sub main()
    Dim oMyObject As Object
    MessageBox.Show(oMyObject.GetType.ToString)
End Sub
```

The compiler will not object (no pun intended) to code like this. However, when this code executes and innocently tries to print out the variable's type, the program crashes with the error shown in Figure 4-2.

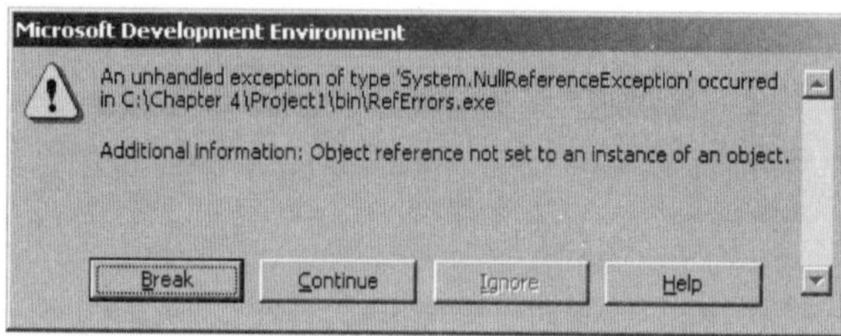

Figure 4-2 Accessing a null reference variable causes a run-time error.

The *String* data type is a sequence of zero or more double-byte (16-bit) Unicode characters. The codes for Unicode characters range from 0 through 65,535. The first 128 (0–127) characters of the Unicode character set correspond to the ASCII character set—the letters and symbols on a standard U.S. keyboard. The second 128 characters (128–255) represent special characters such as Latin-based alphabet letters, accents, currency symbols, and fractions. The remaining characters are used for a wide variety of symbols, including worldwide textual characters, diacritics, and mathematical and technical symbols.

Data Type Features

Visual Basic .NET has a number of features that simplify programming, including strong typing, type safety, and data widening, but the best new feature is probably the *System.Object* class, from which all other classes are derived.

The *System.Object* Class

Almost all modern programming languages have some sort of run-time library that provides common services and ways to access the underlying hardware, operating system, and file storage. In Chapter 2, you learned that the common language runtime is organized into a single hierarchical tree of namespaces. At the root of this tree is the *System* namespace, which contains various objects, including predefined types such as integers, strings, and classes. (The *System.Windows.Forms* namespace we used in Chapter 2 is inherited from the *System* namespace.)

All of the common predefined types can be used from any language the .NET Framework supports. All of the *System* classes are contained in Mscorlib.dll and can be used by all .NET applications. You can use these classes as is or derive your own classes from them.

At the root of all classes (either inherited classes or those we write ourselves) is the *System.Object* class. In Visual Basic .NET, everything implicitly derives from *System.Object*. The *System.Object* class is the ultimate super class of all classes in the .NET Framework—it's the *only* class in the .NET Framework that does not inherit from any other object type. All other object types must either explicitly or implicitly declare support for (inherit from) exactly one other object type. In fact, in Visual Basic .NET it's impossible to use a class that does not inherit from *System.Object*. This fact ensures that every object in Visual Basic .NET inherits *System.Object*'s basic functionality.

All methods defined in the *System.Object* class are available in all of its subclasses, which really means all objects in the system. The *System.Object* class (and therefore every class) has the six basic methods listed in Table 4-3.

Table 4-3 Basic Visual Basic .NET Class Methods

Object.Method	Access	Description
Equals	Public	Takes another object as a parameter and returns a *Boolean* True or False that indicates whether the two objects are equal.
GetHashCode	Public	Returns an integer hash code that represents the object's value. This code is usually used as a key when the object is added to a collection. Two identical objects should generate the same code.
Finalize	Protected	The CLR calls an object's *Finalize* method to notify the object that the object is about to be destroyed. This method really does nothing and is overridden by the class.
MemberwiseClone	Protected	Creates a shallow copy of the object.
GetType	Public	Returns an instance of *System.Type*, which is used to get information about the object through metadata.
ToString	Public	Returns a string representation of the object. The string is not formatted and is almost always overridden by the class implementing it.

Examine Figure 4-3, and notice that neither the *Finalize* method nor the *MemberwiseClone* method is present in the IntelliSense list. (The *Equals*, *GetHashCode*, and *ToString* methods are available but are not in the list.) The methods are absent because they are defined with the *Protected* access modifier in the *System.Object* class; only methods defined with the *Public* access modifier are listed. Remember that methods defined as *Protected* can be accessed only from a child class. When you inherit a class from the *System.Object* class, you will see all five methods.

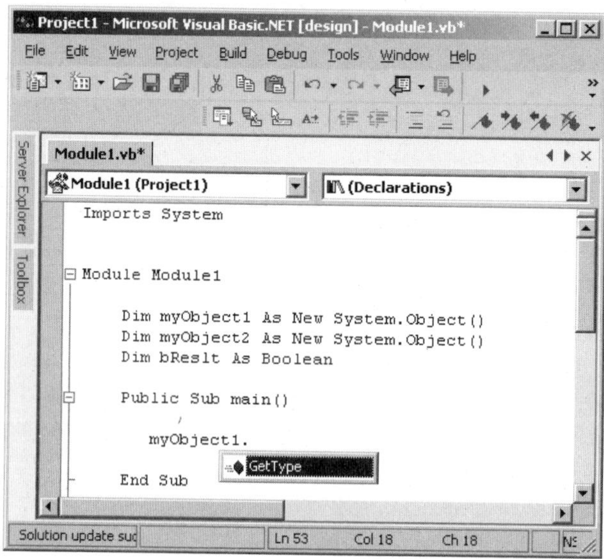

Figure 4-3 The IntelliSense list displays *Public* methods only.

Now let's make use of those methods by extending the code shown in Figure 4-3 as follows:

```
Imports System

Public Module Module1


    Dim myObject1 As New System.Object()
    Dim myObject2 As New System.Object()
    Dim bReslt As Boolean

    Public Sub main()

        myObject1 = "Hello Visual Basic .NET"
        myObject2 = 42

        'What type is this?
        MessageBox.Show(myObject1.GetType.ToString)    'System.String
        'What is the object's HashCode?
```

```
        MessageBox.Show(myObject1.GetHashCode.ToString)     '-1757321832
        'Are the objects equal?
        MessageBox.Show(myObject1.Equals(myObject2).ToString)  'False

        myObject1 = myObject2
        MessageBox.Show(myObject1.Equals(myObject2).ToString)  'True
        MessageBox.Show(myObject1.ToString) '42

    End Sub

End Module
```

> **Note** You must explicitly convert each message box argument to a string. This requirement is an example of the strong typing in Visual Basic .NET, which I'll cover in greater detail later in this chapter.

The *GetType* method of *myObject1* in the first message box prints *System.Object*. The *GetHashCode* method prints -1757321832 on my system, but your result might be different. In a real program, we would override the *GetHashCode* method in a derived class to return some unique number that could be used as, say, a key in a collection.

Next, the *Equals* method of *myObject1* compares *myObject1* to *myObject2*. False is returned, of course, because *myObject1* and *myObject2* are not only different individual objects but the objects themselves contain different values. Because these variables are of type *System.Object*, they readily accept strings, numbers, or any other data type without complaining.

The next line of code sets *myObject1* equal to *myObject2* so that both objects now refer to *myObject2*. The last line prints out the value of *myObject1*. This final message box indicates that both variables reference the same object—a memory location that holds the value 42.

As I mentioned earlier, the *Object* type replaces the *Variant* data type found in previous versions of Visual Basic and can contain anything; for example, a string, a double, or a reference to a Microsoft Word document. Although you'll almost always want to dimension your reference variables as a specific data type, you'll need to dimension a variable as type *Object* in some cases. These cases should be few and far between, however. Why? Because even though a variable declared as type *Object* is flexible enough to contain a reference to any object or data type, calling a method using an *Object* type variable forces late (run-time) binding, which essentially means that each time a program accesses an *Object* variable, the CLR has to determine the variable's type. Not only does this interrogation take CPU cycles, but loose-typed variables can lead to bugs. For example, you might accidentally pass an *Object* that holds a string to a method that's expecting an integer. Mistakes such as these will become apparent only at run time and can cause all sorts of embarrassment when your users get a run-time error.

Because Visual Basic .NET uses strong typing, you should force early (compile-time) binding by dimensioning the variable as a specific object type. And if you can't dimension it as a specific type, you should cast (convert) it to a specific data type wherever possible.

Strong Typing

Strong typing requires you to specify a specific data type for each variable in your program. Strong-typed variables allow IntelliSense to display a variable's properties and methods as you work in the editor. Strong typing also permits the compiler to perform type checking, which ensures that statements that use an improper data type are caught before they can cause subtle run-time errors. Finally, strong typing results in faster execution of your code because the compiler doesn't have to waste CPU cycles determining a variable's type and then performing behind-the-scenes type conversions. Requiring strong typing is one way that .NET forces you to weed out bugs from your code.

In previous versions of Visual Basic, the compiler provided the primitive data types. Recall from Chapter 1, "Visual Basic .NET from the Ground Up," that the primitive data types for all .NET languages are provided by the CLR. The .NET language compilers make a subset of all possible data types available to the various language implementations. The .NET language-specific subset of data types is mapped to the *System.Type* class so that each .NET data type is the same regardless of which language you use—it's guaranteed that the code written in one .NET language can interact seamlessly with code from another .NET language. For those of you that used API function declarations in previous versions of Visual Basic, not having to fiddle with casting data types to the expected C language format will be a welcome relief. The standard .NET data types also facilitate portability so that programs can run (without recompiling) on any operating system that supports the common language runtime.

Type Safety

Visual Basic .NET is a type-safe language. You now know that you can access a variable only through the type associated with that variable—the compiler will bark if you do otherwise because it won't let you mismatch types. This restriction encourages (a nice way to say forces) good program design. It also eliminates potential bugs or security breaches by making the accidental or malicious overwriting of one variable by another impossible. However, if you do not specify a data type when you declare a variable, Visual Basic .NET assigns the *Object* data type to that variable. This default designation is similar to the way Visual Basic 6 assigns the *Variant* data type to variables that you don't specify a data type for.

Visual Basic 6 has the *Option Explicit* directive that forces all variables to be declared. Visual Basic .NET supports this directive and the new *Option Strict* directive, as shown in Table 4-4.

Table 4-4 Visual Basic .NET Type Safety Directives

Directive	Values	Description
Option Explicit	On | Off	Used to force explicit declaration of all variables in a module. This directive is on by default.
Option Strict	On | Off	Restricts implicit data type conversions to widening conversions. This explicitly disallows any data type conversions in which data loss would occur. It also disallows any conversion between numeric types and strings. This directive is off by default.

When the *Option Strict* directive is set to On, all variables must have an *AS* clause that explicitly declares the variable's type. Also, the *&* operator can't be used to concatenate *Object* variables. It's good practice to always use the *Option Explicit* directive in each module to ensure that each variable is explicitly declared using the *Dim*, the *Private*, the *Public*, or the *ReDim* statement—the compiler generates an error for each undeclared variable when *Option Explicit* is turned on. If *Option Explicit* and *Option Strict* are both turned off, you can use an undeclared variable—which would default to type *Object*—as shown here:

```
Option Explicit Off
Option Strict Off

myVariable = "Hello Visual Basic .NET"
```

Apart from the fact that undeclared variables can introduce subtle bugs into your programs, reading the code becomes a challenge because keeping track of undeclared variables is very difficult. Unless you have a really good reason—and I can't think of one off the top of my head—always keep both of these directives turned on. Think of them as free insurance policies.

Here's another example of what happens if you don't declare a data type. If *Option Strict* is off, the following code works fine.

```
Dim myVariable = "Hello Visual Basic .NET"
MessageBox.Show(myVariable & " is type " & _
    myVariable.GetType.ToString())
```

Notice that the *Dim* statement that declares *myVariable* does not include an *AS* clause, so *myVariable* defaults to type *Object*, which can hold any data type. This message box will display the contents of the variable as well as the data type, as shown in Figure 4-4.

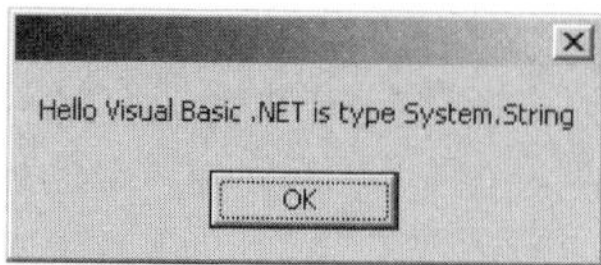

Figure 4-4 In this figure, *myVariable* holds a string.

We could assign a double to the same object variable that just held a string.

```
myVariable = 123.456
MessageBox.Show(myVariable & " is type " & _
    myVariable.GetType.ToString())
```

The message box shown in Figure 4-5 reveals that *myVariable* now holds a double.

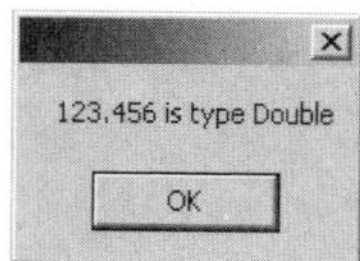

Figure 4-5 In this figure, *myVariable* holds a double.

You might be scratching your head right about now, wondering why this code is legal if Visual Basic .NET is type safe. The answer is that it's not legal unless you specifically turn off the *Option Explicit* directive.

You can still generate the same type of bugs as you can in Visual Basic 6 by turning *Option Explicit* off. For example, you might declare *oMyObject* but later in the code use a variable named *MyObject*. Consider this code fragment:

```
Sub Main()
    Dim oMyObject As Object
    oMyObject = "Hello Visual Basic .NET!"
    MessageBox.Show(MyObject)
End Sub
```

The programmer probably meant to type *oMyObject* in the message box. (It's easy to mistype a variable name.) When he runs the program he expects to see "Hello Visual Basic .NET!" when the message box appears. Because *MyOb-*

ject does not exist, Visual Basic .NET creates it and the message box is empty. Keeping both *Option Strict* and *Option Explicit* on (the default) avoids this problem and is the safe way to go.

Testing for Variable Type

As I've mentioned, Visual Basic .NET gives every data type a default value when the variable is dimensioned. Let's assume a program dimensions an *Object* variable and an *Integer* variable as shown here:

```
Dim myObject1 As New System.Object()
Dim myInteger1 As New Integer()

MessageBox.Show(myObject1.ToString)     'System.Object
MessageBox.Show(myInteger1.ToString)    '0
```

An *Object* variable's default implementation of the *ToString* method returns the fully qualified name of the object's class. Notice that the variable's value is not printed, as it is with the *Integer* variable. Although you'll usually override the *ToString* methods of your objects, the built-in methods are good for debugging purposes.

Value type variables inherit from the *Object.ValueType* class. The *Object.ValueType* class overrides the object's *ToString* method to display the value of the variable. This fact is illustrated by the previous example, which prints the integer variable's value—0—instead of the variable's type.

We can test the type of object by using the built-in function *TypeName*, as shown here:

```
MessageBox.Show(TypeName(myObject1))  'Object
MessageBox.Show(TypeName(myInteger1)) 'Integer
```

A Typical Visual Basic .NET Assignment

Let's consider another example that clearly explains the type system. I know you'll soon run into the challenge of trying to figure out what data type the CLR is looking for in an assignment. For example, you might add a text box control named *txtName* to a form created from *Windows.Forms.Form* to display an employee's name. You might decide to change the text box background color to yellow when the user is editing. Your code might look something like this:

```
txtName.BackColor = "yellow"
```

Unfortunately, the Visual Basic .NET editor knows the code is incorrect and is not shy about telling you so, as shown in Figure 4-6. The problem is that the *BackColor* method of the *txtName* text box is expecting a type *System.Drawing.Color*, and you had the audacity to pass it a string.

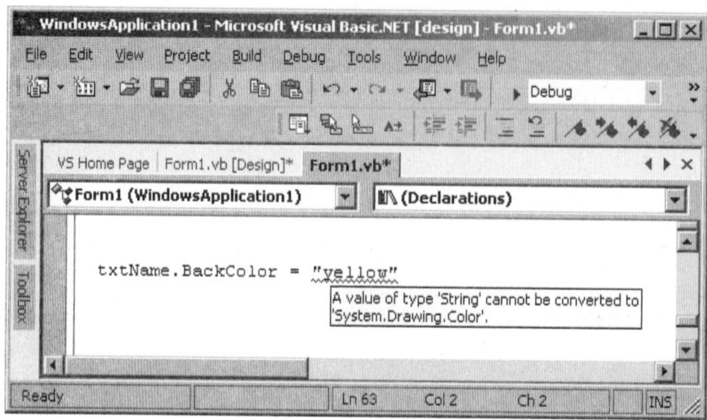

Figure 4-6 The Visual Basic .NET editor warns about data type mismatches.

Take a moment and think about what you're trying to do. Of course, you're trying to set the *BackColor* property of the text box. You can see from the IDE message that the *BackColor* property is expecting a *System.Drawing.Color* data type, not a string. The Visual Basic .NET compiler can't explicitly coerce a string to a data type of *System.Drawing.Color*, nor would we want it to try.

Every data type in the .NET Framework exposes a set of properties and methods. You can solve the problem in this example by using these properties and methods to convert your string to the *System.Drawing.Color* data type that the *BackColor* property expects. The following code does the job nicely. The *Color* class provides a method to do the explicit conversion for us. When you type in *System.Drawing.Color*, the IDE presents you with a rainbow of color choices. We simply select Yellow.

```
txtName.BackColor = System.Drawing.Color.Yellow
```

So you can see that the *System.Drawing.Color* class has various color constants, such as *Yellow*, that we can set. In addition to the color property, the *System.Drawing.Color* class has the useful method *FromName*. If you know the color constants that are predefined, you can use the *FromName* method and pass in a string with the color you want to display.

```
txtName.BackColor = System.Drawing.Color.FromName("blue")
```

These color assignment examples illustrate a typical assignment problem that beginners in Visual Basic .NET will encounter frequently. If you are unfamiliar with how to solve this problem, as we've done here, it can be frustrating. While our problem can be solved in two ways, you are probably thinking that this code looks more like Klingon than Visual Basic. And it also might have crossed your mind that you have no idea where to find all of these classes, let alone understand how they fit together.

Well, don't worry. In the next chapter, we'll examine the .NET Framework in detail and you'll learn how to quickly find what you need. And remember, to help us out the language designers provided the WinCV tool, which we saw in earlier chapters, that presents a hierarchical view that makes finding any class, method, or procedure a snap.

Data Widening

Earlier I mentioned that the *Option Strict* directive restricts implicit data type conversions to widening conversions. This restriction explicitly disallows any data type conversions in which data loss would occur and also disallows any conversion between numeric types and strings.

A widening conversion changes the value to a type that can accommodate data of the same or greater magnitude. Table 4-5 shows the standard data type widening conversions.

Table 4-5 Data Widening Conversions

Data Type	Widens to Data Types
Byte	*Byte, Short, Integer, Long, Decimal, Single, Double*
Short	*Short, Integer, Long, Decimal, Single, Double*
Integer	*Integer, Long, Decimal, Single, Double*
Long	*Long, Decimal, Single, Double*
Decimal	*Decimal, Single, Double*
Single	*Single, Double*
Double	*Double*
Char	*String*
Any type	*Object*

Conversions from *Integer* to *Single*, or from *Long* or *Decimal* to *Single* or *Double*, might result in a loss of precision but never in a loss of magnitude. In this sense, they do not incur information loss because you are storing a value in a larger area. However, the reverse is not the case. Consider this code:

```
Dim iInteger As Integer = 10
Dim lLong As Long

lLong = iInteger       'This works fine; we can safely convert
                       ' an iInteger into a lLong.
iInteger = lLong       'This does not work; we can't safely convert
                       ' a lLong into an iInteger.
```

When this program is run, it generates an error message that states that *Option Strict* disallows implicit conversions from *Long* to *Integer*. *Option Strict* is again helping us stay away from subtle bugs. Of course, turning off *Option Strict* permits implicit conversions, but you should always stay away from doing this. It's easy to accidentally try to fit a number larger than can fit in an *Integer* into a variable named *iInteger*. And because this error happens at run time, you might never encounter the error until your program is deployed in the field. *Option Strict* ensures these overflow bugs can't happen in Visual Basic .NET

Any conversion that does not result in a loss of precision (a narrowing conversion) will not throw an exception. (An exception is a type of error. I'll cover exceptions in greater detail in Chapter 7, "Handling Errors and Debugging Programs.") You can still assign the contents of a *Long* variable to an *Integer* variable by explicitly casting the *Long* to an *Integer*. Of course, the compiler will assume you know what you are doing. Casting an expression means you are going to coerce an expression to a given type. In some programming circles, casting is known as "evil type coercion." Specific cast keywords are used to coerce expressions into the primitive types. The general cast keyword, *CType*, coerces an expression into any type. If no conversion exists from the type of the expression to the specified type, a compile-time error occurs. Otherwise, the result is the value produced by the conversion.

```
CastExpression ::=   CType ( Expression , TypeName ) |
    CastTarget ( Expression )
CastTarget ::=    CBool | CByte | CChar | CDate | CDec |
    CDbl | CInt | CLng | CObj | CShort | CSng | CStr
```

We could cast the contents of our *Long* into an *Integer* by doing the following:

```
iInteger = CType(lLong, Integer)
```

But here's the problem with doing this. Let's say the value of the *Long* is one more than the maximum value that can be held by an *Integer*. As our program runs, it calculates values and unexpectedly holds a value larger than we think. Then we try to cast the value of the *Long* into an *Integer*, as shown here:

```
Dim iInteger As Integer
Dim lLong As Long = 2147483648 'One more than the maximum
                               ' integer value (2,147,483,647)

iInteger = CType(lLong, Integer)
```

Oops! We get a run-time error. You can't predict this error because a *Long* can always hold a larger value than an *Integer*. The only time this error will show up is during run time, as you can see in Figure 4-7.

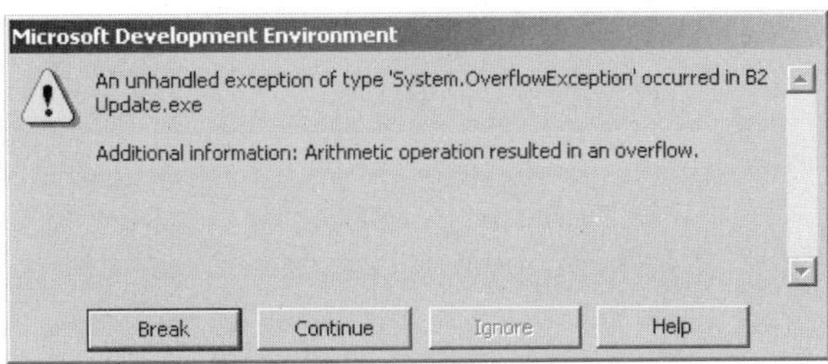

Figure 4-7 There is no way to predict this error.

The *Integer* variable is not explicitly initialized, so the compiler assigns it the default value 0. The code then initializes the *Long* variable *lLong* to a value one greater than the integer can hold. The CLR realizes the value is too large for *iInteger* and throws the exception shown in Figure 4-7.

A run-time error such as this is the worst type of error. A design-time error is easy to fix—in fact, we can't even compile and run the program until we fix it—but a run-time error is much more insidious. The erroneous code might be buried in a deep dark section of your program that rarely gets executed and might have been missed during testing. Or, depending on the sequence of events, a variable might be assigned a large value in an unforeseen way. So you see, the strong typing nature of Visual Basic .NET is really there for your benefit. It forces you to assign one data type to a like data type, or you have to explicitly cast it and accept responsibility for ensuring that no data loss occurs.

The moral of this story is to never shut off the *Option Strict* directive or the *Option Explicit* directive and be sure not to convert a large variable type into a smaller type unless you have an exceptional reason for doing so. And if you have an exceptional reason, you must be sure that the converted value will never exceed the storage capability of the smaller type.

It might seem surprising that a conversion from a derived (inherited) type to one of its base types is considered widening. This convention exists because the derived type contains all the members of the base type, which means the conversion will fully populate the base type. The base type, however, does not have all the members of the derived type, so converting from a base type to a derived type does not fully populate the derived type—it's considered narrowing.

In your programs, you can safely use widening conversions. Widening conversions will always succeed and can always be performed implicitly. However, a narrowing conversion can cause information loss. As we saw, narrowing conversions do not always succeed and might very well fail at run time. That's why the compiler does not allow implicit narrowing—you must explicitly perform this type of conversion.

Garbage Collection: Getting Rid of Our Objects

You've seen how to build and instantiate objects. You also need to know how to get rid of them when you no longer need them. In Visual Basic 6, when you had finished with an object, you had two means to free up memory it occupied. The lazy way was simply to wait for the object to go out of scope. The second and more professional way was to use *SET myObject = Nothing*.

Because Visual Basic 6 relied on COM, whenever a new instance of an object was created or a new reference to an existing object was set, an internal reference counter was incremented. When a reference to the object was released, the internal reference counter was decremented. When all references were released, the object was terminated and its memory and resources were released. At this point, the *Class_Terminate* event would fire predictably. We knew for sure when this event would happen and could place any cleanup code, such as code releasing connections to databases, in that event. This method of clearly terminating an object is known as *deterministic finalization*. Visual Basic 6 programmers always knew exactly when an object would be released.

The Stack and the Managed Heap

When you write a Visual Basic .NET program, the operating system allocates a chunk of memory exclusively for the program's use. The application has many different areas inside its own memory map that are used to store different objects. The program's memory has a code segment (the instructions that tell the computer what to do) and a data segment (in-memory objects, variables, and other temporary storage). The data segment is further broken up into the *stack* (value variables) and the *heap* (reference variables). Now you see why it's important to understand the difference between value and reference variables. The ways they are stored in memory and released when finished are different. A solid understanding of how reference variables are stored can materially help you increase the performance of your code. A depiction of a program's memory map is shown in Figure 4-8.

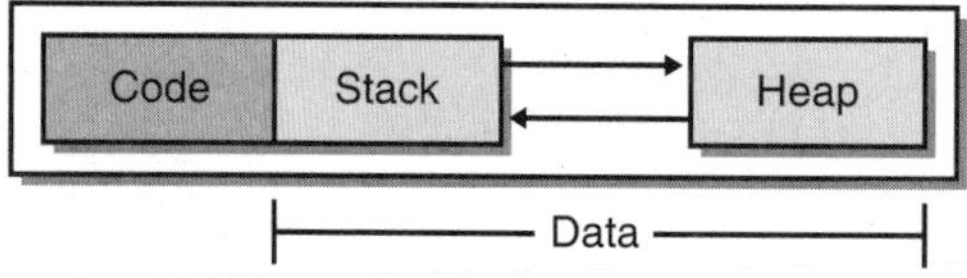

Figure 4-8 A program's memory map.

Value objects, such as integers, are stored on the stack. The stack is also used to hold data passed to functions and methods. As more items are placed on the stack, such as when you pass parameters to a procedure, the stack grows toward the heap. The compiler can determine the size of the stack because it knows the exact size of the value types used in procedures, function calls, and so on. As value variables go out of scope, they are immediately released and memory is freed up, shrinking the stack.

This is not the case with reference variables, which are placed on the managed heap. While we could use *Set myObject = Nothing* in Visual Basic 6 to release memory, Visual Basic .NET operates in a completely different way. In Visual Basic .NET, when an object goes out of scope it is internally flagged for deletion. At some later time, a low-level background thread examines heap memory to see what objects can safely be released. Now it's the system and not the programmer who must manage memory. This memory management is called *nondeterministic finalization*.

While setting an object to *Nothing* in Visual Basic 6 immediately releases memory, in Visual Basic .NET this process might take a while. In some cases, several minutes might elapse before the garbage collector (GC) will get around to releasing objects on the managed heap. The good news is that this delay typically provides a performance benefit. Rather than using CPU cycles to release objects that are no longer needed, the system usually waits until the application is idle, which decreases the impact on the user.

You can trigger garbage collection programmatically by calling *System.GC.Collect*, but this method is used only in rare circumstances when it is imperative to release many large objects immediately. Most programs will never make use of this.

The stack grows toward the heap (and vice versa). If they meet, that application has run out of memory, and once this happens it is just a matter of time before the application crashes. While crashes like these used to be a problem with complex programs, the .NET runtime uses advanced memory allocation algorithms to ensure it won't happen.

Conclusion

As you can see, strong typing is mandatory for all variables in Visual Basic .NET. Enforcement of typing ensures that we know exactly what type of data will be in each variable (which reduces bugs) and that we can optimize memory by using the smallest size data type for the job. Rather than using an *Object* data type to hold a character, we can use the right data type for the job. To all of you pros, this approach is simply common sense.

Reference data types contain a pointer that references another location in memory. This referenced location might contain a large object, a string, or some other data. We can have several reference data types pointing to the same memory location. Changes to anything in that location are reflected in all variables referencing that memory location.

Value types, on the other hand, are primitive types, which contain a data type whose size is known ahead of time, such as an integer. Since an integer will always be 4 bytes, the common language runtime can map the 4-byte memory location that will hold a value. In other words, there is no need to reference another memory location to hold an unknown size variable.

Visual Basic .NET variables are strong typed; each must be dimensioned using the *As* clause, such as *Dim iInteger AS integer*. While some programmers might see this step as unnecessary rigor, most will see strong typing as just good programming.

5

Examining the .NET Class Framework Using Files and Strings

Now that you understand object-oriented programming and have a good understanding of data types, it's time to examine the Microsoft .NET Framework and how you work with it using Microsoft Visual Basic .NET. As you now know, the .NET Framework is an object-oriented, hierarchical class library. The prebuilt functionality in the framework can be tapped into to provide enormous power in a few lines of code. The framework library can be utilized across multiple languages and platforms in a consistent manner.

For over a decade, the Visual Basic language has been a cornerstone of the Microsoft Windows platform. The impact that Visual Basic 1 had on the Windows market was tremendous—for the first time, a programmer could write Windows applications simply and painlessly. This capability came about because the development approach taken with Visual Basic could be grasped by a wide range of programmers. The introduction of support for COM type libraries in Visual Basic 4 helped quickly establish it as the standard object architecture for the Windows platform.

As I mentioned in Chapter 1, "Visual Basic .NET from the Ground Up," Microsoft recognizes that the programming industry is in the middle of a shift from providing software on CDs to providing functionality as Web services via the Internet. The .NET Framework is a key part of Microsoft's strategy to make this transition as painless as possible: the framework is designed from the ground up to enable developers to write and deploy complex Web, network, and stand-alone applications that can run on a variety of hardware platforms.

As this transition to multiple platforms occurs, Visual Basic must retain a certain relevance to developers by becoming a first-class supporter of the .NET Framework. In some cases, the features needed to support the .NET Framework conflict with features in the classic Visual Basic language. But to thoroughly support the framework, Microsoft decided to loosen the bonds of backward compatibility and take the language a step forward in evolution. As you can see throughout this book, the .NET Framework extends the capability of the Windows API and is incredibly powerful, consistent, and easy to use. Of course, you still have access to the Windows API if you require it. However, the .NET Framework is a superset of the API, so the cases in which you'll need to be backward compatible will be rare.

In this chapter, I'll review the organization of the .NET class framework and provide some guidance on how best to locate the classes and functionality you need to include in your programs. Then, using file management classes as an example, we'll continue our investigation of how to work with classes in Visual Basic .NET. Finally, because handling strings is such a critical part of any program, I'll cover how to use the *String* data type in more detail.

What Exactly Is the .NET Framework?

The .NET Framework is the foundation on which you build and run .NET applications. Having such a foundation makes building Visual Basic .NET applications easier, while providing a consistent, simplified programming model. As a Visual Basic 6 developer, you used a programming language that made building a variety of applications easy. The Visual Basic language itself provides the intrinsic data types—such as *Integer*, *Long*, and *String*—as well as some of the most commonly used functions, such as those for string manipulation and data type conversion. As your Visual Basic 6 applications became more sophisticated, you probably used Win32 APIs to perform operations, such as accessing arbitrary registry keys and values, that were not possible with the standard Visual Basic functions. You probably also used the COM component libraries to extend the application's functionality. Probably the most common of these COM objects is the ActiveX Data Objects (ADO) library that your program used for data access. Whenever you added an ADO control, you were using a COM object.

While Visual Basic 6 was flexible enough to offer these different extensibility mechanisms, that flexibility required learning several complex API architectures. First you had to learn how Win32 APIs worked. Next you had to figure out how to call the APIs from Visual Basic 6, which was usually a time-consuming, error-prone task. Next you had to learn how to use various COM components from Visual Basic, which was challenging because each had a different object model.

When you completed a Visual Basic 6 program that utilized Win32 APIs, ADO, and probably many other COM components, you had to think about how to manage the application's deployment along with all the dependent files. A typical nontrivial Visual Basic 6 application's dependency list includes not only the Visual Basic 6 runtime, but also all of the libraries required by the application, such as ADO 2.6. Most times, one or another file was forgotten, only to be discovered when the program crashed on a user's machine.

The idea behind the .NET Framework is to solve these problems. The framework will make it easier for you to develop robust applications without having to learn many different API architectures and without having to deploy and handle versioning for a dozen libraries.

Tapping into the .NET Framework

As you've already seen, you don't have to design all your Visual Basic .NET types from the ground up. The .NET Framework includes classes, interfaces, and value types that help to both expedite and optimize the development process. The framework also gives you tools that allow you to access system functionality. The framework provides types that encapsulate data structures, perform I/O, allow access to information about a loaded class, invoke .NET Framework security checks, encapsulate exceptions, and provide data access. These types make it easy to create rich applications.

It All Starts with the *System* Namespace

The *System* namespace—the root for types in the .NET Framework—includes classes that represent the base data types used by all Visual Basic .NET applications. Remember that these base data types are the *Object* (the root of the inheritance hierarchy), *Byte*, *Char*, *Array*, *Int32*, *String*, and so on. As we discussed in the last chapter, many of these types correspond to the primitive data types that the Visual Basic .NET compiler uses.

Along with the base data types, the *System* namespace contains almost 100 classes that provide functionality ranging from handling exceptions and forming delegates to dealing with core run-time concepts such as application domains and the automatic memory manager. The *System* namespace also contains 25 second-level namespaces, listed in Table 5-1. Take a moment to review the description of each. You can see how the namespace convention logically segregates functionality, making specific classes easy to find.

Table 5-1 Secondary Namespaces in the *System* Namespace

Namespaces	Description
System.CodeDom	Contains classes that can be used to represent the elements and structure of a source code document.
System.Collections	Contains interfaces and classes that define various collections of objects, such as lists, queues, arrays, hash tables, and dictionaries.
System.ComponentModel	Provides classes that are used to implement and license components.
System.Configuration	Provides classes that give system run times, administrative tools, applications, and other consumers of configuration information access to configuration information.
System.Data	Consists mostly of classes that constitute the Microsoft ADO.NET architecture. ADO.NET architecture enables you to build components that manage data from multiple data sources.
System.Diagnostics	Provides classes to debug applications and to trace the execution of code.
System.DirectoryServices	Provides access to Active Directory from managed code. The classes in this namespace can be used with any of the Active Directory service providers such as Internet Information Services (IIS), Lightweight Directory Access Protocol (LDAP), Novell NetWare Directory Service (NDS), and WinNT.
System.Drawing	Provides access to GDI+ basic graphics functionality. Additional advanced functionality is provided in the *System.Drawing.Drawing2D*, *System.Drawing.Imaging*, and *System.Drawing.Text* namespaces.
System.EnterpriseServices	Provides transaction-processing functionality.
System.Globalization	Provides localization information on elements such as the current culture, formatting, date, and time for specific locales.
System.IO	Provides types that allow synchronous and asynchronous reading from and writing to data streams and files.
System.Management	Provides classes for the management of system objects and events.
System.Messaging	Provides classes to connect to message queues on the network, send messages to queues, and receive or *peek* (read without removing) messages from queues.

Table 5-1 Secondary Namespaces in the *System* Namespace *(continued)*

Namespaces	Description
System.Net	Provides a simple programming interface to many of the protocols found on the network today. For example, the *WebRequest* and *WebResponse* classes form the basis of "pluggable protocols." This namespace is an implementation of network services that enables you to develop applications that use Internet resources without worrying about the specific details of the protocol used.
System.Reflection	Contains classes and interfaces that provide a managed view of types, methods, and fields, with the ability to dynamically create and invoke types.
System.Resources	Provides management of resources, such as a resource that contains culture-specific information.
System.Runtime	Provides infrastructure services.
System.Security	Provides the underlying structure of the .NET Framework security system, including interfaces, attributes, exceptions, and base classes for permissions.
System.ServiceProcess	Provides classes to install and run services. Services are long-running executables that do not have a user interface.
System.Text	Contains classes representing ASCII, Unicode, UTF-7, and UTF-8 character encodings; abstract base classes for converting blocks of characters to and from blocks of bytes; and a helper class that manipulates and formats *String* objects without creating intermediate instances of *String*.
System.Threading	Provides classes and interfaces that enable multithreaded programming. This namespace includes a *ThreadPool* class that manages groups of threads, a *Timer* class that enables a delegate to be called after a specified amount of time, a *Mutex* class for synchronizing mutually exclusive threads, and classes for thread scheduling, wait notification, and deadlock resolution.
System.Timers	Provides two components that raise an event on an interval or more complex schedule, the *Timer* and *Schedule* components respectively.

(continued)

Table 5-1 Secondary Namespaces in the *System* Namespace *(continued)*

Namespaces	Description
System.Web	Supplies classes and interfaces that enable browser-server communication. Included are the *HTTPRequest* class that provides extensive information about the current HTTP request, the *HTTPResponse* class that manages HTTP output to the client, and the *HTTPServerUtility* object that provides access to server-side utilities and processes and classes for cookie manipulation, file transfer, exception information, and output cache control.
System.Windows.Forms	Contains classes for creating Windows-based applications (such as a Forms application) and classes for many controls that can be added to forms.
System.Xml	Contains XML classes that provide standards-based support for processing XML.

> **Note** If you are looking for specific functionality, such as file manipulation, go back and scan Table 2-1 to determine which namespace to look in. Because file manipulation is a basic tool, the *System.IO* namespace is grouped under programming basics.

Working with the Windows API is tricky for all types of programmers. Like many classic Visual Basic programmers, I have several dog-eared copies of both 16-bit and 32-bit Windows API reference books on my shelf. These tomes were invaluable for developing all but the simplest Visual Basic programs as I learned to write Windows applications. If an API's parameters were not entered just right, my computer took a trip to General Protection Fault City. Of course, the computer didn't lock up until run time because the API calls were late bound. I had to create buffers of exactly the correct size for return values and had to deal with all sorts of other nuisances because the parameters had to be entered in a way that the C language, not Visual Basic, could understand. In short, the API was like fire—it could either illuminate or burn.

While the classic Visual Basic IDE provided the API viewer with which to copy function declarations to your code, you really had to know what you were looking for before you even started. Of course, the naming conventions were often anti-intuitive, which mandated taking the API book off the shelf and hunting for exactly what you wanted. Luckily, even though the .NET Framework is massive, it is easier to find what you're looking for because of the logical grouping of classes, consistency of use, and a few handy tools.

Learning to Find and Use What You Need

In this section, you'll learn how to find exactly what you need in the .NET Framework. Once you know how to find what you want, we'll take a hands-on approach to understand how to use any class within the framework, using file management classes as an example. This approach will permit you to understand and use every class in the framework. You will soon see that the .NET Framework is not only extremely powerful, but also easy to use once you understand it.

The Windows Class Viewer (WinCV tool) is helpful for locating what we are looking for in the .NET Framework. This tool is located in C:\Program Files\Microsoft VisualStudio .NET\FrameworkSDK\Bin\WinCV.exe.

> **Tip** You'll want to have this tool available each and every time you program, so you can save some time by creating a shortcut to the program. You might want to place the shortcut on your desktop so that you can quickly start WinCV while you're programming Visual Basic .NET.

Start WinCV now. The program should appear as shown in Figure 5-1.

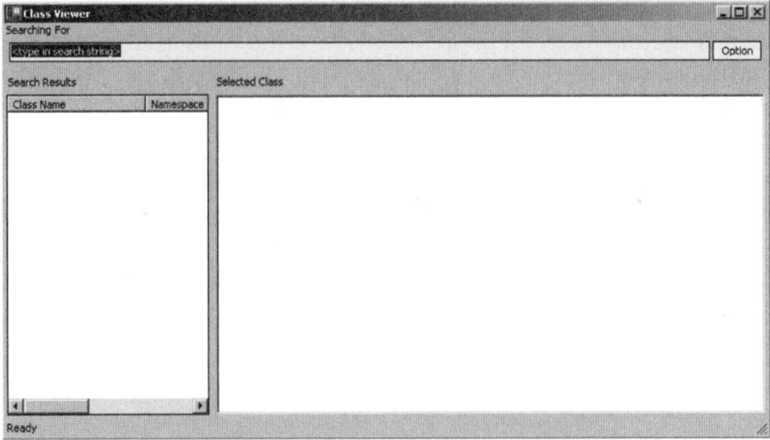

Figure 5-1 The WinCV tool.

Searching in Windows Class Viewer

One of the tasks that every programmer needs to do is read from and write to a file. Performing these operations in .NET is a bit different from how you did them in classic Visual Basic. Rather than just tell you how to do this, let's use the Socratic method with a little help from our friend WinCV.

We want to create a file and then read from and write to it. A programmer new to .NET would probably use the WinCV tool and type in the word *File* because that is what we want to work with. However, this search word causes WinCV to display a cornucopia of various and sundry classes in all sorts of namespaces, as shown in Figure 5-2. That amount of information might be disorienting to a Visual Basic .NET beginner. Where in the world would you start looking for what you need?

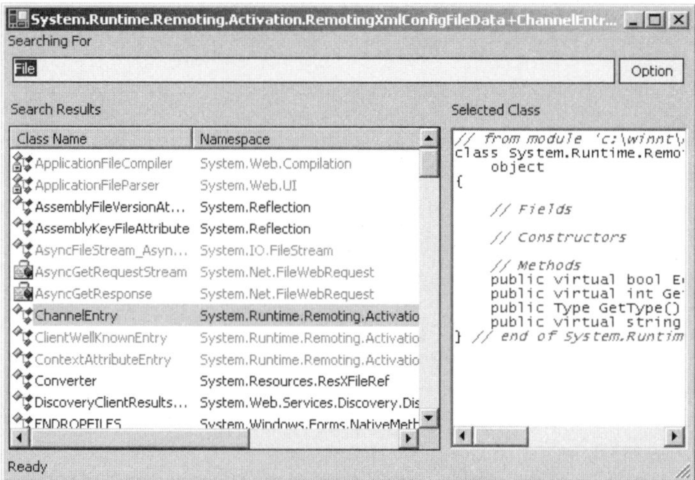

Figure 5-2 Searching on the word "file" causes WinCV to display a lot of information.

Many namespaces and classes within these namespaces contain the word *file*, so when we search on it, we get everything and the kitchen sink in return. While this search is the way many beginning programmers would try to find information about how to handle file access, notice that WinCV shows entries from namespaces such as *System.Web.UI*, *System.Reflection*, *System.Net.File WebRequest*, and many others. For each class in which the literal term *file* is found, an entry is displayed in the WinCV tool.

Using the Namespaces

Recall from Table 5-1 that the namespace *System.IO* contains file access classes. Try searching for *System.IO* instead of the word *file*, as shown in Figure 5-3. Notice that these classes look more like what we want.

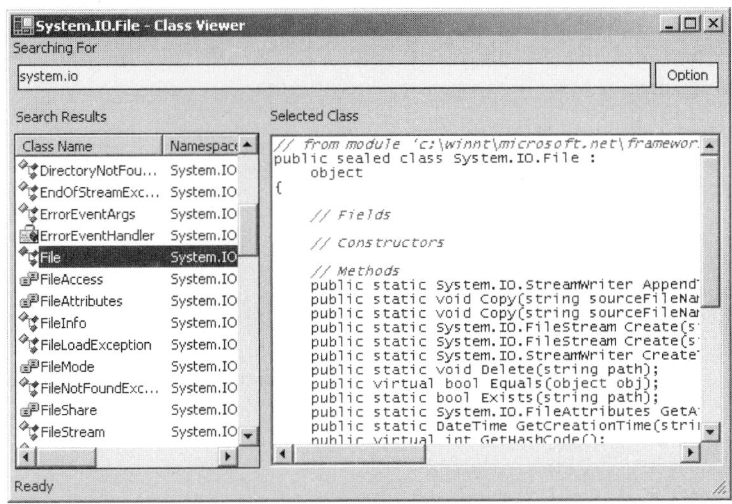

Figure 5-3 Searching for "System.IO" reveals the classes we need.

The *File* class of *System.IO* contains various properties, methods, and events for creating, copying, moving, and deleting files. Select *File* in the Class Name column, and look at the information displayed in the Selected Class area. What we want to do now is fully understand exactly how to read and use this information.

Examining the *File* Class

You should take note of a couple of items in the description of the *File* class. First notice that the class is sealed. In Visual Basic .NET, the *sealed* keyword means that the class is not inheritable. Unless the class itself is static, like this one happens to be, you can create new instances of sealed classes, but you cannot derive other classes from them. Also notice that the *File* class is inherited from *System.Object*.

The class information is shown in C# syntax, so the class information will look just a bit different from what Visual Basic programmers are used to seeing. However, there's really no more than a gnat's eyebrows difference in the syntax of the two languages. We see that this class can be used because it is public, we can't inherit from it because it's sealed, and it happens to be inherited from *System.Object*.

```
public sealed class System.IO.File :
    object
```

> **Note** Remember that when a class is instantiated, it first instantiates its parent and then any parent's parent, and so on up the chain of inheritance to *System.Object*. The chain then starts down, instantiating each child until the original class is reached, which is instantiated after every class it depends on has been initialized. Because each object is ultimately derived from *System.Object*, each class will have the same base of functionality inherited from *System.Object*.

Also notice that the *File* class has neither member fields nor constructors.

```
// Fields

// Constructors
```

How can we even create a new instance of the *File* class if it has no constructor? Well, we can't. If a class has no constructor, we can use the class but we can't create a new instance of it because it is static. Remember how we used static variables to contain a single value across all instances of a class? The *File* class is static, which means that a single instance of the class is shared everywhere in your program.

Notice that the methods of the *File* class are also static and provide for the creation, copying, deletion, moving, and opening of files. Because the *File* class is static, we can't create an instance of the class with the *New* keyword, but we can use the static *File* class as-is without instantiating an object.

```
// Methods
public static System.IO.StreamWriter AppendText(string path);
public static void Copy(string sourceFileName,
    string destFileName);
public static void Copy(string sourceFileName,
    string destFileName, bool overwrite);
```

```
public static System.IO.FileStream Create(string path);
public static System.IO.FileStream Create(string path,
    int bufferSize);
public static System.IO.StreamWriter CreateText(
    string path);
public static void Delete(string path);
```

The *File* class illustrates a twist that will help you understand how to use WinCV with every .NET class. The *File* class is primarily a utility class with static methods that are used to create *FileStream* objects based on absolute file paths. To see how to use the *File* class in our programs, look at its first method, *AppendText*. The signature of *AppendText* tells us exactly how to use the method.

```
public static System.IO.StreamWriter AppendText(string path);
```

You can see that this method is public, so we can access it in our programs. Next, this method is static, so we can't create a new instance of it, but it is available if we declare it. The return parameter, *System.IO.StreamWriter*, tells us that we will have to create a variable of type *StreamWriter* and assign it the return value of *AppendText*. If this process sounds a bit strange at this point, don't worry. Shortly we will use the *AppendText* method so that you can clearly see how these steps are accomplished.

The parameter to *AppendText* is a string that contains the path of the file we want to either create or append to. So, we can call the *AppendText* method of the *File* class and pass in the name and location of a file, and the class will return to us an object of type *StreamWriter*. Now you're probably wondering what a stream is. In Visual Basic .NET, files work hand in hand with streams, so let's take a closer look.

Streams

A stream is essentially an abstraction of a sequence of bytes, such as a file, an input/output device, an interprocess communication pipe, or even a TCP/IP socket. The .NET *Stream* class is the abstract base class of all .NET stream classes. The *Stream* class and its derived classes, such as *FileStream*, provide a generic view of these different types of input and output. The *StreamWriter* class is designed for character output, and subclasses of *Stream* are designed for byte input and output. These classes are incredibly powerful because they isolate the programmer from the specific details of the operating system and the underlying devices.

What's the Difference Between a File and a Stream?

The difference between a file and a stream is not always hard and fast. You can think of a file as an ordered and named collection of a particular sequence of bytes having persistent storage. When we think of files, we think of concepts such as directory paths, disk storage, and file and directory names.

Although streams also provide a way to write and read bytes to and from a backing store, the location can be one of several storage mediums. Just as there are backing stores other than disks, there are several kinds of streams other than file streams. For example, there are network and tape streams. The .NET Framework even provides a *MemoryStream* class that is a nonbuffered stream whose encapsulated data is directly accessible in computer memory. This type of stream has no backing store and may be useful as a temporary buffer.

Streams have some fundamental operations such as reading and writing. Also, streams can support *seeking*, which is the ability to move an internal pointer that indicates the current position in the stream. As with anything else, working with streams includes some exceptions. Depending on the backing store of the stream, only some stream operations might be supported. For example, the *NetworkStream* class does not support seeking. You can access the stream properties *CanRead*, *CanWrite*, and *CanSeek* to determine which operations a specific stream supports.

Reading and Writing Binary, Numeric, or Text Data

As you know, files can contain strings, numeric data types, and binary data. Depending on our needs, we will need to determine what type of stream we need in order to work with the data at hand. The *File* class supports all of these data types and allows you to incorporate data types in files.

The *System.IO* class contains many inherited classes that allow you to read and write characters to and from streams or files, using specific encoding to convert characters to and from bytes. Depending on what we need for the problem at hand, we'll frequently use classes such as *FileStream* to read and write files on a file system, *BinaryReader* and *BinaryWriter* to read and write binary information, *StreamReader* and *StreamWriter* to read and write character information in a specific coding—such as Universal Character Set Transformation Format 8-bit (UTF-8)—and *TextReader* and *TextWriter* to read and write a series of characters.

We will examine the *StreamReader* and *StreamWriter* classes in the examples that follow, but you'll be able to use any of the reader or writer classes because they are implemented in the same way.

Using the *File* and *StreamWriter* Classes in the .NET Framework

When you want to use the *File* class in your programs, import *System.IO* and add a reference to the assembly (if it's not automatically added for you). As we saw earlier, the static *File* class has an *AppendText* method that returns a *StreamWriter* object that handles all the heavy lifting of reading and writing.

```
public static System.IO.StreamWriter AppendText(string path);
```

How do we actually use the *AppendText* method of the *File* class? In the following code example, we first dimension a string variable, *sFileName*, that will hold the name and location of the file we are interested in. Next we dimension a variable, *fStreamWriter*, as type *StreamWriter* and assign it the return value of the *AppendText* method of the *File* class. The *AppendText* method creates a *StreamWriter* object that appends text to a file on the specified path or creates the file if it does not already exist.

```
Dim sFileName As String = "C:\Text.txt"
Dim fStreamWriter As StreamWriter = File.AppendText(sFileName)
With fStreamWriter
    .WriteLine("This is the first line of our file.")
    .WriteLine("The second line of important information.")
    .Flush()
    .Close()
End With
```

Pretty simple, eh? Because both the *StreamWriter* and *File* classes are static, we don't declare new instances of either. We use them as-is and use the *WriteLine* method of the *StreamWriter* object to write some text to the file. Technically, our example doesn't need to call the *Flush* method because the *Close* method calls *Flush* for us. It's better not to rely on the default behavior of the language, however. As a personal preference, I explicitly flush any file contents and then close the file.

Our simple example created a text file and wrote the strings to that file. We can easily see this file in Notepad, as shown in Figure 5-4.

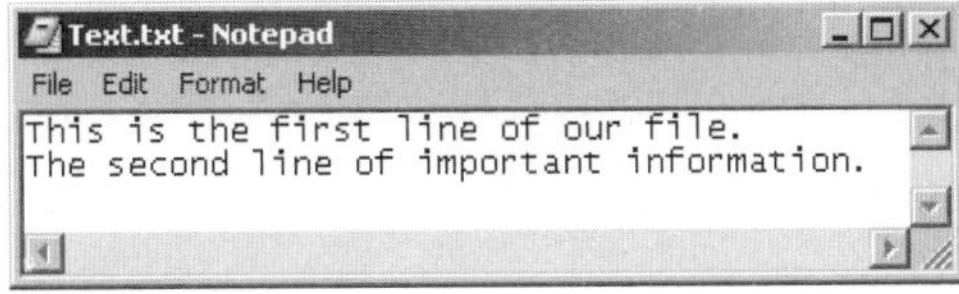

Figure 5-4 The output from our simple example.

Reading Our File

Now that we've created and written information to our Text.txt file and closed it, let's see how to read information from it. To open a file, you need to manipulate the same *System.IO* objects. The *File* class has a number of different methods for opening files, but for this example we will use the *OpenText* method. This particular method returns a *StreamReader* object, which is ideal for reading lines of information from a standard text file.

```
public static System.IO.StreamReader OpenText(string path);
```

Once again, by simply looking at the signatures of the *File* class methods, we can see exactly how to implement code that reads from a text file. The following code demonstrates using the *OpenText* method, passing it the name of the file you intend to open. You should always include a fully qualified path when specifying the file.

```
Dim fStreamReader As StreamReader = File.OpenText(sFileName)
Dim sFileContents As String
sFileContents = fStreamReader.ReadToEnd

fStreamReader.Close()
MessageBox.Show(sFileContents)
```

Here we declare a variable of type *StreamReader* and set it to an open file. Then, using the *ReadToEnd* method of the *StreamReader* object, we assign the file contents to a string variable, *sFileContents*. Because we are not writing to the file, we don't need to explicitly flush its contents. In this example, we simply declare the *StreamReader* on one line and read the entire contents of the file in another line. Two lines of code to read a file—pretty powerful. We then display the file's contents in a message box, as shown in Figure 5-5.

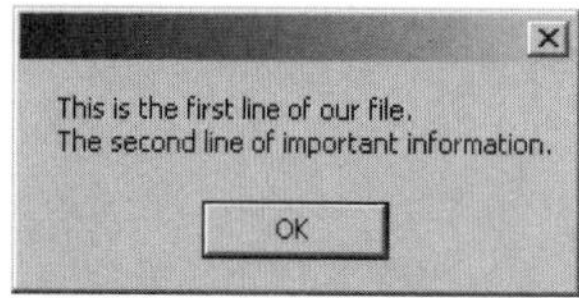

Figure 5-5 The contents of our file.

If you want a better sense of exactly how the *File* and *StreamReader* classes interact, you can dimension the *fStreamReader* in this manner:

```
Dim fStreamReader As New StreamReader( _
    File.Open(sFileName, FileMode.OpenOrCreate))
```

You can see that you must first open a file and pass it as a parameter to the *StreamReader*. Again, pretty simple coding.

Now take a look at the second and third methods of the *File* class, the overloaded *Copy* methods. The first method simply copies a source file to a destination file, and the second overloaded method permits us to pass a Boolean value to indicate whether we want to overwrite the destination file if it exists. Because the return type is *void* (C# terminology for nothing returned), we simply invoke the method. (It might be nice if the method returned an enumerated constant that indicates whether the copy was successful, but there are other ways to check for success, as we will see in a moment.)

```
public static void Copy(string sourceFileName,
    string destFileName);
public static void Copy(string sourceFileName,
    string destFileName, bool overwrite);
```

The *Copy* method is even easier to use than the *AppendText* and *ReadToEnd* methods we just looked at. We simply pass in the name of a valid source file and the name and location of where we want it copied—one line of code.

```
Dim sSource As String = "C:\Text.txt"
Dim sDestination As String = "C:\Copy.txt"
File.Copy(sSource, sDestination, True)
```

In your production code, you would certainly check to see whether the copy operation was successful. As with most .NET classes, we can perform this check with one line of code. The *File.Exists* method takes the name and location of a file and determines whether it exists. You can see that this method returns a *Boolean* True or False.

```
public static bool Exists(string path);
```

As long as we have imported *System.IO* into our code, we can simply use the static *File* object's *Exists* method.

```
If File.Exists(sDestination) Then
    'Do important things
End If
```

The *FileInfo* Class

Because the *File* class is static, we can't use it in every case. We will usually need a class that works with specific instances of a file, which is where the *FileInfo* class comes in handy. For example, we might want to verify that the file we copied contains more than zero bytes. (While the file might be copied, it's very possible that the file's contents weren't copied. The file might exist, but it could be empty. In production code, for example, if we copied a file and there was not enough disk space or a problem writing to disk, we would need to know that and certainly check for it.)

Unlike the static *File* class, the *FileInfo* class permits us to create new instances for individual files. The *FileInfo* class contains most of the same methods of the *File* class for general-purpose uses and also lets us create separate objects for each individual file. Think of the *File* class as a utility class and the *FileInfo* class as the class to use to manipulate specific files. We want to use the *FileInfo* class because it contains all instance methods and can actually perform more tasks than the *File* class. The static methods of the *File* class perform security checks on all methods, so if you are going to reuse an object several times, use the *FileInfo* class instead if the security checks are not necessary.

The *FileInfo* class provides instance methods for the creation, copying, deletion, moving, and opening of files and aids in the creation of *FileStream* objects. Use WinCV to find the *FileInfo* class, as shown in Figure 5-6. You can see that the class includes a constructor, so we can create individual *FileInfo* objects for our files. Notice that *FileInfo* has methods that accomplish the same tasks as the methods in the *File* class.

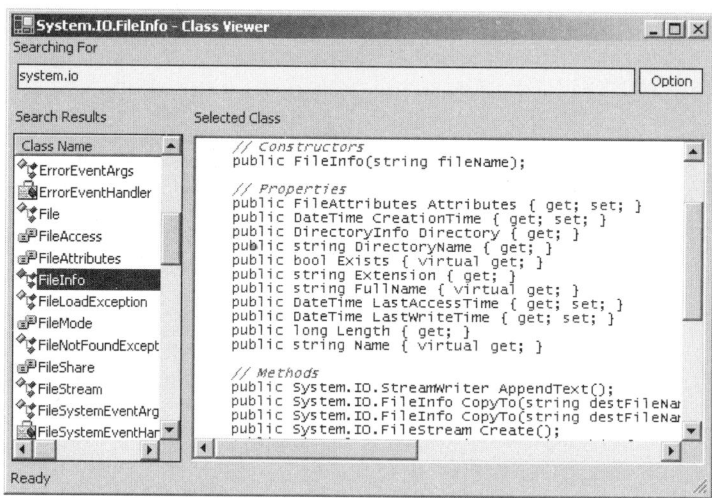

Figure 5-6 The *FileInfo* class in WinCV.

The following code shows how to use the *FileInfo* class to get information about a file.

```
Dim sFileName As String = "C:\Text.txt"
Dim sFileData As String

Dim fInfo As FileInfo = New FileInfo(sFileName)

With fInfo
```

```
    sFileData += "Creation Time: " & _
        .CreationTime.ToLongTimeString CtrlChrs.CrLf
    sFileData += "File Directory: " & _
        .Directory.ToString CtrlChrs.CrLf
    sFileData += "Full Name:  " & .FullName & CtrlChrs.CrLf
    sFileData += "File Size (bytes):  " & _
        .Length.ToString CrlChrs.CrLf
End With

MessageBox.Show(sFileData, "FileInfo Methods", _
    MessageBoxButtons.OK, MessageBoxIcon.Information)
```

Figure 5-7 displays the message box that contains information about the file we created earlier.

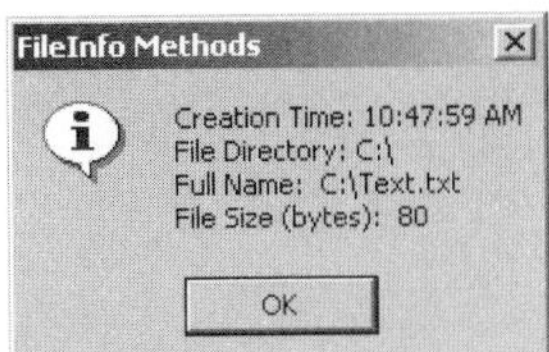

Figure 5-7 You can use the *FileInfo* class to retrieve information about a file.

The return type of the *CreationTime* property must be assigned to a variable of type *DateTime*. This situation is where the strong typing of .NET helps us get away from the nasty run-time errors that result from late binding. The common language runtime knows exactly what data type to expect ahead of time. If we inadvertently try to assign the return value of the *CreationTime* property to a string, the compiler will bark at us during design time, not when the user is running our application.

You can see the benefits of using the *FileInfo* class. Not only can we do the same tasks with it as with the *File* class, but also *FileInfo* contains many properties that permit us to retrieve all sorts of useful information about the file in question.

Creating a New File

Of course, we can also easily create a new file and write to it. The first thing we do is create a new instance of the *FileInfo* class with a string containing the name and location of the file we'd like to create. The following code fragment demonstrates how to use the *FileInfo* class to create and write to a file.

```
Dim sFileName As String = "C:\FileInfo.txt"
Dim fInfo As FileInfo = New FileInfo(sFileName)
Dim fStreamWriter As StreamWriter = fInfo.AppendText
fStreamWriter.WriteLine("Using the FileInfo Class")
```

We create a new instance of the *FileInfo* class, which is held in the *fInfo* variable. Then we use the *AppendText* method of *fInfo*, which returns a *StreamWriter* object. That object is held in our variable *fStreamWriter*. Then, using *fStreamWriter*, we can simply use the *WriteLine* method to write to the file.

Enumerating Directory Entries Using the Framework

The ability to enumerate the files and subdirectories of a directory is essential for many programming tasks. The .NET *FileInfo* and *DirectoryInfo* classes make this task easy. Why not use the *File* and *Directory* classes? Because we usually want to retrieve information such as the size and creation date for a given file. The *File* class focuses on the use of noninstantiated methods, while the *FileInfo* class offers methods based on an instance of a *FileInfo* object. The *Directory* and *DirectoryInfo* classes are similar.

By looking at the signatures of the various properties of the *DirectoryInfo* class, you can easily see whether you can read (get) a property or write (set) that property.

```
// Properties
public FileAttributes Attributes { get; set; }
public DateTime CreationTime { get; set; }
public bool Exists { virtual get; }
public string Extension { get; }
public string FullName { virtual get; }
public DateTime LastAccessTime { get; set; }
public DateTime LastWriteTime { get; set; }
public string Name { virtual get; }
public DirectoryInfo Parent { get; }
public DirectoryInfo Root { get; }
```

To be sure we understand how to use the properties, let's look at the *Attributes* property as an example. You can see that we can both read and write to the *Attributes* property. It also returns a value of type *FileAttributes*. Therefore, we must declare a variable of type *FileAttributes* to hold the object returned from the *Attributes* property. See the pattern? We declare a variable that corresponds to the return type of the property. Once you understand that, you can use any class in the .NET Framework. The following code fragment demonstrates the basics of using the *DirectoryInfo* class to get information about a file.

```
Dim sFileName As String = "C:\Text.txt"


'First create a new instance of a DirectoryInfo object

Dim diDirectoryInfo As DirectoryInfo = _
    New DirectoryInfo(sFileName)
```

```
'Now that we have the DirectoryInfo object, call its
' Attributes property and assign it to a variable of
' type FileAttributes.

Dim diAttributes As FileAttributes = _
    diDirectoryInfo.Attributes

Dim sFileInformation As String

sFileInformation += "File Name: " & sFileName & _
    CtrlChrs.CrLf


If diAttributes = FileAttributes.Normal Then
    sFileInformation += "The file is normal" & CtrlChrs.CrLf
End If

If diAttributes = FileAttributes.Archive Then
    sFileInformation += "The file is not archived" & CtrlChrs.CrLf
End If

If diAttributes = FileAttributes.Hidden Then
    sFileInformation += "The file is hidden" & CtrlChrs.CrLf
Else
    sFileInformation += "The file is not hidden" & CtrlChrs.CrLf
End If

If diAttributes = FileAttributes.Directory Then
    sFileInformation += "The entry is a directory" & _
        CtrlChrs.CrLf
Else
    sFileInformation += "The entry is a file" & CtrlChrs.CrLf
End If

MessageBox.Show(sFileInformation, _
    "DirectoryInfo Properties", MessageBoxButtons.OK, _
    MessageBoxIcon.Information)
```

It's also easy to use the *Attributes* property to change a file's attributes. For example, if we want to make our file hidden, we can simply use the following code.

```
fFile.Attributes = FileSystemAttributes.Hidden

If (fFile.Attributes = FileSystemAttributes.Hidden) Then
    MessageBox.Show("This file is hidden.")
Else
    MessageBox.Show("This file is not hidden.")
End If
```

To reset the file and make it visible again, simply assign the *Normal* attribute.

```
fFile.Attributes = FileSystemAttributes.Normal
```

The *DirectoryInfo* Class Methods

The *DirectoryInfo* class methods are the key to understanding how to enumerate files and subdirectories. Take a moment to examine these methods and see how their signatures determine how they are used.

```
// Methods
public void Create();
public virtual System.Runtime.Remoting.ObjRef
    CreateObjRef(Type requestedType);
public System.IO.DirectoryInfo CreateSubdirectory(string path);
public virtual void Delete();
public void Delete(bool recursive);
public virtual bool Equals(object obj);
public System.IO.DirectoryInfo[] GetDirectories();
public System.IO.DirectoryInfo[] GetDirectories(string
    searchPattern);
public System.IO.FileInfo[] GetFiles();
public System.IO.FileInfo[] GetFiles(string searchPattern);
public System.IO.FileSystemInfo[] GetFileSystemInfos();
public System.IO.FileSystemInfo[]
    GetFileSystemInfos(string searchPattern);
public virtual int GetHashCode();
public virtual object GetLifetimeService();
public Type GetType();
public virtual object InitializeLifetimeService();
public void MoveTo(string destDirName);
public void Refresh();
public virtual string ToString();
```

The following code creates a new instance of the *DirectoryInfo* class and assigns it to *dDirectory*. We use the *GetFiles* method of *dDirectory* to iterate through each file in the current directory and assign the current file to *fFileInfo*, which is an object of type *FileInfo*. We interrogate a few properties, *FullName* for one, and assign them to local variables. We then concatenate the information about each file to a string and display the result in a message box.

```
Dim dDirectory As New DirectoryInfo(".")
Dim fFileInfo As FileInfo
Dim sMessage As String
For Each fFileInfo In dDirectory.GetFiles("*.*")
    Dim fName As String = fFileInfo.FullName
    Dim fSize As Long = fFileInfo.Length
    Dim fCreationTime As DateTime = fFileInfo.CreationTime
```

```
    sMessage += fSize & CtrlChrs.Tab & fCreationTime & _
        CtrlChrs.Tab & fName & CtrlChrs.CrLf
Next fFileInfo

MessageBox.Show(sMessage, "More Framework Examples", _
    MessageBoxButtons.OK, MessageBoxIcon.Information)
```

The output from this code is nicely formatted, as you can see in Figure 5-8. While not terribly complex, these examples illustrate how to use the WinCV tool to discover the framework classes you need to work with.

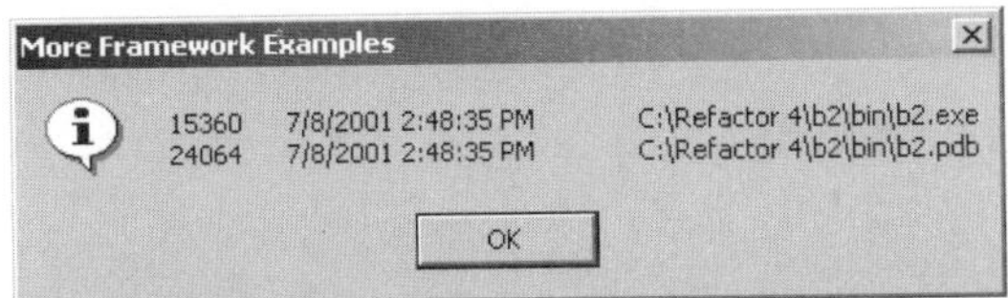

Figure 5-8 The *DirectoryInfo* class makes it easy to enumerate files and subdirectories.

> **Tip** Get to know the framework classes, because understanding the .NET Framework classes is key to professional Visual Basic .NET programming. The WinCV tool makes it easy to discover how to use a framework class: simply find the class in WinCV and scan the constructors, fields, methods, and properties. We used both static and dynamic classes in our examples, so you should not have any problems using either in your own applications.

Let's Talk Strings

Arguably, string manipulation and file manipulation are the two most important facets of computer science. Almost all programs use either or both. Now that we're familiar with file manipulation using the .NET Framework, let's spend some time looking at the new string functionality. Also, in our review of how to work with strings, you will start to see patterns in the .NET Framework classes. Once you master a few of them, the rest follow the same conventions and soon you will feel at home working with them.

It's been said that everything in computer science can be ultimately reduced to string manipulation. While this statement may or may not be true, strings are incredibly important in even the smallest program. The adept string capabilities of classic Visual Basic were the envy of programmers in all languages. Using the classic Visual Basic built-in functions *Mid*, *Left*, and *Right* made string handling a breeze. In many languages, such as C and C++, strings are actually a chore. They're handled as an array, you have to access them just so, and you have to index through them. In fact, most programmers starting out with C++ cut their teeth on the language by writing classes just to handle strings. In short, string manipulation was work.

The good news about strings in Visual Basic .NET is that we have the same capability to manipulate strings as we had in Visual Basic 6. However, we have to change the way we work with strings because they have grown up in Visual Basic .NET. We all became dependent on the string manipulation functions built into the Visual Basic 6 language. While they were simple, elegant, and usually fast, they were built into the compiler and specific to the language.

What's New in Strings?

The *String* data type comes from the *System.String* class. Like the *File* class, the *String* is a sealed class, so you cannot inherit from it. Sealing the *String* class permits the system to perform behind-the-scenes string optimization algorithms. Perhaps the most dramatic new notion associated with strings is that an instance of the *String* class is considered immutable, meaning that a string cannot be modified after it has been created. Wait a moment. If a string is immutable, how can we delete a section from the middle of the string or trim leading or trailing blanks? In fact, how will we use all of the other string manipulation methods? Manipulation implies change.

In Visual Basic .NET, all of the string-manipulation methods *appear* to modify a string, but they actually destroy the original and return a new string containing the modification. The end result is transparent to programmers, so why do we care?

There are several reasons. An immutable string makes threading, ownership, and aliasing of a string object much simpler, for example. Also, .NET maintains a pool of literal strings within the memory space of the running program (known as the *application domain*). All literal strings in the program are automatically part of the pool. This system permits sophisticated algorithms to merge any duplicate strings. Because a string is an object, we can correctly perform reference comparisons (checking the memory location) instead of value comparisons (checking the actual value of the string).

Uninitialized Strings

The first thing to learn about strings is that we have to give them a value before we use them. When a string variable is dimensioned and not given a value, .NET initializes the variable to an empty string. Consider the following line.

```
Dim sString1 As String
```

You can think of *sString1* as a reference variable that points to a string. However, the variable is currently uninitialized because it isn't referring to a string. This oversight was a common misstep in classic Visual Basic.

Now let's say that we try to use the variable in an innocent way, such as displaying it.

```
MessageBox.Show(sString1)
```

Remember that a string is a reference data type, but instead of initializing a string to the NULL of other reference types, Visual Basic .NET initializes the variable to an empty string, or "". Because the *sString1* reference is not NULL, we will not get the dreaded "Attempt to dereference a null object reference" error message if we attempt to access the variable. (In object-oriented programming, dereferencing means attempting to get something from a memory location—think of a reference variable as a pointer in C++. This error message tells us that we attempted to grab something by referencing a memory location, but the object is NULL. Oops. Visual Basic .NET provides another safety net by returning an empty string when you access an uninitialized string variable.)

Working with Strings

Because our strings are objects, they have various manipulation methods built in. All of the handy string manipulation functions in Visual Basic 6 are now methods of the *String* object. For example, if we want to concatenate two strings, we could write code something like the following. The results are shown in Figure 5-9.

```
Dim sString1 As String = "Don't try to shift gears while trying"
Dim sString2 As String = " to put hot sauce on your burrito."

sString1 = sString1.Concat(sString1, sString2)
```

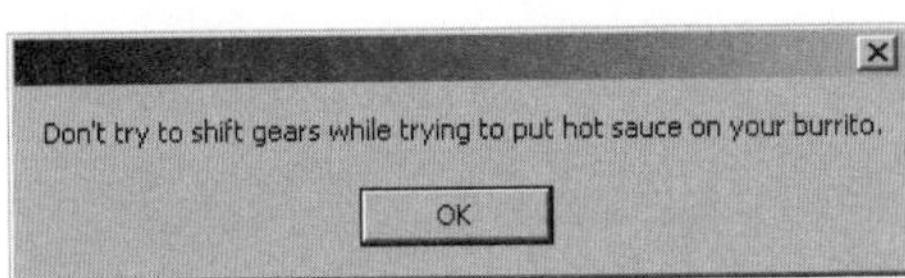

Figure 5-9 The results of our concatenated strings.

Of course, the following two statements accomplish the same thing:

```
sString1 &= sString2
sString1 = sString1 + sString2
```

None of these examples really modifies *sString1* at all. The original string is destroyed, and a new, modified string is created on the fly and assigned to *sString1*. If your program is going to do quite a bit of string manipulation, there will be a lot of creating and throwing away of strings. As you might guess, this process can be slow. If you really need to do some industrial strength string manipulation, use the *StringBuilder* class. *StringBuilder* objects are convenient for situations in which it is desirable to modify a string—perhaps by removing, replacing, or inserting characters—without creating a new string for each modification. The methods contained within this class do not return a new *StringBuilder* object (unless specified otherwise). In the next chapter, we will be using the *StringBuilder* class to build a fun program that mimics a Rogerian psychologist.

The *String* class has several methods that permit you to get substrings, insert and delete substrings, split a string into two substrings, find a string's length, and perform many other operations. For example, the *Split* method takes a delimiter and breaks a string into an array of substrings. Likewise, the *Join* method returns a concatenated string from an array of substrings (similar to those created by the *Split* method). I've written many string parsers over the years to extract fields embedded in a string sent from a legacy mainframe somewhere. The *Split* procedure was added in the Visual Basic 6 language as a built-in function. Now in Visual Basic .NET you can use a single line of code to split a string into substrings.

To determine the length of a string, simply use its *Length* method. Because the *MessageBox* class is expecting a string, you have to call the *ToString* method to convert the numeric value if you want to display the string's length in a message box. (The length returned by the *Length* method is in characters, not bytes.) You can see how this strong typing will save headaches when our program is released.

```
MessageBox.Show(sString1.Length.ToString)    'Displays 71
```

Likewise, finding substrings in a string is also a breeze. If you are looking for a character or substring in a string, call the *IndexOf* method. If the substring (or character) is present, *IndexOf* returns the index of the first occurrence of the substring or character. If the substring is not present, *IndexOf* returns –1.

```
Dim sString1 As String = "Don't try to shift gears while trying"
MessageBox.Show(sString1.IndexOf("s").ToString)  'Displays 13
```

The *Substring* method corresponds to the classic Visual Basic *Mid$* function. The *Substring* method has two overloads. One constructs and returns a substring starting at the specified index to the end of the string. The other extracts and returns a substring at a starting index of the specified length. (Remember that strings start at index 0, not 1.)

Copying and Cloning a String

The *Copy* method of a string object makes a duplicate of a specified string. If the original string is empty, the copy of the string is also empty.

```
sString2 = String.Copy(sString1)
MessageBox.Show(sString2)  'The contents of sString1 are copied
                           ' to sString2
```

Now let's say we want to use the *Clone* method of our *sString1* object. What's the difference between the *Copy* method and the *Clone* method? Whereas *Copy* makes a duplicate string, *Clone* simply returns a reference to the same string.

```
sString2 = sString1.Clone().ToString
MessageBox.Show(sString2)     'sString2 contains a reference
                              ' to sString1
```

The *Equals* method returns True if we compare *sString1* to *sString2* after we either copy or clone *sString1* to *sString2*. We can also use the *Equals* method to compare two unrelated strings.

```
Dim sString1 As String = "You can see the morning, " & _
    "but I can see the light."
Dim sString2 As String = "You can see the morning, " & _
    "but I can see the light."

MessageBox.Show(sString1.Equals(sString2).ToString) 'Returns True
```

As you might imagine, we can also use the comparison operator on strings.

```
If sString1 = sString2 Then
    MessageBox.Show("Strings are equal")
Else
    MessageBox.Show("Strings are not equal")
End If
```

Microsoft .NET provides the handy curly bracket ({}) formatting characters that allow you to insert variables into strings. For example, we might have a program that dynamically presents output. We can use the {} characters to serve as placeholders for variables—{0} represents the first variable in a comma-separated list, {1} represents the second variable, and so on, as shown in the following example.

```
Dim iAdd As Integer = 2

Dim sString As String = String.Format("{0} and {0} = {1}", _
    iAdd, iAdd + iAdd)
MessageBox.Show(sString)
```

The output from this code is shown in Figure 5-10.

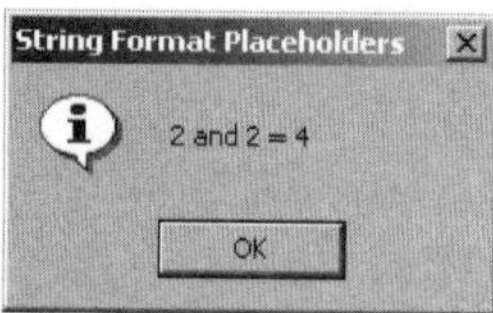

Figure 5-10 The {} formatting characters serve as placeholders for variables.

Using the {} characters is much easier than having to build a string and manually concatenate the variables, as was required in classic Visual Basic.

```
Dim sString As String = iAdd & " and " & iAdd & " = " & _
    (iAdd + iAdd)
```

In addition, you can use the {} characters along with other formatting characters to format a string.

```
Dim iCost As Integer = 954
Dim sString As String = String.Format("Your total is {0:C}.", _
    iCost)
MessageBox.Show(sString, "String Format Placeholders", _
    MessageBoxButtons.OK, MessageBoxIcon.Information)
```

The output from this code is shown in Figure 5-11.

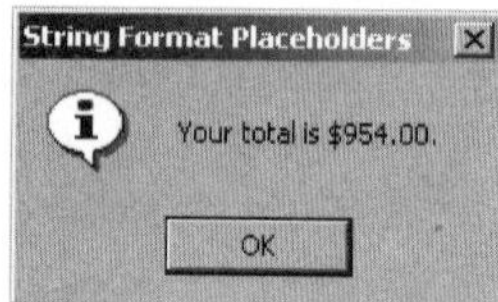

Figure 5-11 Formatting characters make it easy to enhance string output.

For more information about formatting strings see the topics "Creating New Strings" and "Picture Numeric Format Strings" in the Visual Basic .NET help file.

How to Efficiently Use the Help File

All programmers, from novice to guru, will often rely on a product's help file. While this sidebar is about searching the .NET help files, the techniques described here are also helpful when using Internet search engines. Once you know the tricks, you can find whatever you want very quickly, either in the help file or on the Internet.

Let's say you want to find whether the members of the *File* class provide some particular functionality that you need. If you simply search for the characters *ile*, you are soon greeted with 500 or more help entries. Looking through this large number of entries to find what you are looking for would be quite a daunting chore.

If you type **+file +member**, you force the search engine to display only pages that contain both the word *file* and the word *member* on the same page. Or, if you type **+file member**, all pages with the word *file* will be displayed that may or may not contain the word *member*. Although these criteria yield better search results, neither criterion ensure the words are even within a few paragraphs of each other. In many cases this type of search can be helpful, but not when you are looking for a very specific item. If you search for **+"file member"** in quotation marks, however, you force the search engine to display pages where the two words are together, and your search is much more fruitful.

In general, use lowercase in your terms. Many Internet search engines are case sensitive to uppercase letters—if you enter an initial-capped word, such as *File*, only pages that contain the initial-capped word *File* are returned. If you search for *file* with a lowercase *f*, pages that contain both *File* and *file* are returned. The IDE search engine, however, will always change whatever you enter to lowercase. Spend some time poking around the help file. It's probably the best investment of time to start really learning Visual Basic .NET.

Conclusion

In this chapter, we discussed the .NET Framework and some techniques on how to find what we need in the framework to solve a specific problem. The Windows Class Viewer, WinCV, is a helpful tool in this regard. We learned how to read the signatures of the constructors, methods, and properties in the .NET classes. You now have the ability to find and use any class in the entire .NET Framework. We also covered how to use the file handling classes (*File* and *FileInfo*) and the new *String* object.

When thinking about the work you'll do in Visual Basic .NET, keep in mind that computer languages influence how you think about a problem. They also influence how you think about communicating. The limits of a computer language are the limits of one's world. If you don't have a word for "object," for example, you can't think about objects when considering a problem. Because the .NET Framework includes a rich set of classes, developers are provided with productive and elegant tools with which to build solutions. We can stretch our minds and expand our solutions by using prebuilt functionality, which permits us to think about problems in an expanded yet simpler way.

Arrays and Collections in Visual Basic .NET

In most programs, you need to store information in memory. For example, when you dimension a variable in a statement such as *Dim sMyString as string = "Hello Visual Basic .NET"*, you have stored a string in memory. Many times, you'll need to store several strings or numbers together. Let's say you wanted to store a list of cities in the United States so that they could be accessed readily in your program. Most classic Visual Basic programmers would use an array to do this.

In most languages, arrays are the simplest and most common type of structured data. Arrays are handled differently in Visual Basic .NET than in classic Visual Basic. As you probably know, an array is a reference data type that contains variables accessed through indexes. The variables contained in an array, called the *elements* of the array, must all be of the same type, such as all integers or all strings. The elements of an array are created when an instance of the array is created, and, of course, they are extinguished when the instance of the array is destroyed. Each element of an array is initialized to the default value of its type. Because arrays are reference objects, they are allocated out of heap space rather than from the stack.

Arrays allow you to refer to a series of variables by the name of the array and to use a number, called an *index* or *subscript*, to tell them apart. Conceptually an array is like a row of mailboxes, each with a sequential number holding one item of the data type declared with the array. Arrays help you create shorter and simpler code in many situations because you can set up loops that deal efficiently with any number of elements by using the index number.

Collections, on the other hand, are classes that provide controlled access to specific types of variables or objects. For example, Visual Basic .NET has several built-in collections of controls, printers, and forms. If you want to program Microsoft Excel from Visual Basic, you can create an instance of an Excel object and access its collections via Excel's object model. You can create a workbook, grab a worksheet from the worksheet collection, and locate a cell in the worksheet's cell collection. Visual Basic 5 was the first version to provide a built-in collection data type that programmers could use.

When you place an element in a certain position in an array, you can be sure that the element will always be stored in the same position. Collections grow and shrink dynamically, as if they were an array we never have to redimension. While arrays are ordered, collections are unordered—an element's location within the collection can change. Therefore, you usually want to retrieve a collection element by using a key rather than a specific location within the collection. Arrays and collections have other differences that I'll cover as we move through the chapter.

Building Your First Visual Basic .NET Array

The Microsoft .NET Framework class *System.Array* is the base class of all array types. The *System.Array* class has properties for determining the rank, length, and lower and upper bounds of an array, as well as methods for creating, accessing, sorting, searching, and copying arrays. An array type is defined by specifying the element type (such as string or integer), the rank (number of dimensions), and the upper and lower bounds of each dimension of the array. An element is a specific position within an array. The *length* of an array is the number of elements the array can contain.

A Visual Basic .NET array can have one or more dimensions. The *dimensionality* or *rank* of an array corresponds to the number of subscripts used to identify an individual element. For example, if you have *aMyArray(10,3)*, you have a two-dimensional array with 0–9, 0–2 elements. You can actually specify up to 60 dimensions, but I personally get confused after three dimensions, and having more than three dimensions is extremely rare.

Every dimension of an array has a lower bound and an upper bound. The lower bound of an array is the starting index of that dimension and is always 0. You can set an initial value for the upper bound when you create the array. (The upper bound is one less than the number of elements in the array.) The elements of an array are contiguous within these bounds. Visual Basic .NET allocates space for an array element corresponding to each index number, so you should avoid declaring an array larger than necessary—the space will be allocated even if there is no data stored there. If you declare an array of 1000 integers but only store 100, the space required to store the additional 900 integers is still allocated in memory and amounts to wasted space.

A multidimensional array can have different bounds for each dimension. These multidimensional arrays can be used for matrix multiplication. Let's say we want a place to store the various labors of Hercules. What better way to store them than in an array? You can dimension an array in several ways. Let's start out with one that might look familiar.

```
Dim asLaborsOfHercules(13) As String
```

This statement dimensions an array with 13 elements, 0–12. Each of the elements will have a string data type. Because we told the array how many elements we wanted as well as the data type of the elements, each will be initialized to an empty string. As you recall, an empty string is the default initialization for a string data type.

> **Note** By adding *as* to the name of the array *LaborsOfHercules*, I know it is an *a*rray of *s*trings. Naming conventions are like a religion—each has its zealots who are certain that theirs is the correct one. You can use any naming convention you want, but be consistent and clear with whichever convention you use.

Now we want to add strings to each of the elements. You can still use the syntax that's familiar from classic Visual Basic, for example:

```
asLaborsOfHercules(0) = "Kill Nemean Lion"
```

However, because the array we dimensioned has several methods, you can also use the *SetValue* method to add string elements. The syntax for this is as follows:

```
<ArrayName>.SetValue("element contents", element index)
```

To add data to the first element of our array, use this syntax:

```
asLaborsOfHercules.SetValue("Kill Nemean Lion", 0)
```

Let's go ahead and fill our array with the strings we want to store in memory. When you are performing more than two operations on the same object, always remember to use the *With...End With* construct. Rather than using the brute force method of fully qualifying each and every entry to the array, the *With...End With* construct holds the variable reference for us. Not only is the code easier to read, but it's much more efficient. If we fully qualified each entry, Visual Basic would have to look up each nested reference for each new element added. And besides, fully qualifying each entry is a lot of typing, as you can see in the code that follows.

```
asLaborsOfHercules.SetValue("Kill Nemean Lion", 0)
asLaborsOfHercules.SetValue("Slay nine-headed hydra of Lerna", 1)
asLaborsOfHercules.SetValue("Capture elusive Stag of Arcadia", 2)
⋮
```

Every time we use a dot, Visual Basic has to resolve it. If we didn't use the *With...End With* syntax, each time we added a new value, Visual Basic would have to look up the address of our array and resolve any classes it's derived from to ensure it's a valid array for each and every item added.

When you are using a simple array like we are here, the *With...End With* construct is really used for readability and formatting. However, when you get into nested objects with many dots, the performance benefit is material. The more dots in an expression, the deeper you are going in the object model and the better the performance benefit you'll see using the *With...End With* construct if you are frequently accessing the object's elements.

Array Boundaries

We first dimension the array, tell it how many elements to add, and finally specify that it will contain string objects.

```
Dim asLaborsOfHercules(12) As String

With asLaborsOfHercules
    .SetValue("Kill Nemean Lion", 0)
    .SetValue("Slay nine-headed hydra of Lerna", 1)
    .SetValue("Capture elusive Stag of Arcadia", 2)
    .SetValue("Capture wild boar on Mt. Erymantus", 3)
    .SetValue("Clean Stables of King Augeas of Elis", 4)
    .SetValue("Shoot monstrous man-eating birds of the" & _
        " Stymphalian Marshes", 5)
    .SetValue("Capture mad bull of Crete", 6)
    .SetValue("Kill man-eating mares of King Diomedes", 7)
    .SetValue("Steal Girdle of Hippolyta", 8)
    .SetValue("Seize cattle of Geryon of Erytheia", 9)
    .SetValue("Fetch golden apples of Hesperides", 10)
    .SetValue("Retrieve three-headed dog Cerberus from Hell", 11)
    .SetValue("Learn Visual Basic .NET", 12)
End With
```

Our array now contains data for elements 0 through 12, giving us 13 elements. If we attempt to add one more element, for example,

```
asLaborsOfHercules.SetValue("Learn Visual Basic .NET in " & _
    "a single day", 13)
```

we exceed the upper boundary of the array. Whenever this happens, a run-time *System.IndexOutOfRangeException* error is thrown. Because we can access data beyond the bounds of an array only during run time, the faulty program logic that caused this error can't be detected at design time. Many times it's the user that first discovers this mistake at run time, as you can see in Figure 6-1.

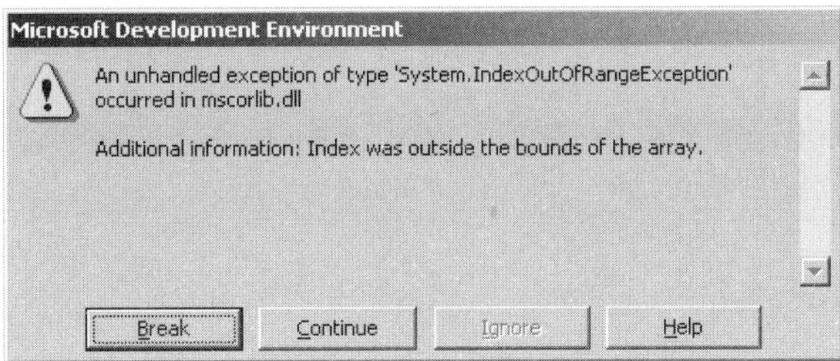

Figure 6-1 This error can't be detected at design time.

To help prevent you from making an error of this sort, the array object contains knowledge of its own structure. You can easily determine the upper and lower bounds of an array, as well as the number of elements it contains, by calling various array methods. Passing in *0* to certain methods gives you information about a one-dimensional array (or the first dimension of a multidimensional array).

For example, *GetLowerBound(0)* returns the lower bound for the indexes of the first dimension of the array, and *GetLowerBound(Rank - 1)* returns the lower bound of the last dimension of a multidimensional array. Why –1? Because if the array contains three dimensions, the first starts at 0, the second at 1, and the third at 2. Here's some code that puts these methods to use. You can see the results in Figure 6-2.

```
Imports Microsoft.VisualBasic.ControlChars
Public Class Form1
    Inherits System.Windows.Forms.Form

    Private Sub Form1_Load(ByVal sender As System.Object, _
        ByVal e As System.EventArgs) Handles MyBase.Load

        Dim sArrayInfo As String
        Dim sArrayInfo As String

⋮

        With asLaborsOfHercules
            .SetValue("Kill Nemean Lion", 0)
            .SetValue("Slay nine-headed hydra of Lerna", 1)
            .SetValue("Capture elusive Stag of Arcadia", 2)
            .SetValue("Capture wild boar on Mt. Erymantus", 3)
```

(continued)

```
            .SetValue("Clean Stables of King Augeas of Elis", 4)
            .SetValue("Shoot monstrous man-eating birds " & _
                "of the Stymphalian Marshes", 5)
            .SetValue("Capture mad bull of Crete", 6)
            .SetValue("Kill man-eating mares of " * _
                "King Diomedes", 7)
            .SetValue("Steal Girdle of Hippolyta", 8)
            .SetValue("Seize cattle of Geryon of Erytheia", 9)
            .SetValue("Fetch golden apples of Hesperides", 10)
            .SetValue("Retrieve three-headed dog Cerberus " & _
                "from Hell", 11)
            .SetValue("Learn Visual Basic .NET", 12)
        End With

        With asLaborsOfHercules
            sArrayInfo = "The lower bound is: " & _
                .GetLowerBound(0) & ControlChars.CrLf
            sArrayInfo += "The upper bound is: " & _
                .GetUpperBound(0).ToString & _
                ControlChars.CrLf
            sArrayInfo += "Number of elements: " & _
                .GetLength(0).ToString & _
                ControlChars.CrLf
            sArrayInfo += "Dimension of array: " & _
                .Rank.ToString & ControlChars.CrLf
        End With
        MessageBox.Show(sArrayInfo, "Array Information")
    End Sub
End Class
```

Figure 6-2 You can determine array information at run time.

As expected, the lower bound is 0 and the upper bound is 12, giving us 13 elements. So when dimensioning a fixed-size array it's helpful to think that the array is dimensioned to the upper bound. But if you are new to zero-based arrays, you must always remember that the array starts at zero (as do arrays in most other languages).

Note At the end of each line in the message box, we want to add a carriage return and line feed character (CrLf). Remember that these constants are referenced in the *Microsoft.VisualBasic.ControlChars* namespace. While we could write something like *Microsoft.VisualBasic.ControlChars.CrLf* to generate the carriage return and line feed characters, there's an easier way. Visual Basic .NET provides a handy means to create an *alias* for a namespace. Aliases let you assign a friendlier name to just one part of a namespace. By defining an alias right in the *Imports* statement and assigning the namespace, you can reference the fully qualified namespace by the shorter name.

```
Imports CtrlChr = Microsoft.VisualBasic.ControlChars
```

Remember what I said about minimizing the dots? Here we reduced two dots to one. This syntax is more efficient and improves readability of the code. Of course, *Imports* statements must always be the first lines in a module.

The major problem some novice programmers have with arrays is either overshooting or undershooting array access. Their code tries to access an element beyond the end of the array, which is known as the *off by one* error. I have read programming books in which the author actually suggests adding an additional element to the end of an array as a "cushion" so that this error won't happen. I find this advice incredibly poor because it not only promotes sloppy programming but, if that end element was actually accessed, invalid data would be there anyway.

If you need to iterate through an array, don't hard-code the boundaries; instead always use the *GetLowerBound* and *GetUpperBound* methods to ensure you don't overshoot or undershoot the array bounds. This defensive programming is not only good style, but it also ensures that you don't attempt to access an element outside of those defined. Doing so inadvertently guarantees a runtime error. In the following code, we simply loop through the array and build a string to output.

```
Dim iIndex As Integer
Dim sArrayContents As String = ""

For iIndex = asLaborsOfHercules.GetLowerBound(0) To _
    asLaborsOfHercules.GetUpperBound(0)

    sArrayContents += _
```

(continued)

```
        asLaborsOfHercules.GetValue(iIndex).ToString & _
        CtrlChr.CrLf

Next
MessageBox.Show(sArrayContents, "Things to do today.")
```

Now we can be sure we never get that nasty run-time error and the code always runs correctly, as shown in Figure 6-3. You can still use the older *LBound(array)* and *UBound(array)* methods from classic Visual Basic, but you should get in the habit of using these newer methods built into the Visual Basic .NET array object.

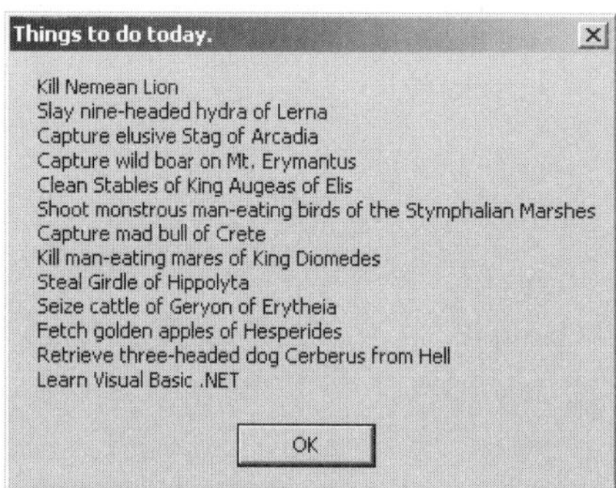

Figure 6-3 *GetLowerBound* and *GetUpperBound* let you work with arrays of all sizes.

Some luminaries in the field of computer science think that you should never access an individual element in an array but should instead always iterate over an entire array sequentially. Their thinking is that random access into an array is conceptually similar to random *GoTo* statements in a program, and we all know that the *GoTo* statement is *verboten* in most professional programming. They state that such random access tends to be undisciplined, error prone, and difficult to prove correct. They suggest that programmers should instead use stacks and queues whose elements can be accessed only sequentially. Luckily, stacks and queues are also built into the .NET Framework; however, I don't subscribe to this belief because at times you do need to randomly retrieve array elements. And because the array object gives us the tools to ensure that we only access legitimate elements, this is not a problem in practice.

Why Arrays Are Based on the *System.Array* Class

Because arrays in Visual Basic .NET are based on the .NET Framework *System.Array* class, several operations that aren't traditionally supported by array types are built into Visual Basic .NET arrays. You can now sort and search arrays, a capability that we old C programmers wished was part of Visual Basic for years.

Sorting Arrays

Classic Visual Basic programmers often needed array data to be sorted, but no built-in routines did this. I've written many bubble-and-heap sort routines to sort arrays. I've also seen voodoo programming where programmers added the contents of an array to an invisible list box, set the list box's *Sort* property to True to sort the data, and then read the data back to the array. While this approach worked, it was slow and used the language in strange and unnatural ways.

We can now use the *System.Array* type and simply pass in the array we want to sort. We can then call the *System.Array Sort* method, and the sorting is quickly done for us with no code. Very nice, as you can see in Figure 6-4.

```
Array.Sort(asLaborsOfHercules)
```

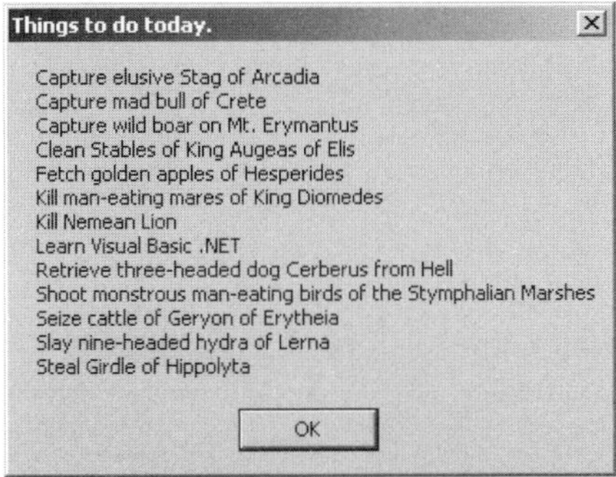

Figure 6-4 The built-in *Sort* method makes it easy to sort arrays.

Reversing the Contents of an Array

In addition to sorting, you can now reverse the contents of an array. Note that reverse does *not* mean a reverse sort, as you might think. Rather, the *Reverse* method indexes the elements of the array in reverse order. As you can see in Figure 6-5, learning Visual Basic .NET is now the easiest of Hercules' tasks.

```
Array.Reverse(asLaborsOfHercules)
```

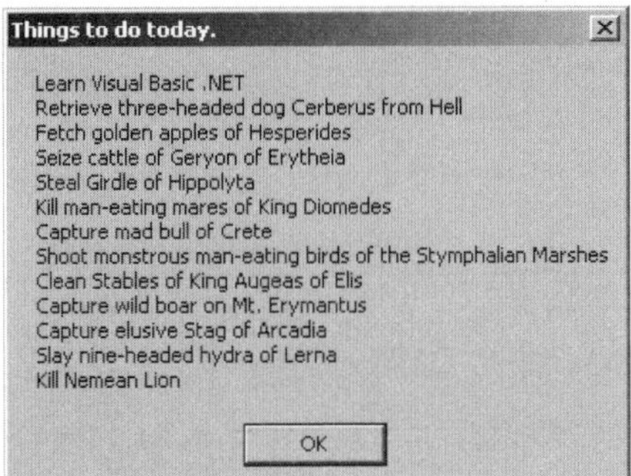

Figure 6-5 The built-in *Reverse* method makes it easy to reverse the order of the elements in an array.

Locating Elements

If you need to find a specific string within an array, you simply use the *IndexOf* method of the *System.Array* class. By passing in the array to search and the string you're looking for, the array index is returned. If the value is not found, –1 is returned. *IndexOf* is overloaded and can search portions of an array. Here's code that locates the index for Hercules' favorite task. Figure 6-6 shows the results.

```
Dim iIndex As Integer

iIndex = Array.IndexOf(asLaborsOfHercules, _
    "Learn Visual Basic .NET")

MessageBox.Show("In element: " & iIndex.ToString, _
    "Where is our string?")
```

Where is our string?

In element: 12

OK

Figure 6-6 The built-in *IndexOf* method returns the index of a specified value.

Binary Search of an Array

For larger arrays, a very efficient binary search method is available. This method works only on a sorted list or array, however. This routine first takes the contents of the middle element and determines whether the value you are searching for is less than or greater than this middle element. If the value is less, the routine just eliminated 50 percent of the items to be searched because it ignores the upper half of the array. The *BinarySearch* method then takes the remaining 50 percent of the array and compares your value to the new middle element. If the value is less than that element, the routine then ignores the top 50 percent of the remaining elements, and so on. You must remember that the *BinarySearch* method works only on sorted arrays. If you forget to sort the array, this method will not find the string. Here's an example of the *BinarySearch* method. Figure 6-7 shows the results.

```
Dim iIndex As Integer
Array.Sort(asLaborsOfHercules)
iIndex = Array.BinarySearch(asLaborsOfHercules, _
    "Learn Visual Basic .NET")
MessageBox.Show("In element: " & iIndex.ToString, _
    "Where is our string?")
```

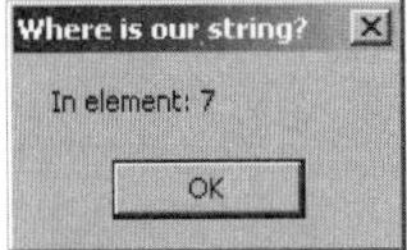

Figure 6-7 The built-in *BinarySearch* method is very efficient.

Arrays in Visual Basic .NET have grown up to provide just about any functionality you might need. With the object-oriented nature of the array object, you simply call a method or property to get what you need. Table 6-1 lists the methods of the *System.Array* class, and Table 6-2 lists the properties.

Table 6-1 Methods of *System.Array*

Method	Description
BinarySearch	Overloaded. This searches a one-dimensional sorted array for a value.
Clear	Sets a range of elements in an array to zero or to a null reference (the equivalent of classic Visual Basic's *Nothing*).
Copy	Overloaded. Copies a section of one array to another array, and performs type downcasting as required.
CreateInstance	Overloaded. Initializes a new instance of the *Array* class.
IndexOf	Overloaded. Returns the index of the first occurrence of a value in a one-dimensional array or in a portion of an array.
LastIndexOf	Overloaded. Returns the index of the last occurrence of a value in a one-dimensional array or in a portion of an array.
Reverse	Overloaded. Reverses the order of the elements in a one-dimensional array or in a portion of an array.
Sort	Overloaded. Sorts the elements in a one-dimensional array.
Clone	Creates a shallow copy of an *Array* object.
CopyTo	Copies all the elements of the current one-dimensional array to the specified one-dimensional array, starting at the specified destination array index.
Equals (inherited from *Object*)	Determines whether the specified object is the same instance as the current object.
GetLength	Gets the number of elements in the specified dimension of the array.

(continued)

Table 6-1 Methods of *System.Array* *(continued)*

Method	Description
GetLowerBound	Gets the lower bound of the specified dimension in an array.
GetUpperBound	Gets the upper bound of the specified dimension in an array.
GetValue	Overloaded. Gets the values of an array's elements at the specified indexes.
Initialize	Initializes every element of the value-type array by calling the default constructor of the value type.
SetValue	Overloaded. Sets the specified array elements to the specified value.
ToString (inherited from *Object*)	Returns a string that represents the current object.

Table 6-2 Properties of *System.Array*

Property	Description
IsReadOnly	Gets a value indicating whether an array is read-only.
IsSynchronized	Gets a value indicating whether access to an array is synchronized (thread-safe).
Length	Gets the total number of elements in all the dimensions of an array.
Rank	Gets the rank (number of dimensions) of an array.

What If I Don't Know How Many Elements I Need Ahead of Time?

In Visual Basic .NET, an array cannot have a fixed size if you want to initialize it with values during the declaration. For example, if you want to declare a specific size for an array, you can use either of the following declarations—they are essentially equivalent:

```
Dim aNumbers(5) As Integer
Dim aNumbers() As Integer = New Integer(5) {}
```

Both of these declarations specify an initial size—in this case 5. But because you specified a size during declaration, Visual Basic .NET will not allow you to initialize the array with values like this:

```
Dim aNumbers(5) as Integer = {0, 1, 2, 3, 4}    ' - Error!
```

Many times you just won't know how many elements will be required in an array. For example, your program might read records from a database and return a varying number of records. Or it might take input from a user that will vary from time to time. You just can't be certain at the time you are coding the program how many elements you will need.

The way to handle this situation is to declare a *dynamic array.* As the name implies, you can modify the size of a dynamic array during execution with the *ReDim* statement. By declaring the array without an index, the array is dynamic.

```
Dim asArray() As String  'Declare a dynamic array
ReDim asArray(5)         'Provide 5 elements
```

You can use the *ReDim* statement to add new elements to the array as needed. Using the *Redim* statement erases the contents of the array and adds more elements. If you need to resize the array but keep the original contents, use *ReDim Preserve.*

```
ReDim asArray(10)                'Erases the contents and
                                 'resizes the array to 10
ReDim Preserve asArray(15) 'Resizes the array but keeps the
                           'previous contents
```

A "gotcha" you have to keep in mind is that if you initialize an array with a specific size, this number is the number of elements, not the upper bound, as was the case in classic Visual Basic. In the preceding example we have 5 elements of integers, but they are indexed from 0 through 4. If you try to exceed the upper limit of an array, you will be presented with the friendly "Index was out of range" error. Again, this error can't be detected during coding but will only show up at execution. So a word to the wise: be extra careful not to address an array element above or below its boundaries.

I would caution you about using the *ReDim Preserve* statement, however. *ReDim* allows you to increase or decrease the array size. When the *ReDim Preserve* keywords are encountered, Visual Basic .NET will create a brand-new array and copy the contents to it. It does this because the array is inherited from *System.Array* and the .NET runtime defined the original fixed size on creation.

If you do declare a dynamic array, you need to write code to hold the current number of elements. Then, when adding a new element, you have to check to see whether this addition will exceed the current boundaries. If it will, you need to write code using the *ReDim Preserve* statement in order to preserve the array and increase the number of elements it contains by some constant. I've performed tons of these operations in previous versions of Visual Basic, and they can get complicated. Also, all of the checks that have to be performed can bog down processing. When I cover collections later in this chapter, you'll see some elegant solutions to this frequent problem. When you need to dynamically resize an array, the new *ArrayList* object makes resizing fast and painless.

Arrays Start at Zero in Visual Basic .NET

As I mentioned, all arrays in the .NET Framework start at zero. The *Option Base* statement that was used in classic Visual Basic is gone. The zero-based array structure was implemented to simplify processing for the common language runtime. While creating arrays with a non-zero base in Visual Basic. NET is possible, don't try to inherit them because it won't work. If you have not been using a zero base for arrays, my suggestion is that you should start now.

If you really need to create a non-zero-based array, you can do so as follows. This syntax creates an array of 5 integers starting at 10. The array has 5 elements from 10 through 14.

```
Dim aBadArray As Array = System.Array.CreateInstance(GetType _
    (Integer), New Integer(){5}, New Integer() {10})
```

Yes, I agree that this declaration looks like neo-Babylonian cuneiform, but you can easily test it by displaying the elements in a message box. By always using the *GetLowerBound* and *GetUpperBound* methods of the array, you can be sure you never walk off either end of the array. But my strong recommendation is don't do this.

> **Note** You can also use non-zero-based arrays in Visual Basic .NET by calling the *NewArray* function in the Visual Basic 6 Compatibility Library. However, I'd recommend resisting this temptation also. Anything in the compatibility class is subject to extinction, and using the *NewArray* function will negatively affect performance. Every reference to the array will require an extra call to the function. Arrays created with the *NewArray* function might not be compatible with other arrays in your project. And as we now know, they do not conform to common language specification standards. Many minuses for keeping a bad habit; it's not worth it.

Initializing the Array During Declaration

If you want to initialize elements when you declare an array, use the following syntax. With this syntax, the array is sized to fit the number of elements by default.

```
Dim aiDays() As Integer = {1, 2, 3, 4, 5, 6, 7}
```

Other array declarations are written like this.

```
Dim a(10) As Integer  'An integer array from 0 - 9
Dim s1(2, 2) As String 'Multi-dimensional 0-1, 0-1

Dim s2(,,) As String  'Multi-dimensional sizes not specified
ReDim s2(3, 4, 5) 'Defines sizes for s2
```

Arrays Are Reference Types

Always remember that arrays are reference types. If you dimension an array with a size and data type, the array is automatically initialized to the default initialization type for that particular data type. For example, the default initialization of a string is an empty string. The following code will create an array of five elements, each with an empty string as its content. The message box will display an empty string because each element contains at least something—an empty string.

```
Dim asArray(5) As String
MessageBox.Show(asArray(0))   'An empty string
```

However, if you use a dynamic array, the compiler has no idea how many elements will be present because you haven't told it. If you inadvertently try to access an element before the array is initialized to the number of elements, you will get a null object reference error.

```
Dim asArray() As String
MessageBox.Show(asArray(0))
```

Because the array is a reference type, we know its default initialization is Null, as you can see in Figure 6-8.

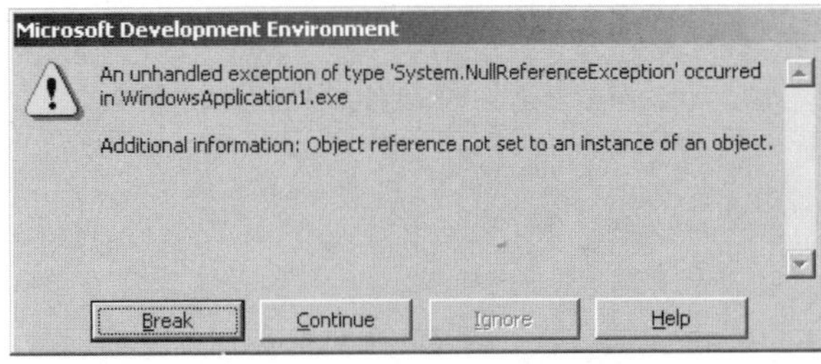

Figure 6-8 References are initialized to Null by default.

Remember that when an array is declared, it is inherited from the *System.Array* class. The *Array* object has knowledge about itself. It knows its data type, its rank, and its upper and lower bounds. When you declare an array of a value data type, such as an integer, double, or some other type, the array itself also contains the data, as you can see here:

```
Dim aiIntegerArray() As Integer = {23, 12, 54, 11}
```

In memory, the array of value types looks like Figure 6-9:

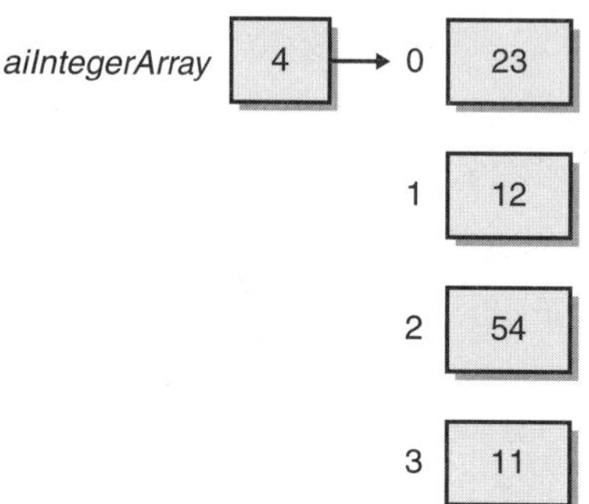

Figure 6-9 An array of value types in memory.

However, if you declare an array of reference types, such as a string, the array will contain references to the string objects and not the strings themselves.

```
Dim asStringArray() As String = {"eenie", "meenie", _
    "minie", "moe"}
```

Arrays of reference types contain an additional level of indirection. The array elements contain references to the string objects. The actual string objects are stored elsewhere, as is shown in Figure 6-10.

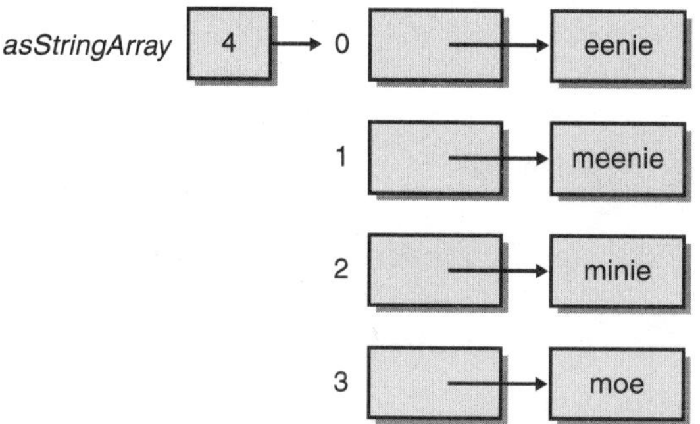

Figure 6-10 Reference types do not store information directly.

While arrays are very useful and fast, like anything else they do have their limitations. An array stores its elements in contiguous memory. Therefore, if you need to access the *i*th element of your array, the operation is very fast. However, because the elements are stored in contiguous memory, inserting a new element in the middle of the array is difficult. You would have to write twisted code to dimension the array again (*ReDim*) and then move all the elements after the one you inserted.

Of course, you could simply create a new, larger array and copy the values. But doing this also involves work and costs precious CPU cycles. If the array is sorted, searching for an element can be fast. If an array is unsorted, you might have to access each element to find your value. So, with an array we trade off speed for flexibility. If you need to add and delete items in a nonsequential order, collections are for you. We will examine collections later in the chapter, after we look at a bit more code.

Arrays in Action: A Roman Numeral Calculator

Let's write a simple program that shows the power of arrays. A good start would be a program that converts a number to its equivalent Roman numeral. The user types in a number, and the program displays the results. Figure 6-11 shows an example.

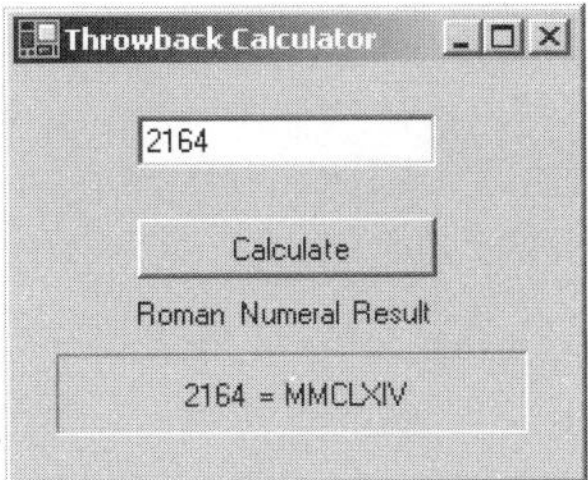

Figure 6-11 A Roman numeral calculator.

To build our Roman numeral calculator, start out by creating a new Visual Basic project. Name the project Throwback, and add a text box, a button, and two labels to Form1. Align the controls to look like the window in Figure 6-11, and then set the following properties with the values listed in Table 6-3.

Table 6-3 Controls and properties for the Throwback program

Object	Property	Value
Text box	*Name*	txtInput
	Text	""
Button	*Name*	cmdCalculate
	Text	Calculate
Label	*Name*	lblDescription
	Text	Roman Numeral Result
	TextAlign	MiddleCenter
Label	*Name*	lblResult
	BorderStyle	Fixed3D
	Text	""
	TextAlign	MiddleCenter

Writing the Code

We want to display the name of the program in several places, such as the form's title bar and various message boxes. Rather than write the name of the program for each place we want to display it, we will dimension a constant value to hold the name. Not only do we save space by declaring this value once, but the value can be computed at compile time, which makes our program marginally faster. Also, if you decide to change the name of the program to Legionnaire's Helper, simply change the value of the constant and recompile and the new name will show up throughout the program. Here's the code:

```
Public Class Form1
    Inherits System.Windows.Forms.Form

#Region " Windows Form Designer generated code "

    Const sProgName As String = "Throwback Calculator"
```

In the *Click* event handler of our cmdCalculate button, add the following code. This code does the heavy lifting for our program.

```
Private Sub cmdCalculate_Click(ByVal sender As System.Object, _
    ByVal e As System.EventArgs) Handles cmdCalculate.Click

    Dim Arabics() As Integer = {1, 4, 5, 9, 10, 40, 50, 90, 100, _
        400, 500, 900, 1000}
    Dim Romans() As String = {"I", "IV", "V", "IX", "X", "XL", _
        "L", "XC", "C", "CD", "D", "CM", "M"}
```

```
    Dim sInput As String = txtInput().Text
    Dim iInput, iCounter As Integer
    Dim sOutPut As String = ""
    Dim ArabicLower As Integer = Arabics.GetLowerBound(0)
    Dim ArabicUpper As Integer = Arabics.GetUpperBound(0)

    lblResult().Text = ""

    iInput = Int32.Parse(txtInput().Text)

    For iCounter = ArabicUpper To ArabicLower Step -1
        While iInput >= Arabics(iCounter)
            iInput -= Arabics(iCounter)
            sOutPut += Romans(iCounter)
        End While
    Next

    lblResult().Text = sInput & " = " & sOutPut

End Sub
```

When the form loads, we can set the title of the form to our program's name. Because *sProgName* refers to our constant, we simply add this value to the *Text* property of the form.

```
Private Sub Form1_Load(ByVal sender As System.Object, _
    ByVal e As System.EventArgs) Handles MyBase.Load

    Me.Text = sProgName

End Sub
```

Examining the Code

In the Throwback program, we've created two arrays, one of integers and one of strings. Remember that arrays must hold the same data type. You can't place a string in an integer array. Our arrays each have 13 elements, indexed from 0 through 12. We've initialized them when they are declared, as you can see here:

```
Dim Arabics() As Integer = {1, 4, 5, 9, 10, 40, 50, 90, 100, _
    400, 500, 900, 1000}
Dim Romans() As String = {"I", "IV", "V", "IX", "X", "XL", _
    "L", "XC", "C", "CD", "D", "CM", "M"}
```

Next the string variable *sInput* is initialized with the contents of the text box. As are the other variables in the *Click* event of our button, *sInput* is a local, or procedure-level, variable, which means that whenever the user clicks the button, this variable is declared and initialized. When the code exits the subroutine, the variable goes out of scope and is destroyed. In other words, *sInput*'s lifetime is only as long as the time that passes when the code is executing in the *Click* event.

```
Dim sInput As String = txtInput().Text
```

Another necessary improvement over classic Visual Basic is the ability to declare like variable data types on the same line. In the declaration below in classic Visual Basic, *iCounter* would be an integer, but *iInput* would be a variant. This difference caused no end of headaches and made tracking down bugs for C programmers coming to Visual Basic difficult. Having this capability in Visual Basic .NET is a major step forward in the maturity of the language. (And because it means less typing for me, all the better.)

```
Dim iInput, iCounter As Integer
```

Note Another important change is that Visual Basic .NET now supports "short circuiting." If we had code like the following in previous versions of Visual Basic, both tests on the *If* line would be conducted, even though we can clearly see that *iInteger* <> 0 is false:

```
Dim iInteger as integer = 0
If ((iInteger <> 0) and (dcConnection = open)) then
    'Do something important
End if
```

Both tests would take place and only then would the test return false. Not only is this inefficient, but it caused many a raised eyebrow from those coming to Visual Basic from other languages. Thankfully, Visual Basic .NET would evaluate the first condition, determine that *iInteger* indeed equals zero, and abandon the test at that point. This approach is how most other languages work.

Caching Our Variables

In the Throwback program, we will loop through both arrays, but going backward this time. We could write the code like this:

```
For iCounter = 12 To 0 Step -1
```

While this code would work, it is considered bad programming form because if we ever added or deleted an array element, our program would crash. A good rule of thumb is to never hard-code any limits if they can be calculated dynamically. This way, if you ever change the number of array elements, your code will still work just fine. To compensate, you could also write code like this.

```
For iCounter = Arabics.GetUpperBound(0) To _
    Arabics.GetUpperBound(0) Step -1
```

Other than more typing, coding like this has a fundamental problem. While we can now add and delete elements from the array and the loop continues to work fine, each time through the loop the program must calculate the upper and lower bounds of the array. While for small arrays this operation might not be noticeable, on larger arrays it can really eat up CPU cycles, constantly calculating array boundary values that won't change each time through the loop.

Whenever you write a loop that has to get an upper and lower bound that can be calculated beforehand, always assign these values to variables. Accessing a local variable in memory is much faster than having the compiler first look up the array and then find the method and then finally return a value. This technique is known as *caching a variable*. We calculate the bounds a single time, assign them to variables, and then use the variables in the loop. This mechanism is very fast.

```
Dim ArabicLower As Integer = Arabics.GetLowerBound(0)
Dim ArabicUpper As Integer = Arabics.GetUpperBound(0)
```

Each time we use our Throwback calculator, we want to be sure the result label is free of old calculations. If a value from a previous calculation is in the result label, we get rid of it. While you might think you could just overwrite the old value with the new result, what if you get an error? An error could really confuse the user by retaining an old value that does not correspond with the new input. Here's the code that solves this problem; it simply clears the text box before the calculation is performed:

```
lblResult().Text = ""
```

When we read a value from the input text box, the result will be a string (note the *Text* property). However, we want an integer, not a string. The Visual Basic .NET way of converting these types is the *Parse* method. The *Parse* method of the int32 data type converts the string representation of a number to its 32-bit signed integer equivalent.

```
iInput = int32.Parse(txtInput().Text)
```

The next part of the code does the heavy lifting for our program. We run through each of the elements of the *Arabics* array backward, from 12 down to 0, decrementing by 1 each time through the loop. As long as the value that the user typed in the text box is larger than or equal to the current value of the *Arabics* array element, we decrement *iInput* by that amount. At the same time, we concatenate the value in Roman numerals from the *Romans* array to our output string, *sOutPut*.

Let's say a user enters 1,000. Because *iInput = 1,000*, which is the value of the last element of the *Arabics* array, *iInput* is decremented by 1000. At the same time, *sOutput* has "M" concatenated to it. The program steps through the rest of the *Arabics* array elements down to 0, but because *iInput* is 0, the *While* loop is never entered again.

```
For iCounter = ArabicUpper To ArabicLower Step -1
    While iInput >= Arabics(iCounter)
        iInput -= Arabics(iCounter)
        sOutPut += Romans(iCounter)
    End While
Next
```

We finally display the results of our calculations in the lblResult label.

```
lblResult().Text = sInput & " = " & sOutPut
```

Now the user can see the Roman numeral display of the Throwback Calculator, as shown in Figure 6-12.

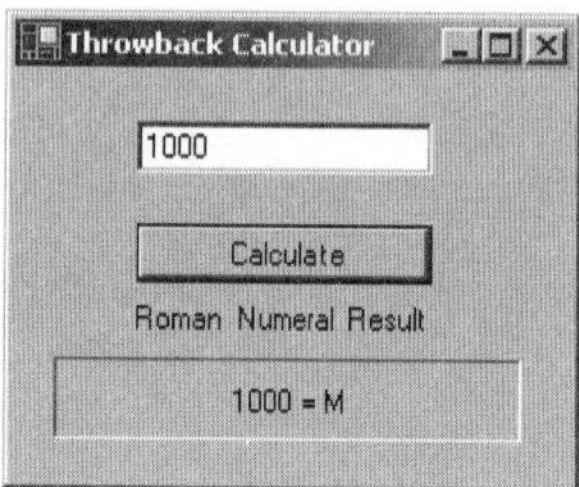

Figure 6-12 The Throwback Calculator in action.

Visual Basic .NET Collections

We covered arrays pretty thoroughly, and now as promised it's time to take a look at collections. In the Visual Basic .NET development environment, the advanced visual tools in the toolbox contain collections. The *TreeView* class has a *Nodes* collection, and the *ListView* class has a *ListItem* collection. In short, you have to understand collections to use the advanced controls and many of the framework classes. Visual Basic .NET also provides several collection classes ready for use.

An array is really considered a simple collection. A collection is just what you think it would be—a group or collection of objects. As an array inherits from the *System.Array* namespace, collections inherit from the *System.Collections* namespace. Collections are so useful that the *System.Collections* namespace contains interfaces and classes that define various collections of objects, such as array lists, hash tables, queues, stacks, and dictionaries. So, you can easily create your own collection of anything you might need. For those of you who have taken a college class in data structures, these terms will be familiar. In any event, I'll briefly touch on some of them to illustrate their differences and describe when you would want to use one over another.

The *ArrayList* Collection

Despite its name, the new *ArrayList* collection type is found in the *System.Collections* namespace. The *ArrayList* type is popular in the Java language, and now the same functionality is available in Visual Basic .NET.

As you can with an array, you can add items to an *ArrayList* collection. However, the first difference to note between an array and an *ArrayList* is that you don't have to provide an index for each item. Why? Collections automatically grow or shrink as you add or delete items. You don't have to keep track of the number of items you are adding and then issue a *ReDim* or *ReDim Preserve* statement to adjust the size of the structure. To give you an idea of an array list, let's convert our list of Hercules' labors from an array to an *ArrayList* collection.

```
Dim salLaborsOfHercules As New ArrayList()

With salLaborsOfHercules
    .Add("Kill Nemean Lion")
    .Add("Slay nine-headed hydra of Lerna")
    .Add("Capture elusive Stag of Arcadia")
    .Add("Capture wild boar on Mt. Erymantus")
    .Add("Clean Stables of King Augeas of Elis")
    .Add("Shoot monstrous man-eating birds of the " & _
        Stymphalian Marshes")
    .Add("Capture mad bull of Crete")
    .Add("Kill man-eating mares of King Diomedes")
    .Add("Steal Girdle of Hippolyta")
    .Add("Seize cattle of Geryon of Erytheia")
    .Add("Fetch golden apples of Hesperides")
    .Add("Retrieve three-headed dog Cerberus from Hell")
    .Add("Learn Visual Basic .NET")
End With
```

Now let's examine some metrics of our *ArrayList* using the code below. The output is shown in Figure 6-13.

```
MessageBox.Show("Array count is: " & _
    salLaborsOfHercules.Count() & _
    "  Array capacity is: " & _
    salLaborsOfHercules.Capacity(), & _
    "To do today")
```

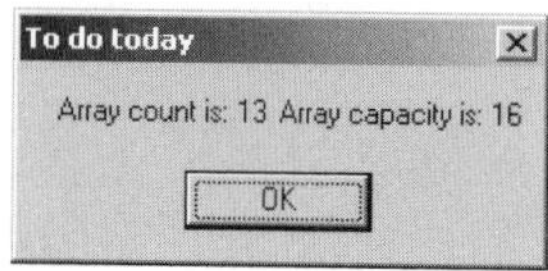

Figure 6-13 *ArrayList* metrics.

The *Capacity* property contains the number of elements that the *ArrayList* is capable of storing. The *Count* property contains the number of elements that are actually in the *ArrayList*. The capacity will always be greater than or equal to the count. If the count exceeds the capacity while you are adding elements, the capacity of the list is immediately doubled by automatically reallocating the internal array.

You can explicitly set the value of the *Capacity* property. When you set the value, the underlying internal array is also reallocated to accommodate the specified capacity. If the capacity is explicitly set to zero, the common language runtime sets it to the default capacity instead. As you can see in Figure 6-13, the default capacity is 16.

Let's say that we add all of the contents to an *ArrayList* and know that no additional elements will be added. We can call the *TrimToSize* method to reduce a list's memory overhead.

```
salLaborsOfHercules.TrimToSize()
```

In Figure 6-14, you can see that the capacity is now the same as the count.

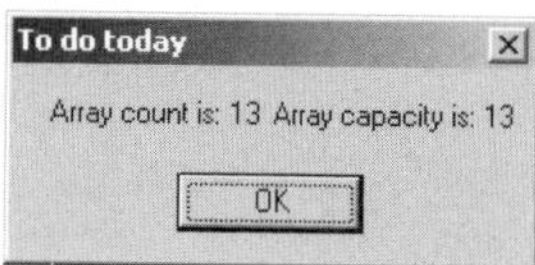

Figure 6-14 *TrimToSize* reduces a list's memory overhead.

To completely clear all the elements from a list, call the *Clear* method before calling *TrimToSize*. Trimming an empty *ArrayList* sets the capacity to the default capacity, not to zero. Figure 6-15 shows the results.

```
salLaborsOfHercules.Clear()         'Clears the contents

salLaborsOfHercules.TrimToSize()    'Resets the capacity
                                    ' to the default

MessageBox.Show("Array count is: " & _
    salLaborsOfHercules.Count() & _
    "Array capacity is: " & _
    salLaborsOfHercules.Capacity(), _
    "To do today")
```

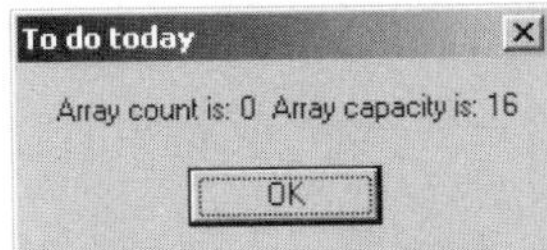

Figure 6-15 The *Clear* method clears all elements from a list. A subsequent call to *TrimToSize* resets the list to the default capacity.

If you want to iterate through a collection such as the *ArrayList*, you simply use a *For Each* statement, as shown here and in Figure 6-16:

```
Dim sCollectionItem As String = ""  'Holds each item in turn
Dim sOutputString As String = ""    'Holds the output of
                                    ' all items

For Each sCollectionItem In salLaborsOfHercules
    sOutputString += sCollectionItem & CtrlChr.CrLf
Next

MessageBox.Show(sOutputString, "Array List Iteration")
```

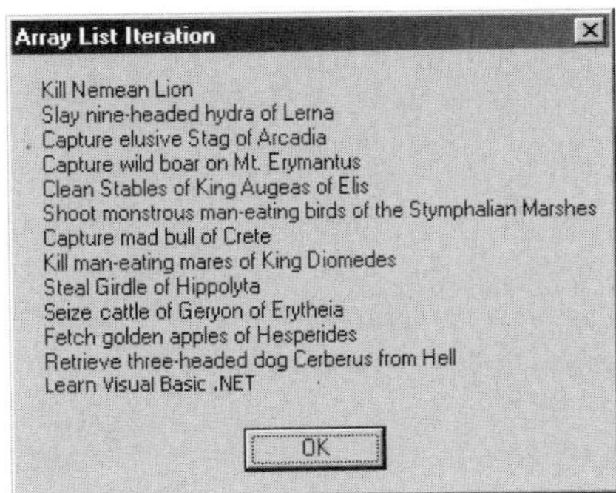

Figure 6-16 The *For Each* statement makes it easy to iterate through a list.

Queues

A queue is a standard data structure that provides a first in/first out (FIFO) capability. Many times an analogy is drawn to a line at a movie theater. Everyone is in line, but the first one in line is the first one admitted to the movie.

Queues are useful for storing messages in the order that they are received for sequential processing. The *Queue* class implements the structure as a circular array, which means that objects stored in a queue are inserted at one end and removed from the other. As with the *ArrayList* collection, when the number of elements in the queue reaches its capacity, the capacity is automatically increased to accommodate more elements.

We use the queue's *EnQueue* method to add an object to the tail of a queue.

```
Dim qWordQueue As New Queue()

With qWordQueue
    .Enqueue("It ")
    .Enqueue("was ")
    .Enqueue("the ")
    .Enqueue("best ")
    .Enqueue("of ")
    .Enqueue("times. ")
End With
```

When you want to retrieve items from the queue, you evoke the *DeQueue* method. This method returns the items in a FIFO sequence. Using the *MoveNext* method, you can ensure that you don't walk off the end of the queue.

```
Dim sTaleOfTwoCities As String = ""

While qWordQueue.GetEnumerator.MoveNext
    sTaleOfTwoCities += qWordQueue.Dequeue.ToString()
End While
```

You also use the *DeQueue* method to remove items from the queue. The item is removed from the head of the queue if it's not empty. Otherwise, as with our friend the array, we get a null reference.

```
MessageBox.Show(sTaleOfTwoCities & _
    "Item count: " & qWordQueue.Count, _
    "Queue - DeQueue")
```

You can see in Figure 6-17 that we have dequeued all of the elements in the queue.

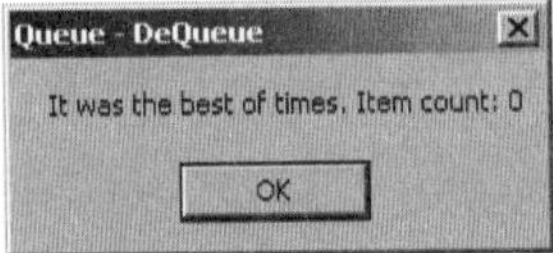

Figure 6-17 The *DeQueue* method removes elements from a queue.

If you want to iterate over a queue without actually eliminating any items, the *For Each* construct works here as well. The following code sample iterates the queue and displays each element without removing it.

```
Dim sQueueItem As String = ""
Dim sTaleOfTwoCities As String = ""

For Each sQueueItem In qWordQueue
    sTaleOfTwoCities += sQueueItem
Next

MessageBox.Show(sTaleOfTwoCities & _
    "Item count: " & qWordQueue.Count, _
    "Queue - For Each")
```

You can see the results in Figure 6-18.

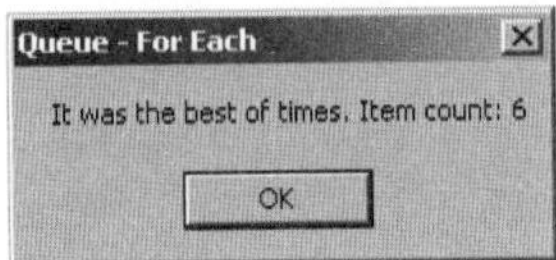

Figure 6-18 The *For Each* statement iterates through queues as well as lists.

You can determine whether a specific object exists in the queue by using the *Contains* method, which returns a Boolean True or False. However, there must be an exact match. Notice in the following code that an empty space appears after the word *was*. If the space were not included, the method would return False.

```
MessageBox.Show(qWordQueue.Contains("was ").ToString()) ' True
```

If you need to take a look at the head of the queue (the first item), use the *Peek* method. The *Peek* method returns the object at the head of the queue without removing it.

```
qWordQueue.Peek()
```

You always want to check a queue's *Count* property before attempting to reference an element to be sure that the queue is not empty. As with an *ArrayList*, if you try to reference an element that is no longer in the queue, a null reference results. However, anticipating that the queue (or the array for that matter) might be empty is simply good defensive programming. Both structures have the information built in to tell you whether accessing a specific element is safe. Always use this information or your user will be greeted with a "Queue empty" message like the one shown in Figure 6-19.

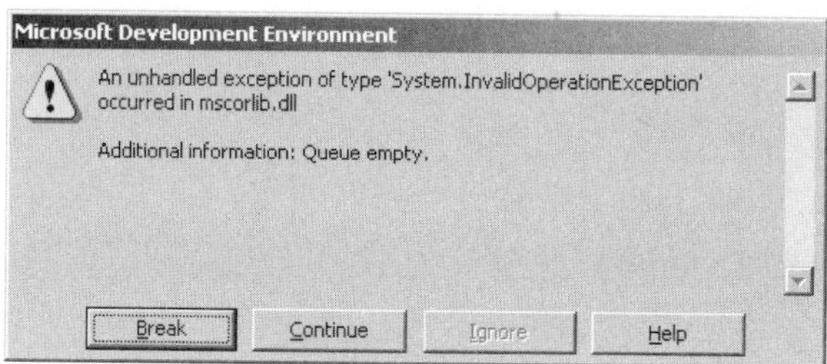

Figure 6-19 Attempting to dequeue an element from an empty queue causes this run-time error.

Stacks

Conceptually, stacks are the opposite of queues. Stacks are last in/first out (LIFO) structures. The analogy used to describe a stack is a spring-loaded plate holder found in school cafeterias. The first plate in is the bottommost and is the last one to be removed. The last plate inserted is at the top and is the first one someone grabs. The terminology used for a stack is to *push* an item onto a stack and to *pop* an item off a stack. Most of what you just learned about queues applies to stacks as well.

```
Dim qWordStack As New Stack()

With qWordStack
    .Push("It ")
    .Push("was ")
    .Push("the ")
    .Push("best ")
    .Push("of ")
    .Push("times. ")
End With

Dim sTaleOfTwoCities As String = ""

While qWordStack.GetEnumerator.MoveNext
    sTaleOfTwoCities += qWordStack.Pop.ToString()
End While
```

The difference between the queue and the stack is that the last item pushed on the stack ("*times.*" in our example) will now be the first one popped off the stack. Internally, the stack is implemented as a circular buffer.

```
MessageBox.Show(sTaleOfTwoCities & _
    "Item count: " & qWordStack.Count, "Stack")
```

Figure 6-20 shows the LIFO order of a stack.

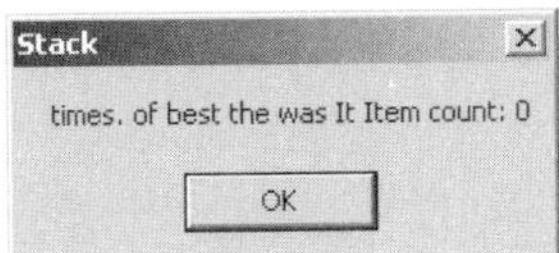

Figure 6-20 A stack processes items in LIFO order.

A stack has a handy *ToArray* method that copies the contents of a stack to an array. The elements are copied to the array in a last-in-first-out order. This order is identical to the one the items would be returned in from a succession of calls to a stack's *Pop* method.

Eliza and the Beginning of Artificial Intelligence

Now that we've covered arrays and collections, let's do something really fun. Let's write a rudimentary artificial intelligence program that will solidify your understanding of arrays and collections and build on your knowledge of how to use the .NET Framework classes.

Back in the dim dark ages of computer science, 1963 to be exact, Dr. Joseph Weizenbaum was working away at MIT, struggling to understand artificial intelligence. He was working on a crude attempt at making a computer understand the English language. Weizenbaum named his program Eliza after George Bernard Shaw's character Eliza Doolittle, from his play *Pygmalion*. The program is simple but can provide what appears to be stunning and profound insight to the uninitiated.

In the program, the patient types a response to a question and presses the Enter key. The program parses each word of the patient's response using the *String* class's *Split* method and places each word in an array element. Our program then quickly scans each word to see whether a match is found in a two-dimensional array in our program. Using arrays and the .NET *String*, *StringBuilder*, *StringCollection*, and *Random* classes, our program displays a response from the doctor that is eerily humanlike.

We know, of course, that the program has no idea what is being typed but is simply manipulating strings. However, users of the program find it strangely compelling. In fact, during the course of developing the original Eliza, some of the "patients" became so attached to the program that Dr. Weizenbaum was appalled. His secretary, for example, saw him developing the program over six months and knew what he was doing. She knew that there was no real intelligence, just word manipulation. Yet, when he asked her to try it out, after a few minutes she started telling Eliza her innermost secrets. She then asked him to leave the room so she could be alone with the program. Dr. Weizenbaum was so upset at how easy it was for humans to turn control over to a machine that he wrote the book *Computer Power and Human Reason,* in which he roundly renounced artificial intelligence.

Be that as it may, Eliza has surfaced again at many college campuses. I wrote a version many years ago in Basic on a Commodore 64 computer and discovered that people had a reaction similar to that Dr. Weizenbaum experienced so many years before. So who knows, after you write Visual Basic .NET Eliza, your friends might actually become attached to your computer.

Eliza in Action

Eliza mimics a nondeterminist Rogerian psychologist. Sometimes the program repeats what the patient says in an open-ended way to encourage more comments. Being from the nondeterminist school, the program does not judge but simply uses the patient's own words to encourage more responses. Eliza also asks unrelated questions that appear to the user to be profound. Figure 6-21 shows the Eliza program.

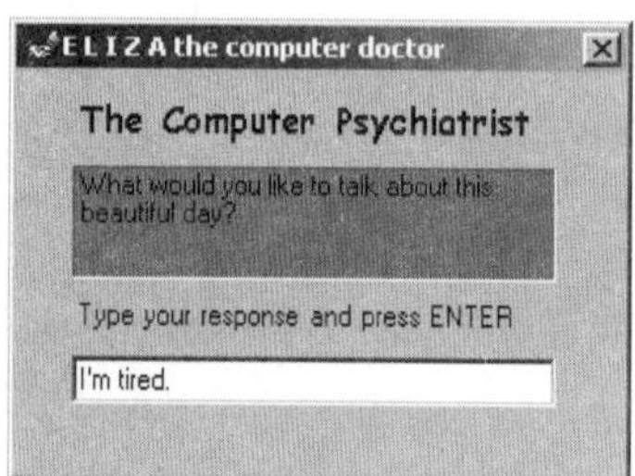

Figure 6-21 Eliza in action.

The program takes what the user says and turns it into a question. It also does some sleight of hand to change a phrase like "I'm tired" into "Why are you tired?", shown in Figure 6-22. This sort of response can give the user the feeling that the program actually understands the context of the question. Of course, we are simply using classes from the .NET Framework for a smoke and mirrors effect.

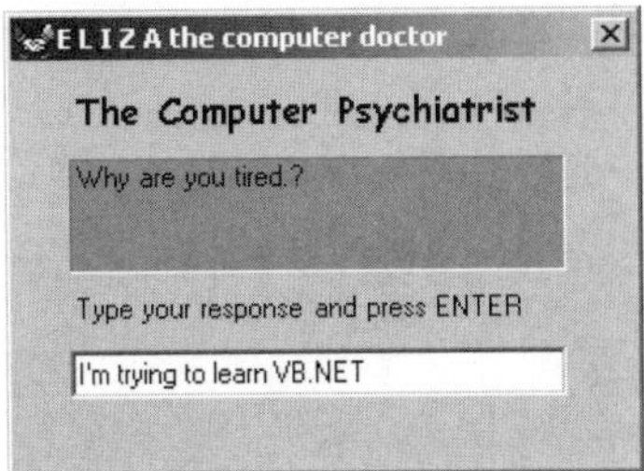

Figure 6-22 Eliza takes the user's text and turns it into a question.

This sample dialog shows that the responses vary just enough so that the user can't be quite sure whether the software is intelligent or not. The program then asks a question from out of left field that the user thinks might have something to do with learning Visual Basic .NET.

Doctor: "Why are you trying to learn Visual Basic .NET?"

Patient: "Why are you so interested?"

Doctor: "Why am I so interested?"

Patient: "Yes, are you a programmer?"

Doctor: "We are discussing you, not me."

Patient: "I'm learning Visual Basic .NET to do great things."

Doctor: "Why are you learning Visual Basic .NET to do great things?"

Patient: "Because it's the next great thing."

Doctor: "Do your friends really like you?"

Patient: "It's hard to tell."

Doctor: "Did you fight with your family?"

The doctor will continue like this as long as the patient keeps typing. The program also has some randomness built in so that at certain times the doctor asks questions about what the patient said earlier in the session. This touch gives the appearance that the program has memory, which it does, thanks to the .NET *StringCollection* class. As you can see, this is a program that you'll have fun building and is an excellent way to understand more about the framework classes and collections.

Note One researcher built a paranoid version of Eliza, which he named Perry. Perry would provide responses that were as paranoid as those of the user. His program would ask questions about horse racing and gambling. Once you have built Eliza, you will find many ways to modify or upgrade the program. You might even stream out the patient-doctor dialogue to a file for later review. And you can certainly expand Eliza's vocabulary to make the program seem brilliant. All in all, you can have some fun with your friends.

Coding Eliza

Start a new Visual Basic .NET Windows program named Eliza. Using the default form, add three labels. The first label is for "The Computer Psychiatrist." The second is to display the doctor's responses. The third is used for the instructions to the user. Add a text box under the instructions. The text box will be used to accept the user's input. Your form should look like the one in Figure 6-23. Once you've set up your form, set the values for the properties listed in Table 6-4.

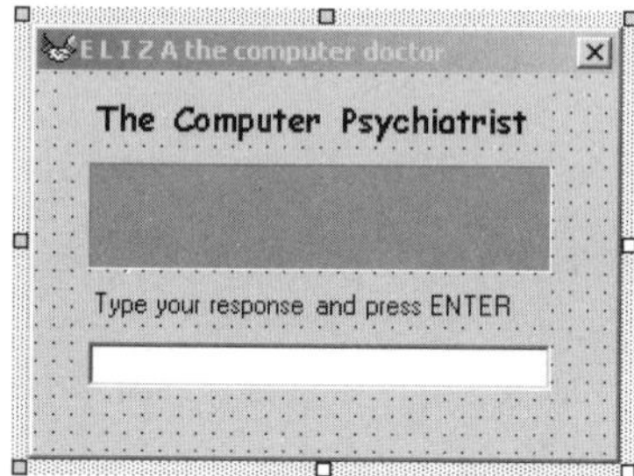

Figure 6-23 The form for the Eliza program.

You might notice that with the newly redesigned Visual Basic .NET controls, both the text box and the label use the *Text* property to display text. Because .NET controls don't have default properties, you can't use statements such as *lblDoctor = "How are you?"*. Instead you must use the fully qualified *lblDoctor.Text = "How are you?"*.

Table 6-4 Properties for the Eliza Program

Object	Property	Value
Form1	*BorderStyle*	FixedDialog
	Icon	Microsoft Visual Studio .NET\Common7\Graphics\Icons\Comm\Handshak
	MaximizeBox	False
	MinimizeBox	False
	Text	ELIZA, the computer doctor
Label1	*Name*	lblCaption
	Font	Comic Sans MS
		Font Style: Bold
		Size: 11
	Text	The Computer Psychiatrist
	TextAlign	MiddleCenter
Label2	*Name*	lblDoctor
	Backcolor	Lime (Pick from Web Tab)
	BorderStyle	Fixed3D
	Text	""
Label3	*Name*	lblInstructions
	Text	Type your response and press Enter
TextBox1	*Name*	txtQuestion
	BorderStyle	Fixed3D
	Text	""

We won't have much code in the form. We will place most of the code in a module that will be the brains of our system. From the main IDE menu, select Project | Add Module. In the Add New Item dialog box, shown in Figure 6-24, select a new module and give it the name Dialog.vb. Click Open to add the new empty code module to your project.

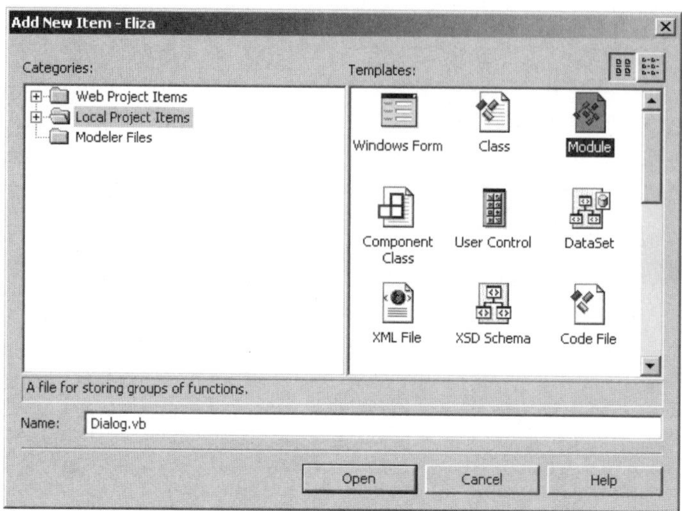

Figure 6-24 Add a new code module to your project.

Topology of Our Dialog.vb Code Module

Our new module will have five main capabilities. The first is a public function, named *getElizaResponse*, that acts as an internal dispatcher. When the user hits the Enter key, the contents of the text box are passed to this function. The first operation the function performs is to stash away the current patient comment in a *StringCollection* object for later use. It also increments a private counter to determine how many times the patient responded to the doctor.

Next *getElizaResponse* tries each of five private routines that attempt to return some profound comment to the user. First it calls *isDiscussingDoctor*, which returns a Boolean. If the patient is discussing the doctor, which we determine by finding the word *you* in the patient's response, an annoyed response is sent back to the patient.

If that routine is not successful in matching a key word, control is passed to the function *getQuickResponse*. Here we determine whether other specific words are in the patient's response. For example, if the code finds the word *mother* in the patient's response, it will return "Tell me more about your family…" This response gives the impression that Eliza understands family dynamics. Nothing but smoke and mirrors, but effective.

If *getQuickResponse* fails, program control is dispatched to the private routine *tryToTranslate*, which attempts to find key words from the patient's response in an array and swaps them with alternate words. For example, if the word "I" is in a response, this routine changes it to *you*. If the user types "I like Visual Basic .NET," this routine finds the word *I* and modifies the program's reply to say "You like Visual Basic .NET?" This routine provides the nondeterministic capability of Eliza.

Another trick up our sleeve is a special piece of code that stores all of the user's responses in another *StringCollection*. Under certain conditions, this code generates a random number between 0 and the number of patient responses so far. You will learn about the framework's *Random* class from this piece of code. When the conditions are met, Eliza says, "Please tell me more about < *one of the user's previous responses*>," giving the appearance of memory and that the program is tying together thoughts from the session.

If that routine comes up empty, we simply display a stock phrase from an array by calling *getStockPhrase*. We keep track of the last stock phrase displayed so we can always provide a new one. All of this management is performed by *getElizaResponse*. The function takes in the patient's response as a parameter and manages the various internal routines to eventually provide a response to the user.

The beauty of this approach is that our module is self-contained. The host (in this case the form) only has to ask for a request. The Dialog.vb module initializes variables and arrays and determines the response to send back. Figure 6-25 shows the sequence in which the appropriate response is generated.

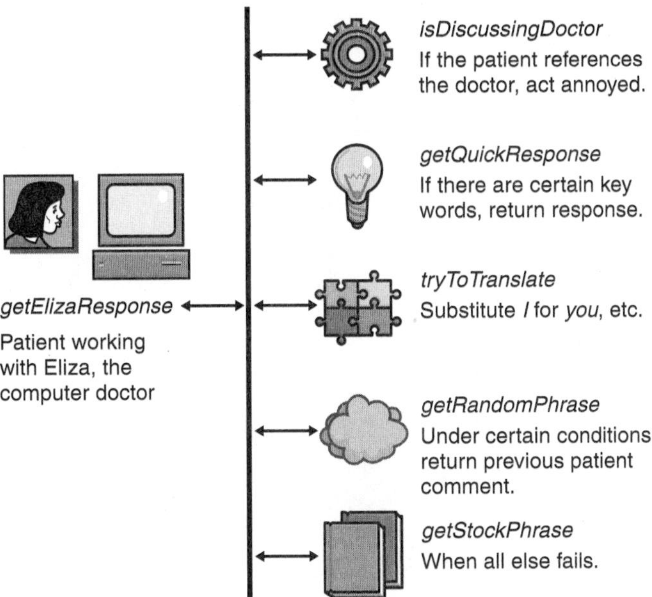

Figure 6-25 How Eliza determines a response.

Code Module vs. Class Module

You might be wondering why I elected to use a code module instead of a class for this project. I could have very easily made this code a class; however, three main architectural reasons favor the module approach. First, the primary reason to build classes is reusability. We won't reuse this code over and over, so we simply placed everything in a module. As you know from working with Visual Basic 6, modules are simply warehouses for code. Second, we won't be instantiating multiple instances of the dialog code. The functionality will simply be imported into our host. Third, we are not setting properties or state in any way from the outside world. The host asks for a response and the module supplies it. As you build more classes and modules, you will find you are making design decisions like this often.

In almost all cases, it's good practice to separate the code from the user interface. In general, with this separation you can modify either the form or the module and the other does not have to be changed. Independence (or *modularity*) is the key to keeping modules from becoming too dependent on each other. The Eliza design is an example of that concept.

Writing the Dialog.vb Code Module

The next step in building the Eliza program is to delete the template code in the Dialog.vb code module and add the code that follows. You'll learn quite a bit about the .NET Framework in this module. Notice that everything is declared private except the *getElizaResponse* function, which is the traffic cop for our module. It dispatches routines and returns the correct response. This approach permits us to keep any knowledge of how Dialog.vb works from the outside world. All that is publicly exposed is *getElizaResponse*.

```
Imports System.Collections
Imports System.Text  ' For StringBuilder


Module Dialog

Private sPatientResponse As String = ""  'Holds patient comment
Private sDoctorResponse As String = ""   'Holds Dr response
Private bInitEliza As Boolean = False    'Is array initialized
Private cBlank() As Char = {CChar(" ")}  'For splitting
                                         ' sentences
```

```
Private aTranslate(,) As String          'Array for swapping
Private iTalkingAboutMe As Integer = 0   'How many times
                                         ' 'you' used
Private iPatientResponseCount As Integer = 0 'Number of patient
                                             ' comments
Private cPatientsResponses As New _
    Collections.Specialized.StringCollection()


Private sStockResponse() As String = _
    {"Do your friends really like you?", _
    "Did you fight with your family?", _
    "Did you have a happy childhood?", _
    "Did you hate your father?", _
    "Are you afraid of your friends?", _
    "Why are you so angry?", _
    "Tell me about your involvement with horse racing.", _
    "Does the name Ruby Begonia mean anything to you?", _
    "Why do you have such dark secrets?", _
    "Why are you obsessed with your mortality?", _
    "Tell me about your criminal background."}


Private Sub initaTranslate()

    '-- This is called to initialize the array to illustrate
    '-- ReDim and another way to init an array.


    ReDim aTranslate(7, 1)

    aTranslate(0, 0) = "i"
    aTranslate(0, 1) = "you"
    aTranslate(1, 0) = "you"
    aTranslate(1, 1) = "I"
    aTranslate(2, 0) = "your"
    aTranslate(2, 1) = "my"
    aTranslate(3, 0) = "my"
    aTranslate(3, 1) = "your"
    aTranslate(4, 0) = "am"
    aTranslate(4, 1) = "are"
    aTranslate(5, 0) = "you"
    aTranslate(5, 1) = "i"
    aTranslate(6, 0) = "are"
    aTranslate(6, 1) = "am"
    aTranslate(7, 0) = "me"
    aTranslate(7, 1) = "you"

End Sub
```

(continued)

```
Public Function getElizaResponse( _
    ByVal patientResponse As String) As String

    '-- This function acts as the dispatcher. It attempts to
    '-- get a response first from tryToTranslate. If that fails,
    '-- it then tries getQuickResponse. Finally, if all else
    '-- fails a call to getStockPhrase is made.

    sDoctorResponse = ""

    '-- No sense going any farther
    If patientResponse.Length = 0 Then
        Return "Please enter a question."
    End If

    '-- Now the response is visible module wide. Make it lower
    '-- case for easier string matching in the routines.
    sPatientResponse = patientResponse.ToLower

    '-- Add the patient's comment for later display
    iPatientResponseCount += 1
    cPatientsResponses.Add(sPatientResponse)


    '-- Has the aTranslate array been initialized? --
    If bInitEliza = False Then
        initaTranslate()
        bInitEliza = True
    End If

    '------------------------------------------------------
    '-- Now we simply call the various functions that will
    '-- build the Dr's response if appropriate. If any of the
    '-- functions return True, then return the phrase.
    '------------------------------------------------------

    '-- See if the patient is talking about the good
    '-- doctor again --
    If isDiscussingDoctor() = True Then
        Return sDoctorResponse
    End If

    '-- Can we get a quick and dirty response? --
    If getQuickResponse() = True Then
        Return sDoctorResponse
    End If

    '-- See if there are any words to substitute --
    If tryToTranslate() = True Then
        Return sDoctorResponse
    End If
```

```
    '-- Can we return an earlier patient phrase? --
    If getRandomPhrase() = True Then
        Return sDoctorResponse
    End If

    '-- When all else fails, get a stock phrase
    sDoctorResponse = getStockPhrase()
    Return sDoctorResponse

End Function

Private Function isDiscussingDoctor() As Boolean

'-- Here we can see if the word 'you' is present. If so,
'-- increment iTalkingAboutMe. Every other time the patient
'-- uses 'you', complain.

If (sPatientResponse.IndexOf("you") > -1) Then
    iTalkingAboutMe += 1

    '-- Display irritation every other time the Dr is mentioned.
    If (iTalkingAboutMe Mod 2 = 0) Then
        If (iTalkingAboutMe < 3) Then
            sDoctorResponse = "We are discussing you, not me"
        Else
            sDoctorResponse = "You have talked about me " & _
                iTalkingAboutMe.ToString & _
                " times. Shall we focus on you?"
        End If
        Return True
    End If

End If
Return False

End Function


Private Function getQuickResponse() As Boolean

'-- Here we see if we can match a word in the patient's
'-- comment. If we can, let's return a response from the Dr.

Dim iIndex As Integer = 0

If (sPatientResponse.IndexOf("yes") > -1) Then
    sDoctorResponse = "Ah...that is positive. Tell me more."
    Return True
```

(continued)

```
ElseIf (sPatientResponse.IndexOf("hate") > -1) Then
    sDoctorResponse = "Why are you so angry?"
    Return True
ElseIf (sPatientResponse.IndexOf("mother") > -1) Then
    sDoctorResponse = "Tell me more about your family..."
    Return True
ElseIf (sPatientResponse.IndexOf("father") > -1) Then
    sDoctorResponse = "Why were you angry at males in " & _
        "your family?"
    Return True
ElseIf (sPatientResponse.IndexOf("sister") > -1) Then
    sDoctorResponse = "Why are you jealous of your sister?"
    Return True
ElseIf (sPatientResponse.IndexOf("brother") > -1) Then
    sDoctorResponse = "Why was your brother liked more " & _
        "than you?"
    Return True
ElseIf (sPatientResponse.IndexOf("you are") > -1) Then
    iIndex = sPatientResponse.IndexOf("you are")
    sDoctorResponse = "I am " & _
        sPatientResponse.Substring(iIndex + 8) & "?"
    Return True
ElseIf (sPatientResponse.IndexOf("i am") > -1) Then
    iIndex = sPatientResponse.IndexOf("i am")
    sDoctorResponse = "Why are you " & _
        sPatientResponse.Substring(iIndex + 5) & "?"
    Return True
ElseIf (sPatientResponse.IndexOf("i'm") > -1) Then
    iIndex = sPatientResponse.IndexOf("i'm")
    sDoctorResponse = "Why are you " & _
        sPatientResponse.Substring(iIndex + 4) & "?"
    Return True
ElseIf (sPatientResponse.IndexOf("we ") > -1) Then
    sDoctorResponse = "Try not to discuss us - " & _
        "tell me about you."
    Return True
ElseIf (sPatientResponse.IndexOf("no ") > -1) Then
    sDoctorResponse = "Why are you so negative?"
    Return True
ElseIf (sPatientResponse.IndexOf("weather") > -1) Then
    sDoctorResponse = "Did you want to be a " & _
        "meteorologist as a child?"
    Return True
Else
    Return False 'No quick response
End If

End Function
```

```
Private Function tryToTranslate() As Boolean

Dim aSentenceWord() As String = _
    sPatientResponse.Split(cBlank)
Dim iWordsLower As Integer = _
    aSentenceWord.GetLowerBound(0)
Dim iWordsUpper As Integer = _
    aSentenceWord.GetUpperBound(0)
Dim iaTranslateLower As Integer = _
    aTranslate.GetLowerBound(0)
Dim iaTranslateUpper As Integer = _
    aTranslate.GetUpperBound(0)
Dim sbDrResponse As New StringBuilder()
Dim iWordLoop As Integer = 0
Dim iTranslateLoop As Integer = 0
Dim sCurrentWord As String = ""
Dim bCanTranslate As Boolean = False
Dim bAddQuestionMark As Boolean = False

'-- Let's see if we can parse the patient's comment and
'-- substitute words from the translate array.

For iWordLoop = iWordsLower To iWordsUpper

    sCurrentWord = aSentenceWord(iWordLoop)
    bCanTranslate = False

    For iTranslateLoop = iaTranslateLower To iaTranslateUpper

    '-- If the current word is in the first aTranslate array
    '-- element, then substitute with the second element

        If aTranslate(iTranslateLoop, _
            0).Equals(sCurrentWord) Then

            If (iWordLoop = 0) Then
                sbDrResponse.Append(aTranslate(iTranslateLoop, _
                    1).TrimStart(cBlank))
            Else
                sbDrResponse.Append(" " & _
                    aTranslate(iTranslateLoop, _
                    1).TrimStart(cBlank))
            End If

            bCanTranslate = True
            bAddQuestionMark = True
            Exit For
        End If
    Next
```

(continued)

```
        '-- If we couldn't swap, add the current word
        If (bCanTranslate = False) Then
            If (iWordLoop = 0) Then
                sbDrResponse.Append(sCurrentWord)
            Else
                sbDrResponse.Append(" " & sCurrentWord)
            End If
        End If

    Next

    '-- If we were successful, append a ? to the
    '-- end and trim any leading blank spaces.
    '-- Recall our brief discussion of short-circuiting.
    '-- If bAddQuestionMark is False, the length of
    '-- sbDrResponse is not checked - the code jumps
    '-- to the Else statement.
    If (bAddQuestionMark = True) And (sbDrResponse.Length > 5) Then

        Dim sFinalResponse As String
        Dim cFirstLetter As Char = CChar(sbDrResponse.Chars(0))

        '-- Extract the first letter and capitalize
        cFirstLetter = cFirstLetter.ToUpper(cFirstLetter)

        '-- Remove the first letter and replace it with cap
        sbDrResponse.Remove(0, 1)
        sbDrResponse.Insert(0, cFirstLetter)

        '-- Add a ? and return the string
        sbDrResponse.Append("?")
        sDoctorResponse = sbDrResponse.ToString
        Return True
    Else
        '-- No luck, return an empty string
        Return False
    End If

    End Function


    Private Function getRandomPhrase() As Boolean

    If (iPatientResponseCount Mod 6 = 0) Then
        Dim iLimit As Integer = cPatientsResponses.Count
        Dim iPickResponse As Integer = 0
        Dim iRandom As New Random()
        Dim sPreviousComment As New StringBuilder() ' Be sure to
                                                    ' use New
```

```
        Dim sComment As String

        '-- Which random response to select from the
        '-- cPatientsResponses collection?
        iPickResponse = iRandom.Next(0, iLimit - 1)


        If (iPickResponse <= cPatientsResponses.Count) Then
            Dim cFirstLetter As Char

            '-- Retrieve the comment to display
            sComment = cPatientsResponses(iPickResponse)

            '-- Take the first letter of the retrieved comment
            cFirstLetter = CChar(sComment.Chars(0))

            '-- Capitalize it
            cFirstLetter = cFirstLetter.ToUpper(cFirstLetter)

            '-- Remove the first letter and replace it with cap
            sComment = sComment.Remove(0, 1)
            sComment = sComment.Insert(0, cFirstLetter)

            '-- Now construct the string for the Dr's response --
            sPreviousComment.Append("Please tell me more about: """)
            sPreviousComment.Append(sComment & """")
            sDoctorResponse = sPreviousComment.ToString
            Return True
        End If
    End If

    Return False

    End Function


    Private Function getStockPhrase() As String

        Static iCurrentStock As Integer = 0

        If iCurrentStock > sStockResponse.GetUpperBound(0) Then
            iCurrentStock = sStockResponse.GetLowerBound(0) + 1
            Return sStockResponse(iCurrentStock - 1)
        Else
            iCurrentStock += 1
            Return sStockResponse(iCurrentStock - 1)
        End If

    End Function
    End Module
```

Examining Our Code

The Eliza program includes a lot of code, so let's look at most of it in detail and solidify our understanding of the operations it performs. Of course we import *System* as usual, but in this case we also import *System.Text*. Importing *System.Text* gives us access to the *StringBuilder* class. Recall from Chapter 5, "Examining the .NET Class Framework Using Files and Strings," that if you are going to do a lot of string manipulation, the *StringBuilder* class is faster than *String* because it allocates a buffer in memory. *StringBuilder* modifies the same memory location for any modifications to the string. When the *String* class is used, we end up destroying the current string and creating a new one for each modification, which is expensive in CPU currency.

Module-Level Variables

We declare several variables at the top of the module so that they have full module scope. For example, both the patient's response and the doctor's response need to be available in all modules. It's cheaper to assign them to module-level variables instead of passing them as parameters to each function that needs them.

There are a couple of items that we need to review. The first is the *cBlank* array of the *Char* data type. In Chapter 5, I described the *String* class's *Split* method, which can take a string and break up its contents into an array. The *Split* method requires a character to use as the separator, and we are using a blank space as that separator. When this separator character is passed to the *Split* method, every word separated by a space will be placed in its own array element. We can then easily examine each word in the patient's response. Finally in this section of the code we dimension a new *StringCollection* object that will be used to hold each of the patient's responses during each session.

```
Private sPatientResponse As String = ""  'Holds patient comment
Private sDoctorResponse As String = ""   'Holds Dr response
Private bInitEliza As Boolean = False    'Is array initialized
Private cBlank() As Char = {CChar(" ")}  'For splitting
                                         ' sentences
Private aTranslate(,) As String          'Array for swapping
Private iTalkingAboutMe As Integer = 0   'How many times
                                         ' 'you' used
Private iPatientResponseCount As Integer = 0 'Number of patient
                                             ' comments
Private cPatientsResponses As New _
    Collections.Specialized.StringCollection()
```

The declaration for the two-dimensional array *aTranslate* might look a bit strange to Visual Basic 6 programmers; the single comma inside the parentheses looks like a mistake. If you are familiar with the Visual Basic 6 *Collection* object, the *StringCollection* concept is similar.

In this sample program, I've used several approaches to dimensioning arrays to illustrate their flexibility. In the following code, I initialize a string array with several strings, separated by commas. When I do this, the array is automatically sized to fit the number of entries. New to Visual Basic .NET are the "{" and "}" characters used to initialize an array, as shown in *sStockResponse*. At any time, you could go back to the source code and add another line or two and the array will compensate and resize itself when the program is run.

```
Private sStockResponse() As String = _
    {"Do your friends really like you?", _
    "Did you fight with your family?", _
    "Did you have a happy childhood?", _
    "Did you hate your father?", _
    "Are you afraid of your friends?", _
    "Why are you so angry?", _
    "Tell me about your involvement with horse racing.", _
    "Does the name Ruby Begonia mean anything to you?", _
    "Why do you have such dark secrets?", _
    "Why are you obsessed with your mortality?", _
    "Tell me your criminal background."}
```

Arrays vs. Collections

We store the patient's responses in a *StringCollection* object. Why didn't we use an array?

```
Private cPatientsResponses As New _
    Collections.Specialized.StringCollection()
```

A collection is not a replacement for an array but a complement. As you saw earlier in the chapter, arrays have a fixed size and structure. If you dimension an array of integers and place the value 42 in element 5, you know that value will be there when you need it. By dereferencing element 5 of our array *(iMeaningOfLife = aCosmic(5))*, we can be sure that our variable will contain 42. However, if you don't know how big to make an array at design time, you have to guess at a size and constantly check to see whether adding another object will overstep the upper bound. Code then needs to be added to redimension the array to accept more items.

Remember that a collection, on the other hand, grows automatically when an object is added. Likewise, when an element is deleted, the collection frees up the memory from the deleted entry automatically. For example, Visual Basic manages a collection of forms you have in a project. You don't have to worry about tracking them; it's done for you. Likewise, each form manages its own collection of the controls it contains. It's important to understand collections because they are used everywhere in the .NET Framework. When you want to grab all of the directories on a machine, a collection is used to hold them. When you need to get all the files in a folder, a collection of folders is interrogated. In the Eliza program, once you understand how to use the *StringCollection* in the *System.Text* namespace, you will be able to use any collection in the .NET Framework.

The Entry Point for Eliza

The public function *getElizaResponse* is used to call our module. The patient's response is passed in as a parameter using *ByVal*. Recall that the default way of passing in a parameter to a procedure in Visual Basic .NET is by using *ByRef*, whereas in classic Visual Basic the default was *ByVal*. When a parameter is passed with *ByVal*, a copy of the object is passed in. You can change it in any way, but because you are only modifying a copy, the original object is unscathed. If we pass in a parameter with *ByRef*, an actual reference (in other words, a pointer to the memory location of the object) is passed in. If you make changes to a *ByRef* variable, the original is also modified because the reference and the original are one and the same.

We initialize *sDoctorResponse* for each call to *getElizaResponse*. It will still contain the doctor's previous response. We then check to see whether the patient actually entered a question. If not, we pass back instructions and exit the dialog. If there is a response, we store the patient's response in the module-level variable *sPatientResponse*. Notice that we cast it to lowercase because we will be doing a boatload of string comparisons for key words. If we know everything is in lowercase, our code is easer to manage because we don't have to check for caps at the beginning of a sentence, for example. Next we increment the number of responses the patient has made so far and then add the current patient's response to our *StringCollection* object.

```
Public Function getElizaResponse( _
    ByVal patientResponse As String) As String

    '-- This function acts as the dispatcher. It attempts to
    '-- get a response first from tryToTranslate. If that fails,
    '-- it then tries getQuickResponse. Finally, if all else
    '-- fails a call to getStockPhrase is made.

    sDoctorResponse = ""

    '-- No sense going any farther
    If patientResponse.Length = 0 Then
        Return "Please enter a question."
    End If

    '-- Now the response is visible module wide. Make it lower
    '-- case for easier string matching in the routines.
    sPatientResponse = patientResponse.ToLower

    '-- Add the patient's comment for later display
    iPatientResponseCount += 1
    cPatientsResponses.Add(sPatientResponse)
```

In a real program, you probably would not initialize an array and then check each time a function is called to see whether it was already initialized. However, I wanted to show you another way to initialize an array. We check whether the Boolean is True. If not, initialize the array and set *bInitEliza* to True so that this block of code will not be executed again. A kludge, but good for illustrating a concept.

```
'-- Has the aTranslate array been initialized? --
If bInitEliza = False Then
    initaTranslate()
    bInitEliza = True
End If
```

Now that the housekeeping has been completed, we simply call each of the five private functions. Each one in turn examines the module-level variable *sPatientResponse* and determines whether it can do something intelligent with it. If it can, that routine sets the module level variable *sDoctorResponse* and returns True. The first function to return True is the response that is returned to the calling form. If the first four routines come up empty, we use *getStockResponse* as our fallback to return a predefined response from an array.

One difference between Visual Basic .NET and classic Visual Basic is the return statement. In classic Visual Basic, you had to assign the return value to the name of the function. Now you can simply use the keyword *Return*. Of course, the return value must be consistent with the function's signature. In this function's signature, we define the return data type as a string.

```
Public Function getElizaResponse( _
    ByVal patientResponse As String) As String
```

When *Return* is encountered, program control is immediately returned to the function caller.

```
'-----------------------------------------------------
'-- Now we simply call the various functions that will
'-- build the Dr's response. If any of the
'-- functions return True, then return the phrase.
'-----------------------------------------------------

'-- See if the patient is talking about the good doctor again --
If isDiscussingDoctor() = True Then
    Return sDoctorResponse
End If

'-- Can we get a quick and dirty response? --
If getQuickResponse() = True Then
    Return sDoctorResponse
End If
```

(continued)

```
        '-- See if there are any words to substitute --
        If tryToTranslate() = True Then
            Return sDoctorResponse
        End If

        '-- Can we return an earlier patient phrase? --
        If getRandomPhrase() = True Then
            Return sDoctorResponse
        End If

        '-- When all else fails, get a stock phrase
        sDoctorResponse = getStockPhrase()
        Return sDoctorResponse

End Function
```

Remember that one of the first operations that *getElizaResponse* performs is to check whether the array *initaTranslate* is initialized using the Boolean *bInitEliza* as a flag. The first time the program is used, the variable is initialized to False, so *initaTranslate* is called. When we declared the array with the module-level variables, we told Visual Basic .NET it would be two-dimensional and hold strings.

```
Private aTranslate(,) As String
```

Notice that we now use the *ReDim* statement to modify the array *aTranslate* so that it holds eight rows and two columns. In production code, always try to stay away from using *ReDim*. As I mentioned earlier, the *ReDim* statement instantiates a new array each time it's used. So, if you are checking to see how many items are in the array and you need to add one more, you use the *ReDim* statement on the array. The original array is deleted and a copy is made with the new bounds. This process is very expensive. And when you use *ReDim*, if by accident you specify a size that's too small, a *System.InvalidCastException* will be thrown when your program attempts to access an out-of-bounds element.

Using the *ReDim* statement with *aTranslate* gives us the first dimension of 8 (0–7) and the second dimension of 2 (0–1). In the first dimension we add a word that the patient might place in a response. If a word is found, the word in the second dimension is returned. If the word *i* is found, we will return *you*. Now you can see why we made the patient response all lowercase. It's easy to compare words. This array is used extensively in the function *tryToTranslate*. Each word in the patient's response is compared to each of the 0th elements for each row. If a match is found, that row's first element is returned and placed in the response.

```
Private Sub initaTranslate()

    '-- This is called to initialize the array to illustrate
    '-- ReDim and another way to init an array.

    ReDim aTranslate(7, 1)

    aTranslate(0, 0) = "i"
    aTranslate(0, 1) = "you"
    aTranslate(1, 0) = "you"
    aTranslate(1, 1) = "I"
    aTranslate(2, 0) = "your"
    aTranslate(2, 1) = "my"
    aTranslate(3, 0) = "my"
    aTranslate(3, 1) = "your"
    aTranslate(4, 0) = "am"
    aTranslate(4, 1) = "are"
    aTranslate(5, 0) = "you"
    aTranslate(5, 1) = "i"
    aTranslate(6, 0) = "are"
    aTranslate(6, 1) = "am"
    aTranslate(7, 0) = "me"
    aTranslate(7, 1) = "you"

End Sub
```

Conceptually, the array looks like the following. A two-dimensional array is much like a spreadsheet. The elements 0 through 7 are the rows, and the elements 0 through 1 are the columns. You simply address the row and column (in that order) to retrieve the value you are looking for.

(0,0) "i"	(0,1) "you"
(1,0) "you"	(1,1) "I"
(2,0) "your"	(2,1) "my"
(3,0) "my"	(3,1) "your"
(4,0) "am"	(4,1) "are"
(5,0) "you"	(5,1) "i"
(6,0) "are"	(6,1) "am"
(7,0) "me"	(7,1) "you"

Is the Patient Discussing the Good Doctor?

We want to be sure our psychiatric session stays on track. One of the first things a new patient does is try to discuss the doctor. We want to be sure the patient knows that this will not help him or her. The conversation should be centered on the patient. This function returns True or False depending on whether the patient discussed the doctor, and takes further action if other conditions are met.

We simply check whether the substring "you" was found in the patient's response, indicating a reference to the doctor. If this is true, we increment the module-level variable *iTalkingAboutMe*. We use this variable to determine whether we should provide an annoyed response to the user.

```
Private Function isDiscussingDoctor() As Boolean

'-- Here we can see if the word you is present. If so,
'-- increment iTalkingAboutMe. Every other time the patient
'-- uses 'you', complain.

If (sPatientResponse.IndexOf("you") > -1) Then
    iTalkingAboutMe += 1
```

We want to provide a response to the user only every other time the word *you* is used. The easiest way to accomplish this is with the *Mod* operator. The modulo operator computes the remainder of the division of two operands. If you have never used the *Mod* operator, you will be amazed at how simple it is. (*Modulus* is a fancy word for remainder.) So, the *Mod* operator divides two numbers and returns only the remainder. If either number is a floating-point number, the result is a floating-point number representing the remainder.

For example, in the following expression, *iResult* (result, i.e., remainder or modulus) equals 2.

```
iResult = 8 Mod 3
```

Using *Mod*, we can easily handle every other occurrence of the patient using the word *you*. We take how many times the patient has mentioned the doctor and divide it by 2. If the remainder is 1, it's either the first, third, fifth (and so on) time the word was used. If the remainder is 0, it's every other time. If we want to respond every fifth time, simply change *Mod 2* to *Mod 5* and check whether the result is equal to 0. By making the doctor respond every other time the word *you* is used instead of every time, we make the doctor appear unpredictable.

```
'-- Display irritation every other time the Dr is mentioned.
If (iTalkingAboutMe Mod 2 = 0) Then
```

The rest of this routine is straightforward. If a response is the first time the patient has referred to the doctor, the doctor simply attempts to redirect the conversation. However, if this happens more than once, the doctor points out exactly how many times he has been mentioned.

```
    If (iTalkingAboutMe < 3) Then
        sDoctorResponse = "We are discussing you, not me"
    Else
        sDoctorResponse = "You have talked about me " & _
            iTalkingAboutMe.ToString & _
            " times. Shall we focus on you?"
    End If
    Return True
    End If

End If
Return False

End Function
```

Can Eliza Return a Quick Response?

If the patient did not discuss the doctor, the next function called is *getQuickResponse*. This function looks for key words within the patient's response. In some cases, if a word is found, a stock response is returned. For example, if the word *mother* is used, the doctor asks to learn more about the family. Sounds profound, eh? Because the doctor's response is visible at the module level, it's set here and can be returned by *getElizaResponse*. If a key word is found, the function returns True and control is returned to the calling function.

```
Private Function getQuickResponse() As Boolean

'-- Here we see if we can match a word in the patient's
'-- comment. If we can, let's return a response from the Dr.

Dim iIndex As Integer = 0

If (sPatientResponse.IndexOf("yes") > -1) Then
    sDoctorResponse = "Ah...that is positive. Tell me more."
    Return True
ElseIf (sPatientResponse.IndexOf("hate") > -1) Then
    sDoctorResponse = "Why are you so angry?"
    Return True
ElseIf (sPatientResponse.IndexOf("mother") > -1) Then
    sDoctorResponse = "Tell me more about your family..."
    Return True
```

(continued)

```
ElseIf (sPatientResponse.IndexOf("father") > -1) Then
    sDoctorResponse = "Why were you angry at males in " & _
        "your family?"
    Return True
ElseIf (sPatientResponse.IndexOf("sister") > -1) Then
    sDoctorResponse = "Why are you jealous of your sister?"
    Return True
ElseIf (sPatientResponse.IndexOf("brother") > -1) Then
    sDoctorResponse = "Why was your brother liked more " & _
        "than you?"
    Return True
```

A few of the key words can be used to turn around a patient's response to provide the nondeterministic aspect of the doctor's replies. For example, if the patient says, "You are a dolt," there is a 50/50 chance that the quick response function will return a message because of the word *you*. However, if the *Mod* operator returns a 1, the function returns False and this function will find the substring "you are". We simply make the doctor's response be "I am," and add the rest of the patient's comments. In this example, the doctor would return, "I am a dolt?"

When we are translating, it's important to get the exact position of the words we are exchanging. For example, if the user enters "Because, I am depressed," we want to grab the start of the string and then add to it the number of spaces in the string and return the remainder. If we didn't do this, our response would pick up fragments of words.

```
ElseIf (sPatientResponse.IndexOf("you are") > -1) Then
    iIndex = sPatientResponse.IndexOf("you are")
    sDoctorResponse = "I am " & _
        sPatientResponse.Substring(iIndex + 8) & "?"
    Return True
ElseIf (sPatientResponse.IndexOf("i am") > -1) Then
    iIndex = sPatientResponse.IndexOf("i am")
    sDoctorResponse = "Why are you " & _
        sPatientResponse.Substring(iIndex + 5) & "?"
    Return True
ElseIf (sPatientResponse.IndexOf("i'm") > -1) Then
    iIndex = sPatientResponse.IndexOf("i'm")
    sDoctorResponse = "Why are you " & _
        sPatientResponse.Substring(iIndex + 4) & "?"
    Return True
```

You can add as many responses as you want to extend Eliza and make the program seem truly intelligent. Be careful when scanning for individual words because they could be contained in larger words. The program looks for the word *we* by adding a space after it. Without this precaution, if the patient entered a substring with the word *welcome*, it would be picked up and an inappropriate response would be returned. And because everyone wants to discuss the weather, we added a response for that as well. If we can't provide a quick response, the function returns False.

```
ElseIf (sPatientResponse.IndexOf("we ") > -1) Then
    sDoctorResponse = "Try not to discuss us - " & _
        "tell me about you."
    Return True
ElseIf (sPatientResponse.IndexOf("no ") > -1) Then
    sDoctorResponse = "Why are you so negative?"
    Return True
ElseIf (sPatientResponse.IndexOf("weather") > -1) Then
    sDoctorResponse = "Did you want to be a " & _
        "meteorologist as a child?"
    Return True
Else
    Return False 'No quick response
End If

End Function
```

Can Eliza Translate the Patient's Response to Make It a Question?

This routine is the most complicated in our module. Essentially we take each word in the patient's response and see whether it is contained in the *aTranslate* array. If it is, a substitution is made.

We pass in the *cBlank* character to the *Split* function of the *sPatientResponse* string. This breaks up the string into each word that is separated by a blank space and returns an array of the words. We store the array of words returned in the *sSentenceWord* array. We then cache the lower and upper bounds of the *aSentenceWord* array in two integer variables for quick looping. Another variable of interest is *sbDrResponse*, which has the data type *StringBuilder*. Because we will do quite a bit of string manipulation to the response in this routine, a *StringBuilder* is made to order.

```
Private Function tryToTranslate() As Boolean

Dim aSentenceWord() As String = _
    sPatientResponse.Split(cBlank)
Dim iWordsLower As Integer = _
    aSentenceWord.GetLowerBound(0)
Dim iWordsUpper As Integer = _
    aSentenceWord.GetUpperBound(0)
Dim iaTranslateLower As Integer = _
    aTranslate.GetLowerBound(0)
Dim iaTranslateUpper As Integer = _
    aTranslate.GetUpperBound(0)
```

(continued)

```
Dim sbDrResponse As New StringBuilder()
Dim iWordLoop As Integer = 0
Dim iTranslateLoop As Integer = 0
Dim sCurrentWord As String = ""
Dim bCanTranslate As Boolean = False
Dim bAddQuestionMark As Boolean = False
```

We now loop through each word in the *aSentenceWord* array and assign each in turn to *sCurrentWord*. We also assume that we can't translate the word, so the Boolean *bCanTranslate* is initialized to False for each time through the loop. This flag is reset when we are successful.

```
'-- Let's see if we can parse the patient's comment and
'-- substitute words from the translate array.

For iWordLoop = iWordsLower To iWordsUpper

    sCurrentWord = aSentenceWord(iWordLoop)
    bCanTranslate = False
```

For each word that is stored in *sCurrentWord*, we compare it to the contents of the first element of the *aTranslate* array to see whether we can substitute for it. Notice that we use the *Equals* method of the *aTranslate* array.

```
For iTranslateLoop = iaTranslateLower To iaTranslateUpper

'-- If the current word is in the first aTranslate array
'-- element, then substitute with the second element

    If aTranslate(iTranslateLoop, 0).Equals(sCurrentWord) Then
```

If the current word matches one of the words in the 0th position of the *aTranslate* array, we append it to the doctor's response, which will be stored in the *StringBuilder* variable *sbDrResponse*. Because *sbDrResponse* is a locally scoped variable, it's created when this function is entered and goes out of scope when the function is exited. Therefore, the first time through the loop, the variable *sbDrResponse* is empty.

If the word that's matched happens to be the first word in the sentence, the returned word is appended to the front of the *StringBuilder*. We take the contents of the *aTranslate* array in row *iTranslateLoop*, column 1, and trim off any blank spaces.

If the matched word is from the body of the patient's response, for example "Because I am depressed," we append it to what is already there. Let's say the user types "Because I am depressed." The first word would not be found, but the second word would be. Because *iWordLoop* would be 1, we append "you" to *sbDrResponse*. Because we found at least one word, we set the two Booleans to True.

```
            If (iWordLoop = 0) Then
                sbDrResponse.Append(aTranslate(iTranslateLoop, _
                    1).TrimStart(cBlank))
            Else
                sbDrResponse.Append(" " & _
                    aTranslate(iTranslateLoop, _
                    1).TrimStart(cBlank))
            End If

            bCanTranslate = True
            bAddQuestionMark = True
            Exit For
        End If
    Next
```

If the current word was not in the *aTranslate* array, it is appended to *sbResponse*; otherwise we add "" before the word.

```
    '-- If we couldn't swap, add the current word
    If (bCanTranslate = False) Then
        If (iWordLoop = 0) Then
            sbDrResponse.Append(sCurrentWord)
        Else
            sbDrResponse.Append(" " & sCurrentWord)
        End If
    End If

Next
```

If we take our example "Because I am depressed," the first time through the loop the word *because* was not found so it is appended to *sbDrResponse*. The next time through the loop the word examined is *I*, which is found. Because *I* is not the first word, *you* is appended to *sbDrResponse*. Our *StringBuilder* variable now equals "because you." We make everything lowercase, so any words we use from the patient's response that have capital letters will need to be fixed. We will do this soon.

The next words in the patient's response, *are depressed*, are not found. That means they are appended to the *StringBuilder* variable as is. As you can see, the result becomes "because you are depressed."

The doctor's response is now built. If we find at least one word in the *aTranslate* array and the length of the doctor's response is greater than 5, we will add the finishing touches. First, we take the first character of the final response, which in our example will be *b*, and assign it to the variable *cFirstLetter*. We then convert this single letter (a character) to uppercase. The *cFirstLetter* variable now contains *B*.

Notice that we have to grab a single character from our response. We use the *Chars* method to indicate which character we want to evaluate. We then cast it to a *CChar* (Cast to CHARacter) and assign it a variable of data type *Char*.

```
'-- If we were successful, append a ? to the
'-- end and trim any leading blank spaces
If (bAddQuestionMark = True) And (sbDrResponse.Length > 5) Then

    Dim sFinalResponse As String
    Dim cFirstLetter As Char = CChar(sbDrResponse.Chars(0))

    '-- Extract the first letter and capitalize
    cFirstLetter = cFirstLetter.ToUpper(cFirstLetter)
```

Using the handy *Remove* and *Insert* methods of the *StringBuilder* data type, we remove the first character of the doctor's response. The first parameter of the *Remove* method, *0*, tells the method where to start removing. The second parameter, *1*, tells the method how many characters to remove. The *Insert* method also takes two parameters. The first indicates where to insert, and the second what to insert. With these two lines we removed the lowercase *b* and inserted an uppercase *B*.

```
'-- Remove the first letter and replace it with cap
sbDrResponse.Remove(0, 1)
sbDrResponse.Insert(0, cFirstLetter)
```

Now, because we've successfully translated the patient's response to a question, let's add a question mark to the end. Finally, we convert the *StringBuilder* data type to a string and assign it to the module-level variable *sDoctorResponse*. We then return True to alert the calling function that we were successful. The variable *sDoctorResponse* now contains "Because you are depressed?" Of course, if no words in the patient's comment are found in the *aTranslate* array, we return False from the function.

```
    '-- Add a ? and return the string
    sbDrResponse.Append("?")
    sDoctorResponse = sbDrResponse.ToString
    Return True
Else
    '-- No luck, return an empty string
    Return False
End If

End Function
```

You can see why we selected a *StringBuilder* data type for building the *sbDrResponse* in this function. We essentially built the response on the fly. Using the *Append*, *Remove*, and *Insert* methods we constructed the response. The *StringBuilder* does all of this in a memory buffer. If we did this with a *String* data type, any change would result in the string being destroyed and a new one constructed reflecting the changes. Finally, we used the *ToString* conversion to assign the final product to the string response that will be sent back to the program using this module.

Return a Previous Patient Phrase

In the event that none of the first three functions returns a doctor response, the program tries the *getRandomPhrase* route. Under certain conditions, this routine replies with a comment made previously by the patient and requests more information about it. This routine not only gives the patient a sense that Eliza has a memory but that the program can see patterns between what was just asked and what was asked several questions ago. This feature is very impressive to the user.

To accomplish this feat, we use our old friend the *Mod* operator. You can see that this function is used rarely. First, all other functions called before must have failed, and when *getRandomPhrase* is called, a previous patient response is returned only when the number of responses is evenly divisible by 6. So this does not occur often, but when it does the patient will find it impressive.

We set the *iLimit* variable to the number of patient responses so far. We also introduce a new class, *Random*. This class represents a pseudo-random number generator, which means that this class produces a sequence of numbers that meet certain statistical requirements for randomness. Pseudo-random numbers are chosen with equal probability from a finite set of numbers. The numbers chosen are not completely random because a definite mathematical algorithm is used to select them, but they are sufficiently random for our purposes. Finally, we also use a *StringBuilder* object to construct our response because we need to do a bit of appending.

```
Private Function getRandomPhrase() As Boolean

If (iPatientResponseCount Mod 6 = 0) Then
    Dim iLimit As Integer = cPatientsResponses.Count
    Dim iPickResponse As Integer = 0
    Dim iRandom As New Random()
    Dim sPreviousComment As New StringBuilder() 'Be sure to
                                                'use new

    Dim sComment As String
```

The *Random* class is overloaded and returns a random number between 0.0 and 1.0. However, we can alter the range by means of the *Next* method, which takes two parameters: lower limit and upper limit. This method returns a random integer within the specified range. Notice that we are generating a random number between 0 and *iLimit* –1. As you know, *cPatientsResponses* is a *StringCollection*. While the string collection might contain eight responses, the first is in position 0. So while the *Count* property assigned to *iLimit* will be 8, the strings are in position 0 through 7. If we used *iLimit*, every once in a while, *Random* would generate *iLimit*, which would be one beyond the last legitimate entry, throwing an exception. This exception is not a good thing, so let's anticipate it.

```
'-- Which random response to select from the
'-- cPatientsResponses collection?
iPickResponse = iRandom.Next(0, iLimit - 1)
```

As a double check we ensure that the number of the string to retrieve is less than the *Count* property of the *StringCollection*. Because each of the patient's responses is stored as lowercase characters, we want to capitalize the first character. We are familiar with how do to this now. First we assign the string from *cPatientsResponses* to a *StringCollection*. Because we are going to manipulate *sComment*, you might be wondering why we didn't use a *StringBuilder*. Well, you can't cast a string (from the *StringCollection*) to a variable of type *StringBuilder*. Yes, you could if you turned off *Option Strict*, but we elected not to do that, so we dimension *sComment* as a string as well to make the assignment cleanly. We then grab the first character of the random previous patient response and capitalize it.

```
If (iPickResponse <= cPatientsResponses.Count) Then
    Dim cFirstLetter As Char

    '-- Retrieve the comment to display
    sComment = cPatientsResponses(iPickResponse)

    '-- Take the first letter of the retrieved comment
    cFirstLetter = CChar(sComment.Chars(0))

    '-- Capitalize it
    cFirstLetter = cFirstLetter.ToUpper(cFirstLetter)
```

I also wanted to use a string to point out another "gotcha." Recall that when we used the *StringBuilder* to remove the first character and insert the capital letter, we could simply do this:

```
'-- Remove the first letter and replace it with cap
sbDrResponse.Remove(0, 1)
sbDrResponse.Insert(0, cFirstLetter)
```

Because *sbDrResponse* is a *StringBuilder* data type, the conversion is done in a memory buffer. There is no need to assign the string to another variable to accomplish the conversion. But this is not the case with a string! You could use the same code above for a string—it will compile fine—however, the changes are simply ignored! We know that when changes are made to a string, the original is destroyed and a new one created. Because this is the case, when working with a string you must assign any *Remove* or *Insert* changes to another string.

We remove the current lowercase first character of the random response and replace it with the uppercase character. Because it's a string, we must assign the change to another string. Behind the scenes, the original *sComment* is automatically destroyed and a new modified string is created.

```
'-- Remove the first letter and replace it with cap
sComment = sComment.Remove(0, 1)
sComment = sComment.Insert(0, cFirstLetter)
```

We want to embed the patient's previous question in quotation marks, and the way to show a quotation mark literal is to have double quotes (""). Double quotes show up as a quotation mark. Notice that the two *Append* lines each have four quotation marks. The first line has a quotation mark at the beginning, one at the end, and two together. Next we append a previous response from the *StringBuilder* and concatenate another quote. This new material is then assigned to the doctor's response and the function returns True. If the conditions are not met, the function returns False.

```
            '-- Now construct the string for the Dr response --
            sPreviousComment.Append("Please tell me more about: """)
            sPreviousComment.Append(sComment & """")
            sDoctorResponse = sPreviousComment.ToString
            Return True
        End If
    End If

    Return False

End Function
```

Notice that not only does this routine return a random previous patient comment, but it capitalizes the first letter and places the entire comment in quotes, as you can see in Figure 6-26.

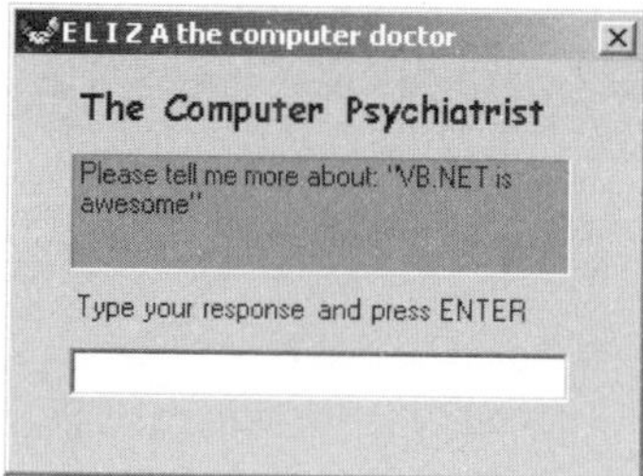

Figure 6-26 Eliza sometimes displays a previous comment in quotation marks.

When All Else Fails

If each of the four previous functions fails to return an incredibly insightful comment, we resort to returning one of our stock phrases. We need a way to keep track of which current stock response the doctor used last so that we can always send a new one. To do this, we need to dimension a variable that keeps track of the last stock phrase that was sent. One way to do this is to declare a module-level variable that stays in scope as long as the program is running. A better way is to declare a local variable that does the same thing.

We know that all local variables come to life when the procedure is entered and are destroyed when the procedure is exited. When we need a local variable that persists from call to call in a procedure, declaring it as *Static* does the trick. This special local variable will retain its value as long as the module is in scope. We declare an integer variable as *Static* and initialize it to 0. When it gets incremented or changed in the *getStockPhrase* procedure, it retains its value.

```
Private Function getStockPhrase() As String

    Static iCurrentStock As Integer = 0
```

The next section of code might look a bit strange. The first time the function is entered, the value of *iCurrentStock* equals *0*. Because *0* is less than the upper bound of the *asStockResponse* array, the *Else* clause is executed. The variable *iCurrentStock* is incremented and now equals *1*. The response in the first array element (i.e., 1 –1) is returned.

This incrementing continues until *iCurrentStock* is larger than the upper bound. When that happens, *iCurrentStock* is set back to *1*. We then send back 1 –0 or the first response all over again. We do this to speed up the code. Remember that when the *Return* keyword is executed, control immediately returns to the caller. There would be nowhere to update *iCurrentStock* after the *If...Else* statement. We would have to increment the counter after we selected a response. This means declaring another temporary variable, assigning the response to it, incrementing the counter, and then returning the response. This was simply a design decision.

```
    If iCurrentStock > asStockResponse.GetUpperBound(0) Then
       iCurrentStock = asStockResponse.GetLowerBound(0) + 1
       Return asStockResponse(iCurrentStock - 1)
    Else
       iCurrentStock += 1
       Return asStockResponse(iCurrentStock - 1)
    End If

End Function
End Module
```

The Dialog.vb module is now complete. Ready to call it from the form?

Calling the Module from the Form

Open up the form you created earlier as the interface. Add the following *Imports* statements to the top of the form as usual, along with an *Imports* statement for the new Eliza dialog box.

```
Imports System.ComponentModel
Imports System.Drawing
Imports System.Windows.Forms
Imports Microsoft.VisualBasic.ControlChars
Imports Eliza.Dialog
```

Now set the *lblDoctor.Text* property, which will be displayed each time Eliza is run.

```
Public Sub New()
    MyBase.New()

    'This call is required by the Windows Form Designer.
    InitializeComponent()

    'Add any initialization after the
    ' InitializeComponent() call

    lblDoctor().Text = "What would you like to talk " & _
        "about this beautiful day?"
    End Sub
```

Now add the *KeyDown* event procedure for our *txtQuestion* text box. What we do is check each key press and determine whether the Enter key was pressed. When you want to check or restrict text from being entered in a text box control, create an event handler for the *KeyDown* event. This will permit you to validate each character entered in the control.

We added *Imports Microsoft.VisualBasic.ControlChars* so that we could easily check for when the Enter key is pressed. The key pressed by the user is in the *KeyEventArgs* parameter passed into the event handler. All we have to do is see whether the key code is equal to the Enter key. If it is not (in most cases), the event handler is simply exited.

If, however, the Enter key was pressed, we know the patient is submitting a response to the good doctor. In that case, we pass in the contents of the *txtQuestion* text box as a parameter to the *getElizaResponse* method of the Dialog module. The value returned is displayed in the *lblDoctor* label on the interface.

An important design feature to note is how we totally decoupled our module from the interface. The interface does not have to know anything about the module. It does not have to initialize it or understand how it is implemented. To the interface, our module is a black box. A patient response is passed in and a doctor response is passed back. This feature is an important point that you should strive to emulate in your designs.

```
Private Sub txtQuestion_KeyDown(ByVal sender As System.Object, _
    ByVal e As System.Windows.Forms.KeyEventArgs) _
    Handles txtQuestion.KeyDown

    '-- If the user doesn't hit Enter, they are not finished
    If (Not e.KeyCode.Equals(keys.Enter)) Then
        Exit Sub
    Else
        lblDoctor().Text = _
            Dialog.getElizaResponse(txtQuestion().Text)
    End If

    txtQuestion().Text = ""

End Sub
```

Also, when we go to hook up the dialog box in our user interface, you can see the benefit of making each of the member variables and procedures private. The user only gets to see the single interface—*getElizaResponse*, as you can see in Figure 6-27. This makes our module pretty foolproof to use.

```
'-- If the user doesn't hit ENTER, they are not finished
If (Not e.KeyCode.Equals(Keys.Enter)) Then
    Exit Sub
Else
    lblDoctor().Text = dialog.
End If
                        getElizaResponse

txtQuestion().Text = ""
```

Figure 6-27 The module's private interfaces are not exposed.

And here is where the strong typing of Visual Basic .NET comes into its own. When the user hooks up the module, it's easy to see that it is expecting a patient response of type *String* and that it will return the favor by passing back a string. No ambiguity here, as you can see in Figure 6-28.

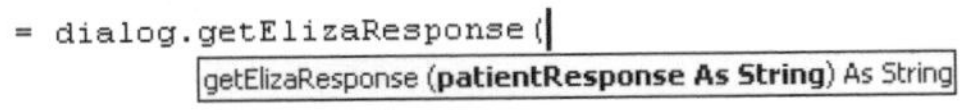

```
= dialog.getElizaResponse (|
        getElizaResponse (patientResponse As String) As String
```

Figure 6-28 Strong typing lets IntelliSense know exactly what parameter types a function expects.

Conclusion

This was an important chapter, and I hope you enjoyed the Eliza program. It's always been one of my favorites. You're now beginning to see how easy it is to use the powerful .NET Framework. Most of the grunt work is taken care of for you. You simply inherit from existing classes and can concentrate on the particular tasks you want your program to perform. In the next chapter, we'll look at how you handle exceptions in your programs and work with the debugger.

7

Handling Errors and Debugging Programs

The Throwback program we wrote in Chapter 6, "Arrays and Collections in Visual Basic .NET," is pretty simple, and you might think that our work with it is done. After all, what could possibly go wrong in such a simple program? We added some error checking to the program by determining the array bounds and converting the text input to an integer value. What else could go wrong? Plenty, actually, so before you congratulate yourself on a job well done, let's take a minute to think about all the ways a user can thwart your hard work.

What Can Possibly Go Wrong?

In the Throwback program, what happens if a user accidentally types a number such as 123Q? Oops. In the design environment, the just-in-time debugger pops up, and we get a nasty error message, as shown in Figure 7-1.

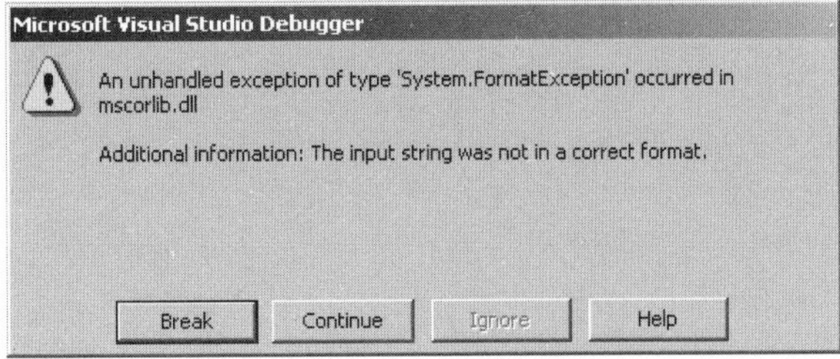

Figure 7-1 An error message displayed by the debugger.

What if the user accidentally types a decimal number, such as 123.45? Another *System.FormatException* error is generated. Now our intrepid user might type 33333333333333? Hmmm. This example illustrates another problem, as shown in Figure 7-2.

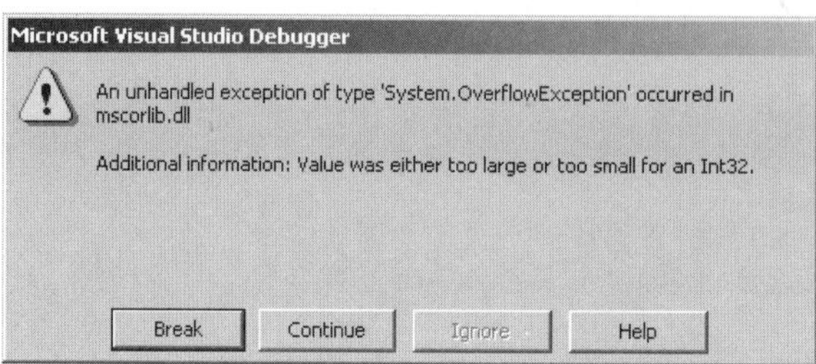

Figure 7-2 Another error message, this one concerning the size of a user-entered value.

A good rule of thumb when thinking about your programs is that if a user can enter wrong data, no matter how remote or improbable that data might be, the user will do so. Said another way, the time it takes a user to enter bad data is inversely proportional to how obscure the error that's generated is. Clearly, we must handle exceptions thrown by our program and handle them gracefully.

When working with production code, you'll find that more than 60 percent of the code is usually devoted to error handling. Including this code—attending to the details of error handling—is what separates a solid, professional program from a fragile one that can crash when something unexpected happens.

What Is an Exception?

An exception is any error condition or unexpected behavior encountered by an executing program. Exceptions can come from both a running program and the run-time environment. As a developer, you are most concerned with program exceptions that can potentially lead to a program crash. Your program might be running perfectly, but when it attempts to save a file, either the disk is unexpectedly full or the floppy drive isn't ready. An exception will be thrown in either case.

To the common language runtime (CLR), an exception is an object that inherits from the *System.Exception* class, the base class from which all exceptions inherit. An exception is thrown from the area of code where a problem occurs to a part of the code designed to catch and handle the error. The type of exception determines which area of code will handle the problem.

While debugging programs is an especially important topic, I've saved my discussion of the subject for this chapter because we've had so much other new information to digest. Like most everything else in Visual Basic .NET, error handling has matured to the level of implementation found in other, more sophisticated languages. But debugging starts not with the debugger but with a solid understanding of what your program does and how the user will interact with it. Writing solid code comes with time and insight. Your objective is to anticipate every possible way your program can go terribly wrong and take measures to handle those errors. The objective is to use the debugger as little as possible.

Job Interviews That Threw Unexpected Errors

There's a story about a famous computer science professor who had an opening for a junior assistant.and had no end of recently minted young PhDs applying for the job. The professor interviewed a promising candidate, who was very nervous and anxious about making a good impression. During the course of the interview, the professor asked the young man how well he knew the debugger. The candidate blurted out, "I know it really well. There is nothing I don't know about it." With that the professor stood up, offered his hand, and declared the interview over. Dismayed, the candidate asked why. "Well," the professor said, "I want someone that rarely needs the debugger; it should be foreign to him." He went on to say that before anyone commits a line of code to the editor, he should have a complete understanding of how each variable will interact with the program, how it's stored in the CPU register, how it's handled in memory, and so on. If a programmer knows these things, the debugger will rarely be used, so it should be alien to the person he hires.

The professor invited the next candidate to dinner for a chat. The professor's wife brought out sizzling steaks for dinner. The candidate, while conversing, reached over for the salt and added a touch to the just delivered steak. The conversation went pleasantly for the duration of dinner, and the trio discussed everything but computer science. At the conclusion of the evening, the professor stood up and declared that the interview was over. Again, the candidate was flustered and asked why. Smiling, the professor noted that the candidate had added salt to her steak before tasting it. Well, what did that have to do with anything, the candidate inquired. The professor smiled and asked how did she know the steak needed salt before she even tasted it. "I want an assistant with no preconceived ideas." Adding salt showed him that this candidate had certain preconceptions about how things are, which was unacceptable in his research. He went on to explain that he expected his assistant to have no

(continued)

Job Interviews That Threw Unexpected Errors *(continued)*

preconceptions because that is what keeps someone from becoming a truly great programmer. Never assume.

In our simple Throwback program, if we failed to anticipate that a user could add a nonnumeric value or add a value that exceeds the bounds of our integer data type, we would be in big trouble. Our objective is to fully understand each and every possible error, from user error to whether a file will not be present or the disk is full and we won't be able to write a value to it. This level of anticipation comes only with much practice and thinking, but if you're aware of what to look for, you can tailor your thinking to ensure that you catch most if not all errors.

Types of Visual Basic .NET Errors

In Visual Basic, errors are *syntax errors*, *run-time errors*, or *logic errors*. Syntax errors are the most common type of error, but they are also the easiest to fix. They appear while you write your code. As you know, Visual Basic .NET checks your code as you type and alerts you if you make a mistake such as misspelling a word or using a language element improperly. Because the compiler barks at you by underlining an error, you can fix it easily in the coding environment as soon as it occurs. As I touched on earlier, in Chapter 4, "Visual Basic .NET Data Types and Features," the *Option Explicit* statement is the best means of avoiding syntax errors. This statement forces a programmer to declare, in advance, all the variables that will be used in the application. When any of the predeclared variables are used in the code, any typographic errors made entering a variable name are caught immediately and can be fixed.

Run-time errors are those that appear only after you compile and run your code. They involve code that appears to be correct because it contains no syntax errors, but these errors cause a program to crash, as in the examples described earlier. For example, the Throwback program works until the user enters a string instead of a number. Run-time errors can be corrected by rewriting the offending code and then recompiling and rerunning your program.

Logic errors are those that appear after the application is in use. These errors usually manifest themselves in the form of unwanted or unexpected results in response to user actions. For example, you might have used the wrong index for your array, and the Throwback calculator displays an X when it should display an M. Logic errors are generally the hardest type of error to fix because their origin is not always clear. And sometimes logic errors are not obvious; the program displays incorrect information that looks as though it might be correct. This sort of situation is one in which a thorough understanding of how a program is expected to be used is important to the programmer.

The Classic Visual Basic *Err* Object Is Gone in Visual Basic .NET

Classic Visual Basic had the *Err* object and used syntax such as *On Error goto myErrorHandler*. No matter how we tried to get away from *goto* statements, because they were part and parcel of error handling in classic Visual Basic, we couldn't escape them entirely. Using the *On Error* statement along with *goto* statements is known as *unstructured error handling*. In unstructured error handling, exception handling is turned on for all code that executes within a procedure by executing an *On Error* statement within that procedure. When an exception is raised in the procedure after the *On Error* statement has been executed, the program branches to the label specified in the *On Error* statement.

The way unstructured error handling worked in classic Visual Basic could be confusing for a novice programmer. If a call were made within one procedure to another procedure and an exception occurred within the called procedure, the exception was propagated back to the calling procedure if the called procedure didn't handle the exception itself. Let's say you have Procedure A and Procedure B in your program. If Procedure A has an error handler, calls Procedure B, and an error occurs, execution immediately branches back from Procedure B to the error handler in Procedure A. When programmers understood how this mechanism worked, everything was fine. However, this approach caused developers to pop open many bottles of aspirin when trying to debug a program. Unstructured error handling using *On Error* statements can actually degrade application performance and result in code that is difficult to debug and maintain.

Thankfully, this primitive and Visual Basic–specific method of unstructured error handling is gone in Visual Basic .NET. It's been replaced by the structured *Try...Catch...Finally* syntax that has been used for years in pre-.NET languages such as C++ and Java.

Try, *Catch*, and *Finally*

When debugging your code and planning where and how to implement error handling, you start by examining your program code and determining which sections of code might throw exceptions. These sections are placed in a *Try* block. The code designed to handle exceptions generated in the *Try* block are placed in a *Catch* block. The *Catch* block is a series of statements beginning with the keyword *Catch*, followed by an exception type and an action to be taken. The *Finally* construct will always execute and can be used for clean-up operations such as closing files or connections.

This manner of handling errors is known as *structured exception handling*. To use this powerful .NET feature, we simply place any code that might fail inside the *Try...Catch* block. With this model, we get quite a bit of functionality, as shown in Figure 7-3.

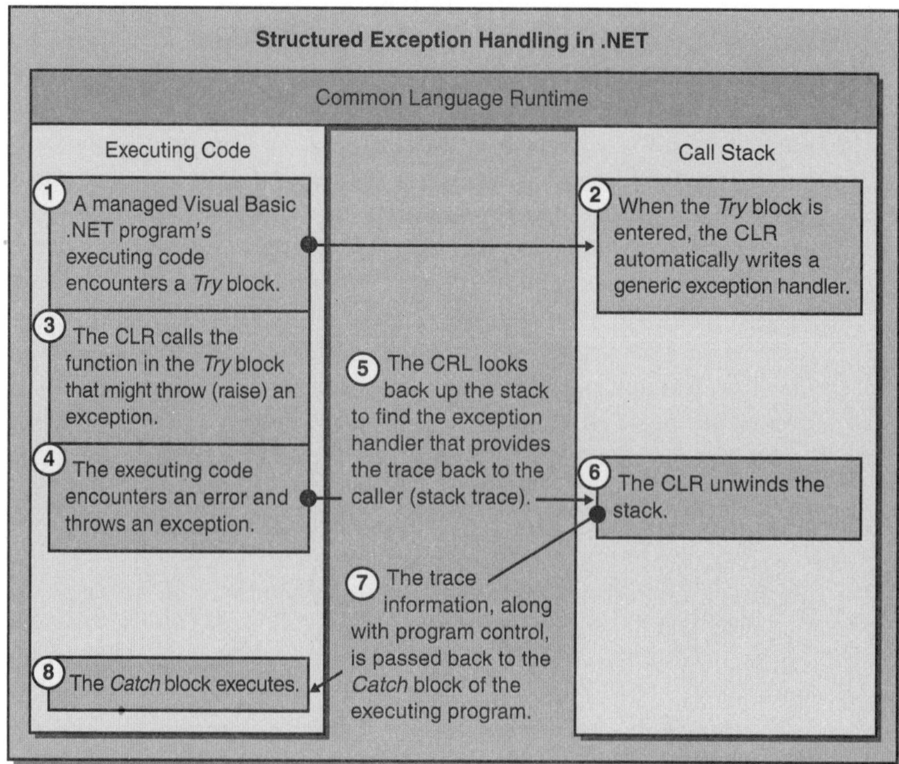
Structured Exception Handling in .NET
Common Language Runtime
Executing Code
Call Stack
1 A managed Visual Basic .NET program's executing code encounters a Try block.
2 When the Try block is entered, the CLR automatically writes a generic exception handler.
3 The CLR calls the function in the Try block that might throw (raise) an exception.
4 The executing code encounters an error and throws an exception.
5 The CRL looks back up the stack to find the exception handler that provides the trace back to the caller (stack trace).
6 The CLR unwinds the stack.
7 The trace information, along with program control, is passed back to the Catch block of the executing program.
8 The Catch block executes.

Figure 7-3 Structured exception handling in the .NET Framework.

Structured exception handling is a service that's built into the core of .NET, so it's available to all languages that target the .NET platform. As you might guess, structured error handling is located in the common language runtime. Very little code is required to fully utilize the features of structured error handling.

When used correctly, structured exception handling in Visual Basic .NET allows your program to detect and usually recover from errors during execution. Visual Basic .NET uses an enhanced version of the *Try...Catch...Finally* syntax already supported by other languages. This form of structured exception handling combines a modern control structure (similar to *Select Case* or *While*) with exceptions, protected blocks of code, and filters.

Structured exception handling is the method recommended for .NET applications and makes creating and maintaining programs with robust, comprehensive error handlers easy. Exceptions that are not caught by a *Catch* block are handled by the common language runtime, but having the runtime handle exceptions is a bad idea. We want to keep it from happening at all costs. Depending on how the common language runtime is configured, having it handle an exception could result in a debug dialog box appearing or in a dialog box appearing with the exception information and the program abruptly stopping execution. These events are not considered good programming form.

As I mentioned earlier, programs need to uniformly handle errors and exceptions that occur during execution. The design of error-tolerant software is greatly assisted by the CLR. The CLR provides a platform for notifying programs of errors in a consistent way, even if the error occurs in a module written in a language different from the language used to write the module catching the error. All .NET Framework methods indicate failure by throwing exceptions. You can now easily catch them when they are thrown and handle them gracefully. Let's see how to add structured error handling to our code.

Adding Structured Error Handling

Open the Throwback Calculator program created in Chapter 6 and add the following lines to it. Remember what I said about devoting more than 60 percent of your code to error handling? This example illustrates the point nicely.

```
Try
    iInput = int32.Parse(txtInput().Text)

    For iCounter = Arabics.GetUpperBound(0) To _
        Arabics.GetLowerBound(0) Step -1

        While iInput >= Arabics(iCounter)
            iInput -= Arabics(iCounter)
            sOutPut += Romans(iCounter)
        End While
    Next

    lblResult().Text = sInput & " = " & sOutPut
    Catch ex As System.Exception When Not _
        IsNumeric(txtInput().Text)

        MessageBox.Show(sInput & " is not a valid number. " & _
            "Please reenter.", sProgName, MessageBoxButtons.OK, _
            MessageBoxIcon.Hand)
        lblResult().Text = ""
```

(continued)

```
    Catch ex As System.FormatException
        MessageBox.Show(sInput & " is not an integer. " & _
            "Please reenter.", sProgName, MessageBoxButtons.OK, _
            MessageBoxIcon.Hand)
        lblResult().Text = ""
    Catch ex As System.OverflowException
        MessageBox.Show(sInput & " is too large or small. " & _
            "Please enter an integer from 1 to 9999.", _
            sProgName, MessageBoxButtons.OK, _
            MessageBoxIcon.Hand)
        lblResult().Text = ""
    Catch ex As System.Exception
        MessageBox.Show(ex.GetType.ToString, sProgName, _
            MessageBoxButtons.OK, MessageBoxIcon.Hand)
        lblResult().Text = ""
    Finally
        txtInput().Clear()
        txtInput().Focus()

End Try
```

The *Try...Catch* Block

The common language runtime supports an exception-handling model that's based on exception objects and protected blocks of code. When an exception occurs, an object is created to represent the exception. Remember that run-time errors do not cause your program to crash, but unhandled run-time errors do. The .NET CLR indicates that an error condition has occurred by executing a *Throw* statement. The statement *throws* an object of a type derived from *System.Exception*. This object provides information about the specific error that has occurred.

If an expression does not evaluate to an instance of a type derived from *System.Exception*, an error occurs at compile time. If at run time an expression evaluates to a null reference, an instance of a *System.NullReferenceException* object is thrown instead.

As I mentioned, the sections of code that might throw exceptions (errors) are placed in a *Try* block. The code designed to handle exceptions generated in the *Try* block are placed in a *Catch* block. The *Catch* block is a series of statements beginning with the keyword *Catch*, followed by an exception type and an action to be taken.

If an exception is thrown within the *Try* block, we want to catch it and handle it. In our example, the first *Catch* clause will fire if a *System.Exception* is thrown when the value entered by the user is not numeric. This *Catch* clause uses a filter to trap when an exception results from a non-numeric value. If we didn't add a filter to specify a particular kind of error, the *Catch* statement would handle each and every instance of *System.Exception*, including all three types we're anticipating.

Of course, we could use a single *Catch* statement to handle all *System.Exception* objects. However, an unfiltered *Catch* statement would not provide the user with helpful information about what happened. Because one of the goals in professional software development is to provide a user with useful and nonthreatening information about the type of error and how to correct it, we've added some detail by using several *Catch* clauses to handle specific errors. In addition, rather than displaying a cryptic .NET runtime message, we want to provide users with an informative message explicitly telling them what went wrong. If a user types a value such as 123Q, our code will handle that particular exception.

Our first *Catch* block will handle only exceptions thrown when the contents of the input text box are not numeric.

```
Catch ex As System.Exception When Not _
    IsNumeric(txtInput().Text)

    MessageBox.Show(sInput & " is not a valid number. " & _
        "Please reenter.", sProgName, MessageBoxButtons.OK, _
        MessageBoxIcon.Hand)
     lblResult().Text = ""
```

Now we can show the user what they entered, tell them it's not a valid number, and ask them politely to try once more, as you can see in Figure 7-4.

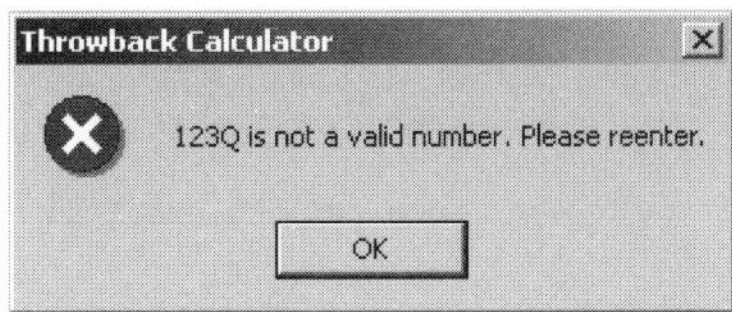

Figure 7-4 The first *Catch* block gracefully handles nonnumeric input.

If some other exception is thrown, the program will bypass the first *Catch* block and go to the next one to see whether it can handle the exception, and so on. We might also want to provide an informative message if a user accidentally types a noninteger, such as 123.45. Here's the *Catch* statement that handles this exception. The error message is shown in Figure 7-5.

```
Catch ex As System.FormatException
    MessageBox.Show(sInput & " is not an integer. " & _
        "Please reenter.", sProgName, MessageBoxButtons.OK, _
        MessageBoxIcon.Hand)
    lblResult().Text = ""
```

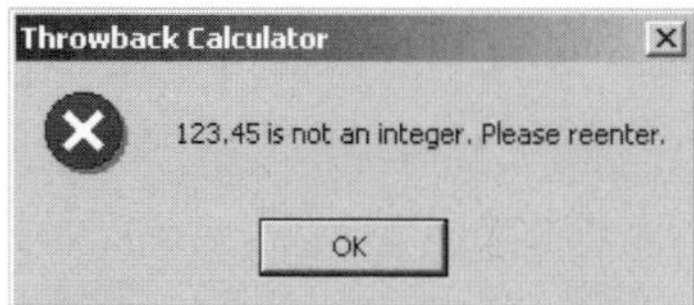

Figure 7-5 The second *Catch* block gracefully handles non-integer values.

Another problem could be that the user enters a very large or small number. Again, we can indicate what's wrong about the data the user entered and provide some guidance, as you can see in Figure 7-6.

```
Catch ex As System.OverflowException
    MessageBox.Show(sInput & " is too large or small. " & _
        "Please enter an integer from 1 to 9999.", _
        sProgName, MessageBoxButtons.OK, _
        MessageBoxIcon.Hand)
     lblResult().Text = ""
```

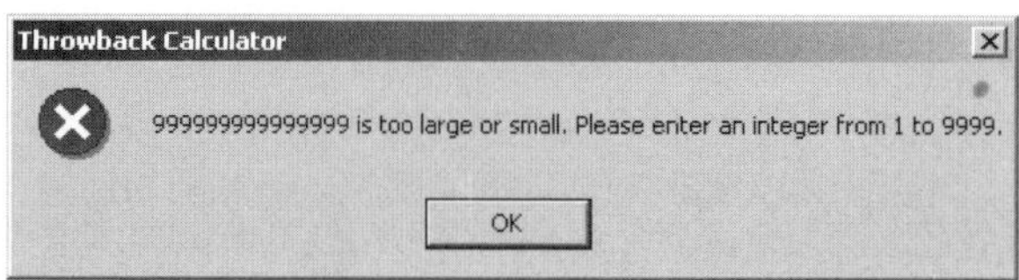

Figure 7-6 The third *Catch* block handles very large and very small values.

When writing your *Catch* clauses, always write the most specific one first and work your way down to the most general. Following this order allows you to handle a specific exception before it's passed to a more general *Catch* block.

Making Our Simple Program Even More Bullet Proof

To put another level of protection in our program, we can easily limit the number of characters a user can enter in a text box. Bring up the properties box for the *txtInput* textbox and set the *MaxLength* property to 4, as shown in Figure 7-7. This setting ensures that the largest number a user can enter is 9999. With this protection, the third *Catch* statement we included is never executed.

We all know that exceptions that we can't predict can be thrown; for example, errors caused by bad hardware, having no memory left, and the like. To handle an error that has not been anticipated, you can use a default *Catch* statement to handle any exceptions not caught by other, more specific statements. In the Throwback program, our default *Catch* statement simply prints out the exception and our program continues unfazed. By using a *Catch* statement, we ensure that the program won't crash and burn.

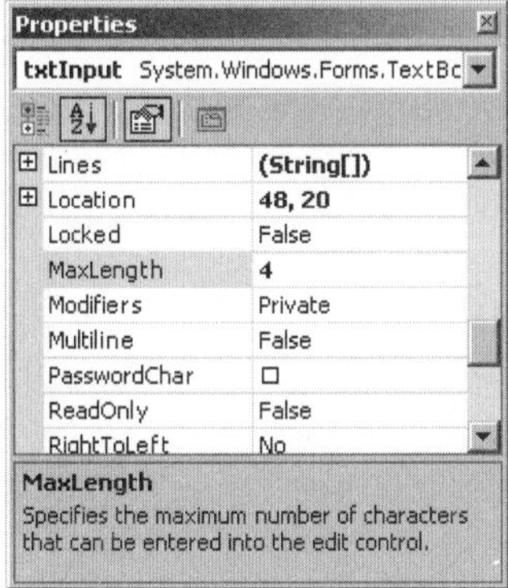

Figure 7-7 Visual Basic .NET lets you limit user input.

```
Catch ex As System.Exception
    MessageBox.Show(ex.GetType.ToString, sProgName, _
        MessageBoxButtons.OK, MessageBoxIcon.Hand)
    lblResult().Text = ""
```

You can derive classes from *System.Exception* and even add additional properties and methods to better explain the error to the code that catches the exception. Two classes that inherit from the *System.Exception* class are *System.Application* (for implementing errors thrown by the application and not the CLR) and *System.SystemException*, which is the base class for all predefined exceptions in the *System* namespace.

The most severe exceptions thrown by the common language runtime are usually nonrecoverable, including *ExecutionEngineException* and *StackOverflowException*. It's not recommended that you throw or catch these two severe errors.

> **Tip** In your programs, you can actually throw your own exceptions. You can programmatically throw as an exception any object that derives from the *Object* class. Developers can create their own exception classes by subclassing the appropriate base exception. You might wonder why in the world you would ever want to throw your own exception. The reason is simple. You could create a class that throws many types of exceptions to see how your program reacts. You could add this class to your programs during your testing. In the class, a timer would throw all sorts of exceptions and you could monitor how your program handles them. Following this approach, you could be pretty sure the final release version was rock solid. Just before release, you would remove the class from the production code.
>
> Another use of a class such as this is to throw an error if a condition is met that will be handled by a *Try...Catch* block located elsewhere in the program. In this way, you can maintain centralized error control.

The *Finally* Block

The *Finally* block is always run when program execution leaves any part of the *Try* statement. No explicit action is required on your part to execute the *Finally* block—when execution leaves the *Try* statement, the system will automatically execute the *Finally* block.

Execution of the *Finally* block occurs regardless of the method in which a program leaves the *Try* statement. The *Finally* block can be reached successfully from the end of the *Try* block, by reaching the end of a *Catch* block, or by executing an *Exit Try* statement. The *Finally* block is usually used for clean-up operations. It is invalid to explicitly transfer execution to a *Finally* block.

We saw in Figure 7-3 that the result of throwing an exception is that the call stack is unwound. If we have a database connection or are using another expensive resource, it will not be finalized and disposed of when the stack is unwound. This problem can be solved by a *Finally* block. Code in the *Finally* block always executes just before the stack is unwound, so this block is a good place to add any resource finalization code you might have.

In our program, we execute the *Clear* method of the text box in the *Finally* block to empty its contents for the next round of user input. We also force focus to the text box so that if the user enters another number, it will be added to the text box automatically—the user will not have to first click the box to give it focus. This detail is a particularly nice touch in professional code.

```
Finally
    txtInput().Clear()
    txtInput().Focus()

End Try
```

A Structured Exception Gotcha

Remember that the *Finally* block always executes no matter what. Many novices find the *Finally* block a bit confusing. Be careful to structure a *Try* block to handle the code you want to execute and use the *Finally* block to perform only operations that will always occur, such as cleanup. In the following code, no matter what number you pass as a parameter, and whether an error occurs or not, the function will always return 0.

(continued)

A Structured Exception Gotcha *(continued)*

```
Private Function squareNumber(ByVal intToSquare As Integer) _
    As Long

    Dim result As Long

    Try
        result = intToSquare * intToSquare
    Catch ex As System.Exception
        MessageBox.Show("There was a slight problem.")
    Finally
        result = 0
    End Try

    Return result

End Function
```

You could easily test this code by calling the function and displaying the result in a message box. Of course, in our *squareNumber* function, we defined the data type of the number to accept as an integer. If you attempted to pass a number such as 5.5, the compiler would bark at you and report "*Option Explicit* disallows implicit conversions from Double to Integer." So strong typing helps you pass the correct data type. But if the logic of the function is malformed, you'll still receive the wrong answer, as shown here.

```
MessageBox.Show(squareNumber(5).ToString)  'prints 0
```

To make this function work correctly, you should place the *result = 0* line in the *Catch* clause. Making this change would return 25, which is what we expected.

Setting a Breakpoint in Your Code

You'll often encounter errors that are not obvious, and you'll need to step through sections of code line by line. To help you step through code, you can add a breakpoint. To set a breakpoint, you first find the line of code you want to start stepping through and then click in the left border of the IDE. A red dot indicates that a breakpoint has been set. If you want to remove the breakpoint, click the dot, and it's removed. Figure 7-8 shows how a breakpoint is represented.

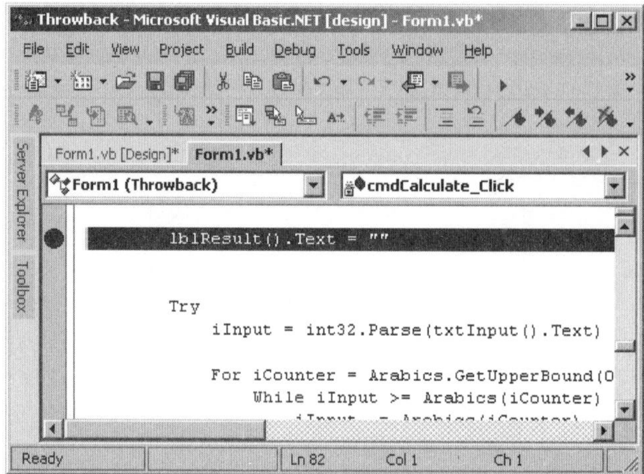

Figure 7-8 Program execution will temporarily halt when it reaches this breakpoint.

You can set breakpoints only on lines of code that are executed. For example, if you tried to set a breakpoint on the declaration of our two integers—*Dim iInput, iCounter As Integer*—the compiler would alert you that setting a breakpoint here is not a good idea. In the first panel of the status bar in the lower left of the IDE window, you would get a message from the compiler, as shown in Figure 7-9.

This is not a valid location for a breakpoint.

Figure 7-9 The compiler warns you if you try to set a breakpoint on a nonexecutable line of code.

Running the Program Using the Debugger

Let's debug our program and get an idea of the wealth of information available to us. First set the breakpoint shown in Figure 7-8, and then press F5 (or select Start from the Debug menu) to run the program so that it will enter the debugger. If you accidentally press Ctrl+F5 or select Start Without Debugging, breakpoints will be ignored.

When the program displays its main form, you can enter a number. Add **123** to the text box, and then click the Calculate button. Because we set a breakpoint inside this event procedure, we can start stepping through our code only at this point. If the Locals window is not displayed, select Debug | Windows | Locals. The Locals window for our program is shown in Figure 7-10. In the Locals window you can see the local variables and the values they contain so far. *Arabics.GetLowerBound(0)* is 0 and *Arabics.GetUpperBound(0)* is 12. If you click the plus sign beside either the *Arabics* or *Romans* array, the display is expanded to show each of the array's elements and their contents. You can also see that *123* was the value entered by examining the *sInput* string variable. Go ahead and click the plus signs and spend a few minutes examining the contents of these variables. You can discover what's happening in your program in the Locals window.

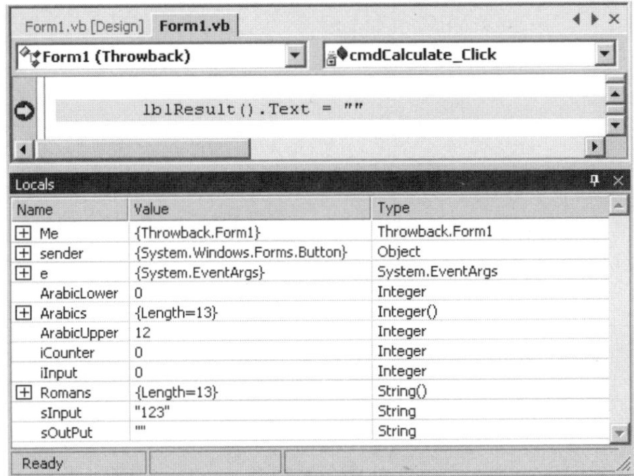

Figure 7-10 The Locals window.

You can even change the value of a variable in the Locals window to test the variable. For example, click the Value column of *sInput* and change the value to **444**, as shown in Figure 7-11. You have just modified the value in memory, and the program will continue on with the new value.

Locals

Name	Value	Type
⊞ Me	{Throwback.Form1}	Throwback.Form1
⊞ sender	{System.Windows.Forms.Button}	Object
⊞ e	{System.EventArgs}	System.EventArgs
ArabicLower	0	Integer
⊞ Arabics	{Length=13}	Integer()
ArabicUpper	12	Integer
iCounter	0	Integer
iInput	0	Integer
⊞ Romans	{Length=13}	String()
sInput	"444"	String
sOutPut	""	String

Ready

Figure 7-11 You can dynamically change variables in the Locals window.

Stepping Through Our Code

You can step through your code using the Start, Break All, Stop Debugging, and Restart buttons on the Debug toolbar in the IDE. If the Debug toolbar, shown in Figure 7-12, is not displayed, right-click the main menu and be sure that the Debug and Debug Location choices are selected. The last three buttons are used for stepping through the code. These buttons are the ones that you'll use most often.

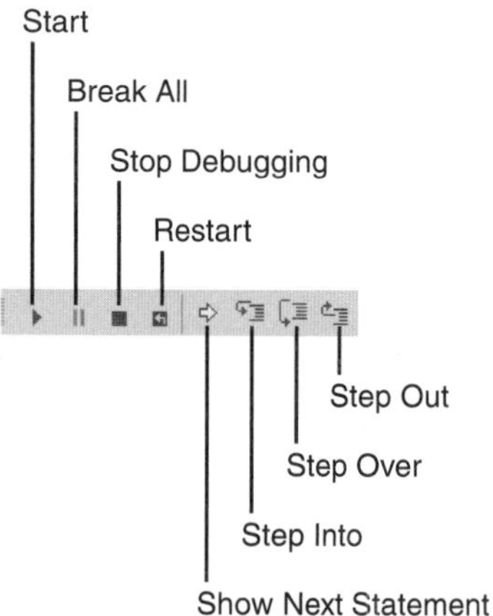

Figure 7-12 The Debug toolbar.

When you click the Start button, the program executes. Clicking the Stop Debugging button halts execution, terminates the program you are debugging, and ends the debugging session. Don't confuse stopping the debugging session with breaking execution, which just temporarily halts execution of the program you're debugging but leaves the debugging session active.

The Step Into button displays an arrow pointing to the next line of code. Use this button to step through lines one by one. (Pressing F8 performs the same operation as the Step Into button and eliminates a mouse click.) As you click the Step Into button, the variables will change in the Locals window as they are updated. You can see what your code is doing at each and every line of code.

The Step Over button shows an arrow pointing to the bottom of a code block. As the name implies, this button is used to step over sections of code. Let's say you have a function that returns a value. You know the function is completely debugged and not part of a problem you're trying to solve. You can use the Step Into button until you get to the line that calls the function. Then, by clicking the Step Over button, the code in the function executes but the debugger continues on as if this block were only a single line of executable code. So Step Into and Step Over differ only in one respect—the way they handle function calls. Each command instructs the debugger to execute the next unit of code. If the next unit contains a function call, Step Into executes only the call itself and then halts at the first unit of code inside the function. Step Over executes the entire function and halts at the first unit outside the function. Use Step Into if you want to look inside the function call. Use Step Over if you want to avoid stepping into functions.

The third step button is the Step Out button. Use the Step Out button when you're working inside a function call and want to return to the calling function. Step Out resumes execution of your code until the function returns and then breaks at the return point in the calling function.

You cannot access any of the step commands if your application is running. They are valid only in break mode or before you start the application.

Helpful Debugging Windows

For a more detailed inspection of your program, the Visual Studio .NET debugger provides a variety of windows and dialog boxes. Select Debug | Windows to select any of the windows described in Table 7-1. Set a breakpoint in the program and step through each line to get a feel for what information the various windows provide.

Table 7-1 The Debugging Windows

Use this debugging window	To view
Autos	Variables in the current and previous statement
Locals	All local variables
QuickWatch	Variables, register contents, and any valid expression recognized by the debugger
Watch	Variables, register contents, and any valid expression recognized by the debugger
Register	Register contents
Memory	Memory contents
Call Stack	Names of functions on the call stack, with the parameter types and values
Disassembly	Assembly code generated by the compiler for your program.
Threads	Information on sequential streams of execution (threads) created by your program
Modules	Modules (DLLs and EXEs) used in your program
Running Documents	List of script code loaded in the current process

Let's take a look in more detail at what some of these windows do for you and at some other details about the debugger.

Disassembly Window

In the Disassembly window you can see how the compiler distills your Visual Basic .NET code into assembly language. The simple assignment of an empty string to the text property of the *lblResult* label generates eight lines of assembly code, ending with the no operation (nop) line, as you can see in Figure 7-13.

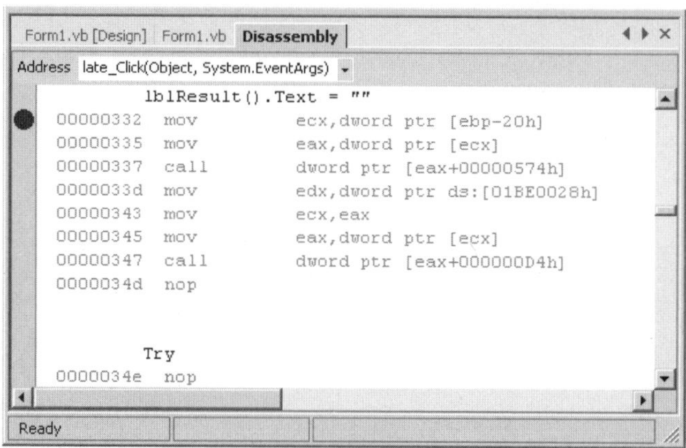

Figure 7-13 The Disassembly window.

The Disassembly window is helpful to view on occasion to remind us of how high level Visual Basic .NET really is. (I remember taking assembly programming back in grad school and actually liking its cold, clear logic, which I'm sure is some sort of personality disorder. Assembly language was actually the first high-level language in which programmers could use meaningful symbols instead of 0s and 1s.) The compiler translates the assembler generated from Visual Basic syntax into the common intermediate language (IL) file that is passed to the CLR.

> **Note** Bill Gates is said to often use the term *no-op* in meetings when he determines that a plan of action is not useful. He will say that this or that idea is a "no-op," referring to the assembly instruction meaning "no operation."

The Debugger Provides an Illusion to the Programmer

In case you're wondering how a program can run in debug mode, most CPUs actually have a special instruction set that is provided explicitly for the debugger. You set a breakpoint and can then step through your running program one line at a time. Single stepping allows the debugger to control the processor executing the program at such a fine level that only a single machine instruction at a time can be executed. After executing a single statement, the processor's debug mode returns control to the debugger program in Visual Basic .NET. The .NET debugger follows the Heisenberg Principle, which means that the debugger must intrude on the debugee program in a minimal way. In other words, we don't want to view our program as it acts when it is being debugged but how it acts during run time. (A great bumper sticker seen around town is "Heisenberg might have been here.")

In the previous section, we looked at the Disassembly window, which contains the assembly code for our program. The Visual Basic .NET compiler's job is to convert the source code into machine instructions. Behind the scenes, the debugger has the nontrivial task of mapping the machine code back to the original source code for us. Because it's the source code and not the machine code that the developer is interested in, the debugger is really a master of illusion. Because the Visual Basic .NET compiler provides extensive debugging information about the source code and how it was mapped to machine code, when we're debugging code it appears to us that it's the Visual Basic code that's executing line by line. In reality, the machine code is executing. However, by opening the various debugging windows, you can see the low-level detail that's taking place. The illusion that the debugger is executing the originally typed source code directly is compelling, but it is completely false. Pay no attention to the man behind the curtain.

If you examine the directory structure of your project, you can see that a Debug subdirectory is created automatically and populated for you, as shown in Figure 7-14. This folder contains the symbol maps that the debugger uses to provide its illusion.

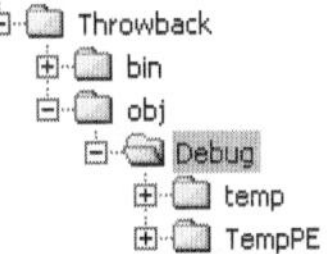

Figure 7-14 Each project contains a Debug subdirectory.

Configuring Your Debugger

In the course of writing any program, you will run into particularly hairy errors that are tough to track down. You can configure the debugger to break on any error, even if the error is handled. For example, you might have a default *Catch* statement such as the last *Catch* statement in our example earlier in the chapter. You might decide not to display a message box or other visible indication that an error has occurred; you include the statement because you simply don't want to crash the system. Having errors occur in these situations is common, but because you are catching the errors you never know they've happened. Not knowing about these errors is another "gotcha" that can result in you spending hours looking for something that won't show up because you protected yourself and the errors are being masked.

Select Exceptions from the Debug menu to display the Exceptions dialog box, shown in Figure 7-15. This dialog box includes four main groups of exceptions: C++, CLR, Native Run Time Checks, and Win32. Each main category can be expanded to show the types of exceptions in each. If you are using only Visual Basic .NET, you need to look at only the CLR exceptions. However, if you have added some unmanaged code such as an ActiveX control to your program, you will also be interested in the Win32 exceptions.

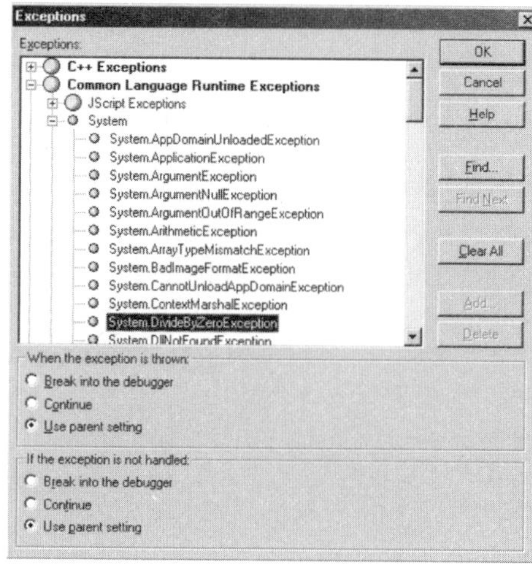

Figure 7-15 The Exceptions dialog box.

Notice the two frames at the bottom of the dialog box. The options in the upper frame configure how the debugger works when an exception is thrown. These options tell the debugger how to handle an exception immediately after it is thrown but before the program you are debugging has a chance to handle it. The options in the lower frame configure how the debugger reacts when an exception is not handled. An exception of this sort occurs after the program you are debugging has tried to handle it and failed.

The option you choose in either frame affects the exception chosen in the Exceptions list. If you were working with a program that does calculations, you would be interested in a divide-by-zero error, for example. If a category is chosen, the option selected will affect all the exceptions in that category, in this case all divide-by-zero errors. Here's more information on each of these options.

- **Break Into The Debugger** Causes the debugger to break execution of your program so that you can examine everything and handle the exception yourself. When this option is selected, the icon next to the exception or category name changes from gray to a large red ball with an X on it.
- **Continue** Allows execution to continue. When this option is selected, the icon next to the exception or category name looks like a large gray ball. This option will permit your exception handler to handle the error.
- **Use Parent Setting** Causes a specific exception to use the setting chosen for the parent node, which would be either Break Into Debugger or Continue. When this option is selected, the icon next to the exception or category name looks like a small gray ball.

The Find button opens a dialog box that allows you to search for an exception name in the Exceptions list. Using the Find button saves you from having to open each individual tree to find the exception name you're looking for. The Find Next button is used to find another occurrence of the exception. The Add button permits you to add a new exception to a selected category. The Delete button removes a user-added exception, and the Clear All button deletes all user-added exceptions.

The QuickWatch Window

Another handy window is the QuickWatch window, shown in Figure 7-16. Simply highlight the variable you want to watch while the debugger is running and press Shift+F9 or select QuickWatch from the Debug menu. You can check the variable you select one time or click Add Watch and the variable will be added to a list of variables on your watch list. This feature is particularly useful for keeping an eye on loop counters or variables that change often under certain circumstances. You can actually see the contents as the program executes.

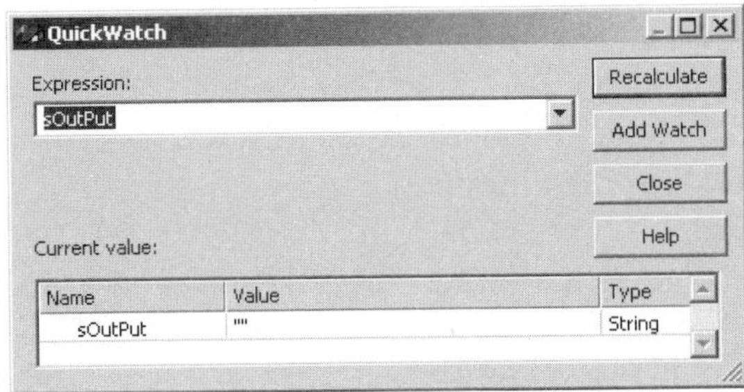

Figure 7-16 The QuickWatch window.

For more complicated programs, you'll find it useful to open several debugging windows simultaneously. Because the Locals window shows you all the local variables, the window can become crowded. If you want to keep tabs on a few specific variables, add them to your watch list, as shown in Figure 7-17. Then, if you need to look at the variables in your watch list, simply click the Watch tab at the bottom of the IDE. Using the watch list lets you isolate specific variables but quickly jump to any object in the entire running program.

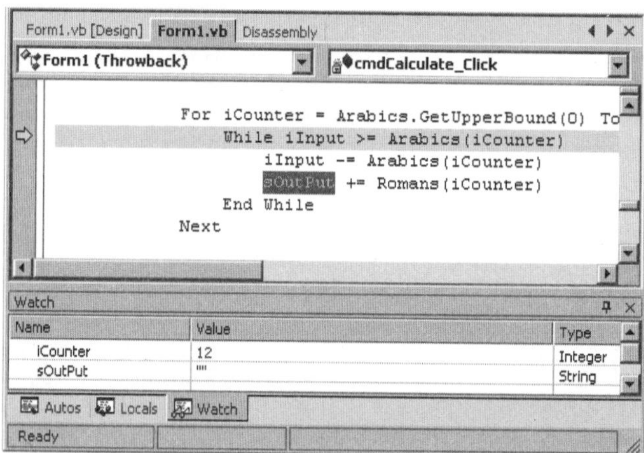

Figure 7-17 The watch list.

The Call Stack

When you add structured error handling to your code, it's important to understand how it works with respect to calling other procedures from within a protected *Try* block. If you call a procedure within a protected *Try* block, code execution transfers to that procedure. If an error occurs in that procedure, it will be handled locally by any defined *Try...Catch* blocks. If, however, no structured handling code is available in the procedure, the code transfers back to the caller. If no error handling is defined in the calling procedure, the code transfers execution up the calling stack until it finds an appropriate handler. If no handler is found, the error is handled (in a rather unfriendly way) by the common language runtime.

Let's say we call *procedure1*, which has a *Try...Catch* block. Then *procedure1* calls *procedure2*, which subsequently calls *procedure3*. Now *procedure3* attempts to divide by zero, which throws an exception.

When the code enters the protected *Try* block in *procedure1*, that error handler becomes active. As the execution transfers to the other procedures and an error is encountered in *procedure3*, the runtime checks whether an active error handler is defined locally. If the runtime doesn't find one, control continues up the call stack until an active handler is found. Consider the following example:

```
Call procedure1()
```

In *procedure1* we have a protected *Try...Catch* block. We will catch any CLR generated exception in that section. When the code completes, the *Finally* block is entered. As soon as code enters the *Try* block in *procedure1*, and until each line within the *Try* block is executing, that handler remains active.

```
Private Sub procedure1()
    Try
        sErrorMessage.Append("In procedure1, calling procedure2" _
            & CtrlChr.CrLf)
        procedure2()
    Catch e As Exception
        sErrorMessage.Append("Catch block in procedure1: " & _
            e.ToString & CtrlChr.CrLf)
    Finally
        sErrorMessage.Append("Finally in procedure1" & _
            CtrlChr.CrLf)
        MessageBox.Show(sErrorMessage.ToString, _
            "Error Stack Example", MessageBoxButtons.OK, _
            MessageBoxIcon.Information)
    End Try

End Sub

Private Sub procedure2()
    sErrorMessage.Append("In procedure2, calling procedure3" & _
        CtrlChr.CrLf)
    procedure3()
    sErrorMessage.Append("In procedure2, returned from " & _
        "procedure3 - never gets here" & CtrlChr.CrLf)
End Sub

Private Sub procedure3()
    Dim iNumerator As Integer = 32
    Dim iDenominator As Integer = 0
    Dim iResult As Integer = 0
    sErrorMessage.Append("In procedure3, generating error" & _
        CtrlChr.CrLf)
    iResult = iNumerator / iDenominator
    sErrorMessage.Append("In procedure3, after error - " & _
        "never gets here" & CtrlChr.CrLf)

End Sub
```

You can see that we go from *procedure1* to *procedure2* to *procedure3* and then generate an error. When the exception is thrown in *procedure3*, there is no active handler, so the code is transferred to *procedure2* and finally to *procedure1*, which does indeed have an active handler. Be sure you understand how the calling stack unwinds until a handler is found. Of course, the *Finally* block will always execute, as shown in Figure 7-18.

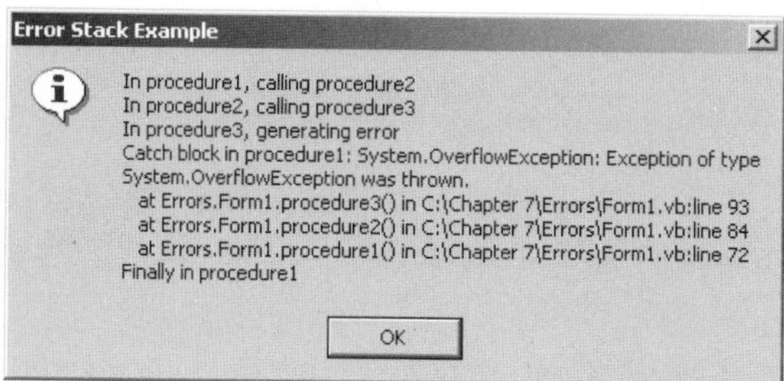

Figure 7-18 The call stack unwinds until a handler is found.

The call stack unwinding feature is great; we get the call stack automatically, which can be quite useful when diagnosing the source of an error. Notice that the source of the error, *procedure3*, is at the top of the stack. The error winds down to *procedure1*, where it is actually caught and handled.

The *Debug* and *Trace* Classes

Visual Basic .NET provides two classes, *Trace* and *Debug*, that contain methods for debugging your code. Both *Trace* and *Debug* are found in the *System.Diagnostics* namespace and have the same properties and methods. They do not derive from each other, however, or from any base class except *Object*. The difference between the two is that *Debug* is active when you define *#DEBUG* statements, and *Trace* is active when you define *#Trace* statements. *Debug* methods are enabled in the debug build of your code, and *Trace* methods are by default enabled in release builds.

Debug.WriteLine

Let's say you want to add a line to your code to see whether a denominator is 0. We never expect this to happen because we would receive a divide-by-zero error. Asserting that the denominator is not 0 will never execute unless, of course, we're wrong. Using *Debug.WriteLine* statements assist in finding any unexpected problems or conditions. You should use the *Debug.WriteLine* statement liberally in your code to ensure that it's behaving as you think it should. Here's an example:

```
Debug.WriteLine(iDenominator <> 0, "The denominator is 0.")
```

When you run the code, the *Debug.WriteLine* statement writes to the Debug window and tells you that the statement is false—the denominator is not 0.

```
'Errors.exe': Loaded 'c:\winnt\assembly\gac\accessibility\
 1.0.2411.0__b03f5f7f11d50a3a\accessibility.dll',
 No symbols loaded.
'Errors.exe': Loaded 'c:\winnt\assembly\gac\microsoft.visualbasic\
 7.0.0.0__b03f5f7f11d50a3a\microsoft.visualbasic.dll',
 No symbols loaded.
'Errors.exe': Loaded 'c:\winnt\assembly\gac\system.xml\
 1.0.2411.0__b77a5c561934e089\system.xml.dll',
 No symbols loaded.
The denominator is 0.: False
The program '[452] Errors.exe' has exited with code 0 (0x0).
```

When you run the *Debug.WriteLine* statement under the debugger, the assertion statement will be evaluated. However, in the release build, the comparison will not be made, so there is no additional overhead.

> **Note** Note: Use *Debug.Write* to write a partial line and *Debug.WriteLine* to have a carriage return and line feed (CrLf) appended to the output. *Debug.Flush* will ensure all text is printed.

Debug.Assert

Another handy method of the *Debug* class is the *Assert* method. This method is a bit more verbose than the *WriteLine* method and will provide the call stack in the output.

```
Private Sub procedure3()
        Dim iNumerator As Integer = 32
        Dim iDenominator As Integer = 0
        Dim iResult As Integer = 0

        Debug.Assert(iDenominator <> 0, "The denominator is 0.")
```

In this example, our assertion fails, and we are told so in no uncertain terms, as you can see in Figure 7-19.

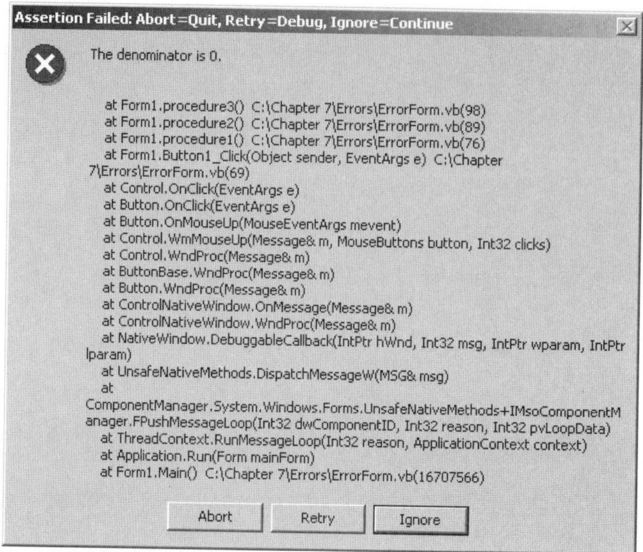

Figure 7-19 A failed assertion.

An assert statement tests a condition that you specify as an argument to the *Assert* method. If the condition evaluates to True, no action occurs. If the condition evaluates to False, the assertion fails. If you are running your program under the debugger, it enters break mode. The *Assert* method can be used from either the *Debug* class or the *Trace* class.

When you are ready to build your program for final release, bring up the properties page of your program by right-clicking the program icon in the Solution Explorer and then selecting Properties. Be sure to clear the Define *DEBUG* Constant check box on the Build page of the Configuration Properties. If you don't do this, the *Debug.Assert* statements will show up to a startled and disoriented user. Both the *DEBUG* and *TRACE* check boxes are checked by default in the debug build, meaning that they are given the value of 1, which is True.

When you modify the configuration for the release version, the *DEBUG* statement is unchecked by default. This will ensure that any *Debug* class methods such as *Assert* or *WriteLine* will be stripped out of the binary. The property page is shown in Figure 7-20.

During development, you can easily include a *#Const Debug = False* statement in your code to turn off any debugging messages as you work. You can then toggle debug messages on and off by changing the *Debug* constant.

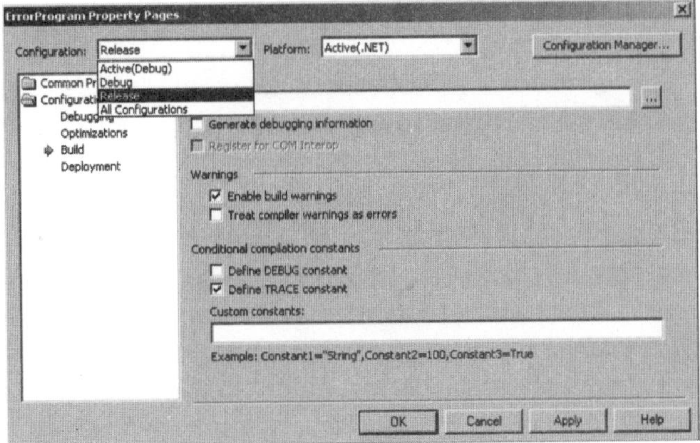

Figure 7-20 A project property page.

When using the *Debug.Assert* method, be sure that any code inside the *Assert* statement does not change the results of the program if the statement is removed. Otherwise, you might accidentally introduce a bug that shows up only in the release version of your program. You want to be especially careful about *Assert* statements that contain function or procedure calls. For example, consider the following line:

```
Debug.Assert (aFunction(iInteger) <> 0 )
```

While this *Debug.Assert* statement might appear safe at first glance, imagine that the function *aFunction* updates a counter each time it is called. When you build the release version, this call to *aFunction* is eliminated, so the counter will not be updated. This is known as a *side effect* because eliminating a call to a function has side effects that result in bugs that appear only in the release version. To avoid such problems, do not place function calls in a *Debug.Assert* statement. To modify the code to eliminate any unwanted side effects, you should use a temporary variable instead, as shown here:

```
iTempInteger = aFunction(iInteger)
Debug.Assert (iTempInteger <> 0)
```

Tracing

You want to use the *Debug* class while developing your application and include *Trace* statements in your deployed application. Placing *Trace* statements in your code permits you to print out information as your program executes and see what's going on in an application that has been deployed. A programmer needs to exercise care to place *Trace* statements strategically for use during run time. If you don't think through what exactly you would like to see in a running application, you could end up adding code that turns out to be useless for diagnosing problems after deployment. You must always consider what tracing information is likely to be needed in a deployed application.

The need for wise planning in your use of *Trace* statements contrasts with the use of debugging messages during testing, where you can place debugging statements almost anywhere in an application under development. Other than placing your *Trace* statements wisely because their presence will incur a slight performance cost, there are no general guidelines for what "strategic" placement of trace statements means. Applications that use tracing vary widely. Wisdom will come with experimentation and practice.

Adding a Tracing Class to Our Code

Developing a generalized class that will handle the output of *Trace* statements for us might make some sense. If we create this class, we won't have to write all the tracing code, check for levels, and so on for each line we want to trace in our application. Instead we will write and include a class called *ErrorTrace*, which *will permit* our application to create an instance of the *ErrorTrace* class and then pass in the information we want to trace. We can leave the determination of the details to the class.

> **Tip** The *ErrorTrace* class is on the companion disc as a class library project named Errors. (The library is a file named Errors.dll.) You can easily import this error tracing assembly to any new .NET program you write. When we discuss assemblies in Chapter 8, "Assemblies in Detail," you'll see how to strongly name and sign the new file so that it can be placed in the global assembly cache. This procedure gives it visibility (scope) to any program on the machine so that no matter which subdirectory you use to write a new Visual Basic .NET program, the Errors.dll file will always be available.

The following *ErrorTrace* class allows you to trace simple errors inside a program. Of course, this class could be greatly expanded; this example is just to get you thinking.

```
Imports System.IO
Imports System.Diagnostics

Public Class ErrorTrace

    Private m_errorFile As StreamWriter
    Private m_fileListener As TextWriterTraceListener
    Private m_sAppName As String = ""
    Private m_tsTraceSwitch As TraceSwitch


    Public Sub New(ByVal sApplication As String)

        Dim sEnv As String = _
            Environment.GetEnvironmentVariable("demoSwitch")


        m_tsTraceSwitch = New TraceSwitch("demoSwitch", _
            "demoSwitch")
        m_tsTraceSwitch.Level = CInt(sEnv)

        If m_tsTraceSwitch.Level = TraceLevel.Off Then Exit Sub

        m_errorFile = File.AppendText("C:\ErrorFile.txt")
        m_fileListener = New TextWriterTraceListener(m_errorFile)

        Trace.Listeners.Add(m_fileListener)


        m_sAppName = sApplication
        Trace.WriteLine(Date.Now & " Application: " & _
            m_sAppName & " started")
        Trace.WriteLine("Application Version: " & _
            Environment.Version.ToString)
        Trace.WriteLine("Current Directory: " & _
            Environment.CommandLine)
        Trace.WriteLine("Machine Name: " & _
            Environment.MachineName)
        Trace.WriteLine("Operating System: " & _
            Environment.OSVersion.ToString)
        Trace.WriteLine("User: " & Environment.UserName.ToString)
        Trace.WriteLine( _
            "-------------------------------------------")
    End Sub

    Public Sub writeError(ByVal eException As System.Exception)

        Trace.WriteLineIf(m_tsTraceSwitch.TraceInfo, _
            "Error: " & eException.Message)
```

(continued)

```
            Trace.WriteLineIf(m_tsTraceSwitch.TraceVerbose, _
                "Stack Trace: ")
            Trace.WriteLineIf(m_tsTraceSwitch.TraceVerbose, _
                eException.StackTrace)
            Trace.WriteLineIf(m_tsTraceSwitch.TraceVerbose, _
                "-----------------------------------")

        End Sub


        Public Sub writeText(ByVal sMessageToWrite As String)
            Trace.WriteLineIf(m_tsTraceSwitch.TraceInfo, _
                sMessageToWrite)
        End Sub


        Public Sub dispose()

            If m_tsTraceSwitch.Level = _
                System.Diagnostics.TraceLevel.Off Then
                Exit Sub
            End If

            Trace.WriteLine(Date.Now & "  Application: " & _
                m_sAppName & " ended")
            m_errorFile.Flush()
            m_errorFile.Close()

        End Sub

    End Class
```

Examining the *ErrorTrace.vb* Code

The *ErrorTrace* class includes four class-scoped variables that are visible to the entire class. The class will create a file that will log each *Trace* statement automatically, provided that a *Trace* variable is set to the level of output. More on this in a moment. First, let's take a look at our class module.

```
Imports System.IO
Imports System.Diagnostics
```

We import the *System.IO* namespace because we will be opening a file in which to write the information. Remember, the *ErrorTrace* class will be used in an application that we have deployed, so we could easily turn tracing on, create the file, and have the user send it to us via e-mail. (Or you could send the file to yourself through a firewall because it will be a simple text file.) The *System.Diagnostics* namespace is where the *Trace* class lives.

The four private member variables have class visibility. We will create an *m_errorFile* file to write our output to. We will then build a listener and a *TraceSwitch* object that will dictate how many entries should be written to the file. Also, because this class is meant to be generalized, *m_sAppName* will hold the name of the application that instantiates our class.

```
Public Class ErrorTrace

    Private m_errorFile As StreamWriter
    Private m_fileListener As TextWriterTraceListener
    Private m_sAppName As String = ""
    Private m_tsTraceSwitch As TraceSwitch
```

The *ErrorTrace.vb* Class Constructor

When we instantiate the class from an application, the constructor takes the name of the application. When we write information to a file, the class writes the name of the application being reported on to the file.

For the *Trace* object to provide the flexibility we want, we use a *TraceSwitch* object that can hold a value from 0 through 4. The *Trace* object will be set to one of these levels at run time, and the value will dictate what, if anything, will be printed to our file. Table 7-2 lists the values and the related outputs.

Table 7-2 TraceSwitch Levels

Enumerated value	Integer value	Type of message displayed (or written to a specified output target)
Off	0	None
Error	1	Only error messages
Warning	2	Warning messages and error messages
Info	3	Informational messages, warning messages, and error messages
Verbose	4	Verbose messages, informational messages, warning messages, and error messages

You can set the *TraceSwitch* level in three ways. The first way is through the registry. This approach is probably not a good idea because to use our class, we would have to write code to add keys to the client's registry. We really don't want users to have to go into the registry and set keys. The other two methods for setting the *TraceSwitch* level are by means of an environment variable. I'll discuss these operations after we wrap up our discussion of the class.

The *TraceSwitch* constructor takes two parameters: a name of the switch and a description of the switch. If the switch (in this case *demoSwitch*) can't be found, the *Trace* class is disabled. I've noticed that getting *TraceSwitch* to read the *demoSwitch* environment variable is erratic, but you can easily grab the value from the environment using *Environment.GetEnvironmentVariable* and passing in the variable you want, in this case our *demoSwitch* value. By using this approach you are guaranteed a foolproof method of reading the value, if any.

We then create the new switch that will be used when we print our information. This switch is assigned to the member variable *m_tsTraceSwitch*. Next we convert the value of *demoSwitch* that we've retrieved from the environment and assign it to the level property of our switch. Finally, if the variable is not set, it will evaluate to *TraceLevel.Off* and we will simply exit the constructor. We don't need to build a file if we are not tracing. Our code can lay dormant until the environment variable is set and we need to perform remote diagnostics.

```
Public Sub New(ByVal sApplication As String)

    Dim sEnv As String = _
        Environment.GetEnvironmentVariable("demoSwitch")


        m_tsTraceSwitch = New TraceSwitch("demoSwitch", _
            "demoSwitch")
        m_tsTraceSwitch.Level = CInt(sEnv)

        If m_tsTraceSwitch.Level = TraceLevel.Off Then Exit Sub
```

If we get past this *If* statement, we know that some level is set for our *m_tsTraceSwitch*. We create a file in the root directory and assign it to *m_errorFile*. Of course, you could enhance the program to create the file right in the directory of the application or on a remote drive.

Once the file is created, we create a *TextWriterTraceListener object*. This object initializes a new instance of the *TextWriterTraceListener* class with *TextWriter* as the recipient of the output. Once that instance is created, we add it to the *Listeners* collection of the *Trace* object. Other listeners permit us to send the output to a stream or to the console. Here we instruct the trace to be sent to the file ErrorFile.txt.

```
m_errorFile = File.AppendText("C:\ErrorFile.txt")
m_fileListener = New TextWriterTraceListener(m_errorFile)

Trace.Listeners.Add(m_fileListener)
```

If any trace level is set, we send some specifics to our log file about the time the application started, its version, where it's located on the user's machine, the current version of the operating system, and the current user. The *WriteLine* method of the *Trace* object sends each piece of information to its own line in the file.

```
m_sAppName = sApplication
    Trace.WriteLine(Date.Now & " Application: " & _
        m_sAppName & " started")
    Trace.WriteLine("Application Version: " & _
        Environment.Version.ToString)
    Trace.WriteLine("Current Directory: " & _
        Environment.CommandLine)
    Trace.WriteLine("Machine Name: " & Environment.MachineName)
    Trace.WriteLine("Operating System: " & _
        Environment.OSVersion.ToString)
    Trace.WriteLine("User: " & Environment.UserName.ToString)
    Trace.WriteLine( _
        "---------------------------------------")
    End Sub
```

Now our class is set up and waiting for any information to be sent from an error. Of course, you should be sure that you place the *writeError* procedure in a *Catch* statement in the running application because it takes an exception as a parameter. Unless *TraceLevel* is set to at least *TraceInfo* (a value of 3), the error message will not be printed. If the *TraceLevel* is verbose (a value of 4), the stack trace will be printed as well.

```
Public Sub writeError(ByVal eException As System.Exception)

    Trace.WriteLineIf(m_tsTraceSwitch.TraceInfo, _
        "Error: " & eException.Message)
    Trace.WriteLineIf(m_tsTraceSwitch.TraceVerbose, _
        "Stack Trace: ")
    Trace.WriteLineIf(m_tsTraceSwitch.TraceVerbose, _
        eException.StackTrace)
    Trace.WriteLineIf(m_tsTraceSwitch.TraceVerbose, _
        "-----------------------------------")

End Sub
```

I've also added a simple procedure that will write a line of text to the file. With this procedure you can easily add information such as "Entering procedure3" to see where the program is at any particular time.

```
Public Sub writeText(ByVal sMessageToWrite As String)
    Trace.WriteLineIf(m_tsTraceSwitch.TraceInfo, _
        sMessageToWrite)
End Sub
```

Finally, when the application that instantiated our class is closed, the *dispose* method is called. With this call, we can log the time the application stopped running and be sure that all entries are flushed to the file. Being good .NET citizens, we then close the file.

```
Public Sub dispose()

    If m_tsTraceSwitch.Level = _
        System.Diagnostics.TraceLevel.Off Then
        Exit Sub
    End If

    Trace.WriteLine(Date.Now & "  Application: " & _
        m_sAppName & " ended")
    m_errorFile.Flush()
    m_errorFile.Close()

End Sub

End Class
```

Setting the Trace Level

Sending any information to the ErrorFile.txt file is predicated on having a trace level set. As I mentioned, you can set the level in several ways. First, you can add an entry to the registry such as this:

```
HKEY_LOCAL_MACHINE\SOFTWARE\Microsoft\COMPlus\Switches\
 <switch name>
```

If any of the entries in this key, for example *Switches*, are not present, you have to add them. Next you add the name of the switch (*demoSwitch* in our case) and a value from 0 through 4. As you can see, asking a user to do this over the phone is a dangerous proposition. You could write a helper program (or add an option to your application's menus) that would add these registry settings programmatically, but setting the trace level by using an environment variable is easier.

To start, simply bring up a command prompt and type **SET demoSwitch=3.** This command will add the variable to the environment. Another, more user friendly, way is to right-click My Computer on the desktop and select Properties from the shortcut menu. Click the Advanced tab, and then click Environment Variables. Under the System Variables box, click New. In the New System Variable dialog box, shown in Figure 7-21, you can add your variable and a value.

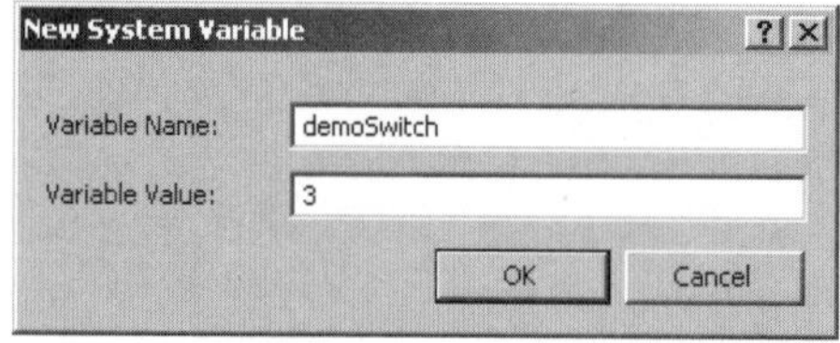

Figure 7-21 You can add a new environment variable and its value in the New System Variable dialog box.

When you click OK, the variable and value are added to the environment, as you can see in Figure 7-22.

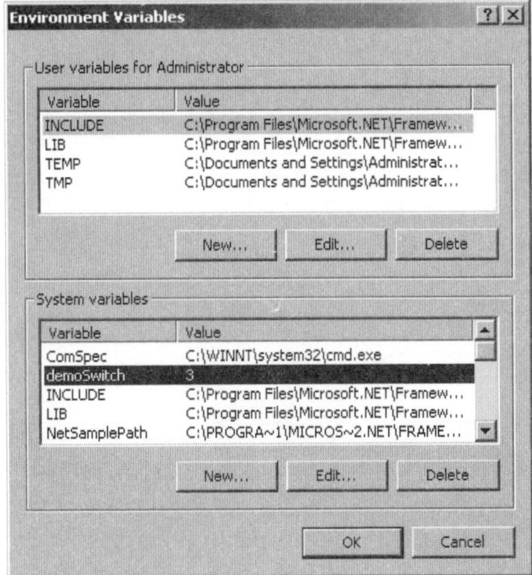

Figure 7-22 The environment variable and its value are added to the environment.

You can display a command prompt and type **set** to see the effects of your work in these dialog boxes. This command shows you all the environment variables. You can see in Figure 7-23 that *demoSwitch* is set to 3.

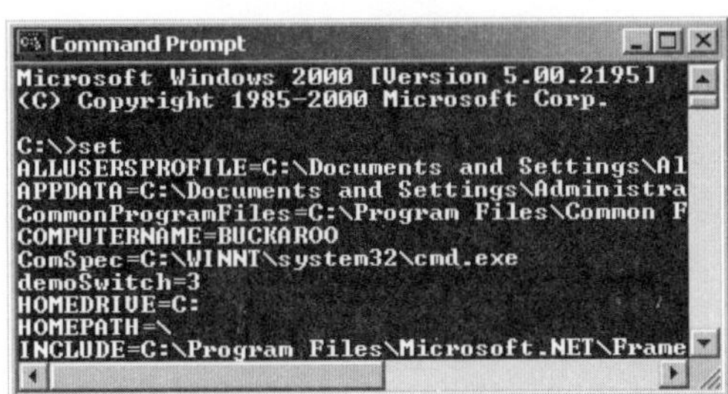

Figure 7-23 The *set* command lists environment variables and their values.

Adding the *Errors.vb* Class to a Program

I'll use the code that generated a divide-by-zero error, presented earlier in the chapter, to demonstrate our new class. The first operation we perform is importing the *Errors.ErrorTrace* namespace. (You'll also need to add a reference to Errors.dll.) This namespace contains the *ErrorTrace* class located in the Errors files we added to the project earlier.

```
Imports Errors.ErrorTrace
```

We also want to import the following two statements.

```
Imports System.Text
Imports CtrlChrs = Microsoft.VisualBasic.ControlChars
```

Remember the discussion about aliasing an imports statement? We want to add a carriage return and line feed after each line. If we imported only the *Microsoft.VisualBasic.ControlChars* namespace, for each carriage return and line feed we would need to write the statement

```
Microsoft.VisualBasic.ControlCharsCtrlChrs.CrLf
```

Instead of the statement

```
CtrlChrs.CrLf
```

If an *Imports* statement does not include an alias name such as *CtrlChrs*, elements defined within the imported namespace can sometimes be used in the module without qualification. However, if an alias name is specified, it must be used as a qualifier for names contained within that namespace.

Next we dimension and create a new instance of our *Errors.ErrorTrace* class and pass in the name of the current application. I've used "Test Error Program" in this example. Be sure that the new *ErrorTrace* object is dimensioned with class scope so that its methods can be seen throughout the class.

```
Dim sErrorMessage As New StringBuilder()
Dim etErrorTracing As _
    New Errors.ErrorTrace("Test Error Program")
```

We want to be sure that any text is flushed to our file and that the file closes properly. One way to be sure these operations occur is to explicitly dispose of our *etErrorTracing* object.

```
Form overrides dispose to clean up the component list.
Protected Overloads Overrides Sub Dispose(ByVal disposing _
    As Boolean)
    If disposing Then
        If Not (components Is Nothing) Then
            components.Dispose()
        End If
    End If

    etErrorTracing.dispose()
    MyBase.Dispose(disposing)
End Sub
```

Let's add a line in a subroutine named *procedure1* that will write the error to our trace file. We simply need to call the *writeError* method of our *etErrorTracing* object and pass in the error object for it to trace.

```
Private Sub procedure1()
    Try
        sErrorMessage.Append("In procedure1, calling " & _
            "procedure2" & CtrlChrs.CrLf)
        procedure2()
    Catch e As Exception

         etErrorTracing.writeError(e)

        sErrorMessage.Append("Catch block in procedure1: " & _
            e.ToString & CtrlChrs.CrLf)
    Finally
        sErrorMessage.Append("Finally in procedure1" & _
            CtrlChrs.CrLf)
        MessageBox.Show(sErrorMessage.ToString, _
            "Error Stack Example", MessageBoxButtons.OK, _
            MessageBoxIcon.Information)
    End Try

End Sub

Private Sub procedure2()
    sErrorMessage.Append("In procedure2, calling procedure3" & _
        CtrlChrs.CrLf)
    procedure3()
    sErrorMessage.Append("In procedure2, returned from " & _
        "procedure3 - never gets here" & CtrlChrs.CrLf)
End Sub
```

Now we can check the *writeText* method by passing it some text. As you can see, with our new class handling the heavy lifting involved in creating files, adding a listener, determining the levels to print, and cleaning up when the application exits, we can simply add lines to the application.

```
Private Sub procedure3()
    Dim iNumerator As Integer = 32
    Dim iDenominator As Integer = 0
    Dim iResult As Integer = 0

    etErrorTracing.writeText("In procedure3 - just " & _
        "before the error.")
    sErrorMessage.Append("In procedure3,generating error" & _
        CtrlChrs.CrLf)
    iResult = iNumerator / iDenominator
    sErrorMessage.Append("In procedure3, after error - " & _
        "never gets here" & CtrlChrs.CrLf)

End Sub
```

When your application is deployed and starts behaving badly, you can set an environmental variable and automatically generate a trace file for your evaluation. Because our *demoSwitch* variable is currently set to 3, we see only informational messages, warning messages, and error messages. If we add a call to *procedure1* in the form's *Load* event and run the program, the output will look like the data shown in Figure 7-24.

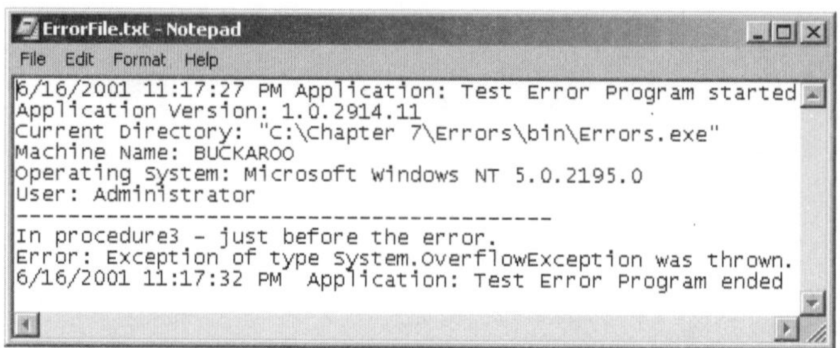

Figure 7-24 The error log receives informational messages, warning messages, and error messages when *demoSwitch* is set to 3.

We can see when the application started and stopped, as well as all sorts of helpful information about the application—where it's located on the drive, machine name, operating system, and the current user. The log shows that the first error occurred in *procedure3*, where an *OverFlowException* error was thrown. We might want to check the call stack and any other information that can be seen in the Verbose mode. Of course, we would have to change the environment variable *demoSwitch* from 3 (Info) to 4 (Verbose).

You can use the Advanced tab of the properties sheet for My Computer and edit the value of *demoSwitch*, changing it from 3 to 4, or you can bring up a command prompt and type **Set demoSwitch=4**. Either technique will change the environment. Unfortunately, you will have to restart Visual Studio .NET to see the change. Also, when the environment variable is read by the .NET common language runtime, the runtime performs some optimizations and reads the variable only once. If the value changes, you have to stop your application and restart it. This situation applies only if you are using an environment variable to hold the switch value. When you change the value of *demoSwitch* to Verbose, the stack trace information is now printed to our file. You can see the results in Figure 7-25.

As I mentioned earlier, the first parameter of the *Trace.WriteLineIf* method is a Boolean that determines whether the line is printed. Because the value of *demoSwitch* is now 4, the complete verbose information such as the stack trace is now printed.

```
Trace.WriteLineIf(m_tsTraceSwitch.TraceVerbose, _
    "Stack Trace: ")
Trace.WriteLineIf(m_tsTraceSwitch.TraceVerbose, _
    eException.StackTrace)
```

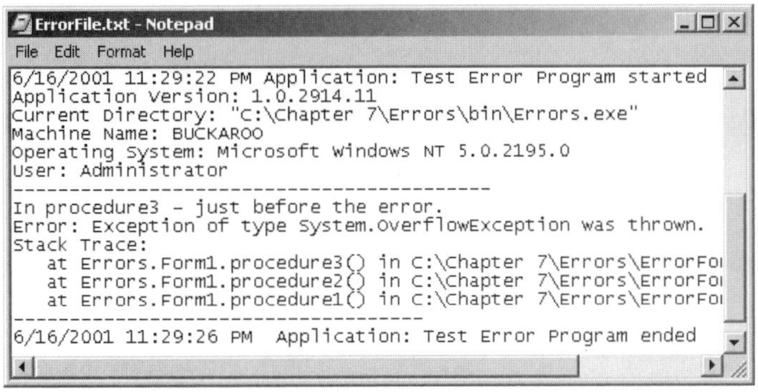

```
ErrorFile.txt - Notepad
File Edit Format Help
6/16/2001 11:29:22 PM Application: Test Error Program started
Application Version: 1.0.2914.11
Current Directory: "C:\Chapter 7\Errors\bin\Errors.exe"
Machine Name: BUCKAROO
Operating System: Microsoft Windows NT 5.0.2195.0
User: Administrator
--------------------------------------
In procedure3 - just before the error.
Error: Exception of type System.OverflowException was thrown.
Stack Trace:
   at Errors.Form1.procedure3() in C:\Chapter 7\Errors\ErrorFo
   at Errors.Form1.procedure2() in C:\Chapter 7\Errors\ErrorFo
   at Errors.Form1.procedure1() in C:\Chapter 7\Errors\ErrorFo
--------------------------------------
6/16/2001 11:29:26 PM  Application: Test Error Program ended
```

Figure 7-25 The error log receives verbose messages when demoSwitch is set to 4.

When you deploy your Visual Basic .NET application, the trace switch is disabled so that users need not observe a lot of irrelevant trace messages appearing on a screen or, in our case, filling up a log file as the application runs. However, if a problem arises in the field, you can stop the application, enable the switches, and restart the application. Once you've done this, the tracing messages will be written to the file.

If the *TraceSwitch* constructor in our class cannot find initial switch settings in the environment, the level of the new switch is set to *TraceLevel.Off*. Also, when your application executes the code that creates an instance of a switch for the first time, it checks the configuration system for trace level information about the named switch. The tracing system examines the configuration system only once for any particular switch: when your application creates the switch for the first time. In a deployed application, you can customize the tracing code by reconfiguring switch objects when the application isn't running. If you are using the registry, making these modifications involves changing the tracing levels and then restarting your application. If you are using the environment to store the values, you usually have to reboot to flush the old value and insert the new.

Adding Event Logging to Your Programs

In keeping with the diagnostics flavor of this chapter, let's see how easy it is to add event logging to a program. If you are running Windows 98, Windows NT 4,

Windows Me, Windows 2000, or Windows XP, you can easily add event-logging features to your programs. You can then see information about the events you log in the Event Viewer, which you open from the Administrative Tools window in Control Panel.

The Event Viewer is used by professional applications to log activity, especially any rogue activity such as errors, the absence of disk space or memory, and so on. We can use our Test Error Program to see how various events could be logged, as shown in Figure 7-26.

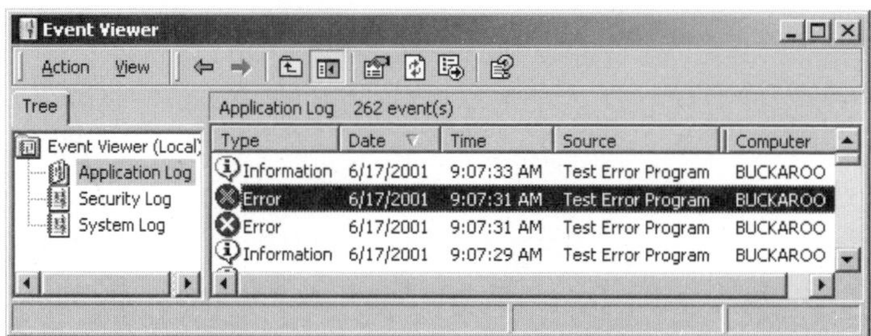

Figure 7-26 The Event Viewer lets you log events in your programs.

Double-clicking on the highlighted error will display that event's properties. The properties include the date, time, and source of the event, as well as a description of what happened, as you can see in Figure 7-27. Because of the power of the .NET Framework, adding this professional touch to your program simply takes a few lines of code.

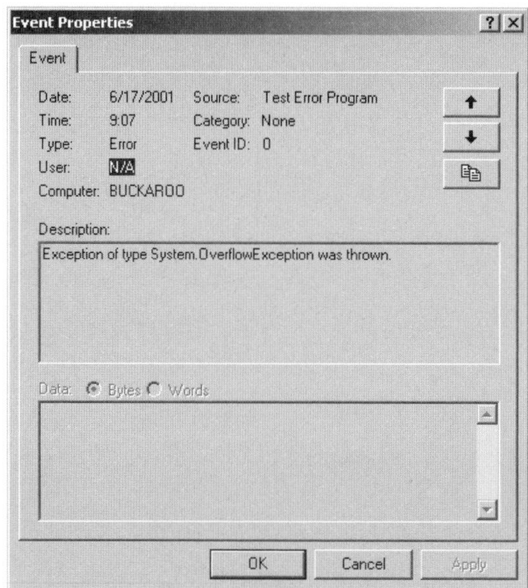

Figure 7-27 Event details.

The Philosophy of Logging Events to the Event Viewer

Event logging in the latest versions of Microsoft Windows provides a standard, centralized way for your Visual Basic .NET applications to record important software and hardware events. For example, when an error occurs, the system administrator or a support technician must determine what caused the error, attempt to recover any lost data, and prevent the error from recurring. As you can imagine, it's helpful if not only applications but also the operating system and other system services record important events. These events might be occurrences such as low-memory conditions or failed attempts to access a disk. The system administrator can use the event log to help determine what conditions caused the error and the context in which it occurred.

The Windows Event Viewer is a standard user interface for viewing these event logs and also a programming interface for examining log entries. In Visual Basic .NET, you use the *EventLog* class, which permits you to easily connect to event logs on both local and remote computers and write entries to these logs. You can also read entries from existing logs and create your own custom event logs.

An *event*, as defined in Windows, is any significant occurrence—whether in the operating system or in an application—that requires users to be notified. Critical events are sent to the user in the form of an immediate message on the screen. Other event notifications are written to one of several *event logs* that record the information for future reference. Every event log entry is classified into one of the following categories: errors, warnings, information, success audits, or failure audits.

Basically, three event logs are available by default on computers running Windows XP, Windows 2000 or Windows NT 4:

- *System log*, which tracks various events that occur on system components, such as drivers
- *Security log*, which tracks security changes and possible breaches
- *Application log*, which tracks events that occur in a registered application, such as the Test Error Program.

In addition to these logs, application services such as Active Directory can create their own default logs. Visual Basic .NET gives you the ability to create your own custom logs using classes in the *System.Diagnostics* namespace.

> **Note** Event logs are installed as part of Windows. You must have either Windows XP, Windows NT version 4, or Windows 2000 installed on the computer on which you do your development work in order to create and test the *EventLog* object.

What to Log as an Event

As you can see, we want to log only major events to the Event Viewer, but we can be more liberal with tracing. You usually only want to spawn messages to the Event Viewer that reflect computer resource problems. For example, if an application enters a low-memory situation that degrades its performance, logging a warning event when memory allocation fails might provide a clue about what went wrong. You also want to consider logging certain information events. For example, a server-based application might use a database to record a user logging on, opening a database, or starting a file transfer. The server can also log error events it encounters such as the inability to access a file, loss of a connection, file corruptions, or FTP success or failure messages. Be judicious about any event sent to the viewer.

Event logging does consume resources such as disk space and processor time. The amount of disk space that an event log requires and the overhead for an application that logs events depend on how much information you choose to log. Therefore, it is important to log only essential information. It is also best to place event log calls in an error path in the code rather than in the main code path, as we did in our example, so as to not reduce performance. Also, if you send several useless messages to the event viewer, not only does that crowd out messages from other applications, but it also creates a false equality—if every message is important then no message is important. In other words, choose your event messages wisely, Grasshopper.

Adding Event Logging to the *ErrorTrace.vb* Class

Open the code module that contains the *ErrorTrace* class, and add a private class member that will hold a reference to the *EventLog* object. (Instead of using the DLL I created earlier, I copied the *ErrorTrace* class file to this project's folder and then added the class to the project.)

```
Public Class ErrorTrace

    Private m_errorFile As StreamWriter
    Private m_fileListener As TextWriterTraceListener
    Private m_sAppName As String = ""
    Private m_tsTraceSwitch As TraceSwitch
    Private m_elEventLog As EventLog

    Private m_isEventWriter As Boolean
```

Because we need to add only a few additional lines to our constructor, we will modify its signature instead of overloading it. The ratio of new lines to the size of the constructor is so small that this is the best design choice. If the user sends *True* as a parameter for the *addEventWriter* variable, our code adds a new *EventLog*. Because the variable *m_elEventLog* is defined with class scope, we can use it anywhere in the class.

```
Public Sub New(ByVal sApplication As String, _
    ByVal addEventWriter As Boolean)

    Dim sEnv As String =  _
        Environment.GetEnvironmentVariable("demoSwitch")

    m_tsTraceSwitch = New TraceSwitch("demoSwitch",  _
        "Testing the TraceSwitch")
    m_tsTraceSwitch.Level = CInt(sEnv)

    If m_tsTraceSwitch.Level = TraceLevel.Off Then Exit Sub

    m_errorFile = File.AppendText("C:\ErrorFile.txt")
    m_fileListener = New TextWriterTraceListener(m_errorFile)

    Trace.Listeners.Add(m_fileListener)

    m_sAppName = sApplication

    m_isEventWriter = addEventWriter 'used when disposing

    '-- Do we want to log info to the event log also?

    If (m_isEventWriter = True) Then
        m_elEventLog = New EventLog("Application", ".", _
            sApplication)
        m_elEventLog.WriteEntry(Date.Now & " Application: " & _
            m_sAppName & " started", EventLogEntryType.Information)
    End If

    '-Write information to our file -
    Trace.WriteLine(Date.Now & " Application: " & m_sAppName & _
        " started")
    Trace.WriteLine("Application Version: " & _
        Environment.Version.ToString)
    Trace.WriteLine("Current Directory: " & _
        Environment.CommandLine)
    Trace.WriteLine("Machine Name: " & Environment.MachineName)
    Trace.WriteLine("Operating System: " & _
        Environment.OSVersion.ToString)
    Trace.WriteLine("User: " & Environment.UserName.ToString)
    Trace.WriteLine("----------------------------------------")
End Sub
```

If the user wants certain events to be logged in the Event Viewer, True is placed in the second parameter of the constructor. If this value is used, we then create a new instance of the *EventLog* object. We pass in three parameters to the *EventLog* constructor:

- The log file that the events will write to. Recall that we looked in the Application Log on the left side of the viewer.
- The machine to log events from. The period (.) provides the default for the current machine. However, you could specify any other machine, such as a web server.
- The description that will show up in the Source column of the event. Traditionally, the application posting the message places its name in this column.

Then we write a simple message stating the time the application started. The *WriteEntry* method is overloaded and permits each message to have a category type, such as *Information*. You'll see in a minute when we write an error that we designate the message as category type *Error* and the appropriate icon is displayed for us.

```
If (addEventWriter = True) Then
    m_elEventLog = New EventLog("Application", ".", _
        sApplication)
    m_elEventLog.WriteEntry(Date.Now & " Application: " & _
        m_sAppName & " started", EventLogEntryType.Information)
End If
```

We could have added our *m_elEventLog* to the *Listeners* collection of the *Trace* object, using a statement such as this:

```
Trace.Listeners.Add(m_elEventLog)
```

However, if we did this, any message that was sent to the trace code based on the *TraceSwitch* would also be sent to the *event log*. As you can imagine, this flood of messages could quickly fill the event log. However, if you ever need to do this, no more code is necessary. All messages printed with *Trace* would send all messages to the listeners, which in our case would be the text file and the event log. As a design decision, we decided to keep trace statements and event logs separate. But in doing so, we have to add a few specialized procedures to accept messages to be logged.

One event we definitely want to log is an error. Simply add this line to the *writeError* procedure. Because this event is an error, pass in the *Error* enumerated category type for the *EventLogEntryType, which* will display the red ball with the X.

```
Public Sub writeError(ByVal eException As System.Exception)

    Trace.WriteLineIf(m_tsTraceSwitch.TraceInfo, _
        "Error: " & eException.Message)
    Trace.WriteLineIf(m_tsTraceSwitch.TraceVerbose, _
        "Stack Trace: ")
    Trace.WriteLineIf(m_tsTraceSwitch.TraceVerbose, _
        eException.StackTrace)
    Trace.WriteLineIf(m_tsTraceSwitch.TraceVerbose, _
        "------------------------------------")

    'Write any error to the event log

    If (m_isEventWriter = True) Then

        m_elEventLog.WriteEntry(eException.Message, _

            EventLogEntryType.Error)

    End If

End Sub
```

Now add the following two procedures to the class. As you can see, one is used for logging an informational message, and the other for a warning message. The *Information* and *Warning* enumerated values are already included, so it's painless to use these procedures from outside the class. Of course, adding the code above already performs the logging of an error.

```
Public Sub writeEventLogInformation(ByVal sMessage As String)
    m_elEventLog.WriteEntry(sMessage, _
        EventLogEntryType.Information)
End Sub

Public Sub writeEventLogWarning(ByVal sMessage As String)
    m_elEventLog.WriteEntry(sMessage, _
        EventLogEntryType.Warning)
End Sub
```

Finally, when our class is disposed of, we are going to write a message to the event log indicating that the program has terminated. By interrogating the Boolean member variable *m_isEventWriter*, we can determine whether the event log is active. If it is, we can write the informational message to it.

```
Public Sub dispose()
    If m_tsTraceSwitch.Level = System.Diagnostics.TraceLevel.Off Then
        Exit Sub
    End If

    Trace.WriteLine(Date.Now & "  Application: " & _
        m_sAppName & " ended")
    If (m_isEventWriter = True) Then
        m_elEventLog.WriteEntry(Date.Now & " Application: " & _
            m_sAppName & " ended.", _
            EventLogEntryType.Information)    End If

    m_errorFile.Flush()
    m_errorFile.Close()
End Sub
```

Using Our New Event Logging Capability

To see how our new event logging capability works, we'll again use the code that generates the divide-by-zero error. First, the signature for the constructor changes, so we have to add a second Boolean parameter to tell our class whether we want to use error logging.

```
Imports System.Text
Imports CtrlChrs = Microsoft.VisualBasic.ControlChars

Public Class Form1
    Inherits System.Windows.Forms.Form

    Dim sErrorMessage As New StringBuilder()
    Dim etErrorTracing As _
        New Errors.ErrorTrace("Test Error Program", _
        True)
```

Now the user of our class can see that the parameter takes either True or False for the *addEventWriter* parameter. As you can see in Figure 7-28, naming parameters with useful names can make using our class a breeze.

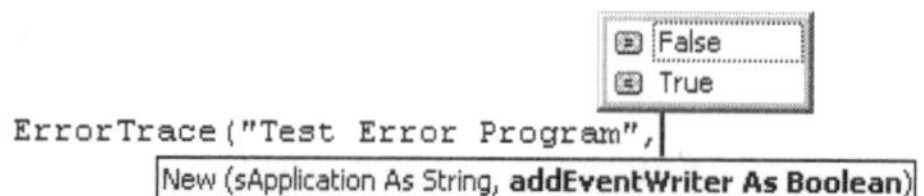

Figure 7-28 Descriptive parameter names simplify the use of our class.

Because we are already writing an error to the event log, we don't need to change the *writeError* method. Recall that our class also logs any error to both the file and the event log automatically.

```
Private Sub procedure1()
    Try
        sErrorMessage.Append("In procedure1, calling " & _
            "procedure2" & CtrlChrs.CrLf)
        procedure2()
    Catch e As Exception
        etErrorTracing.writeError(e)
        sErrorMessage.Append("Catch block in procedure1: " & _
            e.ToString & CtrlChrs.CrLf)
    Finally
        sErrorMessage.Append("Finally in procedure1" & _
            CtrlChrs.CrLf)
        MessageBox.Show(sErrorMessage.ToString, "Error Stack _
        Example", MessageBoxButtons.OK, MessageBoxIcon.Information)
    End Try

End Sub
```

Now, anywhere we want to add an event for either information or warning purposes, we can simply choose the correct method, as you can see in Figure 7-29. Our class will handle the behind the scenes details.

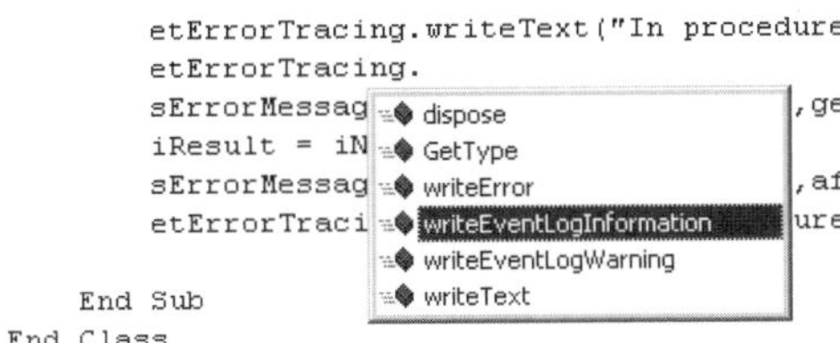

Figure 7-29 Our class makes it easy to add information and warning messages.

Conclusion

That's it. You have just learned how to debug programs and to proactively use structured error and both the *Debug* and *Trace* objects. And we also covered how to write entries to the event log, encapsulating everything in a class. You could easily create another class that simply handles event log entries. By importing the namespace of the class into any of your programs, you are automatically given a powerful way to log important activity in your programs.

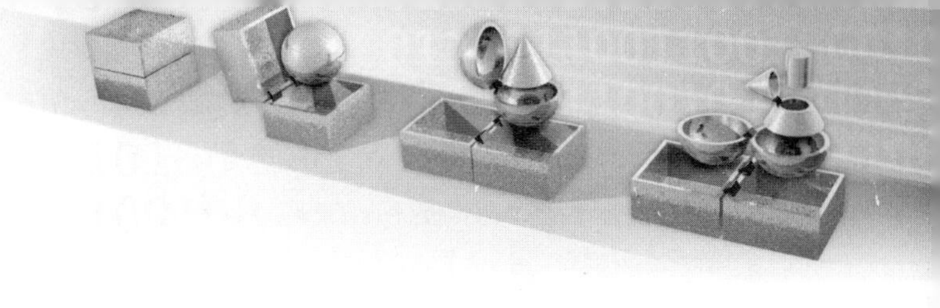

8

Assemblies in Detail

We've used the Microsoft .NET Framework for each of the programs we've written so far, and while I've described how assemblies are used for deployment and you have an idea of what they are, the time has come to dig a bit deeper into assemblies in order to fully understand them. In this chapter, we'll write a program that examines any assembly available to you. In the process of developing this program and learning more about assemblies, you'll also become familiar with a few more of the Visual Basic .NET controls.

The Right to Assemble

As I mentioned previously, assemblies are the building blocks of .NET Framework applications. Assemblies form the fundamental unit for managing deployment, version control, reuse, and security permissions. An assembly is really a collection of types and resources that are built to work together and form a logical unit of functionality. An assembly provides the common language runtime (CLR) with the information it needs to be aware of type implementations in an application. To the runtime, a type does not exist outside the context of an assembly.

We can look closely at assemblies with a technology called *reflection*. If you've accessed COM type libraries in a classic Visual Basic program, the concept of reflection in .NET will be familiar to you. However, reflection is now quite a bit more powerful and much easier to use. When you compile a Visual Basic source file with a .NET compiler, the compiler emits the intermediate language (IL) for the statements in the source file, along with the metadata that fully describes the types defined in the file. It is the metadata that the reflection classes in .NET use to examine the types.

An assembly contains one or more modules. How is this so? A module is a portable executable (PE) file with the extension .dll or .exe that consists of one or more classes and interfaces. A single module can contain multiple namespaces, and a namespace can span multiple modules. Therefore, an assembly is composed of one or more modules.

What makes assemblies different from classic Visual Basic EXE or DLL files is that they contain everything that would usually be found in a type library. As you know, an assembly contains a manifest, which is much like a table of contents. The manifest contains key information such as the assembly's name and version, all the files that make up the assembly (other DLLs, bitmaps, resources, readme files, and so on), and external dependencies.

Because assemblies are self-describing, Visual Basic .NET applications do not rely on registry values, which means that DLL conflicts are reduced and your applications are made more reliable and easier to deploy. To use an assembly, first a reference to the assembly is created and then the *Imports* statement is used to choose the namespaces of the items within the assembly you want to use.

Private Assemblies

Up to now we've been building private assemblies. Private assemblies are stored in the directory of the application and are used exclusively for a specific .NET program. You know that with the older-style DLLs, if a bug fix or enhanced functionality required a new version of the file to be installed, each program that needed this file used the new version automatically. The older version was overwritten by the new DLL. Of course, many times applications that worked just fine mysteriously crashed when another program installed a newer version of a DLL. Because we are storing our assemblies in the same directory as our application, this problem is obviated.

Private assemblies will usually be developed by a single company and will be used by a single application. Disk space is cheap, so storage is not a problem. And because we're in control of our assembly, we don't need to worry about our file being overwritten by a rogue application. If an application uses private assemblies, the application is usually packaged and deployed together with all its assemblies.

Sometimes, however, an assembly written by one company will be used by an application written by another. These companies are probably not coordinating their naming conventions, so the second company could easily develop an assembly that has the same name as the assembly from the first company. If we install two different programs that happen to have the same name, we are courting trouble. Luckily, the .NET Framework has an elegant solution to what was once a thorny problem.

Shared Assemblies

All of the development assemblies used for writing Visual Basic .NET programs are shared assemblies. Shared assemblies are similar to shared DLLs in the \Windows\System directory that are used by classic Visual Basic, Microsoft Windows, Microsoft Access, and other Windows programs. However, .NET ensures that each program uses only the assembly that it was compiled against. How is this accomplished?

Assemblies used in programs targeted for .NET are usually stored in the \Windows\Assembly folder. This folder is for global assemblies (such as *Microsoft.VisualBasic*) that can be used by any .NET program on your machine. When a Visual Basic .NET program is installed on a machine, the Visual Basic namespaces can be referenced automatically from this cache.

For developers using Visual Studio .NET, the public assemblies we just discussed are also stored in the Visual Studio development directories, so you actually have two copies on your machine. However, it's the \Assembly folder that's used to store assemblies on your users' machines for any .NET program you might distribute. Open the \Windows\Assembly folder on your computer—a view of mine is shown in Figure 8-1. You can right-click an assembly to take a look at its properties dialog box.

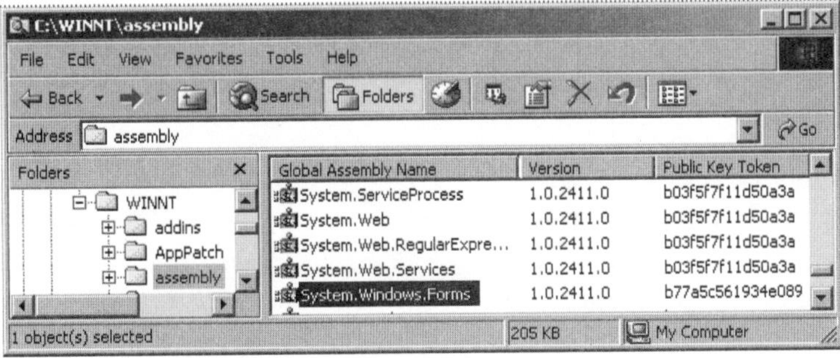

Figure 8-1 The \Windows\Assembly folder contains global assemblies.

Side-by-Side Execution

As I mentioned, the assembly cache contains the set of assemblies available to all applications targeting the .NET Framework. Multiple versions of the same assembly can be placed in the assembly cache, which allows applications that require different versions of the assembly or share the same assembly to execute correctly. The ability to run multiple versions of the same assembly simultaneously is known as *side-by-side execution*. Side-by-side execution puts an end to the so-called DLL Hell that Visual Basic programmers (and Windows users) have had to live with for so long.

Side-by-side execution allows you to create different versions of your assembly that do not need to be backward compatible. Of course, having multiple versions eliminates all sorts of coding and testing of a product and collapses the time you need to get your software to market. The common language runtime provides the infrastructure that allows multiple versions of the same assembly to run on the same computer, or even in the same process. Pretty cool.

To support shared assemblies, Windows has to be able to actually load DLLs that have the same name into a single address space or process. This ability is the method that .NET has for eliminating DLL conflicts. Search your machine for a file called mscorcfg.msc, which is a .NET Admin Tool. It's usually located in C:\Windows\Microsoft.Net\Framework\<*Your version number*>. When you locate the file, double-click mscorcfg.msc and view the assembly cache, shown in Figure 8-2.

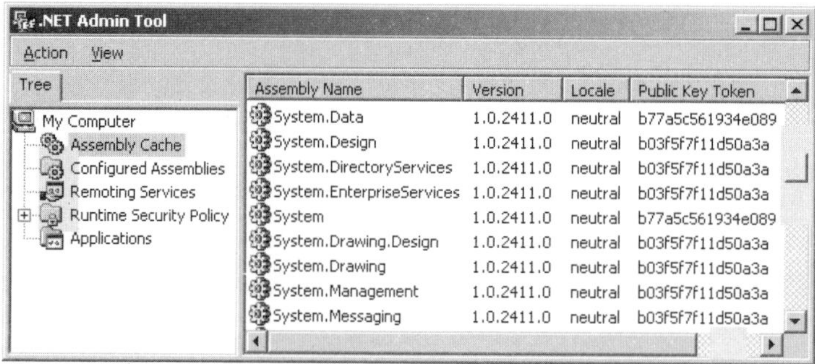

Figure 8-2 The assembly cache.

The Global Assembly Cache

Each computer on which the CLR is installed has a machine-wide code area called the *global assembly cache*. The global assembly cache, or GAC, stores assemblies specifically designated to be shared by several applications on the computer. Usually you should not place an assembly you create in the GAC but should instead keep it in the single directory associated with your program as a private assembly.

However, if you create an assembly that will be used by multiple programs from the GAC, you can no longer replicate or install the application by using the XCOPY command to copy the files to the application's directory—you must move the assembly into the global assembly cache as well. You'll sometimes create a global assembly that acts like a classic Visual Basic DLL or an in-process server. For example, you might create a global assembly that calculates taxes or handles employee information that needs to be shared with other programs that target the .NET Framework. This would be a perfect use for a shared assembly.

But don't do this lightly. You should share assemblies by installing them into the global assembly cache only when you need to. As a general guideline, keep assembly dependencies private and locate assemblies in the application directory unless sharing an assembly is explicitly required. In addition, you do not have to install assemblies into the global assembly cache to make them accessible to unmanaged code or for interoperability with COM. Also, you must have Administrator privileges on a computer to install assemblies into the global assembly cache.

Assemblies deployed in the global assembly cache *must* have a strong name. When an assembly is added to the global assembly cache, the cache performs integrity checks on all files that make up the assembly. The cache performs these checks to ensure that an assembly has not been tampered with (for example, when a file has changed but the manifest does not reflect the change).

Assembly Strong Names

The GAC maintains a database file that contains, among other information, a mapping of where a specific assembly is located. Each company that builds a shared application must have a means to uniquely identify its specific assembly. As I mentioned, two companies naming their production assemblies something like EmployeeTracker is not inconceivable. If we have two assemblies, each from a different software company but both with the name EmployeeTracker, we must have a way to differentiate one from the other. This is where the strong name comes in.

A strong name includes the assembly's identity—its simple text name, version number, and culture information (if provided)—plus a public key and a digital signature. A strong name is generated from an assembly file, which contains the assembly manifest, which, in turn, contains the names and hashes (numeric values derived by applying an algorithm to data) of all the files that make up the assembly. Assemblies with the same strong name are expected to be identical. When you build a Visual Basic .NET application, you can ensure that an assembly name is globally unique by signing an assembly with a strong name. I'll show you how to do that later in the chapter.

Generally, strong names satisfy several requirements of programs that target the .NET platform. For example, strong names guarantee name uniqueness by relying on unique key pairs. No one else can generate the same assembly name that you can because an assembly name generated with one private key is different from an assembly name generated with another private key.

Strong names also protect the version lineage of an assembly. In other words, a strong name can ensure that no one can produce a subsequent version of your assembly. Users can be sure that a version of the assembly that they are loading comes from the same publisher that created the version of the assembly that the application was built with.

Finally, strong names provide a solid integrity check. When a strong-named assembly passes the .NET Framework security checks, the contents of the assembly are guaranteed not to have changed since it was built. Providing a digital signature and supporting certificate adds another level of trust. The signature and certificate are used when you sell or distribute your programs or components over the Internet.

To successfully deploy your Visual Basic .NET application, you must understand how the .NET runtime locates and binds to the assemblies that make up your application. By default, the runtime attempts to bind with the exact version of the assembly that the application was built with.

The common language runtime performs a number of steps when attempting to locate an assembly and resolve an assembly reference. *Probing* is the term used to describe how the runtime locates assemblies. Essentially, the CLR refers to a built-in set of heuristics that is used to locate the assembly on the basis of its name, version, and culture.

As you can see, an assembly contains quite a bit of information. First and foremost the assembly contains metadata—binary information that describes your program whether it is stored in an executable or in memory. When you compile your program, this metadata is stuffed in the file when it is converted to the Microsoft Intermediate Language (MSIL). Essentially, every type and member defined and referenced in a module or assembly is described by the metadata. When your code is executed, the runtime loads metadata into memory and references it to discover information about your code's classes, members, inheritance, and so on. Your program is completely self-describing, and the need to use the registry is unnecessary.

Metadata describes every type and member defined in your code. It contains identity information such as the name, version, culture, and public key to ensure that the assembly has not been modified or corrupted. Also, all of the types that are available and any other dependent assemblies are included in the metadata. Any security permissions are also contained. The assembly is really a self-contained unit that has everything it needs to know to run your program. The metadata is a key part for writing more robust and easily maintainable Visual Basic .NET programs.

The Other Parts of an Assembly

At the top of the diagram shown in Figure 8-3 is the assembly object. As I mentioned, one or more DLLs might make up an assembly, so references to those DLLs are stored in the assembly object. Also, any resources, such as bitmaps, that are used in your program are referenced in this object. Next is the module class. A module references a single DLL, of which there might be more than one for an assembly. Everything the runtime needs to know about that particular DLL module is stored here.

In addition, all type information about the module is stored. It's easy to think of a .NET type as a class. As we will see in our upcoming program, the *Type* class can be used to retrieve all metadata for an object. Each of the type classes has a collection of *Type* objects members. Each type contains members, such as fields, properties, events, methods, constructors, and parameters.

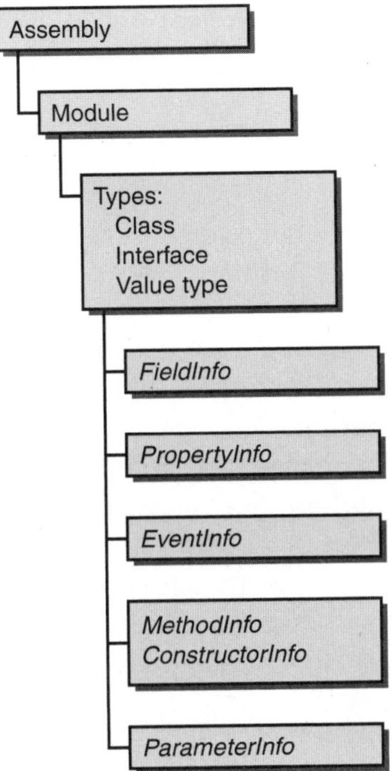

Figure 8-3 The *Assembly* object.

Reflection: How to Go About Examining Assemblies

As you know by now, assemblies provide the infrastructure that allows the common language runtime to understand the contents of an application and to enforce the versioning and dependency rules defined by the application. Assemblies contain modules, and modules contain types. Each type contains members.

The .NET Framework includes classes, known as reflection classes, that provide objects that encapsulate assemblies, modules, and types. By using *System.Reflection* classes, we can spy on the internals of an assembly.

Reflection is a means to find out about objects at run time. The implementation of reflection in Visual Basic .NET is similar to how reflection is implemented in the Java language and, to a larger extent, Runtime Type Information (RTTI) in C++. The *Reflection* namespace contains more than 130 classes and interfaces that provide a managed view of loaded types, methods, and fields, with the ability to dynamically create and invoke types. Reflection can be a complex topic, but I'll cover the important highlights by demonstrating a program that examines all the members of an assembly.

The Assembly Spy Program

In the following sections, we'll write a program we can use to spy on assemblies. In the process of creating this program, you'll solidify your understanding of what assemblies are all about and learn more about how to use Visual Basic .NET controls. Our program will have a menu, a list box at the left that displays namespaces, and a tree view control on the right that enables a hierarchical listing of the internals of each namespace. Because we can't be sure of the length of the names of the namespaces, properties, methods, and other internals, we'll add a splitter bar between the list box and the tree view control. The user can move the splitter in either direction for easier viewing. What's great about the splitter is that we simply set properties—no programming is involved. Once designed, our application window will look like Figure 8-4.

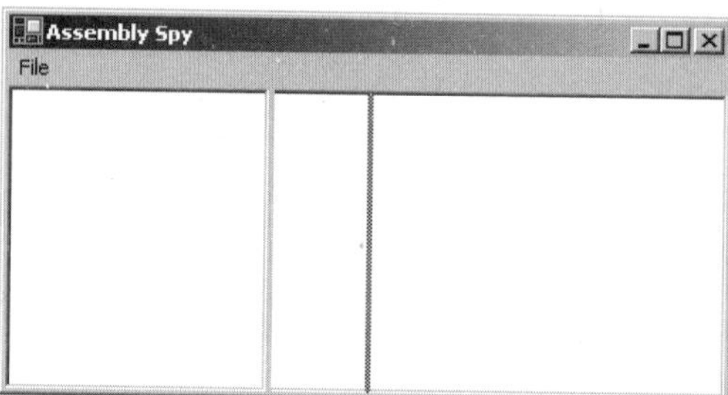

Figure 8-4 The Assembly Spy program.

The menu in our program permits a user to open a new assembly, examine summary assembly information, or quit the program. If no assembly is currently being viewed, the Assembly Information menu option is not available, as you can see in Figure 8-5.

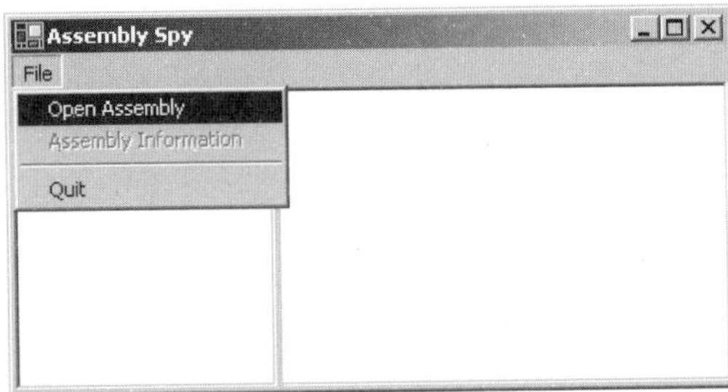

Figure 8-5 When we're not spying on an assembly, the Assembly Information command is not available.

In creating the Assembly Spy program, you'll also learn how to use the new and improved Open File dialog box. When a user clicks Open Assembly on the menu, our customized dialog box appears. As you can see in Figure 8-6, the title bar shows users what they are supposed to do. We also configure the Files Of Type list to display only assembly files.

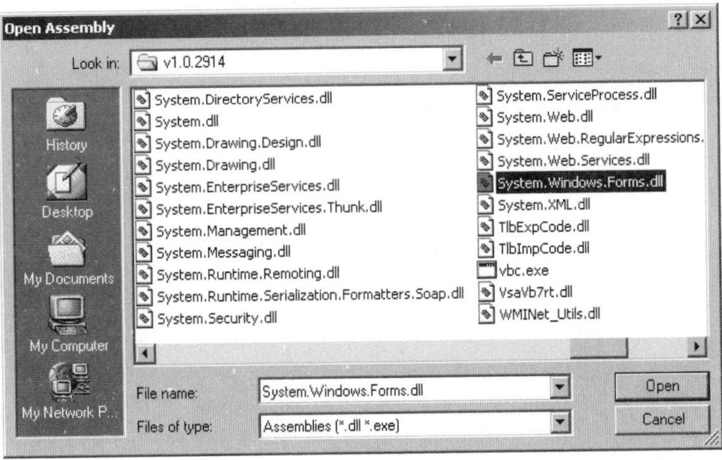

Figure 8-6 In the Assembly Spy program, we customize the Open File dialog box to show only assembly files.

As an example of how the Assembly Spy program works, if we open the C:\WINDOWS\Microsoft.NET\Framework\<*version number*> folder, select Windows.Forms.dll, and click Open, that assembly is loaded into our program. All the namespaces contained in this assembly are listed in alphabetical order on the left. On the right, we list the particular class we are interested in from the namespace at the root of the tree view control. All of the various components of the class, such as constructors, fields, properties and so on are listed. The plus sign (+) tells us whether any of the components have items in a collection.

In Figure 8-7, the Instance Methods item is selected and expanded to reveal the signatures of the methods. The tree view control provides a tool tip that displays the entire contents of a partially hidden entry when the mouse hovers over it. As an added touch, we include the current location and name of the assembly in the title of the form.

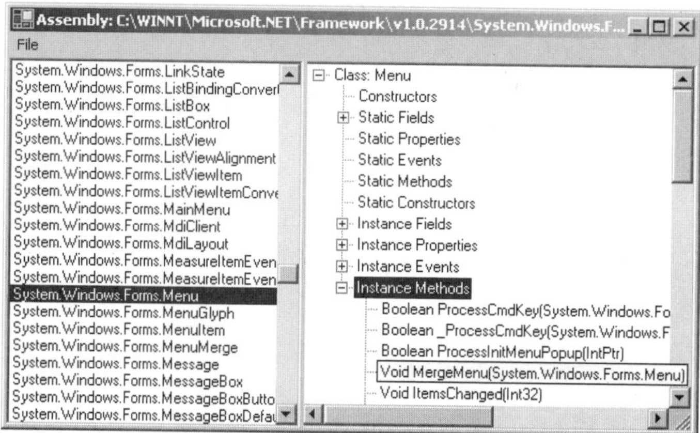

Figure 8-7 The Assembly Spy program in action, showing namespaces on the left and class components on the right.

The signatures of methods in assemblies are written in C#, not in Visual Basic. To us, the signatures look a bit backward. For example, notice in Figure 8-7 that the method highlighted does not return a value (*Void*) but simply takes a menu as a parameter. Notice also that both static and instance fields, properties, events, methods, and constructors are shown. Simply substitute the Visual Basic keyword *Shared* for the C# identifier *Static*, and remember that a shared field or property means that only a single instance is shared among all classes. Instance fields or properties, of course, are unique to an instance of the object.

Because an assembly is currently loaded, selecting Assembly Information from our menu displays a message box with summary information, as shown in Figure 8-8.

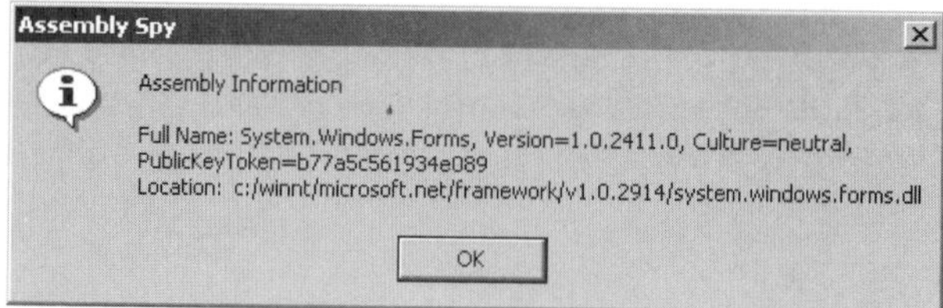

Figure 8-8 Summary information about an assembly produced by the Assembly Spy program.

Building the Assembly Spy Program

Follow these steps to start building the Assembly Spy program yourself.

1. Start a new Windows application project, and name it AssemblySpy.
2. On the default form, add a list box control on the left and a tree view control on the right.
3. Drag a MainMenu and an OpenFileDialog control from the toolbox to the form as well. The only control we still need to add is the splitter, but we have to dock our list box and tree view first, and we'll get to that in a moment. The form should now look something like Figure 8-9. (We'll change the control properties and add commands to the menu in a bit.)

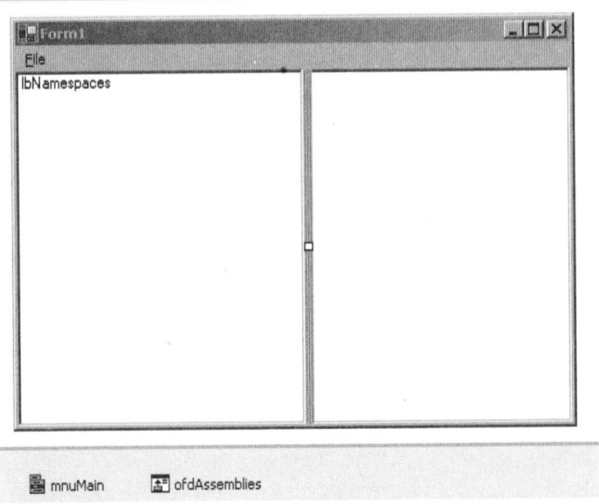

Figure 8-9 The Assembly Spy program starts to take shape.

4. Double-click the form to display the code window. Change the form's class name from the default, Form1, to AssemblySpyForm. Here's how the code should look when you're finished with this step.

```
Public Class AssemblySpyForm
    Inherits System.Windows.Forms.Form
```

5. Set the properties for the controls you've added as shown in Table 8-1.

Table 8-1 Properties and Values for the AssemblySpyForm Controls

Object	Property	Value
MainMenu	*Name*	mnuMain
OpenFileDialog	*Name*	ofdAssemblies
Form1	*Name*	AssemblySpyForm
	Menu	mnuMain
Listbox1	*Name*	lbNamespaces
	Dock	Left
	Sorted	True

You can dock controls at the edges of your form or have them fill the control's container (either a form or a container control). When a control is docked at an edge of its container, it will always be positioned flush against that edge when the container is resized. If more than one control is docked at an edge, the controls will not be placed on top of each other. Once the list box is docked (see Figure 8-10), we can add a splitter control.

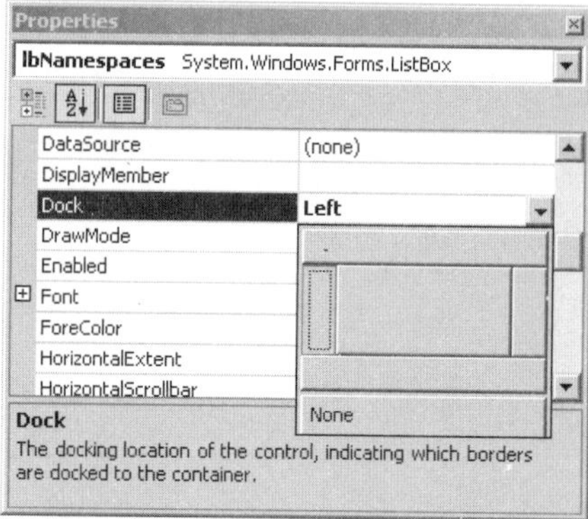

Figure 8-10 Docking the list box control.

6. Now drag a splitter control from the toolbox to the form. Set its *Dock* property to Left. This control will do the heavy lifting in resizing both the list box and the tree view. No code is required to make the splitter operational, but set its properties and the properties of the tree view control as shown in Table 8-2.

Table 8-2 Properties and Values for the Splitter and TreeView Controls

Object	Property	Value
Splitter1	*Dock*	Left
TreeView	*Name*	tvInternals
	Dock	Fill (will fill the remainder of the form)

Adding the Main Menu

The main menu, mnuMain, was associated with our AssemblySpyForm form by setting a property. With the Visual Studio .NET menu editor, you are only required to type in what you want the menu choices to display. Be sure to add the ampersand (&) before the first letter of each menu choice to create a keyboard shortcut for the menu, shown by the underscored characters in Figure 8-11.

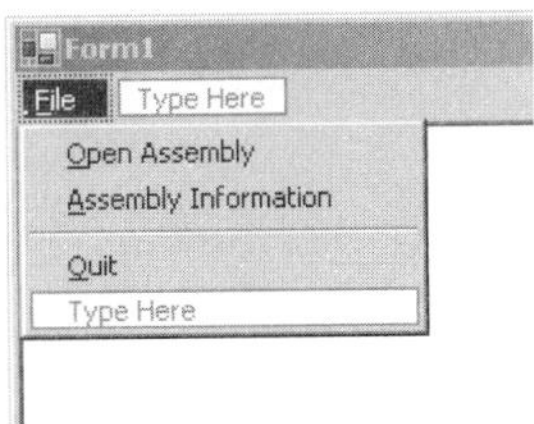

Figure 8-11 The main menu in the Assembly Spy program.

Menu event handlers are not added by default. The easiest way to have Visual Basic .NET add the handler for you is to double-click the menu item. Double-clicking instructs the IDE to add the template for that particular menu item's *Click* event handler.

Let's Write Some Code

All right, let's have a look at the code for this program. I trust you're seeing patterns in writing .NET programs by now and are feeling more comfortable working with the .NET Framework. I'll review only the key concepts as we go through this code.

```
Imports System.Reflection
Imports System
Imports System.Text
Imports CtrlChrs = Microsoft.VisualBasic.ControlChars

Namespace AssemblyView

    Public Class AssemblySpyForm
        Inherits System.Windows.Forms.Form

        Dim tnNode As TreeNode
        Dim tnRootNode As TreeNode
        Const progName As String = "Assembly Spy"

        Dim sAssemblyLocation As String = ""
        Dim aAssembly As [Assembly]
```

(continued)

```
        '--Control declarations omitted...

#Region " Windows Form Designer generated code "
'--Omitted
#End Region


Private Sub loadAssembly(ByVal sAssemblyLocation As String)
    Dim tType As Type

    Try
        Me.Text = "Assembly: " & sAssemblyLocation
        aAssembly = [Assembly].LoadFrom(sAssemblyLocation)
        updateModuleTypes(aAssembly.GetTypes)
        Me.MenuItem3.Enabled = True
    Catch
        Me.MenuItem3.Enabled = False
        MessageBox.Show(sAssemblyLocation & _
            " is not an assembly. ", progName, _
            MessageBoxButtons.OK, _
            MessageBoxIcon.Information)
        sAssemblyLocation = ""
    End Try
End Sub

Private Sub updateModuleTypes(ByRef tTypes() As Type)
    Dim tType As Type

    lbNamespaces.BeginUpdate()
    Cursor.Current = System.Windows.Forms.Cursors.WaitCursor

    For Each tType In tTypes
        If tType.IsPublic Then
            lbNamespaces.Items.Add(tType.FullName)
        End If
    Next

    lbNamespaces.EndUpdate()
    Cursor.Current = System.Windows.Forms.Cursors.Default
End Sub

Private Sub lbNamespaces_SelectedIndexChanged( _
    ByVal sender As System.Object, _
    ByVal e As System.EventArgs) _
    Handles lbNamespaces.SelectedIndexChanged

    Dim tType As Type = _
        aAssembly.GetType(lbNamespaces.SelectedItem)
```

```
    tnRootNode = New TreeNode()
    tnRootNode.Text = "Class: " & tType.Name

    With tvInternals
        .Nodes.Clear()
        .Nodes.Add(tnRootNode)
        .SelectedNode = tnRootNode
    End With

'-- Add Categories and Elements --
    addCategory("Constructors")
    Dim ciConstructorInfo() As ConstructorInfo = _
        tType.GetConstructors(BindingFlags.Static Or _
        BindingFlags.NonPublic Or BindingFlags.Public)
    printElements(ciConstructorInfo)

    addCategory("Static Fields")
    Dim fFields() As FieldInfo = _
        tType.GetFields(BindingFlags.Static Or _
        BindingFlags.NonPublic Or BindingFlags.Public)
    printElements(fFields)

    addCategory("Static Properties")
    Dim piStaticPropertyInfo() As PropertyInfo = _
        tType.GetProperties(BindingFlags.Static Or _
        BindingFlags.NonPublic Or BindingFlags.Public)
    printElements(piStaticPropertyInfo)

    addCategory("Static Events")
    Dim eiStaticEventInfo() As EventInfo = _
        tType.GetEvents(BindingFlags.Static Or _
        BindingFlags.NonPublic Or BindingFlags.Public)
    printElements(eiStaticEventInfo)

    addCategory("Static Methods")
    Dim miStaticMethodInfo() As MethodInfo = _
        tType.GetMethods(BindingFlags.Static Or _
        BindingFlags.NonPublic Or BindingFlags.Public)
    printElements(miStaticMethodInfo)

    addCategory("Static Constructors")
    Dim ciStaticConstructorInfo() As ConstructorInfo = _
        tType.GetConstructors(BindingFlags.Static Or _
        BindingFlags.NonPublic Or BindingFlags.Public)
    printElements(ciStaticConstructorInfo)

    addCategory("Instance Fields")
    Dim fiFieldInfo() As FieldInfo = _
```

(continued)

```
            tType.GetFields(BindingFlags.Instance _
            Or BindingFlags.NonPublic Or BindingFlags.Public)
        printElements(fiFieldInfo)

        addCategory("Instance Properties")
        Dim piPropertyInfo() As PropertyInfo = _
            tType.GetProperties(BindingFlags.Instance _
            Or BindingFlags.NonPublic Or BindingFlags.Public)
        printElements(piPropertyInfo)
        addCategory("Instance Events")
        Dim eiEventInfo() As EventInfo = _
            tType.GetEvents(BindingFlags.Instance _
            Or BindingFlags.NonPublic Or BindingFlags.Public)
        printElements(eiEventInfo)

        addCategory("Instance Methods")
        Dim miMethodInfo() As MethodInfo = _
            tType.GetMethods(BindingFlags.Instance Or _
            BindingFlags.NonPublic Or BindingFlags.Public)
        printElements(miMethodInfo)
    End Sub

    Private Sub printElements(ByVal miElements() As MemberInfo)
        Dim miElement As MemberInfo

        For Each miElement In miElements
            tnNode = New TreeNode()
            tnNode.Text = Convert.ToString(miElement)
            tvInternals.SelectedNode.Nodes.Add(tnNode)
        Next
    End Sub

    Private Sub addCategory(ByVal sTitle As String)
        'A string is passed in and a node is added to the tree
        tnNode = New TreeNode()
        tnNode.Text = sTitle
        With tvInternals
            .SelectedNode = tnRootNode
            .SelectedNode.Nodes.Add(tnNode)
            .SelectedNode = tnNode
        End With
    End Sub

    Private Sub MenuItem2_Click(ByVal sender As System.Object, _
        ByVal e As System.EventArgs) Handles MenuItem2.Click

        With ofdAssemblies
            'The InitialDirectory property of the dialog box references
            'the build on my machine. Your build number will be different.
```

```
            .InitialDirectory = _
                "C:\WINNT\Microsoft.NET\Framework\v<your version number>\"
            .Filter = "Assemblies (*.dll *.exe)|*.dll; *.exe"
            .FilterIndex = 1
            .RestoreDirectory = True
            If .ShowDialog = DialogResult.OK Then
                sAssemblyLocation = .FileName
                lbNamespaces.Items.Clear()
                tvInternals.Nodes.Clear()
                loadAssembly(sAssemblyLocation)
            End If
        End With
    End Sub

    Private Sub MenuItem3_Click(ByVal sender As System.Object, _
        ByVal e As System.EventArgs) Handles MenuItem3.Click

        Dim sAssemblyInfo As New StringBuilder()

        With sAssemblyInfo
            .Append("Assembly Information" & _
                CtrlChrs.CrLf & CtrlChrs.CrLf)
            .Append("Full Name: " & _
                aAssembly.FullName & CtrlChrs.CrLf)
            .Append("Location:  " & _
                aAssembly.Location & CtrlChrs.CrLf)
        End With

        MessageBox.Show(sAssemblyInfo.ToString, progName, _
            MessageBoxButtons.OK, MessageBoxIcon.Information)
    End Sub

    Private Sub MenuItem5_Click(ByVal sender As System.Object, _
        ByVal e As System.EventArgs) Handles MenuItem5.Click

        Application.Exit()
    End Sub

    Private Sub Form1_Load(ByVal sender As System.Object, _
        ByVal e As System.EventArgs) Handles MyBase.Load

        Me.Text = progName
        Me.MenuItem3.Enabled = False
    End Sub

    End Class

    End Namespace
```

Examining the Code

We first import the assemblies needed in the program. The *Reflection* classes are the meat and potato classes for this program. We'll dynamically build a string that will contain the summary information about the assembly being viewed, so a *StringBuilder* object is just what's needed. These objects live in the *System.Text* namespace, so we include an *Imports* directive for it. Finally, we use our little imports alias trick to reference control characters, using the alias *CtrlChrs* instead of the fully qualified name of the namespace. We also want to add a namespace to our program even though it has only a single class. We add the namespace to illustrate how namespaces are displayed in our program.

```
Imports System.Reflection
Imports System
Imports System.Text
Imports CtrlChrs = Microsoft.VisualBasic.ControlChars

Namespace AssemblyView

    Public Class AssemblySpyForm
        Inherits System.Windows.Forms.Form
```

When you use a tree view control, you actually have to add a node to the tree for each item. Many beginning Visual Basic programmers find the tree view control complicated because of this extra piece. A node is simply an object that is instantiated from the *TreeNode* class. Once instantiated, the node can then contain various items such as the text to display in the tree view, the font to use for the text, an image to render, a background color, and so on. The *Node* object is also aware of its parents, siblings, and any child nodes it might have. It knows whether it's visible and other aspects of its state. Each node is really a class that has several properties and events, such as expanding and collapsing, that give it quite a bit of functionality. We add the node to the *Nodes* collection of the tree view control. A *TreeNode* object can't exist independently of a tree view control. Because we'll be displaying our program's name in the title bar of the form and in the message box with an assembly's summary information, dimensioning the title as a constant makes sense. When our program loads the assembly in question, its location on disk has to be known. We store that in the *sAssemblyLocation* string variable. Finally, we dimension a variable *aAssembly* of type *Assembly*. Be sure to add the square brackets ([ ]) around the keyword *Assembly*.

Each of these variables (and the constant) is declared with class-level scope. Because they are declared at the top of the class, they can be seen and referenced anywhere within our class.

```
Dim tnNode As TreeNode
Dim tnRootNode As TreeNode
Const progName As String = "Assembly Spy"

Dim sAssemblyLocation As String = ""
Dim aAssembly As [Assembly]
```

Let's examine the rest of the code in the sequence in which it will be called.

When the form is loaded, we set the *Text* property of the form to the name of the program. Next we disable *MenuItem3*, which permits the user to select the Assembly Information command. Of course, there is no assembly loaded yet, so this is another example of defensive programming. If the command does not make sense in this context, don't give it to the user.

```
Private Sub Form1_Load(ByVal sender As System.Object, _
    ByVal e As System.EventArgs) Handles MyBase.Load

    Me.Text = progName
    Me.MenuItem3.Enabled = False
End Sub
```

When the form is displayed, the user can use the menu to bring up the Open File dialog box. Let's see how that's accomplished. The *OpenFileDialog* control has several properties that we can set to customize it for our application. For the sake of simplicity, we set the *InitialDirectory* property of the *ofdAssemblies* dialog box to the directory on my machine where the development assemblies are stored. Because we want only DLLs or EXEs to be displayed, we can set the *Filter* property to return these types of files. To add this detail, we simply add a text string. We first add the types of files we want displayed in the Files Of Type box. The user thus knows which types of files will be displayed. Then a bar character (|) is added as a delimiter to separate the types of files we want to display. Notice that a semicolon appears after each specific type of file. Next we set the *FilterIndex* property to 1. This property gets or sets the current filename filter string, which determines the choices that appear in the Files Of Type list in the dialog box. We have only one selection, but we could easily have added more specific types of files, such as text files, Microsoft Word files, or all files. Setting the *RestoreDirectory* property to True sets a value indicating whether the dialog box restores the current directory before closing. Because we will usually use this directory for assemblies, setting this property reduces some mouse clicks if we have to navigate back.

The *ShowDialog* method displays the dialog box modally. We check to see whether the return value is *DialogResult.OK*. This value tells us that a valid file has been returned. If the result is any other value, we bypass the rest of the *If* statement and the operation is canceled.

If the user picks a valid file (which may or may not be an assembly), the class-level string variable *sAssemblyLocation* is set to the *FileName* property of the dialog box. To be sure neither the list box nor the tree view contains any information from a previous operation, we simply clear both controls. Finally, we call the procedure *loadAssembly* with the fully qualified name of the assembly we want to open.

```
Private Sub MenuItem2_Click(ByVal sender As System.Object, _
    ByVal e As System.EventArgs) Handles MenuItem2.Click

    With ofdAssemblies
        .InitialDirectory = _
            "C:\WINNT\Microsoft.NET\Framework\v<your version number>\"
        .Filter = "Assemblies (*.dll *.exe)|*.dll; *.exe"
        .FilterIndex = 1
        .RestoreDirectory = True
        If .ShowDialog = DialogResult.OK Then
            sAssemblyLocation = .FileName
            lbNamespaces.Items.Clear()
            tvInternals.Nodes.Clear()
            loadAssembly(sAssemblyLocation)
        End If
    End With
End Sub
```

We'll try to open the assembly here. I say *try* because the user could have easily selected an EXE or a DLL that happens not to be an assembly. The protected block of code in the *Try* construct will be executed and, if a file that's not an assembly is loaded, an exception will be thrown.

Setting the form's *Text* property to the name of the assembly ensures that the user knows which file is open. Then we try to load an assembly using the [*Assembly*].*LoadFrom* method in our class-level variable *aAssembly*, which is of type *Assembly*.

At this point, things could go south quickly if the user has selected an executable by mistake. If an exception is thrown, our code jumps to the unfiltered handler, *Catch*. Because we didn't use a filtered *Catch* construct, our handler will catch any and all errors. Here we simply catch the exception, ensure the user can't select the Assembly Information menu option, and display a message box stating that the selection was not an assembly. You can see an example of our friendly message in Figure 8-12.

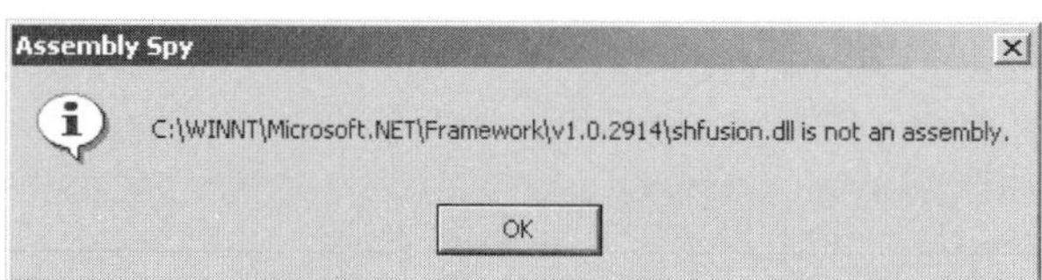

Figure 8-12 If a user of Assembly Spy selects a file that isn't an assembly, the user will see a message like this one.

If a valid assembly was loaded, it is assigned to our reference *aAssembly* variable of type *Assembly*. Because we want to extract all the types from the assembly, we access the *aAssembly.GetTypes* method, which returns an array of *Types*. We pass that array of types as a parameter to the *updateModuleTypes* routine.

```
Private Sub loadAssembly(ByVal sAssemblyLocation As String)
    Dim tType As Type

    Try
        Me.Text = "Assembly: " & sAssemblyLocation
        aAssembly = [Assembly].LoadFrom(sAssemblyLocation)
        updateModuleTypes(aAssembly.GetTypes)
        Me.MenuItem3.Enabled = True
    Catch
        Me.MenuItem3.Enabled = False
        MessageBox.Show(sAssemblyLocation & _
            " is not an assembly. ", progName, _
            MessageBoxButtons.OK, MessageBoxIcon.Information)
        sAssemblyLocation = ""
    End Try
End Sub
```

In this code, we pass an array of type *Type* to *updateModules* from the loaded assembly that contains objects for all the types defined in this assembly. As I mentioned, a type represents type declarations: class types, interface types, array types, value types, and enumeration types. *Type* is the root of all reflection operations and the object that represents a type inside the system. *Type* is an abstract base class that allows multiple implementations.

We now populate the left side of our form with the namespaces contained within the loaded assembly. Because some assemblies—*System.dll* is one of them—have quite a few namespaces, we set the *Sorted* property of the list box to True, so there can be some overhead when the list box is populated. If an assembly contains a lot of namespaces, updating the list box in a sorted order can be a bit costly in CPU cycles. To help speed things up, use the *BeginUpdate* and *EndUpdate* methods of the list box. These methods enable a programmer to add a large number of items without the control being repainted each time an item is added to the list. And because populating this control might take a second or two, don't forget to set the cursor to an hourglass to provide a visual clue that the program is busy. Again, it's attention to detail that gives comfort to the users.

Next we iterate through the *tTypes* collection of *Types* passed in to the subroutine. If the type is public, we add its full name to the list box. Otherwise, we will get many private types that we don't have access to. When all the namespaces have been added, we call *EndUpdate* to refresh the list box and reset the cursor.

```
Private Sub updateModuleTypes(ByRef tTypes() As Type)
    Dim tType As Type

    lbNamespaces.BeginUpdate()
    Cursor.Current = System.Windows.Forms.Cursors.WaitCursor

    For Each tType In tTypes
        If tType.IsPublic Then
            lbNamespaces.Items.Add(tType.FullName)
        End If
    Next

    lbNamespaces.EndUpdate()
    Cursor.Current = System.Windows.Forms.Cursors.Default
End Sub
```

At this point, the namespaces in the assembly are loaded into the list box. Because they're sorted, finding a specific namespace is easy. You could easily extend this program by adding a Find dialog box. You could also easily add the built-in *InPutBox* and have the user enter a partial namespace, such as *Clipboard*. When the user clicks OK in the input box, simply use the *FindString* or *FindStringExact* method of the list box to search for a namespace in the list that contains a specific search string.

If we want to take a look at the namespaces located in *System.Windows.Forms*, we select that assembly from our common dialog box. Notice in Figure 8-13 that the name of the assembly is displayed in the form's caption area.

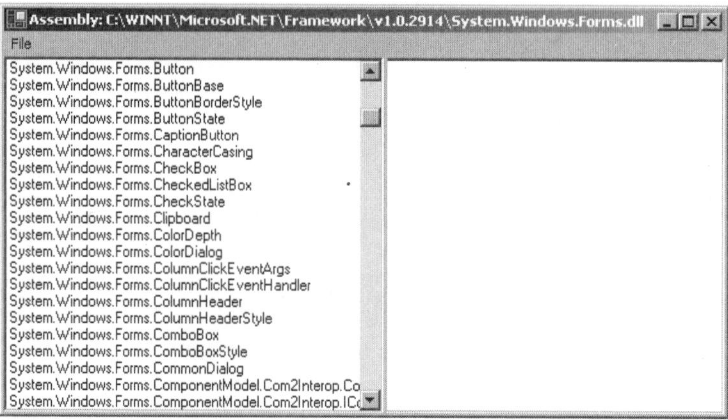

Figure 8-13 Examining the namespace *System.Windows.Forms* in the Assembly Spy program.

Now the user can either use the menu to view the summary information about the assembly or click a namespace to view its contents. Remember that when the assembly was successfully loaded, we enabled *MenuItem3*, which permits the user to view assembly information. Gathering this information is simply a matter of reading a few properties from our *aAssembly* variable. Because we build a string dynamically, now is a good time to use our friend the *StringBuilder*.

```
Private Sub MenuItem3_Click(ByVal sender As System.Object, _
    ByVal e As System.EventArgs) Handles MenuItem3.Click

    Dim sAssemblyInfo As New StringBuilder()

    With sAssemblyInfo
        .Append("Assembly Information" & _
            CtrlChrs.CrLf & CtrlChrs.CrLf)
        .Append("Full Name: " & _
            aAssembly.FullName & CtrlChrs.CrLf)
        .Append("Location:  " & _
            aAssembly.Location & CtrlChrs.CrLf)
    End With

    MessageBox.Show(sAssemblyInfo.ToString, progName, _
        MessageBoxButtons.OK, MessageBoxIcon.Information)
End Sub
```

A message box is a good device for displaying this sort of information, as you can see in Figure 8-14.

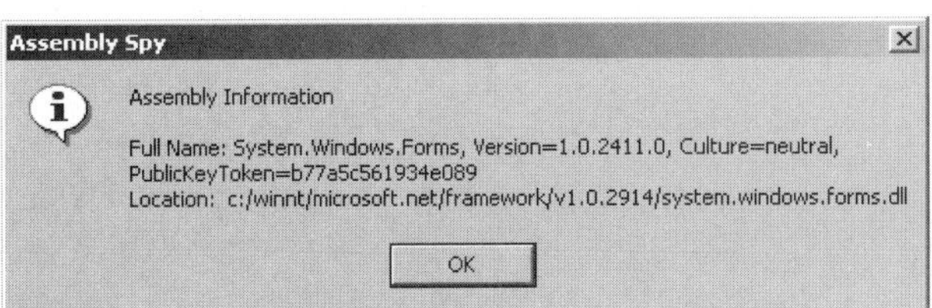

Figure 8-14 The summary information produced by Assembly Spy.

To display the internal types of any of the namespaces, a user can simply click the list box. Of course, the *SelectedIndexChanged* event fires when this occurs, and we can place our code in the event handler to add the components of the namespace to the tree view on the right.

Using the *GetType* method of our loaded assembly, we can pass in the name of the namespace the user selected and assign it to our local variable *tType* of *Type*. The *System.Type* class is central to reflection. The common language runtime creates the *Type* object for a loaded type when the *Reflection* class requests it. We can then use the *Type* object's methods, fields, properties, and nested classes to find out everything about that type.

The first item we want to add to the root of the tree view is the name of the namespace class currently being viewed. To make this addition, we create a new *TreeNode* object called *tnRootNode* so that we can distinguish it from the other child nodes. We can assign the name property of the *tType* variable (which is the namespace) to the *Text* property of the new node.

```
Private Sub lbNamespaces_SelectedIndexChanged( _
    ByVal sender As System.Object, _
    ByVal e As System.EventArgs) _
    Handles lbNamespaces.SelectedIndexChanged

    Dim tType As Type = _
        aAssembly.GetType(lbNamespaces.SelectedItem)

    tnRootNode = New TreeNode()
    tnRootNode.Text = "Class: " & tType.Name
```

Because this is a new namespace, let's clear out any nodes that might have been in the tree previously. Then we add the root node we just created, *tnRootNode*, to the *Nodes* collection of the tree view. Finally, we make that node the selected node. If you have used the tree view control in previous versions of Visual Basic, you need to know that the way nodes are added in Visual Basic .NET is fundamentally different. In classic Visual Basic, you pass in several parameters to designate where the node should be placed, whether it is a child or sibling, the parent node, and so forth. In Visual Basic .NET, when you want to add a child node, you simply make the parent the selected node. You can then add child nodes to the *SelectedNode.Nodes* collection.

```
With tvInternals
    .Nodes.Clear()
    .Nodes.Add(tnRootNode)
    .SelectedNode = tnRootNode
End With
```

Adding the Categories to the Tree View

We want to add all of the constructors, fields, properties, events, and methods of the loaded assembly to the tree view in an ordered and structured way. To streamline the process, we add two helper functions, *addCategory* and *printElements,* that can be called for each category. Let's examine the first items we'll add—the constructors in the namespace.

After we add the title "Constructors," the constructor information is retrieved. *ConstructorInfo* is used to discover the attributes of a constructor by returning an array of *ConstructorInfo* information. Notice that we dimension our *ciConstructorInfo* variable as an array of *ConstructorInfo* objects. Using the

GetConstructors method on our variable *tType,* which contains a reference to the namespace that we're examining, we retrieve the constructor information. Our code uses the information gathering methods of the *Reflection* class along with *BindingFlags*. *BindingFlags* permits us to list the members (constructors, fields, properties, events, and methods) of the specified class, dividing the members into static and instance categories. By putting them together with an *Or* operation, we can retrieve the static constructors that are both nonpublic and public.

```
'-- Add Categories and Elements --
addCategory("Constructors")
Dim ciConstructorInfo() As ConstructorInfo = _
    tType.GetConstructors(BindingFlags.Static Or _
    BindingFlags.NonPublic Or BindingFlags.Public)
printElements(ciConstructorInfo)
```

Our program repeats this approach for each category by retrieving the *FieldInfo*, *PropertyInfo*, *EventInfo*, and *MethodInfo* properties. Notice the *BindingFlags.Static* flag. This flag ensures that we retrieve only the static members for this call. After each of the static members is added, we add the instance members. The *BindingFlags* flags for these are *Instance*.

```
addCategory("Instance Fields")
Dim fiFieldInfo() As FieldInfo = _
    tType.GetFields(BindingFlags.Instance _
    Or BindingFlags.NonPublic Or BindingFlags.Public)
printElements(fiFieldInfo)
```

The Helper Procedures

For each category we want to add to the tree view, we pass in a string with a value of something like *"Constructors"*. In the *addCategory* subroutine, a new *TreeNode* object is created and its *Text* property is set to the *sTitle* string variable passed in as a parameter. Remember that when we added the namespace to the tree view, we created a special node called *tnRootNode* that has class scope. Because we want to add each category as a child under the root node, we assign *tnRootNode* as the value of *SelectedNode* for the tree view. We can now simply add our new *tnNode* to the *SelectedNode.Nodes* collection. I like this much simpler approach to adding a child node.

Of course, the next step is to add the various elements, such as any constructors, under that category. Therefore, we set the newly added node as the *SelectedNode*. We can now add the constructors to the *SelectedNode.Nodes* collection, which will place the actual constructor information under the Constructor category we just added.

```
Private Sub addCategory(ByVal sTitle As String)

    ' A string is passed in and a node is added to the tree
    tnNode = New TreeNode()
    tnNode.Text = sTitle
    With tvInternals
        .SelectedNode = tnRootNode
        .SelectedNode.Nodes.Add(tnNode)
        .SelectedNode = tnNode
    End With
End Sub
```

If we add a category for static constructors, for example, the next line retrieves the constructors and places them in the *ciConstructorInfo* array of *ConstructorInfo* types.

```
Dim ciConstructorInfo() As ConstructorInfo = _
    tType.GetConstructors(BindingFlags.Static Or _
    BindingFlags.NonPublic Or BindingFlags.Public)
```

Then the array is passed to the helper subroutine *printElements* as a parameter:

```
printElements(ciConstructorInfo)
```

The array is one of the generic *MemberInfo* objects describing each of the members of the current type. We can set the parameter of the signature of *printElements* to accept an array of *MemberInfo* objects. The *MemberInfo* class is the abstract base class of the classes used to obtain information about all members of a class (constructors, events, fields, methods, and properties). We can use this class to generically accept arrays of constructors, events, fields, methods, and properties.

Conceptually this subroutine is similar in structure to the *addCategory* procedure. However, this time we want to iterate through each of the items in the array, add its description to a node, and insert it under the appropriate category. We dimension a variable of type *MemberInfo* so that we can hold each item in turn and display it.

For each *miElement* in the *miElements* array, a new *TreeNode* object is instantiated. Because we want to display the entire contents of the description, we must use the *Convert.ToString* method on each *miElement* so that it can be displayed. And remember that in the *addCategory* subroutine, we made the current category (in this case *"Constructors"*) the currently selected node. So now it's just a matter of adding each of the elements to the *SelectedNode.Nodes* collection, and they become children of the current category.

```
Private Sub printElements(ByVal miElements() As MemberInfo)
    Dim miElement As MemberInfo

    For Each miElement In miElements
        tnNode = New TreeNode()
        tnNode.Text = Convert.ToString(miElement)
        tvInternals.SelectedNode.Nodes.Add(tnNode)
    Next
End Sub
```

Self-Examination: Contemplating Our Own Assembly

Now, what fun would it be if we didn't use this program to examine the assembly we just created? Select Build | Build to create AssemblySpy.exe in the bin directory of your project. Run the program, navigate to the bin folder and load your new assembly in Assembly Spy. The filename of the assembly is AssemblySpy. The program has a namespace, *AssemblyView*, and within that namespace we have a single class, *AssemblySpyForm*.

```
Namespace AssemblyView
    Public Class AssemblySpyForm
```

In the list box, as shown in Figure 8-15, we see our fully qualified namespace, *<Assembly> <NameSpace> <Class within the namespace>*. Clicking the list box reveals the current class within the namespace, *AssemblySpyForm*. When the categories are expanded, we can see our constant program name, *progName,* under the Static Fields category. We can also poke around and see the various variables, such as *tnNode* and *tnRootNode*. Very self-referential, eh?

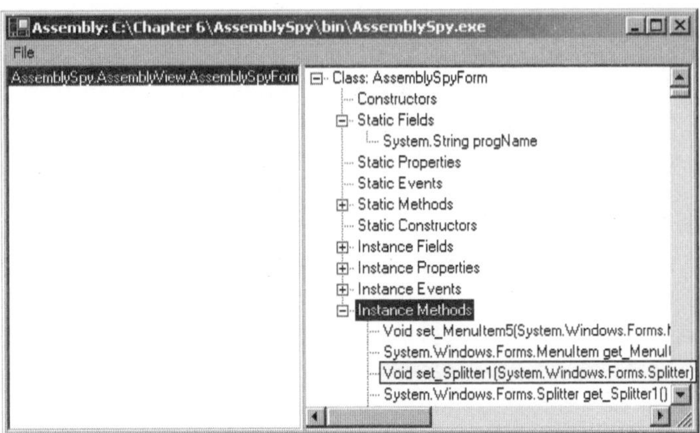

Figure 8-15 Looking at our own assembly in the Assembly Spy program.

In the following sections, we'll use our own assembly to add to our understanding of some of the concepts that I touched on briefly earlier in the chapter. I'll cover code signing and strong names and then return to the global assembly cache. You'll learn how to provide an assembly with a strong name, register it in the global assembly cache, and administer how it can be used.

Code Signing

Remember that when you distribute your .NET component or program, you'll want to assure your users that you are the author, that the code is safe and can be trusted, and that the identity of the assembly can be verified. You accomplish these guarantees by *signing* your code. You can sign an assembly in two ways.

The first way is to use a digital certificate, also called *signcode.* To sign your assembly using signcode, you go to a third-party authority and prove your identity. At that time you obtain a digital certificate that guarantees you are the originator of the component. All secure Web sites use a digital certificate to ensure visitors that they are connecting to the site they think they're connecting to. Likewise, you can sign your program or component to ensure that you are the author.

Another way to sign your code is to assign your assembly a *strong name.* As I described earlier in the chapter, a strong name consists of the assembly's identity plus a public key and a digital signature. A strong name is guaranteed to be a unique name, and thereby ensures the identity of your assembly. Although providing a strong name for your assembly guarantees its identity, it by no means guarantees that the code can be trusted. Put another way, a strong name uniquely identifies and guarantees the identity of an assembly, but it does not guarantee that you wrote it. However, a trust decision can reasonably be made on the basis of a strong-name identity alone. If you are selling or distributing components in the wild, you will want to look into getting a digital certificate.

Creating a Strongly Named Assembly

When you build an assembly as we just did, it is not strongly named by default. To sign an assembly with a strong name, you must have a public-private key pair. These public and private keys are a cryptographic key pair that's used during compilation to create the strong name for an assembly. You create a key pair using the Strong Name tool (Sn.exe). Key pair files usually have an .snk file extension. We'll put Sn.exe to work shortly.

The *StrongName* class represents evidence of a unique, cryptographically strong name of a code assembly. The strong name consists of a public key, a given name, and version parts. The public key corresponds to the publisher's private key, which is kept secret and with which the assembly must be signed in order for the strong name to be valid.

Let's take a few minutes and create a strong name for our assembly.

1. Right-click Form1.vb in the Solution Explorer and rename the form file AssemblySpyForm.vb, as shown in Figure 8-16.

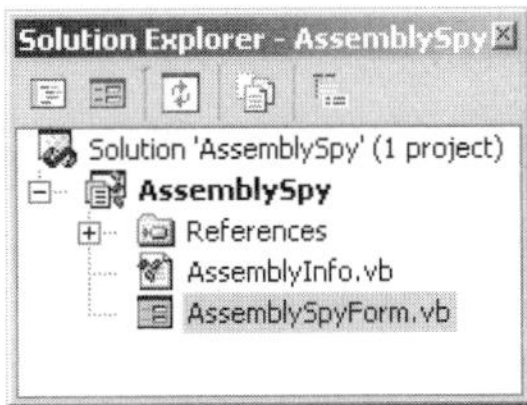

Figure 8-16 Use the Solution Explorer to rename the form file AssemblySpyForm.vb.

2. Open the AssemblyInfo.vb file. Notice that it includes general information about various attributes of the assembly. Add the title, description, and a fictitious company name if you want.

Notice that the assembly also contains a globally unique ID, or GUID, that is used to register your program in the Windows registry if it interacts with COM.

```
Imports System.Reflection
Imports System.Runtime.InteropServices

' General information about an assembly is controlled through
' the following set of attributes. Change these attribute values
' to modify the information associated with an assembly.

' Review the values of the assembly attributes.

<Assembly: AssemblyTitle("Assembly Spy")>
<Assembly: AssemblyDescription("Examine Assemblies")>
<Assembly: AssemblyCompany("Solidstate Software, Inc.")>
<Assembly: AssemblyProduct("")>
<Assembly: AssemblyCopyright("2001")>
<Assembly: AssemblyTrademark("")>
<Assembly: CLSCompliant(True)>

' The following GUID is for the ID of the typelib if this
' project is exposed to COM
<Assembly: Guid("FB159EAB-6F6C-4661-AA62-86442266C725")>

' Version information for an assembly consists of the following
' four values:
'
'      Major Version
'      Minor Version
'      Build Number
```

(continued)

```
'       Revision
'
' You can specify all the values or you can default the Build
' and Revision Numbers
' by using the '*' as shown below:

<Assembly: AssemblyVersion("1.0.*")>
```

Now that we have updated our metadata, let's add a strong name. You can give an assembly a strong name by using a command line program. First you use the Sn.exe utility to generate a public and private key pair. Next we indicate to our assembly where the key file is located, and then rebuild the assembly.

1. Locate Sn.exe on your drive. You use the command parameters *sn –k <file name>* to create a key pair. We'll name our key file asKey.snk.
2. At the command prompt, type **sn –k asKey.snk.** You will see the following message on your screen:

   Microsoft (R) .NET Framework Strong Name Utility Version 1.0.2914.11

   Copyright (C) Microsoft Corp. 1998-2001. All rights reserved.

   Key pair written to asKey.snk
3. We want to add the key file we just generated, so you have to open AssemblyInfo.vb and add the AssemblyKeyFile command yourself. Pass in the fully qualified path to the file you just created with the key pair, as shown here.

```
Imports System.Reflection
Imports System.Runtime.InteropServices

' General information about an assembly is controlled
' through the following set of attributes. Change these
' attribute values to modify the information associated
' with an assembly.

' Review the values of the assembly attributes.

<Assembly: AssemblyTitle("Assembly Spy")>
<Assembly: AssemblyDescription("Examine Assemblies")>
<Assembly: AssemblyCompany("Solidstate Software, Inc.")>
<Assembly: AssemblyProduct("")>
<Assembly: AssemblyCopyright("2001")>
<Assembly: AssemblyTrademark("")>
<Assembly: CLSCompliant(True)>
<Assembly: AssemblyKeyFile("C:\VB .NET Coding Techniques
 \Chap08\AssemblySpy\asKey.snk")>
```

```
' The following GUID is for the ID of the typelib if this
' project is exposed to COM
<Assembly: Guid("FB159EAB-6F6C-4661-AA62-86442266C725")>

' Version information for an assembly consists of the follow-
' ing four values:
'
'       Major Version
'       Minor Version
'       Build Number
'       Revision
'
' You can specify all the values or you can default the
' Build and Revision Numbers
' by using the '*' as shown below:

<Assembly: AssemblyVersion("1.0.*")>
```

4. Rebuild your project by clicking Build | Rebuild Solution. That's it!

The Global Assembly Cache Revisited

Earlier in the chapter we looked at the mscorcfg.msc program, which permits us to examine the global assembly cache. If we attempt to add an assembly that does not have a strong name to the global cache, it will bark at us, as you can see in Figure 8-17.

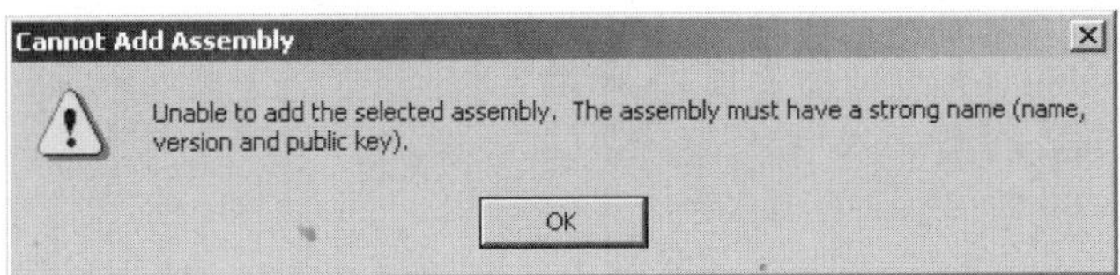

Figure 8-17 You can't add an assembly that doesn't have a strong name to the global assembly cache.

However, now that our AssemblySpy assembly has a strong name, we can click the Assembly Cache to give it focus and click Action | Add, navigate to the directory that contains our assembly, and then add our assembly to the global cache. Figure 8-18 shows that our assembly now has a public key token that is the hexidecimal representation of the public key that is the cryptographic public key for the assembly. Cool. (If no culture is defined, such as English or French or Chinese, the Locale is neutral.)

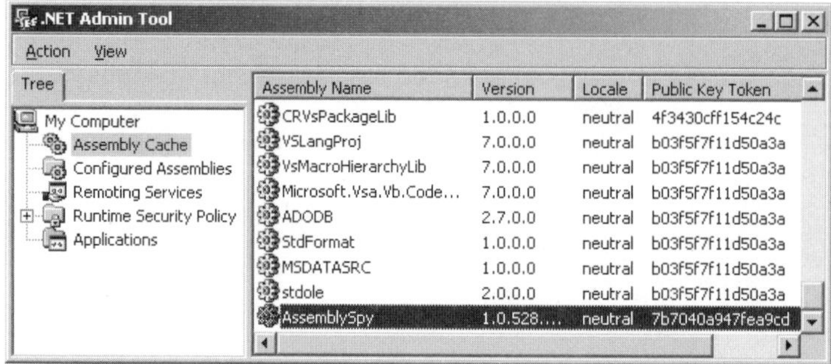

Figure 8-18 Our assembly is now part of the global cache.

Use Windows Explorer to navigate to the folder where your program is located, right-click the program, and select Properties. As you can see in Figure 8-19, the General tab lists information about the program. Notice that our AssemblySpy program is under 20,000 bytes. The compiler does a good job at providing trim, streamlined programs. Because our assembly relies on the .NET Framework, our programs are reasonably small because most of the code is shared from framework assemblies in the global assembly cache.

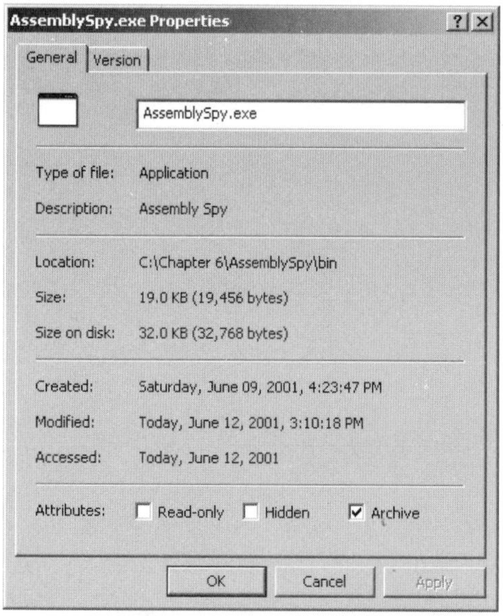

Figure 8-19 The General tab.

On the Version tab, shown in Figure 8-20, you can see that the information we placed in the AssemblyInfo.vb module can be viewed by the public. Simply add any legal trademarks or other identifying information, and the information will be readily available when you distribute your assembly.

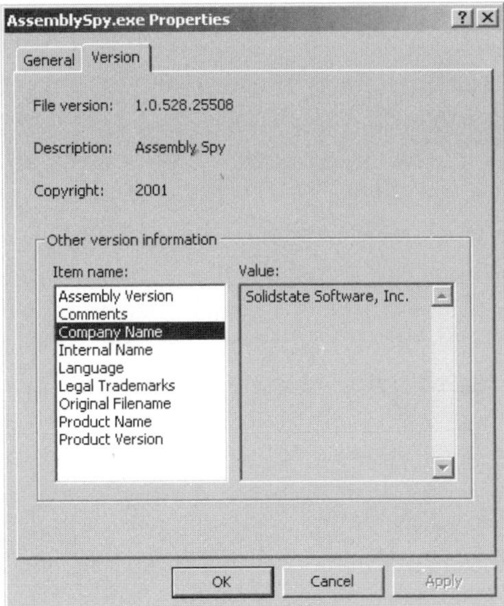

Figure 8-20 The Version tab.

Assembly Versioning

Microsoft recommends that programmers avoid sharing assemblies if at all possible. Also, you should get into the habit of providing even your private assemblies with strong names. And, once an application is deployed, you should resist the temptation to update an assembly file. Sometimes, however, a bug is discovered (gasp!), and something must be done. In situations such as this, assembly versioning comes into play.

Remember that in our assembly file in the Solution Explorer we had this line.

```
<Assembly: AssemblyVersion("1.0.*")>
```

When you need to modify or otherwise update a deployed assembly, you should update the version before you recompile. Every assembly has a version number associated with it. An assembly's version consists of information such as the following:

Assembly Version Major Number	Assembly Version Minor Number	Build Number	Revision Number
1	5	432	2

Using the sample values, we have an assembly with the version number 1.5.432.2. The first two numbers, 1.5, make up the logical assembly version. The third number, 432, represents the build number of the assembly. If you rebuild your assembly each day, this number should be incremented appropriately. The last number, 2, represents the revision of the current build.

The common language runtime considers assemblies with different versions to be different assemblies even though several assemblies with the same name might exist. How the runtime understands assemblies can have some unpleasant consequences. Let's say that a Visual Basic .NET program is compiled with version 1.5.432.2 of your assembly, but this version has been deleted from the global assembly cache. Only version 2.0.0.0 is available. When the program that was compiled with the earlier version is run, the CLR will not bind with the new version of the assembly and the program will fail. (This behavior is how binding occurs by default. Binding can be changed using an administrative override.)

If the runtime sees two assemblies with the same name and the same major and minor versions, it will attempt to bind to the assembly with the latest build and revision numbers.

> **Note** Versioning applies only to strongly named global assemblies. When using a private assembly, the runtime will use whichever assembly it can find. The version information is not used.

Load the .NET Admin Tool mscorcfg.msc once again. Click Configured Assemblies, and then click Configure An Assembly on the right. The Configure An Assembly dialog box, shown in Figure 8-21, is displayed.

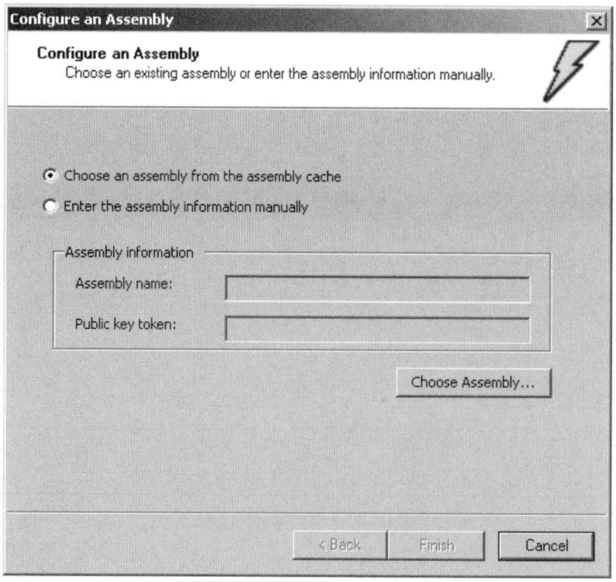

Figure 8-21 The Configure An Assembly dialog box.

Click the Choose Assembly button to display the Choose Assembly From Assembly Cache dialog box, shown in Figure 8-22. Select AssemblySpy, click Select, and then click Finish in the Configure An Assembly dialog box.

When you click Finish, the AssemblySpy Properties dialog box is displayed, shown in Figure 8-23. The first tab shows the name of our assembly and the public key token. To conserve storage space, the CLR hashes the full public key and takes the last eight bytes of the hashed value. This reduced value has been statistically determined to be unique, so it is safe to use. The reduced value of the public key is called the *public key token* and is stored in the AssemblyRef table mentioned earlier.

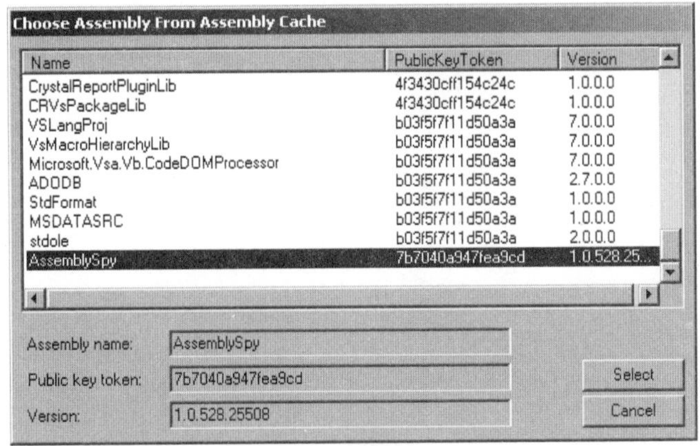

Figure 8-22 The Choose Assembly From Assembly Cache dialog box.

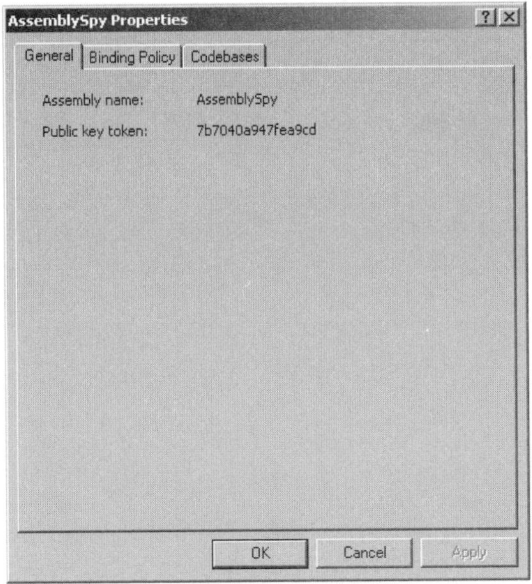

Figure 8-23 The Assembly Spy program properties dialog box.

The second tab, Binding Policy, shown in Figure 8-24, provides options for an administrator to tell the runtime how to bind to assemblies with newer version numbers. These settings let you administer exactly how the runtime uses various versions of the assembly.

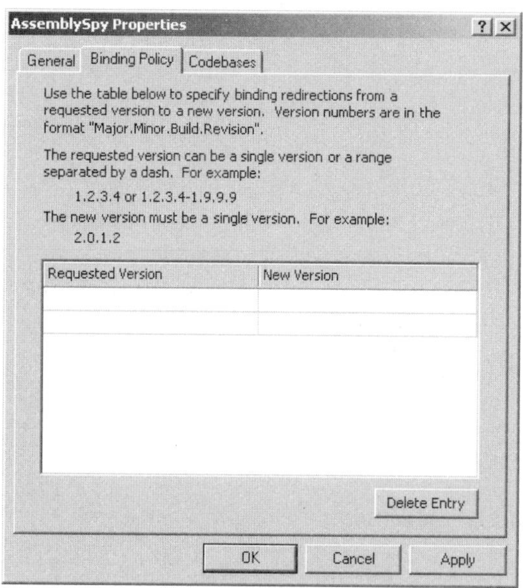

Figure 8-24 The Binding Policy tab provides options for overriding the default binding behavior.

New Variable Scoping in Visual Basic .NET

Now that we've had a chance to contemplate one of the key features of programming in .NET, let's take a look at another new item we need to come to grips with—variable scoping. While you probably understood this very well in classic Visual Basic, the rules have changed a bit for .NET. Thankfully, the way scoping works now gives us more power and is actually more intuitive.

The *scope* of a variable, constant, or procedure refers to its availability for reference by other parts of your code. Scope is also simply known as the visibility of a variable or procedure. The scope of a declared element is the set of all code that can refer to that element without qualifying its name or making it available through an *Imports* statement.

The scope of a variable in Visual Basic .NET can be at one of four levels. The most limited level is block-level and the greatest visibility is project-level.

- **Block-level.** Available only within the code block in which it is declared
- **Procedure-level.** Available only within the procedure in which it is declared
- **Module-level.** Available to all procedures within the module, class, or structure in which it is declared
- **Project-level.** Available to all procedures in the project or application

Consider the module shown below. Module-level scope applies equally to modules, classes, and structures. You can declare elements at this level by placing the declaration statement outside any procedure or block within the module, class, or structure. The code below shows a module-level variable, *sModuleLevelScope,* and a project-level variable, *sProjectLevelScope.*

```
Private sModuleLevelScope As String = ""

Public sProjectLevelScope As Integer = 5

Public Function myFunction(ByVal N As Integer) As Integer
    Dim sLocalScope As String = "Hello"

    If N < 1291 Then
        Dim bBlockScope As Integer

        bBlockScope = n ^ 3
    End If
    Return bBlockScope
End Function
```

Elements with module-level scope, such as *sModuleLevelScope*, that you declare with the *Private* keyword are available for reference to every procedure in that module. Of course, an element such as this is not available to any code in a different module. The *Dim* statement at module level defaults to *Private* access, so it is equivalent to using the *Private* statement. However, I recommend that you make scope and access more obvious by using the keyword *Private.*

The other variable, *sProjectLevelScope*, is declared as *Public,* which means it is visible anywhere in our project. It can also be read or written to from the outside world.

When you make a declaration at module level, the access you choose determines the scope. The namespace that contains the module, class, or structure also affects the scope.

The variable *sModuleLevelScope* can be seen only anywhere within the procedure *myFunction*. This level of visibility is quite similar to classic Visual Basic.

What's new in Visual Basic .NET is the *block-scoped variable*. We dimension *bBlockScope* within the *If-End If* block. Essentially, a block is a set of statements terminated by an *End, Else, Loop,* or *Next* statement; for example, within a *For...Next* or *If...Then...Else...End If* construction. An element such as *bBlockScope* that's declared within a block can be used only within that block. In our example, the scope of the *bBlockScope* integer variable is the block between *If* and *End If*. Therefore, *bBlockScope* can be seen only within the *If...End If* block and can no longer be referenced when execution passes out of that block. This level of access is the most restrictive level of scope and should be used whenever possible.

Namespace Scope

Namespace scope is a variation of module-level scope. For example, if you declare an element at module level using the *Friend* or *Public* statement, it becomes available to all procedures throughout the namespace in which the element is declared. Namespace scope also includes nested namespaces. An element available from within a namespace is also available from within any namespace nested inside that namespace.

If your project does not contain any *Namespace* statements, everything in the project is in the same namespace. In this case, namespace scope can be thought of as project scope. Elements declared as public in a module, class, or structure are also available to any project that references their project. This is how our variable *sProjectLevelScope* works.

Determining the Scope of a Variable

Knowing how to scope a variable is important in any language, and Visual Basic .NET is no exception. When considering the scope of a variable, keep in mind that local variables are a good choice for any kind of temporary calculation. They consume memory only when their procedure is running, and their names are not susceptible to conflict with other parts of your program.

For example, you can create several different procedures containing a variable named *iTempCounter*. As long as each *iTempCounter* object is declared as a local variable, each procedure recognizes only its own version of *iTempCounter*. Any one procedure can alter the value of its local *iTempCounter* without affecting the other variables with the same name in other procedures.

As a rule of thumb, always scope each variable with the narrowest scope possible. This technique not only shows good programming habits, but it will eliminate many subtle bugs and make the most efficient use of memory.

Conclusion

As always, we covered quite a bit of territory in this chapter. You now have an in-depth knowledge of assemblies and can start building both private and public assemblies. You also know more about the new scoping rules in .NET. These rules help ensure that our programs are as bug free and efficient as possible. In the next chapter, we'll look at ways to monitor files on a network and how to create a Windows Service application. If your work involves any sort of network administration, you'll be interested.

9

File System Monitoring

I've come across applications that are designed to wait for files to show up in a particular directory and then process them—for example, an application that imports data from a file into a database. Data files can be downloaded from a mainframe or transferred to an input directory by some other means, and then an application imports them into a database. Instead of constantly polling the directory for new files, the application can wait for notifications indicating that a new file has been created. You can create programs with this capability in Visual Basic 6, but you have to use and understand Win32 APIs. This task becomes trivial in Visual Basic .NET by using the .NET Framework classes. The implementation of such a program in Microsoft .NET is also consistent with the way you do everything else in .NET, so the learning curve is minimal.

The .NET Framework has a built-in class named *System.IO.FileSystemWatcher* that a program can use to watch the file system. This class provides properties that let you set which path to monitor and specify whether you are interested in changes at the file or subdirectory level. The *System.IO.FileSystemWatcher* class also lets you specify which filenames and types to watch for. (For example, **.txt* is the instruction you use to watch for changes to all text files.) Finally, you can even specify the types of changes you're interested in monitoring—for instance, new file creations, changes to file attributes, or changes to file size.

After you establish what to watch and what to watch for, you can wire in event handlers for the various events that interest you. The *FileSystemWatcher* class events that we can trap are *Changed*, *Created*, *Deleted*, *Error*, and *Renamed*. To handle an event, you write an event handler with the same declaration as the *FileSystemEventHandler* delegate and then add this handler to the *FileSystemWatcher* class. (The program we build in this chapter will illustrate the use of delegates.) This delegate-based architecture lets you add multiple handlers for the same event or use one handler for multiple events, which you couldn't do in Visual Basic 6.

The File Sentinel Program

The File Sentinel program will help you learn more about the .NET Framework and will be immediately useful to you if your work involves network administration. This program runs in the background and monitors any directory or file changes. If you help administer a network, you probably want to keep an eye on certain files and be notified if they are changed. You might also want to run a program such as File Sentinel on your Web server to notify you if someone (a.k.a., a hacker) is tampering with files on your server. Or you might want to have this program monitor your cookies directory to see whether there is any unauthorized access to your PC.

Many times, network managers in larger organizations create a dummy file with a tempting name such as salary.xls or passwords.bin and check to see whether anyone tampers with it. This technique is called placing a "honey pot" on the network. Like a high-tech sting operation, the honey pot is posted for any snooping user to attempt to view. The File Sentinel program could be set to monitor the honey pot file and notify you when someone tampers with it. If a user tries to take the honey, our File Sentinel program helps sting them.

The File Sentinel program can monitor files on either a local machine or across a network. In the process of creating this program, you'll learn more about creating and writing to files, events, and the new .NET delegate. In Visual Basic 6, events were acts of God—you could use only what you were given. Visual Basic .NET delegates permit us to add our own events to a program.

Note The File Sentinel program works only with Windows 2000 or Windows NT 4. Unfortunately, the .NET Framework does not have the plumbing for this particular program for Windows 9*x* or Windows Me. Also, the *FileSystemWatcher* class can watch disks as long as they are not switched or removed. *FileSystemWatcher* does not raise events for CDs and DVDs because time stamps and properties cannot change. Remote machines must have one of these operating system platforms installed for the component to function properly. Unfortunately, however, you cannot watch a remote Windows NT 4 computer from a Windows NT 4 computer. Hopefully, these limitations will be removed in later editions of the .NET Framework.

How the File Sentinel Program Works

Before we write the code for this program, let's take a look at what it does. In File Sentinel, the user selects either a file or a folder to monitor. Notice in Figure 9-1 that the Disable Sentinel button is disabled. The user must first select either a file or a directory to monitor before the program can actually do anything. But, just in case a user has a quick trigger finger and clicks Enable Sentinel before making a selection, we default to the current drive. As always, we protect the user from simple or thoughtless mistakes.

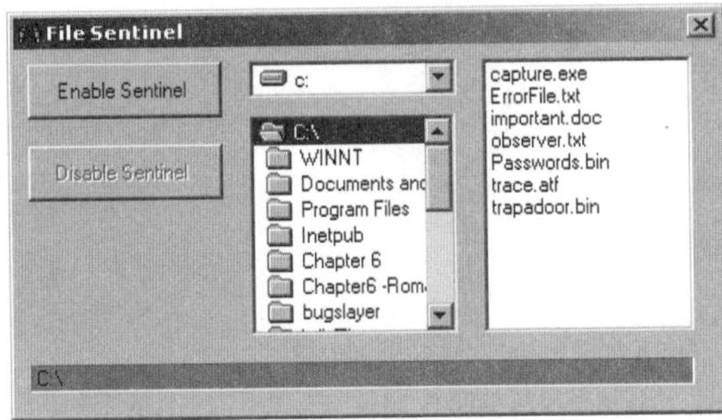

Figure 9-1 The File Sentinel program. Nothing happens until the user selects a file or a folder.

The program also includes a few tooltips to ensure that our users know how to operate the software, as shown in Figure 9-2. A tooltip is extremely easy to implement—it takes only a single line of code—and it provides an application with a professional, finished look. In earlier versions of Visual Basic, we used the *Tag* property of a control to hold a string with Help information about the control. Then, through the convoluted use of a timer and the *Mouse_Move* event, we added code to manually display a tooltip. In Visual Basic .NET, we now have a much easier way to display tooltips.

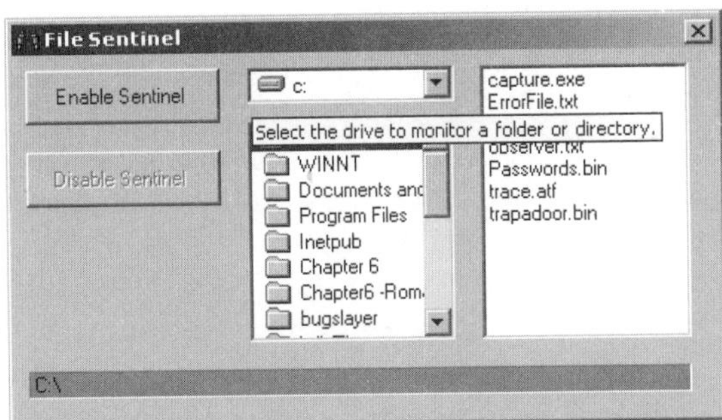

Figure 9-2 We implement a tooltip to help users know what to do.

We will write the output generated by the program to a simple text file. Of course, you could easily design the program to send e-mail messages to your machine or even page you with a message if someone tampers with files on the server. But for now, a simple text file will do nicely.

The program will write the date and time of the tampering, the file or files affected, and what type of activity was detected. If we open the output file in Notepad, we can see the date and time of each monitored access. Figure 9-3 shows that a file named trapdoor.bin was renamed to trash.doc and then examined. I think you'll agree that this program can be useful to you right away.

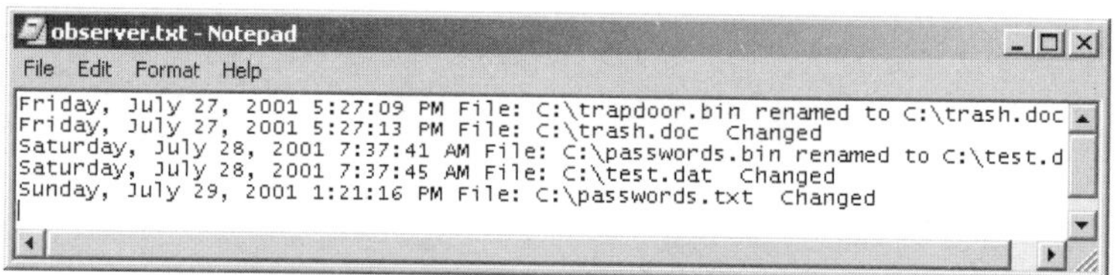

Figure 9-3 Output from the File Sentinel program is written to a text file.

Starting to Write the File Sentinel Program

As I've mentioned in previous chapters, the three steps in writing a Visual Basic .NET program are:

1. Draw the interface.
2. Set the properties of the controls.
3. Write the code.

Unlike the days before visual languages such as Visual Basic and Visual C++, when the user interface was thrown on as an afterthought, in Visual Basic .NET, building the interface is the first step we want to perform. Even though the File Sentinel program is a small one, building the interface first is a low-rent way to prototype its look and feel. We want to get the interface right from the start. Remember, to the user, the interface is the program.

Adding Controls to the Toolbox

We need to add three controls to the toolbox: the DirListBox, DriveListBox, and the FileListBox. These controls are old friends from classic Visual Basic that have been revamped to work in .NET. To add the controls, right-click the toolbox and then select Customize Toolbox. Click the .NET Framework Components tab, shown in Figure 9-4, select the controls, and then click OK.

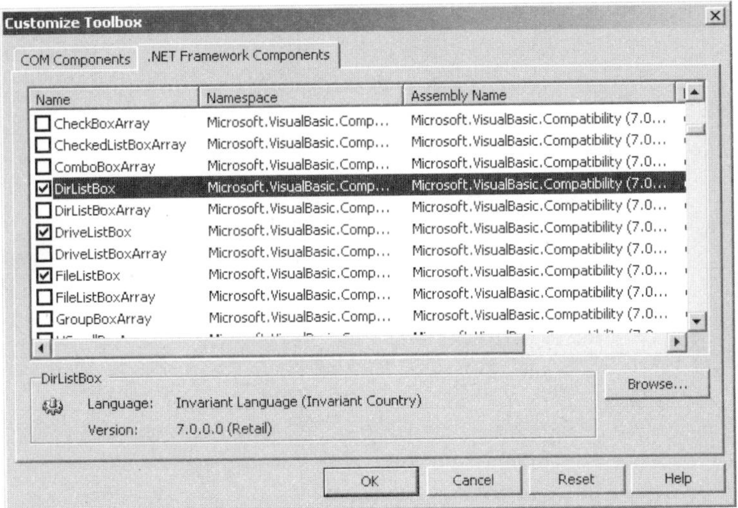

Figure 9-4 These three controls will be added under the Windows Forms tab of your toolbox.

Building the User Interface and Setting the Properties

Create a new Visual Basic .NET Windows project named FileSentinel, add the controls listed in Table 9-1 to the default form, and set the values for the properties listed. Your form should look similar to Figure 9-5 in design mode.

Table 9-1 Controls and Property Settings for the File Sentinel Program

Control	Property	Value
Button	*Name*	btnEnable
	Text	&Enable Sentinel
Button	*Name*	btnDisable
	Text	&Disable Sentinel
Label	*Name*	lblWatching
	BackColor	Lime
	BorderStyle	Fixed3D
Form	*FormBorderStyle*	FixedDialog
	Icon	*<Your choice>*
	Text	File Sentinel

(continued)

Table 9-1 Controls and Property Settings for the File Sentinel Program *(continued)*

Control	Property	Value
	StartPosition	CenterScreen
	Locked	True
ToolTip	*Name*	ttTip
DriveListBox	*Name*	DriveListBox1
DirListBox	*Name*	DirListBox1
FileListBox	*Name*	FileListBox1

> **Note** As I mentioned in Chapter 2, "Object-Oriented Programming in Visual Basic .NET," because the tooltip is not visible in the finished product, the control is placed in the trough below the form, where controls such as a ToolTip, the Error Provider, the Timer, and others that are not visible are placed. The trough is a nice touch because in the Visual Studio .NET IDE, controls you put there don't take up any valuable real estate on the form as you design the user interface.

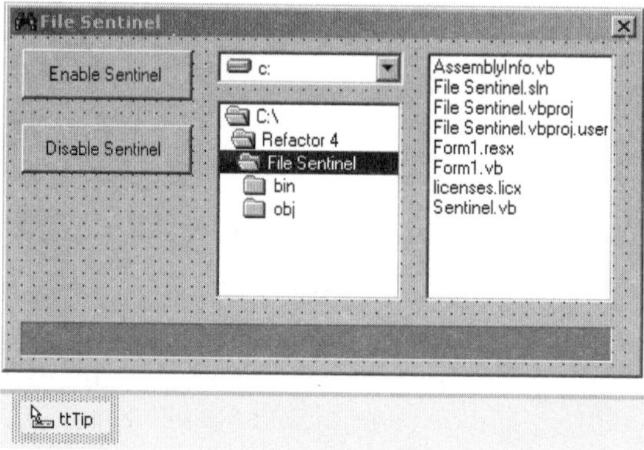

Figure 9-5 The File Sentinel form with the interface controls added.

Now that we've drawn the controls and set their properties, it's time to roll up our sleeves and write some code. We're going to encapsulate the functionality of the File Sentinel program in a class. The form we just drew will be its face to the outside world.

A Word on Legacy ActiveX Controls

You might be wondering why we don't use any of the COM ActiveX .ocx controls we're familiar with. Remember that the common language runtime (CLR) manages all code that runs inside the .NET Framework. Code that executes under the control of the CLR is called *managed* code. Conversely, code that runs outside the CLR is called *unmanaged* code. COM components, ActiveX interfaces, and Win32 API functions are all unmanaged code.

Of course, you might have built some custom COM controls or have purchased several expensive controls that are not yet available for .NET. In many cases, it is neither practical nor necessary to upgrade a COM component simply to incorporate its features into your managed application. Accessing existing functionality through interoperation services provided by the CLR often makes more sense.

.NET Windows forms can only host controls that are part of *System.Windows.Forms.Control*. For .NET to use a legacy ActiveX control, you need to make it appear as a Windows Forms control. By the same token, the ActiveX control does not expect to be hosted by .NET but instead by an ActiveX container. Fortunately, the *System.Windows.Forms.AxHost* class does the trick here. This class is really a Windows Forms control on the outside and an ActiveX control container on the inside. Essentially, the *AxHost* class creates a *wrapper* class that exposes its properties, methods, and events. Some ActiveX controls will work better than others, but if you really need to use a legacy control, fire up the WinCV program we reviewed earlier in Chapter 5, "Examining the .NET Class Framework Using Files and Strings," and see what it's all about.

Adding the *Sentinel* Class to Our Program

The .NET Framework *FileSystemWatcher* class is so handy that it's provided as a component in the toolbox. While we could add a FileSystemWatcher control to our form and set some properties, we're instead going to build our own component in a class. We take this step because we want to inherit from the built-in framework class and then add functionality, such as writing to a file and permitting the user to select files or directories to monitor. You can see the FileSystemWatcher component in Figure 9-6, under the Components tab of the toolbox.

Figure 9-6 The Components tab of the toolbox.

Adding a Class to Our Project

The class that implements our FileSystemWatcher component does all the heavy lifting for our program. When we finish the class, we will wire it into the user interface. But for now, let's understand how the class works.

1. Select Project | Add Class.
2. Select Class from the templates available, name the class Sentinel.vb, and click Open. Delete the skeleton code placed in the class, and then add the following code:

```
Imports System
Imports System.Diagnostics
Imports System.IO
Imports System.Threading

Namespace SystemObserver

    Public Class sentinel

        Private m_Watcher As System.IO.FileSystemWatcher
        Private m_ObserveFileWrite As StreamWriter
        Private fiFileInfo As FileInfo

        Public Sub New(ByVal sToObserve As String)
            m_Watcher = New FileSystemWatcher()
            fiFileInfo = New FileInfo(sToObserve)
```

```
        If (fiFileInfo.Exists = False) Then

            If (Not sToObserve.EndsWith("\")) Then
                sToObserve.Concat("\")
            End If

            With m_Watcher
                .Path = sToObserve
                .Filter = ""
                .IncludeSubdirectories = False
            End With
        Else
            With m_Watcher
                .Path = fiFileInfo.DirectoryName.ToString
                .Filter = fiFileInfo.Name.ToString
                .IncludeSubdirectories = False
            End With
        End If

        m_Watcher.NotifyFilter = _
            NotifyFilters.FileName Or _
            NotifyFilters.Attributes Or _
            NotifyFilters.LastAccess Or _
            NotifyFilters.LastWrite Or _
            NotifyFilters.Security Or _
            NotifyFilters.Size Or _
            NotifyFilters.CreationTime Or _
            NotifyFilters.DirectoryName

        AddHandler m_Watcher.Changed, AddressOf OnChanged
        AddHandler m_Watcher.Created, AddressOf OnChanged
        AddHandler m_Watcher.Deleted, AddressOf OnChanged
        AddHandler m_Watcher.Renamed, AddressOf OnRenamed
        AddHandler m_Watcher.Error, AddressOf onError

        m_Watcher.EnableRaisingEvents = True
        m_ObserveFileWrite = _
            New StreamWriter("C:\observer.txt", True)
    End Sub

    Private Sub OnChanged(ByVal source As Object, _
        ByVal e As FileSystemEventArgs)

        Dim sChange As String

        Select Case e.ChangeType
            Case WatcherChangeTypes.Changed : _
                sChange = "Changed"
            Case WatcherChangeTypes.Created : _
                sChange = "Created"
            Case WatcherChangeTypes.Deleted : _
```

(continued)

```
                    sChange = "Deleted"
            End Select

            If (Len(sChange) > 0) Then
                If (e.FullPath.IndexOf("observer.txt") > 0) _
                    Then

                    Exit Sub
                End If
            End If

            writeToFile("File: " & e.FullPath & _
                "  " & sChange)
        End Sub

        Private Sub OnRenamed(ByVal source As Object, _
            ByVal e As RenamedEventArgs)

            writeToFile("File: " & e.OldFullPath &  _
                " remaned to " & e.FullPath)
        End Sub

        Private Sub onError(ByVal source As Object, _
            ByVal errevent As ErrorEventArgs)

            writeToFile("ERROR: " & _
                errevent.GetException.Message())
        End Sub

        Private Sub writeToFile( _
            ByRef observeString As String)
            Dim sRightNow As String = _
                Date.Now.ToLongDateString() & _
                " " & Date.Now.ToLongTimeString()

            Try
                m_ObserveFileWrite.WriteLine(sRightNow & _
                    " " & observeString)
                m_ObserveFileWrite.Flush()
            Catch
            End Try
        End Sub

        Public Sub dispose()
            m_Watcher.EnableRaisingEvents = False
            m_Watcher = Nothing
            m_ObserveFileWrite.Close()
        End Sub

    End Class

End Namespace
```

How the Code Works

We want to import these four namespaces:

```
Imports System
Imports System.Diagnostics
Imports System.IO
Imports System.Threading
```

Next we wrap our class in the *SystemObserver* namespace. The name of our class within the namespace is *sentinel*. We declare three private class member variables. The first is the variable *m_Watcher*, of type *FileSystemWatcher*. The *FileSystemWatcher* framework class lives in the *System.IO* namespace.

Because we want to write our output to a file, we also create a member variable *m_ObserveFileWrite* as type *StreamWriter*. The third variable we include is needed to check whether we will be monitoring a file or a directory. The *fiFileInfo* variable of type *FileInfo* will provide the methods we need. Because these variables are scoped at the top of the class, they are visible to the entire class.

```
Namespace SystemObserver

    Public Class sentinel

        Private m_Watcher As System.IO.FileSystemWatcher
        Private m_ObserveFileWrite As StreamWriter
        Private fiFileInfo As FileInfo
```

When we instantiate a *sentinel* object, we will pass into the class's constructor as a string the path of either the file or the directory we want to monitor. A new instance of the *FileSystemWatcher* class is instantiated, but at this point we don't know whether the string variable *sToObserve* contains a file or a directory to monitor. We use the *FileInfo* class to determine which it is.

```
Public Sub New(ByVal sToObserve As String)
    m_Watcher = New FileSystemWatcher()
    fiFileInfo = New FileInfo(sToObserve)
```

Configuring the *FileSystemWatcher*

We need to set several properties of the *FileSystemWatcher* class that affect how it behaves. These properties determine what directories and subdirectories the object will monitor and the exact occurrences within those directories that will raise events.

The first two properties that determine what directories *FileSystemWatcher* should watch are *Path* and *IncludeSubdirectories*. The *Path* property indicates the fully qualified path of the root directory to watch. The property's value can be set in standard directory path notation (c:\directory) or in UNC format

(\\server\directory). The *IncludeSubdirectories* property indicates whether subdirectories within the root directory should be monitored. If this property is set to True, the component watches for the same changes in the subdirectories as it does in the main directory that it is watching. However, you will not be happy to find that if you set *IncludeSubdirctories* to True, each event you want to watch might generate an additional 10 to 15 unwanted events. The Windows operating system generates tons of messages on all sorts of internal files each and every time a user changes a file. I've found that it's better to leave *IncludeSubdirectories* set to False if you are monitoring the root directory of the drive.

If the user passes in the fully qualified path of a file, the *fiFileInfo.Exists* method returns True. If the path is a directory, the *Exists* method returns False. So, let's first check for any directories.

If the user selects a directory path such as "C:\", we have no problem. However, if the user selects a path such as "C:\Program Files\Common Files," we want to place a backslash (\) to delimit the directory. Using two methods of the *String* object makes doing this a snap. If the string *sToObserve* does not end with a backslash, we concatenate one. Couldn't be easier.

When a directory is selected, we set the path to the variable *sToObserve*. If the user wants to monitor all the files in the directory "C:\Program Files\Common Files," we would have added a trailing backslash character and set the *Path* property.

To monitor changes in all files, set the *Filter* property to an empty string (""). We do that here because we want to monitor all files in the selected directory. To monitor a specific file, set the *Filter* property to the filename. For example, to watch for changes in the file Passwords.bin, set the *Filter* property to "Passwords.bin". You can also watch for changes in a certain type of file. For example, to watch for changes in any Microsoft Word files, set the *Filter* property to "*.doc".

When a user selects a file instead of a directory to monitor, we know that the *fiFileInfo* object has all the information about the file we need. It's easy to set the *Path* property of our *FileSystemWatcher* object by setting it to *fiFileInfo.DirectoryName.ToString*. This call returns the fully qualified directory name where the file is located. Likewise, the *Name* property provides the name of the file to monitor. In both cases—monitoring files or directories—we have set *IncludeSubDirectories* to False. This setting makes our log file cleaner. It will contain only relevant entries on the files in question.

```
If (fiFileInfo.Exists = False) Then

    If (Not sToObserve.EndsWith("\")) Then
        sToObserve.Concat("\")
    End If
```

```
    With m_Watcher
        .Path = sToObserve
        .Filter = ""
        .IncludeSubdirectories = False
    End With
Else
    With m_Watcher
        .Path = fiFileInfo.DirectoryName.ToString
        .Filter = fiFileInfo.Name.ToString
        .IncludeSubdirectories = False
    End With
End If
```

Now that we have set the *Path*, *Filter*, and *IncludeSubdirectories* properties of the *FileSystemWatcher* object, we will specify which changes to watch for in a file or folder by setting the *NotifyFilter* property.

```
m_Watcher.NotifyFilter = NotifyFilters.FileName Or _
    NotifyFilters.Attributes Or _
    NotifyFilters.LastAccess Or _
    NotifyFilters.LastWrite Or _
    NotifyFilters.Security Or _
    NotifyFilters.Size Or _
    NotifyFilters.CreationTime Or _
    NotifyFilters.DirectoryName
```

In our program, we are going to look for all types of changes by bundling them together with *Or* statements. Because these values are enumerated (in other words, represented by a number under the hood), using *Or* simply adds them together. Table 9-2 describes the different values for *NotifyFilters*.

Table 9-2 Values for the *NotifyFilters* Property

Member Name	Description
Attributes	The attributes of the file or folder
CreationTime	The time the file or folder was created
DirectoryName	The name of the directory
FileName	The name of the file
LastAccess	The date the file or folder was last opened
LastWrite	The date the file or folder last had anything written to it
Security	The security settings of the file or folder
Size	The size of the file or folder

We combined all the members of this enumeration in order to watch for all changes. You can easily select only one or two of the *NotifyFilters* properties by simply *Or*ing them together as we did. For example, you can monitor changes in the size of a file or folder and for changes in security settings.

```
m_Watcher.NotifyFilter = NotifyFilters.FileName Or _
    NotifyFilters.Attributes Or NotifyFilters.LastAccess Or _
    notifyFilters.LastWrite Or NotifyFilters.Security Or _
    NotifyFilters.Size or NotifyFilters.CreationTime Or _
    NotifyFilters.DirectoryName
```

Now you are probably wondering just how the events we want to monitor are wired to the event handlers. That's where the concept of a delegate comes in.

Delegates

As you know, an event is nothing more than a message sent by something to let whatever is listening know that something has happened. This may shock you, but in .NET, the object that triggers an event is known as the *event sender*, and the object that is listening is known as the *event receiver*. The problem we need to address is whether the event receiver knows what to listen for. We can send events all day long, but if no receiver is listening it does us little good.

Although the event sender does not need to know who is listening and the event receiver does not need to know who is sending, we still need to link the sender with a receiver to ensure that the event message is passed correctly. To do this, we use a delegate. A delegate formalizes the process of declaring a procedure that will respond to an event.

A delegate is used to communicate the message (of the event being triggered) between the source and the listener. A receiver registers the delegate with a sender, letting the sender know that the receiver will respond to the sender's events. Another powerful feature of delegates is *multicast functionality*, which means that a single sender can be dispatched to several receivers, acting as a one-to-many relationship. We are going to implement the reverse and use a delegate in a situation in which messages from several senders are sent to a single receiver. In this situation, we can easily determine which sender sent the message, making our code more streamlined and easier to read.

The *FileSystemWatcher* object knows how to raise four different events, depending on the types of changes that occur in the directory or file it is watching. These events are:

- *Created*, which is raised whenever a directory or file is created.
- *Deleted*, which is raised whenever a directory or file is deleted.
- *Renamed*, which is raised whenever the name of a directory or file is changed.

- *Changed*, which is raised whenever changes are made to the size, system attributes, last write time, last access time, or NTFS security permissions of a directory or file. Of course, as we have just seen, we can use the *NotifyFilter* property to limit the amount of events the *Changed* event raises.

For each of these four *FileSystemWatcher* events, we define handlers that call methods when a change occurs. Each event handler provides two parameters that allow you to handle the event properly—the *sender* parameter, which provides an object reference to the object responsible for the event, and the *e* parameter, which provides an object for representing the event and its information.

We know that an event is a message sent by an object to signal the occurrence of an action. The action might be caused by user interaction such as a mouse click, or it might be triggered by some other program logic or even the operating system itself. In our case, an event will be generated when a user performs an action such as renaming a file, for example.

The *FileSystemWatcher* component is the event sender in our example. The object or procedure that captures and responds to the event is the event receiver. In event communication, however, the event sender class does not know which object or method will receive (handle) the events it raises. Therefore, what is needed is an intermediary between the source and the receiver. The .NET Framework defines a special type, or *Delegate*, which provides this functionality.

In our example, we will add a handler for the *Changed*, *Created*, *Deleted*, *Renamed*, and *Error* events that can be raised by *m_Watcher*. We do this by using the *AddressOf* operator, which we use to create a function delegate. This delegate points to the function specified by the procedure name of the operator. Whenever our *m_Watcher* object triggers a *Changed* event, we want to know about it and probably do something. So, we can add an event handler, *OnChanged*, that will receive each *Changed* event. The following line from our program tells us that we are adding a handler to the *m_Watcher.Changed* event and that this handler can be found at the location specified by the *AddressOf* operator for the procedure *OnChanged*.

```
AddHandler m_Watcher.Changed, AddressOf OnChanged
```

After we add the delegate that instructs *m_Watcher* where to send any *Changed* events, we have to write the *OnChanged* event procedure itself. We make these procedures private so that they can be seen only in our class.

```
Private Sub OnChanged(ByVal source As Object, _
    ByVal e As FileSystemEventArgs)

'Do things when a file or directory is changed

End Sub
```

As I mentioned, we use the Visual Basic .NET *AddressOf* operator to create a function delegate that points to the function specified by *procedurename*, in this case *OnChanged*. I've used shorthand notation for creating our delegate; however, both of the following lines are equivalent:

```
AddHandler m_Watcher.Changed, AddressOf OnChanged
AddHandler m_Watcher.Changed, _
    New EventHandler(AddressOf OnChanged)
```

With this code we have registered the receiver, *OnChanged*, with the sender of the message, *m_Watcher.Changed*. Each time our object *m_Watcher* raises a *Changed* event, it will be captured by the *OnChanged* event handler.

Notice that we are going to handle all five events that can be fired by the *m_Watcher* object. However, the *Changed*, *Created*, and *Deleted* events will all be handled by the *OnChanged* event handler, which shows our many-to-one relationship. The following code defines and registers the delegates:

```
AddHandler m_Watcher.Changed, AddressOf OnChanged
AddHandler m_Watcher.Created, AddressOf OnChanged
AddHandler m_Watcher.Deleted, AddressOf OnChanged
AddHandler m_Watcher.Renamed, AddressOf OnRenamed
AddHandler m_Watcher.Error, AddressOf onError
```

We wrap up our constructor code by setting the *EnableRaisingEvents* property to True. The object will not start operating until you have set both the *Path* and *EnableRaisingEvents* properties. (We covered writing to files in Chapter 5, so the *StreamWriter* object is an old friend by now.)

```
m_Watcher.EnableRaisingEvents = True
m_ObserveFileWrite = _
    New StreamWriter("C:\observer.txt", True)
```

At this point, the *m_Watcher* object is ready and waiting for any relevant events to trap and write to our text file, C:\observer.txt.

Handling the *Changed*, *Created*, and *Deleted* Events

As I mentioned above, when the *Changed*, *Created*, or *Deleted* events are fired, each will be handled by the *OnChanged* event handler. The *source* parameter tells us who sent the event. The *FileSystemEventArgs* parameter contains information about the specific message. The *ChangeType* property of *FileSystemEventArgs* tells us what type of change occurred. We can simply interrogate *FileSystemEventArgs* to find out what occurred.

Let's take a brief detour, visit our friend the WinCV tool again, and search for *FileSytemEventArgs*. We will interrogate these properties to find out the type of change that occurred in the *ChangeType* property as well as the file affected in the *FullPath* property. Again, spend time with the WinCV tool not only for practice in reading the .NET classes, but also for finding out exactly what the classes can do.

```
public class System.IO.FileSystemEventArgs :
    EventArgs
{

    // Fields

    // Constructors
    public FileSystemEventArgs(
        System.IO.WatcherChangeTypes changeType,
        string directory, string name);

    // Properties
    public WatcherChangeTypes ChangeType { get; }
    public string FullPath { get; }
    public string Name { get; }

    // Methods
    public virtual bool Equals(object obj);
    public virtual int GetHashCode();
    public Type GetType();
    public virtual string ToString();
} // end of System.IO.FileSystemEventArgs
```

When one of these three events (*Changed*, *Created*, or *Deleted*) is fired by *m_Watcher*, the *OnChanged* event handler is called. We can determine which of the three events occurred and write a string literal to our local string variable, *sChange*.

```
Private Sub OnChanged(ByVal source As Object, _
    ByVal e As FileSystemEventArgs)

    Dim sChange As String

    Select Case e.ChangeType
        Case WatcherChangeTypes.Changed : _
            sChange = "Changed"
        Case WatcherChangeTypes.Created : _
            sChange = "Created"
        Case WatcherChangeTypes.Deleted : _
            sChange = "Deleted"
    End Select
```

We now know what event was fired. When we write to our file, an event will also be fired for this change. We want to ignore changes to the observer.txt file.

```
If (Len(sChange) > 0) Then
    If (e.FullPath.IndexOf("observer.txt") > 0) _
        Then

        Exit Sub
    End If
End If
```

Finally, we can write the change to our file by calling our routine *writeToFile*. By passing in the *FullPath* property of the file and the type of change, we will know exactly what happened.

```
writeToFile("File: " & e.FullPath & "  " & sChange)
```

Handling the *Renamed* and *Error* Events

These event handlers are similar to those we learned about in the previous section. As another exercise, take a look at the WinCV tool and check out *RenamedEventArgs*. You can see that you can read the *FullPath*, *OldFullPath*, and *OldName* properties to know exactly what the file was renamed to.

```
public class System.IO.RenamedEventArgs :
    System.IO.FileSystemEventArgs
{

    // Fields

    // Constructors
    public RenamedEventArgs(
        System.IO.WatcherChangeTypes changeType,
        string directory, string name, string oldName);

    // Properties
    public WatcherChangeTypes ChangeType { get; }
    public string FullPath { get; }
    public string Name { get; }
    public string OldFullPath { get; }
    public string OldName { get; }

    // Methods
    public virtual bool Equals(object obj);
    public virtual int GetHashCode();
    public Type GetType();
    public virtual string ToString();
} // end of System.IO.RenamedEventArgs
```

Here we simply interrogate the *RenamedEventArgs* parameter to determine everything we need to know about a renamed file. Likewise, by interrogating *ErrorEventArgs*, we can see what type of error was generated. Both of these handlers build a string and pass it into our *writeToFile* routine to log the renaming and error events.

```
Private Sub OnRenamed(ByVal source As Object, _
    ByVal e As RenamedEventArgs)

    writeToFile("File: " & e.OldFullPath &  _
        " remaned to " & e.FullPath)
End Sub

Private Sub onError(ByVal source As Object, _
    ByVal errevent As ErrorEventArgs)

    writeToFile("ERROR: " & errevent.GetException.Message())
End Sub
```

Writing to Our Log File

Having a timestamp for changes we are interested in can be helpful, so we dimension a string and grab the current time and date. The *Try…Catch* block was described in Chapter 7, "Handling Errors and Debugging Programs," so that part of the code should be familiar to you. Because we might have trouble writing to a file, we place the file-access code in the protected *Try* block. *Catch* is empty, but it will catch any error and not cause our program to crash and burn if there is any difficulty writing to our file. We then use the *WriteLine* method of the *StreamWriter* object being held in the private member variable *m_ObserveFileWrite*. After we write the entry, calling the *Flush* method ensures that the line is immediately written to disk.

```
Private Sub writeToFile(ByRef observeString As String)
    Dim sRightNow As String = _
        Date.Now.ToLongDateString() & _
        " " & Date.Now.ToLongTimeString()

            Try
                m_ObserveFileWrite.WriteLine(sRightNow & _
                    " " & observeString)
                m_ObserveFileWrite.Flush()
            Catch
            End Try

End Sub
```

Of course, when our object is released, the *dispose* method of the class is called. We turn off capturing events by setting *EnableRaisingEvents* to False, set the object to *Nothing*, and then close the file.

Note Remember that setting our object to *Nothing* only flags the object for deletion but, unlike in Visual Basic 6, does not immediately release memory and resources. These operations are performed the next time the garbage collector makes its rounds. It will see that our object is flagged for deletion and remove it, but its removal could be up to several minutes later.

```
Public Sub dispose()
    m_Watcher.EnableRaisingEvents = False
    m_Watcher = Nothing
    m_ObserveFileWrite.Close()
End Sub
```

That wraps up our class that monitors important events in files and directories. Now let's wire it to our user interface.

Wiring Up the User Interface

Ready to write some code? In the Visual Basic .NET IDE, switch to the Form1.Vb tab so that you can start writing the code required to use our file sentinel. As usual, we really don't have to write much code for what this program does. The functionality we get even without writing much code again illustrates how powerful the .NET Framework is. Add the following code to Form1.vb:

```
Imports FileSentinel.SystemObserver.sentinel

Public Class Form1
    Inherits System.Windows.Forms.Form

    Private m_sFilesToScan As String
    Private m_fsSentinel As _
        FileSentinel.SystemObserver.sentinel

    Public Sub New()
        MyBase.New()

        ' This call is required by the Windows Form Designer.
        InitializeComponent()

        ' Add any initialization after the
        ' InitializeComponent() call

        lblWatching Text = DriveListBox1.Drive.ToUpper & "\"
```

```
    '-- Call our private routine that initializes the GUI
    InitializeGUI()

End Sub

Private Sub InitializeGUI()

'-- Disable the options until a legitimate Dir/File
' selection is made
    btnEnable.Enabled = True
    btnDisable.Enabled = False

    ttTip.SetToolTip(btnEnable, _
        "Enable the File Sentinel to monitor a folder " & _
        "or directory. ")
    ttTip.SetToolTip(btnDisable, _
        "Stop monitoring a folder or directory.")
    ttTip.SetToolTip(DriveListBox1, _
        "Select the drive to monitor a folder or " & _
        "directory.")
End Sub

Private Sub btnDisable_Click( _
    ByVal sender As System.Object, _
    ByVal e As System.EventArgs) _
    Handles btnDisable.Click

    m_fsSentinel.dispose()
    btnEnable.Enabled = True
    btnDisable.Enabled = False
    DriveListBox1.Enabled = True
    DirListBox1.Enabled = True
    FileListBox1.Enabled = True
End Sub

Private Sub DriveListBox1_SelectedIndexChanged( _
    ByVal sender As System.Object, _
    ByVal e As System.EventArgs) _
    Handles DriveListBox1.SelectedIndexChanged

    Try
        DirListBox1.Path = DriveListBox1.Drive
        lblWatching.Text = DriveListBox1.Drive
    Catch
        DriveListBox1.Drive = DirListBox1.Path
    End Try

End Sub
```

(continued)

```
Private Sub DirListBox1_SelectedIndexChanged( _
    ByVal sender As System.Object, _
    ByVal e As System.EventArgs) _
    Handles DirListBox1.SelectedIndexChanged

    Try
        FileListBox1.Path = DirListBox1.Path
        lblWatching.Text = DirListBox1.Path
    Catch
    End Try
End Sub

Private Sub FileListBox1_SelectedIndexChanged( _
    ByVal sender As System.Object, _
    ByVal e As System.EventArgs) _
    Handles FileListBox1.SelectedIndexChanged

    If FileListBox1.Path.EndsWith("\") Then
        lblWatching.Text = FileListBox1.Path & _
            FileListBox1.FileName
    Else
        lblWatching.Text = FileListBox1.Path & _
            "\" & FileListBox1.FileName
    End If

End Sub

Protected Sub startWatching()

    '-- Initialize the Tool Tips
    '-- Create a new instance of the File Sentinel
    m_fsSentinel = _
        New FileSentinel.SystemObserver.sentinel( _
            m_sFilesToScan)

    '-- Update the UI --
    btnEnable.Enabled = False
    btnDisable.Enabled = True
    DriveListBox1.Enabled = False
    DirListBox1.Enabled = False
    FileListBox1.Enabled = False
End Sub

Private Sub btnEnable_Click( _
    ByVal sender As System.Object, _
    ByVal e As System.EventArgs) _
    Handles btnEnable.Click

    startWatching()
End Sub
```

```
    Private Sub lblWatching_TextChanged( _
        ByVal sender As Object, _
        ByVal e As System.EventArgs) _
        Handles lblWatching.TextChanged

        m_sFilesToScan = lblWatching.Text
    End Sub

    ' Other Windows Form Designer generated code omitted.

End Class
```

How the Interface Code Works

The first task we need to take care of is importing the *SystemObserver* class. Once we've imported our new class, we can reference the object in our user interface.

```
Imports FileSentinel.SystemObserver.sentinel
```

At the top of our *Form1* class, we add two private variables. The first, *m_sFilesToScan,* is used to hold the file or directory selected for monitoring. The second variable, *m_fsSentinel*, will of course hold a reference to an instance of our *sentinel* class.

```
Public Class Form1
    Inherits System.Windows.Forms.Form

    Private m_sFilesToScan As String
    Private m_fsSentinel As _
        File_Sentinel.SystemObserver.sentinel
```

In the form constructor, we want to initialize a value to display in the label named lblWatching. If the user clicks the Enable Sentinel button immediately after the program starts, at least some default value is included and our program won't crash. Next we call our built-in routine *InitializeGUI*, which sets up the user interface. Notice that we set the label after the built-in *InitializeComponent* routine is called. This order ensures that all the controls are sited and the form is completely built and displayed. We can then write to the form, or to any controls contained in it, and not get an error. Be sure that any code that manipulates a visible part of a form is executed after the *InitializeComponent* routine.

```
Public Sub New()
    MyBase.New()

    ' This call is required by the Windows Form Designer.
    InitializeComponent()
```

(continued)

```
        ' Add any initialization after the
        ' InitializeComponent() call
        lblWatching.Text = DriveListBox1.Drive.ToUpper & "\"

        '-- Call our private routine that initializes the GUI
        InitializeGUI()

    End Sub
```

The ToolTip Control

When the form is loaded, built, and displayed, our routine *InitializeGUI* is called. In this routine, we activate the Enable Sentinel button and construct our tooltips. We add a tooltip to both the Enable Sentinel and Disable Sentinel buttons, as well as to the DriveListBox control. The tooltip is very easy to set by using the following format:

```
ToolTipControl.SetToolTip(controlToAssociate, _
    "Message to display")
```

You can get fancy with a tooltip by setting some of the control's properties. For example, you can set multiple delay values for the Windows Forms ToolTip control. The unit of measure for these properties is milliseconds. The *InitialDelay* property determines how long the user must point at the associated control before the tooltip string appears. The *ReshowDelay* property sets the number of milliseconds that pass for subsequent tooltip strings to appear as the mouse moves from one tooltip-associated control to another. The *AutoPopDelay* property determines the length of time the tooltip string is shown. You can set these values individually or by setting the value of the *AutomaticDelay* property, which will then set the other delay values in a fixed ratio to the value set for *AutomaticDelay*. (When *AutomaticDelay* is set to a value of *N*, *InitialDelay* is set to *N*, *ReshowDelay* is set to *N*/5, and *AutoPopDelay* is set to 5*N*.) We are going to use the default values because they are fine for our program.

```
Private Sub InitializeGUI()

    '-- Disable the options until a legit Dir/File
    ' selection is made
    btnEnable.Enabled = True
    btnDisable.Enabled = False

    '-- Initialize the ToolTips
    ttTip.SetToolTip(btnEnable, _
        "Enable the File Sentinel to monitor a folder " & _
        "or directory. ")
    ttTip.SetToolTip(btnDisable, _
        "Stop monitoring a folder or directory.")
```

```
    ttTip.SetToolTip(DriveListBox1, _
        "Select the drive to monitor a folder " & _
        "or directory.")
    End Sub
```

When the user enables the File Sentinel, the Enable Sentinel button is disabled and the Disable Sentinel button is enabled. We also enable the drive, directory, and file list boxes to permit the user to make a selection.

```
Private Sub btnDisable_Click( _
    ByVal sender As System.Object, _
    ByVal e As System.EventArgs) _
    Handles btnDisable.Click

    m_fsSentinel.dispose()
    btnEnable.Enabled = True
    btnDisable.Enabled = False
    DriveListBox1.Enabled = True
    DirListBox1.Enabled = True
    FileListBox1.Enabled = True
End Sub
```

We want the user to be able to select any drive that the computer can see, whether local or remote. The Visual Basic 6 DriveListBox control was usually used to select or change drives in a File Open or a Save dialog box. Unfortunately, Visual Basic .NET has no equivalent for the DriveListBox control. If you upgrade older Visual Basic programs to Visual Basic .NET, any existing DriveListBox controls are upgraded to the VB6.DriveListBox control that is provided as a part of the compatibility library (*Microsoft.VisualBasic.Compatibility*). We'll use this control for our program because it was converted to .NET and is considered to be managed code. Of course, when we added the control it was listed within the .NET Framework Components tab of the Customize Toolbox dialog box.

When the user selects a drive, we want to set the directory list box to the new drive. However, if the user selects, say, drive A and no disk is inserted, we will get an error. By placing the following line within a protected *Try* block, we can handle any error:

```
DirListBox1.Path = DriveListBox1.Drive
```

If the drive is legitimate, we set the directory list box to the new drive and display the current drive in the label. If, however, the change in drives throws an error, the *Catch* block is executed and we reset the drive to the previously good drive from the directory list box. This simple technique will prevent a runtime error.

```
Private Sub DriveListBox1_SelectedIndexChanged( _
    ByVal sender As System.Object, _
    ByVal e As System.EventArgs) _
    Handles DriveListBox1.SelectedIndexChanged

    Try
        DirListBox1.Path = DriveListBox1.Drive
        lblWatching.Text = DriveListBox1.Drive
    Catch
        DriveListBox1.Drive = DirListBox1.Path
    End Try
End Sub
```

If the drive selected is available, the directory list box is set to the path of the new drive letter. If this change does not cause an error, we display the new directory in the label *lblWatching*. As with the DriveListBox control, Visual Basic .NET does not include a .NET version of the DirListBox control.

```
Private Sub DirListBox1_SelectedIndexChanged( _
    ByVal sender As System.Object, _
    ByVal e As System.EventArgs) _
    Handles DirListBox1.SelectedIndexChanged

    Try
        FileListBox1.Path = DirListBox1.Path
        lblWatching.Text = DirListBox1.Path
    Catch
    End Try
End Sub
```

If the directory list box does not throw an error, the file list box is updated. As I mentioned, we want to terminate the string with a back slash if the character is not there.

```
Private Sub FileListBox1_SelectedIndexChanged( _
    ByVal sender As System.Object, _
    ByVal e As System.EventArgs) _
    Handles FileListBox1.SelectedIndexChanged

    If FileListBox1.Path.EndsWith("\") Then
        lblWatching.Text = FileListBox1.Path & _
            FileListBox1.FileName
    Else
        lblWatching.Text = FileListBox1.Path & "\" & _
            FileListBox1.FileName
    End If

End Sub
```

Whenever a legitimate drive, directory, or folder is selected, the label *lbl-Watching* is updated. This update fires the *TextChanged* event of the label. We set the class-level private variable *m_sFilesToScan* to the contents of the label's *Text* property.

```
Private Sub lblWatching_TextChanged( _
    ByVal sender As Object, _
    ByVal e As System.EventArgs) _
    Handles lblWatching.TextChanged

    m_sFilesToScan = lblWatching.Text
End Sub
```

When a file or directory is successfully selected, the user clicks the Enable Sentinel button we created with the name *btnEnable*. This event simply calls the procedure *startWatching*.

```
Private Sub btnEnable_Click( _
    ByVal sender As System.Object, _
    ByVal e As System.EventArgs) _
    Handles btnEnable.Click

    startWatching()
End Sub
```

When the sentinel is enabled, we create a new instance of our *sentinel* class. Then, to ensure that the user does not start clicking other buttons or drives when the sentinel is enabled, the Enable Sentinel button and the drive, directory, and file list boxes are disabled, which avoids confusion on the part of the user. We gently guide them through what they can and cannot select in the context of the running program.

```
Protected Sub startWatching()

    '-- Create a new instance of the File Sentinel
    m_fsSentinel = _
        New File_Sentinel.SystemObserver.sentinel( _
            m_sFilesToScan)

    '-- Update the UI --
    btnEnable.Enabled = False
    btnDisable.Enabled = True
    DriveListBox1.Enabled = False
    DirListBox1.Enabled = False
    FileListBox1.Enabled = False
End Sub
```

Because we encapsulated all of the code in our class—following good design practice—within our user interface we can see only the *dispose* and *GetType* methods. Everything else is hidden, as you can see in Figure 9-7.

Figure 9-7 All we see in the interface are the *dispose* and *GetType* methods.

Possible Enhancements to the File Sentinel

If you were using the File Sentinel program in a work environment, you might want to give the user more granularity in what to monitor. To do this, you could add three *WriteOnly* properties: *WatchAttributes*, *WatchFileSize*, and *WatchLastAccess*. Our program watches these properties by default, but you can give the user the option if you want to by adding these to the *sentinel* class. While we added all of them, you could add only a few default filters, such as *LastWrite*, *Security*, *CreationTime*, and *DirectoryName*.

```
m_Watcher.NotifyFilter = NotifyFilters.FileName Or _
    NotifyFilters.LastWrite Or _
    NotifyFilters.Security Or _
    NotifyFilters.CreationTime Or _
    NotifyFilters.DirectoryName
```

Then you could add three custom *WriteOnly* properties to your class. If the user wanted to monitor additional events, such as monitoring the attributes, file size, or last access of a file, these properties would be set to True within your class. Because the *NotifyFilters* property is enumerated, simply add whichever attribute you want by adding the enumerated data type to the *NotifyFilters* property of the class.

You can combine the members of the *NotifyFilter* enumeration to watch for more than one kind of change because it allows a bitwise combination of its member values. For example, you can watch for changes in the size of a file or folder and for changes in security settings. This raises an event any time a change in size or security settings of a file or folder occurs. Table 9-3 lists the members of *NotifyFilters*.

Table 9-3 *NotifyFilters* Members

Member Name	Description
Attributes	The attributes of the file or folder
CreationTime	The time the file or folder was created
DirectoryName	The name of the directory
FileName	The name of the file
LastAccess	The date the file or folder was last opened
LastWrite	The date the file or folder last had anything written to it
Security	The security settings of the file or folder
Size	The size of the file or folder

Here are three custom *WriteOnly* properties that you might add to your class to watch for changes in file attributes, file size, and file access:

```
WriteOnly Property WatchAttributes() As Boolean
    Set(ByVal Value As Boolean)
        If (value = True) Then
            m_Watcher.NotifyFilter += _
                IO.NotifyFilters.Attributes
        End If
    End Set
End Property

WriteOnly Property WatchFileSize() As Boolean
    Set
        If (value = True) Then
            m_Watcher.NotifyFilter += _
                IO.NotifyFilters.Size
    End Set
End Property

WriteOnly Property WatchLastAccess() As Boolean
    Set
        If (value = True) Then
            m_Watcher.NotifyFilter += _
                IO.NotifyFilters.LastAccess
        End If
    End Set
End Property
```

Then, within your user interface, you could add three check boxes. If the user checked one or more of the optional items to watch, you simply set that particular class property to True.

```
If chkAttributes.Checked = True Then _
    m_fsSentinel.WatchAttributes = True
If chkSize.Checked = True Then _
    m_fsSentinel.WatchFileSize = True
If chkAccess.Checked = True Then _
    m_fsSentinel.WatchLastAccess = True
```

That's it for our File Sentinel class, or is it? You might be wondering why we didn't add extensive user interface capabilities (such as displaying notification messages in a dialog box) to the class. Well, the reason is that we are going to convert our class into a Windows service, and services don't have a user interface.

> **Note** The DriveListBox, DirListBox, and FileListBox legacy controls behave somewhat erratically in the .NET platform—when the File Sentinel program is running, you might need to click the controls several times before they display the proper elements.

Introduction to Windows Services

Microsoft Windows services, formerly known as NT services, enable you to create long-running executable applications that run in their own Windows sessions. Service applications can be set up to start when the computer boots, and they can be paused and restarted.

These services do not have any user interface, which makes converting our class to a service for use on a server (or wherever you need long-running functionality that does not interfere with other users working on the same computer) quite easy. You can also run services in the security context of a specific user account that is different from the logged-on user or the default computer account.

You create a service by creating an application that is installed as a service. If we want to use the *sentinel* class as a service, we can convert it to run on a server in the background. And because we used object-oriented programming, we can simply use the class as-is, giving real meaning to reusability.

The Life and Death of a Service

A service goes through several internal states in its lifetime. First the service is installed onto the system on which it will run, such as your Web server. This process executes the installers for the service project and loads the service into the Windows Service Control Manager (SCM) for that computer. The SCM is the central utility provided by Windows to administer services. It can be configured to run automatically when booted or can be started and stopped at will. A running service can exist in this state indefinitely until it is either stopped or paused or until the computer shuts down. A service can exist in one of three basic states: running, paused, or stopped.

Unlike some types of projects, for a service you must create installation components for the service application. The installation components install and register the service on the server and create an entry for your service with the SCM. Luckily, .NET makes this task very easy, and I'll cover the steps in detail.

Windows service applications run in a different Windows station—a secure object that contains a clipboard, a set of global atoms, and a group of desktop objects—than other applications. Because of this, dialog boxes raised from within a Windows service application will not be seen and will probably even cause your program to stop responding. Therefore, you want to be sure to write all messages, including error messages, to a file rather than raise any messages in the user interface by means of something such as a message box.

Building Our File Sentinel into a Windows Service

Start a new Visual Basic project, and this time select the Windows Service template, shown in Figure 9-8. Name the project vbFileMonitorService. Of course, the IDE will create a new directory with that name under the directory listed in the Location text box.

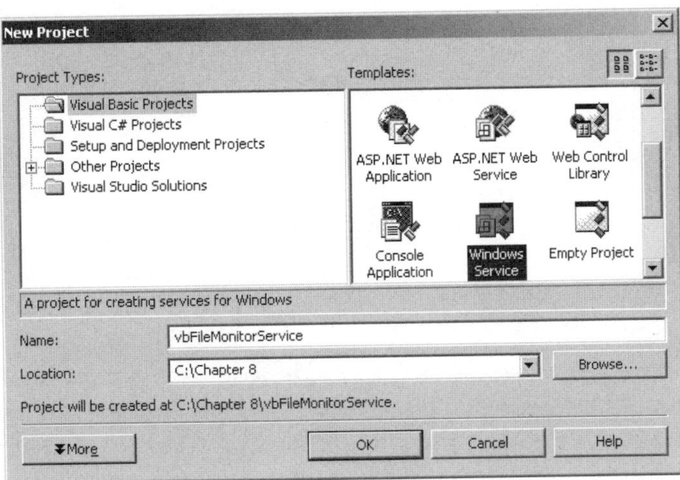

Figure 9-8 Use the Windows Service project icon to create a Windows service application.

When the project is created, you'll see a blank designer screen. Click the hyperlink that reads "click here to switch to code view," shown in Figure 9-9. The IDE adds the service template for us, but we'll need to add a few lines of code in order to include our *sentinel* class and also to write to an event log file.

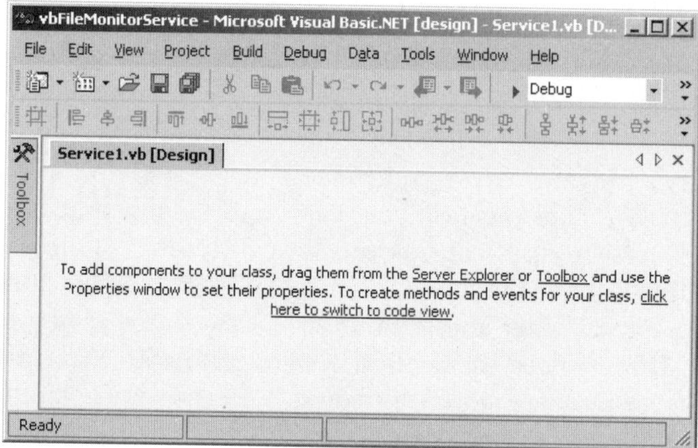

Figure 9-9 Use the hyperlink to switch to code view.

Adding Our *Sentinel* Class to Our Service

We're going to add the *sentinel* class we built earlier in this chapter to this project to illustrate object-oriented class reusability. We will make this addition in the easiest way—using Windows Explorer to copy the file Sentinel.vb in the directory of your last project to the vbFileMonitorService directory. Sentinel.vb is the text file that contains the code with the namespace *SystemObserver* and the public class *sentinel*.

After the file is in the vbFileMonitorService directory, we want to add the file to our current project.

1. From the Visual Studio .Net IDE, Select Project | Add Existing Item.
2. When the Add Existing Item dialog box comes up, select Sentinel.vb to include our class file in the vbFileMonitorService project. Now the file is physically in our current project directory and is added to our project solution file.
3. Click the Sentinel.vb tab to display the code for our *sentinel* class. Comment out the *EnableRaisingEvent* property line. We are going to add two properties to turn this event on and off. Also change the name of the log file to vbFMS.txt. With separate names, we can keep both log files on disk and use them for different purposes.

```
        AddHandler m_Watcher.Changed, AddressOf OnChanged
        AddHandler m_Watcher.Created, AddressOf OnChanged
        AddHandler m_Watcher.Deleted, AddressOf OnChanged
        AddHandler m_Watcher.Renamed, AddressOf OnRenamed
        AddHandler m_Watcher.Error, AddressOf onError

        ' m_Watcher.EnableRaisingEvents = True

        m_ObserveFileWrite = _
            New StreamWriter("C:\vbFMS.txt", True)
```

Remember that the *OnChanged* event handler checks to see whether the log file was being modified. If it was, we ignored the event. Because we changed the name of our log file to vbFMS.txt, add this name in lowercase characters to the *IndexOf* property. This setting will prevent our log from recording each and every write to the file.

```
If (Len(sChange) > 0) Then
    If (e.FullPath.IndexOf("vbfms.txt") > 0) Then
        Exit Sub
    End If
End If
```

Finally, add the following two public properties to the class. With these properties, when our service starts and stops, we can instruct the *sentinel* class to start and stop logging changes to files.

```
Public Sub StartLogging()
    m_Watcher.EnableRaisingEvents = True
End Sub

Public Sub StopLogging()
    m_Watcher.EnableRaisingEvents = False
End Sub
```

With these minor changes, we're able to import our *sentinel* class and quickly change it from a Windows application to a Windows service.

Updating the Service1.vb File

As with other project templates, the Visual Studio .NET project template Windows Service does much of the work of building a service for you. It references the appropriate classes and namespaces, sets up the inheritance from the base class for services, and overrides several of the methods you're likely to want to override.

With this work done for you, at a minimum you must do the following to create a functional service:

- Set the *ServiceName* property.
- Create the necessary installers for your service application.
- Override and specify code for the *OnStart* and *OnStop* methods to customize the ways in which your service behaves.

Click the Service1.vb tab to switch to the service template code generated by the IDE. In the interest of space, I'll simply highlight the lines of code that you have to add. Because we are referencing our File Sentinel program, we had to first add it to our project.

```
Imports System.ServiceProcess
Imports vbFileMonitorService.SystemObserver.sentinel


Public Class Service1
    Inherits System.ServiceProcess.ServiceBase

    Dim vbFMS As vbFileMonitorService.SystemObserver.sentinel

#Region " Component Designer generated code "

    Public Sub New()
        MyBase.New()

        ' This call is required by the Component Designer.
        InitializeComponent()

        ' Add any initialization after the
        ' InitializeComponent() call
        EventLog.EnableRaisingEvents = True
        Me.AutoLog = True
        Me.CanStop = True

        vbFMS = New _
            vbFileMonitorService.SystemObserver.sentinel("C:\")

    End Sub

    ' The main entry point for the process
    Shared Sub Main()
        Dim ServicesToRun() As _
            System.ServiceProcess.ServiceBase

        ' More than one NT Service may run within the same
        ' process. To add another service to this process,
        ' change the following line to create a second
        ' service object. For example,
        '
```

```
        '    ServicesToRun = New _
        '        System.ServiceProcess.ServiceBase ()
        '       {New Service1, New MySecondUserService}
        '
        ServicesToRun = New _
            System.ServiceProcess.ServiceBase () _
            {New Service1}

        System.ServiceProcess.ServiceBase.Run(ServicesToRun)
    End Sub

    ' Required by the Component Designer
    Private components As System.ComponentModel.Container

    ' NOTE: The following procedure is required by the
    ' Component Designer.
    ' It can be modified using the Component Designer.
    ' Do not modify it using the code editor.
    <System.Diagnostics.DebuggerStepThrough()> _
    Private Sub InitializeComponent()
        components = New System.ComponentModel.Container()
        Me.ServiceName = "vbFileMonitorService"
    End Sub

#End Region

    Protected Overrides Sub OnStart(ByVal args() As String)
        ' Add code here to start your service. This method
        ' should set things in motion so your service can
        ' do its work.
        vbFMS.StartLogging()
        EventLog.WriteEntry("Started logging files.")
    End Sub

    Protected Overrides Sub OnStop()
        ' Add code here to perform any tear-down
        ' necessary to stop your service.
        vbFMS.StopLogging()
        EventLog.WriteEntry("Stopped logging files.")
    End Sub

End Class
```

How Our Service Works

The *Main* method for our service application must use the Run command for the services your project contains. The *Run* method loads the services into the SCM on the appropriate server. Because we used the Windows Services project template, the *Run* method is written for us. Keep in mind that loading a service is not the same operation as starting a service.

We first have to import our class that contains the File Sentinel. Because we are including the class in our vbFileMonitorService project, we add the following *Imports* statement:

```
Imports vbFileMonitorService.SystemObserver.sentinel
```

We now add a class-level variable that contains a reference to an instance of the *sentinel* class.

```
Dim vbFMS As vbFileMonitorService.SystemObserver.sentinel
```

Logging Events to the Event Viewer

Event logging in Microsoft Windows provides a standard, centralized way to have applications record important software and hardware events. For example, when an error occurs, the system administrator must determine what caused the error. It is helpful if applications, the operating system, and other system services record important events such as low-memory conditions or failed attempts to access a disk. The system administrator can then use the event log to help determine what conditions caused the error and the context in which it occurred.

Windows supplies a standard user interface for viewing these event logs, the Event Viewer, shown in Figure 9-10, and a programming interface for examining log entries. In Visual Basic 6, you could perform limited write operations to some event logs, but you could not easily read or interact with all the logs available to you.

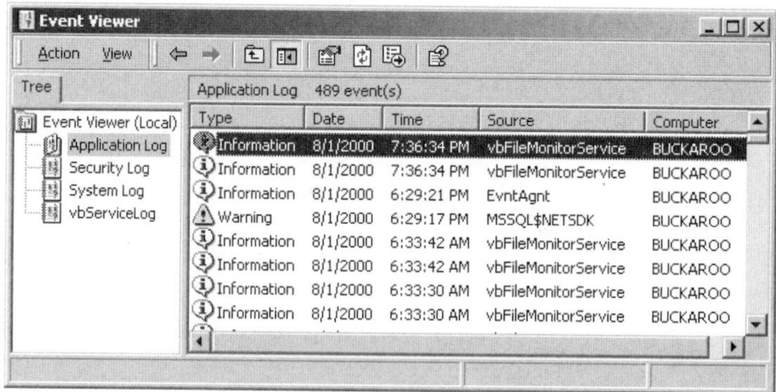

Figure 9-10 The Windows Event Viewer.

In .NET, however, we simply use the *EventLog* component, which allows us to connect to event logs on both local and remote computers and then write entries. You can also read entries from existing logs and create your own custom event logs. In our class, we will simply write to the standard application log. As our service executes, we can have it write events to the application log for any event we deem important. By default, the event type is set to Information if you do not specify otherwise. However, you can set the type of event by using a parameter on an overloaded form of the *WriteEntry* method of the *EventLog* object.

By double-clicking one of the events in the Event Viewer, you can see the event's Event Properties dialog box. In Figure 9-11, you can see one of our custom messages logged to the Application log.

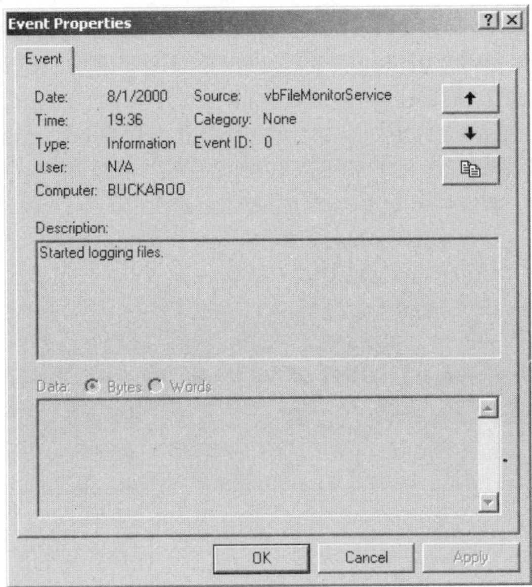

Figure 9-11 The Event Properties dialog box.

The *EnableRaisingEvents* property determines whether the *EventLog* object raises events when entries are written to the log. When the property is True, components receiving the *EventWritten* event will receive notification any time an entry is written to the log. If *EnableRaisingEvents* is False, no events are raised. In our example, we set this property to True but don't check for the event. I did it this way in the example simply to illustrate the concept and syntax.

```
EventLog.EnableRaisingEvents = True
```

You must be prudent when writing to the log file because it can easily become so filled with messages that the messages become meaningless to whoever is viewing them. In full production services, we want to write entries for resource problems. For example, if your application is in a low-memory situation (caused by a code bug or inadequate memory) that degrades performance, logging a warning event when memory allocation fails might provide a clue about what went wrong. We can also log information events. A server-based application (such as a database server) might want to record a user logging on, opening a database, or starting a file transfer. The server can also log error events it encounters (failed file access, host process disconnected, and so on), corruptions in the database, or whether a file transfer was successful.

By default, all Windows Service projects can interact with the Application event log by writing information and exceptions to it. Use the *AutoLog* property to indicate whether you want this built-in functionality in your application. By default, logging is turned on for any service you create with the Windows Service project template. In our project, we use a static form of the *EventLog* class to write service information to a log. We don't have to create an instance of an *EventLog* component or manually register a source.

If you want to write to an event log other than the Application log, you must set the *AutoLog* property to False, create your own custom event log within your services code, and register your service as a valid source of entries for that log.

```
Me.AutoLog = True
```

At times, we might want to stop logging file changes. In case of maintenance or normal file access, we can simply turn off our service when needed. When *Stop* is called on a service, the SCM verifies whether the service accepts Stop commands using the value of *CanStop*. For most services, the value of *CanStop* is True, but some operating system services do not allow the user to stop them.

If *CanStop* is True, the Stop command is passed to the service and the *OnStop* method is called, as it is in our service. However, if we don't define an *OnStop* method, the SCM handles the Stop command through the empty base class method *ServiceBase.OnStop*.

```
Me.CanStop = True
```

The next line should be familiar. With it we instantiate a new instance of our *sentinel* class. The root directory of drive C is passed into the constructor as a parameter. Because Windows services do not have a user interface, we have to pass in a value manually and not from a UI. You might want to code this parameter as the root directory that holds your Web pages or some other location of importance. But for now, we will monitor all files in the root directory.

```
vbFMS = New _
    vbFileMonitorService.SystemObserver.sentinel("C:\")
```

In the next line of code from the *InitializeComponent* procedure, we change the service name to something that is meaningful to our program.

```
Me.ServiceName = "vbFileMonitorService"
```

We then add two one-line methods to our file sentinel. The methods, *StartLogging* and *StopLogging,* will turn on and off the *EnableRaisingEvents* property of the *FileSystemMonitor* object. When the service is started, we set the property to True, and when it's stopped, we toggle the value to False.

After each call to our class for turning on and off the events, we write to the event log to track when our service starts and ends. We use the *WriteEntry* method of the static *EventLog*. It will automatically time stamp the entry for us.

```
Protected Overrides Sub OnStart(ByVal args() As String)
    ' Add code here to start your service. This method
    ' should set things in motion so your service can
    ' do its work.
    vbFMS.StartLogging()
    EventLog.WriteEntry("Started logging files.")
End Sub

Protected Overrides Sub OnStop()
    ' Add code here to perform any tear-down
    ' necessary to stop your service
    vbFMS.StopLogging()
    EventLog.WriteEntry("Stopped logging files.")
End Sub
```

The *Main* method for the vbFileSystemMonitor service application issues the Run command for the services your project contains. Because we used the Windows Services project template, this method is provided for us. Once the service is loaded, we will manually start and stop the service from the SCM.

```
Shared Sub Main()
    Dim ServicesToRun() As System.ServiceProcess.ServiceBase

    ServicesToRun = New _
        System.ServiceProcess.ServiceBase () _
            {New Service1}
    System.ServiceProcess.ServiceBase.Run(ServicesToRun)
End Sub
```

Adding an Installer to Our Windows Service

We have to add an installer to our Windows service, which we don't have to do with a standard Windows program. The installer is responsible for doing the heavy lifting required to register our new service with the SCM. The *ServiceInstaller* class does work specific to the service with which it is associated. It is used by the installation utility we will add to the service to write registry values associated with the service to a subkey within the *HKEY_LOCAL_MACHINE\System\CurrentControlSet\Services* registry key.

The service is identified by its *ServiceName* within this subkey. The subkey also includes the name of the executable or DLL to which the service belongs. If you are interested, use Regedit.exe to examine the registry entry of the service after we install it. You can see in Figure 9-12 that the registry contains the fully qualified name of our service in the ImagePath key.

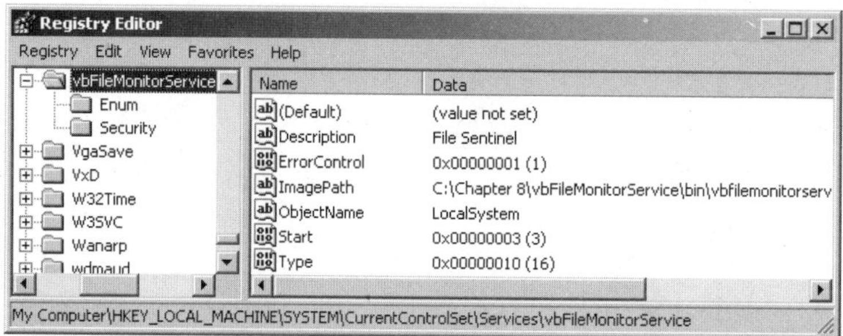

Figure 9-12 Viewing our registered service in the Registry Editor.

Adding the *ServiceInstaller*

Adding a *ServiceInstaller* to our Windows service is pretty straightforward. Go to the Service1.vb [Design] tab, and then right-click. On the pop-up menu, select the Add Installer option, shown in Figure 9-13.

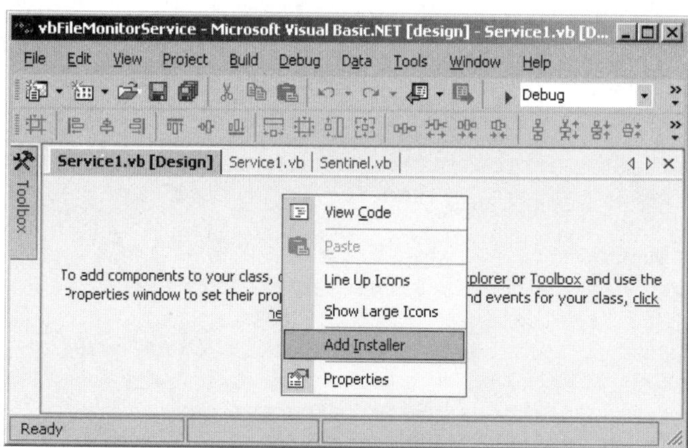

Figure 9-13 Adding a *ServiceInstaller*.

As you can see in Figure 9-14, the IDE adds both a *ServiceProcessInstaller* and a *ServiceInstaller*. Most of the code for these objects will be added for us. When we run the installer program, InstallUtil.exe, it will read this code and install the vbService as a Windows service for us.

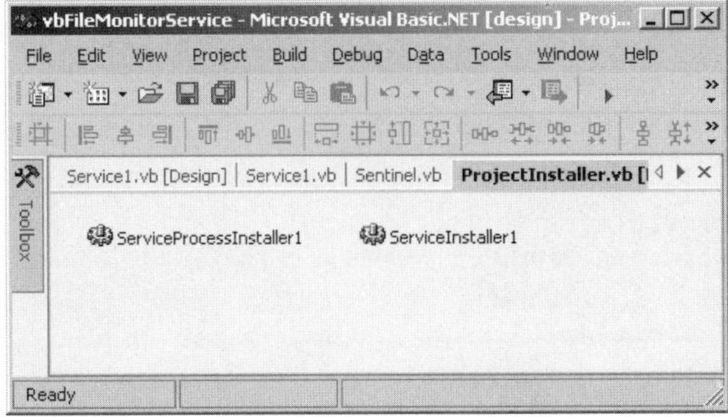

Figure 9-14 The IDE adds a *ServiceProcessInstaller* and a *ServiceInstaller.*

Double-click both ServiceProcessInstaller1 and the ServiceInstaller1 on the ProjectInstaller.vb [Design] tab in the IDE. The template code does the bulk of the work, but we need to add a few lines of code to make the installer functional for our program. Again, in the interest of space, only the lines you need to add are highlighted.

```
Imports System.ComponentModel
Imports System.Configuration.Install

<RunInstaller(True)> Public Class ProjectInstaller
    Inherits System.Configuration.Install.Installer

#Region " Component Designer generated code "

    Public Sub New()
        MyBase.New()

        ' This call is required by the Component Designer.
        InitializeComponent()

        ' Add any initialization after the
        ' InitializeComponent() call

    End Sub
    Friend WithEvents ServiceProcessInstaller1 As _
        System.ServiceProcess.ServiceProcessInstaller
    Friend WithEvents ServiceInstaller1 As _
        System.ServiceProcess.ServiceInstaller

    ' Required by the Component Designer
    Private components As System.ComponentModel.Container

    ' NOTE: The following procedure is required by the
    ' Component Designer
```

(continued)

```
    ' It can be modified using the Component Designer.
    ' Do not modify it using the code editor.
    <System.Diagnostics.DebuggerStepThrough()> _
    Private Sub InitializeComponent()
        Me.ServiceProcessInstaller1 = New _
            System.ServiceProcess.ServiceProcessInstaller()
        Me.ServiceInstaller1 = New _
            System.ServiceProcess.ServiceInstaller()
        '
        ' ServiceProcessInstaller1
        '
        Me.ServiceProcessInstaller1.Account = _
            System.ServiceProcess.ServiceAccount.LocalSystem
        Me.ServiceProcessInstaller1.Password = Nothing
        Me.ServiceProcessInstaller1.Username = Nothing
        '
        ' ServiceInstaller1
        '
        Me.ServiceInstaller1.ServiceName = _
            "vbFileMonitorService"
        '
        ' ProjectInstaller
        '
        Me.Installers.AddRange(New _
             System.Configuration.Install.Installer() _
             {Me.ServiceProcessInstaller1, Me.ServiceInstaller1})

    End Sub

#End Region

    Private Sub ServiceInstaller1_AfterInstall( _
        ByVal sender As System.Object, _
        ByVal e As _
            System.Configuration.Install.InstallEventArgs) _
        Handles ServiceInstaller1.AfterInstall

    End Sub

    Private Sub ServiceProcessInstaller1_AfterInstall( _
        ByVal sender As System.Object, _
        ByVal e As _
            System.Configuration.Install.InstallEventArgs) _
        Handles ServiceProcessInstaller1.AfterInstall

    End Sub
End Class
```

How the Installation Code Works

In this code, we are telling the *ServiceProcessInstaller* which local account process space under which to run. By default, the service will start manually. Another option is to have the service start automatically when the machine boots. When you get your service up and running, you might want to change this setting. For now, a manual start is what we want.

```
Me.ServiceProcessInstaller1.Account = _
    System.ServiceProcess.ServiceAccount.LocalSystem
```

As before, we give our service the name that we want to show up in the Services window.

```
Me.ServiceInstaller1.ServiceName = _
    "vbFileMonitorService"
```

When logging is turned on, the installer for our service registers the service as a valid source of events with the Application log on the computer where the service is installed. The service logs information each time the service is started, stopped, paused, resumed, installed, or uninstalled. It also logs any failures that occur. You do not need to add any code to write entries to the log when using the default behavior. The service handles these details for you. Pretty cool, eh?

Installing Our Service

Now we're ready to install our service. Build the project by selecting Build | Build from the IDE. This creates the file vbFileMonitorService in the \bin directory.

After you create and build the application, you install the service by running the command-line utility InstallUtil.exe and passing the path to the service's executable file. The easiest way to do this is to use Windows Explorer to find InstallUtil.exe on your drive. Copy the file to the directory where your service executable is located. On my drive, the file is located under C:\Chapter 9\vbFileMonitorService\bin. If you install the companion disc files to the default location, your path will be C:\Coding Techniques for Visual Basic .NET\Chap09\vbFileMonitorService\bin.

Bring up an MS-DOS command prompt window, run *installutil,* and pass it the full name of the service. You will see several messages printed to the command window. Here's what the installation process will look like:

```
C:\Chapter 9\vbFileMonitorService\bin>installutil
 vbfilemonitorservice.exe
Microsoft (R) .NET Framework Installation utility
Copyright (C) Microsoft Corp 2001. All rights reserved.
```

(continued)

```
Running a transacted installation.

Beginning the Install phase of the installation.
See the contents of the log file for the C:\Chapter
 8\vbFileMonitorService\bin\vbfilemonitorservice.exe
 assembly's progress.
The file is located at C:\Chapter
 9\vbFileMonitorService\bin\vbfilemonitorservice.InstallLog.
Call Installing. on the C:\Chapter
 9\vbFileMonitorService\bin\vbfilemonitorservice.exe assembly.
Affected parameters are:
   assemblypath = C:\Chapter
 9\vbFileMonitorService\bin\vbfilemonitorservice.exe

   logfile = C:\Chapter
 9\vbFileMonitorService\bin\vbfilemonitorservice.InstallLog
Installing service vbFileMonitorService...
Service vbFileMonitorService has been successfully installed.
Creating EventLog source vbFileMonitorService in log
 Application...

The Install phase completed successfully, and the Commit
 phase is beginning.
See the contents of the log file for the C:\Chapter
 9\vbFileMonitorService\bin\vbfilemonitorservice.exe
 assembly's progress.
The file is located at C:\Chapter
 9\vbFileMonitorService\bin\vbfilemonitorservice.InstallLog.
Call Committing. on the C:\Chapter
 9\vbFileMonitorService\bin\vbfilemonitorservice.exe assembly.
Affected parameters are:
   assemblypath = C:\Chapter
 9\vbFileMonitorService\bin\vbfilemonitorservice.exe

   logfile = C:\Chapter
 9\vbFileMonitorService\bin\vbfilemonitorservice.InstallLog

The Commit phase completed successfully.

The transacted install has completed.
```

> **Note** To uninstall the service, you must first close the Service Management Console. If the console is open, it must be closed and reopened to allow the uninstall to complete. Use the syntax *installutil /u vbFileMonitorService.exe* to perform this operation.

Looking at vbMonitorService in the Services Window

Now that the service has been installed, we can start to use it.

1. Bring up the Services window by clicking Start | Programs | Administrative Tools | Services on the Windows task bar. (In Windows 2000 Professional, open the Control Panel, double-click Administrative Tools, and then double-click Services.) In the Services dialog box, shown in Figure 9-15, you'll see our new service registered with the other system services.

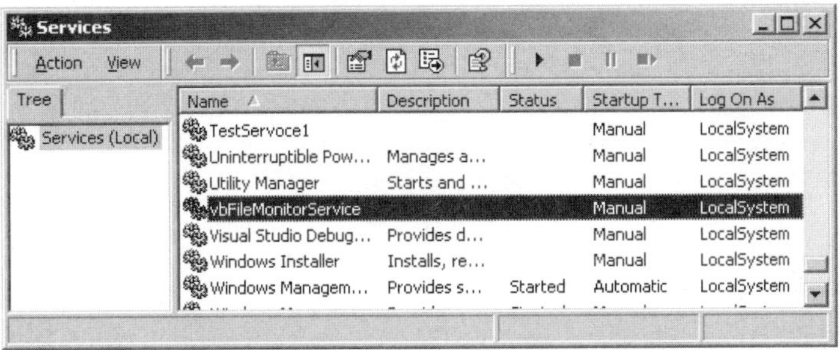

Figure 9-15 Our service among the others in the Services window.

2. Double-click vbMonitorService to display the properties dialog box, shown in Figure 9-16. Add the name *File Sentinel* to the Description text box. This name will show up in the Description column of the Services window. Note that if you are running Windows XP, the description text cannot be changed.

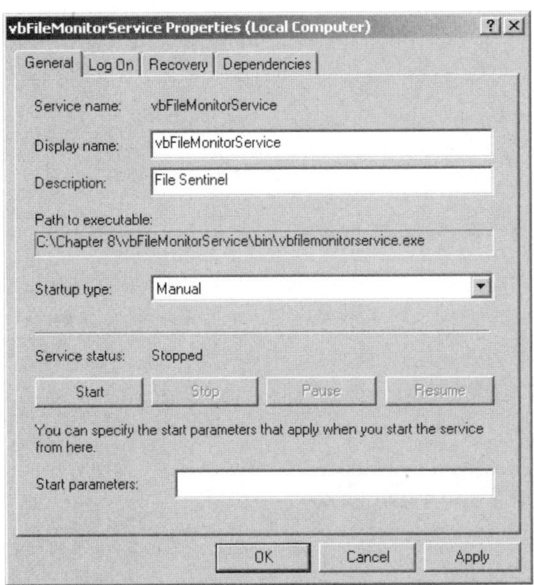

Figure 9-16 The properties dialog box for vbFileMonitorService.

3. Click Apply to add the description to the service.
4. Now we're ready to start running our new service and put it to work. Click the Start Service button. A Service Control dialog box with a progress bar will be displayed for a few seconds while our service is started, as shown in Figure 9-17.

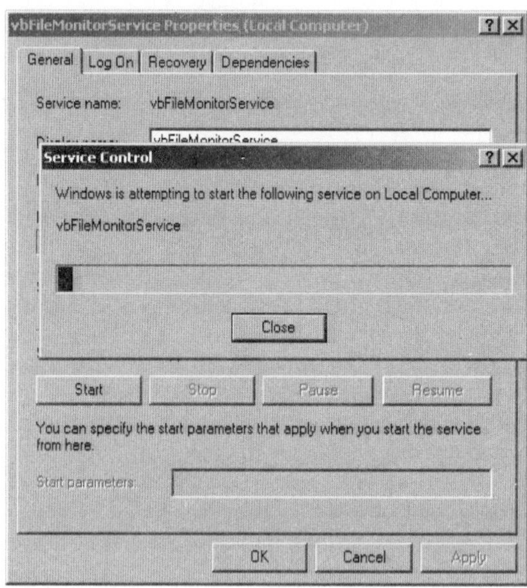

Figure 9-17 A progress bar is displayed while our service starts running.

By examining the Services window, shown in Figure 9-18, you can see that the description of our service has been added and that it is also now running. As the service runs, it will monitor any changes to files in the root directory of the C drive.

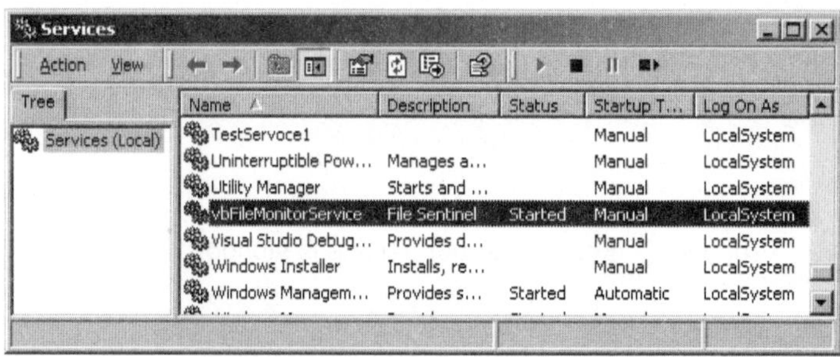

Figure 9-18 Our service is running.

We can examine the vbFMS.txt file and see whether any suspicious file modifications occurred. A quick look at the text file might reveal some interesting changes.

```
Monday, July 30, 2001 9:33:13 PM File: C:\passwords.exe
 renamed to C:\trash.exe
Monday, July 30, 2001 9:33:13 PM File: C:\trash.exe  Changed
Monday, July 30, 2001 9:33:18 PM File: C:\trash.exe  Changed
Monday, July 30, 2001 9:33:39 PM File: C:\trash.exe  Deleted
Monday, July 30, 2001 9:34:08 PM File: C:\salaries.xls  Changed
Monday, July 30, 2001 9:34:08 PM File: C:\salaries.xls  Changed
Monday, July 30, 2001 9:34:18 PM File: C:\passwords.txt  Changed
```

When we want to stop our service, we simply double-click vbFileMonitorService in the Services window and then click Stop. A Service Control dialog box is displayed again (see Figure 9-19), and the service is stopped for us. Now you can see why we wanted to add those two methods, *StartLogging* and *StopLogging,* to the *sentinel* class. These methods make turning our service on and off pretty trivial.

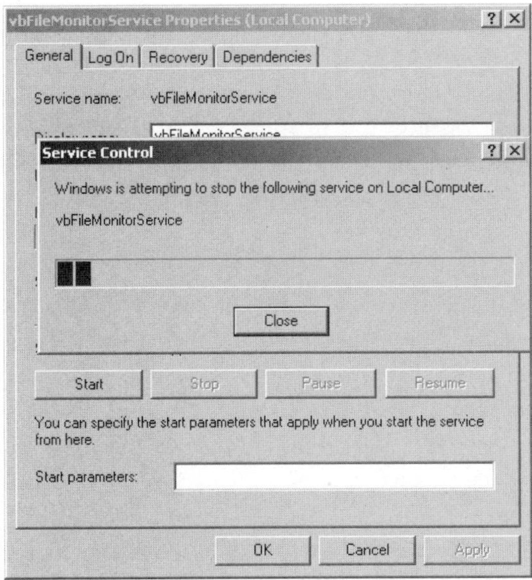

Figure 9-19 Progress is made while our service is stopped.

Debugging a Windows Service

As you've just seen, after we finish writing our service, the compiled executable file must be installed on the computer where it will run before the project can function in a meaningful way. In addition, you cannot debug or run a service application by pressing F5 or F11 in the IDE. Because of the nature of services, you cannot immediately run a service or step into its code.

Because a service must be run within the context of the SCM rather than within Visual Studio .NET, debugging a service is not as straightforward as debugging other Visual Studio application types. To debug a service, you must start the service and then attach a debugger to the process in which it is running. You can then debug your application by using all the standard debugging functionality of the Visual Studio IDE.

> **Note** You should not attach to a process unless you know what the process is and understand the consequences of attaching to and possibly killing that process. For example, if you attach to the WinLogon process and then stop debugging, the system will halt because it cannot operate without WinLogon.

You can only attach the debugger to a running service. As you might expect, the attachment process interrupts the functioning of your service instead of stopping or pausing the service's processing—that is, if your service is running when you begin debugging it, the service is still technically in the started state as you debug it, but its processing has been suspended.

Attaching a debugger to the service's process allows you to debug most but not all of the service's code. For example, because the service has already been started, you cannot debug the code in the service's *OnStart* method, nor can the code in the *Main* method that is used to load the service be debugged. Both procedures have already been executed to get the service loaded.

One way to work around this limitation is to create a temporary second service within your service application that exists only to aid in debugging. You can install both services and then start the dummy service to load the service process. After the temporary service has started the process, you can use the Debug menu in Visual Studio .NET to attach to the service process.

After attaching to the process, you can set breakpoints and use these to debug your code. Once you exit the dialog box you use to attach to the process, you are effectively in debug mode. You can use the SCM to start, stop, pause, and continue your service, thus hitting the breakpoints you've set. Remove the dummy service later after debugging is successful.

When you are ready to start debugging your service, use the SCM to start the service. Once the service is running, you can start debugging.

1. Select Debug | Process from the IDE to display the Processes dialog box. Be sure to check the Show System Processes check box, which is cleared by default. Because we wrote a system process, if this option were not checked we would not see the process. Of course, our service does not have a user interface, so there is no title for our application to display in the Title column, as you can see in Figure 9-20.

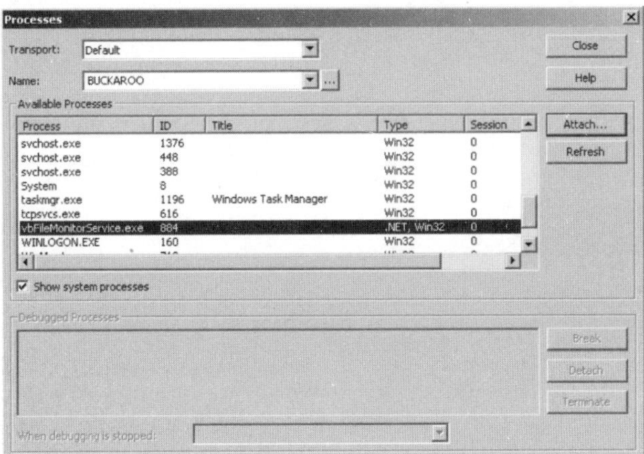

Figure 9-20 Attaching to a process to debug our service.

2. Double-click the vbFileMonitorService process to display the Attach To Process dialog box, shown in Figure 9-21. Check the Common Language Runtime option, and then click OK to attach the debugger to this process.

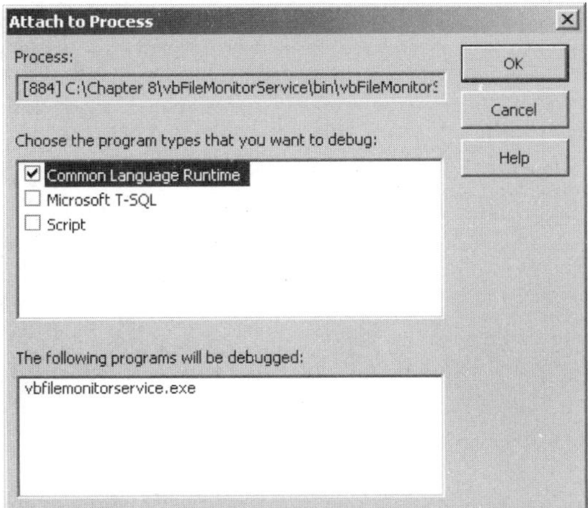

Figure 9-21 The Attach To Process dialog box.

3. We've now successfully attached the debugger to our vbFileMonitorService process, as you can see in Figure 9-22. Click Close to dismiss the Processes dialog box.

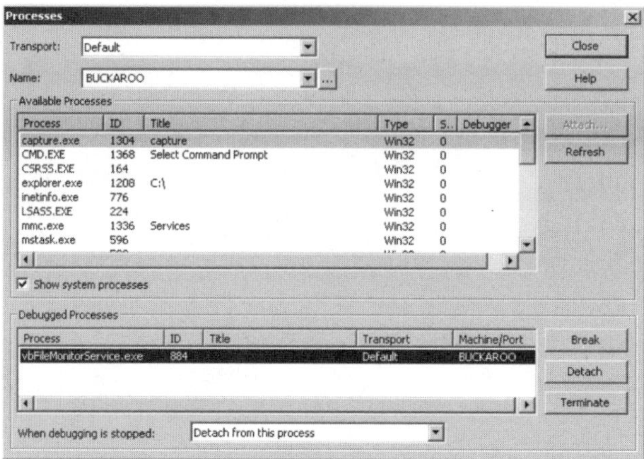

Figure 9-22 Success—we've attached the debugger to our service's process.

You are now in debug mode. Go ahead and set any breakpoints you want to use in your code. Run the SCM and work with your service, sending stop, pause, and continue commands to hit your breakpoints.

Conclusion

Well, this was a pretty important chapter. We learned more about the .NET Framework and how to build classes in Visual Basic .NET. In the process, we learned about delegates and also used our knowledge of stream writers to log events. In addition, we converted the class to an interfaceless Windows service.

These first nine chapters have provided you with the techniques you use to work with Visual Basic .NET and how to use any framework class in any namespace. Armed with this knowledge, we'll now move on to learn about ADO.NET, putting our knowledge to use by understanding and using the .NET database access methodologies.

10

Data Access with ADO.NET

Three versions of Visual Basic were released before any database access capabilities were provided with the program. Data Access Objects (DAO) technology was added with the release of Visual Basic 3. DAO enabled programmers to access local databases in the Microsoft Jet Database Engine format, which were primarily ISAM (Indexed Sequential Access Method) files. With DAO you could also access databases on a server, but I always found performance between a client and a server to be poor because DAO was optimized for local access.

After DAO came Remote Data Objects (RDO) and then ActiveX Data Objects (ADO). These data access technologies were designed for the client/server paradigm. With the movement away from a client/server model to an n-tier, loosely coupled design, a new data access methodology is required.

ADO.NET components have been designed from the ground up for faster data access and data manipulation in an n-tier environment. Two central components of ADO.NET accomplish this: the in-memory *DataSet* object and the .NET data provider. The data provider is a set of components that include the *Connection*, *Command*, *DataReader*, and *DataAdapter* objects. I'll go into more detail about the *DataSet* object and the data provider objects shortly. First let's see how ADO and ADO.NET compare.

From ADO to ADO.NET

Many of you are familiar with ADO from your work with classic Visual Basic. A main feature in ADO is the *Recordset* object. ADO recordsets allow enough flexibility that an application can navigate between records and apply filters and bookmarks with ease. Recordsets also provide sorting, automatic pagination, and persistence. They can even be worked with when an application is disconnected from the data source. In short, the ADO recordset provides a rich and attractive programming interface.

Recordsets can also be marshaled very efficiently across tiers or the wire in a COM environment because of their native and compact binary format, the Advanced Data Table Gram (ADTG) format. This efficiency is possible because the ADO recordset is based on COM, however, only COM objects can use ADO recordsets. In a homogeneous architecture, where COM and DCOM (Distributed COM) are used exclusively, the reliance on COM is a nonissue. The Internet, however, has many environments that use neither COM nor Windows.

ADO recordsets quickly become rather unusable in a distributed and heterogeneous environment in which varied platforms are involved. Today's Web-based systems require significant interoperability and scalability. When we need to communicate with Unix systems or mainframes, work comes to a screeching halt when we use COM objects. While ADO is powerful for manipulating data in a Windows and COM–based scenario, it has quickly lost its appeal as systems have moved in the direction of total Internet interoperability. The ADO recordset had to evolve to meet the challenges of the Internet. Enter ADO.NET.

ADO.NET from 50,000 Feet

At the heart of ADO.NET is the *DataSet* object, the successor to the ADO *Recordset* object. A data set is an in-memory resident representation of data that provides a consistent relational programming model regardless of the source of the data it contains. A *DataSet* object can model data logically or abstractly because, unlike the *Recordset*, the *DataSet* is not a data container that can hold only rows of data. The *DataSet* can actually hold multiple tables and the relationships between them.

Let's say we perform a join on two tables in Microsoft's well-known sample database, Northwind Traders. We could write an SQL query that retrieved the current products; for example:

```
SELECT DISTINCTROW Products.*,
    Categories.CategoryName
FROM Categories
    INNER JOIN Products
    ON Categories.CategoryID = Products.CategoryID
    WHERE (((Products.Discontinued)=No));
```

We would get back a recordset that looks like the one shown in Figure 10-1. Notice that the Supplier and Category columns contain quite a bit of repeated data, which is pretty wasteful and somewhat limiting. To retrieve information for a specific supplier or category, we would have to write code that looked for the next unique supplier or write another query looking for unique items.

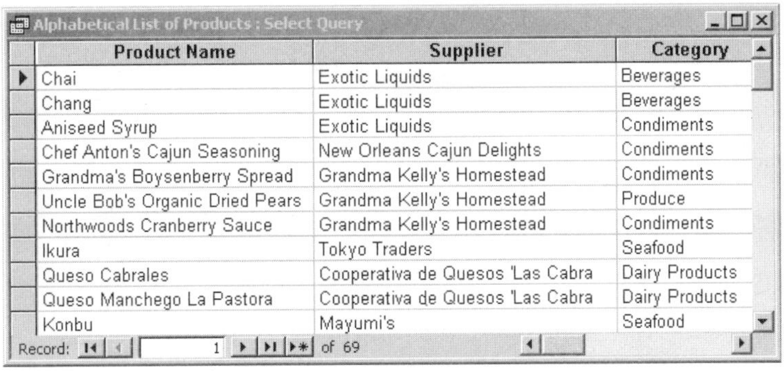

Alphabetical List of Products : Select Query

Product Name	Supplier	Category
Chai	Exotic Liquids	Beverages
Chang	Exotic Liquids	Beverages
Aniseed Syrup	Exotic Liquids	Condiments
Chef Anton's Cajun Seasoning	New Orleans Cajun Delights	Condiments
Grandma's Boysenberry Spread	Grandma Kelly's Homestead	Condiments
Uncle Bob's Organic Dried Pears	Grandma Kelly's Homestead	Produce
Northwoods Cranberry Sauce	Grandma Kelly's Homestead	Condiments
Ikura	Tokyo Traders	Seafood
Queso Cabrales	Cooperativa de Quesos 'Las Cabra	Dairy Products
Queso Manchego La Pastora	Cooperativa de Quesos 'Las Cabra	Dairy Products
Konbu	Mayumi's	Seafood

Record: 1 of 69

Figure 10-1 This recordset contains duplicate information.

Individual Tables, Not the Join, Are in a *DataSet*

Unlike an ADO recordset, an ADO.NET data set would actually contain both the Products and Categories tables in memory, not just the results of the join that are shown in Figure 10-1. You would create the joins and constraints and relationships within the data set itself, after the tables were contained in memory.

Figure 10-2 depicts data flow from a data source to a data consumer using ADO.NET. First we connect to and retrieve tables from a relational database. The tables are each placed in an in-memory *DataSet* object using *DataSetCommand* objects. These *DataSetCommand* objects specify the tables (or a subset thereof) that we are interested in. After the *DataSet* is filled, the connection to the database is immediately closed. We build the relationship between the individual tables within the *DataSet* itself. We can then send the data, via text-based XML, to any client application.

Because data sets can be constructed entirely from XML, we can build local data sets in either a Windows or a Web-based .NET application. We might also want to work with Electronic Data Interchange (EDI) by passing the XML file to a vendor's Web service.

As you can see, the old notion of client/server doesn't apply to the .NET world. Instead we use an n-tier paradigm in which each tier accomplishes a specific task. In a Windows Forms application, we pass the data in XML to a data set within our application. Because the XML data has a schema that fully describes its contents, we can construct a data set within our application from the XML. The user can then edit or otherwise manipulate the data within the data set contained in the application. When the user wants to update the data source, an XML file is constructed from the application's *DataSet* object and sent back through an intranet or the Internet to the business tier. Here the *DataSet* object is updated, and it then updates the data source. Keep in mind that all of the data passing though an intranet or the Internet is passed in XML. Getting your mind around these concepts might take a while, but the programming that's required is actually easier than using COM objects.

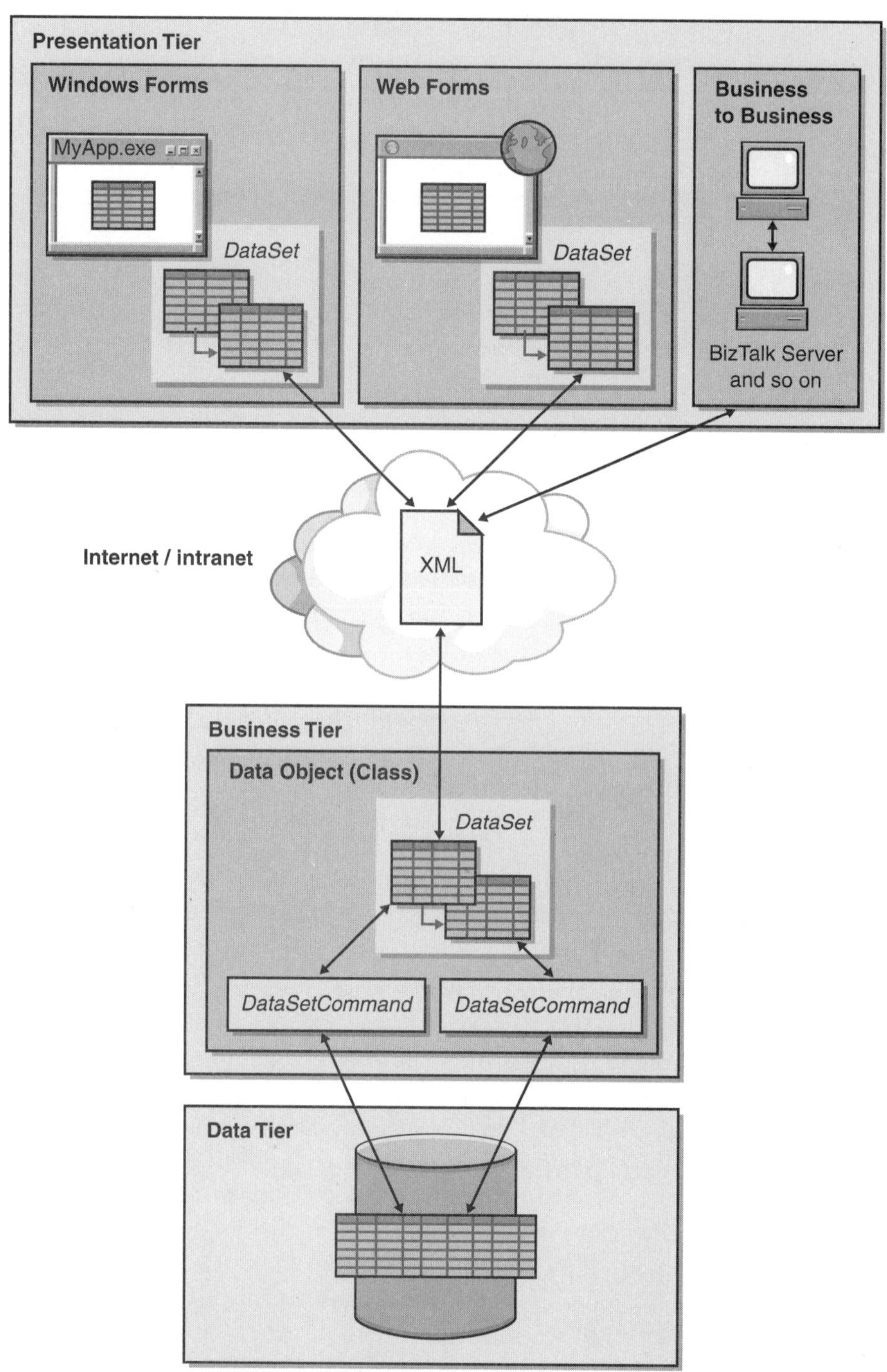

Figure 10-2 ADO.NET data flow.

The biggest difference between an ADO *Recordset* and an ADO.NET *DataSet* is that the *DataSet* is disconnected from the data source. To use the *DataSet* you simply connect to a data source, execute one or more queries to get the data you want, and then immediately disconnect. The *DataSet* itself contains all the logic required to scroll, edit, and manipulate the data inside. When the user (program or human) is finished manipulating the data in the *DataSet*, the object has the built-in ability to reconnect to and update the data source. The data logic and the user interface are completely separate. In Figure 10-2, we have a data tier, a business tier, and a presentation tier. Each tier is separated from the others, which permits us to scale an application for use by thousands of users around the globe.

> **Note** As you've learned in previous chapters, the .NET Framework uses strong typing, and ADO.NET is no exception. Typed programming is easier to read, of course, but it is also easier to use in a program. For example, with ADO.NET we can now write code like this:
>
> ```
> DataSet.Employee("Smith").EmployeeID
> ```
>
> Contrast this statement with earlier syntax, such as this:
>
> ```
> Table("Employee")("Smith").Column("EmployeeID")
> ```

Comparing Classic ADO and ADO.NET

A good way to understand the advantages of ADO.NET over classic ADO as used in Visual Basic 6 is to compare their features. One glance at the information in Table 10-1 shows you that ADO.NET is an improvement over ADO.

Table 10-1 A Comparison of ADO and ADO.NET Features

Feature	ADO	ADO.NET
Memory-resident data	Uses the *Recordset* object, which looks like a single table.	Uses the *DataSet* object, which can contain one or more tables represented by *DataTable* objects.
Relationships between multiple tables	Requires the JOIN query to assemble data from multiple database tables in a single result table.	Supports the *DataRelation* object to associate rows in one *DataTable* object with rows in another *DataTable* object.
Accessing data	Scans *Recordset* rows sequentially.	Permits nonsequential access to rows in a table. Follows relationships to navigate from rows in one table to corresponding rows in another table.

(continued)

Table 10-1 A Comparison of ADO and ADO.NET Features *(continued)*

Feature	ADO	ADO.NET
Disconnected access	Provided by the *Recordset* object, but generally supports connected access represented by the *Connection* object. Communicates with a database with calls to an OLE DB provider.	Communicates to a database with standardized calls to a *DataSetCommand* object.
Programmability	Uses the *Connection* object to transmit commands.	Uses the strictly typed programming characteristic of XML. Data is self-describing. Underlying data constructs such as tables and rows do not appear in the XML, making code easier to read and to write.
Sharing disconnected data between tiers or components	Uses COM marshaling to transmit a disconnected recordset. Supports only those data types defined by the COM standard.	Transmits a *DataSet* with an XML file. The XML format places no restrictions on data types and requires no type conversions.
Transmitting data through firewalls	Problematic because firewalls are typically configured to prevent system-level requests such as COM marshaling of binary objects.	No problem because the ADO.NET *DataSet* object uses text-based XML, which can pass through firewalls.
Scalability	Database locks and active database connections for long durations contend for limited database resources.	Disconnected access to database data limits contention for limited database resources.

Another significant difference between the *Connection* object in ADO and ADO.NET is that the ADO.NET *Connection* object does not have a *CursorLocation* property. The absence of this property is not a bug but a database design issue. ADO.NET has no explicit implementation of cursors, but of course they are there. The implementation of cursors in ADO.NET is unlike classic ADO, in which you had to set cursors on either the server or the client. While the more sophisticated *DataSet* object looks like a static cursor, the *DataReader* object is the equivalent of the ADO read-only cursor. In fact, ADO.NET does not have explicit support for server-side cursors. One exception, however, is the *DataReader* object, which simply performs a record-by-record read. If you need to perform data manipulation on the server, classic ADO is still the way to go.

An application can establish its result sets either within the application process (client side) or within the data source (server side). Client-side cursors are supported in ADO.NET by the *DataSet* object. These cursors permit the management of data, such as scrolling and updating. Client-side cursors are generally a good choice for any type of impromptu user interaction with the data because a round trip to the server is not necessary for each action.

Server-side cursors are supported in ADO.NET by the *DataReader* object. Server-side cursors should be used cautiously, however, because nonsequential scrolling and the updating of results through a server-side cursor might hold locks and cause resource contention that greatly limits the scalability of an application. Instead of using a scrollable, updateable server-side cursor, an application can usually benefit from using stored procedures for procedural processing of results on the server.

You should also consider using a scrollable, updateable server-side cursor in either classic ADO or OLE DB in either of the following two situations.

- Your data source does not support stored procedures.
- The result set is too large for a client-side cursor and you expect relatively few concurrent users for a particular set of data.

A Closer Look at the Foundation of ADO.NET: The *DataSet* Object

The *DataSet* object provides a common way to represent and manipulate data. It's important not to think of a *DataSet* object as a database but as a cache of data from any source. You use a *DataSet* not only when querying a database, but anytime you need to move data around. A data set can be created programmatically and filled with data, and then the data can be sent on its way via XML.

A data set is already in XML format, but like light, a data set has a dual nature. Consider that light is composed of both particles and waves simultaneously. A data set can be a binary object, programmable through the .NET classes, while at the same time it can be raw XML. While the *DataSet* is itself binary, it contains XML and can read and write XML. In fact, it is XML.

To distribute records over the network, you now have an inherently portable solution—use the XML representation of the data set. Target modules will receive XML and use it as best they can. If we take a peek at the map of the .NET Framework shown in Figure 10-3, we can see that data access and XML are in the same logical block.

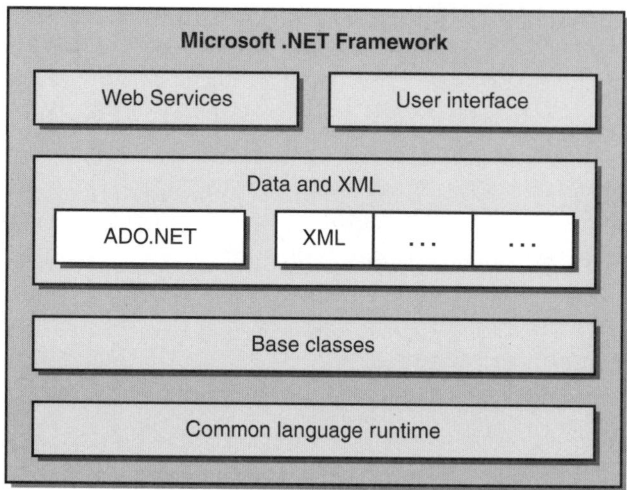

Figure 10-3 ADO.NET and XML together in the .NET Framework.

The *DataSet* object in ADO.NET resides in the *System.Data* namespace. As its name implies, this namespace is all about data. It contains classes and methods for manipulating data within a *DataSet*. Table 10-2 lists the key objects in the *System.Data* namespace.

Table 10-2 Important Objects in *System.Data*

Object	Description
DataSet	In-memory container for data.
DataTable	Used to retrieve the *TablesCollection,* which holds any *DataTable* object added to a *DataSet.*
DataRow	Used to retrieve the *RowsCollection,* which holds any *DataRow* object in a *DataTable.*

The *DataTable* Object

You can easily add a *DataTable* from a data source such as Microsoft SQL Server 2000 or create your own *DataTable* within a *DataSet*. Table 10-3 lists the important properties of the *DataTable* object.

If you programmatically create a *DataTable* using a *DataSet*, you create a *DataColumn* by providing the column name and data type. Then you add the *DataColumn* to the *DataTable*. Using the *DataSet.Tables* property, the *DataTable* is added to the *DataSet*. You repeat adding *DataColumn* and *DataTable* objects until you are satisfied with the result. I'll examine this procedure a bit more in the next chapter.

Table 10-3 *DataTable* Object Properties of Interest

Property	Description
Columns	Retrieves the columns as a collection. Returns the *DataColumnCollection*, which contains any or all *Column* objects.
Rows	Retrieves the rows in the *DataTable* by returning a *DataRowCollection* of *DataRow* objects.
ParentRelations	Returns a *DataRelationCollection* of all logical relationships between the tables.
Constraints	Returns a *ConstraintCollection* of the table constraints.
DataSet	Returns the *DataSet* to which the *DataTable* belongs.
PrimaryKey	Gets or sets the primary key of the table using an array of *DataColumn* objects. The objects make up the table's primary key.

The *DataSet* Object and XML

The *DataSet* object can use any data type. This openness is accomplished through the use of XML. As I touched on earlier in this chapter, the *DataSet* is capable of reading and writing its data and schema as XML. Of course, this ability permits you to both create and modify data in a data set using XML or an XML-enabled solution such as SQL Server 2000.

If you've thought you could get along without learning XML, your time is up. ADO.NET, as well as the entire .NET Framework infrastructure, makes extensive use of XML. XML is essentially a plain text representation of data, which means that it can pass through firewalls just like HTML. Unlike with binary data (such as COM or COM+ objects), firewalls can inspect XML data and recognize that it is simply text. Therefore, the data can be passed in and out of port 80 on a server, which is the HTTP port. In fact, you can take XML (which describes the data) and combine it in an HTML envelope (which formats the data) to exchange data between heterogeneous systems on the Internet. This mechanism is what underlies a format known as SOAP, for Simple Object Access Protocol. We will discuss SOAP in Chapter 12, "ASP.NET and XML Web Services." Table 10-4 lists the XML methods for the *DataSet* object.

Table 10-4 XML Methods of Interest for the *DataSet* Object

Methods	Description
ReadXML	Reads an XML schema and data into the *DataSet*.
ReadXMLSchema	Reads an XML schema into the *DataSet*.
WriteXML	Writes an XML file from the *DataSet*.
WriteXMLSchema	Writes an XML schema from the *DataSet*.

DataView Objects

Using a *DataView* object, you can create multiple views of any given table. For example, you might have an Employees table with both a department and a skills column. You could create two different views of the data—one for departments, and another for skills. The *DataView* object is designed so that it can be directly bound to either a Windows form or a Web Form. Table 10-5 lists some important properties of the *DataView* object.

Table 10-5 *DataView* Object Properties of Interest

Property	Description
Table	Gets or sets the source *DataTable* for the view.
Sort	Gets or sets the sort column and the sort order, either descending or ascending.
RowFilter	Gets or sets the expression used to filter which rows are displayed.
RowStateFilter	Gets or sets the row state filter, which could include *CurrentRows*, *Deleted*, *ModifiedCurrent*, *None*, *ModifiedOriginal*, *New*, *OriginalRows*, or *Unchanged* enumerated values.

Managed Providers in ADO.NET

To get our data from the data source (a relational database, a text file, an e-mail message, and so on), we need a managed provider. Managed providers include a collection of classes for accessing various data sources.

A .NET Framework data provider serves as a bridge between an application and a data source. It is used for connecting to a data source, executing commands, and retrieving results. Those results can then be either processed directly or placed in an ADO.NET *DataSet*. When the data is placed in a *DataSet*, it can be exposed to the user in an ad-hoc manner, combined with data from multiple sources, or remoted between tiers, as we saw in Figure 10-2. A data provider is also used to reconcile changes to the data back to the data source.

The .NET data provider is designed to be lightweight, creating a minimal layer between the data source and your code, increasing performance while not sacrificing functionality. ADO.NET includes two .NET data providers:

- **SQL Server .NET data provider**, for Microsoft SQL Server 7 or later.
- **OLE DB .NET data provider**, for data sources exposed via OLE DB.

The managed providers have similar objects, as shown in Table 10-6. The only difference is the prefix SQL or OLEDB; otherwise, the programming is essentially the same. The providers abstract the functionality and handle all the heavy lifting under the hood. Both of the providers live in the *System.Data* namespace.

Table 10-6 .NET Data Providers

SQL Server .NET Data Provider	OLE DB .NET Data Provider
SqlCommand	*OleDbCommand*
SqlConnection	*OleDbConnection*
SqlDataAdapter	*OleDbDataAdapter*
SqlDataReader	*OleDbDataReader*
SqlParameter	*OleDbParameter*

As managed providers, these provider objects themselves contain objects that represent the core elements of the .NET provider model: the *Connection*, *Command*, *DataReader*, and *DataAdapter* objects. Table 10-7 describes each of these objects.

Table 10-7 .NET Data Provider Objects

Provider Object	Description
Connection	Establishes a connection to a specific data source.
Command	Executes a command at a data source. Exposes parameters and can enlist a transaction from a connection.
DataReader	Reads a forward-only, read-only stream of data from a data source.
DataAdapter	Populates a *DataSet* and resolves updates with the data source.

You can see in Figure 10-4 that the *DataSetCommand* object of a managed provider gets the data from the data source and passes it to the data set. Likewise, when the data set is modified and the user is ready to update the original data source with the changes, a *DataSetCommand* object from the managed provider accomplishes this operation as well.

Figure 10-4 The *DataSetCommand* is a bridge between a data set and a data source.

In the past, data processing relied primarily on a two-tier architecture and was connection based. As data processing increasingly uses multitier architectures, programmers are switching to a disconnected approach to data processing to provide better scalability for their applications. The *DataSetCommand* provides an important tool in this approach for ADO.NET. As Figure 10-4 illustrates, a *DataSetCommand* loads a *DataSet* object and provides the bridge between the *DataSet* object and its data source for retrieving and saving data. It accomplishes this by invoking the appropriate SQL commands against the data source.

As I noted earlier, the .NET Framework includes the SQL Server .NET data provider and the more generic OLE DB .NET data provider. In our examples, we'll use the SQL Server data provider. However, the syntax for the OLE DB provider is almost identical. Many beginners will be scratching their heads wondering which provider to use. Table 10-8 lists some tips on which managed provider to choose for your task at hand.

Table 10-8 Recommended Uses of the ADO.NET Managed Data Providers

Provider	Recommended Uses
SQL Server .NET data provider	■ Middle-tier applications using Microsoft SQL Server 7 or later. ■ Single-tier applications using Microsoft Data Engine (MSDE) or Microsoft SQL Server 7 or later. ■ Recommended over the OLE DB Provider for SQL Server (SQLOLEDB) with the OLE DB .NET data provider. Note: For Microsoft SQL Server 6.5 and earlier, you must use the OLE DB Provider for SQL Server with the OLE DB .NET data provider.
OLE DB .NET data provider	■ Middle-tier applications using Microsoft SQL Server 6.5 or earlier or Oracle. ■ Single-tier applications using Microsoft Access databases. ■ Use of the OLE DB .NET data provider with a Microsoft Access database for a middle-tier application is not recommended. Note: Support for the OLE DB Provider for ODBC (MSDASQL) is disabled.

A Common Provider Model

As should be evident to you, ADO.NET exposes a common model for .NET data provider objects. A single set of code can be used regardless of the .NET data provider you choose. For example, the following code, shown only for purposes of illustration, will work with either the SQL Server .NET or the OLE DB .NET data provider. The code shows how you could implement a *Command* object by creating a class that implements *IDbCommand*. The *IDataReader* interface allows an inheriting class to implement a *DataReader* class, which provides a means of reading one or more forward-only streams of result sets.

```
Dim cmdCommand As IDbCommand = myConn.CreateCommand()
cmdCommand.CommandText = "SELECT * FROM Customers"
Dim drReader As IDataReader = cmdCommand.ExecuteReader()

Do While drReader.Read()
    Console.WriteLine("{0}" & vbTab & "{1}", & _
        drReader.GetString(0), drReader.GetString(1))
Loop
```

As I noted, this example is for illustration only. We will be using the SQL Server data provider in our examples in this chapter.

Enough Talk, Let's Look at Some Code

We've been discussing the *DataSet* object and how it is the cornerstone of ADO.NET. However, the *DataSet* has a smaller and faster cousin known as the *DataReader* object. This object is optimized to retrieve a read-only, forward-only stream of data from a database and is used for displaying data. It's fast and increases your application's performance, but you can't edit the data it returns and it handles only one record at a time. In spite of these limitations, however, the *DataReader* is much easier to understand than the *DataSet,* so we'll use the *DataReader* in our first example. The concepts are the same.

Many times in our applications we might simply want to grab data from a data source and fill a data grid for display. The *DataReader* is the perfect choice for this task, and the *DataReader* is a member of a .NET managed provider. You need to understand and perform three operations when working with ADO.NET:

- A *connection* to a data source. This is a physical connection to a data source such as SQL Server, Oracle, an Access database, an XML file, a flat file, an e-mail store, or whatever.
- A *command* that represents a directive to retrieve (select) or manipulate (insert, update, or delete) the data in the data source.
- A *DataSet* or *DataReader* object to hold the data that is retrieved from the data source.

Connecting to Our Data Source

To move data between a data source and your application, you must first have a connection to that data source. In ADO.NET, you can create and manage a connection using one of the two connection objects: the *SqlConnection* object, which manages a connection to a data source running SQL Server version 7 or later, or the *OleDbConnection* object, which manages a connection to any data source accessible via OLE DB.

The *SqlConnection* object is optimized for use with SQL Server 7 or later by bypassing the OLE DB layer, among other things. The *OleDbConnection* object interacts with OLE DB to expose a consistent API for a variety of data sources, everything from simple text files to spreadsheets and, of course, full-featured databases.

As I mentioned earlier, both of these connection objects expose roughly the same members. However, the specific members available with a given *OleDbConnection* object depend on what data source it is connected to. In other words, not all data sources support all members of the *OleDbConnection* class.

The primary property associated with a connection object is the *ConnectionString* property. This property consists of a string with attribute-value pairs holding the information required to point to a specific database and log on to it. A typical *ConnectionString* property looks something like the following:

```
Dim sqlConn As SqlConnection = New _
    SqlConnection("server=(local)\NetSDK;uid=QSUser; " & _
        "pwd=QSPassword;database=northwind")
```

The most common attribute-value pairs used by an *SqlConnection* object are the server, the user ID, the password, and the data source to connect to. When working with a connection object, you can either set the *ConnectionString* property as a single string, as shown in the previous code example, or you can set individual connection properties. (If your data source requires connection string values that are not represented by individual properties, you must set the *ConnectionString* property.)

The two primary methods for managing connections are *Open* and *Close*. The *Open* method uses the information in the *ConnectionString* property to contact the data source and establish an open connection. The *Close* method tears the connection down. Closing connections is essential because most data sources support only a limited number of open connections, and open connections take up valuable system resources.

Commands to Manipulate Data from the Data Source

After establishing a connection to a data source with a connection object, you can execute commands and return results from the data source using a *Command* object. A *Command* object can be created using the *Command* constructor, as we do in the following code example, or by calling the *CreateCommand* method of the connection object. If you are connecting to an SQL Server database, an *SqlCommand* object might be configured to look like this.

```
Dim cmdSqlCommand As SqlCommand = _
    New SqlCommand("SELECT CustomerID, " & _
        "CompanyName FROM Customers", sqlConn)
```

When creating a *Command* object using the *Command* constructor, you specify an SQL statement to execute at the data source as the first parameter and a connection object as the second parameter.

Now that we've built our connection string to specify which data source we are interested in and constructed our command on the data we want to retrieve, we simply execute the *Open* method of the connection object to establish the connection.

```
sqlConn.Open()
```

Creating the *DataReader* Object

Now we need someplace to hold the data that is retrieved from the database, which is how we'll use the *DataReader* object. After creating an instance of a *Command* object, you create a *DataReader* by calling the *ExecuteReader* method on the command. This method retrieves rows from a data source as specified in the *Command* object. At this point the *DataReader* is filled with records from the database.

```
Dim drSqlDataReader As SqlDataReader = _
    cmdSqlCommand.ExecuteReader()
```

Now that our *DataReader* is filled with records, we can display them. In this example, we get the first and second columns from each record (remember the first column is 0, the next 1, and so on) and send them to the output box.

You can get at the data in each column of the returned row in two ways. You can either provide the name of the field you want to retrieve, or you can use the ordinal reference of the column, as we do in the code example that follows. To get the best performance from the *DataReader*, you can use a series of methods to access column values in their native data types (*GetDateTime*, *GetDouble*, *GetGuid*, *GetInt32*, and so on). We use *GetString* so that the system doesn't need to look up the data type and then handle displaying the strings. This is an example of a lean-and-mean, no-frills data output machine.

When the *DataReader* is first filled, it is positioned to a Null record until its *Read* method is called for the first time. This approach is different from classic ADO logic in which the first record in a result set is pointed to by default. In this example, we loop through each record and display the two fields in the output console.

The *DataReader* object does not have a *MoveNext* method. Not surprisingly, many developers often forget to add the *MoveNext* statement and then complain about performance because their code never terminates. The *DataReader.Read* method now automatically advances the cursor to the next record and returns False if there is no more data to read. Notice that the next example simply uses a *Do While Loop* construct to read each record, one at a time.

While the *DataReader* permits direct, high-performance access to the database, it provides only read-only and forward-only access to the data. The results it returns are not memory resident, and it can access only one record at a time. While these limitations put less load on the server's memory requirements, you can use the *DataReader* only to display data. Remember, though, that many applications need just this display of data, so when you can, use the *DataReader* because it provides the best performance.

```
Do While drSqlDataReader.Read()
    Console.WriteLine(vbTab & "{0}" & vbTab & "{1}", _
        drSqlDataReader.GetString(0), drSqlDataReader.GetString(1))
Loop
```

Finally we close both the *DataReader* object and the connection to the database.

```
drSqlDataReader.Close()
sqlConn.Close()
```

Putting the Pieces of Our *DataReader* Together

Now that we've looked at the pieces, let's put them together in a simple program. Start a new Visual Basic Windows Application project and add the following statements.

```
Imports System.Data
Imports System.Data.SqlClient
Imports System
```

The rest of the code could easily be placed in the *Click* event handler of a button if you are interested in running it. The first step we'll take is to dimension an *SqlConnection* object to define the database we are interested in and an *SqlCommand* object that defines the table and records from that table we want to retrieve. Then we dimension an *SqlDataReader* object that will hold the data. Finally the records are iterated and written to the console. As good practice, we close both the *DataReader* and the connection. That's all there is to it. Here's the code:

```
'Note that you must adjust the following connection
'parameters for your Microsoft SQL Server connection
Dim sqlConn As SqlConnection = New _
    SqlConnection("Initial Catalog=Northwind;" & _
        "Data Source=localhost;Integrated Security=SSPI")
```

```
Dim cmdSqlCommand As SqlCommand = New _
    SqlCommand("SELECT CustomerID, CompanyName " & _
        "FROM Customers", sqlConn)

sqlConn.Open()

Dim drSqlDataReader As SqlDataReader = _
    cmdSqlCommand.ExecuteReader()


Console.WriteLine("---------")
Do While drSqlDataReader.Read()
    Console.WriteLine(vbTab & "{0}" & vbTab & "{1}", _
        drSqlDataReader.Item(0).ToString(), _
        drSqlDataReader.GetString(1))
Loop

drSqlDataReader.Close()
sqlConn.Close()
```

When we run the program, the results are piped to the output box (which is the console during design mode). In these few lines of code, we've examined the key elements of retrieving data and displaying it, as you can see in Figure 10-5.

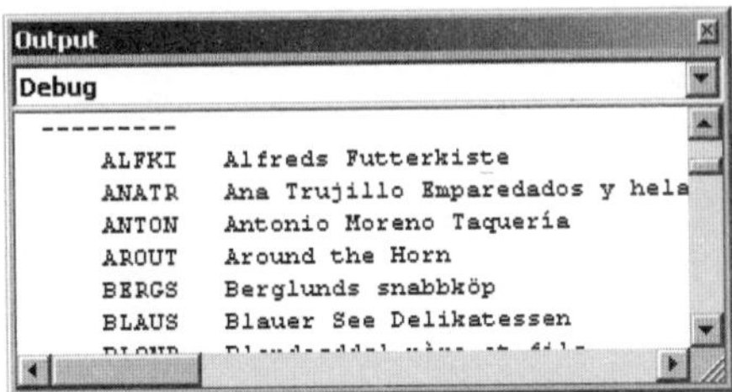

Figure 10-5 Data retrieved through a *DataReader* object.

This program has no frills, but it got our feet wet with the ADO.NET *DataReader*. While the *DataReader* is fast and useful in certain situations, many times we just need more functionality. Our application might need to permit a user to scroll through or edit the data that's retrieved. And when the user makes changes, we want to update the data source from which the original data was retrieved. In these cases, we need to use the *DataSet* object.

Writing a Simple *SQLClient* Class *DataSet* Program

Our next sample program, SQLDataGrid, will not only show you how the *DataSet* object works, it will also drive home the concept of how integral XML is to ADO.NET. SQLDataGrid retrieves all the records from the Customers table of the Northwind database and displays them in a DataGrid control. We can then scroll through the records and edit them. When we're finished, we can commit the changes to the original database. We can examine the records retrieved and also look at the XML representation of the data schema that defines the table within the data set.

While the OleDB classes are more generic for ADO, we'll use the SQLClient classes for our first *DataSet* example. As I've mentioned, the *System.Data.SQLClient* classes are optimized for SQL Server 2000. However, the SQL managed provider supports named parameters and not positional parameters, so the syntax for the SQL provider is just a bit more involved than that required for the OleDB provider. Luckily, the Visual Studio .NET IDE provides a few wizards to take care of the grungy code. We have to write only a few lines to build a fully operational program. The finished product will look like Figure 10-6.

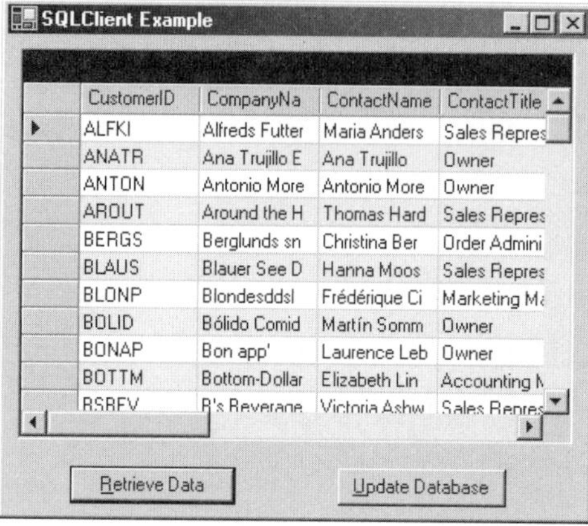

Figure 10-6 Our SQLDataGrid program in action.

Getting Started

Start a new Windows Application project in Visual Studio .NET and name it SQLDataGrid. The next step we take is to add a connection to the Northwind database. In the next chapter, we will add a connection manually, but for now let's use the Data Link Properties box.

1. Select View | Server Explorer from the main IDE menu. The Data Connections collection holds connections to various databases we might use. We want to add a new connection to the Northwind database and then select the records in the Customers table. To add a new connection, right-click Data Connections and then click Add Connection, as shown in Figure 10-7.

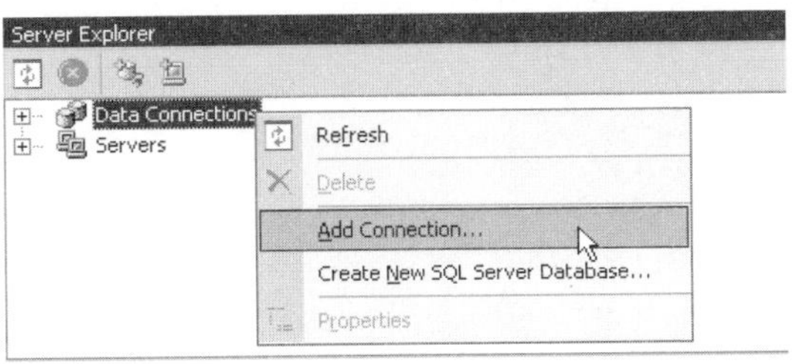

Figure 10-7 Adding a connection to the Northwind database.

2. We will be using our local machine in this example, so, in the Data Link Properties dialog box, enter "**host**" (or your SQL Server name) for the server name. Next, select the option for Use Windows NT Integrated Security. (You could also select the Use A Specific User Name And Password option and enter appropriate information such as QSUser for the user name and QSPassword for the password.) Click the Refresh button to make sure that the server's name is legitimate and you didn't make a typo. If you type the name incorrectly, when you attempt to retrieve the available databases, you will get a data link error message, shown in Figure 10-8.

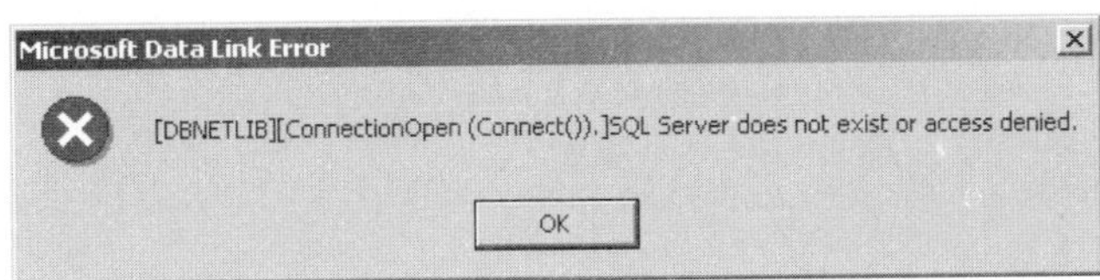

Figure 10-8 If a server name isn't valid, you get a data link error.

If you get a data link error, a message box notifies you that the catalog of databases for the local server can't be retrieved, as shown in Figure 10-9.

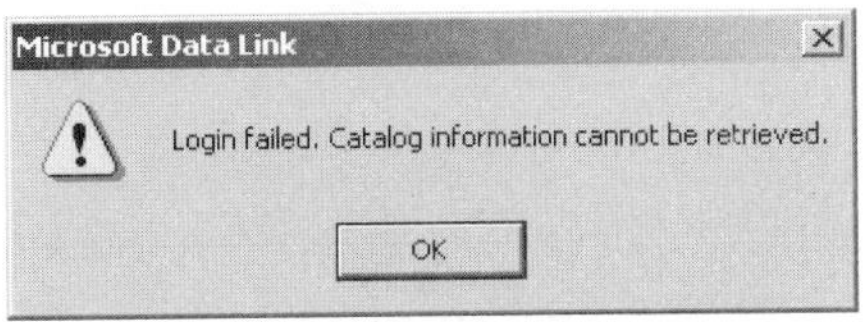

Figure 10-9 The database catalog error message.

When the server name is resolved correctly, you'll see the databases installed on your PC. Click the drop-down list and select Northwind, shown in Figure 10-10.

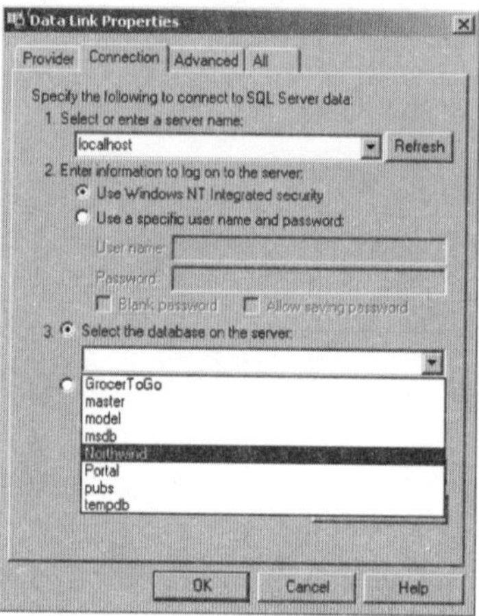

Figure 10-10 Selecting the Northwind database in the Data Link Properties dialog box.

3. To be sure that we can connect to the Northwind database, click the Test Connection button. The message box indicates that the test connection succeeded. Life is good, as Figure 10-11 clearly shows.

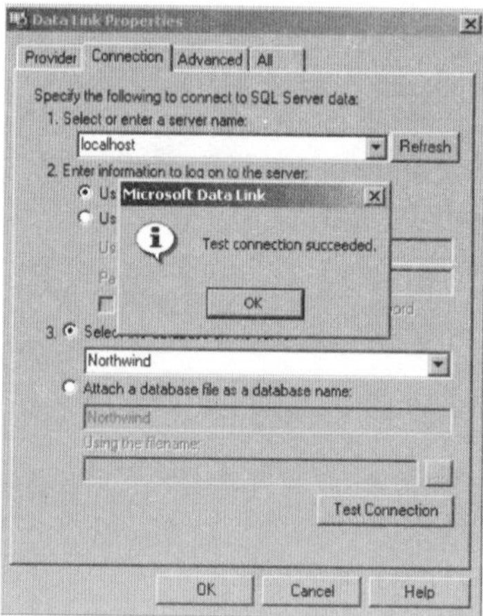

Figure 10-11 Our connection succeeded.

Before dismissing the Data Link Properties dialog box, click the Provider tab. The Microsoft OLE DB Provider for SQL Server is selected by default, as shown in Figure 10-12. You can see, however, that several other managed OLE

DB providers are listed. After the .NET Framework is released and more programmers migrate to this platform, you'll see more and more providers become available. Click the OK button. The connection information required to connect to the Northwind database will be written for us.

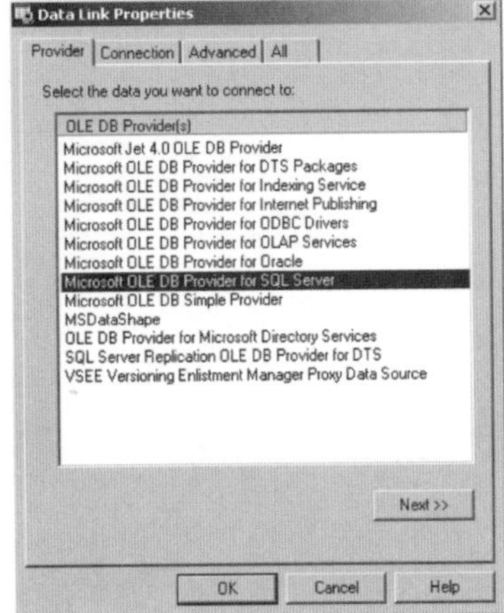

Figure 10-12 The Provider tab of the Data Link Properties dialog box.

Now we need to add an *SqlConnection* object to the program.

1. In the toolbox, click the Data tab and double-click the SqlConnection control to add a new *SqlConnection* object to our project. The default name is SqlConnection1.
2. Right-click on the *SqlConnection1* object and select Properties. We need to provide our new connection object with the connection string it needs to connect to the database. Click the ConnectionString drop-down box and select the Northwind connection we just created, as shown in Figure 10-13.

> **Note** You could have first added an *SqlConnection* object and then selected New Connection, and the Data Link Properties dialog box from the previous procedure would have been displayed. Also note in the top drop-down box that our connection lives in the *System.Data.SqlClient* namespace within the .NET Framework.

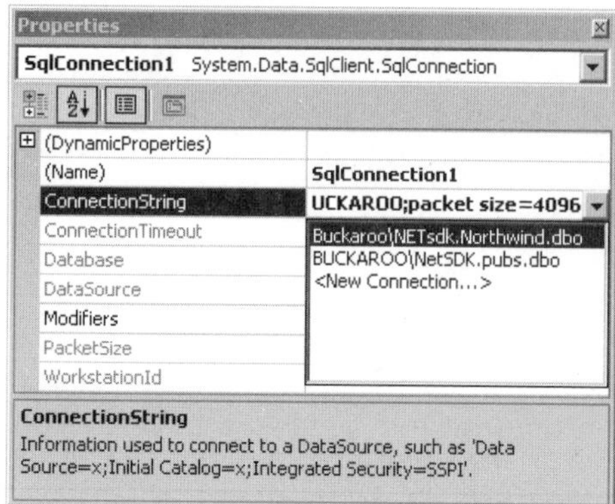

Figure 10-13 Designating our connection string.

In case you were wondering, here's the code that Visual Basic .NET added on my machine when I chose the connection in the ConnectionString drop-down box. (The code will be slightly different on your machine.) Notice that the *SqlConnection* object's *ConnectionString* property shows which server to use, which database we're connecting to, some security information, and information about the workstation and packet transfer size.

```
Me.SqlConnection1.ConnectionString = _
    "data source=localhost;initial catalog=Northwind;" & _
    "integrated security=SSPI;persist security info=False;" & _
    "workstation id=localhost;packet size=4096"
```

Adding a *DataAdapter* Object to Our Program

The *DataAdapter* is the object that connects to the database to fill the memory resident *DataSet*. Then the *DataAdapter* connects to the database again to update the data on the basis of the operations performed while the *DataSet* held the data.

In the past, data processing has been primarily connection-based. Now, in an effort to make multitiered applications more efficient, data processing is turning to a message-based approach that revolves around chunks of information. At the center of this approach is the *DataAdapter*, which provides a link between a *DataSet* and its data source that's used to retrieve and save data. It accomplishes these processes by means of requests to the appropriate SQL commands made against the data source.

1. In the toolbox, double-click the SqlDataAdapter control to add a *SqlDataAdapter* to our program. When the *SqlDataAdapter* is added, the Data Adapter Configuration Wizard is displayed, as shown in Figure 10-14. Click Next, and follow the steps to configure the new *SqlDataAdapter*.

Figure 10-14 The opening screen for the Data Adapter Configuration Wizard.

2. Select the database connection to the Northwind database we just built, as shown in Figure 10-15. (Notice that at this point you can still create a new connection by clicking New Connection.) Click Next.

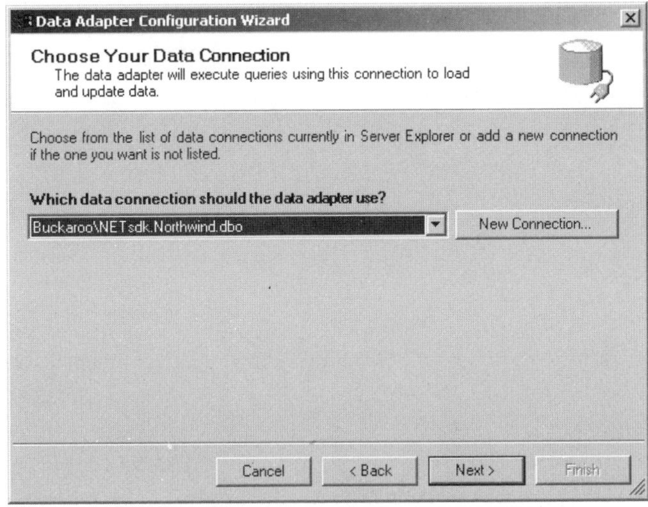

Figure 10-15 Selecting our database connection in the wizard.

Remember when I mentioned that the SQLClient *DataAdapter* is a bit trickier to set up than the OleDB *DataAdapter*? This is where the wizard earns its pay. We'll let the wizard add the SQL statements by selecting the Use SQL Statements option, shown in Figure 10-16. Click Next to continue.

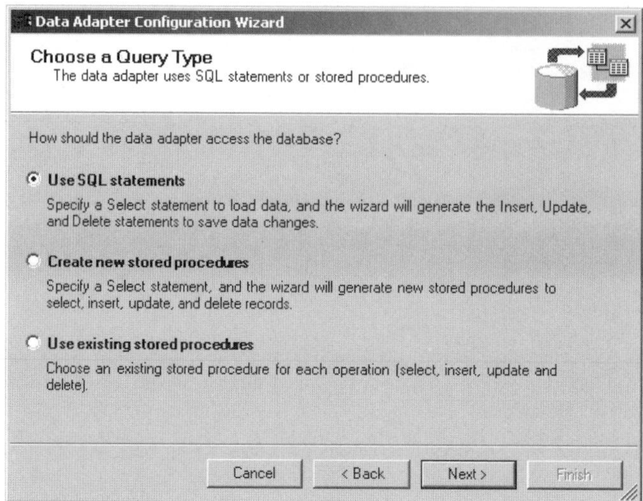

Figure 10-16 Letting the wizard do the work.

3. The next screen, shown in Figure 10-17, lets us use a standard SQL statement to select the data we want the *DataAdapter* to retrieve from the database. In this case, type in the *SELECT* statement shown in Figure 10-17, which selects all the records and all the fields from the Customers table in the Northwind database.

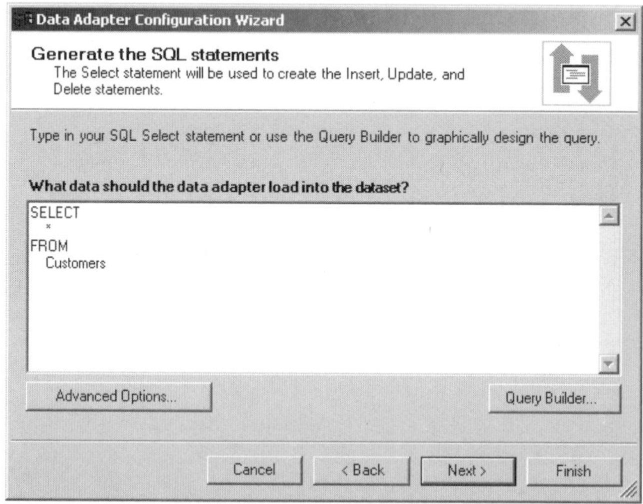

Figure 10-17 Selecting the data we want to retrieve.

4. Click the Advanced Options button. You'll see the Advanced SQL Generation Options dialog box, shown in Figure 10-18. Leave the three options checked by default. You can see that the wizard will

generate all the SQL statements for us and also take care of the details of detecting changes between the data in the database and our data set.

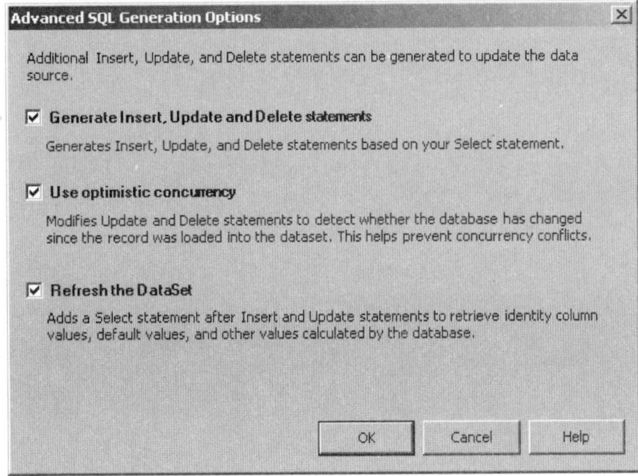

Figure 10-18 Advanced options in the wizard.

5. Click OK to close the Advanced SQL Generation Options dialog box. Now click the Query Builder button to display the Query Builder, shown in Figure 10-19. You can see that all columns for all records are selected. If you wanted to modify the conditions for retrieving data from the database, you would do that here. Let's keep things simple for our first example and leave the *SELECT* statement as is.

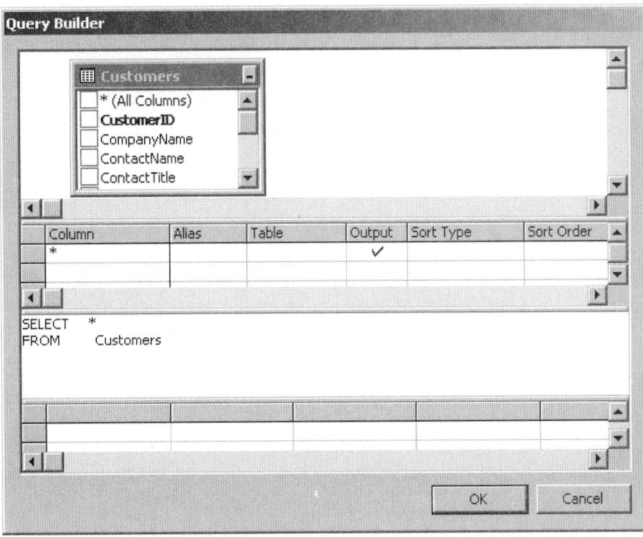

Figure 10-19 The Query Builder.

6. Click OK to close the Query Builder dialog box, and then click Next in the configuration wizard. Using our instructions, the wizard now goes to work constructing the underpinnings of the SQL connection and commands.

7. Click Finish to dismiss the wizard, whose work is now done. We'll soon see that the work was not trivial.

I described the *SqlDataAdapter* as a bridge between the data source and the memory-resident data set. The wizard added the commands for that bridge, which are illustrated in Figure 10-20.

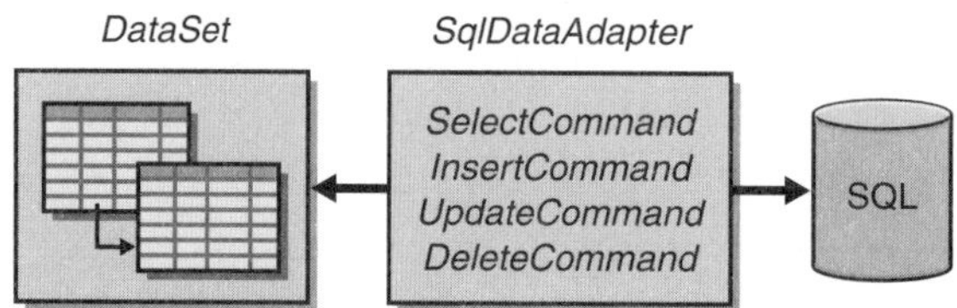

Figure 10-20 The wizard builds its bridge.

Finishing the User Interface

Before we look at the data and the program's code in more detail, let's finish the interface for our form. Add a DataGrid component from the Windows Forms tab of the toolbox to the form and also two command buttons. Set the properties for the controls as listed in Table 10-9.. Your form should now look something like Figure 10-21.

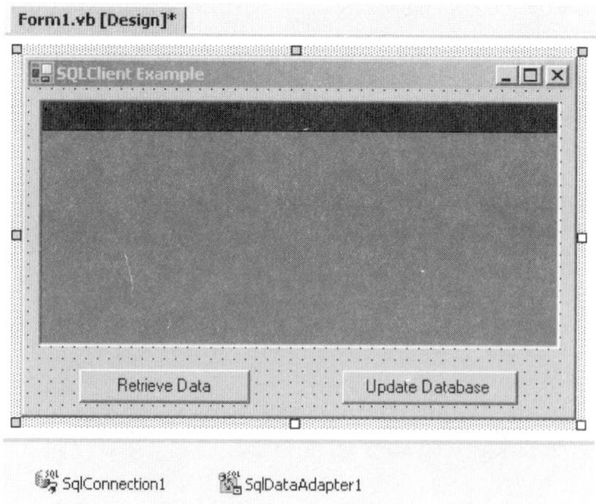

Figure 10-21 Adding interface controls to our form.

Table 10-9 Properties for the SQLDataGrid Form

Object	Property	Value
Form	*Text*	SQLClient Example
DataGrid		Defaults
Button	*Text*	&Retrieve Data
	Name	btnRetrieve
Button	*Text*	&Update Database
	Name	btnUpdate

> **Tip** Take a moment and bring up the properties sheet for the DataGrid control. Click the AutoFormat hyperlink displayed under the list of properties. An Auto Format dialog box will be displayed. Click a few of the formats to get an idea of how you can display your data. When you've finished exploring the various built-in formats, click Cancel to stick with the default view. When you start writing your own .NET database programs for production, you can add a lot of eye candy options for free.

A Sneak Preview of Our Data from the *DataAdapter*

Let's take a quick look at the data that we'll retrieve. Right-click on the form, and then select Preview Data. You can see the data that will be displayed when our program comes to life.

1. In the Data Adapter Preview dialog box, be sure that SqlDataAdapter1 is selected in the Data Adapters list, as shown in Figure 10-22, and then click the Fill Dataset button. This dialog box provides all sorts of information, including how large the data set will be in bytes.

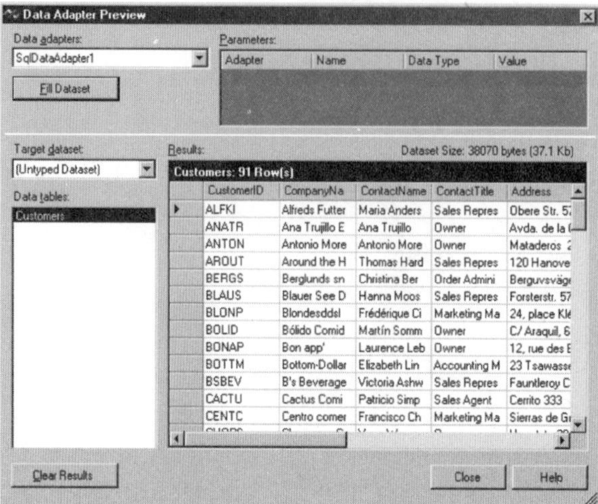

Figure 10-22 Previewing our data in the Data Adapter Preview dialog box.

2. Close the Data Adapter Preview dialog box, right-click the form again, and select Generate Dataset to display the Generate Dataset dialog box, shown in Figure 10-23. Accept the defaults, and then click OK.

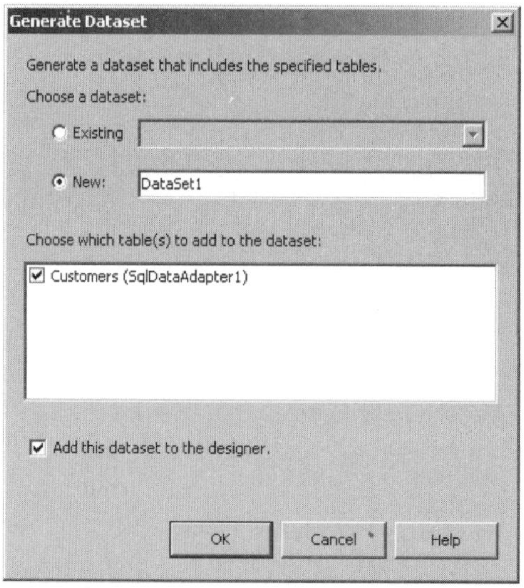

Figure 10-23 The Generate Dataset dialog box.

When you dismiss the Generate Dataset dialog box, a new *DataSet* object will be added to your program. Right-click on the

DataSet object to display its properties dialog box, shown in Figure 10-24.

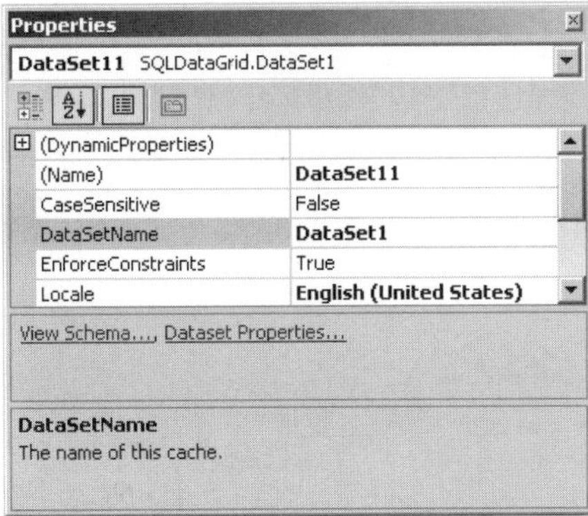

Figure 10-24 The properties dialog box for the new *DataSet* object.

Notice the two hyperlinks at the bottom of the properties dialog box. One leads you to a view of the database schema; the other shows a view of the data set properties.

3. Click the View Schema hyperlink. You'll see the database schema, which is the template of the table our data adapter will use to pull the records from the database. The schema is shown in Figure 10-25.

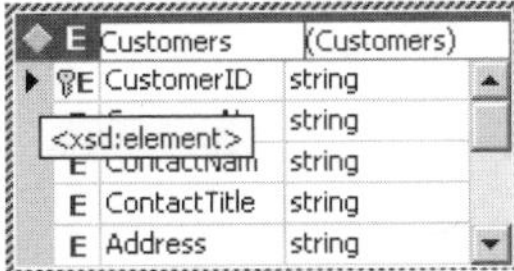

Figure 10-25 The database schema.

XML Schema for the Customers Table

Our program shuttles data between the data source (the Customers table in the Northwind database) and our data set via the data adapter. The schema provides the rules for how the data will be represented in our data set and the ground rules for how tables, records, and columns relate to one another.

Now either right-click the schema and select View XML Source or click the XML tab at the bottom left of the IDE. Either of these actions will display the XML representation of the schema that the data set will use. You can see that the XML schema is human readable (in other words, it is not binary). It is nested and case sensitive. The elements show each of the fields that the data set is expecting as well as the field's data type attribute.

```
<xsd:schema id="DataSet1"
 targetNamespace="http://www.tempuri.org/DataSet1.xsd" xmlns="http://
www.tempuri.org/DataSet1.xsd" xmlns:xsd=http://www.w3.org/2001/
XMLSchema
 xmlns:msdata="urn:schemas-microsoft-com:xml-msdata"
 attributeFormDefault="qualified"
 elementFormDefault="qualified">
<xsd:element name="DataSet1" msdata:IsDataSet="true">
<xsd:complexType>
 <xsd:choice maxOccurs="unbounded">
  <xsd:element name="Customers">
   <xsd:complexType>
    <xsd:sequence>
     <xsd:element name="CustomerID" type="xsd:string" />
     <xsd:element name="CompanyName" type="xsd:string" />
     <xsd:element name="ContactName" type="xsd:string"
      minOccurs="0" />
     <xsd:element name="ContactTitle" type="xsd:string"
      minOccurs="0" />
     <xsd:element name="Address" type="xsd:string"
      minOccurs="0" />
     <xsd:element name="City" type="xsd:string"
      minOccurs="0" />
     <xsd:element name="Region" type="xsd:string"
      minOccurs="0" />
     <xsd:element name="PostalCode" type="xsd:string"
      minOccurs="0" />
     <xsd:element name="Country" type="xsd:string"
      minOccurs="0" />
     <xsd:element name="Phone" type="xsd:string"
      minOccurs="0" />
     <xsd:element name="Fax" type="xsd:string"
      minOccurs="0" />
   </xsd:sequence>
  </xsd:complexType>
 </xsd:element>
</xsd:choice>
</xsd:complexType>
<xsd:unique name="Constraint1" msdata:PrimaryKey="true">
<xsd:selector xpath=".//Customers" />
<xsd:field xpath="CustomerID" />
</xsd:unique>
</xsd:element>
</xsd:schema>
```

Just Add Code

Now that we've taken the grand tour of the *SqlConnection*, *SqlDataAdapter*, and *SqlDataSet* objects, we can write a few lines of code to make our program fully functional. Add the following lines of code to both the btnRetrieve and btnUpdate *Click* event handlers. Remember that structured error handling that would ordinarily be added to any production code is omitted for the sake of clarity.

```
Private Sub btnRetrieve_Click(ByVal sender As System.Object, _
    ByVal e As System.EventArgs) Handles btnRetrieve.Click

    SqlDataAdapter1.Fill(DataSet11, "Customers")

    With DataGrid1
        .DataSource = DataSet11
        .AllowSorting = True
        .AlternatingBackColor = System.Drawing.Color.Bisque
        .SetDataBinding(DataSet11, "Customers")
    End With
End Sub

Private Sub btnUpdate_Click(ByVal sender As System.Object, _
    ByVal e As System.EventArgs) Handles btnUpdate.Click

    DataGrid1.Update()
    SqlDataAdapter1.Update(DataSet11)
End Sub
```

Running Our Program

Go ahead and run the program. Click the Retrieve Data button. A connection is established with the data source, and the data grid is populated. The *AlternatingBackColor* property gives the grid a more professional look. The *AllowSorting* property is set to True by default, but I wanted to illustrate how easy it is to give your grid superhuman properties with a single line of code.

Click the first column heading in the grid. Notice the recessed up arrow at the right side of the heading, shown in Figure 10-26. This arrow is a cue that this column can be sorted and that it is sorted in ascending order.

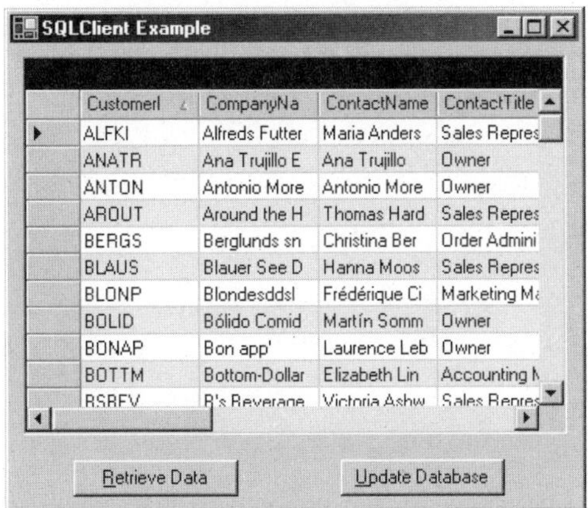

Figure 10-26 Sorting our data set.

Now click the ContactName column heading. Clicking sorts the records in the data set in ascending order. Click again and our program sorts the data set in descending order. You can click the column headings a few times until you get bored. At times you might need to sort on multiple columns. For example, you might need to show all customers sorted alphabetically by city. While the data grid can sort only on a single column, *DataView objects* have more flexibility.

Editing Our Data

Our grid not only displays our data easily, it also permits editing. If you select the first record and make a change, as illustrated in Figure 10-27 with the ContactName column, the leftmost cell icon changes from an arrow to a pencil, indicating that the current row is being edited. The data grid and the underlying data set hold any changes we might make to the data. Because we don't currently have a connection to the underlying database, the data source is not updated—yet.

Figure 10-27 Editing data in the data grid.

If you want to commit the changes to the underlying database table, clicking the Update Database button does the trick. Be careful because clicking this button will actually change the Northwind Customers table if you commit any changes. And this update is accomplished with two lines of code! Now that is powerful.

How the Code Works

When the user clicks the Retrieve Data button, the data set is filled with the records from the database. Populating the data set is pretty simple. We call the

Fill method of the *SqlDataAdapter* and pass in the data set to be filled and the name of the table. Remember that the data adapter is already configured with the connection and it knows the SQL statements required to extract the records from the Customers table.

```
Private Sub btnRetrieve_Click(ByVal sender As System.Object, _
    ByVal e As System.EventArgs) Handles btnRetrieve.Click

    SqlDataAdapter1.Fill(DataSet11, "Customers")
```

This is all the code that's required to connect to the database with the connection object, grab the data with the *DataAdapter* object, and fill the memory-resident data set.

Remember that the *DataSet* object is independent of the data source, which means it does not require a persistent connection to the database. The connection is opened to get the data and closed once the *DataSet* has been filled. The *Fill* method retrieves rows from the data source by using the *SELECT* statement specified by an associated *SelectCommand* property. In our case, the wizard wrote that statement for us. If you look at the code the wizard wrote, it simply selects each field in the Customers table for us.

```
Me.SqlSelectCommand1.CommandText = "SELECT CustomerID, " & _
    "CompanyName, ContactName, ContactTitle, Address, " & _
    "City, Region, PostalCode, Country, Phone, Fax " & _
    "FROM Customers"
```

The *Connection* property of the *SqlSelectCommand* was also taken care of for us.

```
Me.SqlSelectCommand1.Connection = Me.SqlConnection1
```

The connection object associated with the *SELECT* statement must be valid, but it does not need to be open. If the connection is closed before *Fill* is called, it is opened to retrieve data and then closed. If the connection is manually opened before *Fill* is called, it remains open. In other words, if we were to add *SqlConnection1.Open* to our code, we would have to explicitly close the connection. Otherwise, letting the *DataAdapter* open and close the connection as necessary is more efficient.

The *Fill* operation then adds the rows to the destination *DataTable* object in the *DataSet*, creating the *DataTable* objects if they do not already exist. The *DataSet* stores data using .NET Framework data types. For most applications, these types provide a convenient representation of data source information, as we saw in the database schema shown earlier. However, this representation might cause a problem when the data type in the data source is an SQL Server decimal. The .NET Framework decimal data type allows a maximum of 28 significant digits, while the SQL Server decimal data type allows 38 significant digits. If the *SqlDataAdapter* determines, during a fill operation, that the precision of an SQL Server decimal field is greater than 28 characters, the current row will not be added to the *DataTable*. Instead the *FillError* event will occur, which enables you to determine whether a loss of precision will occur and respond appropriately.

So, we just filled the *DataSet* with a single command. Now we want to configure our *DataGrid* and bind it to the data set so that our data can be displayed. We really only need to set the *DataSource* property and invoke the *SetDataBinding* method of the *DataGrid* object to display our information. However, we will also set the *AllowSorting* property to True, allowing the *DataGrid* to now sort individual columns. And setting the *AlternatingBackColor* property gives a nice aesthetic look to the final product.

```
With DataGrid1
    .DataSource = DataSet11
    .AllowSorting = True
    .AlternatingBackColor = System.Drawing.Color.Bisque
    .SetDataBinding(DataSet11, "Customers")
End With
```

Updating the Data Source

When the user wants to commit the changes made in the data grid back to the underlying data source, clicking the Update Database button does the job in only two lines of code. The first line updates the data grid control. This operation is for cosmetic reasons. The *DataGrid.Update* method forces the control to paint any currently invalid areas. Next the *SqlDataAdapter.Update* method is called, which does the heavy lifting to update the data source. The *Update* method calls the respective *INSERT*, *UPDATE*, or *DELETE* statement for each inserted, updated, or deleted row in the specified *DataSet*.

```
Private Sub btnUpdate_Click(ByVal sender As System.Object, _
    ByVal e As System.EventArgs) Handles btnUpdate.Click

    DataGrid1.Update()
    SqlDataAdapter1.Update(DataSet11)
End Sub
```

When our application calls the *SqlDataAdapter* object's *Update* method, the data adapter examines the *RowState* property and executes the required *INSERT*, *UPDATE*, or *DELETE* statement on the basis of the order of the indexes configured in the *DataSet*.

For example, *Update* might first execute a *DELETE* statement, followed by an *INSERT* statement, and then another *DELETE* statement because of the ordering of the rows in the *DataTable* that resides in the *DataSet*. An application can call the *GetChanges* method in situations in which you must control the sequence of statement types (for example, an *INSERT* before an *UPDATE*).

If *INSERT*, *UPDATE*, or *DELETE* statements have not been specified, the *Update* method generates an exception. If you don't want to use the wizard and instead write the code yourself, you can create a *SqlCommandBuilder* object to automatically generate SQL statements for single-table updates by using the *SelectCommand* property of a .NET data provider. Then the *CommandBuilder* generates any additional SQL statements required. However, this magical generation logic requires key column information to be present in the *DataSet*.

If you feel like writing code manually and you're working with a keyed, single table, you can write the following code to generate the required SQL commands.

```
Dim daDataAdapter As SqlDataAdapter = _
    New SqlDataAdapter("SELECT * FROM Customers", _
    sqlConn)
Dim sqlCommandBuilder As SqlCommandBuilder = _
    New SqlCommandBuilder(daDataAdapter)

'-- We explicitly open the database connection.
'-- Of course, we would also have to code that.
sqlConn.Open()

Dim dsDataSet As DataSet = New DataSet

daDataAdapter.Fill(dsDataSet, "Customers")

'-- Code to modify data in DataSet here.

'-- Without the SqlCommandBuilder, this line would fail.
custDA.Update(dsDataSet, "Customers")

sqlConn.Close()
```

The wizard, however, added all of the commands needed. If you were to look at the code the wizard provided, you would see something like this.

```
Friend WithEvents SqlConnection1 As _
    System.Data.SqlClient.SqlConnection
Friend WithEvents SqlDataAdapter1 As _
    System.Data.SqlClient.SqlDataAdapter
Friend WithEvents SqlSelectCommand1 As _
    System.Data.SqlClient.SqlCommand
Friend WithEvents SqlInsertCommand1 As _
    System.Data.SqlClient.SqlCommand
Friend WithEvents SqlUpdateCommand1 As _
```

(continued)

```
    System.Data.SqlClient.SqlCommand
Friend WithEvents SqlDeleteCommand1 As _
    System.Data.SqlClient.SqlCommand
Friend WithEvents DataGrid1 As _
    System.Windows.Forms.DataGrid
Friend WithEvents btnRetrieve As _
    System.Windows.Forms.Button
Friend WithEvents btnUpdate As _
    System.Windows.Forms.Button
Friend WithEvents DataSet11 As SQLDataGrid.DataSet1
```

The wizard also added the following *UPDATE* statement for us using the database schema we looked at earlier as its guide. Now, while a wizard many times has a dark side, in this case it really did provide much of the low-level, tedious code we would have to work with otherwise.

```
Me.SqlUpdateCommand1.CommandText = "UPDATE Customers " & _
    "SET CustomerID = @CustomerID, CompanyName = " & _
    "@CompanyName, ContactName = @ContactName, " & _
    "ContactTitle = @ContactTitle, Address = Address, " & _
    "City = @City, Region = @Region, PostalCode = " & _
    "@PostalCode, Country = @Country, Phone = @P" & _
    "hone, Fax = @Fax WHERE (CustomerID = " & _
    "@Original_CustomerID) AND (Address = @Origi" & _
    "nal_Address OR @Original_Address1 IS NULL AND " & _
    "Address IS NULL) AND (City = @Original_City OR " & _
    "@Original_City1 IS NULL AND City IS NULL) AND " & _
    "(CompanyName = @Original_CompanyName) AND " & _
    "(ContactName = @Original_ContactName OR " & _
    "@Original_ContactName1 IS NULL AND ContactName " & _
    "IS NULL) AND (ContactTitle = @Original_ContactTitle " & _
    "OR @Original_ContactTitle1 IS NULL AND ContactTitle " & _
    "IS NULL) AND (Country = @Original_Country OR " & _
    "@Original_Country1 IS NULL AND Country IS NULL) " & _
    "AND (Fax = @Original_Fax OR @Original_Fax1 IS NULL " & _
    "AND Fax IS NULL) AND (Phone = @Original_Phone " & _
    "OR @Original_Phone1 IS NULL AND Phone IS NULL) AND " & _
    "(PostalCode = @Original_PostalCode OR " & _
    "@Original_PostalCode1 IS NULL AND PostalCode IS " & _
    "NULL) AND (Region = @Original_Region OR " & _
    "@Original_Region1 IS NULL AND Region IS NULL); " & _
    "SELECT CustomerID, CompanyName, ContactName, " & _
    "ContactTitle, Address, City, Region, PostalCode, " & _
    "Country, Phone, Fax FROM Customers WHERE " & _
    "(CustomerID = @Select_CustomerID)"
```

The wizard puts in quite a bit of additional code for us. When you get a moment, poke through the form and take a look. In the next chapter, we'll write some examples using the OleDB managed provider. Luckily, these classes are easier to work with when hand coding.

Conclusion

In this chapter you learned how to set up a connection to a database and retrieve data. That data was brought into an in-memory data set via a data connector. We modified the data and sent it back to update its source. The main objects that we became friends with were the following:

- *Connection.* For connecting to and managing transactions against a database.
- *Command.* For issuing SQL commands against a database.
- *DataReaders.* For reading a forward-only stream of data records from an SQL Server data source.
- *DataSets.* For storing, remoting, and programming against flat data, XML data, and relational data.
- *DataAdapters.* For pushing data into a *DataSet* and reconciling data against a database.

Now we are ready to move on to explore some of the finer parts of ADO.NET.

11

Data Sets in Detail

After reading the last chapter, you should have a good idea of how a data provider connects to a data source and places the information retrieved in an in-memory *DataSet* object. In this chapter, we'll continue looking at how ADO.NET and Visual Basic .NET work together by reviewing data tables, relationships, and the *DataView* object in more detail.

Looking Again at the ADO.NET Object Model

Before we jump in, take a moment to look over Figure 11-1, which shows the ADO.NET object model. The ADO.NET object model has been streamlined significantly so that it is much easier to understand and work with than classic ADO.

ADO.NET is represented in the Microsoft .NET Framework by the namespace *System.Data*, as well as all of *System.Data*'s child namespaces. ADO.NET's object model is an all-purpose, generalized data access model that's designed to support accessing and writing to a wide variety of data sources.

The data provider communicates with a data source such as a database, an e-mail store, a Microsoft Excel spreadsheet, a text file, and so on. The beauty of the data provider approach is that we have only to configure the data provider and program the uniform *DataSet* object model. We don't have to worry about how the data gets to the data set. Once it's there, we have a uniform object model that works the same regardless of where the data came from.

Remember that the data provider connects to the data source on behalf of ADO.NET. All of the connections are encapsulated. The data provider has several key objects contained in it, which we looked at briefly in Chapter 10, "Data Access with ADO.NET."

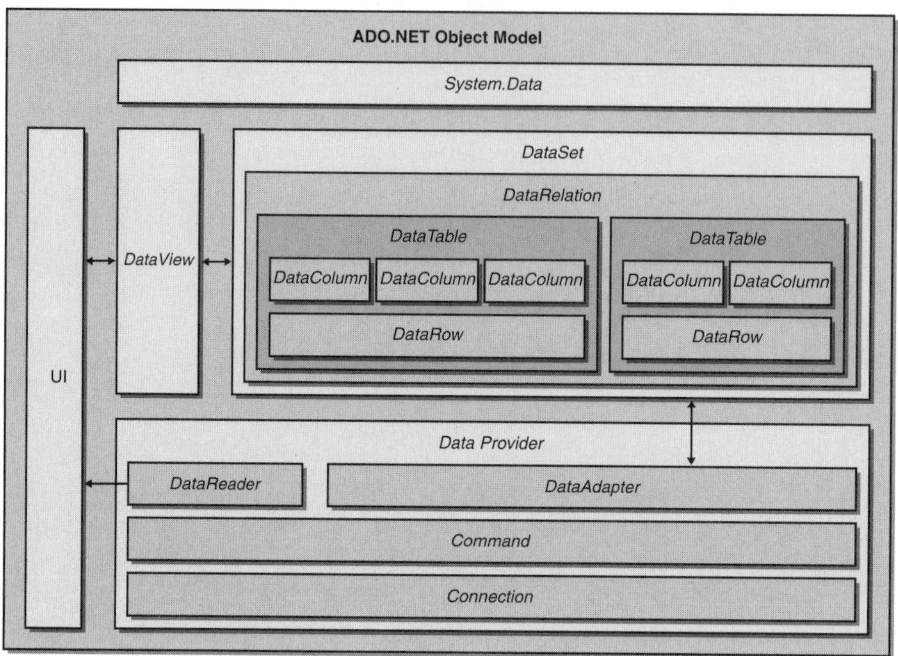

Figure 11-1 The ADO.NET object model.

- *Connection*. Used to connect to the data source. *Connection* objects are represented by the provider-specific classes *SqlConnection* and *OleDbConnection*. Connections are opened either explicitly by calling the *Open* method on the connection or implicitly by using a *DataAdapter*.

- *Command*. Contains information that is submitted to a data source as a query. *Command* objects are represented by the specific classes *SqlCommand* and *OleDbCommand*. Functionally, commands travel over connections, and query results are returned in the form of streams, which can then be accessed by a *DataReader* object or passed into a *DataSet* object via a *DataAdapter*.

- *DataAdapter*. Provides a set of methods and properties to retrieve and save data, forming a bridge between a data set and its data source. The *DataAdapter* encapsulates a set of data commands and a connection that is used to fill a data set as well as to update the data source. The *Fill* method calls the SELECT command, while the *Update* method calls INSERT, UPDATE, or DELETE commands for each changed row.

- *DataReader*. Provides methods and properties that deliver a forward only stream of data rows from a data source.

The *DataSet* object represents a cache of data that contains tables, columns, relationships, and various constraints. While it behaves much like a database, a *DataSet* object does not interact directly with a database. That is what the data provider is for. As I mentioned, this approach allows a Visual Basic .NET developer to work with a consistent object model, regardless of the source of the data. Data can easily be placed into a *DataSet* from a database, an XML file, generated code, or user input. The *DataSet* object's consistent programming model works easily with flat, relational, or hierarchical data storage.

The *DataSet* tracks changes made to the data it contains before updating the source. You can use the *GetChanges* method of a *DataSet* to create a second *DataSet* that contains only the changes to the original data. The *DataSet* object holding the changes can be used by a *DataAdapter* to update the original source.

The *DataView* object provides methods and properties that enable various user interface objects—such as a data grid—to bind to a data set and view its contents in various meaningful ways. The *DataView* is really very simple, and we will explore its use later in the chapter. The *DataView*, however, can be used only in conjunction with a *DataSet* and never a *DataReader*.

We wrote a program in Chapter 10 that used the *DataReader* object, which, as you can see in Figure 11-2, is contained in the data provider. The *DataReader* is an extreme optimization of the ADO.NET object model because it eliminates the need for a *DataSet*. By eliminating parts of the ADO.NET object model, it provides lightning fast and efficient data access.

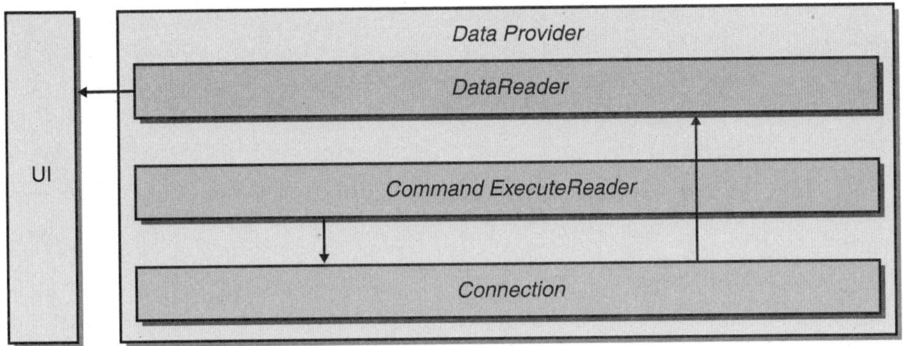

Figure 11-2 The *DataReader* object.

The *ExecuteReader* method of the *Command* object sends the *Command.CommandText* call to the *Connection* object. The *Connection* object then builds the *DataReader* and sends the result set to the UI via a stream. As I mentioned in the last chapter, be sure to use a *DataReader* when you need only to display but not update data.

Data Sets and XML

In this chapter, we will explore a bit more how to use a data set to generate XML. Because our data is represented in memory as text-based XML, the entire result set can be sent over the Internet to any server. To see how this works, we will write a program that retrieves the records from the Categories table in the Northwind database and places them in a data grid. Figure 11-3 shows how we would expect to see the data in a grid control, which isn't any different from how we'd view data if we were using classic Visual Basic.

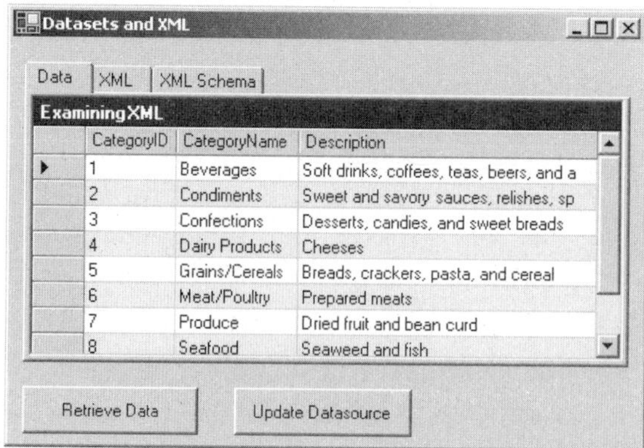

Figure 11-3 A view of data in a data grid.

Figure 11-4 shows the XML representation of the same data. As you know, this XML format is how the data is stored in memory. XML is also the format in which the data is passed around from tier to tier—pure text instead of a binary object. This approach is the way e-business can be conducted, by sending XML through the HTTP Port 80 on a Web server. No complicated specialized formats or special value added networks (VANS) are needed to transmit the file. Using XML, the data can be shipped safely to anywhere in the world with no special setups or handshakes agreed upon up front.

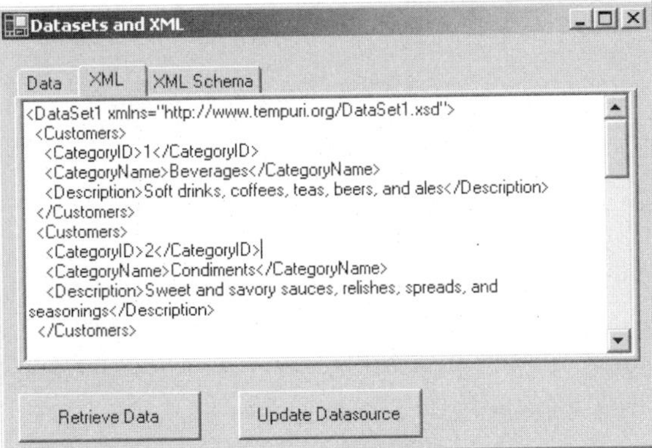

Figure 11-4 The data is stored in memory as text-based XML.

Finally, we can examine the schema of the XML file. The XML schema is the self-describing part of a data set, shown in Figure 11-5. With the schema, disparate and heterogeneous systems can know what an XML file contains without ever seeing the structure before. The XML schema (XML schema definition, or XSD) supports data types and the use of XML syntax, is able to be processed by XML processors, and supports global and local scope as in the use of identical element names within nested elements. So the XSD is itself an XML document.

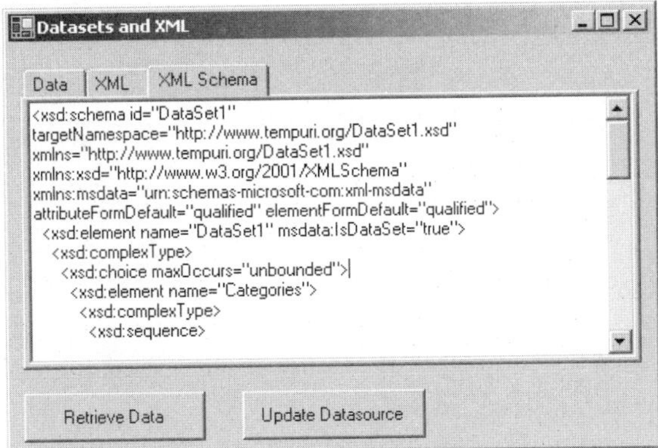

Figure 11-5 A data set describes itself in an XML schema.

Building the Data Set and XML Viewer Project

Create a new Windows project, and call it SqlXMLExample. On the default form, add a tab control. We will be adding a data grid to the first tab and text boxes to the next two tabs so that we can have different views of the same data. To create the rest of the project, follow these steps:

1. Right-click the tab control, and select Properties. In the Properties window, click the button with three dots in the *TabPages* property to display the TabPage Collection Editor, shown in Figure 11-6. The editor permits us to modify the appearance of each of the tab objects in the tab collection. Add two additional tabs by clicking the Add button. Change the *Text* property of the TabPage1 tab to Data, as shown in Figure 11-6, the TabPage2 tab to XML, and the TabPage3 tab to XML Schema.

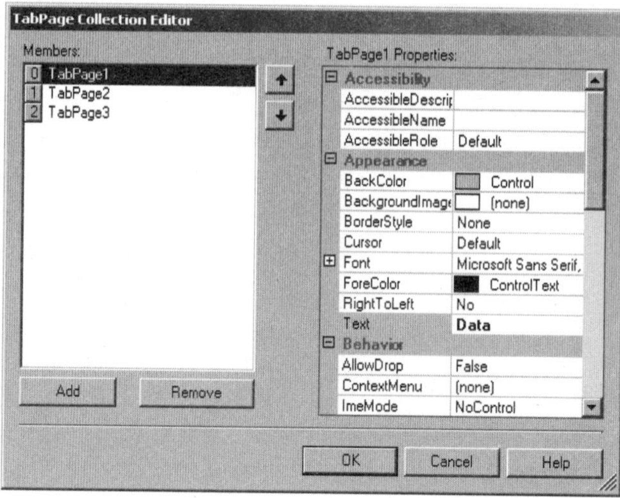

Figure 11-6 Use the TabPage Collection Editor to add tabs and set their properties.

2. Add a data grid control to the first tab. Set the *Dock* property of the data grid to Fill. This setting will expand the control to fill the entire container of the tab, as shown in Figure 11-7. Change the name of the control to dgDataGrid.

3. Add two buttons to the form as shown in Figure 11-7. Name the first one btnRetrieve, and set its *Text* property to &Retrieve Data. Name the second button btnUpdate, and set its *Text* property to &Update Datasource.

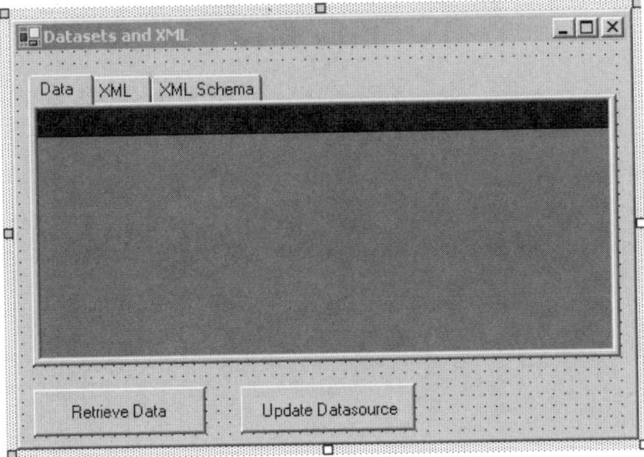

Figure 11-7 The data grid control fills the tab control.

4. Click the second tab, and add a text box control. Do the same thing for the third tab. Table 11-1 lists the properties to set for the form and its controls.

Table 11-1 Properties to Set for SqlXMLExample

Control	Property	Value
Form	*Text*	Datasets and XML
Tab control	*Name*	tcTabControl
	TabCollection	Add tabs as described in step 1
Data grid on tab 1	*Name*	dgDataGrid
	Dock	Fill
Text box on tab 2	*Name*	txtXML
	Dock	Fill
	MultiLine	True
	ScrollBars	Both
Text box on tab 3	*Name*	txtXMLSchema
	Dock	Fill
	MultiLine	True
	ScrollBars	Both
Button	*Name*	btnRetrieve
	Text	&Retrieve Data
Button	*Name*	btnUpdate
	Text	&Update Datasource

Adding the *Connection*, *Data Adapter*, and *DataSet* Objects

I won't spend a lot of time on this aspect of building the program because I covered it in depth in the last chapter. I'll only discuss the modifications to the objects.

1. Add a *SqlConnection* object to your program. Right-click the *SqlConnection* object and select Properties. In the drop-down list for the *ConnectionString* property, select the Northwind.dbo connection we built in Chapter 10.

2. Add a *SqlDataAdapter* object to your program. The Data Adapter Configuration Wizard starts when you drop the object on the form; click Next on the Welcome screen. The Northwind.dbo connection will be selected on the next screen, so simply keep that and click Next. Leave the Use SQL Statements option selected, and then click Next. The SQL statement will be different from the example in Chapter 10. Add *"SELECT CategoryID, CategoryName, Description FROM Categories"* in the text box, as shown in Figure 11-8. (We don't select all the records in this example because a link to a picture object is also stored in the Categories table.)

   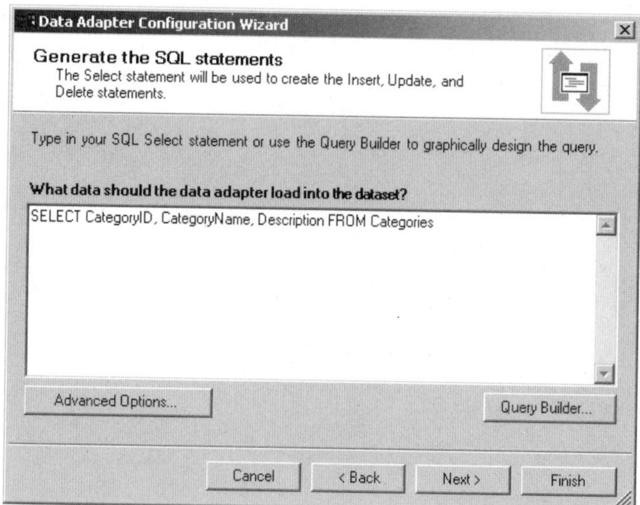

   Figure 11-8 This SQL statement selects the fields we want.

   Click Next, and the wizard will do its magic. Then click Finish to complete the configuration of the data adapter.

3. Right-click the form, and then select Generate Dataset. Keep the default settings in the dialog box, and then click OK. This will add the object to the program. Simply by using the wizards, all of the internal mechanisms to connect to the database are in place. We now just have to add a few lines of code to wire everything together.

Adding Code to Our Program

At the top of the form class, add the namespaces that we will use for our SQL connection, data adapter, and data set. We also need to add a class-level *Boolean* variable that will be set to True when data is placed into our data grid. Unfortunately, there is no easy way to clear the grid manually, so we will simply use the *Boolean* variable to skip the code that updates the grid if it has already been filled. Simple, yet effective. Of course, we could disable the Retrieve button after the data has been added, thus preventing the user from double or triple populating the grid with the same data. Here's the code to add:

```
Imports System
Imports System.Data.SqlClient

Public Class Form1
    Inherits System.Windows.Forms.Form

    Dim bDataAdded As Boolean = False
```

Now add the following code to the btnRetrieve *Click* event handler. By now, this code should be second nature to you.

```
Private Sub btnRetrieve_Click(ByVal sender As System.Object, _
    ByVal e As System.EventArgs) Handles btmRetrieve.Click

    If bDataAdded = True Then Exit Sub

    Try

        SqlDataAdapter1.Fill(DataSet11, "Categories")

        With dgDataGrid
            .CaptionText = "Examining XML"
            .DataSource = DataSet11
            .AllowSorting = True
            .AlternatingBackColor = System.Drawing.Color.Bisque
            .SetDataBinding(DataSet11, "Categories")
        End With

        '-- Update the XML tab
        txtXML.Text = DataSet11.GetXml

        '-- Update the XML Schema tab
        txtXMLSchema.Text = DataSet11.GetXmlSchema

        bDataAdded = True

    Catch ex As Exception
        Console.WriteLine(ex.ToString())
    End Try
End Sub
```

Now add this code to the btnUpdate *Click* event handler.

```
Private Sub btnUpdate_Click(ByVal sender As System.Object, _
    ByVal e As System.EventArgs) Handles btnUpdate.Click

    Try
        dgDataGrid.Update()
        SqlDataAdapter1.Update(DataSet11)
    Catch ex As SystemException
        MessageBox.Show(ex.Message)
    End Try
End Sub
```

That's all there is to it. If you are so inclined, examine the regions of code in the form and spend a few minutes reviewing the code the wizard added for us. Contrast that with the few lines that we had to add to wire everything together. This example is a good illustration of just how productive programmers will be using Visual Basic .NET. Run the program, and examine the output placed in the XML and XML Schema tabs.

How It Works

As you now know, the *SqlDataAdapter* object manages getting data to and from the database by using the appropriate Transact-SQL statements against the data source. Recall that the *SqlClient* classes are optimized for Microsoft SQL Server 7 and later. Therefore, the *SqlDataAdapter* object is used in conjunction with the *SqlConnection* and *SqlCommand* objects to increase performance when connecting to a SQL Server database. Because there's a chance that our database won't be available, we want to put the code that accesses it (in the btnRetrieve *Click* event handler) in a structured *Try* block.

```
Try

    SqlDataAdapter1.Fill(DataSet11, "Categories")

    With dgDataGrid
        .CaptionText = "Examining XML"
        .DataSource = DataSet11
        .AllowSorting = True
        .AlternatingBackColor = System.Drawing.Color.Bisque
        .SetDataBinding(DataSet11, "Categories")
    End With
```

Next, we set a few properties of the data grid and then bind it to our data set. The only new property here is *CaptionText*, which places a header on the data grid—a nice detail that you should consider using in your production code.

Generating XML from Our Data Set

With Visual Basic .NET, displaying the XML representation and the XML schema of the data contained in our data set is pretty trivial. Simply set the *Text* property of each text box to the appropriate and self-describing methods of our *DataSet* object.

```
'-- Update the XML tab
txtXML.Text = dsDataSet.GetXml

'-- Update the XML Schema tab
txtSchema.Text = dsDataSet.GetXmlSchema
```

If everything in the *Catch* block works as expected, we set the form-level variable to True so that if the user clicks the Retrieve button again, the code simply exits the procedure.

```
bDataAdded = True
```

Now, if everything works as advertised, the data grid is populated with records. In the unlikely event of a water landing—or an exception—the code will jump to the *Catch* block and be displayed, preventing our program from crashing.

```
Catch ex As Exception
    Console.WriteLine(ex.ToString())
End Try
```

Updating the Data Source

When you work with a disconnected data set, updates require two stages: you first place new data in the data set, and then, after the user is finished editing the fields, you reconnect and send the data back from the data set to the source database. The data adapter can perform this second step with its *Update* method, which examines every record in the specified data table in the data set and, if a record has changed, sends the appropriate UPDATE, INSERT, or DELETE command to the database. Calling the *Update* method of the *SqlDataAdapter* object does all of this for us automatically using its existing connection object.

```
Private Sub btnUpdate_Click(ByVal sender As System.Object, _
    ByVal e As System.EventArgs) Handles btnUpdate.Click

    Try
        dgDataGrid.Update()
        SqlDataAdapter1.Update(DataSet11)
    Catch ex As SystemException
        MessageBox.Show(ex.Message)
    End Try
End Sub
```

In our example, we accomplished the first step in the update process by using the data grid control. If your application is concerned only with the data set—for example, after updating the data set you simply send its contents via XML to another application—you're finished at this point.

However, if you are updating the original data source with changes, you have to send the changes from the data set to the original data source. That is, you must explicitly update the data source by using the *Update* method, as we do in the preceding code.

XML in .NET

XML was developed by an XML working group (originally known as the SGML Editorial Review Board) formed under the auspices of the World Wide Web Consortium (W3C) in 1996. Since then, XML has rapidly grown in acceptance as a standard for digital information markup. XML allows information (data, metadata, documentation, and resources of any kind) to be expressed in a structured, flexible, and easily parsible manner. XML also allows for content-based tagging of any information resource, and consequently it allows for powerful, focused, and efficient contents-based search and retrieval of information.

While you might be familiar with HTML, XML is very different. Even though both use tags enclosed in brackets (<>), HTML is used as a markup to describe how to show data on a browser. For example, you might do something like *<B>*This is in Bold*</B>*. However, HTML knows nothing about what it is displaying. XML, on the other hand, is used to represent and describe the data it contains. XML is designed to deliver structured content over the Web and, with a schema (XSD), to fully describe itself to the recipient.

Unlike HTML, XML allows users to structure and define the information in their documents. And while HTML has a finite collection of tags, XML allows users to create their own tags to meet their requirements, hence the extensibility. XML is a core technology substrate in .NET. All parts of the .NET Framework (ASP.NET, Web services, and so on) use XML as their native data representation format. The .NET Framework XML classes are also tightly coupled with managed data access in ADO.NET. If you have worked with data sources in the past, you know that traditionally there have always been different programming models for working with relational versus hierarchical data. By placing our data in XML, .NET breaks that tradition by offering a more deeply integrated programming model for all types of data.

ADO.NET and XML

Let's take a moment to examine the XML information generated by our data set. Rather than trying to wade through all of the records, I'm simply going to modify our SELECT command to retrieve a single record. There is no need for you to do this, but we can examine the XML output a bit easier this way.

```
'SqlSelectCommand1
'
Me.SqlSelectCommand1.CommandText = _
    "SELECT CategoryID, CategoryName, Description " & _
    "FROM Categories Where CategoryID = '1'"
Me.SqlSelectCommand1.Connection = Me.SqlConnection1
```

Because we created the *DataSet* object automatically, the default name DataSet1 is provided. If you want to change the name, simply rename the *DataSetName* property in the data set properties dialog box. If you decide to hand-code a *DataSet* instead of having the wizard add one as we did, the default name will be NewDataSet. However, the *DataSet* constructor is overloaded. If you want to give the data set a unique name, you do this when you instantiate the *DataSet* object. Give it a name with no spaces when you instantiate it.

```
Dim dsDataSet As DataSet = New DataSet("ADO_Example")
```

The XML file will be created with the name you give it.

```
<ADO_Example>
  <Customers>
    ⋮
  </Customers>
</ADO_Example>
```

Examining Our Program's XML Output

The following is an XML file generated from a single returned record and displayed on the XML tab. Spend a moment looking at this XML file. As you can see, it's pretty straightforward to understand. The data is structured and presented hierarchically. The tags are self-explanatory.

```
<DataSet1 xmlns="http://www.tempuri.org/DataSet1.xsd">
  <Categories>
    <CategoryID>1</CategoryID>
    <CategoryName>Beverages</CategoryName>
    <Description>Soft drinks, coffees, teas, beers,
      and ales</Description>
  </Categories>
</DataSet1>
```

In order to keep our XML file unique, we have an XML namespace (*xmlns*) that uniquely identifies our file. DataSet1.xsd is the schema file that defines the elements of our XML file.

The first, or root, element is the *<Categories>* tag, and all of the descendant child elements are between that tag and the closing *</Categories>* tag. Elements in XML are case sensitive, unlike tags in HTML. You can see that the three elements in *Categories—CategoryID*, *CategoryName*, and *Description*—are the three fields that were retrieved from the Categories table.

The XML Schema Output

Now that we've seen the XML file, let's spend a moment looking at the schema generated for our single record. The name, or ID, of the schema is the following:

```
<xsd:schema id="DataSet1"
 targetNamespace="http://www.tempuri.org/DataSet1.xsd"
 xmlns="http://www.tempuri.org/DataSet1.xsd"
 xmlns:xsd="http://www.w3.org/2001/XMLSchema"
 xmlns:msdata="urn:schemas-microsoft-com:xml-msdata"
 attributeFormDefault="qualified"
 elementFormDefault="qualified">
```

Notice that the target namespace is the same as our XML file, which is how the schema is associated with the XML file. Next, the root element of the schema is the name of the data set, *DataSet1<xsd:element name="DataSet1" msdata:IsDataSet="true">*

The *xmlns:xsd* element shows that the file uses the XSD namespace that conforms to the latest W3C XML schema recommendation.

```
xmlns:xsd="http://www.w3.org/2001/XMLSchema"
```

After the root name and its various elements are listed, we see that this schema is considered a complex type.

```
<xsd:complexType>
```

Complex types are user-defined data types that can include other elements or attributes. Complex types can contain elements defined as either simple or complex. Complex types can also include attributes and groups. Complex types are defined using the *complexType* element and typically contain combinations of element, attribute, and group declarations, as well as references to globally declared elements and groups. A complex type can be thought of as a minischema that defines the valid structure and data contained within a specific element.

You can see that the elements within this complex type are nested. The basic building blocks of XML schemas are elements and attributes. Data types define the valid content that elements and attributes contain. When you create XML schemas, you define the individual elements and attributes and assign valid types to them. The first child element, *CategoryID*, is a data type of *String* and can have zero or more occurrences of this field. A basic element definition consists of a name and a data type. Elements with the *minOccurs = "0"* attribute are considered optional columns. You can see that the *CategoryID* element is read-only, auto-incremented, and an integer data type. This information is used when a data set is reconstituted from an XML file.

```
<xsd:element name="CategoryID" msdata:ReadOnly="true"
 msdata:AutoIncrement="true" type="xsd:int" />
```

Taking a look at the *Description* element, it's easy to see that it is a *String* data type and optional (because it includes the attribute *minOccurs="0"*).

```
<xsd:element name="Description" type="xsd:string"
 minOccurs="0" />
```

A *maxOccurs="unbounded"* attribute tells us that this element can occur any number of times. Many novices find the occurrences attribute confusing. Table 11-2 describes how the *minOccurs* and *maxOccurs* attributes work.

Table 11-2 *minOccurs* and *maxOccurs* Element Descriptions

minOccurs	*maxOccurs*	Description
0	1	The element is optional, but it can only contain one element.
1	1	There must be only a single occurrence of the element.
0	Unbounded	There can be any number of occurrences of this element.
1	Unbounded	There must be at least one occurrence of this element.
2	7	There must be at least two occurrences of this element, but no more than seven.

Toward the end of the file, the *Constraint1* element was added. In this case, the constraint is showing that the CategoryID field is the primary key. The schema contains all the information needed to fully describe the content of the associated XML file.

```
<xsd:unique name="Constraint1" msdata:PrimaryKey="true">
  <xsd:selector xpath=".//Categories" />
  <xsd:field xpath="CategoryID" />
</xsd:unique>
```

So now you have a general sense of how an XML schema works. A complete schema contains enough information for .NET to reconstitute the format of the SQL table we retrieved, and the XML file fills in the data, as shown here.

```
<xsd:schema id="DataSet1"
 targetNamespace="http://www.tempuri.org/DataSet1.xsd"
 xmlns="http://www.tempuri.org/DataSet1.xsd"
 xmlns:xsd="http://www.w3.org/2001/XMLSchema"
 xmlns:msdata="urn:schemas-microsoft-com:xml-msdata"
 attributeFormDefault="qualified"
 elementFormDefault="qualified">
  <xsd:element name="DataSet1" msdata:IsDataSet="true">
    <xsd:complexType>
      <xsd:choice maxOccurs="unbounded">
        <xsd:element name="Categories">
          <xsd:complexType>
            <xsd:sequence>
              <xsd:element name="CategoryID"
                msdata:ReadOnly="true"
                 msdata:AutoIncrement="true" type="xsd:int" />
              <xsd:element name="CategoryName"
               type="xsd:string" />
              <xsd:element name="Description"
               type="xsd:string" minOccurs="0" />
            </xsd:sequence>
          </xsd:complexType>
        </xsd:element>
      </xsd:choice>
    </xsd:complexType>
    <xsd:unique name="Constraint1" msdata:PrimaryKey="true">
      <xsd:selector xpath=".//Categories" />
      <xsd:field xpath="CategoryID" />
    </xsd:unique>
  </xsd:element>
</xsd:schema>
```

Persisting Our XML Information

Let's write our XML file of the data set to disk. We can persist the file and reconstitute it in this or another data set. Add another button to the program's form, and name it btnWriteXML. Add &Write XML as the *Text* property. Within the *Click* event handler of our new button, add the following two lines of code. This code permits us to write both the XML file with a built-in schema as well as a *DiffGram*, which notes only the differences between the original data and what we have changed.

```
Private Sub btnWriteXML_Click(ByVal sender As System.Object, _
    ByVal e As System.EventArgs) Handles btnWriteXML.Click

    DataSet11.WriteXml("C:\SqlXML.xml", _
        XmlWriteMode.WriteSchema)
    DataSet11.WriteXml("C:\SQLChanges.xml", _
        XmlWriteMode.DiffGram)
End Sub
```

When writing XML to disk, you have three options. The enumerated *XmlWriteMode* provides quite a bit of flexibility here, as shown in Table 11-3.

Table 11-3 *XmlWriteMode* Enumerated Values

XmlWriteMode	Description
IgnoreSchema	Writes the current contents of the *DataSet* as XML data, without an XSD schema. This is the default value.
WriteSchema	Writes the current contents of the *DataSet* as XML data with the relational structure as an inline XSD schema.
DiffGram	Writes the entire *DataSet* as a *DiffGram*, including original and current values.

Testing Our Persistence Code

To illustrate how the code we added to persist the XML file works, I modified the description for the dairy products category and then deleted record number 6, as you can see in Figure 11-9. (However, I didn't commit these changes via the Update Datasource button because it would modify the original Northwind table.) After I made these two changes, I clicked the Write XML button to serialize the output to XML files on disk.

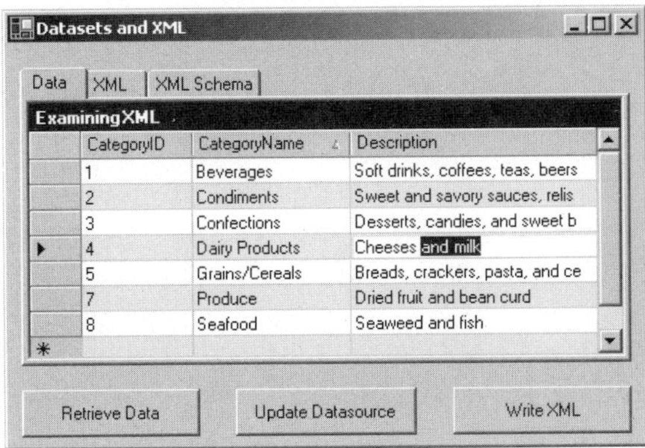

Figure 11-9 The modified data set.

After clicking the Write XML button, examine the contents of the directory where the XML files were written. You will have two .xml files on your drive. In the first file, SqlXML.xml in this example, we wrote the XML file with the enumerated *XmlWriteMode.WriteSchema*. This instructs our program to write both the XML file and an inline schema. If you examine this file, you will note that the dairy products category has been modified. In addition, item number 6 is no longer there because we just deleted it. The header contains a new line with the version number. This line is called the declaration, and although it's optional, every written XML file should begin with an XML declaration. Here's the XML written to the file.

```
<?xml version="1.0" standalone="yes" ?>
- <DataSet1 xmlns="http://www.tempuri.org/DataSet1.xsd">
- <xsd:schema id="DataSet1"
 targetNamespace="http://www.tempuri.org/DataSet1.xsd"
 xmlns="http://www.tempuri.org/DataSet1.xsd"
 xmlns:xsd="http://www.w3.org/2001/XMLSchema"
 xmlns:msdata="urn:schemas-microsoft-com:xml-msdata"
 attributeFormDefault="qualified"
 elementFormDefault="qualified">
- <xsd:element name="DataSet1" msdata:IsDataSet="true">
- <xsd:complexType>
- <xsd:choice maxOccurs="unbounded">
- <xsd:element name="Categories">
- <xsd:complexType>
- <xsd:sequence>
  <xsd:element name="CategoryID" msdata:ReadOnly="true"
   msdata:AutoIncrement="true" type="xsd:int" />
  <xsd:element name="CategoryName" type="xsd:string" />
  <xsd:element name="Description" type="xsd:string"
   minOccurs="0" />
  </xsd:sequence>
  </xsd:complexType>
  </xsd:element>
  </xsd:choice>
  </xsd:complexType>
- <xsd:unique name="Constraint1" msdata:PrimaryKey="true">
  <xsd:selector xpath=".//Categories" />
  <xsd:field xpath="CategoryID" />
  </xsd:unique>
  </xsd:element>
  </xsd:schema>
- <Categories>
  <CategoryID>1</CategoryID>
  <CategoryName>Beverages</CategoryName>
  <Description>Soft drinks, coffees, teas, beers,
   and ales</Description>
```

```
  </Categories>
- <Categories>
  <CategoryID>2</CategoryID>
  <CategoryName>Condiments</CategoryName>
  <Description>Sweet and savory sauces, relishes,
   spreads, and seasonings</Description>
  </Categories>
- <Categories>
  <CategoryID>3</CategoryID>
  <CategoryName>Confections</CategoryName>
  <Description>Desserts, candies, and sweet
   breads</Description>
  </Categories>
- <Categories>
  <CategoryID>4</CategoryID>
  <CategoryName>Dairy Products</CategoryName>
  <Description>Cheeses and milk</Description>
  </Categories>
- <Categories>
  <CategoryID>5</CategoryID>
  <CategoryName>Grains/Cereals</CategoryName>
  <Description>Breads, crackers, pasta, and
   cereal</Description>
  </Categories>
- <Categories>
  <CategoryID>7</CategoryID>
  <CategoryName>Produce</CategoryName>
  <Description>Dried fruit and bean curd</Description>
  </Categories>
- <Categories>
  <CategoryID>8</CategoryID>
  <CategoryName>Seafood</CategoryName>
  <Description>Seaweed and fish</Description>
  </Categories>
  </DataSet1>
```


Examining the *DiffGram*

A *DiffGram* is an XML serialization format that includes the original and current data of an element. It also includes a unique identifier that associates the original and current versions with one another. *DiffGram* objects are used for marshaling the data within a *DataSet* across a network connection so that different versions (original or current) and *RowState* values (added, modified, deleted, unchanged, detached) of the *DataRow* objects persist. Many times, you will add another data set to your program and insert a *DiffGram* from the original *DataSet*. You can examine and clean up an errors collection before committing the data to the source. When the errors are fixed, the *DiffGram* data set is merged with the original, the changes accepted, and the original data set updated.

If you examine the SQLChanges.xml file after making the changes I describe (the file is listed at the bottom of this page), you'll notice that the original records are listed first. The *DiffGram* gives each element a unique identifier—in this case Categories4 for the first change. It also adds the *hasChanges* attribute value of *modified*.

```
-
 <Categories diffgr:id="Categories4" msdata:rowOrder="3" diffgr:hasCha
nges="modified">
  <CategoryID>4</CategoryID>
  <CategoryName>Dairy Products</CategoryName>
  <Description>Cheeses and milk</Description>
  </Categories>
```

Later in the file, a hierarchical grouping starting with *<diffgr: before>* occurs. Between this tag and the delimiter, *</diffgr: before>*, are any changes to the original. This grouping contains both the modifications for dairy products and the deleted record. The *DiffGram* uses the *id* attribute to tie the original to the modified data. Because the ID Customers6 is not present in the original, it is implied that the record was deleted.

```
<diffgr:before>
-
 <Categories diffgr:id="Categories4" msdata:rowOrder="3" xmlns="http:/
/www.tempuri.org/DataSet1.xsd">
  <CategoryID>4</CategoryID>
  <CategoryName>Dairy Products</CategoryName>
  <Description>Cheeses</Description>
  </Categories>
-
 <Categories diffgr:id="Categories6" msdata:rowOrder="5" xmlns="http:/
/www.tempuri.org/DataSet1.xsd">
  <CategoryID>6</CategoryID>
  <CategoryName>Meat/Poultry</CategoryName>
  <Description>Prepared meats</Description>
  </Categories>
</diffgr:before>
```

It's easy to see how the *DiffGram* flags differences between the original and modified data. And of course, it's all text.

```
<?xml version="1.0" standalone="yes" ?>
- <diffgr:diffgram
   xmlns:msdata="urn:schemas-microsoft-com:xml-msdata"
   xmlns:diffgr="urn:schemas-microsoft-com:xml-diffgram-v1">
- <DataSet1 xmlns="http://www.tempuri.org/DataSet1.xsd">
- <Categories diffgr:id="Categories1" msdata:rowOrder="0">
  <CategoryID>1</CategoryID>
  <CategoryName>Beverages</CategoryName>
  <Description>Soft drinks, coffees, teas, beers,
   and ales</Description>
```

```
  </Categories>
- <Categories diffgr:id="Categories2" msdata:rowOrder="1">
  <CategoryID>2</CategoryID>
  <CategoryName>Condiments</CategoryName>
  <Description>Sweet and savory sauces, relishes, spreads,
   and seasonings</Description>
  </Categories>
- <Categories diffgr:id="Categories3" msdata:rowOrder="2">
  <CategoryID>3</CategoryID>
  <CategoryName>Confections</CategoryName>
  <Description>Desserts, candies, and sweet
   breads</Description>
  </Categories>
- <Categories diffgr:id="Categories4" msdata:rowOrder="3"
   diffgr:hasChanges="modified">
  <CategoryID>4</CategoryID>
  <CategoryName>Dairy Products</CategoryName>
  <Description>Cheeses and milk</Description>
  </Categories>
- <Categories diffgr:id="Categories5" msdata:rowOrder="4">
  <CategoryID>5</CategoryID>
  <CategoryName>Grains/Cereals</CategoryName>
  <Description>Breads, crackers, pasta, and
   cereal</Description>
  </Categories>
- <Categories diffgr:id="Categories7" msdata:rowOrder="6">
  <CategoryID>7</CategoryID>
  <CategoryName>Produce</CategoryName>
  <Description>Dried fruit and bean curd</Description>
  </Categories>
- <Categories diffgr:id="Categories8" msdata:rowOrder="7">
  <CategoryID>8</CategoryID>
  <CategoryName>Seafood</CategoryName>
  <Description>Seaweed and fish</Description>
  </Categories>
  </DataSet1>
- <diffgr:before>
- <Categories diffgr:id="Categories4" msdata:rowOrder="3"
   xmlns="http://www.tempuri.org/DataSet1.xsd">
  <CategoryID>4</CategoryID>
  <CategoryName>Dairy Products</CategoryName>
  <Description>Cheeses</Description>
  </Categories>
- <Categories diffgr:id="Categories6" msdata:rowOrder="5"
   xmlns="http://www.tempuri.org/DataSet1.xsd">
  <CategoryID>6</CategoryID>
  <CategoryName>Meat/Poultry</CategoryName>
  <Description>Prepared meats</Description>
  </Categories>
  </diffgr:before>
  </diffgr:diffgram>
```

Leveraging Our XML File for New Classes

Visual Studio .NET contains a handy XML schema definition tool that generates XML schema or common language runtime classes from XDR (Microsoft Extensible Data Reduced Schema Language), XML, and XSD files, or from classes in a runtime assembly. The tool, Xsd.exe, allows you to manipulate only XML schemas that follow the XML schema definition (XSD) language proposed by the W3C. (For more information on the XML schema definition proposal or the XML standard, see *http://w3c.org*.) We can first generate a stand-alone XML schema definition (XSD) from our SqlXML.xml file and then generate classes in Visual Basic .NET that we can use to build a program. Interested? Let's take a look.

The Xsd.exe Program

Locate the Xsd.exe file on your computer. On my machine it's located at C:\Program Files\Microsoft Visual Studio .NET\FrameworkSDK\Bin\Xsd.exe. Copy the file to the C:\ root directory where we wrote our XML files.

The first task we want to perform is to build the XSD file. Simply pass the name of the SqlXML.xml file as a command-line parameter to Xsd.exe.

```
C:\>xsd sqlxml.xml
Microsoft (R) Xml Schemas/DataTypes support utility
[Microsoft (R) .NET Framework, Version 1.0.3319.11]
Copyright (C) Microsoft Corp. 1998-2001. All rights reserved.

Writing file 'C:\sqlxml.xsd'
```

The Sqlxml.xsd file just created will be used to build our common language runtime Visual Basic .NET classes. Because the default language for class declarations is C#, we must tell Xsd.exe to spit out the file in Visual Basic .NET format. We pass in the name of our new .xsd file and use the command line directive */c* to instruct Xsd.exe to build classes for us, and */l:vb* to tell it to use the Visual Basic .NET language.

```
C:\>xsd sqlxml.xsd /c /l:vb
Microsoft (R) Xml Schemas/DataTypes support utility
[Microsoft (R) .NET Framework, Version 1.0.2914.11]
Copyright (C) Microsoft Corp. 1998-2001. All rights reserved.
Writing file 'C:\sqlxml.vb'
```

This file will be created in the directory where you build the program. The file created is called Sqlxml.vb and is constructed from our data set.

Visual Basic .NET generated a similar file, DataSet.vb, for the SqlXMLExample project. (Recall that when we built our inline schema, it had the default name DataSet1.) The code for the automatically generated new file spreads across acres of pages, so in the interest of brevity, I'll show only a small portion of it here. The important point to understand is that once you have a schema, all the information is present to automatically build Visual Basic .NET common language runtime classes that can be immediately imported into any Visual Basic .NET program.

```
'------------------------------------------------------------------------------
' <autogenerated>
'     This code was generated by a tool.
'     Runtime Version: 1.0.2914.11
'
'     Changes to this file may cause incorrect behavior and
'     will be lost if the code is regenerated.
' </autogenerated>
'------------------------------------------------------------------------------

Option Strict Off
Option Explicit On

Imports System
Imports System.Data
Imports System.Runtime.Serialization
Imports System.Xml


<Serializable(), _
System.ComponentModel.DesignerCategoryAttribute("code")> _
Public Class DataSet1
    Inherits System.Data.DataSet

    Private tableCategories As CategoriesDataTable

    Public Sub New()
        MyBase.New
        Me.InitClass
    End Sub

    Private Sub New(ByVal info As SerializationInfo, _
        ByVal context As StreamingContext)

        MyBase.New
        Me.InitClass
        Me.GetSerializationData(info, context)
    End Sub

<System.ComponentModel.Browsable(false), _
System.ComponentModel.DesignerSerializationVisibilityAttribute( _
    System.ComponentModel.DesignerSerializationVisibility.Content)>
```

(continued)

```
    Public ReadOnly Property Categories As CategoriesDataTable
        Get
            Return Me.tableCategories
        End Get
    End Property

    Protected Overrides Function ShouldSerializeTables() _
        As Boolean

        Return false
    End Function

    Protected Overrides Function ShouldSerializeRelations() _
        As Boolean

        Return false
    End Function

    Protected Overrides Sub ReadXmlSerializable(ByVal reader _
        As XmlReader)

        Me.ReadXml(reader, XmlReadMode.IgnoreSchema)
    End Sub
```

If you scan the code, you'll see all of the properties required, such as those for getting and setting the *Description* property. Some sophisticated structured error-trapping code is also added for us. Following is the *Description* property code. Everything was written for us to both read and write the description of a category name. Pretty interesting, eh?

```
Public Property Description As String
    Get
        Try
            Return _
                CType(Me( _
                    Me.tableCategories.DescriptionColumn), _
                    String)
        Catch e As InvalidCastException _
            Throw New StrongTypingException( _
                "Cannot get value because it is DBNull.", e)
       End Try
    End Get
    Set
        Me(Me.tableCategories.DescriptionColumn) = value
    End Set
End Property
```

How might a class like this be used? I could send you an XML file without you having any previous knowledge of its contents. You would run it through the XSD program to build the XSD file, which you would then run through the Xsd.exe program again to build a robust Visual Basic .NET class that manages all of the editing for you. This new class could then be imported into a Visual Basic .NET program, and you could start handling all of the data I passed you in the XML file. (But we wouldn't learn much if we let all the code be written for us, would we?)

Examine this code some more to understand its finer points. For now, let's return to our program and see if we can enhance it a bit.

Adding a Relationship to Our Program

In any except the most trivial database program, you need to examine multiple tables in a parent/child format. The .NET data grid comes into its own in this situation. You can hand code the relationships between tables or have it done for you. To illustrate just how easy it is to show a parent/child relationship between tables, we will expand the program we built at the start of this chapter.

The *DataSet* object model contains a *DataRelations* collection that will hold any table relationships we define and add to this collection. The *DataSet* also has a *DataTables* collection that contains all the tables currently in memory. Each of the *DataTables* has a *DataColumn*, *DataRow*, and *Constraints* collection. The *DataSet* object model is shown in Figure 11-10.

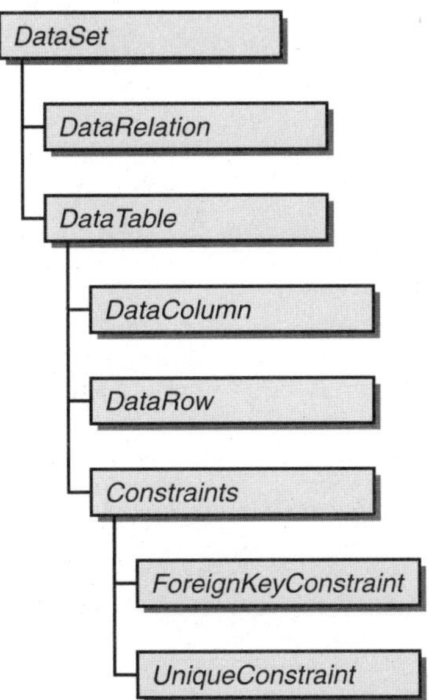

Figure 11-10 The *DataSet* object model.

The Data Sets and XML Program

In the Northwind database, the Categories table has a primary key on the CategoryID field. The Products table has a CategoryID field as its foreign key. This example will link the child Products table to the parent Categories table. Notice in Figure 11-11 that each category record has a plus sign beside it, indicating that each record has one or more child records associated with it.

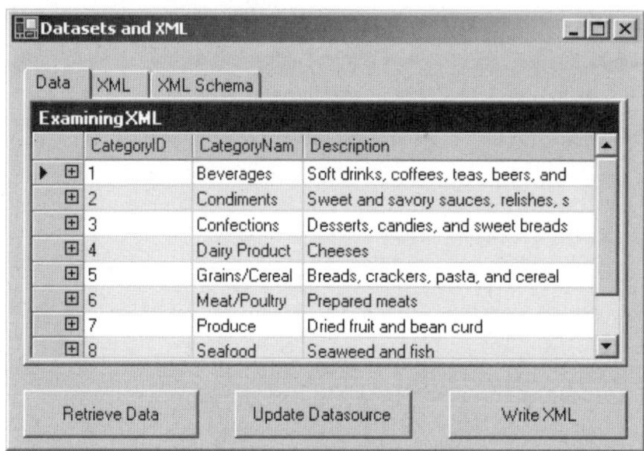

Figure 11-11 The plus sign indicates that child records are associated with the parent record.

By expanding a record, we can see a relationship named CategoriesProducts that was created for us. (The .NET convention for naming relationships is *ParentTableNameChildTableName*.) Clicking the CategoriesProducts link, shown in Figure 11-12, displays all of the child records associated with that category.

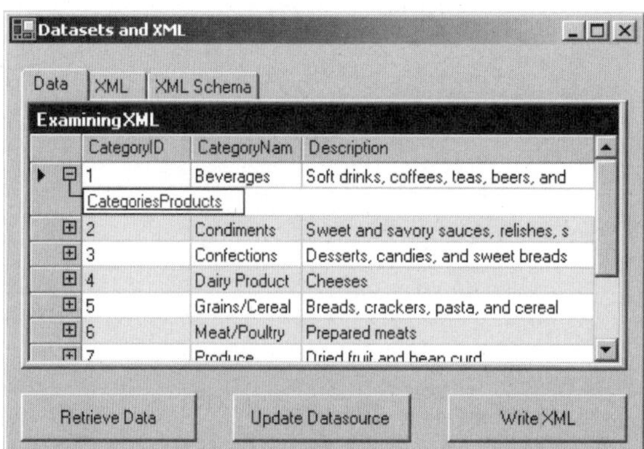

Figure 11-12 Expanding a record shows a link to the child records.

> **Note** When the child records are displayed, note that the data grid actually adds two icons. Clicking the white box with the up and down arrows on the right side of the data grid's caption bar will display or hide the Categories bar. When the Categories bar is displayed, each of the fields of the parent record is displayed. If there are more fields than can be displayed, as in our example, black arrows permit horizontal scrolling. Clicking the white box again will hide this row. To return to the parent Categories table, click the white left-pointing arrow next to the box on the right side of the data grid. This is a compelling approach to displaying complex relationships of data.

Creating the Parent/Child Relationship

The first operation we want to perform is to add a second *SqlDataAdapter* to the form. We already have a connection to the Northwind database, a data adapter with which to grab the information we want from the Categories table, and a data set in which to place the records. Essentially we are going to use the second data adapter to get the records from the Products table and place them in the existing data set. Recall from Chapter 10 that a data set can contain multiple tables and that the relationships are built within the data set.

1. Add a second data adapter to your program.
2. Accept the defaults the wizard presents for the connection and the Use SQL Statements option. On the Generate The SQL Statements screen, add the following SQL statement. We are simply retrieving each of the fields with the exception of the Discontinued field from the Products table. Also, by using the WHERE clause, only products that are not discontinued will be retrieved.

   ```
   SELECT ProductID, ProductName, SupplierID, CategoryID,
       QuantityPerUnit, UnitPrice, UnitsInStock, UnitsOnOrder,
       ReorderLevel FROM Products WHERE (Discontinued = 0)
   ```

   Click Next, and the wizard informs you that *SqlDataAdapter2* has been configured successfully. Click Finish.
3. We now want to add the records retrieved from the Products table to our existing data set. Right-click *SqlDataAdapter2,* and select Generate Dataset. Use the existing dataset, SqlXMLExample, and select the Products table. Be sure to clear the Add This Dataset To The Designer check box because we are using the existing DataSet1, as shown in Figure 11-13. Click OK to generate commands to add the Products table to the existing data set.

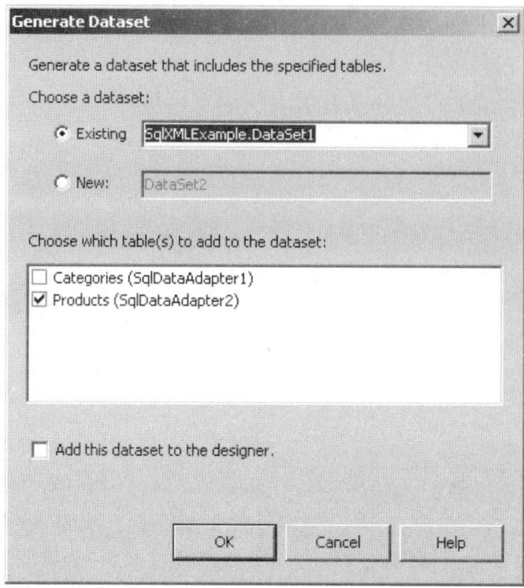

Figure 11-13 Be sure to clear the Add This Dataset To The Designer check box before you click OK.

Now right-click the form, and select Generate Dataset. We want to have both tables, Categories from *SqlDataAdapter1* and Products from *SqlDataAdapter2*, placed in DataSet1. Leave the default options unchanged, and click OK to generate the data set.

4. The schema Dataset1.xsd has been added to the Solution Explorer. Open the Solution Explorer, and double-click Dataset1.xsd to display the graphical representation of the schema. Note that both of the tables, Categories and Products, are now resident in the single dataset in the XML Designer, as you can see in Figure 11-14.

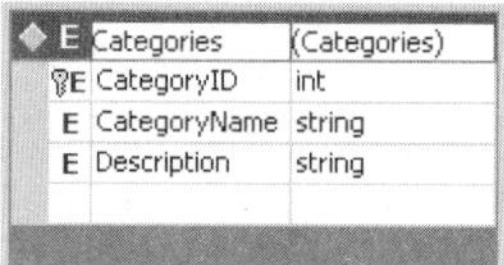

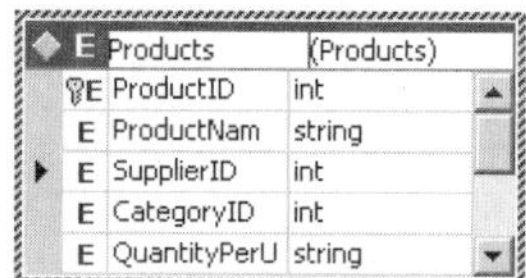

Figure 11-14 The Categories and Products tables are now resident in the single data set.

Adding a Relationship to Our Tables

Let's take a moment to consider how relationships are built in .NET versus traditional database theory. This concept is one of those that you need to get down right away.

If we wanted to retrieve all the orders placed by each of our employees, we would write an inner join in SQL that looks like this.

```
SELECT Employees.EmployeeID, Employees.LastName,
    Employees.FirstName, Employees.Title, Orders.*
FROM Employees
    INNER JOIN Orders
    ON Employees.EmployeeID = Orders.EmployeeID;
```

This query would return a recordset that merges the column (EmployeeID) that we need to work with into a single result. Our INNER JOIN statement ends up returning rows with a certain quantity of duplicated data. For example, for each of the orders placed by Nancy Davolio, we get the entire Employee table fields duplicated. We certainly don't need to repeat her name, title, and so forth for each order she sold, but there it is in the returned tabular structure from the result set, as you can see in Figure 11-15.

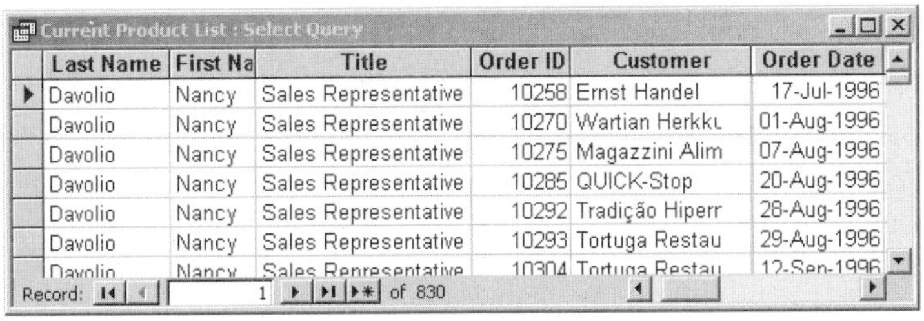

Current Product List : Select Query

Last Name	First Na	Title	Order ID	Customer	Order Date
Davolio	Nancy	Sales Representative	10258	Ernst Handel	17-Jul-1996
Davolio	Nancy	Sales Representative	10270	Wartian Herkku	01-Aug-1996
Davolio	Nancy	Sales Representative	10275	Magazzini Alim	07-Aug-1996
Davolio	Nancy	Sales Representative	10285	QUICK-Stop	20-Aug-1996
Davolio	Nancy	Sales Representative	10292	Tradição Hiperr	28-Aug-1996
Davolio	Nancy	Sales Representative	10293	Tortuga Restau	29-Aug-1996
Davolio	Nancy	Sales Representative	10304	Tortuga Restau	12-Sep-1996

Record: 1 of 830

Figure 11-15 Employee information is repeated in this inner join.

Now you need to create a relationship between the tables. Select both tables, right-click one of the tables and choose Add | New Relation. Confirm that the values shown in Table 11-4 are set in the Edit Relation dialog box, shown in Figure 11-16. Click OK when you're finished.

Table 11-4 Edit Relation Values

Setting	Value
Name	CategoriesProducts (You will need to know this name later so, if you change it, be sure you make a note of the new name.)
Parent Element	Categories
Child Element	Products
Key	Constraint1
Key Fields	CategoryID
Foreign Key Fields	CategoryID
Create Foreign Key Constraint Only	Not selected

Edit Relation

Name: CategoriesProducts

To define a relationship (keyref), select the parent element and key, select the child element, and then select the child field corresponding to each parent field.

Parent element: Categories

Child element: Products

Key: Constraint1

New...

Fields:

Key Fields	Foreign Key Fields
CategoryID	CategoryID

Dataset Properties

Create foreign key constraint only

Update rule: (Default)

Delete rule: (Default)

Accept/Reject rule: (Default)

OK Cancel Help

Figure 11-16 The Edit Relation dialog box.

A relation icon is displayed between the two tables in the XML Designer, as shown in Figure 11-17. If you need to change relationship settings, you can right-click the relationship line and choose Edit Relation.

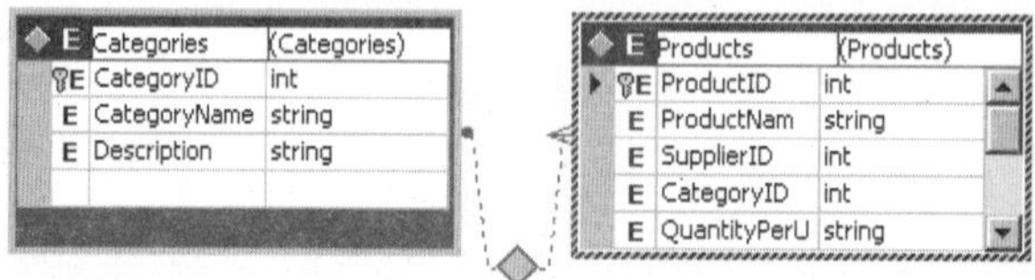

Figure 11-17 The XML Designer shows the new relationship.

At this point, you have set up everything you need in order to get information out of the database and into a data set. The only step left for us to take is to execute the *Fill* method of *SqlDataAdapter2* and pass in the Products table to the *DataSet* object. Add the following line to the Retrieve button's *Click* event handler.

```
Private Sub btnRetrieve_Click(ByVal sender As System.Object, _
    ByVal e As System.EventArgs) Handles btmRetrieve.Click

    If bDataAdded = True Then Exit Sub
```

```
    Try

        SqlDataAdapter1.Fill(DataSet11, "Categories")
        SqlDataAdapter2.Fill(DataSet11, "Products")

        With dgDataGrid
            .CaptionText = "Examining XML"
            .DataSource = DataSet11
            .AllowSorting = True
            .AlternatingBackColor = System.Drawing.Color.Bisque
            .SetDataBinding(DataSet11, "Categories")
        End With

        '-- Update the XML tab
        txtXML.Text = DataSet11.GetXml

        '-- Update the XML Schema tab
        txtXMLSchema.Text = DataSet11.GetXmlSchema

        bDataAdded = True

    Catch ex As Exception
        Console.WriteLine(ex.ToString())
    End Try

End Sub
```

That's all there is to it. A little wizardry and a single line of code gives us our parent/child relationship. And because we bind the single data set to the data grid, it knows how to display both of the tables. Before you leave this project, click the Write XML button to write a file that contains both the Categories and Products tables, along with the relationship between the two. Now take a moment to examine the new SqlXML.xml written to disk. We will shortly be using this file to populate a data grid in a new program.

Examining *DataSet* Properties

It's easy to see the contents of our data set. Right-click DataSet11 in the Forms Designer, and select Dataset Properties. Note that our data set now contains both the Categories and Products tables. Expand all of the nodes to display the fields. The Categories table contains the CategoriesProducts relationship, which contains the Products table as a child. The *Constraint1* in each table represents their respective primary keys. The Dataset Properties dialog box is shown in Figure 11-18.

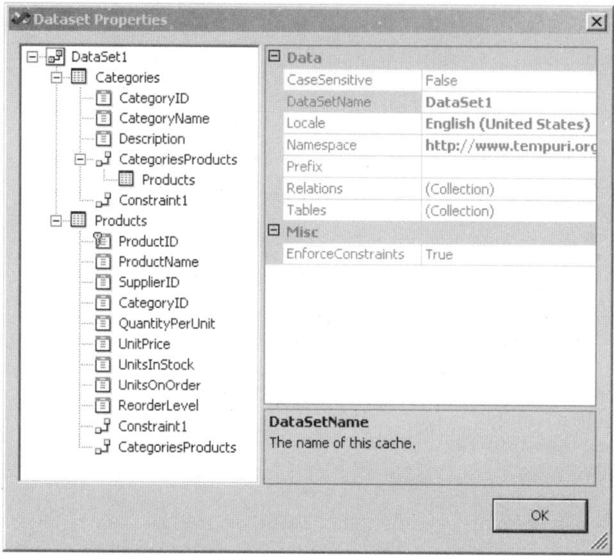

Figure 11-18 The Dataset Properties dialog box.

Populating a Data Grid from a Persisted XML File

Just to prove that the XML file we wrote contains enough information to fully describe our data, we will populate a data grid from the SqlXML.xml file from the last example. Create a new Windows project named ReadFromXML, and then follow these steps:

1. Add a data grid, and name it dgDataGrid. Add a button named btnPopulate, and set its *Text* property to "&Populate from XML." Set the form's *Text* property to "Read from XML."

2. Right-click the data grid, and select Auto Format. In the Auto Format dialog box, select Colorful 1 as the new style. We might as well add a bit of glitz because it's so easy to do. Click OK to format the data grid.

3. Now add the following code to the btnPopulate button's *Click* event handler. We create new *DataSet*, *FileStream*, and *XmlTextReader* objects. The SqlXML.xml file we created from the last example will then be read into the data set. Finally, we bind the data set to the data grid.

```
Private Sub btnPopulate_Click(
    ByVal sender As System.Object, _
    ByVal e As System.EventArgs) Handles btnPopulate.Click

    Dim dsDataSet As New DataSet()
```

```
        'Set the file path and name.
        Dim sFilename As String = "C:\SqlXML.xml"

        'Create a FileStream object with the file path and name.
        Dim fsFileStream As New System.IO.FileStream _
            (sFilename, System.IO.FileMode.Open)

        'Create a new XmlTextReader object with the FileStream.
        Dim XmlTReader As _
            New System.Xml.XmlTextReader(fsFileStream)

        'Read the XML and schema into the DataSet
        'and close the reader.
        dsDataSet.ReadXml(XmlTReader)
        XmlTReader.Close()

        With dgDataGrid
            .CaptionText = "Populated from XML"
            .DataSource = dsDataSet
            .AllowSorting = True
            .AlternatingBackColor = System.Drawing.Color.Bisque
            .SetDataBinding(dsDataSet, "Categories")
        End With
    End Sub
```

Run the Program

Run the program, and then click the Populate From XML button. Remember that the file contains not only the data from the two tables but also an inline schema as well. The schema is read first and sets up the columns in the data grid. Then the XML file populates the columns with data. Because the relationships are fully described in the schema, the child records can also be displayed, as you can see in Figure 11-19.

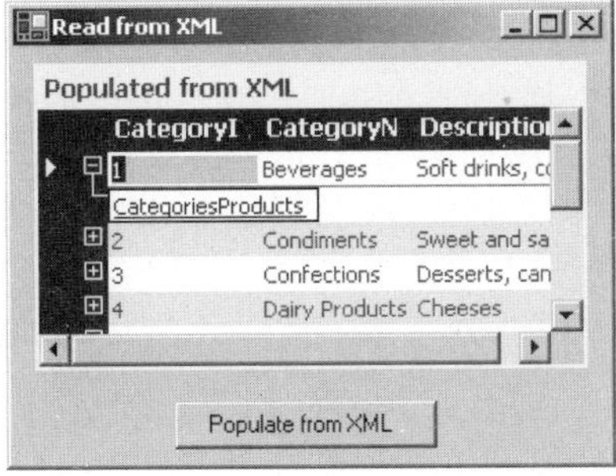

Figure 11-19 The data grid populated from our XML file.

Expand the records, and then select the CategoriesProducts link. All of the child Products records will be displayed, just as though we read the data from the database. This example clearly illustrates just how powerful text-based XML is. From the single text file, all of the data, plus the metadata contained in the schema, is enough to reconstitute the data grid. You now see how a text-based XML file can be passed through a firewall on a Web-based server to construct a data set. Of course, this data set can be edited and then passed back to the source if you want.

How the Program Works

Let's take a look at the code in a little more detail. First a new data set is created. The name and location of our Sqlxml.xml file is placed in the *sFileName* string variable. A *FileStream* object is used to connect to our text file and open it from disk.

```
Dim dsDataSet As New DataSet()

' Set the file path and name.
Dim sFilename As String = "C:\SqlXML.xml"

' Create a FileStream object with the file path and name.
Dim fsFileStream As New System.IO.FileStream _
    (sFilename, System.IO.FileMode.Open)
```

The *XmlTextReader* class provides a fast parser that enforces rules such as that the XML file must be well-formed XML. Because our file was originally created from the data set in our last program, we know that the file will be well formed.

```
' Create a new XmlTextReader object with the FileStream.
Dim XmlTReader As _
    New System.Xml.XmlTextReader(fsFileStream)
```

We are now ready to read the file. Use the *ReadXml* method of the data set to read an XML document that includes both a schema and data. To read the data from an XML document that contains only data into a data set, use the *ReadXml* method. To read just the schema from an XML document, use the *ReadXmlSchema* method of the data set.

If an inline schema is specified as in our file, the inline schema is used to extend the existing relational structure prior to loading the data. If there are any conflicts (for example, the same column in the same table defined with different data types) an exception is raised. If no inline schema is specified, the relational structure is extended through inference, as necessary, according to the structure of the XML document. But because we don't want any nasty surprises, it's easy to include an inline schema as we did. So the XML file is read and then the *XmlTextReader* object is closed because all the data is now transferred into the data set.

```
' Read the XML and schema into the DataSet
' and close the reader.
dsDataSet.ReadXml(XmlTReader)
XmlTReader.Close()
```

The rest of the code is familiar, so I won't review it here. I simply wanted to show you how powerful XML is and also how easily XML can be manipulated with the built-in .NET class framework.

Hand Coding a Simple Program

If you would like to manually code a simple data retrieval program, you can do it with a few lines of code. However, there are some caveats. First, only a single table can be retrieved. Second, that table must have a primary key. These restrictions are pretty important from where I stand, but it's good to know exactly how to hand code a program.

Create a new Windows project, and name it AutoGenerateCommands. Add a data grid control, and set its *Name* property to dgDataGrid. Add a button with the name btnRetrieve, and set its *Text* property to &Retrieve Data. Add a second button with the name btnUpdate, and set its *Text* property to &Update Source. Your familiar-looking form is shown in Figure 11-20.

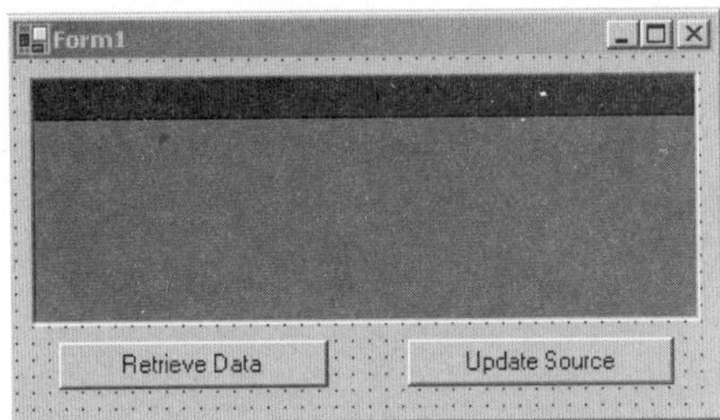

Figure 11-20 The beginnings of our hand-coded program.

Add the following form-level variable declarations.

```
Dim sqlDataAdapter1 As SqlClient.SqlDataAdapter
Dim dsDataSet As New DataSet()
```

Now add the following code to the btnRetrieve button's *Click* event handler. This code will do the heavy lifting of creating the connection to the database.

```
Private Sub btnRetrieve_Click(ByVal sender As System.Object, _
    ByVal e As System.EventArgs) Handles btnRetrieve.Click

    Dim sConnString = "Initial Catalog=Northwind;" & _
        "Data Source=localhost;" & _
        "Integrated Security=SSPI;" & _
        "persist security info=False"

    Dim sqlConn As New SqlClient.SqlConnection(sConnString)

    sqlDataAdapter1 = _
        New SqlClient.SqlDataAdapter( _
        "Select * from Categories", sqlConn)

    Dim sqlCmdBuilder As SqlClient.SqlCommandBuilder

    sqlCmdBuilder = _
        New SqlClient.SqlCommandBuilder(sqlDataAdapter1)

    sqlDataAdapter1.Fill(dsDataSet, "Categories")

    With dgDataGrid
        .CaptionText = "Auto Command Generation"
        .AllowSorting = True
        .AlternatingBackColor = System.Drawing.Color.Bisque
        .SetDataBinding(dsDataSet, "Categories")
    End With
End Sub
```

Add the following code to the btnUpdate button's *Click* event handler:

```
Private Sub btnUpdate_Click(ByVal sender As System.Object,  _
    ByVal e As System.EventArgs) Handles btnSave.Click

    Try
        sqlDataAdapter1.Update(dsDataSet, "Categories")
    Catch ex As Exception
        MessageBox.Show("Error: " & ex.ToString)
    End Try
End Sub
```

Run the program, and the data will be displayed as you'd expect. Again, this method of data retrieval can display only a single, keyed table, so it really makes sense to use the wizard to put in all of the commands required for a more robust program.

Data Binding

Now we are going to take a look at data binding, which permits us to bind data from a data set to a control. In the sample program we'll construct in this section, we'll examine both data binding and the new *DataView* object.

A common scenario might be one in which we have our employees' names listed in a drop-down box. When an employee is selected, a data grid is populated with all the orders that the employee has taken. One way to program this functionality is to bind the Employees.LastName field to a combo box. We could then bind the Employees.Title field to a text box and the Employees.EmployeeID to another text box. Then, when a name is selected from the combo box, we use a *DataView* object to filter for only those records in the child Orders table that pertain to the selected employee. With the built-in functionality of the data grid, we still have the ability to sort on any column. The program is shown in Figure 11-21.

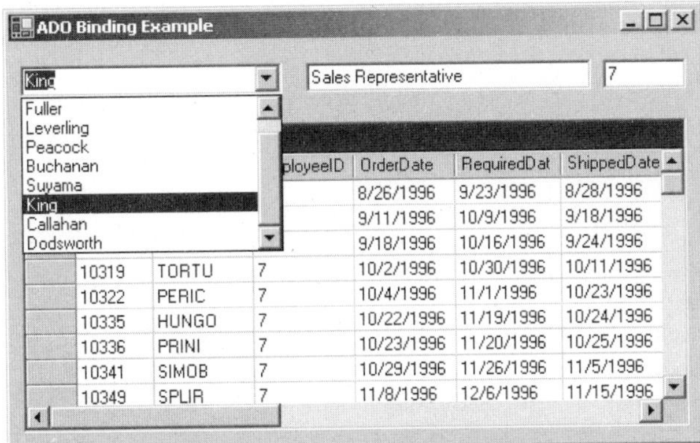

Figure 11-21 The ADO.NET data binding sample program.

Creating the Program

Let's put our program together and see how it works.

1. Start a new Windows project, and name it DataBinding. On the default form, add a combo box, two text boxes, and a data grid, as shown in Figure 11-22. Set the properties for the form and its controls as shown in Table 11-5.

Table 11-5 Properties and Values for the DataBinding Sample

Object	Property	Value
Form	*Text*	ADO Binding Example
Combo box	*Name*	cbEmployee
	Text	""
Text box	*Name*	tbTitle
	Text	""
Text box	*Name*	tbEmployeeID
	Text	""
Data grid	*Name*	dgDataGrid

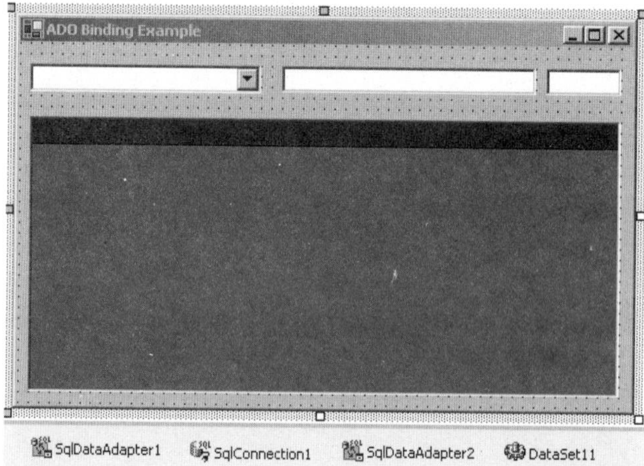

Figure 11-22 The default form with controls added for the data binding sample.

2. After you add the controls, add a *SqlDataAdapter* object from the Data tab of the toolbox. Select the Northwind connection we've been using in the other sample programs. Keep the Use SQL Statements option selected for the Query Type. In the text box on the Generate The SQL Statements screen, add *"Select * From Employees"* and complete the wizard's screens. Notice that both the data adapter and the new *SqlConnection1* objects have been added.

3. Add a second *SqlDataAdapter* object and use the same defaults, except add *"Select * From Orders"* for the SQL statement. Our first data adapter will hold the contents of the Employees table, and the second data adapter will hold the Orders table records.

4. Right-click the form, and select Generate Dataset. Keep the default name, and be sure that both *SqlDataAdapter* objects are selected. Be sure that Add This Dataset To The Designer is also selected. Click OK to add the new DataSet11.

Adding the Code That Wires the Controls to the Data Set

Because we will be accessing our *DataView* object from various procedures, we need to give it class-level scope. Add the *dvDataView* reference variable at the top of our form class.

```
Public Class Form1
    Inherits System.Windows.Forms.Form

    Dim dvDataView As DataView
```

In the form's *New* constructor routine, call *setupdata,* which initializes our controls and fills the data set. As soon as we're sure that the form and controls are sited and ready to be accessed, we can start building our data elements.

```
'Add any initialization after the
' InitializeComponent() call
setupdata()
```

Next add the subroutine named *setupdata*. This subroutine will do the hard work of first filling our data set with the Employees and Orders table records. Then it initializes our two *DataTable* objects. After that it dimensions and initializes two *DataColumn* objects and then builds the parent/child relationship between the tables. The combo box and text boxes are bound to fields in the Employees table after that. And finally our *DataView* object is created.

```
Private Sub setupdata()
    Dim tEmployeesTable As DataTable
    Dim tOrdersTable As DataTable
    Dim drDataRelation As DataRelation

    SqlDataAdapter1.Fill(DataSet11, "Employees")
    SqlDataAdapter2.Fill(DataSet11, "Orders")

    tEmployeesTable = DataSet11.Tables("Employees")
    tOrdersTable = DataSet11.Tables("Orders")

    Dim colParent As DataColumn
    Dim colChild As DataColumn

    colParent = _
        DataSet11.Tables("Employees").Columns("EmployeeID")
```

(continued)

```
        colChild = _
            DataSet11.Tables("Orders").Columns("EmployeeID")

        '--Build the Relationship
        drDataRelation = New DataRelation("EmployeesOrders", _
            colParent, colChild)
        DataSet11.Relations.Add(drDataRelation)

        '--Complex Binding --
        cbEmployee.DataSource = tEmployeesTable
        cbEmployee.DisplayMember = "LastName"

        '-- Simple Binding --
        tbTitle.DataBindings.Add("Text", tEmployeesTable, "Title")
        tbEmployeeID.DataBindings.Add("Text", tEmployeesTable, _
            "EmployeeID")

        dvDataView = New DataView(tOrdersTable)
    End Sub

    Private Sub setUpGrid()
        dvDataView.RowFilter = "EmployeeID = '" & _
            tbEmployeeID.Text & "'"
        dgDataGrid.DataSource = dvDataView
    End Sub

    Private Sub Form1_Activated(ByVal sender As System.Object, _
        ByVal e As System.EventArgs) Handles MyBase.Activated

        setUpGrid()
    End Sub

    Private Sub TbEmployeeID_TextChanged( _
        ByVal sender As System.Object, _
        ByVal e As System.EventArgs) _
        Handles tbEmployeeID.TextChanged

        setUpGrid()
    End Sub
```

Run the Program

You can now click the drop-down combo box to select an employee. When a new employee is selected, the person's title and EmployeeID are automatically updated in the respective text boxes because we bound them to the Employees table, as you can see in Figure 11-23. Then the data grid is updated to display orders made by that employee. Of course, you can click any column of the data grid to sort the records.

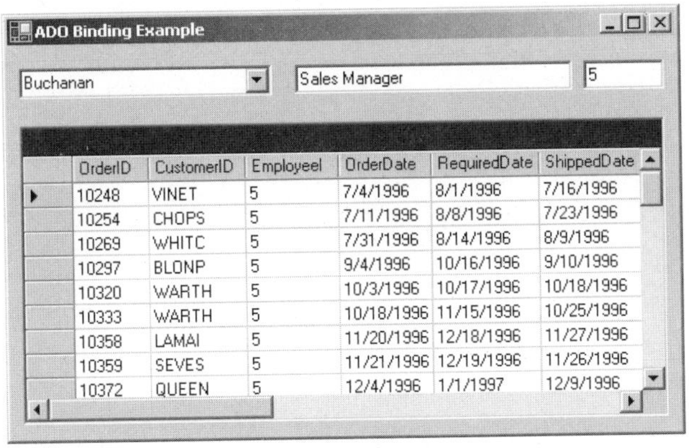

ADO Binding Example

Buchanan | Sales Manager | 5

OrderID	CustomerID	EmployeeI	OrderDate	RequiredDate	ShippedDate
10248	VINET	5	7/4/1996	8/1/1996	7/16/1996
10254	CHOPS	5	7/11/1996	8/8/1996	7/23/1996
10269	WHITC	5	7/31/1996	8/14/1996	8/9/1996
10297	BLONP	5	9/4/1996	10/16/1996	9/10/1996
10320	WARTH	5	10/3/1996	10/17/1996	10/18/1996
10333	WARTH	5	10/18/1996	11/15/1996	10/25/1996
10358	LAMAI	5	11/20/1996	12/18/1996	11/27/1996
10359	SEVES	5	11/21/1996	12/19/1996	11/26/1996
10372	QUEEN	5	12/4/1996	1/1/1997	12/9/1996

Figure 11-23 Employee information is displayed in controls bound to fields in the table.

How It Works

We know that our form's constructor calls its base constructor to ensure that each of the parent classes is fully initialized. Next the form calls its own *InitializeComponent* routine to create and initialize the visible controls—the text boxes, combo box, data grid, and various SQL commands inserted by our *DataAdapter*. When this work is complete, control of the program returns to the constructor and the *setupdata* routine is called.

```
Public Sub New()
    MyBase.New()

    'This call is required by the Windows Form Designer.
    InitializeComponent()

    'Add any initialization after the
    ' InitializeComponent() call
    setupdata()

End Sub
```

The *setupdata* routine fills our data sets; builds and initializes the *DataTable*, *DataColumns*, and *DataRelation* objects; binds controls; and creates and initializes the *DataView* object. We will create two tables from the data in our data set as well as a relationship between them.

> **Note** A *DataTable* object represents one table of in-memory data. The *DataTable* is a central object in the ADO.NET library. Other objects that use the *DataTable* include the *DataSet* and the *DataView*. A bit of esoterica about *DataTable* objects: they are conditionally case sensitive. By that I mean that if one *DataTable* is named "dtdatatable" and another is named "dtDataTable", a string used to search for one of the tables is regarded as case sensitive. However, if "dtdatatable" exists and "dtDataTable" does not, the search string is regarded as case insensitive.

The schema of a table is defined by the *DataColumnCollection*, the collection of *DataColumn* objects. The *DataColumnCollection* is accessed through the *Columns* property. The *DataTable* also contains a collection of *Constraint* objects that can be used to ensure the integrity of the data. Constraints are rules that are applied when rows are inserted, updated, or deleted in a table. You can define two types of constraints:

- A unique constraint, which checks that the new values in a column are unique in the table.
- A foreign-key constraint, which defines rules for how related child records should be updated when a record in a master table is updated or deleted.

To determine when changes are made to a data table, use the *RowChanged*, *RowChanging*, *RowDeleting*, or *RowDeleted* event.

We also dimension a *DataRelation* object. As you know, there are many times when your application needs to work with related tables. Although our data set contains tables and columns as in a database, it does not inherently include the database's native ability to relate tables. To accomplish this, we create *DataRelation* objects that establish a relationship between a parent and a child table based on a common key. This is done in memory on the client side.

```
Private Sub setupdata()
    Dim tEmployeesTable As DataTable
    Dim tOrdersTable As DataTable
    Dim drDataRelation As DataRelation
```

We have used the *Fill* method of data adapters before. Here we are simply adding both the Employees and Orders tables to DataSet11.

```
SqlDataAdapter1.Fill(DataSet11, "Employees")
SqlDataAdapter2.Fill(DataSet11, "Orders")
```

Next we initialize our two *DataTable* objects. The *DataSet* class includes the *Tables* collection of data tables. The *DataTable* class includes the *Rows* collection of table rows, the *Columns* collection of data columns, and the *ChildRelations* and *ParentRelations* collections of data relations.

```
tEmployeesTable = DataSet11.Tables("Employees")
tOrdersTable = DataSet11.Tables("Orders")
```

A *DataTable* contains a collection of *DataColumn* objects referenced by the *Columns* property of the table. This collection of columns, along with any constraints, defines the schema, or structure, of the table. You create *DataColumn* objects within a table by using the *DataColumn* constructor or by calling the *Add* method of the *Columns* property of the table, which is a *DataColumnCollection*. We need a column in each table to use as a basis for the parent/child relationship.

```
Dim colParent As DataColumn
Dim colChild As DataColumn

colParent = _
    DataSet11.Tables("Employees").Columns("EmployeeID")
colChild = _
    DataSet11.Tables("Orders").Columns("EmployeeID")
```

Now that we have the parent column in the Employees table and the child column in the Orders table defined, we are ready to build the relationship between the tables. In the constructor, we first give the relationship a name, EmployeesOrders, and then the two columns that we want to relate. When the *DataRelation* is built, it's added to the *Relations* collection of DataSet11.

```
'-- Build the Relationship
drDataRelation = New DataRelation("EmployeesOrders", _
    colParent, colChild)
DataSet11.Relations.Add(drDataRelation)
```

Now we want to bind the LastName column of the Employees table to the combo box. This way, it will automatically be populated with the employees' last names. There are two types of binding—simple and complex. *Simple data binding* means a single value within a data set is bound to something such as a property of a control or a form. Any property of a component, such as the *Text* property of a text box, can be bound to any value in a data set. *Complex data binding*, on the other hand, means components are able to bind to a data set. So our simple binding of the two text boxes will display a single field, and the combo box complex binding will display all of the values of that field. Some components that can take advantage of complex binding include the data grid and the combo box controls.

```
'-- Complex Binding --
cbEmployee.DataSource = tEmployeesTable
cbEmployee.DisplayMember = "LastName"

'-- Simple Binding --
tbTitle.DataBindings.Add("Text", tEmployeesTable, "Title")
tbEmployeeID.DataBindings.Add("Text", tEmployeesTable, _
    "EmployeeID")
```

Finally we want to call the constructor of our class-visible *DataView* object. A *DataView* can be customized to present a subset of data from the *DataTable*. You might want to have two *DataView* objects bound to the same *DataTable* but with each showing a different view of the data. For example, one control might be bound to a *DataView* showing all the rows in the table, while a second might be configured to display only the rows that have been deleted from the *DataTable*. The *DataTable* also has a *DefaultView* property that returns the default *DataView* for the table.

```
dvDataView = New DataView(tOrdersTable)
```

We want the *DataView* to show only orders for a specific employee, so we set the *RowFilter* property on the *DataView* when the user selects a specific employee from the combo box.

We just saw how our procedure *setupdata* is called when the form is initialized. When the form's *Activated* event handler is fired, we can be sure that all the visible controls on the form have been built, sited, and initialized. If you ever want to programmatically place data in a text box or other control, you should always do this from the *Activated* event handler. When the *Activated* event handler fires, signaling that everything is set up, we call the *setUpGrid* routine to display the order records for the currently selected employee.

```
Private Sub Form1_Activated(ByVal sender As System.Object, _
    ByVal e As System.EventArgs) Handles MyBase.Activated

    setUpGrid()
End Sub
```

When the form is initialized, the first employee record will be the current record. When *setUpGrid* is called, we take the contents of the bound tbEmployeeID text box as part of our *DataView.RowFilter* string. This string will retrieve only the records in the Orders table for that particular employee. The *DataView* and *DataSet* are independent objects. The *DataView* holds a link to the parent table, Employees in our example. The *DataView* does not cache the table, nor does it make an internal copy of the data. The *DataView* object simply contains information about the way and the order in which the content of the table must be shown. Once we define the filter for the data we want to be shown, the *dvDataView* object is set as the *DataSource* property of the grid.

```
Private Sub setUpGrid()
    dvDataView.RowFilter = "EmployeeID = '" & _
        tbEmployeeID.Text & "'"
    dgDataGrid.DataSource = dvDataView
End Sub
```

The *DataView* is an interesting animal because in classic ADO there was no way to get an independent view of our data. The filtered recordset in classic ADO was really always the same object, except that it displayed fewer records than were in the recordset. Here we can dim two *DataView* objects, for example, and have each provide a completely different view of our data source. Not only that, but each view can have its own set of properties, methods, and events. In our example, we build our *DataView* to show only those orders that are tied to the current salesperson. We could build another to show only those records in the beverage category, for example. Both could be managed independently. Figure 11-24 illustrates the workings of the *DataView* object.

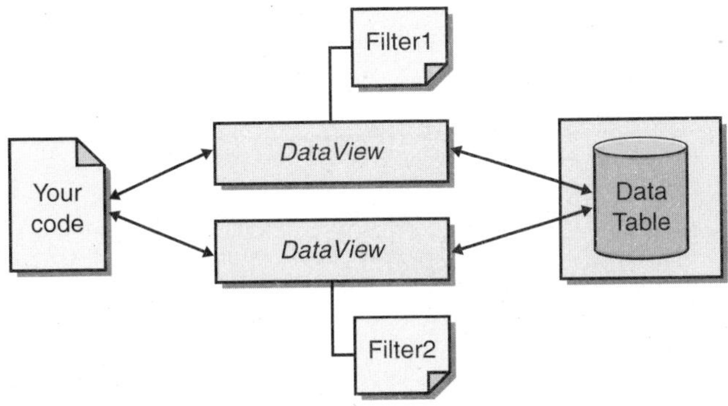

Figure 11-24 The workings of the *DataView* object.

Of course, you can only use a *DataView* when it is linked to a non-empty data table. The *DataView* constructor gives you a *DataView* object based on a data table. The *DefaultView* property of a data table returns a *DataView* object that is initialized on all the records of that table. The two properties you will use the most often with a *DataView* are *Rowfilter* and *Sort*. The filter string is really a concatenation of expressions. You take any column name that can be compared against a literal, a number, a date, or even another column. The wildcard characters * and % are supported. I find that I use them often with the LIKE command. So you could do something like this:

```
DvDataView.Rowfilter = "Lname LIKE Sm*th"
```

This statement would return records with names such as Smith and Smyth.

Updating Our Data Grid

Because the tbEmployeeID text box is bound to the EmployeeID field of the Employees table, the EmployeeID for the current Employee will automatically be displayed. We can simply call the *setUpGrid* routine whenever the *TextChanged* event handler fires. When the user selects another employee from the combo box, the tbEmployeeID field will change, so *setUpGrid* is called to display only the records for that employee.

```
Private Sub TbEmployeeID_TextChanged( _
    ByVal sender As System.Object, _
    ByVal e As System.EventArgs) _
    Handles tbEmployeeID.TextChanged

    setUpGrid()
End Sub
```

Conclusion

In this chapter, you've learned more about XML, XML schemas, persisting and reconstituting XML files, and a bit about *DataView* objects, auto-generating command filters, and simple and complex data binding, to name just a few of the topics covered. In the next chapter, we'll look some more at data binding.

12

ADO.NET Data Binding

In this chapter, we'll wrap up our discussion of ADO.NET by looking at data binding a bit more closely. This more detailed examination will ensure that you understand how data binding works for your production programs. We will also examine how to build and manipulate a data table programmatically, for those times when a bound control is not required.

The *BindingContext* Object

Each Visual Basic .NET Windows form has at least one *BindingContext* object. For each data source associated with a Windows form (such as a table or a collection), there is a single associated *CurrencyManager* object, as shown in Figure 12-1. The *BindingContext* object manages the *CurrencyManager* object or objects for the form. Because multiple data sources may be associated with a Windows form, you can use the *BindingContext* object to retrieve the particular *CurrencyManager* object associated with a data source.

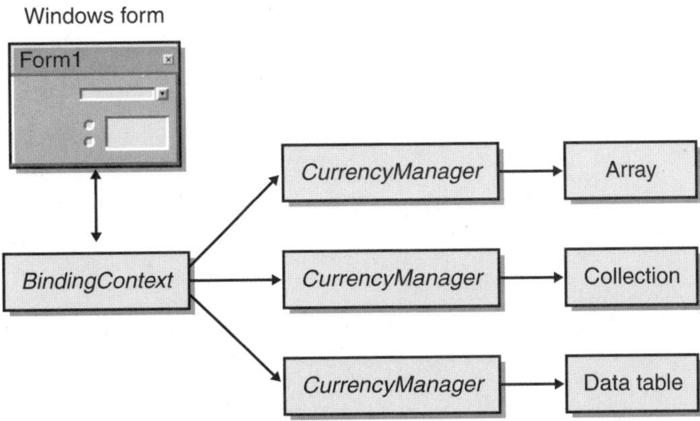

Figure 12-1 The *BindingContext* object supports multiple data sources.

In Chapter 11, "Data Sets in Detail," we added controls to a form and bound them to columns in a data table. Remember the text box that displayed the EmployeeID field? When we added the text box control to the form and bound it to the EmployeeID column of the Employees table in a data set, that control communicated with the *BindingContext* object for the form. The *BindingContext* object communicates with the specific *CurrencyManager* object for that data association. For example, if you need to know which record's data is being displayed in a bound text box, querying the *Currency-Manager* object's *Position* property will report the current record for the data source to which the text box control is bound. Here's code in which we bind a text box control named tbTitle to the Title column of tEmployeesTable through the *BindingContext* object for the form the control is on.

```
tbTitle.DataBindings.Add("Text", tEmployeesTable, "Title")
```

In the following code, we add a second text box control, tbEmployeeID, to the form and bind it to the EmployeeID column of tEmployeesTable in the same data set.

```
tbEmployeeID.DataBindings.Add("Text", _
    tEmployeesTable, "EmployeeID")
```

The *BindingContext* object is aware of the first binding (tbTitle to tEmployees.Title), so it uses the same *CurrencyManager* object for the second binding (tbEmployeeID to tEmployees.EmployeeID) because both text boxes are bound to the same table (tEmployeesTable). Simple data binding is accomplished by adding *Binding* objects—objects that maintain a simple binding between the property of a control and either the property of an object or the property of the current object in a list of objects—to a *ControlBindingsCollection*. Any object that inherits from the *Control* class can access the *ControlBindingsCollection* through the *DataBindings* property.

If you want to programmatically use a bound control to navigate to a specific record, you first set the *DataSource* and *DisplayMember* properties, as you can see here:

```
cbEmployee.DataSource = tEmployeesTable
cbEmployee.DisplayMember = "LastName"
```

Then, by communicating with the *Position* property of the *BindingContext* object, you could move through the records.

```
Me.BindingContext(tEmployeeTable, "Employees").Position = 1
```

The *CurrencyManager* Object

The *CurrencyManager* object is used to keep data-bound controls synchronized with one another, essentially ensuring that each shows data from the same record. The *CurrencyManager* object accomplishes this magic by managing a collection of the bound data supplied by a single data source.

Because more than one data source can be associated with a form, the *BindingContext* object manages all the *CurrencyManager* objects for any particular form. Not only forms, but also all container controls have at least one *BindingContext* object to manage their *CurrencyManager* objects.

Record Navigation

We need to understand how to bind controls to data sources because within Visual Basic .NET, data sources do not have any idea of a control's position within the data source. Unlike classic ADO, which maintained the current record and provided ways for you to navigate to other records, we need to use a different approach when working with ADO.NET. Some Visual Basic .NET programmers might be surprised to see that the data no longer "knows" where the current record itself is. ADO.NET doesn't use the notion of a cursor in our disconnected recordsets. But there is an upside to this approach. Because of the absence of a cursor, you can have multiple positions set on the same store of data.

When you need to know where you are in a data source, you must examine the *Position* property of the *CurrencyManager* object. Just remember that the term *currency* is used to refer to the *currentness* of position within a data structure. You can easily use the *Position* property of the *CurrencyManager* class to determine the currency of all controls bound to the same *CurrencyManager* object.

Consider the two text boxes, tbTitle and tbEmployeeID, mentioned previously. These text boxes are bound to the same table, but they are bound to different columns. When the *Position* property of the common *CurrencyManager* object is set to the fourth position within that data source (corresponding to the fifth record because the position is zero-based), both controls display the appropriate values (the fifth "Title" and the fifth "EmployeeID") for that position in the table.

A Simple Example

Most any production program requires code that lets users or the program itself navigate through records. This navigational code is fairly easy to write, but as I mentioned, in the .NET world navigation is quite different from how navigation was accomplished in classic ADO. Here's a simple program that loads the Employees table from the Northwind database and permits a user to scroll through the records. The finished program is shown in Figure 12-2.

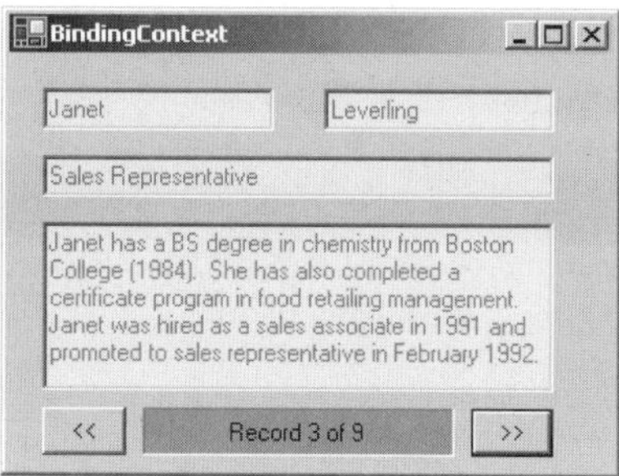

Figure 12-2 The BindingContext program in action.

To start, create a new Windows application project named BindingContext. Draw four text boxes, two buttons, and a label on the default form, as shown in Figure 12-3.

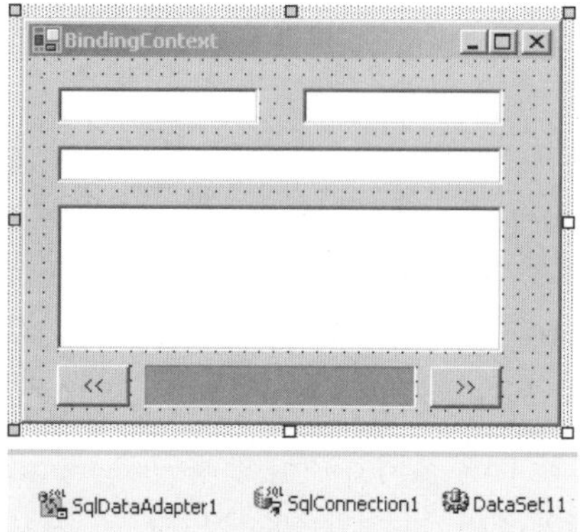

Figure 12-3 The BindingContext form.

Add a *SqlDataAdapter* object, use the Northwind connection we created in Chapter 10, "Data Access with ADO.NET," and select all the fields from the Employees table. *SqlConnection1* will automatically be added for us. Right-click the *SqlDataAdapter* object, select Generate Dataset, and then click OK in the Generate Dataset dialog box, which will insert the *DataSet11* object for us. Now set the properties for the controls you added to the form as indicated in Table 12-1.

Table 12-1 Properties and Values for the BindingContext Controls

Object	Property	Value
Text box	*Name*	tbFirstName
	Text	""
Text box	*Name*	tbLastName
	Text	""
Text box	*Name*	tbTitle
	Text	""
Text box	*Name*	tbNotes
	MultiLine	True
	Text	""
Button	*Name*	btnPrevious
	Text	<<
Button	*Name*	btnNext
	Text	>>
Label	*Name*	lblPosition
	Backcolor	Lime
	Text	""
	TextAlign	MiddleCenter

Add the Code

We need to check the current position as well as the number of records in various routines. To accomplish this, we'll define two class-level variables in the program. Here's the code to add:

```
Public Class Form1
    Inherits System.Windows.Forms.Form

    Dim iRecordCount As Integer
    Dim iCurrentPosition As Integer
```

When the form class is loaded, we want to bind our controls as well as add two event handlers. The routine *setUpData* is called once do to this, and then the *updateLabel* routine is called to display the current number of records present.

```
Public Sub New()
    MyBase.New()

    'This call is required by the Windows Form Designer.
    InitializeComponent()

    'Add any initialization after the
    'InitializeComponent() call
    setUpData()
    updateLabel()
End Sub

Private Sub setUpData()

    'Fill our dataset
    SqlDataAdapter1.Fill(DataSet11, "Employees")

    '--Bind the text boxes
    tbLastName.DataBindings.Add("Text", DataSet11, _
        "Employees.LastName")
    tbFirstName.DataBindings.Add("Text", DataSet11, _
        "Employees.FirstName")
    tbTitle.DataBindings.Add("Text", DataSet11, _
        "Employees.Title")
    tbNotes.DataBindings.Add("Text", DataSet11, _
        "Employees.Notes")

    Dim tbBackground() As Control = {tbLastName, tbFirstName, _
        tbTitle, tbNotes}
    Dim tbCtrl As Control

    For Each tbCtrl In tbBackground
        With tbCtrl
            .BackColor = System.Drawing.Color.BlanchedAlmond
            .ForeColor = System.Drawing.Color.DarkGray
            .Enabled = False
        End With
    Next

    'Add handlers to check button navigation
    AddHandler btnNext.Click, AddressOf Me.ValidateRecords
    AddHandler btnPrevious.Click, AddressOf Me.ValidateRecords
End Sub

Private Sub ValidateRecords(ByVal sender As System.Object, _
    ByVal e As System.EventArgs) Handles btnPrevious.Click

    '-- Get status
    iRecordCount = Me.BindingContext(DataSet11, _
        "Employees").Count
```

```
    iCurrentPosition = Me.BindingContext(DataSet11, _
        "Employees").Position + 1

    '-- Reasonability check for buttons --
    If iRecordCount <= 1 Then
        btnPrevious.Enabled = False
        btnNext.Enabled = False
        updateLabel()
        Exit Sub
    End If

    'Back button pressed
    If (sender.Equals(btnPrevious)) Then
        'Can we go backwards?
        If iCurrentPosition > 1 Then
            Me.BindingContext(DataSet11, _
                "Employees").Position -= 1
        Else
            btnPrevious.Enabled = False
        End If
    End If

    'Forward button pressed
    If (sender.Equals(btnNext)) Then
        If iRecordCount > iCurrentPosition Then
            Me.BindingContext(DataSet11, _
                "Employees").Position += 1
        Else
            btnNext.Enabled = False
        End If
    End If

    '-- Get Status after move --
    iCurrentPosition = Me.BindingContext(DataSet11, _
        "Employees").Position + 1

    If iRecordCount = iCurrentPosition Then
        btnNext.Enabled = False
    Else
        btnNext.Enabled = True
    End If

    If iCurrentPosition = 1 Then
        btnPrevious.Enabled = False
    Else
        btnPrevious.Enabled = True
    End If

    updateLabel()
End Sub
```

(continued)

```
Private Sub updateLabel()

    iRecordCount = Me.BindingContext(DataSet11, _
        "Employees").Count
    iCurrentPosition = Me.BindingContext(DataSet11, _
        "Employees").Position + 1

    If iRecordCount <= 1 Then
        lblPosition.Text = "No Records"
    Else
        lblPosition.Text = "Record " & iCurrentPosition & _
            " of " & iRecordCount
    End If

End Sub
```

How the Code Works

The *setUpData* routine is called only once, when the form is loaded. The *DataSet* object is filled, and the text boxes are bound to their respective columns.

```
Private Sub setUpData()

    'Fill our dataset
    SqlDataAdapter1.Fill(DataSet11, "Employees")

    '-Bind the text boxes
    tbLastName.DataBindings.Add("Text", DataSet11, _
        "Employees.LastName")
    tbFirstName.DataBindings.Add("Text", DataSet11, _
        "Employees.FirstName")
    tbTitle.DataBindings.Add("Text", DataSet11, _
        "Employees.Title")
    tbNotes.DataBindings.Add("Text", DataSet11, _
        "Employees.Notes")
```

I added this *setUpData* routine to give you some ideas for your own applications. We dimension the *tbBackground* array of type *Control*. The four text boxes are then added as elements of the array. Then we iterate through the text box controls in the array and set three properties for each. We could have set these properties in the property box in the IDE, but seeing this example might give you ideas for other applications. In classic Visual Basic, I always used control arrays to streamline code that had to perform similar operations on several visual controls. Because Visual Basic .NET no longer provides a control array, we can easily build our own.

```
Dim tbBackground() As Control = {tbLastName, tbFirstName, _
    tbTitle, tbNotes}

Dim tbCtrl As Control
For Each tbCtrl In tbBackground
    With tbCtrl
        .BackColor = System.Drawing.Color.BlanchedAlmond
        .ForeColor = System.Drawing.Color.DarkGray
        .Enabled = False
    End With
Next
```

Next we want to add two event handlers, one for the *Click* event of each button. When the user clicks either the btnPrevious or btnNext button, the *ValidateRecords* event will fire.

```
'Add handlers to check button navigation
AddHandler btnNext.Click, AddressOf Me.ValidateRecords
AddHandler btnPrevious.Click, AddressOf Me.ValidateRecords
```

As I noted, the *ValidateRecords* routine is called when either button is clicked. We want to let the *ValidateRecords* routine handle record navigation so that we don't have to duplicate code in both of the buttons' *Click* events. Notice that the *ValidateRecords* routine's signature is the same as a *Click* event. The first operation the routine performs is to update the class-level variables that hold the number of records that are in the table and indicate which is the current record.

Notice also that we retrieve both the number of records as well as the current position within the table from the *BindingContext* object. We tell the *BindingContext* object which data source we are interested in. The *BindingContext* object, and not the data set in our case, manages all of the positional information.

```
Private Sub ValidateRecords(ByVal sender As System.Object, _
    ByVal e As System.EventArgs) Handles btnPrevious.Click

    '-- Get Status
    iRecordCount = Me.BindingContext(DataSet11, _
        "Employees").Count
    iCurrentPosition = Me.BindingContext(DataSet11, _
        "Employees").Position + 1
```

If the table doesn't have any records, the buttons are disabled, the label is updated, and the routine is exited.

```
'-- Reasonability check for buttons --
If iRecordCount <= 1 Then
    btnPrevious.Enabled = False
    btnNext.Enabled = False
    updateLabel()
    Exit Sub
End If
```

Either button's *Click* action can call the *ValidateRecords* routine. We can easily tell which button fired the event by calling the *sender.Equals* method and passing in the button as a parameter. If the user clicked the previous record button, the code block determines whether the current position is greater than the first record. If it is, the button is enabled and we go back a record. If the current record is the first record, however, we have nowhere to go, so the button is disabled to give the user a visual cue of the position. When we move between records, *BindingContext* is the object that moves the internal cursor to the next record and performs the synchronization.

```
'Back button pressed
If (sender.Equals(btnPrevious)) Then
    'Can we go backwards?
    If iCurrentPosition > 1 Then
        Me.BindingContext(DataSet11, _
            "Employees").Position -= 1
    Else
        btnPrevious.Enabled = False
    End If
End If
```

The same logic checks are made to determine whether the btnNext button was clicked. If the current record is less than the total records, the *BindingContext* object moves to the next record within the table.

```
'Forward button pressed
If (sender.Equals(btnNext)) Then
    If iRecordCount > iCurrentPosition Then
        Me.BindingContext(DataSet11, "Employees").Position += 1
    Else
        btnNext.Enabled = False
    End If
End If
```

After the navigation, the current position is checked, and if we are at the first record, the btnPrevious button is disabled. Likewise, if the last record is current, the btnNext button is disabled. Finally the *updateLabel* routine is called to provide visual feedback about where we are within the table.

```
'-- Get status after move --
iCurrentPosition = Me.BindingContext(DataSet11, _
    "Employees").Position + 1

If iRecordCount = iCurrentPosition Then
    btnNext.Enabled = False
Else
    btnNext.Enabled = True
End If


If iCurrentPosition = 1 Then
    btnPrevious.Enabled = False
Else
    btnPrevious.Enabled = True
End If

updateLabel()
```

The *updateLabel* routine simply updates the label to show the position within the table as the navigation buttons are clicked.

```
Private Sub updateLabel()

    iRecordCount = Me.BindingContext(DataSet11, _
        "Employees").Count
    iCurrentPosition = Me.BindingContext(DataSet11, _
        "Employees").Position + 1

    If iRecordCount <= 1 Then
        lblPosition.Text = "No Records"
    Else
        lblPosition.Text = "Record " & iCurrentPosition & _
            " of " & iRecordCount
    End If

End Sub
```

Now we know how the mechanics of binding controls to data sources work in a bit more detail. Another piece of information you need to understand is how to programmatically read and write from and to tables, columns, and fields in a data source. While we've seen some examples of updating data using the DataGrid control, we will certainly need to update data from a program as well.

The *DataTable*, *DataRow*, and *DataColumn* Objects

I've been discussing data tables and how to bind columns to visual controls. Now I want to describe how to programmatically retrieve or write values from and to rows and columns in a table. I will also describe how to create our own tables on the fly from a program.

As we saw in Chapter 11, the *DataTable* object is a central object in the ADO.NET library. We saw how objects that use the *DataTable* object include the *DataSet* and *DataView* objects. It will probably come as no surprise that the *DataRow* and *DataColumn* objects are primary components of a *DataTable*. A programmer will use the *DataRow* object with its properties and methods to manipulate values in the table. The *DataRow* object is used to retrieve and evaluate values as well as to insert, delete, and update records. Of course, a record is represented as a *DataRow*. Internally, the *DataRowCollection* represents the actual *DataRow* objects in the *DataTable*. The *DataColumnCollection*, of course, contains the *DataColumn* objects that describe the schema of the *DataTable*. We can use the *DataColumnCollection* object's overloaded *Item* property to read or write a value to a *DataColumn*.

Examining the *DataTable* Schema

If we want to examine the fields and data types of those fields in a table, we can do so by using the *DataColumnCollection*. By its name, we can tell that the collection contains each of the *DataColumn* objects in the table. We dimension a variable, *dccCollection*, to hold the collection, as well as the variable *dcDataColumn* to hold each *DataColumn* object as we iterate through the collection. We will stick with the Employees table from the Northwind database in this example. If we wrote a program and used an *SqlDataAdapter* object to retrieve all the fields from the Employees table, the following code would let us iterate through each of the fields and look at its data type.

```
Dim dccCollection As DataColumnCollection
Dim dcDataColumn As DataColumn
Dim sDescription As String
    Dim tEmployeesTable As DataTable

tEmployeesTable = DataSet11.Tables("Employees")
dccCollection = tEmployeesTable.Columns

For Each dcDataColumn In dccCollection
    sDescription += "Name: " & dcDataColumn.ColumnName & _
        CtrlChrs.Tab & CtrlChrs.Tab & " DataType:  " & _
        dcDataColumn.DataType.ToString & CtrlChrs.CrLf
Next
```

```
MessageBox.Show(sDescription, "Employees Table Column " & _
    "Collection", MessageBoxButtons.OK, _
    MessageBoxIcon.Information)
```

When we run this code, we can see that the fields are listed along with their data types, as you can see in Figure 12-4. Again, each of these fields can be accessed individually and is stored in the *DataColumnCollection* of the table.

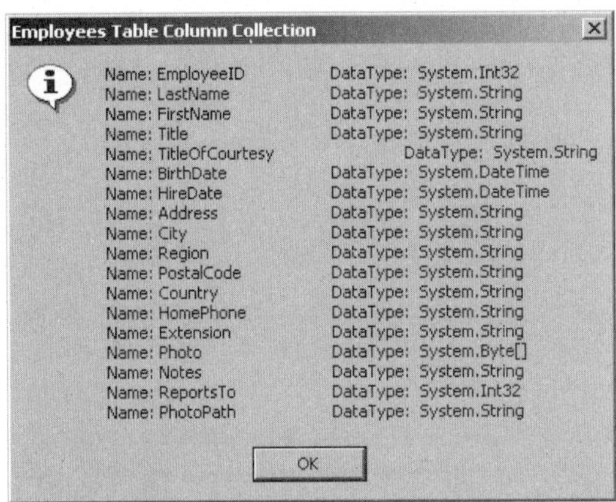

Figure 12-4 The fields in the Employees table.

Now that we've seen the columns of a data table and their respective data types, let's take a look at the contents of the columns. We can easily do this by examining the *Item* property of a *DataRow* object. The *Item* property is passed in the name of the column to be displayed.

```
Dim drDataRow As DataRow

SqlDataAdapter1.Fill(DataSet11, "Employees")

tEmployeesTable = DataSet11.Tables("Employees")

sDescription = "There are " & tEmployeesTable.Rows.Count & _
    " rows in the Employees table" & CtrlChrs.CrLf

For Each drDataRow In tEmployeesTable.Rows
    sDescription += "ID: " & drDataRow.Item("EmployeeID") & _
        CtrlChrs.Tab & "Last Name: " & _
        drDataRow.Item("LastName")& CtrlChrs.CrLf
Next

MessageBox.Show(sDescription, "Employees Table Data Rows", _
    MessageBoxButtons.OK, MessageBoxIcon.Information)
```

We can see the two fields that we retrieved by column name in Figure 12-5.

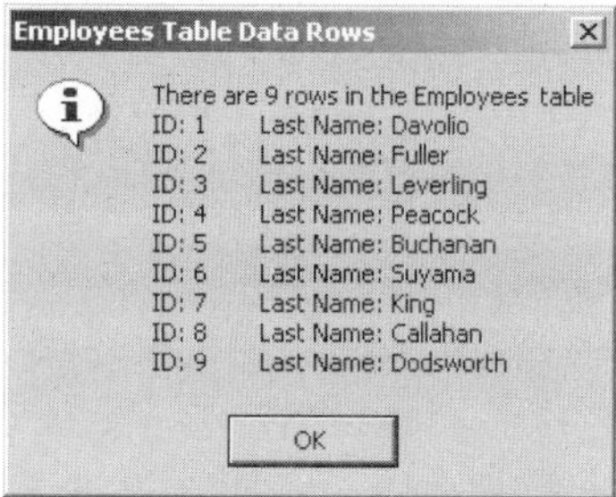

Figure 12-5 The contents of the ID and the LastName columns in the Employees table.

It's straightforward to select any column within a row if we know its name. But if you don't know the column name you want to access but do know its position within the row, you can pass the ordinal value of the column. So, if we printed out *drDataRow(0)*, the contents of the first column of our table would be printed.

Building a Table Programmatically

At times, you'll need to build a table on the fly or you'll need to search for specific records in a data table. Let's spend a moment looking at how to do these chores because the technique for doing so with Visual Basic .NET and ADO.NET is different from classic ADO. Here's the code we'll be examining.

```
Dim dtDataTable as DataTable
' Create a new DataTable
dtDataTable = New DataTable("tbLanguageTable")

' Declare a variable for the DataRow object
Dim dcDataRow As DataRow

' Create new DataColumn, set DataType, ColumnName
' and add it to our new DataTable
dcDataColumn = New DataColumn()
With dcDataColumn
    .DataType = System.Type.GetType("System.Int32")
    .ColumnName = "Sequence"
    .ReadOnly = True
    .AutoIncrement = True
End With

' Finally, add the Column to the DataColumnCollection
dtDataTable.Columns.Add(dcDataColumn)
```

```
' Create second column
dcDataColumn = New DataColumn()
With dcDataColumn
    .DataType = System.Type.GetType("System.String")
    .ColumnName = "ParentItem"
    .AutoIncrement = False
    .ColumnName = "Language"
    .ReadOnly = False
    .Unique = False
End With

' Add the column to the table
dtDataTable.Columns.Add(dcDataColumn)

' Make the ID column the primary key column
Dim PrimaryKeyColumns(0) As DataColumn
PrimaryKeyColumns(0) = dtDataTable.Columns("Sequence")
dtDataTable.PrimaryKey = PrimaryKeyColumns

dcDataRow = dtDataTable.NewRow()
dcDataRow(1) = "VB .NET"
dtDataTable.Rows.Add(dcDataRow)

dcDataRow = dtDataTable.NewRow()
dcDataRow(1) = "C#"
dtDataTable.Rows.Add(dcDataRow)

dcDataRow = dtDataTable.NewRow()
dcDataRow(1) = "C++"
dtDataTable.Rows.Add(dcDataRow)

Dim dsDataSet As DataSet
' Instantiate the DataSet variable
dsDataSet = New DataSet()
' Add the new DataTable to the DataSet
dsDataSet.Tables.Add(dtDataTable)
```

How the Code Works

We first create a new reference variable named *dtDataTable* of type *DataTable*. The *dtDataTable* variable is a handle to our new but currently empty table.

```
' Create a new DataTable
dtDataTable = New DataTable("tbLanguageTable")

' Declare a variable for the DataRow object
Dim dcDataRow As DataRow
```

The new table is empty of any content. Let's add two columns to it. The first column, to be named Sequence, will hold an *Integer* type and will increment itself automatically. Because this *DataColumn* object increments itself, you want to make it read-only.

```
' Create new DataColumn, set DataType, ColumnName
' and add it to our new DataTable
dcDataColumn = New DataColumn()
With dcDataColumn
    .DataType = System.Type.GetType("System.Int32")
    .ColumnName = "Sequence"
    .ReadOnly = True
    .AutoIncrement = True
End With

' Finally add the Column to the DataColumnCollection
dtDataTable.Columns.Add(dcDataColumn)
```

Using a shorthand syntax, we can both add and define a column by writing this statement:

```
dtDataTable.Columns.Add("Sequence", _
    Type.GetType("System.Int32"))
```

Of course, we still have to set the other properties, such as *ReadOnly* and *AutoIncrement.*

Next we create another column and set the primary key. Both of these tasks are self-explanatory. Now we're ready to add some data, so let's add three rows of data to the two columns we've defined. Because the Sequence field (field 0) is auto-incrementing and read-only, it will take care of itself. Using the *NewRow* method of our table object, we create a new row and add a language value in the second field (field 1) of each. Then we add each new row to the *Rows* collection of our table.

> **Note** The maximum number of rows that a *DataTable* object can store is 16,777,216.

Notice that adding a row to a *DataTable* by using the *NewRow* method returns a new *DataRow* object. The *NewRow* method returns a new row following the schema of our *DataTable.* The definition of the table's schema is contained in the table's *DataColumnCollection.* The *DataColumnCollection* is accessed through the *Columns* property.

```
dcDataRow = dtDataTable.NewRow()
dcDataRow(1) = "VB .NET"
dtDataTable.Rows.Add(dcDataRow)

dcDataRow = dtDataTable.NewRow()
dcDataRow(1) = "C#"
dtDataTable.Rows.Add(dcDataRow)

dcDataRow = dtDataTable.NewRow()
dcDataRow(1) = "C++"
dtDataTable.Rows.Add(dcDataRow)
```

Next we create a new data set and add our table to it. We learned how to do this in Chapter 10.

```
Dim dsDataSet As DataSet
' Instantiate the DataSet variable
dsDataSet = New DataSet()
' Add the new DataTable to the DataSet
dsDataSet.Tables.Add(dtDataTable)
```

Finding Specific Records

The way you find records in a data set is different in Visual Basic .NET than in classic ADO. We first define a string that specifies the records we want to find and then pass the string to the *Select* method of our table. The *Select* method returns an array of *DataRow* objects for each of the rows that contain the string we're looking for. The objects are in order of primary key (or lacking a primary key, in order of addition). After we have the records we are looking for, the values can be edited.

```
Dim sFind, sMessage As String
Dim iCounter As Integer
Dim foundRows() As DataRow  'an array of DataRows

sFind = "Language = 'VB .NET'"

foundRows = dtDataTable.Select(sFind)

For iCounter = 0 To foundRows.GetUpperBound(0)
    sMessage = "Item: " & foundRows(iCounter).Item(1)
    foundRows(iCounter).Item(1) = "Visual Basic .NET"
    sMessage += " is now " & foundRows(iCounter).Item(1)
Next
MessageBox.Show(sMessage, "Finding Records", _
    MessageBoxButtons.OK, MessageBoxIcon.Information)
```

In this code, we searched our table for a field that contains the string "VB .NET". In this case, only a single *DataRow* entry was placed in the *foundRows* array. We then grabbed the original value of "VB .NET" and changed it to "Visual Basic .NET". You can see the results in Figure 12-6.

Figure 12-6 Values of "VB .NET" are changed to "Visual Basic .NET".

We now want to find all records that contain the string "C++" and delete them. We again use the *Select* method and then use the *Delete* method on the *DataRow* objects we want to extinguish. After successfully deleting the record, we do another search to ensure that the record has been deleted.

```
sFind = "Language = 'C++'"

foundRows = dtDataTable.Select(sFind)

For iCounter = 0 To foundRows.GetUpperBound(0)
    sMessage = "Item: " & foundRows(iCounter).Item(1) & _
        " found." & ctrlchrs.CrLf
    foundRows(iCounter).Delete()
    sMessage += "C++ was successfuly deleted" & ctrlchrs.CrLf
Next

foundRows = dtDataTable.Select(sFind)
If foundRows.Length < 1 Then
    sMessage += "C++  not found" & ctrlchrs.CrLf
End If

MessageBox.Show(sMessage, "Finding Records", _
    MessageBoxButtons.OK, MessageBoxIcon.Information)
```

Notice how the record was deleted from the array containing the specific *DataRow* object returned from the *Select* method. Our successful results are confirmed in Figure 12-7.

Figure 12-7 We can successfully find and delete records.

Conclusion

As you now see, ADO.NET is very different from the classic ADO we have been used to. The *BindingContext* object of a form manages the various *CurrencyManager* objects used to bind a table, a collection, or an array to a visual control. The *BindingContext* object ensures each of the individual *CurrencyManager* objects are synchronized when a new record is selected. To navigate through records, we manipulate the *Position* property of the *BindingContext* object. To bind a control to a column in a table, we simply add the table and field to the *DataBindings* collection of the individual control. Using this new knowledge, we learned how to navigate through a data table.

We also learned how to dynamically build a data table. Our example included building new columns and specifying their properties, such as the data type it will hold and its name. Next we went on to add data to our new table on the fly and then learned how to find individual records that contained specific values. These are all the things that we are used to doing with classic ADO, but you will no doubt agree that the way we approach the tasks in ADO.NET is very different.

This chapter wraps up our discussion of ADO.NET. You are now armed with the knowledge of accessing any data store. There were several new concepts we covered in the past three chapters—not the least of which is the disconnected nature of ADO.NET. As you think about this new paradigm, you will no doubt see how you can use this knowledge in new and previously unthought-of ways. Learning about Visual Basic .NET gives you all sorts of new perspectives on manipulating data.

13

ASP.NET and Web Services

So far, we've seen how Visual Basic .NET can render data with Windows Forms and in console applications. We're now going to look at how we can render Web pages, using the same techniques we've learned when building a Windows Forms application. I'll also describe Web services, which are used to communicate with interfaces of remote components. If the use of Web services sounds strange, hang on until you reach the second part of the chapter. Web services are going to become the next big thing on the Internet, and Microsoft .NET is poised to make this happen.

Web Forms (the controls and classes .NET provides for building Web pages) and Web services (programmable application logic accessible by standard Internet protocols) are part of the framework for Internet functionality included in Visual Basic .NET and are known by the umbrella term ASP.NET. If you have previously worked with Active Server Pages (ASP), you will be surprised at how much different and more efficient ASP.NET is. ASP.NET encompasses a completely new programming object model. It replaces the Visual Basic 6 WebClasses and DHTML pages. Not only that, but the ASP.NET programming model is also more consistent and easier to use.

A Look Back at ASP

ASP is a powerful model and is the right tool for most jobs. The information systems department I manage has written and has running more than 100 ASP pages that clients (internal and external) use to access various pieces of functionality within our organization. But if you've had the chance to work with ASP, you know that it has some drawbacks. You know that you have to write code to perform any operation, and you quickly notice that you are dealing with spaghetti code. The unstructured nature of ASP code—where everything is placed in an ASP page—often offends purists. Yes, you can use *include* statements, but doing that requires more work. You usually find ASP logic script code mixed with HTML tags for presentation. This mix, of course, does not help readability or debugging, and because ASP uses interpreted script, performance problems arise in some cases. But in spite of the difficulties, ASP has evolved to become the foremost tool in the Windows-oriented Web programmer's toolbox.

One thing that always bites Web developers is the need for multiple browser support. When we design ASP pages for external clients, we must either program to the lowest common denominator of browser or write extra classes to support each browser the clients might use. Not only that, but no state management is available unless the programmer writes acres of code to persist values from page to page. Of course, ASP has the *Application* and *Session* objects, but there are two potential problems with these. First, they make scaling a high-volume site difficult. Second, because they are run on the server, if the host has a server farm, you can't be sure that the next page won't be served from a completely different machine. Luckily, ASP.NET solves these thorny problems.

Why ASP.NET?

The compelling nature of ASP.NET will draw Web programmers toward its orbit for the following reasons:

- **Language independence.** ASP.NET allows you to use compiled languages, providing better performance and cross-language compatibility.
- **Simplified development.** ASP.NET makes even the richest pages straightforward and easy to write.
- **Separation of code and content.** Each Web Form has a code module with the same name but with the extension .vb. This so-called *code behind the page* contains the program logic code, while the Web Form contains the visual components.
- **Improved scalability.** New session-state features make it easy to create Web Forms that work on Web server farms (multiple servers).
- **Support for multiple clients.** ASP.NET controls can automatically detect the client and optimize themselves for a consistent look and feel. You no longer have to write separate code for different browsers.

- **New Web Forms controls.** The new controls can output HTML 3.2 for down-level browsers while taking advantage of the runtime libraries for enhanced interactivity on richer clients. Our programs can now output to a whole new range of platforms such as wireless phones, palm pilots, and handheld pagers and devices.
- **Server-side processing.** ASP.NET changes each page into a server-side object. More properties, methods, and events can be used with your code to create content dynamically. The *runat="server"* attribute converts the HTML element into a server-side control that is visible and therefore programmable within ASP.NET on the server. Events raised by Web Form controls are detected, and the appropriate code is executed on the server in response to these events.

> **Note** ASP.NET is written entirely in the new C# language. All ASP.NET pages have the .aspx file extension, which allows both .asp and .aspx files to be run on the same machine under the existing ASP runtime.

Getting from There to Here

In some ways, everything you've learned in this book up to now has poised us to write ASP.NET programs. You will soon see how similar that is to creating Windows Forms programs in .NET. You drag and drop controls and set properties in the same manner you do with Windows Forms. You use the technologies you've learned about so far—the .NET Framework; object-oriented programming; events, properties, and methods; ADO.NET; and XML—and put them together in Web Forms.

When I hire a new programmer, I'm amazed at how many applicants are proud to say they understand Visual Basic. The applicants describe how they know various esoteric uses of items such as control arrays or undocumented memory pointers. What they fail to realize is that I'm looking for someone that understands database design, n-tier architecture, ActiveX Data Objects (ADO), XML, HTML, Dynamic HTML (DHTML), object-oriented programming, Transmission Control Protocol/Internet Protocol (TCP/IP), the Open Systems Interconnection (OSI) protocol stack, custom ActiveX control construction, network security, firewalls, and so

(continued)

Getting from There to Here *(continued)*

on. Many of these technologies and concepts are implemented in Visual Basic. Learning the language is only the first part—not the be-all and end-all, but rather a beginning.

While it's easy to find people who know Visual Basic, it's difficult to find people who understand the gestalt of how programs operate in a distributed environment. And if you look back at how much ground we've covered in this book to get to this point, you might be pleasantly surprised at how most of what you've learned will be directly applicable to writing ASP.NET programs.

Several years ago, when graphical tools such as Visual Basic came on the scene, many software developers were concerned that programming would become so easy that they would be out of a job. After all, even accountants could drag buttons to a form and set properties. However, quite the opposite has happened. Programming has become exponentially more abstract. It turns out that we need the graphical capabilities so that we can concentrate on application design and fitting the pieces together. A Visual Basic .NET program has many moving parts—especially programs running on the Internet. Luckily, Visual Basic .NET provides some very powerful graphical tools that help get Web sites up and running quickly.

Our First Web Form

To give you an immediate sense of how powerful Web Forms are, we'll create a simple program that uses the new calendar control. The program will display a calendar from which the user must select a date before submitting the page. If a date is not selected, a field validator will notify the user and the page won't be sent.

Start a new ASP.NET Web application project with the name WebForms, as shown in Figure 13-1. Notice that the location of the file will be the local host. If you are running Internet Information Services (IIS) or Personal Web Server on the same machine as Visual Studio .NET, the local host will usually be C:\Inetpub\wwwroot.

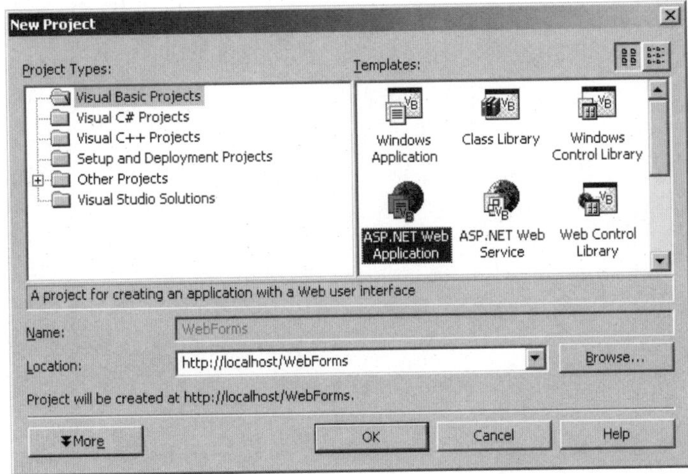

Figure 13-1 Create an ASP.NET Web application named WebForms.

The default workspace for an ASP.NET Web application, shown in Figure 13-2, looks a bit different from what we're used to seeing. The toolbars are slightly different, and the design surface is white, but the overall feel is the same. (The message you see on the form is not part of our application; it's simply a note from Visual Basic .NET telling us which layout mode is being used.)

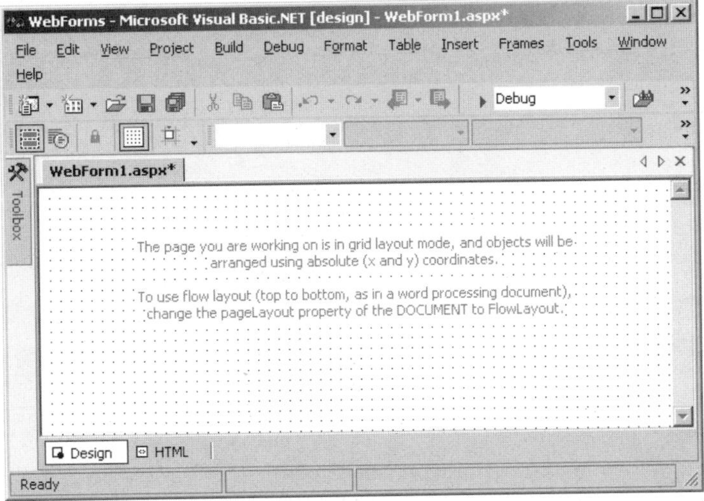

Figure 13-2 The default ASP.NET Web application workspace.

Tip To change the layout of the ASP.NET Web application workspace, right-click on the display area and select Properties. When the Document Property Pages dialog box appears, you can change the page layout. The page layout options you use will be primarily a matter of preference. The FlowLayout setting allows the user to add text and hard paragraph breaks to the page, which is converted into HTML code. When the default GridLayout setting is selected, the controls are placed on the surface of the page but are not interspersed with HTML code, as happens in FlowLayout. If you have ever used Microsoft FrontPage, you are familiar with the WYSIWYG style, which is a huge improvement over earlier designs.

The Solution Explorer reveals that a few more files are required when developing Web Forms rather than Windows Forms, as you can see in Figure 13-3. The classes that include the visual components are located in the *System.Web* namespace. Table 13-1 lists and describes the files in our WebForms project.

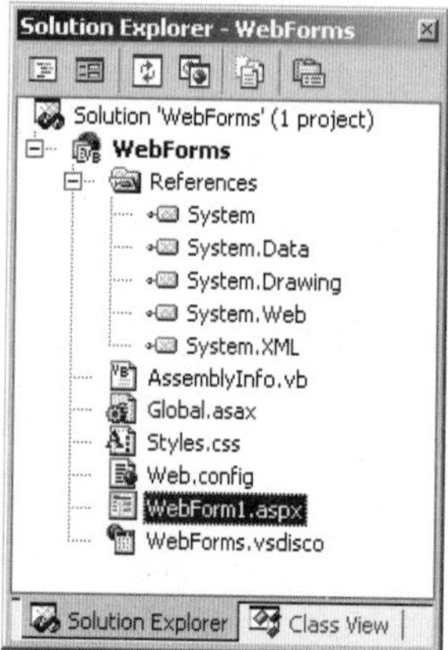

Figure 13-3 Web Forms applications have more files than Windows Forms applications.

Table 13-1 The Files in Our WebForms Project

File	Description
AssemblyInfo.vb	An optional project information file that contains metadata about the assemblies in a project, such as name, version, and culture information.
Web.config	An XML-based file that contains configuration information for ASP.NET resources.
Global.asax	An optional file for handling application-level events. This file resides in the root directory of an ASP.NET application. When deployed, this project's WebService1.dll file will contain the "code-behind" file associated with the .asax file. I'll be covering code-behind files shortly.
WebForms.vsdisco	An optional XML-based file that contains links (URLs) to resources providing discovery information for a Web service.
WebForm1.aspx	The user interface file we are now working with.

New Server Controls

If you take a look at the Web Forms tab in the toolbox, shown in Figure 13-4, you can see the names of quite a few new controls. These controls are referred to as *server controls* and are similar to the Windows Forms controls we've been working with. Each control provides a consistent set of properties and methods. In addition, these controls manage state, can be manipulated in code, and provide a limited set of events to which we can add our program logic.

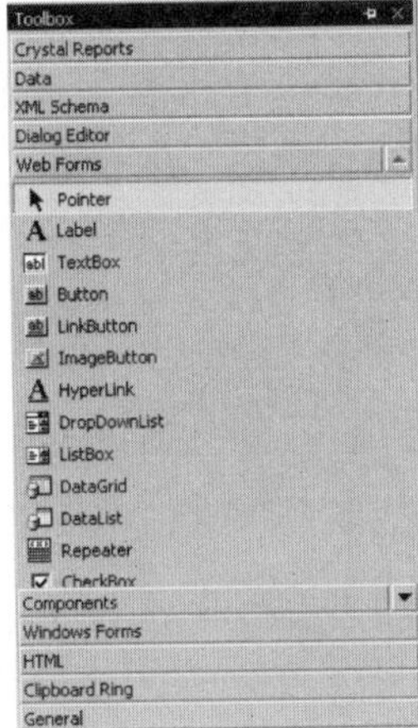

Figure 13-4 Web Forms server controls.

Another set of controls available for Web Forms appears on the HTML tab, shown in Figure 13-5. These controls are referred to as *HTML server controls*. Each of these controls is basically a one-to-one match for the HTML controls found on current Web pages. These controls are not sophisticated and have no intelligence for handling how they appear with various browsers. HTML server controls were provided to update existing pages to the new server controls. Unless you are updating pages already created, I'd suggest you stick with the server controls on the Web Forms tab.

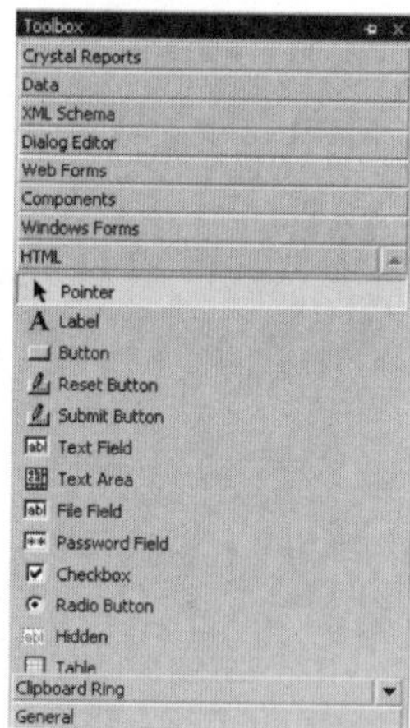

Figure 13-5 HTML server controls.

ASP.NET server controls are incredibly powerful. They have a more consistent and flexible object model than the ASP object model that is familiar to classic Visual Basic programmers. When a control is served to the client, it is rendered in HTML automatically. Server controls contain automatic browser detection logic and can customize and optimize their output. The new controls can also perform data binding.

In addition to the HTML server controls and the Web Forms server controls, we also have new validation controls. Field validation has always been the bane of ASP developers. Addressing the problem required a few more acres of code, but that's no longer the case. The validation controls are wired to a control such as a text box, and they take care of our needs, such as constraints on numeric-only or required fields.

Let's go ahead and add controls from the Web Forms tab to our designer. Add a text box, a calendar, a button, and a RequiredFieldValidator. Position the controls roughly as shown in Figure 13-6.

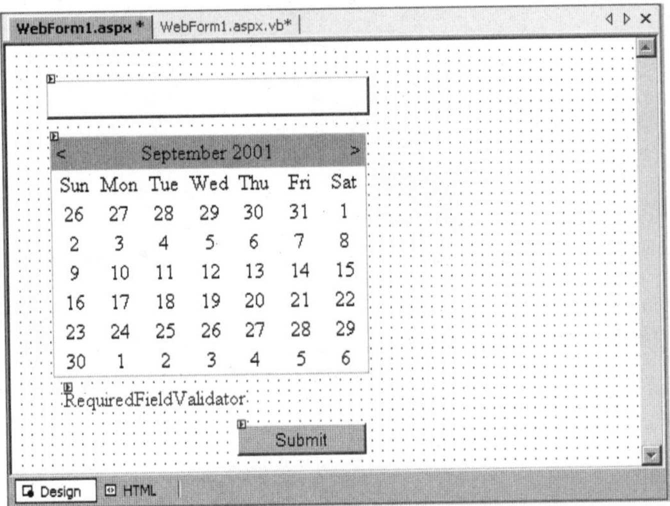

Figure 13-6 Add the controls shown here.

The HTML Presentation Template

Notice the Design and HTML options at the bottom of the designer window. A Web Form consists of two pieces: an HTML-based template that contains the layout of the page, and a code module that contains the code behind the page. Click the HTML tab to see the following code that will be sent to a browser. The code will look familiar to those of you who have worked with ASP. You really don't need to know how to read HTML, but this code provides insight into how Web Forms do their magic.

```
<%@ Page Language="vb" AutoEventWireup="false"
  Codebehind="WebForm1.aspx.vb" Inherits="WebForms.WebForm1"%>
<!DOCTYPE HTML PUBLIC "-//W3C//DTD HTML 4.0 Transitional//EN">
<HTML>
  <HEAD>
    <title></title>
    <meta name="GENERATOR" content=
      "Microsoft Visual Studio.NET 7.0">
    <meta name="CODE_LANGUAGE" content="Visual Basic 7.0">
    <meta name="vs_defaultClientScript" content="JavaScript">
    <meta name="vs_targetSchema"
      content="http://schemas.microsoft.com/intellisense/ie5">
  </HEAD>
  <body MS_POSITIONING="GridLayout">
```

(continued)

```
    <form id="Form1" method="post" runat="server">
      <asp:TextBox id="TextBox1" style="Z-INDEX: 101;
        LEFT: 32px; POSITION: absolute; TOP: 27px"
        runat="server" Width="233px"></asp:TextBox>
      <asp:Calendar id="Calendar1" style="Z-INDEX: 102;
        LEFT: 35px; POSITION: absolute; TOP: 61px"
        runat="server" Width="233px"></asp:Calendar>
      <asp:RequiredFieldValidator id="RequiredFieldValidator1"
        style="Z-INDEX: 103; LEFT: 44px; POSITION: absolute;
        TOP: 263px" runat="server"
        ErrorMessage="RequiredFieldValidator">
      </asp:RequiredFieldValidator>
      <asp:Button id="Button1" style="Z-INDEX: 104;
        LEFT: 150px; POSITION: absolute; TOP: 295px"
        runat="server" Width="112px" Text="Submit"></asp:Button>
    </form>
  </body>
</HTML>
```

The Structure of a Web Form

Visual Basic .NET Web Forms are based on a Microsoft ASP.NET technology in which code that runs on the server dynamically generates Web page output to the client browser. Take a look at the first line with the *@Page* directive.

```
<%@ Page Language="vb" AutoEventWireup="false"
  Codebehind="WebForm1.aspx.vb" Inherits="WebForms.WebForm1"%>
```

Web Forms pages are built on the ASP.NET Page framework, which means that each Web Forms page is an object that derives from the ASP.NET *Page* class. *Page* objects are compiled and automatically cached.

A *Page* object also acts as a container for the various controls. When a user requests a Web Forms page from a server, the Page framework runs the Web Forms *Page* object and all the individual controls on it. It then converts the output of the *Page* class and of the controls to HTML that can be rendered in a browser. In addition, the Page framework supports controls that can be programmed for user interaction with your Web Forms pages. User actions in a form are captured and processed by the Page framework in a way that lets you treat them as standard events.

The *@Page* directive tag also defines characteristics of the page. First of all, the directive indicates that the language will be Visual Basic (instead of C#, for example). *AutoEventWireUp* determines whether the *Page_Load* event handler is automatically wired to the *OnPageLoad* event. Setting the value to False means that we need to provide our own code for this handler if required.

The next statement is the rather cryptic *Codebehind = "WebForm.aspx.vb"*. This statement is necessary because the code that drives the page is actually placed in another file. This file is the code behind the interface defined in WebForm1.aspx. I'll examine that file in detail shortly, but briefly, it contains a class definition that is used as the base class for the Web Forms page. This particular base class will be used in conjunction with code in this file to generate the HTML that reaches the user. Web Forms essentially separate the user interface (WebForm.aspx) from the code that implements it (WebForm.aspx.vb). The Web Forms Page framework and the relationships between these files are shown in Figure 13-7.

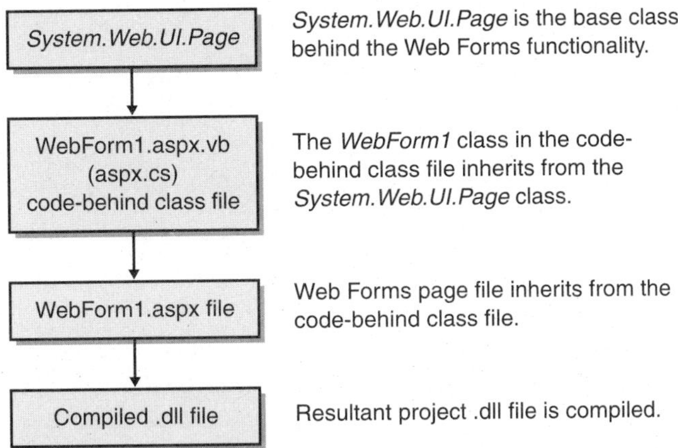
System.Web.UI.Page
System.Web.UI.Page is the base class behind the Web Forms functionality.
WebForm1.aspx.vb (aspx.cs) code-behind class file
The WebForm1 class in the code-behind class file inherits from the System.Web.UI.Page class.
WebForm1.aspx file
Web Forms page file inherits from the code-behind class file.
Compiled .dll file
Resultant project .dll file is compiled.

Figure 13-7 The relationships between the Web Forms Page framework files.

Within the ASP.NET *Page* class model, the entire Web Forms page is really an executable program that generates output that is then sent to the browser. The ASP.NET *Page* class model makes developing a Web Forms application identical to developing a Windows Forms application, and it is a quantum leap in functionality for ASP developers. Separating our class, WebForm1.aspx.vb, as the code-behind file is not only easier to debug (trust me on this one), but you can now let the designers work on the user interface for a Web page while the programmers work on the code behind it all.

Our code-behind class *WebForm1* inherits from the *Page* class that lives in the *System.Web.UI* namespace. The *Page* class contains the properties, methods, and events in the Web Forms page framework.

```
Public Class WebForm1
    Inherits System.Web.UI.Page
```

Our user interface file, WebForm1.aspx, inherits from the code-behind class.

```
<%@ Page Language="vb" AutoEventWireup="false"
  Codebehind="WebForm1.aspx.vb" Inherits="WebForms.WebForm1"%>
```

Both files are then compiled into a DLL that is run from the server.

The Controls

Web Forms server controls are referenced with the syntax *<asp:ControlName>*. All of the properties of the control are set within the *<asp:ControlName ....>* and *</asp:ControlName>* tags. The calendar control is given an ID of Calendar1, the default name of the calendar when it's drawn on the form. Then some style and location properties are set. Finally the critical *runat="server"* attribute is provided, which makes all of this code work.

```
<asp:Calendar id="Calendar1" style="Z-INDEX: 102;
  LEFT: 35px; POSITION: absolute; TOP: 61px"
  runat="server" Width="233px"></asp:Calendar>
```

If the *runat="server"* attribute is left out, we are effectively providing client-side code, which will fail miserably if the control uses any server-side style coding. Note that the syntax for controls is based on XML, so you'll get an error if you inadvertently omit the closing tags.

The beauty of Web Forms server controls is that we have full access to their properties and events through the Properties window (just as we do with their Windows Forms brethren) and can receive instant feedback in the code or design environment whenever we make changes.

Viewing the Code-Behind File

Return to Design mode and choose Code from the View menu to display the code-behind file, WebForm1.aspx.vb. This file is where the Visual Basic .NET code we use to handle the logic for the page lives. By now you should be quite familiar with this code, so I won't spend time on it here.

```
Public Class WebForm1
    Inherits System.Web.UI.Page
    Protected WithEvents Calendar1 As _
        System.Web.UI.WebControls.Calendar
    Protected WithEvents TextBox1 As _
        System.Web.UI.WebControls.TextBox
    Protected WithEvents Button1 As _
        System.Web.UI.WebControls.Button
    Protected WithEvents RequiredFieldValidator1 As _
        System.Web.UI.WebControls.RequiredFieldValidator

#Region " Web Form Designer Generated Code "

    'This call is required by the Web Form Designer
```

```
    <System.Diagnostics.DebuggerStepThrough()> _
    Private Sub InitializeComponent()

    End Sub

    Private Sub Page_Init(ByVal sender As System.Object, _
        ByVal e As System.EventArgs) Handles MyBase.Init
        'CODEGEN: This method call is required by the
        ' Web Form Designer.
        'Do not modify it using the code editor.
        InitializeComponent()
    End Sub

#End Region

    Private Sub Page_Load(ByVal sender As System.Object, _
        ByVal e As System.EventArgs) Handles MyBase.Load
        'Put user code to initialize the page here
    End Sub
End Class
```

Setting the Properties on Our Web Page

Return to the design WebForm1.aspx form, and right-click the calendar control. Select Auto Format to bring up the Calendar Auto Format dialog box, shown in Figure 13-8. Select the Professional 1 scheme, and then click OK. Setting this property will make our page look pretty sophisticated.

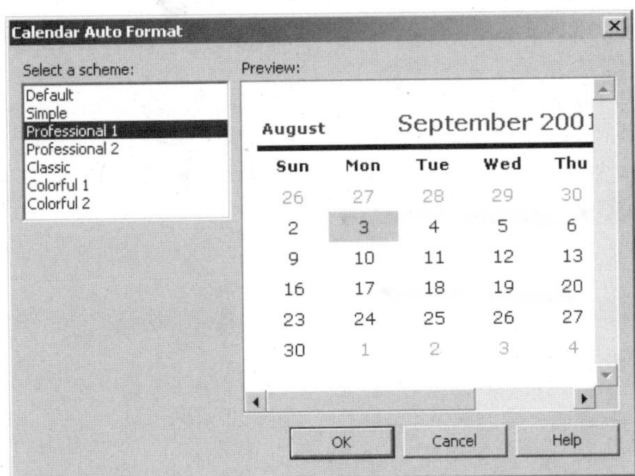

Figure 13-8 The Professional 1 scheme provides a sophisticated look for a Web page.

Arrange the controls as shown in Figure 13-9, and then set the properties for the controls as listed in Table 13-2.

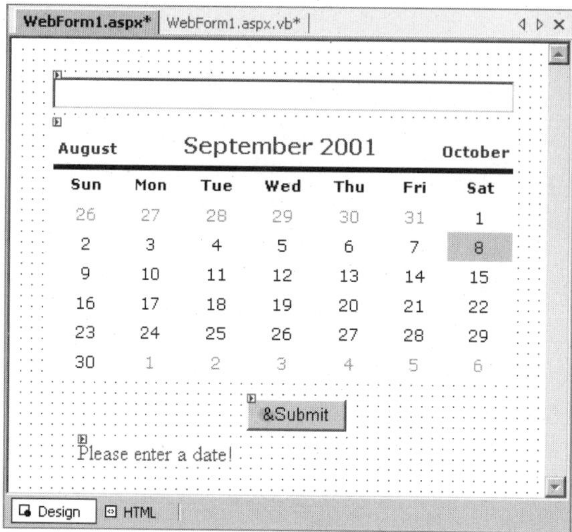

Figure 13-9 Arrange the controls as shown here.

Table 13-2 Properties for the WebForm Controls

Object	Property	Value
Text box	*ID* (like *Name* in Windows)	tbDate
Calendar	Keep defaults	
Button	*ID*	btnSubmit
	Text	&Submit
RequiredFieldValidator1	*ControlToValidate*	tbDate (from the drop-down list)
	ErrorMessage	"Please enter a date!"

Adding the Calendar Control Code

Double-click the calendar control. The template for the *SelectionChanged* event handler will be created automatically. Add a single line of code that will take the date the user selects and display it in the text box. Notice that several built-in formats are available for us. In this example, we'll use the *ToLongDateString* format.

```
Private Sub Calendar1_SelectionChanged( _
    ByVal sender As System.Object,_
    ByVal e As System.EventArgs) _
    Handles Calendar1.SelectionChanged

    tbDate.Text = Calendar1.SelectedDate.ToLongDateString

End Sub
```

Running the Web Form

Go ahead and run the Web Form by pressing F5. The browser is invoked, and your page is displayed, as you can see in Figure 13-10. Click the Submit button without selecting a date. Notice that the RequiredFieldValidator becomes visible and displays our error message. No code was required to accomplish this, which will make any grizzled ASP programmer smile. We were able to display this page—with a sophisticated calendar, text box, button, and field validation control—with only a single line of code. This is nothing short of amazing.

Figure 13-10 The WebForms application in action.

When the Submit button is clicked, the date is submitted back to the server. By default, a button control on a Web Form application is a submit button that posts data back to the server. You can provide an event handler for the *Click* event to programmatically control the actions performed when a submit button is clicked. In our case, we didn't write any code for the button. Still, when it is pressed, it attempts to post data back to the server. It couldn't here because the required field *tbDate* is empty.

Now select a date from the calendar, and click the Submit button once more. This time we are successful. The date is displayed in the text box in the long date format, as you can see in Figure 13-11.

Figure 13-11 The text box shows dates in the long date format.

Examining the HTML Sent to the Browser

Run the WebForms application again, but before you select a date, click the View Source menu option from Internet Explorer. I mentioned that ASP.NET pages and controls can remember their state between calls to the server. Let's see how this magic is accomplished. Examine the first few lines of the HTML our program sent to the browser.

```
<!DOCTYPE HTML PUBLIC "-//W3C//DTD HTML 4.0 Transitional//EN">
<HTML>
  <HEAD>
    <title></title>
      <meta name="GENERATOR" content="Microsoft Visual
        Studio.NET 7.0">
      <meta name="CODE_LANGUAGE" content="Visual Basic 7.0">
      <meta name="vs_defaultClientScript"
        content="JavaScript">
      <meta name="vs_targetSchema"
        content="http://schemas.microsoft.com/intellisense/ie5">
  </HEAD>
  <body MS_POSITIONING="GridLayout">
    <form name="Form1" method="post" action="WebForm1.aspx"
      language="javascript" onsubmit="ValidatorOnSubmit();"
      id="Form1">
<input type="hidden" name="__VIEWSTATE" value="dDwtMzQ0NzE0MzI4Ozs" />
```

Notice the text string in the hidden input field with the name *_VIEWSTATE*. It is the hidden *_VIEWSTATE* field that encapsulates the state of the form. This information is used when the form is posted back to the server to re-create the user interface, keep track of changes, and so on. Essentially it holds the state of the form and controls.

Click a date on the calendar, and examine the source code from the browser again. Notice that the *_VIEWSTATE* string has grown quite a bit. It contains the selected date, changes to the calendar, and other information. As you can imagine, on sophisticated Web forms, this string can grow quite large.

```
<input type="hidden" name="__VIEWSTATE" value="dDwtMzQ0NzE0M
zI403Q802w8aTwxPjs+02w8dDw7bDxpPDM+0z47bDx0PEAwPHA8cDxsPFNE0
z47bDxsPFN5c3RlbS5EYXRlVGltZSwgbXNjb3JsaWIsIFZlcnNpb249MS4wL
jI0MTEuMCwgQ3VsdHVyZT1uZXV0cmFsLCBQdWJsaWNLZXlUb2tlbjl1NzdhN
WM1NjE5MzRlMDg5PDIwMDEtMDktMjY+0z47Pj47Pjs70zs70zs70zs+0zs+0
z4+0z4+0z4=" />
```

The *_VIEWSTATE* string will remember the form's state and thus any values that have been submitted. It's important to keep in mind that the server has nothing to do with maintaining this state information. Remembering the values is performed entirely by the *_VIEWSTATE* string. The server requires no resources to maintain the form's state and absolutely no state is being stored on the server. Instead, the values are posted to the server using standard methods. When the server posts back to the page, the *_VIEWSTATE* string prepopulates the form with the previous values.

The *_VIEWSTATE* string is an elegant method of storing a Web page's state. Because HTTP is a stateless protocol, Web pages are created from scratch each and every time a round trip between the server and the client occurs. After a Web page is served, the server is finished with the page and no further connection with the client is maintained. Web pages are stateless, and no values from Web page variables are maintained on the server. Not only that, but also in a Web server environment in which a user might get one page from one server and the next page from a totally different server (because of load balancing), using *_VIEWSTATE* permits the page to hold its own state. ASP.NET gets around this serious limitation and behaves as though the server remembers each and every detail of each page.

The Web Form state information is tokenized, which means it is translated into a compressed form. And because HTTP does not permit binary objects to be sent, the tokens are all text based. Preliminary tests at Microsoft have revealed that even with very long *_VIEWSTATE* strings, performance is comparable to other more complex state management techniques.

> **Note** ASP.NET does not support Visual Basic Scripting Edition. The default language is Visual Basic. ASP.NET code is compiled into intermediate language and then executed by the common language runtime.

If you look at the rest of the source code that's sent to the browser, you'll notice that each of our Web Forms controls is converted to HTML for display in the browser. We drew the text box on the Web Form, but the ASP.NET run-time engine did all the coding for us.

```
<input name="tbDate" type="text" readonly="readonly"
  id="tbDate" style="border-style:Outset;height:26px;
  width:350px;LEFT: 38px; POSITION: absolute; TOP: 34px" />
```

For the sake of brevity, I'll show only a portion of the HTML used to generate the calendar. We are several levels of abstraction removed from having to provide all this code ourselves. We can now program a consistent object model of a graphical control, yet the ASP.NET run-time engine will take our graphical calendar control and convert it to HTML 3.2 to ensure that it can be consistently displayed on even older browsers. We can draw a calendar control on our Web Form, and that control is converted to HTML for us. Cool.

```
<table id="Calendar1" cellspacing="0" cellpadding="2"
  bordercolor="White" border="0" style="color:Black;
  background-color:White;border-color:White;border-width:1px;
  border-style:solid;font-family:Verdana;font-size:9pt;
  height:190px;width:350px;border-collapse:collapse;LEFT: 34px;
  POSITION: absolute; TOP: 72px">
<tr><td colspan="7" style="background-color:White;
  border-color:Black;border-width:4px;border-style:solid;">
  <table cellspacing="0" border="0" style="color:#333399;
  font-family:Verdana;font-size:12pt;font-weight:bold;
  width:100%;border-collapse:collapse;">
    <tr><td valign="Bottom" style="color:#333333;font-size:8pt;
      font-weight:bold;width:15%;">
```

Building a Loan Payment Calculator

Where I work, we've built a Web-based loan origination system. Clients can enter various parameters and see which loan products they qualify for. Then we pass some XML files to Fannie Mae for credit analysis and receive our response in XML. This data is parsed, and an e-mail message is sent back to the client. We then use Simple Object Access Protocol (SOAP) to pass e-mail messages around to the various internal departments. This system reduces the time it takes to return an acknowledgment to the user from days to a few minutes. Best of all, this system is available 24 hours a day, 7 days a week.

Let's build a very simple online calculator that includes user interaction. The program will let users enter the amount they want to borrow, an interest rate, and the term (in months) over which they want to repay the loan. The finished product is shown in Figure 13-12.

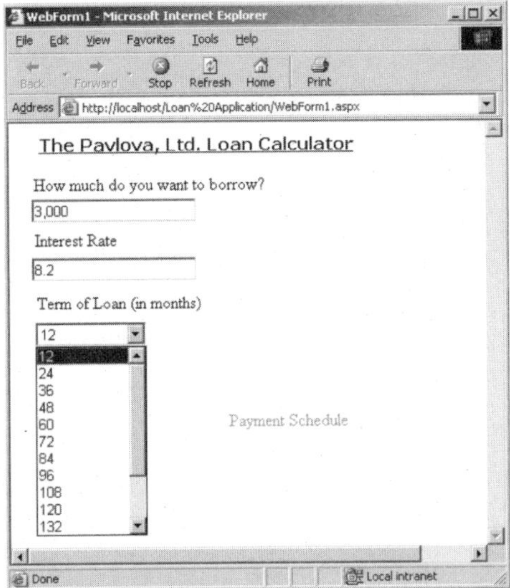

Figure 13-12 The finished online calculator application.

We will have to write some validation code to ensure the information the user enters is valid. We will also add a hyperlink control to enable navigation to another page, one that displays the loan payment schedule. The hyperlink will be disabled until legitimate information is entered and a monthly payment is calculated. When the user clicks the Calculate button and the payment is calculated, the Payment Schedule hyperlink is enabled and the user can navigate to another page, as shown in Figure 13-13.

Notice in Figure 13-14 that on the loan schedule page, the values from the first page are retained and are used to populate a Web Forms data grid. We can show some useful information such as how much of the payment goes to principal and how much to interest. The PrincipalRemaining and PaidToDate columns provide a good roadmap of how much of the loan is left to be paid. We will build a table from scratch, populate it with the loan information, and bind it to the data grid. This program will also demonstrate how to navigate from page to page as well as how to cache variables from one page to use on another.

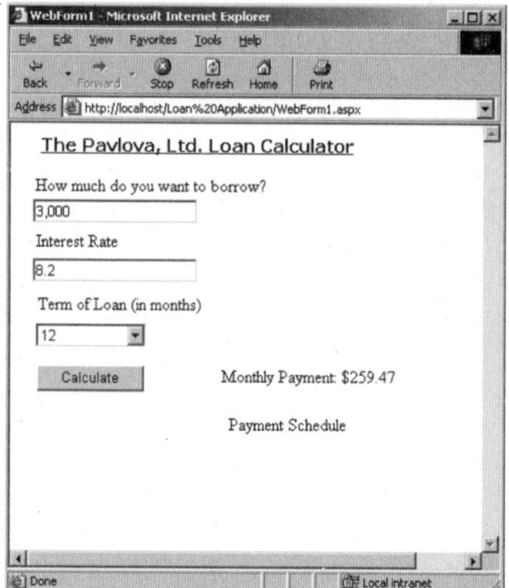

Figure 13-13 The calculator application enables the Payment Schedule hyperlink after it calculates a payment.

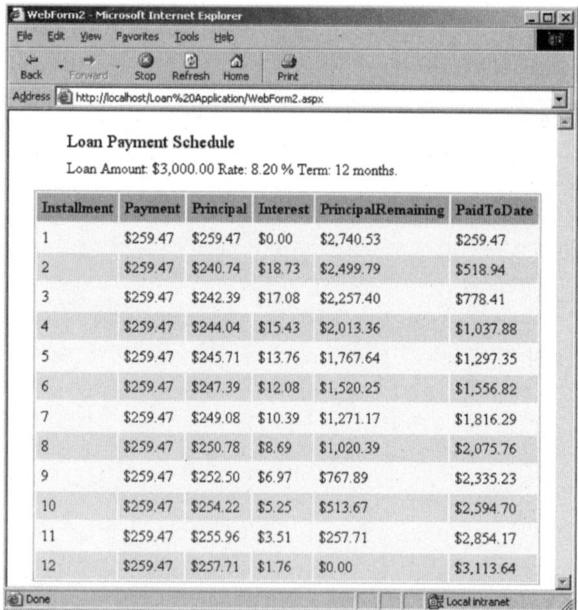

Installment	Payment	Principal	Interest	PrincipalRemaining	PaidToDate
1	$259.47	$259.47	$0.00	$2,740.53	$259.47
2	$259.47	$240.74	$18.73	$2,499.79	$518.94
3	$259.47	$242.39	$17.08	$2,257.40	$778.41
4	$259.47	$244.04	$15.43	$2,013.36	$1,037.88
5	$259.47	$245.71	$13.76	$1,767.64	$1,297.35
6	$259.47	$247.39	$12.08	$1,520.25	$1,556.82
7	$259.47	$249.08	$10.39	$1,271.17	$1,816.29
8	$259.47	$250.78	$8.69	$1,020.39	$2,075.76
9	$259.47	$252.50	$6.97	$767.89	$2,335.23
10	$259.47	$254.22	$5.25	$513.67	$2,594.70
11	$259.47	$255.96	$3.51	$257.71	$2,854.17
12	$259.47	$257.71	$1.76	$0.00	$3,113.64

Figure 13-14 The calculated values populate a Web Forms data grid.

Building Our Loan Application Project

Start a new Web Forms project and call it Loan Application. On the default form, add the controls listed in Table 13-3 and set their properties as described. The form should look something like Figure 13-15.

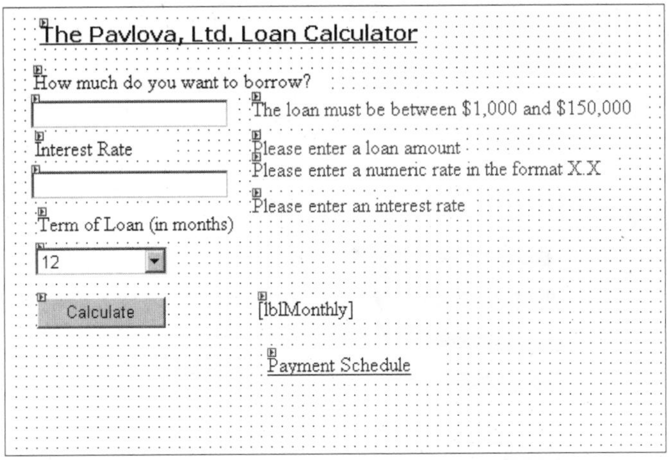

Figure 13-15 Your form should look similar to this.

Table 13-3 Properties for the Loan Application Controls

Object	Property	Value
Label	*Name*	lblTitle
	Font	Verdana
	Bold	True
	Underlined	True
	Text	The Pavlova, Ltd. Loan Calculator
Label	*Name*	lblAmount
	Text	How much do you want to borrow?
Text box	*Name*	tbAmount
	Text	""
Label	*Name*	lblRate
	Text	Interest Rate
Text box	*Name*	tbRate
	Text	""

(continued)

Table 13-3 Properties for the Loan Application Controls *(continued)*

Object	Property	Value
Label	*Name*	lblTerm
	Text	Term of Loan (in months)
Drop-down list	*Name*	ddlTerm
Button	*Name*	btnCalculate
	Text	Calculate
Label	*Name*	lblMonthly
	Text	""
Range validator	*ID*	rvAmount
	ControlToValidate	tbAmount
	MaximumValue	150000
	MinimumValue	1000
	ErrorMessage	The loan must be between $1,000 and $150,000
	Type	Currency
Required field validator	*ID*	rfvAmount
	ControlToValidate	tbAmount
	ErrorMessage	Please enter a loan amount
Regular expression validator	*ID*	revRate
	ControlToValidate	tbRate
	ErrorMessage	Please enter a numeric rate in the format X.X
	ValidationExpression	\d*[.]{0,1}\d*
Required field validator	*ID*	rfvRate
	ControlToValidate	tbRate
	ErrorMessage	Please enter an interest rate
Hyperlink	*ID*	hlSchedule
	Text	Payment Schedule

We want to add the months in which to repay the loan to the drop-down list. Right-click the drop-down list, and then select Properties. Select the Items property box and then click the ellipsis to display the ListItem Collection Editor dialog box. Add the numbers shown in Figure 13-16, representing 15 years—from 12 through 180 months.

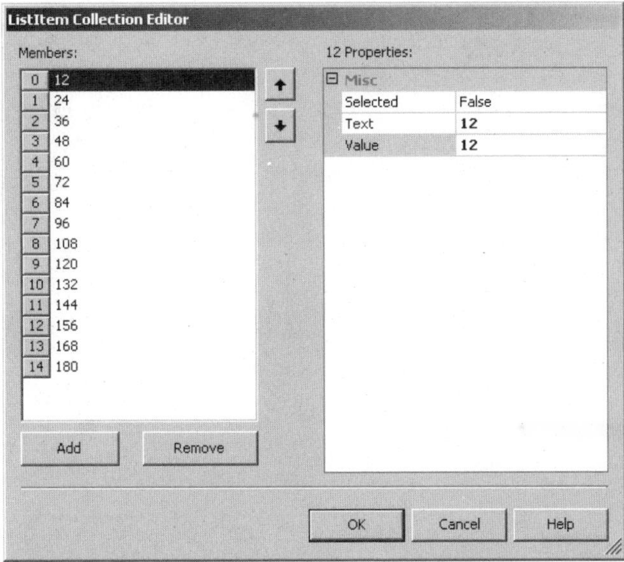

Figure 13-16 Add these values.

Adding Code to the Code-Behind Form

Right-click on the designer surface and select View Code to open the file WebForm1.aspx.vb, which is our code-behind form. Each .aspx Web Form that we create has its associated .aspx.vb code module behind it. This module contains our business logic. The relationship between the two forms is shown in Figure 13-17.

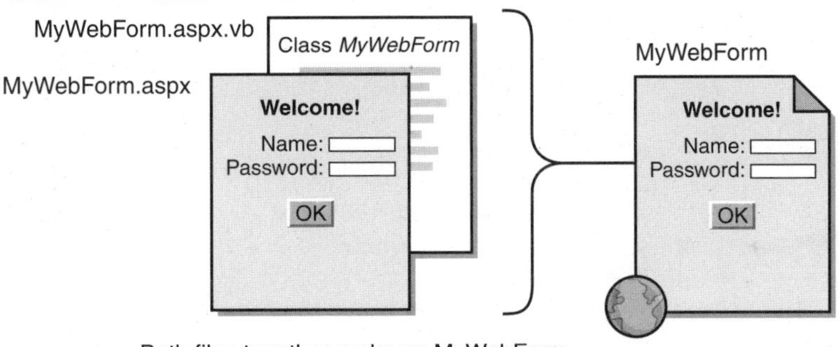

Figure 13-17 The relationship between a Web Form and its code-behind form.

WebForm1.aspx.vb contains the code that responds to events fired from the Web Form. Add these two *Imports* statements before the WebForm1 class statement.

```
Imports System.Math
Imports System.Web.Caching

Public Class WebForm1
    Inherits System.Web.UI.Page
```

Now add the following code to the *Page_Load* event handler. This code simply initializes our drop-down list and disables the hyperlink.

```
Private Sub Page_Load(ByVal sender As System.Object, _
    ByVal e As System.EventArgs) Handles MyBase.Load

    'Put user code to initialize the page here

    If Not IsPostBack Then
        ddlTerm.SelectedIndex = 0
        hlSchedule.Enabled = False
    End If
End Sub

Private Sub btnCalculate_Click(ByVal sender As System.Object, _
    ByVal e As System.EventArgs) Handles btnCalculate.Click

    calculatePayment()
    hlSchedule.Enabled = True
End Sub

Private Sub calculatePayment()
    Dim iLoanAmount As Integer = CInt(tbAmount.Text)
    Dim sRate As Single = (CSng(tbRate.Text) / 100)
    Dim iterm As Integer = CInt(ddlTerm.SelectedItem.Value)

    Dim sPayment As Single = Pmt(sRate / 12, iterm, _
        -iLoanAmount, 0, DueDate.BegOfPeriod)

    lblMonthly.Text = "Monthly Payment: " & _
        Math.Round(sPayment, 2).ToString("C")

    Cache("LoanAmount") = iLoanAmount
    Cache("Rate") = sRate
    Cache("Term") = iterm
    Cache("Payment") = Math.Round(sPayment, 2)
End Sub
```

The Life of a Web Form

A Web Form has four basic states in its life cycle—initialization, loading the page, event handling, and clearing up resources.

- **Page initialization.** The *Page_Init* event is fired when a page is initialized. At this point, controls perform all initialization required to create and set up each instance.
- **Page load.** The *Page_Load* event occurs after initialization. Here the page checks to see whether it is being loaded for the first time. It also performs data binding, reads and updates control properties, and restores the state saved from a previous client request.
- **Event handling.** Every action on a Web Form fires an event that goes to the server. Essentially there are two views of a Web Form—client view and server view. All processing of data is performed on the server. When an event is fired, the event goes to the server and returns the corresponding data.
- **Cleanup.** This stage is the last one to occur when a form is ready to be discarded. The *Page_Unload* event fires and does such cleanup work as closing files, closing database connections, and discarding objects.

How Our Program Works

When the *Page_Load* event fires, all the controls have been instantiated. There are tasks (such as initializing controls) that we want to perform only when the page first loads. Using the *Page* class's *IsPostBack* property, we can do just that. *IsPostBack* gets a value indicating whether the page is being loaded in response to a client postback or whether it is being loaded and accessed for the first time. If the page load is not in response to a client postback, we know that the page is being loaded for the first time. Here we simply select the first item in our drop-down list (so that we have a current value) and disable the hyperlink control.

```
Private Sub Page_Load(ByVal sender As System.Object, _
    ByVal e As System.EventArgs) Handles MyBase.Load

    'Put user code to initialize the page here

    If Not IsPostBack Then
        ddlTerm.SelectedIndex = 0
        hlSchedule.Enabled = False
    End If
End Sub
```

When the user clicks the Calculate button, our validation controls perk up their ears. If any field is empty or contains an invalid value, the user is prompted to fix whatever is wrong and the code in the button's *Click* event does not fire. When all the validation criteria are met, the routine *calculatePayment* is called. We know that when this routine is called, we will receive a solid value because we validated each of the fields.

I like to use controls such as drop-down lists with predefined values. The man-machine interface is the most difficult to program because users can do anything imaginable—and many things unimaginable. But by populating a drop-down list with valid data, users can select only a valid value.

```
Private Sub btnCalculate_Click(ByVal sender As System.Object, _
    ByVal e As System.EventArgs) Handles btnCalculate.Click

        calculatePayment()
        hlSchedule.Enabled = True
End Sub
```

The *calculatePayment* routine does the heavy lifting. We can initialize the first three variables based on values in the form's controls. Remember, these variables are stored as text values, so we simply cast them as the correct numeric values of integer or single. The rate must be divided by 100 because a rate of 8.2 is really 0.082 when used in calculations.

```
Private Sub calculatePayment()
    Dim iLoanAmount As Integer = CInt(tbAmount.Text)
    Dim sRate As Single = (CSng(tbRate.Text) / 100)
    Dim iterm As Integer = CInt(ddlTerm.SelectedItem.Value)
```

Determining the payment is simple because Visual Basic .NET has a built-in financial function named *Pmt*. This function returns a *Double* value (we use a *Single* in our code) specifying the payment for an annuity on the basis of periodic, fixed payments and a fixed interest rate. We pass in the value of the variables taken from the Web Form and place them as parameters to the *Pmt* function. The loan amount is given a negative sign because it returns a negative amount, so we make it positive. There is no future value so that value is 0.

```
PMT(RATE, Number of Periods, Loan Amount, _
    Future Value, Due Date)
```

We again take advantage of the new Visual Basic .NET feature of dimming and initializing this variable on the same line.

```
Dim sPayment As Single = Pmt(sRate / 12, iterm, _
    -iLoanAmount, 0, DueDate.BegOfPeriod)
```

We imported the Math library because we wanted the *Round* method that it includes. This method will display our value with only two decimal values instead of 10, which would normally be shown. Rounding values like this is an added touch that separates professional software from the rest.

```
lblMonthly.Text = "Monthly Payment: " & _
    Math.Round(sPayment, 2).ToString("C")
```

It's necessary to retain the values we got from this form and pass them to another form that will display the payment schedule. That bit of work is simple with the *Cache* class, which implements the cache for a Web Forms application. One instance of this class is created per application domain, and it remains valid as long as the application domain remains active. As long as our program is running, its *Cache* object remains intact. We simply add to the *Cache* with the following syntax:

```
Cache("Key") = value
```

Here's the relevant code from our program:

```
Cache("LoanAmount") = iLoanAmount
Cache("Rate") = sRate
Cache("Term") = iterm
Cache("Payment") = Math.Round(sPayment, 2)
```

You can improve your application's performance by storing your objects and values in the cache. The cache is global to the ASP.NET application, is thread safe, and implements automatic locking so that it is safe for you to access your cached objects and values concurrently from more than one page.

Taking a Closer Look at Our Drop-Down List

Take a look at the HTML code behind our WebForm1.aspx file by clicking HTML in the lower left side of the designer. You can see that the drop-down list control has the *asp:* directive along with various attributes that deal with its size and position.

```
<asp:dropdownlist id="ddlTerm" style="Z-INDEX: 107;
  LEFT: 24px; POSITION: absolute; TOP: 188px"
  runat="server" Height="22px" Width="104px">
    <asp:ListItem Value="12">12</asp:ListItem>
    <asp:ListItem Value="24">24</asp:ListItem>
    <asp:ListItem Value="36">36</asp:ListItem>
    <asp:ListItem Value="48">48</asp:ListItem>
    ⋮
</asp:dropdownlist>
```

Remember that when the form is run, we programmatically select the first element in the drop-down list to ensure that we have a valid value. If you look at the HTML source within the browser as your page is displayed, you can see that the item is selected in the HTML code.

```
<option selected="selected" value="12">12</option>
<option value="24">24</option>
<option value="36">36</option>
<option value="48">48</option>
```

Then, when the user selects a value from the drop-down list and clicks the Calculate button and a postback occurs, the code is changed to show that the user selected a new value.

```
<option value="12">12</option>
<option value="24">24</option>
<option value="36">36</option>
<option value="48">48</option>
<option selected="selected" value="60">60</option>
<option value="72">72</option>
```

Adding the Payment Schedule Page

Now it's time to add another Web Form to our program. This page will hold the payment schedule. After we have this page set up, we can set the hyperlink property for our control on the input page so that it will navigate to the payment schedule page. Click Project | Add Web Form, select the Web Form template, and keep the default name WebForm2.aspx, as shown in Figure 13-18.

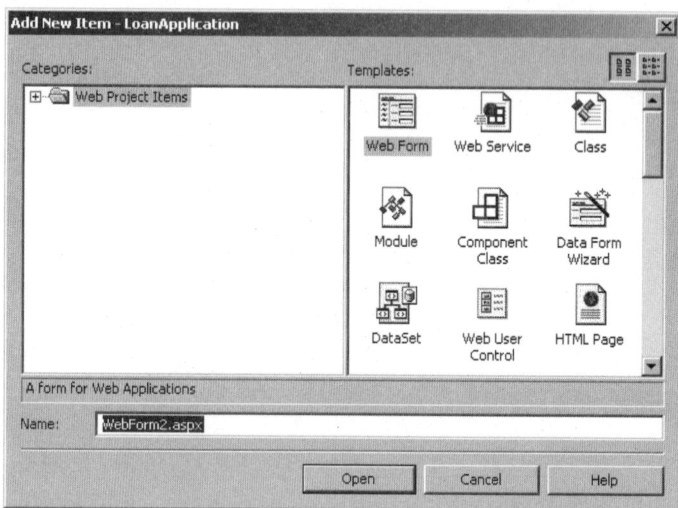

Figure 13-18 Add another Web Form to the program.

Return to the WebForm1 main page to complete our remaining task—assigning the *NavigateURL* property of our hyperlink control. Right-click on the control and select Properties. Click the ellipsis next to NavigateURL to display the Select URL dialog box, shown in Figure 13-19. Select WebForm2.aspx.

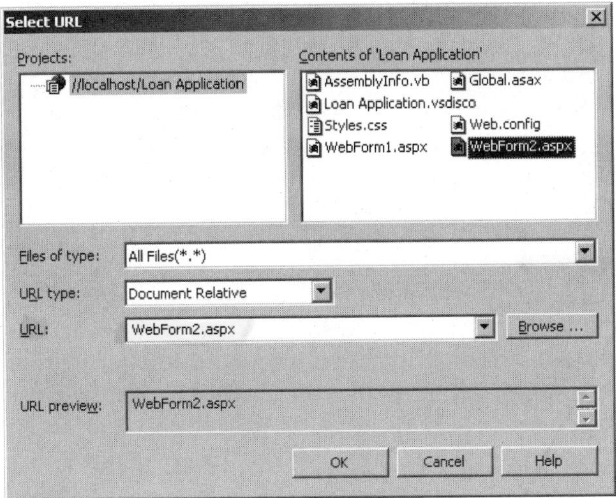

Figure 13-19 Select WebForm2.aspx in the Select URL dialog box.

Return to the payment schedule form (WebForm2.aspx), and add two labels and a data grid. We want to change the default look of the form to something a bit more interesting. Right-click on the data grid, and select Auto Format. Select the Colorful 5 scheme. Our form is shown in Figure 13-20.

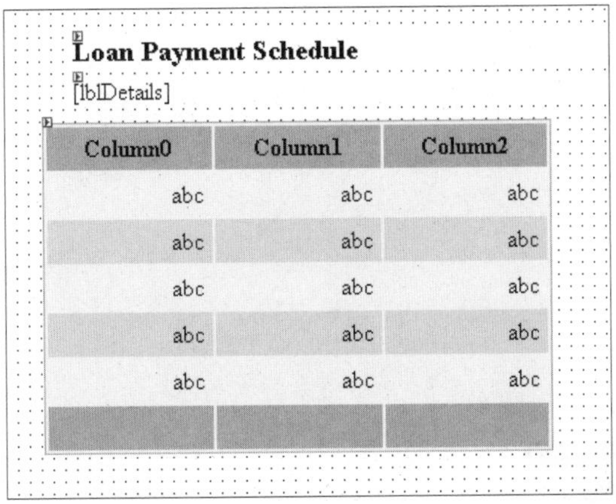

Figure 13-20 Add two labels and a data grid.

Set the properties of the labels and data grid as shown in Table 13-4.

Table 13-4 Properties for the WebForm2.aspx Controls

Object	Property	Value
Label	*ID*	lblTitle
	Font/Size	Larger
	Text	Loan Payment Schedule
Label	*ID*	lblDetails
	Text	""
Data grid	*ID*	dgSchedule
	CellPadding	5
	CellSpacing	2

Right-click on the designer, and then select View Code. The second code-behind form, this one named WebForm2.aspx.vb, is added to your project.

Adding Our Class Code

Add the following two *Imports* statements at the top of the class:

```
Imports Loan_Application.WebForm1

Imports System.Web.Caching

Public Class WebForm2
    Inherits System.Web.UI.Page
    Protected WithEvents dgSchedule As _
        System.Web.UI.WebControls.DataGrid
    Protected WithEvents lblTitle As _
        System.Web.UI.WebControls.Label
    Protected WithEvents lblDetails As _
        System.Web.UI.WebControls.Label
```

After the class and control definitions, add the following variables and routines. We will be using some of these variables in more than one location, so place them in the class-level area so that they can be seen throughout the entire class.

```
Dim dsSchedule As DataSet
Dim tblTable As DataTable
Dim iLoanAmount As Integer
Dim sRate As Single
Dim iTerm As Integer
Dim sPayment As Single
```

```
Dim colColumn1 As DataColumn
Dim colColumn2 As DataColumn
Dim colColumn3 As DataColumn
Dim colColumn4 As DataColumn
Dim colColumn5 As DataColumn
Dim colColumn6 As DataColumn


Private Sub Page_Load(ByVal sender As System.Object, _
    ByVal e As System.EventArgs) Handles MyBase.Load
    'Put user code to initialize the page here

    iLoanAmount = Cache("LoanAmount")
    sRate = Cache("Rate")
    iTerm = Cache("Term")
    sPayment = Cache("Payment")
    lblDetails.Text = "Loan Amount: " & _
        iLoanAmount.ToString("C") & "    Rate:  " & _
        sRate.ToString("P") & "    Term:  " & _
        iTerm.ToString & " months."
    'Build the dataset and table
    constructTable()
    calculateSchedule()
End Sub

Private Sub calculateSchedule()

    Dim iInstallment As Integer
    Dim drDataRow As DataRow
    Dim sPrincipal As Single
    Dim sPaidToDate As Single = 0
    Dim sTotalPrincipal As Single = iLoanAmount

    For iInstallment = 1 To iTerm
        drDataRow = dsSchedule.Tables("Schedule").NewRow
        dsSchedule.Tables("Schedule").Rows.Add(drDataRow)
        drDataRow("Installment") = iInstallment
        drDataRow("Payment") = sPayment.ToString("C")

        sPrincipal = PPmt(sRate / 12, iInstallment, iTerm, _
            -iLoanAmount, 0, DueDate.BegOfPeriod)
        drDataRow("Principal") = Math.Round(sPrincipal, _
            2).ToString("C")

        drDataRow("Interest") = (sPayment - _
            sPrincipal).ToString("C")

        sTotalPrincipal -= sPrincipal
```

(continued)

```
            drRataRow("PrincipalRemaining") = _
                sTotalPrincipal.ToString("C")

            sPaidToDate += sPayment
            drDataRow("PaidToDate") = sPaidToDate.ToString("C")

            dsSchedule.AcceptChanges()
        Next

        With dgSchedule
            .PageSize = iTerm
            .DataSource = _
                New DataView(dsSchedule.Tables("Schedule"))
            .DataBind()
        End With
    End Sub

    Private Sub constructTable()
        'Instantiate the dataset and table
        dsSchedule = New DataSet("PaymentSchedule")
        tblTable = New DataTable("Schedule")
        dsSchedule.Tables.Add(tblTable)

        colColumn1 = New DataColumn("Installment")
        colColumn1.DataType = System.Type.GetType("System.Int32")

        colColumn2 = New DataColumn("Payment")
        colColumn2.DataType = System.Type.GetType("System.String")

        colColumn3 = New DataColumn("Principal")
        colColumn3.DataType = System.Type.GetType("System.String")

        colColumn4 = New DataColumn("Interest")
        colColumn4.DataType = System.Type.GetType("System.String")

        colColumn5 = New DataColumn("PrincipalRemaining")
        colColumn5.DataType = System.Type.GetType("System.String")

        colColumn6 = New DataColumn("PaidToDate")
        colColumn6.DataType = System.Type.GetType("System.String")

        With tblTable.Columns
            .Add(colColumn1)
            .Add(colColumn2)
            .Add(colColumn3)
            .Add(colColumn4)
            .Add(colColumn5)
            .Add(colColumn6)
        End With

    End Sub
```

How the Calculator Works

When the page loads, we read the values we stuffed in the cache and assign them to our class-level variables. The details of the loan are displayed in the lbl-Details label. Note that we can use the formatting method of the *ToString* method to quickly and painlessly format our output.

```
Private Sub Page_Load(ByVal sender As System.Object, _
    ByVal e As System.EventArgs) Handles MyBase.Load
    'Put user code to initialize the page here

    iLoanAmount = Cache("LoanAmount")
    sRate = Cache("Rate")
    iTerm = Cache("Term")
    sPayment = Cache("Payment")
    lblDetails.Text = "Loan Amount: " & _
        iLoanAmount.ToString("C") & "    Rate:  " & _
        sRate.ToString("P") & "    Term:  " & _
        iTerm.ToString & " months."
    'Build the dataset and table
    constructTable()
    calculateSchedule()
End Sub
```

In our *constructTable* routine, a *DataSet* object and table are instantiated. The table is then added to the new data set. Six columns are created and given names that will be shown as the column titles. The first column will hold an integer because this column will display the payment number. However, we want to format the rest of the fields and display them as currency, so they are all made to hold the *String* data type. Finally, each of the six columns are added to the table columns collection.

```
Private Sub constructTable()
    'Instantiate the dataset and table
    dsSchedule = New DataSet("PaymentSchedule")
    tblTable = New DataTable("Schedule")
    dsSchedule.Tables.Add(tblTable)

    colColumn1 = New DataColumn("Installment")
    colColumn1.DataType = System.Type.GetType("System.Int32")

    colColumn2 = New DataColumn("Payment")
    colColumn2.DataType = System.Type.GetType("System.String")

    colColumn3 = New DataColumn("Principal")
    colColumn3.DataType = System.Type.GetType("System.String")

    colColumn4 = New DataColumn("Interest")
    colColumn4.DataType = System.Type.GetType("System.String")
```

(continued)

```
    colColumn5 = New DataColumn("PrincipalRemaining")
    colColumn5.DataType = System.Type.GetType("System.String")

    colColumn6 = New DataColumn("PaidToDate")
    colColumn6.DataType = System.Type.GetType("System.String")

    With tblTable.Columns
        .Add(colColumn1)
        .Add(colColumn2)
        .Add(colColumn3)
        .Add(colColumn4)
        .Add(colColumn5)
        .Add(colColumn6)
    End With
End Sub
```

Now that the table has been dynamically created and added to the data set, it can be populated. The procedure-level variables are dimmed—no surprises here.

```
Private Sub calculateSchedule()

    Dim iInstallment As Integer
    Dim drDataRow As DataRow
    Dim sPrincipal As Single
    Dim sPaidToDate As Single = 0
    Dim sTotalPrincipal As Single = iLoanAmount
```

Essentially, we loop through from 1 to the number of months, perform calculations, and then bind the information to the data grid. For each iteration of the loop, a new *DataRow* object is added, created from the Schedule table in the data set. That new empty row is then added to the Schedule table. Recall that we gave each of the columns names such as “Installment” and “Payment” when we created the table. Now that we have a new data row, we can easily access the columns in the row by their names. The Installment column will contain the number of months from 1 to the term of the loan. The Payment column will always contain the same value—the fixed payment each month—so we simply add that value. Again, notice that we format the value by converting it to “C”, for currency.

```
For iInstallment = 1 To iTerm
    drDataRow = dsSchedule.Tables("Schedule").NewRow
    dsSchedule.Tables("Schedule").Rows.Add(drDataRow)
    drDataRow("Installment") = iInstallment
    drDataRow("Payment") = sPayment.ToString("C")
```

Visual Basic has another handy built-in financial function, *PPmt*. This function returns a value specifying the principal payment for a given period of an annuity based on periodic, fixed payments and a fixed interest rate. By passing in the rate (divided by 12 to represent a single month), the payment, the term of the loan, the amount, 0, and whether the payment is due at the beginning or end of the period, we get the principal amount. That amount is then rounded, formatted, and placed in the Principal column of that row.

```
sPrincipal = PPmt(sRate / 12, iInstallment, iTerm, _
    -iLoanAmount, 0, DueDate.BegOfPeriod)
drDataRow("Principal") = Math.Round(sPrincipal, _
    2).ToString("C")
```

We can easily deduce how much of the payment goes toward interest by simply subtracting the principal from the payment.

```
drDataRow("Interest") = (sPayment - _
    sPrincipal).ToString("C")
```

The total principal to be paid (that is, the loan amount) is decremented by the principal paid for this single payment. The amount is formatted and added to the remaining principal column of the row.

```
sTotalPrincipal -= sPrincipal
drDataRow("PrincipalRemaining") = _
    sTotalPrincipal.ToString("C")
```

We initialize how much we have paid to date to 0 at the beginning of the routine and then increment it for each payment made. The user can then see how much he or she has paid into the loan for each payment. That value is then added to the correct column of the row. Finally we add the changes to the data set for that new row.

```
sPaidToDate += sPayment
drDataRow("PaidToDate") = sPaidToDate.ToString("C")

dsSchedule.AcceptChanges()
```

We wrap up the routine by setting how many rows the data grid displays to the number of months of the loan. A *DataView* object that contains the Schedule table with all the new rows is assigned to the *DataSource* property of the data grid. Finally we bind the *DataView* object to the data grid and it is displayed.

```
With dgSchedule
    .PageSize = iTerm
    .DataSource = New _
        DataView(dsSchedule.Tables("Schedule"))
    .DataBind()
End With
```

After all this, you should make an important note. All this code is for logic processing and none for displaying the data on the Web Form. On our Web Forms, we used the same object models for the controls that we used in Windows Forms. And the code behind is just like Windows Forms code. This is a milestone in Web development. Programming for the Web is nearly identical to programming for Windows!

Tracing Our Program

A useful way to find out what is happening in our program is to enable tracing. In the HTML section of the WebForm1.aspx form, add the attribute *Trace="True"* to the first line.

```
<%@ Page Language="vb"  AutoEventWireup="false"
  Codebehind = "WebForm1.aspx.vb" Trace="True"
  Inherits = "Loan_Application.WebForm1"%>
```

By adding this attribute, you can get some handy information about the page, including its Session ID and the timing information to display the page. This information is shown in Figure 13-21. (The *Visible* property of each control on the page was temporarily set to False to capture the figure.)

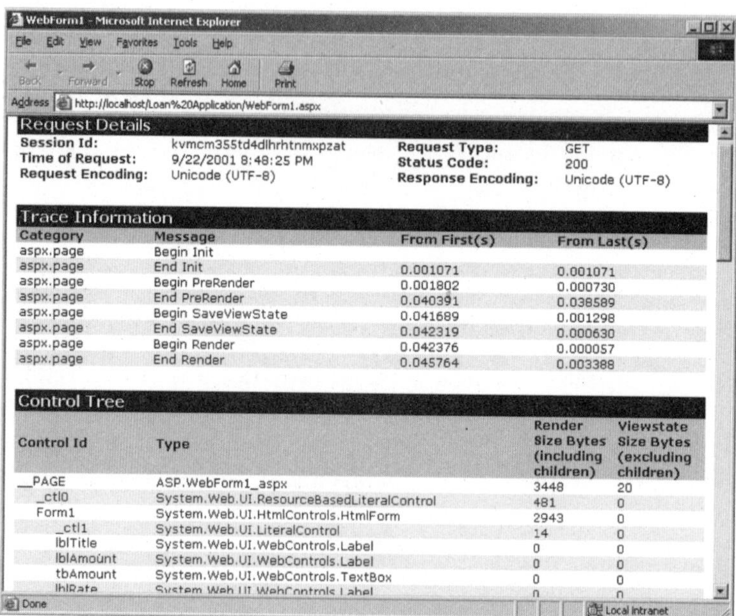

Figure 13-21 Enable tracing to get a wealth of information about the page.

Web Services: The New Marketplace

As we all know, the Internet represents both value and reach for businesses of all sizes by providing opportunities to find new customers, streamline supply chains, provide new services, and secure financial gain. A major impediment has held back the enormous potential of the Internet marketplace to open up trade worldwide. This roadblock is not only in the way of those already conducting business-to-business (B2B) e-commerce but also in the way of businesses that are not yet players in the digital economy. This roadblock is one of design. Most Internet services currently in place take divergent paths to connect buyers, suppliers, marketplaces, and service providers, which means that without large investments in their technology infrastructure, a furniture manufacturer in North Carolina might have a difficult time working with a specialized fittings supplier in Borneo. Also, the furniture manufacturer can only work with global trading partners it knows about, so there has to be a mechanism for the supplier to make its presence widely known. E-commerce participants have not yet agreed on one standard or backbone on which to communicate their services, which makes finding and working with potential trading partners severely limited. This situation, however, is rapidly changing.

What Are Web Services?

In very general terms, ASP.NET pages are for human interaction with a Web server, and Web services are for programmatic interaction with a Web server. Web services are a general model for building applications that can be implemented for any operation that supports communication over the Internet. Web services combine both component-based development models and the Web. Of course, component-based object models such as Distributed Component Object Model (DCOM), Remote Method Invocation (RMI), and Internet Inter-Orb Protocol (IIOP) have been around for some time. The down side of these models is that they depend on a protocol that's particular to the object model. Web services, on the other hand, extend these models a bit further to communicate using SOAP and XML, which essentially eradicates the object model–specific protocol barrier. The nature of a Web service is shown in Figure 13-22.

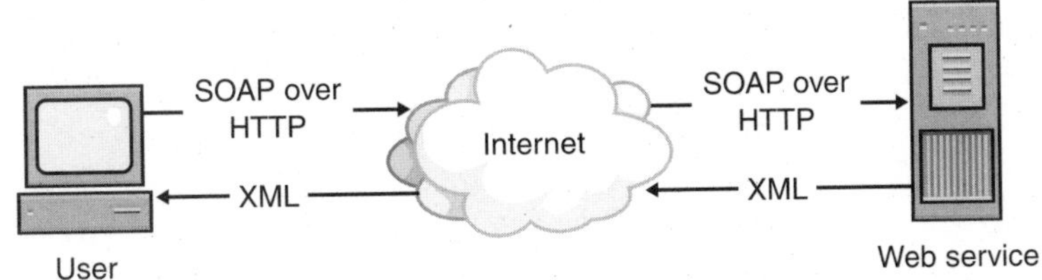

Figure 13-22 High-level view of the Web service model.

As you can see in the illustration, SOAP calls are remote function calls that invoke code-method executions on Web services components. The output from these methods is rendered as XML and passed back to the user. This magic can be accomplished because Web services basically use text-based HTTP and SOAP to make business data available on the Web. A Web service exposes business objects (such as COM objects, Java Beans, and so on) to SOAP calls over HTTP and then executes remote function calls on their receipt. Consumers of Web services can easily invoke method calls on remote objects using SOAP and HTTP and have their data returned via text-based XML. This is an elegant and compelling scenario.

OK, Now How Do We Communicate?

Let's say that the North Carolina–based furniture manufacturer wants to communicate with the Borneo-based fittings supplier. How does the furniture manufacturer become aware of the semantics required to actually use the fittings supplier's Web service?

This question is easily answered—by conforming to a common standard. A few of these standards are the Service Description Language (SDL), SOAP Contract Language (SCL), and Network Accessible Service Specification Language (NASSL), which are XML-like languages built to facilitate communication between a client and a server. IBM and Microsoft, however, recently agreed on the Web Services Description Language (WSDL) as a Web service standard. Therefore, in order to dynamically communicate, each Web service exposes the structure of its components using WSDL.

WSDL is a general-purpose XML language for describing the interface, protocol bindings, and deployment details of network services. WSDL defines XML grammar for describing network services as collections of communication endpoints capable of exchanging messages. WSDL service definitions provide documentation for distributed systems and automate the details involved in communications between applications. Like XML, WSDL is extensible to allow the description of endpoints and their messages, regardless of what message formats or network protocols are used to communicate. WSDL can be used to design specifications to invoke and operate Web services on the Internet and to access and invoke remote applications and databases.

Visual Basic .NET makes it easy to create Web services with components that communicate using HTTP GET, HTTP POST, and SOAP. Consumers of a Web service don't need to know anything about the platform, object model, or programming language used to implement the service. Consumers only need to understand how to send and receive SOAP messages (HTTP and XML).

The decentralized nature of Web services enables both the client and the Web service to function as autonomous units. This provides limitless ways to consume a Web service—for example, a call to a Web service that might be included in your Web application, or from a middleware component, or even from another Web service, as in our furniture supplier example.

Finding Out Who Is Offering What in the Global Marketplace

To address the problems of finding what Web services are out there and how to communicate to them, a group of technology and business leaders have come together to develop the Universal Discovery, Description, and Integration (UDDI) specification. The UDDI service is an industry-wide effort to bring a common standard to B2B integration. It defines a set of standard interfaces for accessing a database of Web services. This initiative creates a platform-independent, open framework to enable businesses to accomplish several goals at once. The UDDI data structure provides a framework for the description of basic business and service information and also architects an extensible mechanism to provide detailed service access information.

- Businesses can discover each other.
- The definition of how businesses interact over the Internet is defined.
- Businesses can easily share information in a global registry.

UDDI is the name of a group of Web-based registries that expose information about a business or other entity and its technical interfaces (APIs). This way, UDDI provides a way for businesses to publish information about their own services as well as find services they need from other businesses.

The UDDI specifications take advantage of World Wide Web Consortium (W3C) and Internet Engineering Task Force (IETF) standards such as XML, HTTP, and Domain Name System (DNS) protocols. Also, cross-platform programming features are addressed by adopting early versions of the SOAP messaging specifications found at the W3C Web site. There are three steps in how the UDDI works:

1. Software companies, standards bodies, and programmers populate the registry with descriptions of different types of services they support.
2. The UDDI Business Registry assigns a programmatically unique identifier to each service and business registration.
3. Marketplaces, search engines, and business applications query the registry to discover services at other companies.

Conceptually, the information provided in a UDDI business registration consists of three components. There are the "white pages," which include the business address, contact, and known identifiers. Next are the "yellow pages," which include industrial categorizations. And finally there are the "green pages," which contain technical information about services that are exposed by the business.

As you might guess, it's the green pages that allow us to automatically discover how to use the service because they include references to specifications for the Web services as well as support for pointers to various file and URL-based discovery mechanisms—if required.

Once a Web service is found, there must be a mechanism to determine exactly what methods (essentially that service's API) it exposes. For example, a client needs to know that the service has a method named *getProductDescription* that takes a long and returns a string. The client can accomplish this task using the WSDL, which is conceptually similar to a COM type library. Using WSDL, a C++ or Java client can understand the parameters of the *getProductDescription* API and build the correct SOAP message to invoke the service. Essentially, WSDL is a specification for using XML schemas to fully describe the service's API.

The third Web service standard is the use of XML schema definition language (XSD). XSD defines a pretty large set of data types that should cover most application's needs. The standard data types ensure that the data passed between service and client, such as integers and dates, are interpreted and laid out in memory the same way on each side. However, if absolutely necessary, XSD permits you to define your own data types when required. Since XSD is used, both the client and the service can agree on what is a string, a long, and so on.

The vocabulary surrounding Web services is that a Web service *provides* services by exposing its API while a client *consumes* those services, as shown in Figure 13-23. So a client first finds out about a service from UDDI, then uses WSDL to determine how to communicate with the service, and then contacts the service.

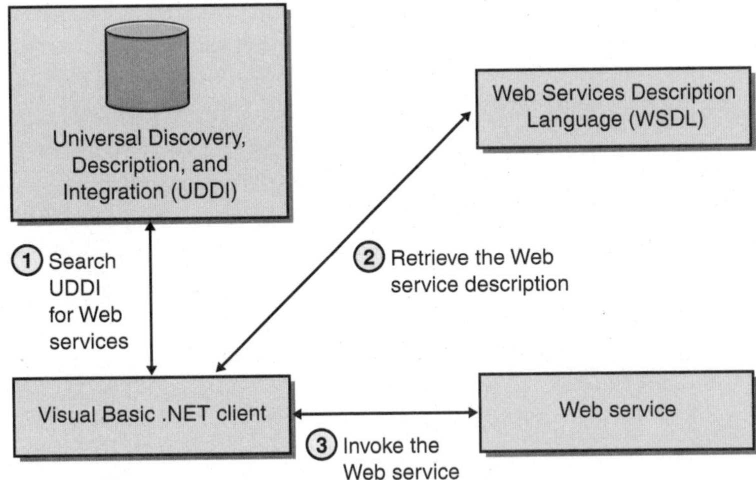

Figure 13-23 How a client discovers and communicates with a Web service.

Where Are Web Services Going?

Web services are quickly becoming the programmatic backbone for electronic commerce. In Chapter 1, "Visual Basic .NET from the Ground Up," I referred to a fictitious Web service that calculates arbitrage rates for cross-currency wire transfers. Another example is where one company calls another's Web service to send a purchase order directly via an Internet connection. Another service might be one that calculates the cost of shipping a package of a certain size or weight over so many miles via a specific carrier.

The future looks bright for Web service technology developed with Visual Basic .NET. However, Microsoft is not alone in the race for Web services technology. Both Sun and IBM are also very interested. In addition, SOAP toolkits are available for Apache and Java Web servers. Although the discovery process is still in the embryonic stages, Web services have the potential to introduce new concepts to the Internet. For example, it would be easy to construct Web sites that generate revenue for each request serviced to a user. This micro-billing would charge by use, not by a flat monthly fee. It's easy to see how searches on sites for periodical publications might charge $1.50 to view any article over 5 years old.

In Chapter 1, I touched on federations of Web services, a situation in which my Web service might call on another Web service to provide value. For example, if my Web service sends foreign denominated wire transfers, behind the scenes I might call on one Web service to validate the user and another to provide the real-time currency exchange rates. By using others' services, my service can concentrate on formatting the instructions correctly and efficiently to send the wire instruction to the Federal Reserve or S.W.I.F.T. When looked at in this light, Web services can be described as the "plug and play" building blocks of B2B Web solutions.

Building a Web Service

With all the daily decisions Visual Basic .NET programmers have to make, wouldn't it be helpful if there were an oracle of sorts we could turn to for sage development advice? If there were a Web service we could query for answers to our thorny problems, life would be so much simpler. So, let's create such a Web service for the betterment of all.

Start a new project and select ASP.NET Web Service. Name the project MagicEightBall. The New Project dialog box for our Web service is shown in Figure 13-24.

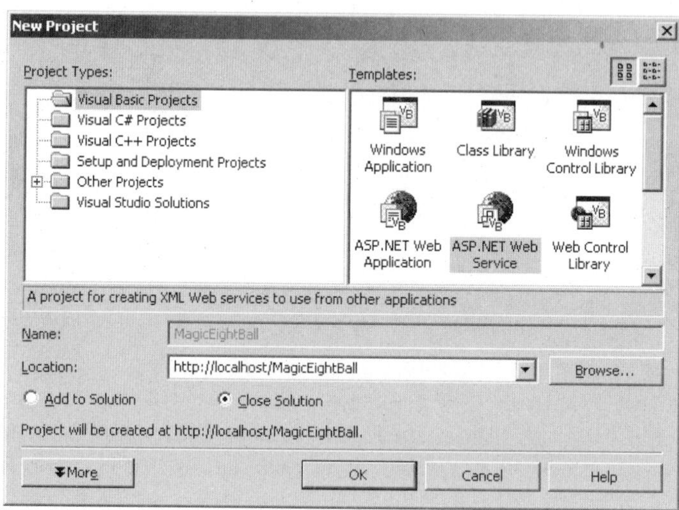

Figure 13-24 Create an ASP.NET Web Service project named MagicEightBall.

You'll be presented with a blank designer screen with the Service1.asmx.vb tab. Right-click the designer, and select Properties. Change the name from Service1 to Magic8Ball. This change will also change the name of the class in the code-behind from Service1 to Magic8Ball.

Bring up the Solution Explorer, and then right-click the Service1.asmx file. Rename the file Magic8.asmx. Right-click the designer again, and then select View Code to bring up the code window. Next change the URL to *http://www.solidstatesoftware.com/webservices/* in the code before the class declaration. This statement provides a unique namespace for our Web service. The code should look like this:

```
<System.Web.Services.WebService(Namespace:= _
    "http://www.solidstatesoftware.com/webservices/")>
Public Class Magic8Ball
    Inherits System.Web.Services.WebService
```

Add the following code to the template:

```
Private possibleFutures() As String = _
    {"The answer is unclear", _
     "Uncertain at this time", _
     "I have no idea", _
     "Absolutely yes!", _
     "Ask again later", _
     "Emphatically No!", _
     "Buy Microsoft short"}

<WebMethod(Description:="Provides an answer")> _
Public Function getFuture() As String

    Dim rndRandom As System.Random = New System.Random()
    Dim iLower = possibleFutures.GetLowerBound(0)
    Dim iUpper = possibleFutures.GetUpperBound(0)

    Return possibleFutures(rndRandom.Next(iLower, iUpper))

End Function

<WebMethod(Description:="Ask me a question")>  _
Public Function getAnswer(ByVal Question As String) As String

    Dim rndRandom As System.Random = New System.Random()
    Dim iLower = possibleFutures.GetLowerBound(0)
    Dim iUpper = possibleFutures.GetUpperBound(0)
    Dim sAnswer As String

    sAnswer = Question & "?  " & _
        possibleFutures(rndRandom.Next(iLower, iUpper))

    Return sAnswer
End Function
```

The first member is a class-level array of strings, named *possibleFutures*. This array is private so that it can't be seen from outside the Web service. Next are two Web methods, *getFuture* and *getAnswer*. By prefacing each with the

<*WebMethod()*> directive, we expose both of these methods to the outside world. The templates for the Web methods will show *WebMethod()*. By adding the description, users querying your Web service can see a useful message showing what each method is used for. Also notice that we used *Question* as the parameter for the *getAnswer* method instead of *sQuestion*. We used this name because *Question* will show up when our service is queried, making it crystal clear what the purpose of the method is. We keep our Web service simple, but just simple enough to provide sage advice to anyone who cares to query for it.

The first Web method, *getFuture*, returns an answer. The second, *getAnswer*, takes a specific question from the user and appends the answer. As you can see, we generate a random number between 0 and the number of entries in the *possibleFutures* array. A random response will be returned to the client using our service. If you want any helper functions, simply make them private so that they can't be seen by the outside world. We won't spend any more time on these methods because they should be very familiar by now.

Run the Program

Web services have no visual interface; they simply expose methods. Without writing any additional code, the screen shot shown in Figure 13-25 is displayed, showing the name of the Web service and the two services it currently offers.

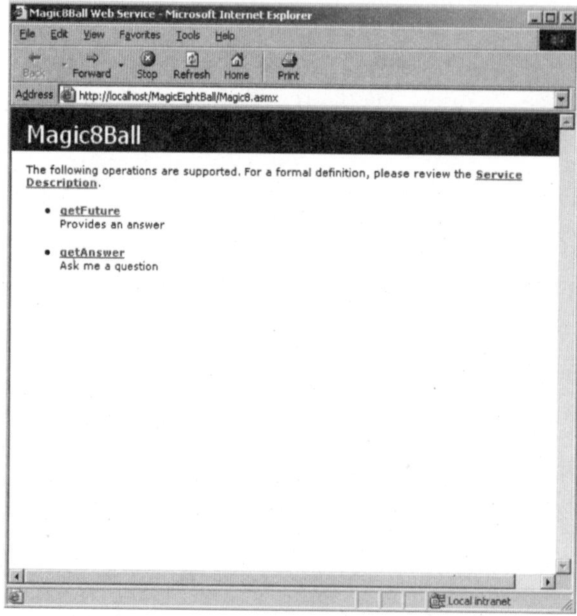

Figure 13-25 The MagicEightBall application in action.

Click on *getFuture* to see information about the method along with a button you can click to invoke the method, shown in Figure 13-26. In addition, a sample SOAP request and response are provided.

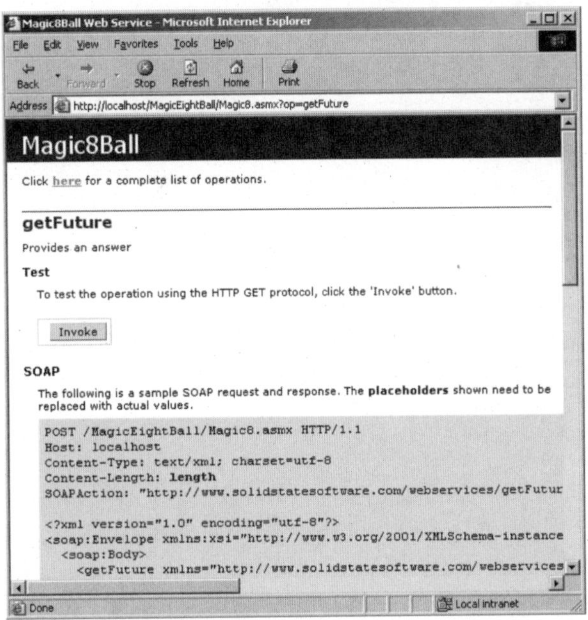

Figure 13-26 Information about the *getFuture* method.

Click the Invoke button. A new browser window is displayed with the XML formatted response from the Magic8Ball Web service. We can see that an example answer is "Uncertain at this time." This text is what would be returned to a program on the Internet that invoked the *getFuture* method of our Web service.

```
<?xml version="1.0" encoding="utf-8" ?>
<string xmlns="http://www.solidstatesoftware.com/webservices/">
Uncertain at this time</string>
```

Close the second browser window, click the back button on the first browser, and click *getAnswer*. This method requires a string to be entered, so the name of the parameter, *Question*, is displayed as a prompt with a text box to enter our query. Now you can see why we used *Question* instead of the traditional *sQuestion* we would normally use when humans do not see parameters. Even though most programmers are human, they don't count in this context. Enter a question in the text box, and click Invoke, as shown in Figure 13-27.

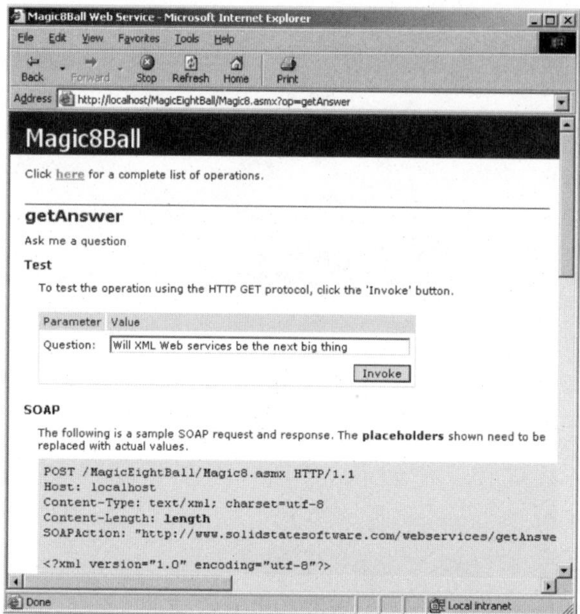

Figure 13-27 Type in a question before you invoke the *getAnswer* method.

Another browser window is opened, and our answer is provided in XML. The service works as advertised. The question is displayed along with the answer.

```
<?xml version="1.0" encoding="utf-8" ?>
<string xmlns="http://www.solidstatesoftware.com/webservices/">
Will Web services be the next big thing? Uncertain
 at this time</string>
```

Now close the second browser window, click the back button in the first browser window, and click Service Description. A small portion of the WSDL for our Web service is shown in Figure 13-28.

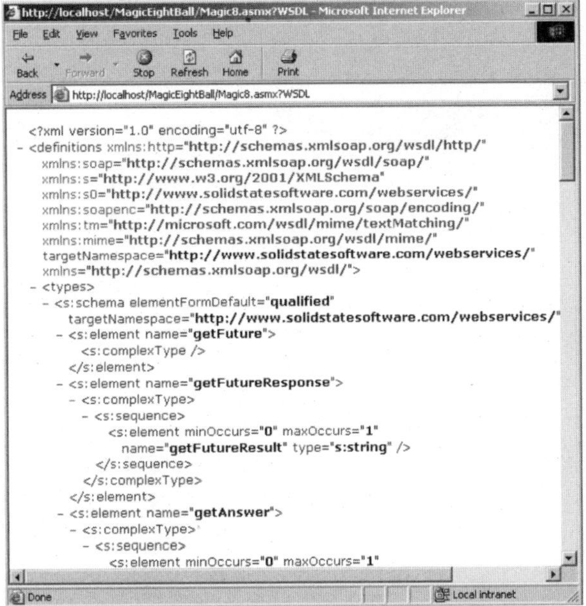

Figure 13-28 A small portion of the WSDL for our Web service.

This WSDL file will be used to build a proxy class in a client that consumes our Web service.

Consuming the MagicEightBall Web Service

Start a new Windows application project named ConsumeEightBall. To keep things simple while illustrating each of the important concepts in this topic, our client will exercise both exposed Web methods of the MagicEightBall Web service. One button will retrieve an answer, and a second button will accept a question in the text box and return the question and answer. Our client is shown in Figure 13-29.

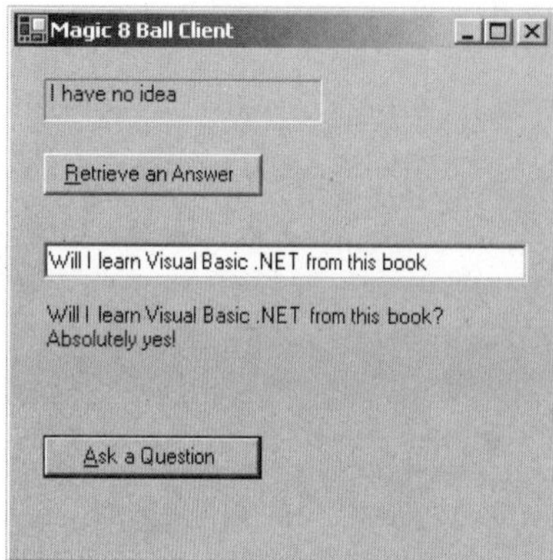

Figure 13-29 The ConsumeEightBall application in action.

One of the key questions you might have is, "Does a client actually execute methods on the Web service's Web server?" As you can imagine, doing that would be a serious security threat. Web masters don't want anyone to use their Web resources in a way that could do malicious damage to sensitive data, not to mention chewing up bandwidth. We also have to keep in mind that Web services are distributed applications. With distributed applications, we have to be concerned about the marshaling of data.

To get around these problems, we actually replicate the object behavior locally on the user's machine. In our example, we will replicate the MagicEightBall Web service functionality on the client's program. It sounds strange, but stay tuned. We do this replication by creating a proxy object to act on behalf of the original Web service. The proxy object has all the publicly available data interfaces that the original Web service does.

How do we get the publicly available data interface? Recall that we used the <*WebMethod()*> directive in our MagicEightBall service. Only Web methods will be replicated at the proxy object. This limitation protects our service from exposing sensitive business logic to malicious hackers at the client end. So we program to the proxy object in our program, and it takes care of sending the SOAP messages to and from the real Web service, as shown in Figure 13-30.

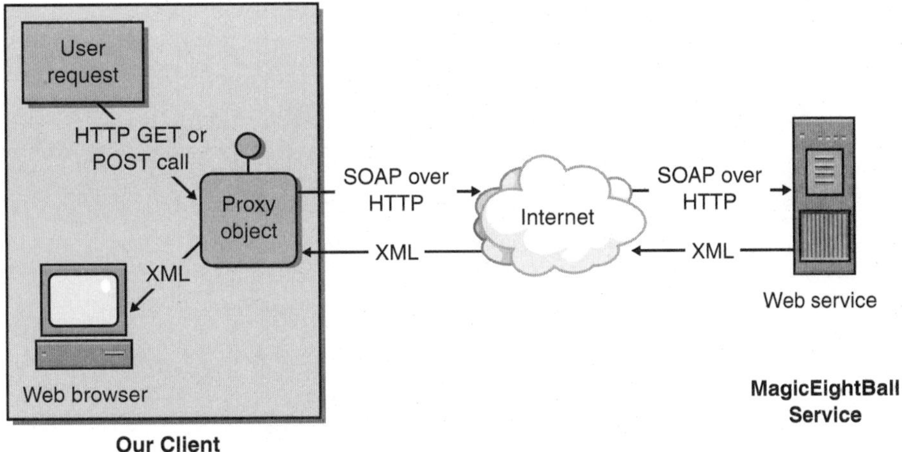

Figure 13-30 The proxy object takes care of sending the SOAP messages to and from the real Web service.

Building Our Web Services Client Program

Add two labels, two buttons, and a text box to the ConsumeEightBall default form, as shown in Figure 13-31.

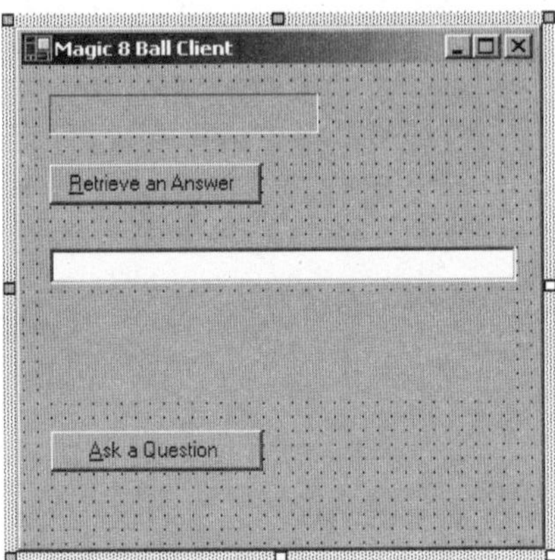

Figure 13-31 Add these controls to the form.

Set the properties for each of the controls and the form as shown in Table 13-5.

Table 13-5 Properties for the ConsumeEightBall Controls

Object	Property	Value
Form1	*Text*	Magic 8 Ball Client
Label	*Name*	lblRetrieveAnswer
	BorderStyle	Fixed3D
	Text	""
Button	*Name*	btnRetrieve
	Text	&Retrieve an Answer
Text box	*Name*	txtQuestion
	Text	""
Label	*Name*	lblQuestion
	Text	""
Button	*Name*	btnAskQuestion
	Text	&Ask a Question

Adding a Proxy Class to Our Program

To access the MagicEightBall Web service, we have to add a proxy class. You can add a proxy through the command line with a program called Wsdl.exe, but this approach is pretty difficult. I won't cover it, but if you are interested, you can check out the online help. Instead, we will do it the easy way.

Choose Add Web Reference from the Project menu to bring up the Add Web Reference dialog box. Click Web References On Local Web Server to display all the .vsdisco files in the InetPub\wwwroot directories. Click the .vsdisco file for our MagicEightBall service, as shown in Figure 13-32.

Click View Contract at the right side of the Add Web Reference dialog box to examine the XML formatted .disco discovery file. Click the Add Reference button to add this file to the project. Now take a look at the Solution Explorer. Notice in Figure 13-33 that the Web References folder contains the WSDL file of our Web service. This file is what's used to create the proxy that our program will use.

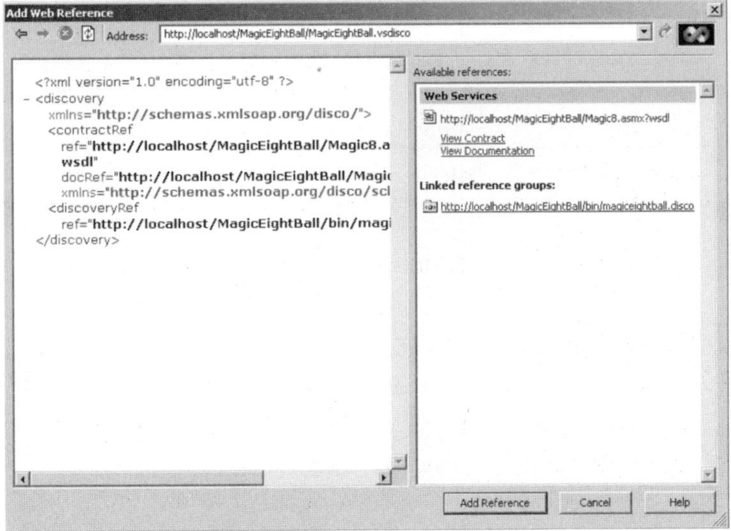

Figure 13-32 Click the .vsdisco file for our MagicEightBall service.

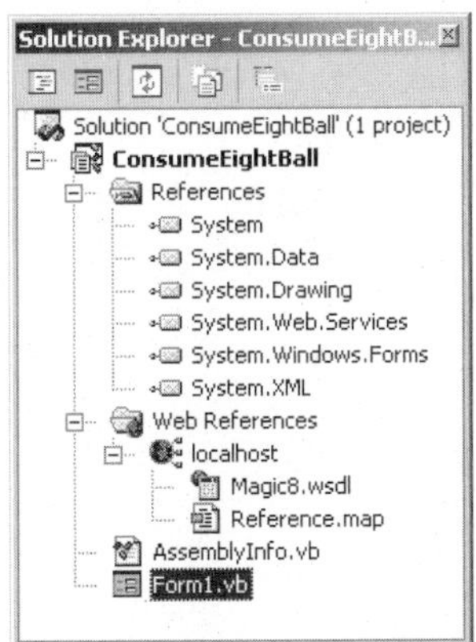

Figure 13-33 The Web References folder contains the WSDL file of our Web service.

Adding Code to Get Our Magic Eight Ball Answers

First right-click the form and choose View Code. Next add the *Imports* statement that will reference the local host folder in our Solution Explorer. This statement gives us the reference to the proxy class that was automatically built for us.

```
Imports ConsumeEightBall.localhost
```

Now add the code for the two buttons.

```
Private Sub btnRetrieve_Click(ByVal sender As System.Object, _
    ByVal e As System.EventArgs) Handles btnRetrieve.Click

    Dim Magic8 As New localhost.Magic8Ball()
    lblRetrieveAnswer.Text = Magic8.getFuture
End Sub

Private Sub btnAskQuestion_Click(ByVal sender As System.Object, _
    ByVal e As System.EventArgs) Handles btnAskQuestion.Click

    Dim Magic8 As New localhost.Magic8Ball()

    If (txtQuestion.Text.Length < 2) Then
        MessageBox.Show("Please enter a question to submit.", _
            "Magic 8 Ball Client", MessageBoxButtons.OK, _
            MessageBoxIcon.Question)
    Else
        lblQuestion.Text = Magic8.getAnswer(txtQuestion.Text)
    End If
End Sub
```

As you can see, all we have to do is create a reference to the *Magic8Ball* proxy that we just added. In both procedures, we created a local variable, *Magic8*, that is a new instance of the *Magic8Ball* proxy class. When the first button is clicked, we simply display the answer from the *getFuture* Web method, and when the second button is clicked, we pass in a question from the text box to the *getAnswer* Web method. As you can see, we simply have to get a reference to the proxy class *Magic8Ball*, as we would from any other class we might use from the .NET Framework or build ourselves. Then we can reference it. What could be easier?

Conclusion

To me, Web services are the most exciting offering of the entire .NET experience. In this chapter alone, you've learned how to build sophisticated, multipage, data-validated ASP.NET pages. You also learned how to both build and then consume Web services. That shows how easy these powerful technologies have become with Visual Basic .NET.

14

Visual Inheritance and Custom Controls

In this last chapter, I want to bring together many of the coding techniques and practices we've covered throughout this book. We'll cover some additional topics and build a sample program that illustrates how what we've learned comes together in Microsoft Visual Basic .NET.

We will first use our knowledge of object-oriented programming to inherit a standard class and that class's visual rendering as a form. We will then move on to build our own Microsoft .NET custom control. After that, we will bring all of our .NET knowledge together to write our final project, Sticky Notes, an electronic version of the ubiquitous and helpful tool for providing reminders and notes. We can stick these notes to our screen. When we finish with that program, we'll wrap up the book by writing an installation program that will enable you to deploy the Sticky Notes program to your friends.

Visual Inheritance

Back in this book's early chapters, we learned about object-oriented programming and how to inherit objects from prebuilt classes. We learned that each form is nothing more than a class that inherits from *System.Windows.Forms.Form*. Taking the concept of inheritance a step further, we can easily inherit from a base form to create identical child forms. Why is the ability to do this so great? How many times have you had to re-create the look and feel of a form for your company? Now this task becomes trivial using visual inheritance.

Let's say you have a form that your company wants to use to present a common look and feel throughout its applications. You could develop a base form that you can inherit from and make any specific changes on child forms that inherit from the base. In a base company form, we might have an About button that's private and can't be overridden in a child form. This way we can have a consistent About statement on all forms. We could also provide a link to our Web site that can't be overridden in a child form. On the other hand, it might be helpful to inherit the Help button in child forms so that context-sensitive help can be provided on each child form. Our base form might look something like Figure 14-1.

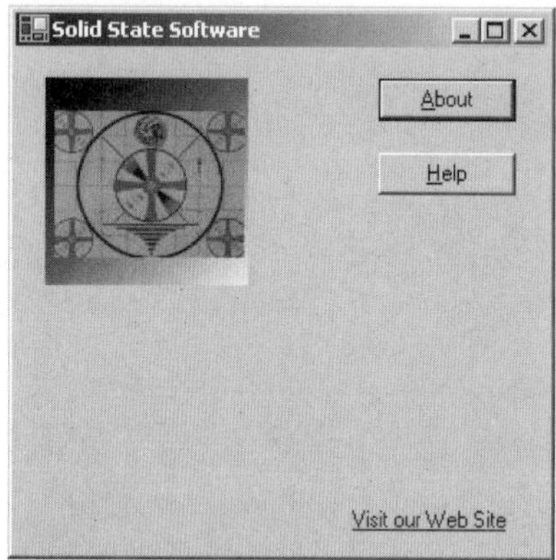

Figure 14-1 Our base form.

Building a Base Form

Here are the steps we'll take to build our base form and inherit from it.

1. Create a Windows project and name it CompanyBase. Add an image that represents a company logo, two buttons as shown in Figure 14-1, and a LinkLabel control that will point to your company's Web site. Set the control properties as shown in Table 14-1.

Table 14-1 Properties for the CompanyBase Form and Controls

Object	Property	Value
Form	*Name*	CompanyForm
	Text	Solid State Software
PictureBox	*Name*	pbLogo
Button	*Name*	btnAbout
	Text	&About
Button	*Name*	btnHelp
	Text	&Help
LinkLabel	*Name*	llWebSite
	Text	Visit our Web Site

2. Add a message in the btnAbout button's *Click* event. The signature for this event is private, so the message can't be overridden in any child form. When the user clicks the About button, code in the base form will execute.

```
Private Sub btnAbout_Click(ByVal sender As System.Object, _
    ByVal e As System.EventArgs) Handles BbtnAbout.Click

    Dim sMessage As String = _
        "Developing .NET Solutions since 2001"

    MessageBox.Show(sMessage, "Solid State Software, Inc.", _
        MessageBoxButtons.OK, MessageBoxIcon.Information)
End Sub
```

3. Change the signature of the *Click* event procedure for the btnHelp button to be *Protected Overridable*. This procedure can be overridden by an identically named procedure in a derived class.

```
Protected Overridable Sub btnHelp_Click(ByVal sender As  _
    System.Object, ByVal e As System.EventArgs) _
    Handles btnHelp.Click

End Sub
```

4. In order to inherit from our base form, we have to change the output type from a Windows Application to a Class Library. Right-click the CompanyBase project, and select Properties. Change the Output Type setting to Class Library and the Startup Object setting to None. Now our form is a class file that can be inherited from. Notice in Figure 14-2 that the form will be compiled as CompanyBase.dll.

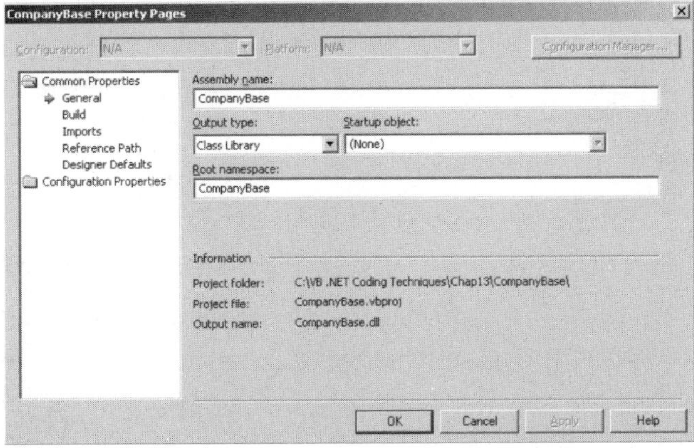

Figure 14-2 Change the output type to Class Library.

5. Before we can inherit from our form, we have to build it. Select Build | Build Solution to compile our new class. You can only inherit forms if they are compiled into a DLL.

Adding the Inherited Form

In the next set of steps, we'll add an inherited form to the project so that you can see visual inheritance at work.

1. Bring up the Solution Explorer and click CompanyBase. Right-click and select Add | Add Inherited Form. The Add New Item dialog box, shown in Figure 14-3, will be displayed. Select Inherited Form, and then rename the form to ChildForm.vb.

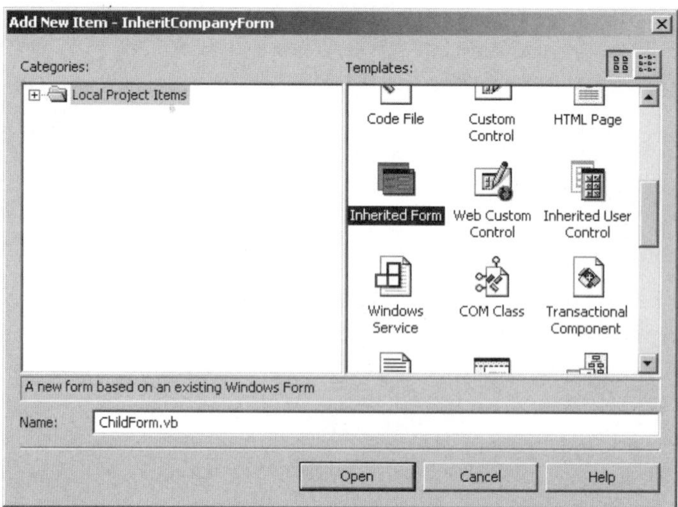

Figure 14-3 Add an inherited form named ChildForm.vb.

2. Click Open, and the Inheritance Picker dialog box will be displayed, shown in Figure 14-4. Select the form you want to inherit from, CompanyForm in this case, and click OK. If you take a look at the Solution Explorer, you can see that we now have two projects in our solution.

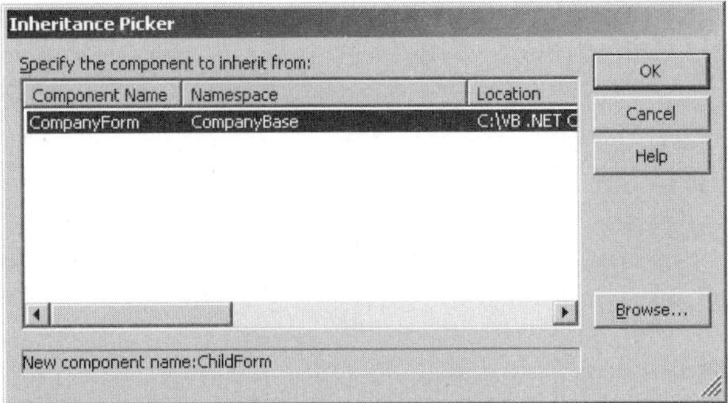

Figure 14-4 Select CompanyForm in the Inheritance Picker dialog box.

Now look closely at the inherited ChildForm in the IDE. Notice that each of the controls that have been inherited is displayed with an arrow in a white box, as you can see in Figure 14-5. This cue tells us that these controls are inherited from the base form.

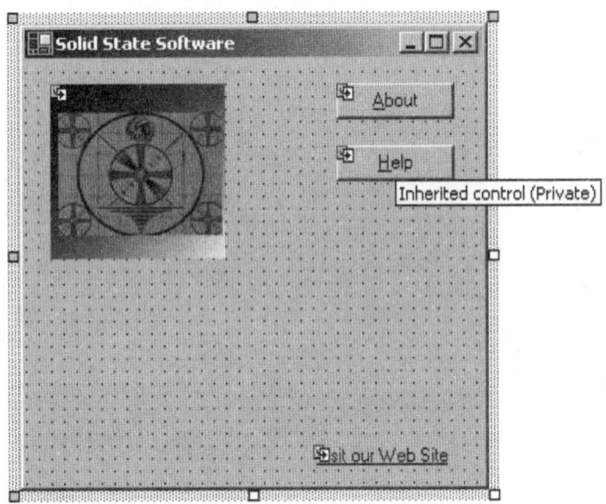

Figure 14-5 Inherited controls on the form are distinguished by an arrow in a white box.

3. Double-click the child form to bring up the code window. You'll see in the code that ChildForm inherits from *CompanyBase.CompanyForm*.

```
Public Class ChildForm
    Inherits CompanyBase.CompanyForm
```

4. We want to provide context-sensitive help that is specific to each child form. We can now easily do this by overriding the *Click* event of the Help button of the parent form. The signature of the event in each child form must be identical to the base form's, so you might want to simply cut and paste the subroutine from the parent to the child. Modify the signature to add *Protected Overrides* before the *Sub*.

```
Protected Overrides Sub btnHelp_Click( _
    ByVal sender As System.Object, _
    ByVal e As System.EventArgs) Handles btnHelp.Click

    Dim sMessage As String = "Context Sensitive Help"
    MessageBox.Show(sMessage, "Child Form", _
        MessageBoxButtons.OK, MessageBoxIcon.Information)
End Sub
```

5. Add a few controls to the child form. You can use these controls for code that performs operations such as getting a login ID and password, getting employee information, displaying database information, and so on. A modified child form is shown in Figure 14-6.

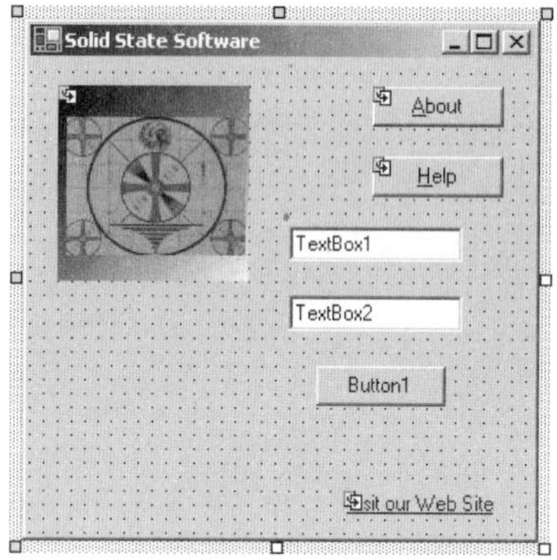

Figure 14-6 Add some controls to the child form.

6. The last step we have to take is to indicate in the project which form should be used as the startup form. We can't run the base form because it is now a class library, so we will select the child form. Right-click CompanyBase in the Solution Explorer, and select Properties. Select Windows Application as the output type and ChildForm as the startup object.

7. Press F5 to start the program. Click the About button. The code in the base form is executed. Now click the Help button, and the overridden *Click* event in the child form is executed. You can easily see how you can neatly package code that is common to all forms in the base and then use child-specific code in each inherited child form.

Creating a Custom Control

With Visual Basic .NET, you have the ability to create custom, managed controls. If you've ever built ActiveX controls in Visual Basic 6, you already know how to accomplish this. I'll briefly touch on the highlights of control construction by illustrating how to build a simple control that raises an event in the host.

Changing the Background Color of a Text Box

As you know, a control cannot exist on its own but instead needs a host container such as a form to exist. In this example, we'll create a control that contains a context menu and permits the user to change the control's background color. The example is admittedly simple and contrived, but all of the main points are illustrated. A sample of our control is shown in Figure 14-7.

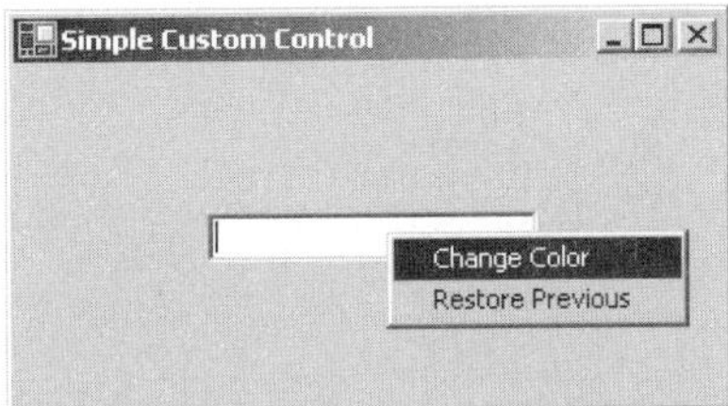

Figure 14-7 This control permits the user to change the control's background color.

When Change Color is selected, a common dialog box is displayed with all the colors available on that computer. The user can select a color to change the text box's background color property. The common dialog is contained in the custom control. The Windows Forms ColorDialog control is a preconfigured dialog box that allows the user to select a color from a palette and add custom colors to that palette. It is the same dialog box that you see in other Windows applications, such as the Display control panel. We will use the common dialog box within our control in lieu of configuring our own dialog box.

When the color is changed in our custom control, the control fires an event in the host container. The program displays a message box, shown in Figure 14-8, that indicates the new color. Simple, but this example illustrates how events can be fired in the host. In addition, parameter values such as the color the text box was changed to can also be passed back to the host quite easily.

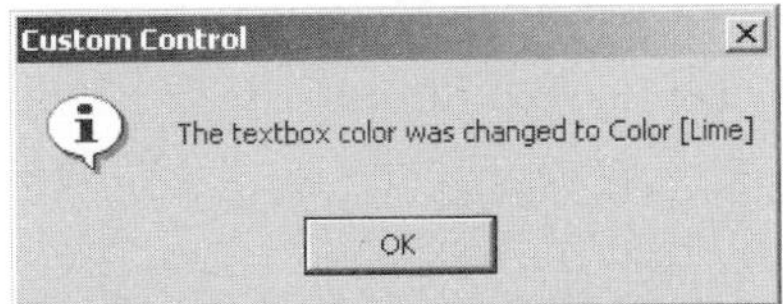

Figure 14-8 A message box is displayed when the control fires an event.

Building Our Control

Start a new project, but this time select a Windows Control Library project. Name the new project Custom Text Control. When a Windows Control Library project is started, a user control designer window is added to the IDE, which looks much like a form but is actually the substrate on which we will build our control. You can see the control designer in Figure 14-9.

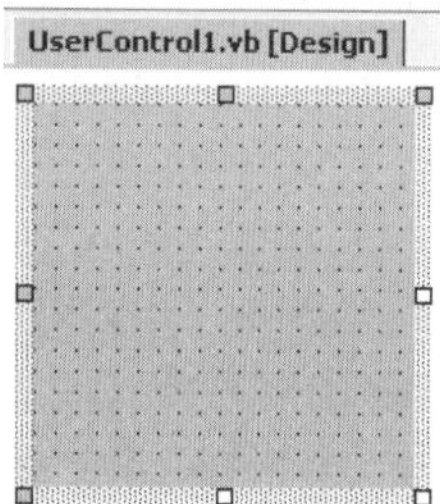

Figure 14-9 A blank control designer.

Add a text box to the user control, set its *Text* property to an empty string, and resize the substrate to the size shown in Figure 14-10. (Make the control substrate as small as possible.) When we draw our control on the host form, the substrate and any controls on that substrate are included. Using the toolbox, add a ColorDialog control to the control.

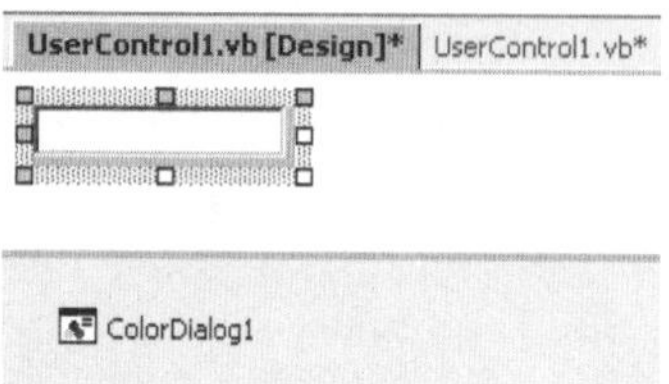

Figure 14-10 Resize the substrate and add a ColorDialog control.

Adding Code to Our Control

We want to add two class-scoped items to our control. The first is a variable, *cPreviousColor*, that will hold the color of the text box before the user changes the color. With this variable, we can add an undo feature so that if the user makes a terrible mistake, he or she can simply reset the color to its previous value. The other item is an event procedure declaration, *colorChanged*, that will be visible in any host that uses our control. We will pass in the value of the new text box background color as a parameter to this event. Later in the code, we will raise this event when certain conditions are met.

```
Public Class UserControl1
    Inherits System.Windows.Forms.UserControl

    Dim cPreviousColor As System.Drawing.Color

    Public Event colorChanged( _
        ByVal color As System.Drawing.Color)
```

Once these items are defined, the next job is to call a procedure that sets up our text box's context menu. This procedure is called immediately after the control sites and initializes any of its own controls.

```
Public Sub New()
    MyBase.New()

    'This call is required by the Windows Form Designer.
    InitializeComponent()

    setUpContextMenu()
End Sub
```

Add the *setUpContextMenu* procedure as well as the two routines that handle the *Click* event for each of the menu items. Here's the code:

```
Sub setUpContextMenu()
    Dim cmContextMenu As New ContextMenu()
    Dim mnuItem1 As New MenuItem("Change Color")
    Dim mnuItem2 As New MenuItem("Restore Previous")

    With cmContextMenu
        .MenuItems.Add(mnuItem1)
        .MenuItems.Add(mnuItem2)
    End With

    TextBox1.ContextMenu = cmContextMenu

    AddHandler mnuItem1.Click, AddressOf menuItem1Click
    AddHandler mnuItem2.Click, AddressOf menuItem2Click
End Sub

Sub menuItem1Click(ByVal sender As System.Object, _
    ByVal e As System.EventArgs)

    With ColorDialog1
        .AllowFullOpen = True
        .AnyColor = True
        .SolidColorOnly = False
        .ShowHelp = True
        .Color = TextBox1.BackColor
```

(continued)

```
            cPreviousColor = .Color
            .ShowDialog()
            TextBox1.BackColor = .Color
            RaiseEvent colorChanged(.Color)
        End With
    End Sub

    Sub menuItem2Click(ByVal sender As System.Object, _
        ByVal e As System.EventArgs)

        TextBox1.BackColor = cPreviousColor
    End Sub
```

Build the project before you continue.

Adding Our Custom Control to the Host Form

We need to add another project to our solution, so select File | Add Project | New Project to display the Add New Project dialog box. Select a Windows Application project, and name it Host.

Now open the toolbox and scroll to the bottom of the Windows Forms tab. You'll see that a UserControl is now on the list. Drag this control to the Host form as you would any other control. If you look closely at the control on the form, you can see the substrate boundaries, as shown in Figure 14-11.

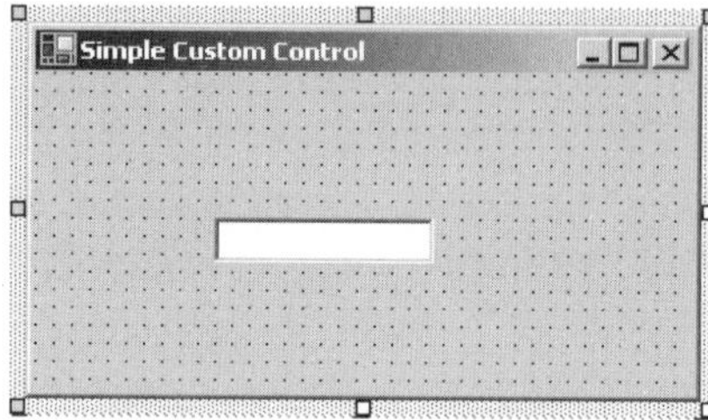

Figure 14-11 Add the custom control to the form.

Now look at the Solution Explorer. You'll see that Visual Basic .NET automatically adds a reference to the control, as shown in Figure 14-12.

We only need to add a single line of code to the host. The message box alerts us to the fact that the control raised the *colorChanged* event. And because we passed in the value of the new color, we will show that as well.

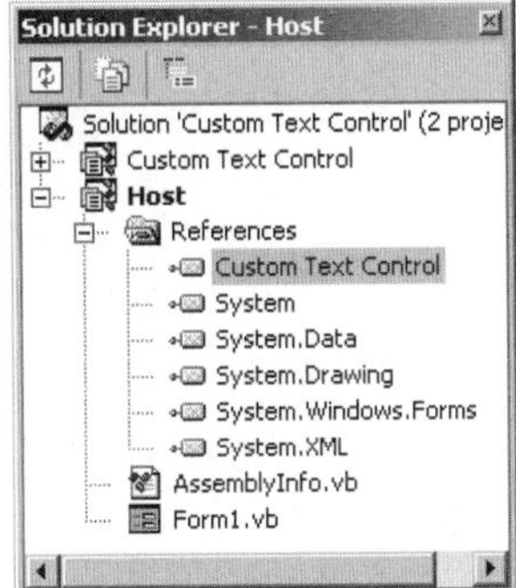

Figure 14-12 Visual Basic .NET automatically adds a reference to the control.

```
Private Sub UserControl11_colorChanged(ByVal color As _
    System.Drawing.Color) Handles UserControl11.colorChanged

    MessageBox.Show("The textbox color was changed to " _
        & color.ToString, "Custom Control", _
        MessageBoxButtons.OK, _
        MessageBoxIcon.Information)
End Sub
```

The last step that's required is to set the host form as the project's startup object. Bring up the Solution Explorer, select the Host project, right-click, and select Set As Startup Project. Now press F5 and run the new control in its host form.

How It Works

I'll cover context menus and event handlers in more detail in our next project, but suffice it to say that in this project we first dimension a context menu, create two new menu items (using the overloaded constructor that permits us to add the text when we build them), and then add each menu item to the *MenuItems* collection of the context menu.

```
Sub setUpContextMenu()
    Dim cmContextMenu As New ContextMenu()
    Dim mnuItem1 As New MenuItem("Change Color")
    Dim mnuItem2 As New MenuItem("Restore Previous")

    With cmContextMenu
        .MenuItems.Add(mnuItem1)
        .MenuItems.Add(mnuItem2)
    End With
```

After the context menu is built, it's added to the text box's *ContextMenu* property. Of course, the menu items can't do anything until we build event handlers for them. When the *Click* event is fired, the respective delegate for menu item one or two will be fired. Again, we will cover this a bit more in the next project.

```
    TextBox1.ContextMenu = cmContextMenu

    AddHandler mnuItem1.Click, AddressOf menuItem1Click
    AddHandler mnuItem2.Click, AddressOf menuItem2Click
End Sub
```

When the user clicks the Change Color menu item, the handler refers the code to the *menuItem1Click* delegate to handle it. Before we display the Color dialog box we want to first set the *Color* property to the current background color of the text box. We do this so that if the user cancels the Color dialog box without selecting a color, the new color will be the same as the current color. The *ShowDialog* method displays the Color dialog box. Because this dialog box is displayed modally, control won't be returned to our code until the user dismisses the dialog. When that happens, the background color of the text box is set to either a new color or the existing color, if the operation is canceled.

The next item of interest is the *RaiseEvent* command, which fires the event we declared at the top of the control class. This event in turn fires the event in the host and passes in the *Color* value as a parameter.

```
Sub menuItem1Click(ByVal sender As System.Object, _
    ByVal e As System.EventArgs)

    With ColorDialog1
        .AllowFullOpen = True
        .AnyColor = True
        .SolidColorOnly = False
        .ShowHelp = True
        .Color = TextBox1.BackColor
        cPreviousColor = .Color
        .ShowDialog()
        TextBox1.BackColor = .Color
        RaiseEvent colorChanged(.Color)

    End With
End Sub
```

If the user clicks Restore Previous, we set the background color of the text box to the value stored in *cPreviousColor*.

```
Sub menuItem2Click(ByVal sender As System.Object, _
    ByVal e As System.EventArgs)

    TextBox1.BackColor = cPreviousColor
End Sub
```

This code has been kept to a minimum so that I could illustrate the important points of control construction. As you see, you already know how to write a control because the methodology is almost the same as for a standard Windows form. What's important to keep in mind is that you are working with a different audience when developing controls. The audience for your control is not a user but a programmer. The goal is to make your controls as general as possible, and providing many events and properties in your controls accomplishes this. A programmer can respond to whichever events are appropriate for the task at hand and ignore the rest.

Putting It Together: What We've Learned So Far

For our final program in *Coding Techniques for Microsoft Visual Basic .NET*, let's have a bit of fun while at the same time reinforcing many of the concepts we've learned throughout the previous chapters. We will build a program that creates sticky notes and allows us to add these electronic notes to our screen. Most programmers I know keep notes scattered on scraps of paper around their desks. Well, this program will put the scraps of paper right on the screen.

The program will be operated from a notify icon in the system tray at the bottom of the screen. From here, the user can add a new note, show or hide all of the notes, or quit the program. We will create a *serialize* class that will manage an internal *ArrayList* object of sticky note forms. Each sticky note form will in turn have its own menu permitting the user to hide or delete an individual note, or even keep it on top of all other windows.

When the user dismisses the program, we will store the contents of each note in an XML file on disk. When the program is restarted, each note will be displayed with the size and location it had when the user last used the program. An internal data set and data table will be built dynamically to assist in the serialization and deserialization of the XML file for saving and reconstituting each of the notes.

A context menu will be added to the notify icon, and we will add handlers that respond when one of the menu items is clicked. Finally, we will have a "driver" form that builds the context menu and instantiates the *serialize* class. Remember that a .NET program has to have a main form to keep running. However, we don't want this driver form to be visible, so we will use the new *Opacity* property of .NET forms. By setting the *Opacity* property to 0 percent, the form will run but be invisible. So, as you can see, our program has quite a few moving parts. But I know this is one program that you'll use daily and probably want to distribute to your friends. Soon your screen will look like Figure 14-13.

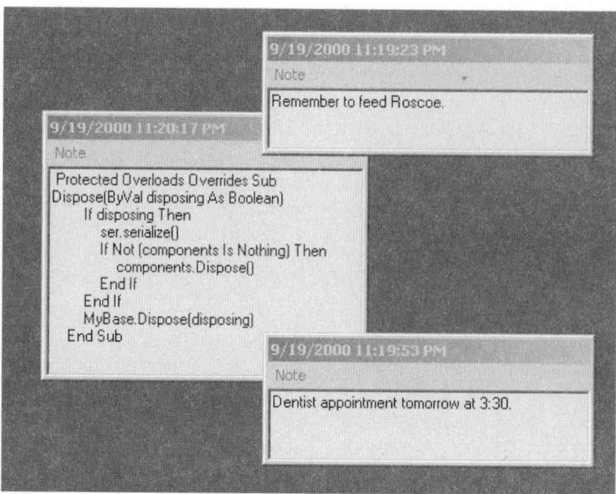

Figure 14-13 The sticky note program in action.

How Do We Save the Notes? XML, Of Course

Our program uses XML to store information so that when the program is run, each form is reconstituted exactly as it was when the user quit. We will use streams and files for our file I/O. Here's the XML file for three notes created when the user quits the program. Notice that we save the title, the message in the note, and the location and size of the form.

```
<NewDataSet>
- <tblSticky>
  <Title>9/19/2000 11:19:23 PM</Title>
  <Message>Remember to feed Roscoe.</Message>
  <Location>{X=408,Y=80}</Location>
  <Size>{Width=248, Height=93}</Size>
  </tblSticky>
- <tblSticky>
  <Title>9/19/2000 11:19:53 PM</Title>
  <Message>Dentist appointment tomorrow at 3:30.</Message>
  <Location>{X=410,Y=305}</Location>
  <Size>{Width=248, Height=100}</Size>
  </tblSticky>
- <tblSticky>
  <Title>9/19/2000 11:20:17 PM</Title>
  <Message>Protected Overloads Overrides Sub Dispose(ByVal
 disposing As Boolean) If disposing Then ser.serialize() If Not
 (components Is Nothing) Then components.Dispose() End If
 End If MyBase.Dispose(disposing) End Sub</Message>
  <Location>{X=242,Y=140}</Location>
  <Size>{Width=248, Height=203}</Size>
  </tblSticky>
  </NewDataSet>
```

As I mentioned, the program is run from a notify icon in the tool tray that has an icon of a note. As you can see in Figure 14-14, when a user right-clicks the icon, a context menu is displayed with options for the user. Our approach keeps the program out of the way but also readily accessible.

Figure 14-14 Right-click the notify icon to see the program's options.

Each individual sticky note also has its own menu. We can select individual notes to stay on top of all other windows by clicking the Keep On Top menu choice. Clearing the menu item allows the window to be arranged in the normal z-order with all others. As you can see in Figure 14-15, a user can also hide or delete individual notes. All in all, this is not only useful but also pretty cool.

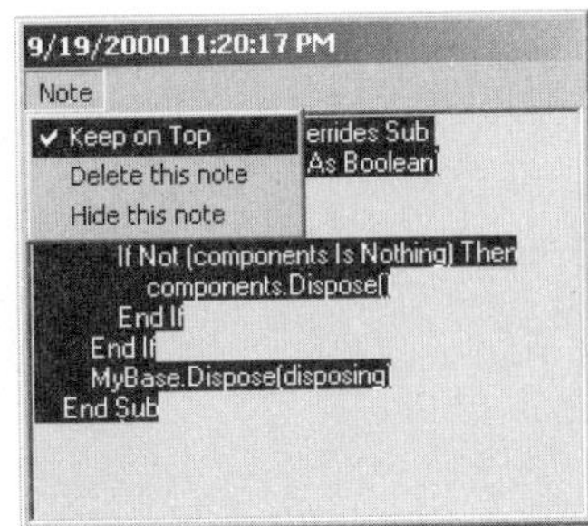

Figure 14-15 You can ensure that a sticky note stays on top of other windows.

While on the surface the Sticky Notes program looks simple, it illustrates quite a few important concepts. I mentioned the message loop and the *Opacity* property of .NET forms. To respond to menu clicks, we will add delegates and wire them to the *Click* events of the menu items. When a new form is added, we will inherit from a form that represents a new note, named BaseNote. Each *BaseNote* form will also contain its own menu, and each of the new *BaseNote* forms will be managed by using a shared *ArrayList* object to track all active notes. Also, an in-memory data set and data table will be built dynamically to permit using the *WriteXML* method of the data set for saving the contents of the notes. We will cover two new data types, *Point* and *Size*, and character arrays will be covered as well as the *TrimStart* and *TrimEnd* methods of a *String* object. Finally, we'll use streams and files when we read and write the contents of the notes to disk. Before we add any code to our default form, we'll build our *serialize* class. This class will be instantiated by the default form.

Building the Sticky Notes Program

Start a new Visual Basic .NET Windows application and give it the name Sticky. The default form will actually be our driver for the program. Now follow these steps:

1. Add a NotifyIcon control to the form and set its *Name* property to niIcon.
2. Select Project | Add Class. Click the Class icon and name the class *serialize.vb*. Click Open to add the new class template to your project.
3. Add the following code to the *serialize* class. We will be doing quite a bit in this class, from reading and writing XML to building a data set and data table in memory.

```
Imports System
Imports System.Collections
Imports System.IO

Public Class serialize


    Dim dsDataSet As New DataSet()
    Dim tblDataTable As DataTable
    Dim dcDataColumn As DataColumn
    Dim dcDataRow As DataRow
    Shared aArraylist As New ArrayList()
    Dim bSerialized As Boolean = False

    Sub New()
        ' Create a new DataTable.
        tblDataTable = New DataTable("tblSticky")

        tblDataTable.Clear()

        ' Declare variables for DataColumn and
        ' DataRow objects.
        Dim dcDataColumn As DataColumn
        dcDataColumn = New DataColumn()

        With dcDataColumn
            .DataType = System.Type.GetType("System.String")
            .ColumnName = "Title"
        End With
        tblDataTable.Columns.Add(dcDataColumn)

        dcDataColumn = New DataColumn()
```

```
        With dcDataColumn
            .DataType = System.Type.GetType("System.String")
            .ColumnName = "Message"
        End With
        tblDataTable.Columns.Add(dcDataColumn)

        dcDataColumn = New DataColumn()
        With dcDataColumn
            .DataType = System.Type.GetType("System.String")
            .ColumnName = "Location"
        End With
        tblDataTable.Columns.Add(dcDataColumn)

        dcDataColumn = New DataColumn()
        With dcDataColumn
            .DataType = System.Type.GetType("System.String")
            .ColumnName = "Size"
        End With
        tblDataTable.Columns.Add(dcDataColumn)

        dsDataSet.Tables.Add(tblDataTable)
    End Sub

    Sub addNewSticky(ByVal sticky As BaseNote)
        aArraylist.Add(sticky)
    End Sub

    Sub showAll()
        Dim fSticky As Sticky.BaseNote

        For Each fSticky In aArraylist
            fSticky.Show()
        Next
    End Sub

    Shared Sub delete(ByVal sticky As BaseNote)
        aArraylist.Remove(sticky)
    End Sub

    Sub hideAll()
        Dim fSticky As Sticky.BaseNote

        For Each fSticky In aArraylist
            fSticky.Hide()
        Next
    End Sub

    Sub serialize()
        If bSerialized = True Then Exit Sub
```

(continued)

```
        Dim fSticky As Sticky.BaseNote

        '--Remove older data
        tblDataTable.Clear()

        For Each fSticky In aArraylist
            dcDataRow = tblDataTable.NewRow()
            dcDataRow(0) = fSticky.Text
            dcDataRow(1) = fSticky.txtNote.Text
            dcDataRow(2) = fSticky.Location
            dcDataRow(3) = fSticky.Size
            tblDataTable.Rows.Add(dcDataRow)
        Next

        Dim strStream As Stream = File.Open("c:\sticky.xml", _
            FileMode.Create, FileAccess.ReadWrite)
        dsDataSet.WriteXml(strStream)

        strStream.Close()
        bSerialized = True
    End Sub

    Sub deserialize()
        Dim strStream As Stream
        Try
            strStream File.Open("c:\sticky.xml", _
                FileMode.OpenOrCreate, FileAccess.Read)
            Dim xmlrXmlReader As New _
                System.Xml.XmlTextReader(strStream)

            dsDataSet.ReadXml(xmlrXmlReader)
            xmlrXmlReader.Close()

            Dim dtDataTable As DataTable
            Dim drDataRow As DataRow
            Dim dcDataColumn As DataColumn
            Dim sPoint As String    'Hold  {Width=248,
                                    ' Height=184}
            Dim sLocation As String 'Hold "248,184"

            For Each dtDataTable In dsDataSet.Tables
                For Each drDataRow In dtDataTable.Rows

                    Dim fSticky As BaseNote = New BaseNote()

                    fSticky.Text = drDataRow(0)
                    fSticky.txtNote.Text = drDataRow(1)
```

```
                sPoint = drDataRow(2)
                fSticky.Location = formatPoint(sPoint)

                sPoint = drDataRow(3)
                fSticky.Size = formatSize(sPoint)

                fSticky.Show()
                aArraylist.Add(fSticky)

            Next
        Next
    Catch

    End Try
    StrStream.Close()

    If (aArraylist.Count = 0) Then
        MessageBox.Show("No notes - please right " & _
            "click icon in tray", "Sticky Notes", _
            MessageBoxButtons.OK, _
            MessageBoxIcon.Information)
    End If
End Sub

Function formatPoint(ByVal sPoint As String) As Point
    Dim sFormattedPoint As String
    Dim pPoint As New Point()

    Dim aPoint() As String = sPoint.Split(",")

    Dim cStart As Char() = {"{"c, "X"c, "="c}
    pPoint.X = aPoint(0).TrimStart(cStart)

    Dim cEnd As Char() = {"Y"c, "="c}
    sFormattedPoint = aPoint(1).TrimStart(cEnd)

    pPoint.Y = sFormattedPoint.Trim("}"c)

    Return pPoint
End Function

Function formatSize(ByVal sPoint As String) As Size
    Dim sFormattedPoint As String
    Dim sSize As New Size()

    '<Size>{Width=248, Height=184}</Size>

    Dim aPoint() As String = sPoint.Split(",")
```

(continued)

```
            Dim cWidth As Char() = {"{"c, "W"c, "i"c, "d"c, _
                "t"c, "h"c, "="c}
            sSize.Width = aPoint(0).TrimStart(cWidth)


            Dim cHeight As Char() = {" "c, "H"c, "e"c, "i"c, _
                "g"c, "h"c, "t"c, "="c}
            sFormattedPoint = aPoint(1).TrimStart(cHeight)
            sSize.Height = sFormattedPoint.Trim("}"c)

            Return sSize
        End Function
    End Class
```

4. Now that we have the *serialize* class built, it can be instantiated from our default form. Return to the default form code window, Form1.vb, and add an *Imports System* statement.

5. The context menu as well as the menu items that will be added will have class-level scope, so add these lines right after the *#Region* added by the IDE.

```
#Region " Windows Form Designer generated code "

    Dim cmContextMenu As New ContextMenu()
    Dim mnuItem1 As New MenuItem("New Note")
    Dim mnuItem2 As New MenuItem("Hide All")
    Dim mnuItem3 As New MenuItem("Show All")
    Dim mnuItem4 As New MenuItem("Quit Program")

    Shared ser As New serialize()

    Public Sub New()
        MyBase.New()

        'This call is required by the Windows Form Designer.
        InitializeComponent()

        'Add any initialization after the
        ' InitializeComponent() call
        addContextMenu()
        ser.deserialize()
    End Sub
```

6. In the *Dispose* procedure, add the following line that will call the *Serialize* method of the *ser* class. When the main form, Form1, is disposed of, all existing notes will be written to a stream.

```
Protected Overloads Overrides Sub Dispose( _
    ByVal disposing As Boolean)

    If disposing Then
        ser.serialize()
        If Not (components Is Nothing) Then
            components.Dispose()
        End If
    End If
    MyBase.Dispose(disposing)
End Sub
```

7. Now add the following procedures.

```
Private Sub addContextMenu()
    With cmContextMenu
        .MenuItems.Add(mnuItem1)   ' New Note
        .MenuItems.Add(mnuItem2)   ' Hide All
        .MenuItems.Add(mnuItem3)   ' Show All
        .MenuItems.Add(mnuItem4)   ' Quit Program
    End With

    niIcon.ContextMenu = cmContextMenu

    AddHandler mnuItem1.Click, AddressOf mnuItem1Click
    AddHandler mnuItem2.Click, AddressOf mnuItem2Click
    AddHandler mnuItem3.Click, AddressOf mnuItem3Click
    AddHandler mnuItem4.Click, AddressOf mnuItem4Click
End Sub

Sub mnuItem1Click(ByVal sender As System.Object, _
    ByVal e As System.EventArgs)

    '--Create a new note--
    Dim fSticky As Form = New BaseNote()

    With fSticky
        .Text = Now
        .Show()
    End With

    ser.addNewSticky(fSticky)
End Sub

Sub mnuItem2Click(ByVal sender As System.Object, _
    ByVal e As System.EventArgs)

    ser.hideAll()
End Sub
```

(continued)

```
Sub mnuItem3Click(ByVal sender As System.Object, _
    ByVal e As System.EventArgs)

    ser.showAll()
End Sub

Sub mnuItem4Click(ByVal sender As System.Object, _
    ByVal e As System.EventArgs)

    Me.Dispose()
End Sub
```

Constructing a Sticky Note

Of course, a sticky note is really just a form. Select Project | Add Windows Form, name the form BaseNote.vb, and then click Open. We will design this new form to be a note, and then, because forms are classes, we will instantiate as many of these forms as we need as new notes.

1. Add a text box control to the form. Next drag a MainMenu control from the toolbox to the design area. Set the properties of our form and its text box control as shown in Table 14-2.

Table 14-2 Properties for BaseNote Form and Controls

Object	Property	Value
Form	*Name*	BaseNote
	ControlBox	False
	Icon	\Program Files\Microsoft Visual Studio .NET\Common7\Graphics\Icons\Writing\Note02.ico
	MaximizeBox	False
	Menu	MainMenu1
	ShowInTaskBar	False
	MinimizeBox	False
	StartPosition	Manual
Text box	*Name*	TxtNote
	BackColor	Yellow
	Dock	Fill
	MultiLine	True

> **Note** Each note is a form and would usually be displayed in the taskbar. If 10 or 20 notes are either displayed or hidden, having them all show up in the taskbar can be distracting. Setting the *ShowInTaskBar* property to False fixes this problem.

2. Click the MainMenu control on the BaseNote form. On the top level, add &Note as a menu item. Next add three sublevel menu items—&Keep on Top; &Delete this note; &Hide this note. You can see the results in Figure 14-16.

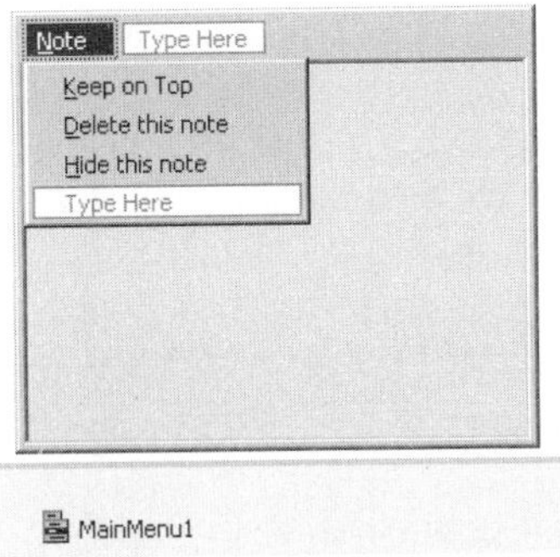

Figure 14-16 Add these menu items.

Adding Code to the Sticky Note

Surprisingly, we don't need a lot of code in this form. We will instantiate a *BaseNote* form for each new note, but adding, saving, and other operations will be performed in the *serialize* class. First, add these imports statements.

```
Imports System.Windows.Forms
Imports Sticky.Form1
Imports Sticky.serialize
```

As I mentioned, users can and will try to close various *BaseForm* sticky note forms. If they close a note form, it will not be available when we attempt to serialize all notes at the time the program is terminated. This is an easy problem to fix: we don't let users close a form because we eliminated the close button in the upper right corner and also the default form menu. We will simply hide the form, but not close it.

Intercepting the *Close* Event

You may in your programs find a need to programmatically stop the user from closing a form. To do this, when the user closes the form, you can intercept the *Close* event and hide the form instead by placing code in the *Closing* event. Because a form's *Closing* event template is not included by default, we could write it ourselves or let the IDE do it for us. Select Base Class Events in the drop-down list to the left in the IDE. Click the drop-down box to the right, and you'll see all the event handlers that the form knows how to respond to. Click *Closing* and the template will be written for us, as you see in Figure 14-17.

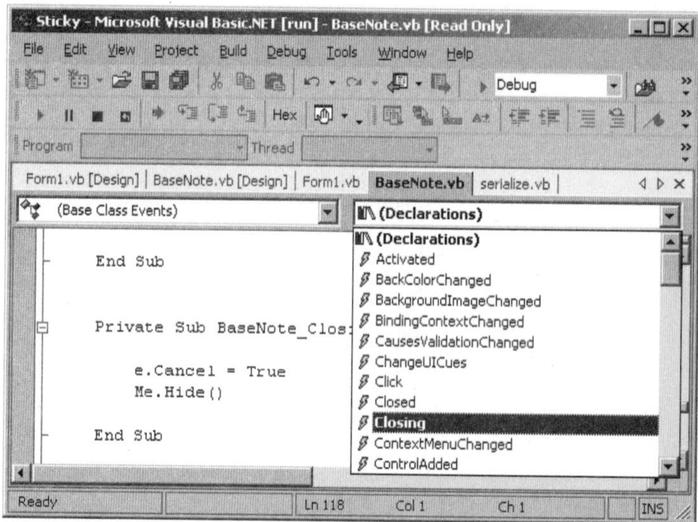

Figure 14-17 Click *Closing* to force the IDE to write a template for the *Closing* event.

If you ever need to stop a user from closing a form, intercept the *Closing* event and set the *CancelEventArgs* property to True. You might want to do this for a form in which a user enters data and might accidentally close the form. Most word processing or data capture forms contain a Boolean, *bIsDirty*, which is set to False when the form is loaded. If the user changes any information on the form, *bIsDirty* is set to True. When the user closes the form, the value of *bIsDirty* is checked. If the value is True, and the data was not yet saved, a message box is displayed alerting the user and asking whether the data should be saved before closing the form. Again, you don't need to add this code to our sample program. I'm showing it for illustrative purposes only.

Intercepting the *Close* Event *(continued)*

```
Private Sub AForms_Closing(ByVal sender As Object, _
    ByVal e As System.ComponentModel.CancelEventArgs) _
    Handles MyBase.Closing

    e.Cancel = True   'Cancels the form's closing
End Sub
```

Go ahead and add the code to handle the three child menu click events.

```
Private Sub MenuItem2_Click(ByVal sender As System.Object, _
    ByVal e As System.EventArgs) Handles MenuItem2.Click

    MenuItem2.Checked = Not MenuItem2.Checked

    If MenuItem2.Checked = True Then
        Me.TopMost = True
    Else
        Me.TopMost = False
    End If
End Sub

Private Sub MenuItem3_Click(ByVal sender As System.Object, _
    ByVal e As System.EventArgs) Handles MenuItem3.Click

    Dim iResult As Integer = MessageBox.Show("Delete this note?", _
        "Yellow Sticky", MessageBoxButtons.YesNoCancel, _
        MessageBoxIcon.Question)

    If iResult = DialogResult.Yes Then
        serialize.delete(Me)
        Me.Close()
        Me.Dispose()
    End If
End Sub

Private Sub MenuItem4_Click(ByVal sender As System.Object, _
    ByVal e As System.EventArgs) Handles MenuItem4.Click

    MenuItem2.Checked = False
    Me.Hide()
End Sub
```

How Does It Work?

Let's start with the sequence of how the code will execute. When our start up form is run, a context menu along with four menu items are dimensioned. Of course, this form will be invisible; we are using it only to display the menu and run the message loop. All of the menu items have class-level scope. The menu items are overloaded, so passing in the title we want in the menu prevents us from having to set the *Text* property of each later on.

```
Dim cmContextMenu As New ContextMenu()
Dim mnuItem1 As New MenuItem("New Note")
Dim mnuItem2 As New MenuItem("Hide All")
Dim mnuItem3 As New MenuItem("Show All")
Dim mnuItem4 As New MenuItem("Quit Program")
```

The next step is to instantiate an instance of our *serialize* class. We do this by assigning a new instance to our reference variable *ser*. Note that *ser* is shared. We shared this variable because we want to access this class from both this form and each individual *BaseNote* form. Therefore, we want only a single instance of *serialize* to be shared among entities in the program. The *serialize* class maintains an *ArrayList* of all forms currently active in our program, so we want to be sure that all forms work with this single *ArrayList*. Setting the access to *Shared* ensures that only a single copy of *serialize* will exist.

```
Shared ser As New serialize()
```

Now we call the routine *addContextMenu* to build our context menu for the program. Because the opacity of the form Form1 is 0 percent, it is invisible. The context menu is the only interface to our program. After the context menu is built, the *deserialize* method of the *serialize* class is called. This method reads an XML file that contains any current sticky note information.

```
'Add any initialization after the
' InitializeComponent() call
addContextMenu()
ser.deserialize()
```

The *addContextMenu* routine adds each of the four menu items we declared above to the *MenuItems* collection of the context menu. The *MenuItems* property contains the entire menu structure for the control. For the context menu, the *MenuItems* property contains the list of submenu items associated with the context menu. With the reference to the collection of menu items for the menu (provided by this property), you can add and remove menu items, determine the total number of menu items, and clear the list of menu items from the collection.

```
Private Sub addContextMenu()
    With cmContextMenu
```

```
        .MenuItems.Add(mnuItem1)    ' New Note
        .MenuItems.Add(mnuItem2)    ' Hide All
        .MenuItems.Add(mnuItem3)    ' Show All
        .MenuItems.Add(mnuItem4)    ' Quit Program
    End With
```

Now that the context menu has been built, we can assign it to the notify icon's *contextMenu* property.

```
niIcon.ContextMenu = cmContextMenu
```

We next have to add event handlers to manage the *Click* event of each menu item. *AddHandler* takes two arguments: the name of an event from an event sender such as *menuItem1*, and an expression that evaluates to a delegate such as *mnuItem1Click*. You do not need to explicitly specify the delegate class when using *AddHandler* because the *AddressOf* statement always returns a reference to the delegate.

```
AddHandler mnuItem1.Click, AddressOf mnuItem1Click
AddHandler mnuItem2.Click, AddressOf mnuItem2Click
AddHandler mnuItem3.Click, AddressOf mnuItem3Click
AddHandler mnuItem4.Click, AddressOf mnuItem4Click
```

Adding Event Handler Delegates

The delegates' event handlers are where all of the action takes place in Form1. We added a handler for the *mnuItem1.Click* event and pointed it to the address of the *mnuItem1Click* event handler, which we must build on our own. Remember that *mnuItem1* is for adding a new sticky note. When the user clicks this item, the *mnuItem1Click* delegate that was wired to that event is fired. We first instantiate a new instance of *BaseNote* and assign it to the reference variable *fSticky*. With the new form, we add the current time to the title and then immediately display the new note. After the new sticky note form is displayed, the form is passed to the *addNewSticky* method of the *serialize* class, which inserts the form in an *ArrayList*. We will soon visit the *serialize* class to see how this is done.

```
Sub mnuItem1Click(ByVal sender As System.Object, _
    ByVal e As System.EventArgs)

    '--Create a new note--
    Dim fSticky As Form = New BaseNote()

    With fSticky
        .Text = Now
        .Show()
    End With

        ser.addNewSticky(fSticky)
End Sub
```

The next menu item permits the user to hide all of the sticky notes on the screen. A simple call to the *hideAll* method in the *serialize* class handles this.

```
Sub mnuItem2Click(ByVal sender As System.Object, _
    ByVal e As System.EventArgs)

    ser.hideAll()
End Sub
```

The same concept applies when the user clicks the Show All menu item. The *showAll* method is called from the *serialize* class.

```
Sub mnuItem3Click(ByVal sender As System.Object, _
    ByVal e As System.EventArgs)

    ser.showAll()
End Sub
```

When the user clicks the fourth menu item, Quit Program, we must take care to save all of the current notes to disk. To accomplish this, the *Dispose* method of Form1 is called. Because Form1 is invisible, this call is the only way to dismiss the program short of the task manager.

```
Sub mnuItem4Click(ByVal sender As System.Object, _
    ByVal e As System.EventArgs)

    Me.Dispose()
End Sub
```

In this built-in method, we add a call to the *serialize* method of the *serialize* class. This method is responsible for writing all of the notes to disk. Only when serialization is accomplished is program control returned and the form dismissed.

```
Protected Overloads Overrides _
Sub Dispose(ByVal disposing As Boolean)
    If disposing Then
        ser.serialize()
        If Not (components Is Nothing) Then
            components.Dispose()
        End If
    End If
    MyBase.Dispose(disposing)
End Sub
```

It's easy to see that all of the sticky note form manipulation was encapsulated in the *serialize* class. When we want to add, hide, or show the notes, methods in *serialize* are called. Likewise, when the program starts, the *deserialize* method of the *serialize* class reads notes from disk. When the program ends, the *serialize* method writes the sticky notes to disk again. The *serialize* class juggles all of the notes and acts as a traffic cop for each one of them.

The *serialize* Class in More Detail

The *serialize* class builds a data table and adds it to an in-memory data set to store the information from each sticky note. The *ArrayList* that holds the forms will be accessed both from the driver form (Form1) when we add a new form and from each of the sticky notes as well. The sticky note (a *BaseNote* form) will need to access the *ArrayList* that contains it when a user deletes that particular form. Making the *ArrayList* shared ensures that all the forms in the program use a single copy.

```
Imports System
Imports System.Collections
Imports System.IO

Public Class serialize

    Dim dsDataSet As New DataSet()
    Dim tblDataTable As DataTable
    Dim dcDataColumn As DataColumn
    Dim dcDataRow As DataRow
    Shared aArraylist As New ArrayList()
    Dim bSerialized As Boolean = False
```

The *New* subroutine is the constructor of the *serialize* class and is called from our driver form, Form1. When a new, shared instance of this class is instantiated, we build a new *DataTable* object with the name *tblSticky*. The *DataTable* is then cleared just for good form.

```
Sub New()
    'Create a new DataTable
    tblDataTable = New DataTable("tblSticky")

    tblDataTable.Clear()
```

Of course, we have to add columns to the new table in which to store information from our sticky notes. After a new *DataColumn* class is instantiated and referenced with the reference variable *dcDataColumn*, we give the column a data type and a name. This new column is then added to the *Columns* collection of our new table.

```
'Declare variables for DataColumn and DataRow objects.
Dim dcDataColumn As DataColumn
dcDataColumn = New DataColumn()

With dcDataColumn
    .DataType = System.Type.GetType("System.String")
    .ColumnName = "Title"
End With
tblDataTable.Columns.Add(dcDataColumn)
```

When we want to store a form, we could stream the entire form to disk with a *BinaryFormatter* class. However, this approach would be overkill for our purposes. It's much easier to simply store our information in XML. So because we are not storing the entire *BaseForm* class but only its important information, we want to create fields for the actual message of the note, the location of the note, and the size of the note, in addition to the sticky note's title. With this critical information we can re-create as many notes as required. This table will be used when we save each note.

```
dcDataColumn = New DataColumn()
With dcDataColumn
    .DataType = System.Type.GetType("System.String")
    .ColumnName = "Message"
End With
tblDataTable.Columns.Add(dcDataColumn)

dcDataColumn = New DataColumn()
With dcDataColumn
    .DataType = System.Type.GetType("System.String")
    .ColumnName = "Location"
End With
tblDataTable.Columns.Add(dcDataColumn)

dcDataColumn = New DataColumn()
With dcDataColumn
    .DataType = System.Type.GetType("System.String")
    .ColumnName = "Size"
End With
tblDataTable.Columns.Add(dcDataColumn)

dsDataSet.Tables.Add(tblDataTable)
```

As soon as a new shared instance of the *serialize* class is instantiated from Form1, we call the *deserialize* method. The purpose of this method is to read an XML file that might contain sticky notes that were previously saved. The XML file is read from disk into the data set we created in the constructor. For each saved note, we create a new instance of the sticky note and reconstitute its message, size, and location.

When we dismiss the Sticky program, the *serialize* method writes any notes to a file, Sticky.xml. In *serialize* we open a stream. As mentioned earlier in the book, the *Stream* class and its derived classes provide a generic view of data sources and repositories, isolating the programmer from the specific details of the operating system and underlying devices. When we open the file and assign it to the stream, we use the *FileMode* and *FileAccess* parameters to specify that the operating system should open a file if it exists or create a new file if one does not. We could have first used the *File.Exists("c:\sticky.xml")* method, but using that method would mean another line of code and another Boolean check. So using *FileMode* is simply a design decision.

Once *strStream* points to the XML file containing our saved notes, we can read the XML file into our data set by passing in the stream as a parameter to a new *XmlTextReader*. The *XmlTextReader* object represents a reader that provides fast, noncached, forward-only access to XML data. The *XmlReader* checks that the XML is well formed and throws *XmlExceptions* if an error is encountered. It can read a stream or a document, and it implements the namespace requirements outlined in the recommendation provided by the W3C, located at *www.w3.org/TR/REC-xml-names*.

As you might recall from our discussion of ADO.NET, to read just the schema from an XML document, use the *ReadXmlSchema* method. To read the data from an XML document that contains only data into a data set, use the *ReadXml* method. Once the XML file has been read into the data set, we close the *XmlTextReader* and free up its resources. Using *Try...Catch...End Try* structured error handling protects us in the event that we can't read the file or errors occur when assigning properties.

```
Sub deserialize()
    Dim strStream As Stream
    Try
        strStream = File.Open("c:\sticky.xml", _
            FileMode.OpenOrCreate, FileAccess.Read)
        Dim xmlrXmlReader As New _
            System.Xml.XmlTextReader(strStream)

        dsDataSet.ReadXml(xmlrXmlReader)
        xmlrXmlReader.Close()
```

Now that the data set has been populated, we know that a single table is defined in the XML file. This code dimensions *DataTable*, *DataRow*, and *DataColumn* objects so that we can read what's in the data set. In addition, when we save the location and size of the form, these values are saved as groups of data. However, when we try to assign this data back to a new form to set its location and size, we have to format the information differently. The sticky note's *Location* property requires a *Point* data type and the *Size* property requires a *Size* data type, while we are storing this information in strings in our XML file.

```
<Location>{X=408,Y=80}</Location>
<Size>{Width=248, Height=131}</Size>
```

We can easily get the table we want by iterating through the tables collection of our data. We, however, know there is only a single table, *tblDataTable*. Next we loop through each of the rows in the *Rows* collection of the data table. Each row represents all the information about a single sticky note. On looping through a new row, a new *BaseNote* class (a sticky note) is instantiated. We know that the first row contains the contents of the title of the form, which we set to the time the note was created. The second field is the actual message of the note. This field is assigned to the *Text* property of the *txtNote* text box on the form.

```
<NewDataSet>
- <tblSticky>
  <Title>9/19/2000 11:19:23 PM</Title>
  <Message>Remember to feed Roscoe.</Message>
  <Location>{X=408,Y=80}</Location>
  <Size>{Width=248, Height=131}</Size>
  </tblSticky>
```

```
Dim dtDataTable As DataTable
Dim drDataRow As DataRow
Dim dcDataColumn As DataColumn
Dim sPoint As String    'Hold  {Width=248,
                        ' Height=184}
Dim sLocation As String 'Hold "248,184"

    For Each dtDataTable In dsDataSet.Tables
        For Each drDataRow In dtDataTable.Rows

            Dim fSticky As BaseNote = New BaseNote()

            fSticky.Text = drDataRow(0)
            fSticky.txtNote.Text = drDataRow(1)
```

The location of the form is stored as an *x*, *y* coordinate. However, this represents a *Point* data type, which contains both an *X* and a *Y* property that needs to be set. If you expand the *Location* property on the properties window of the *BaseNote* form, you can see the two properties, as shown in Figure 14-18.

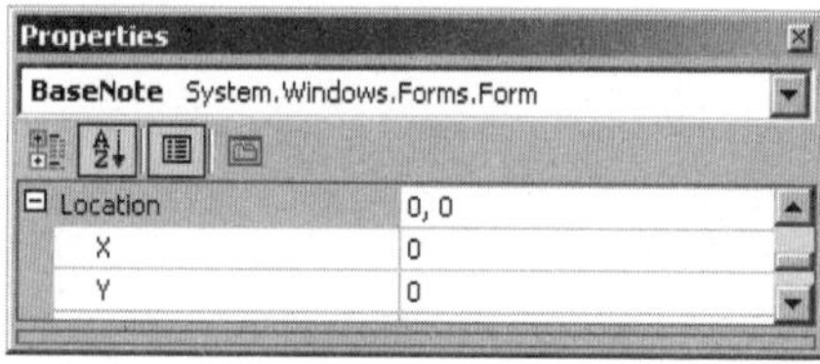

Figure 14-18 The two properties of the *Point* data type.

```
sPoint = drDataRow(2)
fSticky.Location = formatPoint(sPoint)
```

We take the contents of the third element of the record and assign it to the string *sPoint*. The string will look something like this:

```
<Location>{X=408,Y=80}</Location>
```

The string will have to be converted to a type *Point*. Our function, *formatPoint*, is passed the string containing the location. The function returns a *Point* data type that can now be assigned safely to the *Location* property of the new sticky form.

The same concept applies when we want to set the *Size* property. We take the fourth column and assign it to a string variable. This column's contents will look something like this:

```
<Size>{Width=248, Height=131}</Size>
```

We created another function, *formatSize*, that will take the size record stored in the fourth column and return a properly formatted *Size* data type that can safely be assigned to the *Size* property of our sticky note.

```
sPoint = drDataRow(3)
fSticky.Size = formatSize(sPoint)
```

When the new sticky form's properties are all set, the form is displayed and added to our *ArrayList*, which manages all of the current sticky notes during a session.

```
            fSticky.Show()
            aArraylist.Add(fSticky)

        Next
    Next
Catch
End Try
StrStream.Close()
```

In the event no sticky notes are stored on the hard drive, a message is displayed alerting the user to that fact. The *Count* property of our *ArrayList* can be interrogated to determine how many sticky forms have been created and stored for this session.

```
If (aArraylist.Count = 0) Then
    MessageBox.Show("No notes - please right " & _
        "click icon in tray", "Sticky Notes", _
         MessageBoxButtons.OK, _
         MessageBoxIcon.Information)
End If
```

During a session, the user can right-click the notify icon and select New Note. In that case, our driver form, Form1, instantiates a new *BaseNote* object and calls *serialize.AddNewSticky*. As you can see, that call simply inserts the new form into our *ArrayList*.

```
Sub addNewSticky(ByVal sticky As BaseNote)
    aArraylist.Add(sticky)
End Sub
```

If the user wants to display all of the notes—as some might have been hidden previously during a session—the *showAll* method is called from Form1 when the Show All menu item is clicked. Here we simply iterate through each of the sticky note forms stored in the *ArrayList* and call the *Show* method.

```
Sub showAll()
    Dim fSticky As Sticky.BaseNote

    For Each fSticky In aArraylist
        fSticky.Show()
    Next
End Sub
```

Remember that the user can delete an individual note by selecting Delete This Note from the menu for that individual note. This procedure is shared so that the same procedure can be accessed from all of the sticky notes to ensure that all forms add themselves to and remove themselves from the same *ArrayList*. The individual note is passed as a parameter and removed from the *ArrayList*. Because the *ArrayList* manages all existing forms, removing a note ensures that the deleted note will not be serialized to disk when the program is exited.

```
Shared Sub delete(ByVal sticky As BaseNote)
    aArraylist.Remove(sticky)
End Sub
```

The *hideAll* procedure is conceptually like *showAll*. When the user clicks the Hide All menu selection, this subroutine is invoked, the *ArrayList* containing all the sticky notes is iterated through, and the *Hide* method is called on each, effectively hiding each form in turn.

```
Sub hideAll()
    Dim fSticky As Sticky.BaseNote

    For Each fSticky In aArraylist
        fSticky.Hide()
    Next
End Sub
```

When the User Quits the Sticky Notes Program

When the Sticky Notes program is terminated, the *serialize* method is called from the *dispose* method of Form1. Remember that we added this line to be sure our *serialize* class saved all the notes properly before returning control to the *dispose* method.

```
Protected Overloads Overrides _
Sub Dispose(ByVal disposing As Boolean)
```

```
    If disposing Then
        ser.serialize()
        If Not (components Is Nothing) Then
            components.Dispose()
        End If
    End If
    MyBase.Dispose(disposing)
End Sub
```

The *serialize* method essentially iterates through each sticky note form that is stored in the *ArrayList*, assigns its important properties to a new row in the data table we created in the constructor, and then uses the *WriteXML* method of the data set to stream out the contents of our sticky notes. Depending on when this routine is called, it might be called twice. To prevent an error, we set the Boolean *bSerialized* to True the first time through; if it is called again, program control simply exits.

A variable of type *Sticky.BaseNote* has been declared and assigned to the reference variable *fSticky*. We want to be sure that the data table is empty before we save our current notes; invoking the *Clear* method of the table handles this for us.

```
Sub serialize()
    If bSerialized = True Then Exit Sub

    Dim fSticky As Sticky.BaseNote

    '--Remove older data
    tblDataTable.Clear()
```

Next we build new rows for the data table and then add each to the *Rows* collection. This lets us use the *WriteXML* method of the data set to create our file.

```
For Each fSticky In aArraylist
    dcDataRow = tblDataTable.NewRow()
    dcDataRow(0) = fSticky.Text
    dcDataRow(1) = fSticky.txtNote.Text
    dcDataRow(2) = fSticky.Location
    dcDataRow(3) = fSticky.Size
    tblDataTable.Rows.Add(dcDataRow)
Next
```

When the important information for each form in the *ArrayList* has been translated into a new row in our data table, we open another stream to our Sticky.xml file. By passing the stream to the *WriteXML* method of the data set, our file is created for us. The stream is closed and the Boolean is set to True, indicating that serialization has already been accomplished.

```
Dim strStream As Stream = File.Open("c:\sticky.xml", _
    FileMode.Create, FileAccess.ReadWrite)
dsDataSet.WriteXml(strStream)

strStream.Close()
bSerialized = True
```

Our *formatPoint* function takes in a string and returns a *Point* data type. In this simple function, we cover some important concepts about strings and arrays. First, we dimension variable *pPoint* as type *Point*. Next we dimension an array, *aPoint*, and assign it on the same line. Because we know that the *sPoint* string passed into the function looks like *{X=408,Y=80}*, we need to do something because we want the result to be 408,80 so that we can convert these values to a .NET *Point* data type. Because we are now dealing with a string, using the *Split* method of *sPoint* and the comma as a delimiter, the *aPoint* array will contain two elements. The *Split* method returns a zero-based, one-dimensional array containing a specified number of substrings. Now our array will contain two elements. The first element is *{X=408* and the second element is *Y=80}*.

```
Function formatPoint(ByVal sPoint As String) As Point
    Dim sFormattedPoint As String
    Dim pPoint As New Point()

    Dim aPoint() As String = sPoint.Split(",")
```

We want to get rid of a few characters at the beginning of the first array element. Using the built-in *TrimStart* method does the trick. This method removes characters from the beginning of a string specified by an array of characters. By dimensioning and initializing the *cStart* array of characters that we want to remove, we can pass that array as a parameter of the *TrimStart* method. Each character is designated with a *c* after the quoted character, which ensures that each symbol is cast as a character and not a byte. Each character is stored in the *cStart* array. The *pPoint* variable has an *X* and a *Y* property. Because we know the *X* position is stored in the first array element, that is assigned to our *Point* data type variable. *TrimStart* effectively removes the *{X=* from the element and leaves only the 408 to be assigned to *pPoint.X*.

```
Dim cStart As Char() = {"{"c, "X"c, "="c}
pPoint.X = aPoint(0).TrimStart(cStart)
```

We perform the same operation with the second *aPoint* array element. That element will look something like *Y=80}*. Therefore the *cEnd* array contains the first two characters and the *TrimStart* method removes them and assigns the result to the *sFormattedPoint* string. However, the result will contain an ending bracket and look like *80}*.

```
Dim cEnd As Char() = {"Y"c, "="c}
sFormattedPoint = aPoint(1).TrimStart(cEnd)
```

Removing the curly bracket is simply a matter of using the *Trim* method of the *sFormattedPoint* string and assigning the resulting *"80"* to the *Y* property of the *pPoint* variable. The *pPoint Point* variable is then returned to the caller and assigned to the sticky form's *Location* property.

```
pPoint.Y = sFormattedPoint.Trim("}"c)

Return pPoint
```

The only difference between the *formatPoint* and *formatSize* routines is that we are returning different data types. Except for the specific details, the concepts are identical.

```
Function formatSize(ByVal sPoint As String) As Size
    Dim sFormattedPoint As String
    Dim sSize As New Size()

    '<Size>{Width=248, Height=184}</Size>

    Dim aPoint() As String = sPoint.Split(",")

    Dim cWidth As Char() = {"{"c, "W"c, "i"c, "d"c, "t"c, _
        "h"c, "="c}
    sSize.Width = aPoint(0).TrimStart(cWidth)


    Dim cHeight As Char() = {" "c, "H"c, "e"c, "i"c, _
        "g"c, "h"c, "t"c, "="c}
    sFormattedPoint = aPoint(1).TrimStart(cHeight)
    sSize.Height = sFormattedPoint.Trim("}"c)

    Return sSize
End Function
```

How the *BaseNote* Sticky Yellow Form Works

Our *BaseNote* form has only a few lines of code, so let's take a close look at them. Sometimes the user will want to keep one or two notes on top of all the other windows. Topmost forms are always displayed at the highest point in the z-order of an application. A program such as one that uses a Find and Replace window also might keep its windows on top of others. In our application, we will check the menu item to provide a visual cue that the window is on top, as you can see in Figure 14-19.

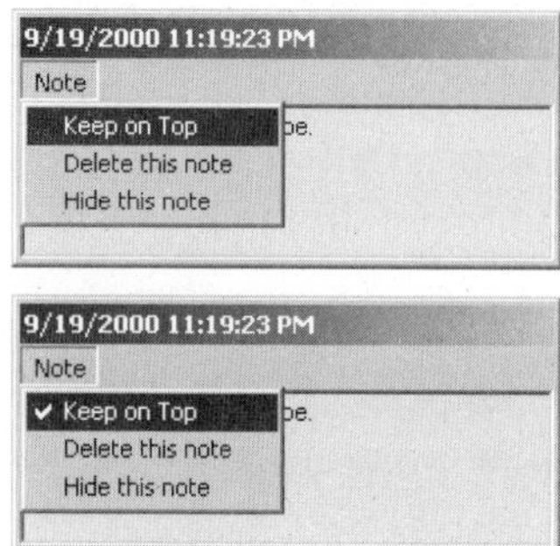

Figure 14-19 The Keep On Top menu item is checked when the *Top-Most* property is True.

Because the menu item can be either checked or unchecked, we will use a little technique that toggles between the two. We can accomplish this in a single line of code.

```
MenuItem2.Checked = Not MenuItem2.Checked
```

When the user clicks the menu for the first time, it is not checked (the *Checked* property is False), so the Not operator sets the *Checked* property to True and the menu becomes checked. Likewise, when the menu item is clicked again, because the *Checked* property is True, the Not operator sets it to False. This mechanism simply toggles between checked and unchecked each time the user clicks the menu item. This is much cleaner than writing code that first checks the current value of the property, then uses an *If* statement to check to see if the menu item is checked, and then unchecks the item. If the menu item is checked, the *Topmost* property of the form is set to True; otherwise it is False.

```
Private Sub MenuItem2_Click(ByVal sender As System.Object, _
    ByVal e As System.EventArgs) Handles MenuItem2.Click

    MenuItem2.Checked = Not MenuItem2.Checked

    If MenuItem2.Checked = True Then
        Me.TopMost = True
    Else
        Me.TopMost = False
    End If
End Sub
```

If the user wants to delete a specific note, the *MenuItem3_Click* event procedure handles this. First, we display a message box to confirm the action, shown in Figure 14-20.

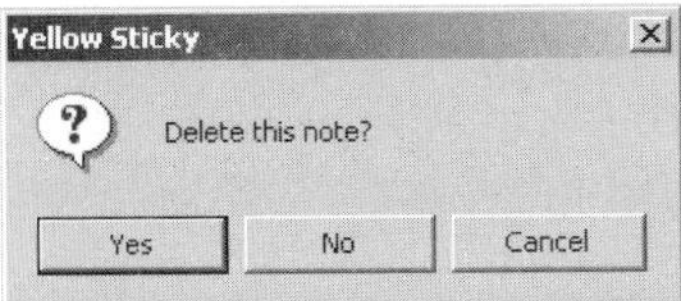

Figure 14-20 We ask for confirmation before deleting a note.

The message box returns an integer that contains one of several enumerated values. Because the message box is a variation of a dialog box, the return values are the same. Each return value is an integer, but they are enumerated, so you can simply test for the English value. To determine what the user selected, we assign the result from the message box to an integer variable, *iResult*. This variable can be checked to see whether the user clicked the Yes button. If the user clicked Yes, the *delete* method of the *serialize* class is called with the current form as a parameter. Remember that the *delete* method simply removes that particular form from the shared *ArrayList*. Recall also that certain fields, methods, and properties can be associated with the class itself rather than with an instance of the class. As mentioned before, our *ArrayList* is allocated in memory only once for the entire class and is shared by all instances of the *BaseNote* form.

```
Private Sub MenuItem3_Click(ByVal sender As System.Object, _
    ByVal e As System.EventArgs) Handles MenuItem3.Click

    Dim iResult As Integer = MessageBox.Show("Delete this note?", _
        "Yellow Sticky", MessageBoxButtons.YesNoCancel, _
        MessageBoxIcon.Question)

    If iResult = DialogResult.Yes Then
        serialize.delete(Me)
        Me.Close()
        Me.Dispose()
    End If

End Sub
```

If the user wants to hide a note but keep it around, we simply make sure that the Keep On Top menu item is unchecked (in case it was previously checked) and then hide the form.

```
Private Sub MenuItem4_Click(ByVal sender As System.Object, _
    ByVal e As System.EventArgs) Handles MenuItem4.Click

    MenuItem2.Checked = False
    Me.Hide()
End Sub
```

Deploying Our Sticky Notes Program

We now have this pretty handy program and want to give it to our friends. Some of our friends might not have the .NET files installed on their computers yet, but the files' absence causes no problem because we can add the required files right in our installation program.

The first step is to add another project to our solution that contains a Setup Wizard. From the main IDE menu, select File | Add Project | New Project. When the Add New Project dialog box is displayed, select Setup And Deployment Projects in the Project Types list and then select Setup Wizard in the group of templates. Give the project the name Sticky Notes.

Visual Studio .NET provides several options that make assembling program files, assemblies, and any resources simple and consistent. The Setup Wizard creates an executable that performs the installation tasks to get the program up and running quickly. Table 14-3 lists some guidelines for choosing the correct type of deployment project to add to your project.

Table 14-3 Types of Deployment Projects

Setup Template	Description
CAB Project	Creates a compressed cabinet archive file that contains multiple smaller files. This could also be used with the other types of projects if many files are included with your project. CAB projects allow you to create a .cab file to package ActiveX components that can be downloaded from a Web server to a Web browser.
Merge Module Project	When several projects use common files, this permits creation of an intermediate module that can be integrated into other setup projects. The resulting .msm files can be included in any other deployment project.
Setup Project	Creates a setup file that automatically installs files and resources on the target client computer.
Setup Wizard	Creates any of these project types with the help of a wizard to walk through the steps.
Web Setup Project	Builds an installer for a Web application.

For a setup project, the installer will install files into a Program Files directory on a target computer. For a Web Setup project, the installer will install files into a Virtual Root directory on a Web server. Note that once a project is created, the type of a project can't be changed from Web to standard or vice versa. If you have created a standard deployment project and decide later to deploy the project to a Web site, you will need to create a new setup project.

After adding the setup project, the Setup Wizard is displayed. The wizard will walk us through deploying any of the types of projects. Click Next on the introductory screen. On the second screen, keep the default value for creating a setup for a Windows application, shown in Figure 14-21.

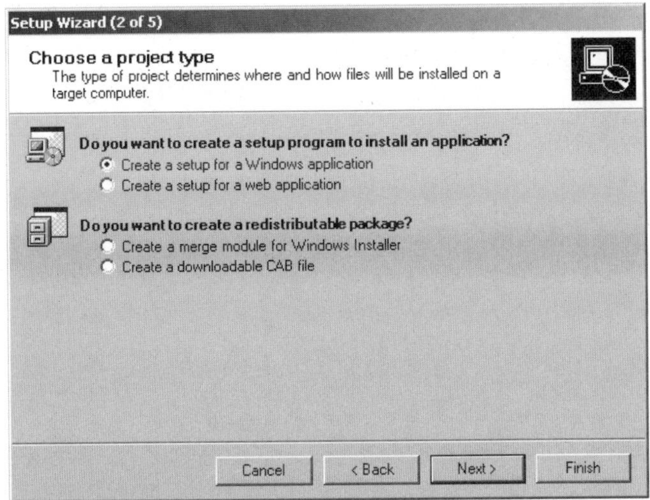

Figure 14-21 Keep the default value for creating a setup for a Windows application.

Click Next, and select Primary Output From Sticky, which will be the executable for our compiled program. Click Next again. The fourth screen permits the addition of any help or readme files, bitmaps, or any other resource files you want to include with the program. Our program is so simple we don't need any help files. Click Next to display the last page of the Setup Wizard, shown in Figure 14-22.

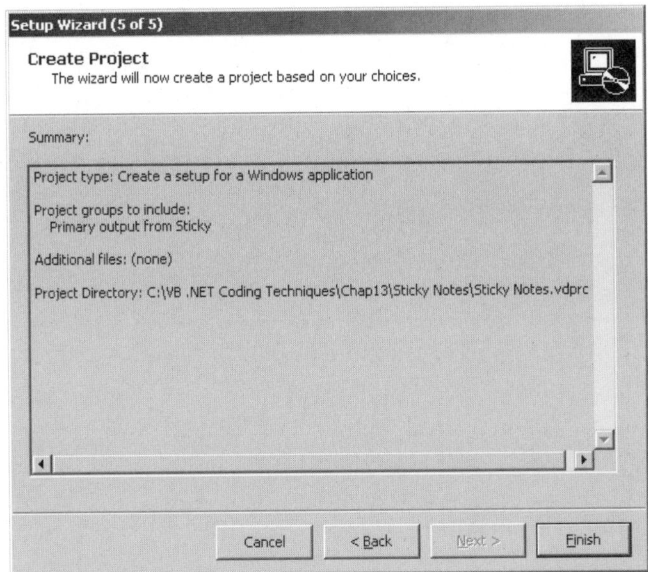

Figure 14-22 The summary information of the Setup Wizard.

After reviewing the summary information, click Finish. The new setup project will be added to the Solution Explorer. Either right-click the entry for the primary output from Sticky and select Properties or select the entry and click the Properties button in the upper left of the Solution Explorer, shown in Figure 14-23.

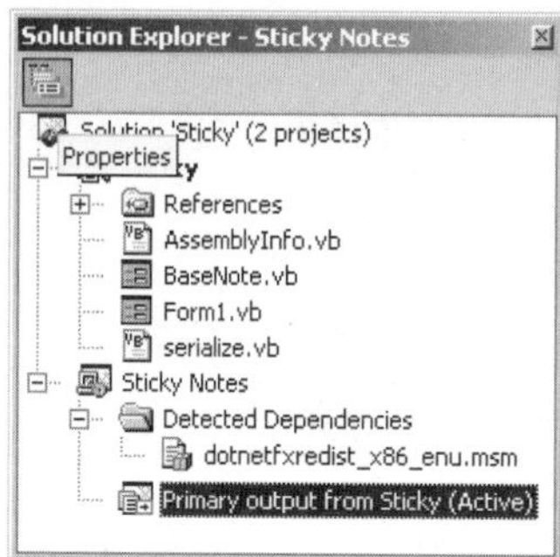

Figure 14-23 Open the Properties window for the primary output from our program.

Take a few minutes to review the properties for the output of the program. Expand the KeyOutput node, shown in Figure 14-24, and examine the entries to gain a sense of what will be included in the build. Clicking Dependencies displays a dialog box showing all the files required to run the Sticky Notes program. Clicking the ellipsis button in the Files entry opens the Files dialog box that will show Sticky.exe. If any readme files had been included, they would also be displayed here.

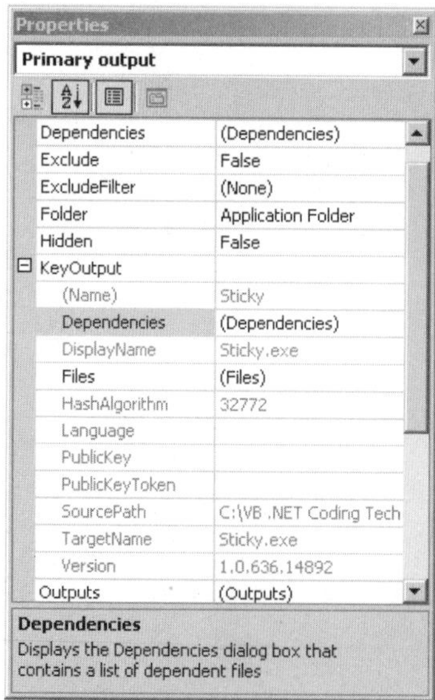

Figure 14-24 Expand the KeyOutput node.

You can customize the installation process for your own company. Bring up the Solution Explorer, and click the Sticky Notes setup project. Notice the new icons displayed in the Explorer. These icons provide options for you to customize the installation process. Click the fourth button, for the User Interface Editor, shown in Figure 14-25.

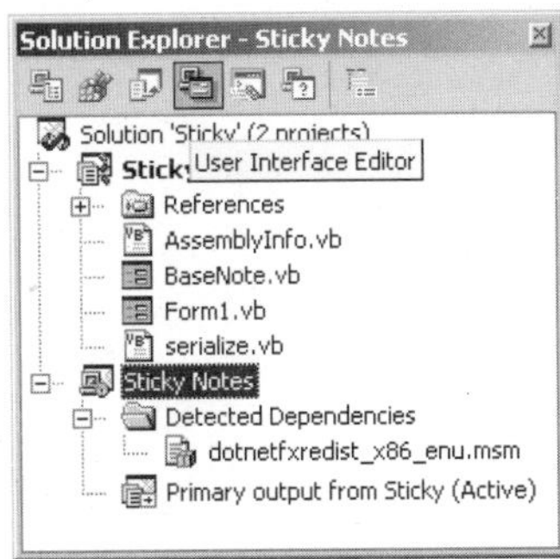

Figure 14-25 Click the User Interface Editor button.

A User Interface tab will be displayed in the IDE. Expand all the nodes in the install tree. The properties of each of these items can be selected and customized. The User Interface Editor is used to specify and edit dialog boxes that are displayed during installation on a target computer. Dialog boxes are included for most common installation functions such as gathering user information or reporting progress, but you can also add your own custom dialog boxes.

Right-click the Progress item, and select Properties Window. Here you can suppress the progress bar or even add a bitmap to be displayed during installation, as shown in Figure 14-26.

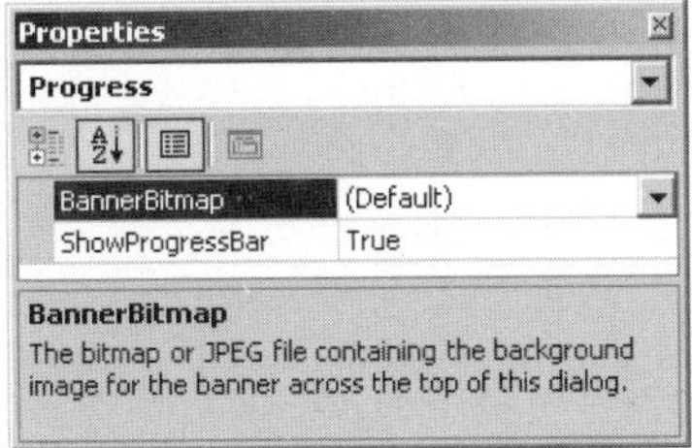

Figure 14-26 The Properties window for the Progress item.

Now we want to finally build our Sticky Notes project, so let's change the build type from Debug to Release. From the main IDE menu select Build | Configuration Manager. Change the configuration options to Release, and select the Build check box for the Sticky Notes project, shown in Figure 14-27, and then close the window.

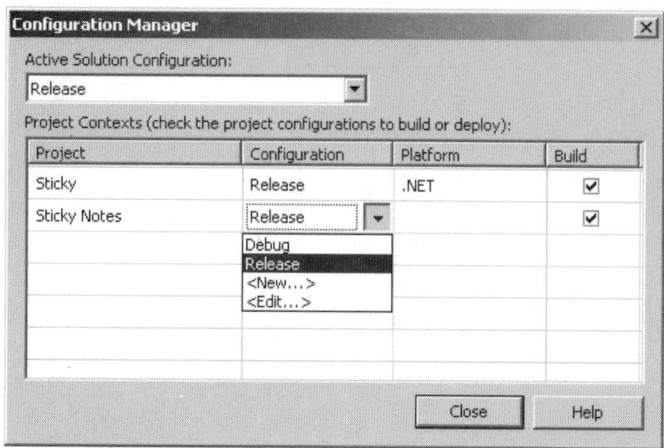

Figure 14-27 Change the configuration options to Release, and select the Build check box for the Sticky Notes project.

From the main menu, select Build | Build Solution. The Build window of the Output form displays the progress as our program is being compiled. Notice how all the dependent files are also included in the build.

Installing Our Program on a Client Machine

To find our setup file, navigate to the directory in which you built the program. In the example, we called the setup project Sticky Notes, so a directory was created with the name Sticky Notes. The Sticky Notes.msi file is in the release subdirectory of the Sticky Notes directory, *<drive>DirectoryCreatedIn*\Sticky Notes\Release.

DLL conflicts will be eliminated as advertised with .NET. All of the files required to run our program are installed in the directory along with our .msi file. In theory you could use the venerable MS-DOS XCOPY command to copy all these files into a single directory, without having to worry about registry entries or shared DLLs in the system directory. Everything needed to run Sticky Notes is contained in the single directory. Even Mscorlib.dll, which contains the common language runtime, is included. That is how the magic is accomplished.

Right-click the Sticky Notes.msi install program, and select Properties. As you can see in Figure 14-28, the program is over 15 megabytes because of all the support files that were installed in the CAB file.

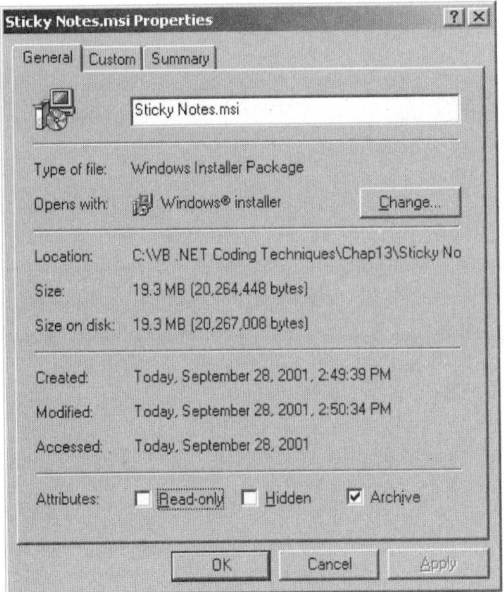

Figure 14-28 The Sticky Notes program's properties dialog box.

Install the Sticky Notes Program

Double-click the Sticky Notes installation icon to install the program on the client machine. The setup program starts its work, as you can see in Figure 14-29.

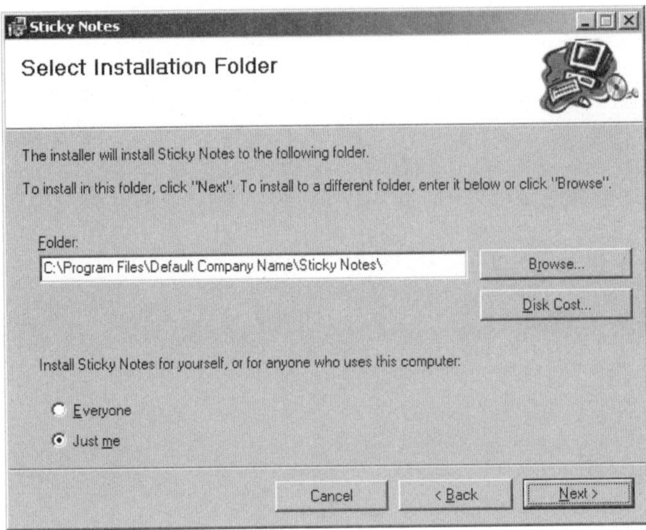

Figure 14-29 Installing the Sticky Notes program.

To find your program, navigate to <*Drive*>\Program Files*Default Company Name*\Sticky Notes. The file Sticky.exe is in that directory. Right-click Sticky.exe, select Create Shortcut, and then drag the shortcut icon to the desktop so that it will always be available. Run the Sticky Notes program to see your work in action. It's as simple as that.

Conclusion

Bill Gates has commented that moving from traditional programming to the .NET Framework will be a bigger shift for programmers than was the move from MS-DOS to Windows. Based on what you have learned in this book, I can only imagine that you will agree. You are now ready to start using Visual Basic .NET in a meaningful way. In addition, you are now equipped with the knowledge of how to expand your understanding of this incredibly powerful and far-reaching technology. I hope you had as much fun reading *Coding Techniques for Microsoft Visual Basic .NET* as I had writing it. We are now poised on the verge of the .NET revolution.

Appendix

Some Helpful ADO.NET Wizards

Many grizzled programmers have a pathological distrust of software wizards, and many wizards have definitely had a dark side to them. They were often buggy and incomplete. The wizards provided in Visual Studio .NET, however, are powerful, robust, and rich with features. Although I've been one of those who distrusted wizards, with Microsoft .NET we should see them for what they are—timesaving tools on the one hand, and teaching mechanisms on the other.

In this appendix, I'll briefly examine two of the most powerful wizards used with ADO.NET, the Data Form Wizard and the Crystal Report Wizard. The Data Form Wizard allows you to easily build a fully functional database application without writing a single line of code. The Crystal Report Wizard helps build reports about the information in these database applications that can be shown on the screen or exported in several formats and distributed via e-mail.

Using the Data Form Wizard

I'm including a discussion of the Data Form Wizard for two reasons. First, Visual Studio .NET is full of great features and this gem will be easy to overlook. You can't use its power if you don't know it exists. Second, this wizard generates very clean and robust code. It will be instructive for you to build a program with the Data Form Wizard and then review the code it generates. You'll understand data sets and data connections more fully by doing so. This wizard also uses the *OleDB* classes instead of the *SqlClient* classes (which I demonstrated in Chapter 10) because the wizard is more general in its connection targets.

The Data Form Wizard is used to generate different configurations of forms, both Web Forms pages and Windows Forms. The code that it generates is designed to handle a variety of situations, including various combinations of controls on the form and various data sources. The Data Form Wizard is a well-constructed wizard and can also provide some useful insight to solidify your knowledge of how to communicate with various data sources. In fact, one of the purposes of the wizard is to generate code that you can study to learn how to create your own data-bound forms. Of course, you should be aware of where the wizard-generated code might differ from your own code that is optimized for particular form requirements. Let's spend a few minutes reviewing how simple it is to use the Data Form Wizard.

1. Start a new Visual Basic project, choosing the Empty Project template. Name the project DataFormWiz. Click OK.

2. If the Start Page tab is visible, right-click the Start Page tab and then select Hide to dismiss that page. From the main IDE menu, select Project | Add New Item to display the Add New Item dialog box, shown in Figure A-1. Now we'll add a Data Form Wizard to our project.

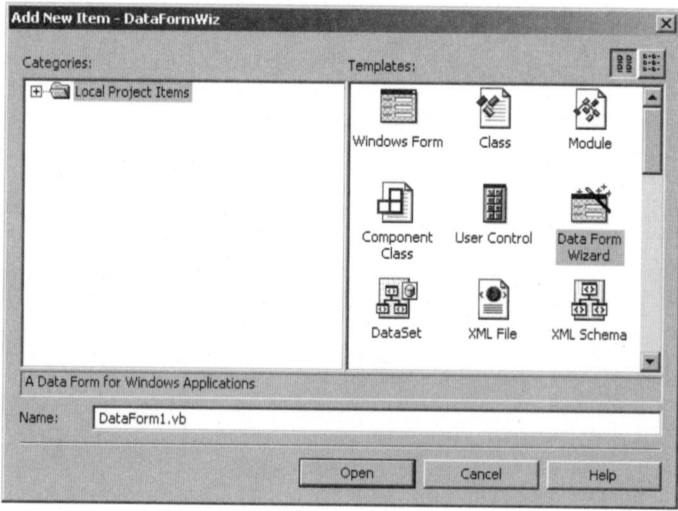

Figure A-1 The Add New Item dialog box.

3. Select Data Form Wizard, and leave the default name DataForm1.vb. Click Open to have the Data Form Wizard added to the empty project. As soon as you click Open, the Data Form Wizard starts. Click Next.

4. We want to provide a name for a new data set, so give it the name dsDataWizard, as shown in Figure A-2. Click Next.

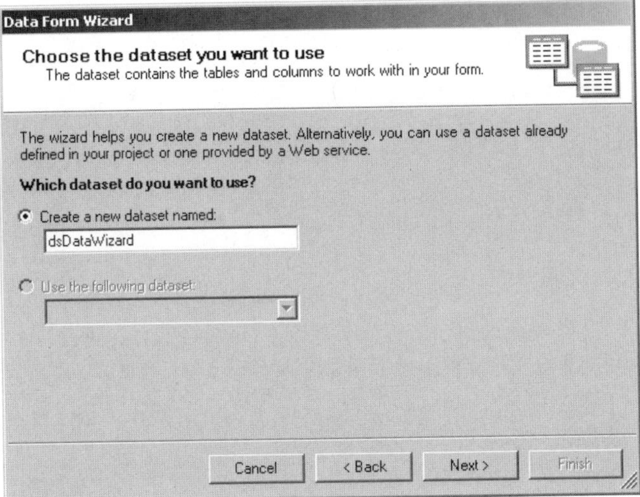

Figure A-2 Create a new data set named dsDataWizard.

5. We could create a new connection at this point, but instead just select the Northwind connection we built in Chapter 10, as shown in Figure A-3. Click Next to continue.

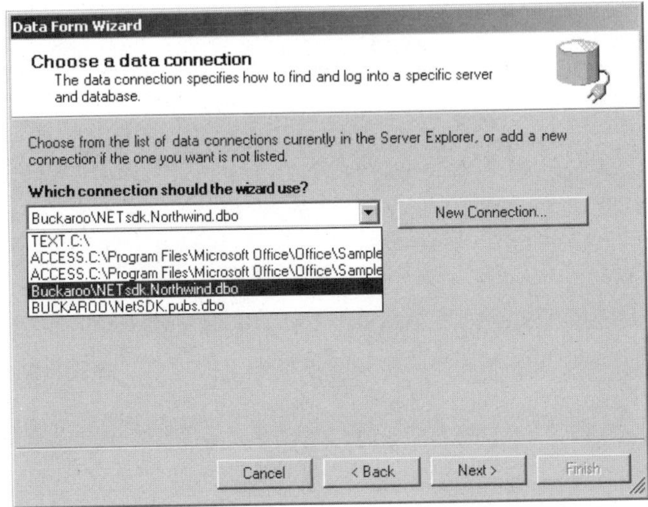

Figure A-3 Select the Northwind connection we built in Chapter 10.

6. Add the Categories table and the Products table to the Selected Item(s) list, as shown in Figure A-4. Click Next.

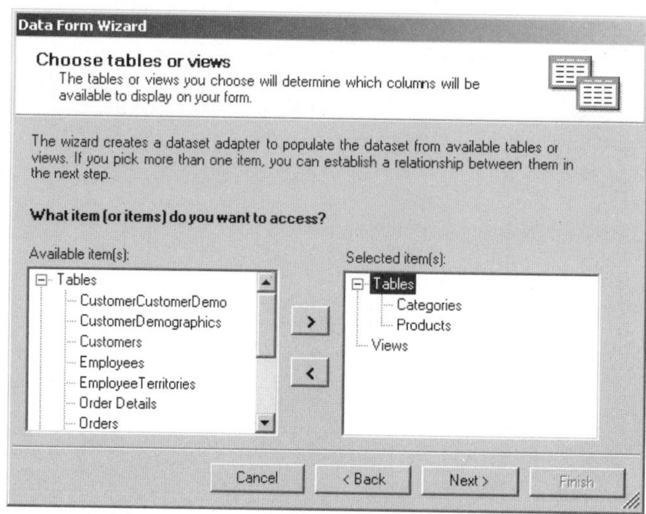

Figure A-4 Add the Categories table and the Products table.

We need to name the relationship between the tables. Enter CategoriesProducts in the Name text box. Categories is the parent table using its CategoryID primary key. Products is the child table with its foreign key CategoryID used as the link, as shown in Figure A-5. When this information is added, click the > button to add this relationship to the Relations box on the right. Click Next.

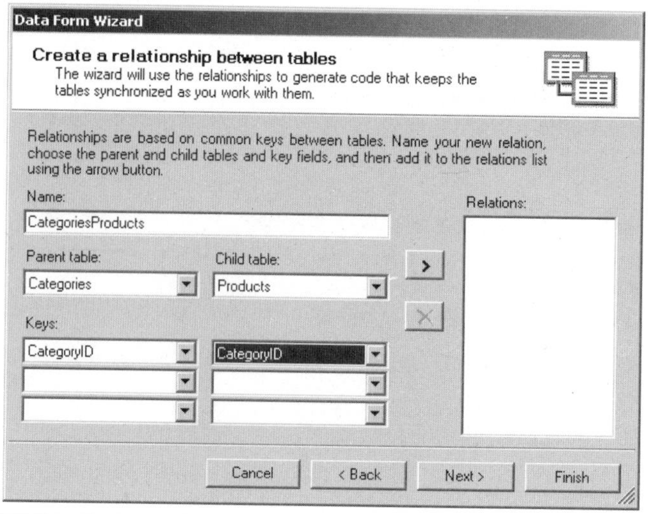

Figure A-5 Create this relationship.

7. In the next window, we select the tables and fields we want to display. Leave all the fields except the picture field in the Categories table checked, as shown in Figure A-6. Click Next.

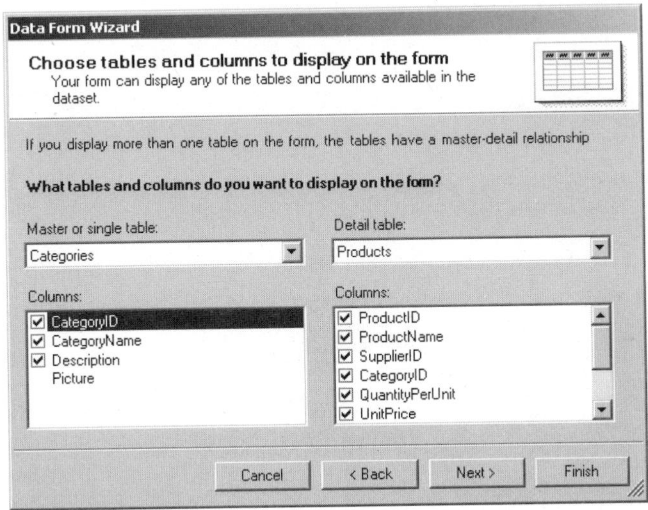

Figure A-6 Select the tables you want to display.

8. Let's display all of the records in a grid for now, so leave the default settings as shown in Figure A-7. Click Finish to have the wizard do its magic and generate our working application.

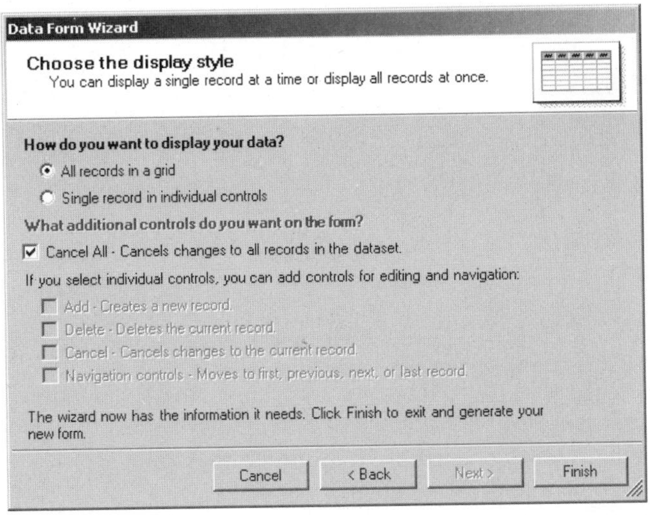

Figure A-7 Leave the default display style settings unchanged.

After a few seconds of disk whirring, the new DataForm will be constructed and displayed, as shown in Figure A-8. Although the result is a pretty utilitarian-looking interface, the more complex internals are also present. You can use the wizard to build your application and then spiff up the user interface yourself.

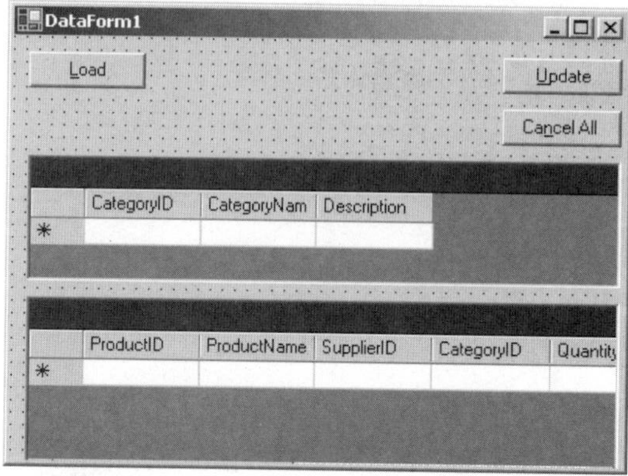

Figure A-8 The new DataForm.

You won't be surprised at what the wizard has added to our program. We have the dsDataWizard data set, the *OleDB* connection to Northwind, and the *OleDb* data adapters for each of the two tables in our example. If you try to run the program now, however, an error will be generated. You must first tell the project that you want the new Data Form Wizard form to be the startup object. Bring up the Solution Explorer, and then right-click the project named DataFormWiz, and select Properties. Select DataForm1 from the Startup Object drop-down list. Click OK to close the dialog box.

Run the Program

Press F5 to run the newly created program. Click the Load button, which then establishes a connection to the database and retrieves the data, as shown in Figure A-9. Scroll through the top Categories table, and select a record. Notice how the bottom Products table changes because of the relationship we built. You can change any of the fields in any of the records. If Update is clicked, all the changes made in the data grids will be propagated back to the Northwind data source. And all without writing a single line of code.

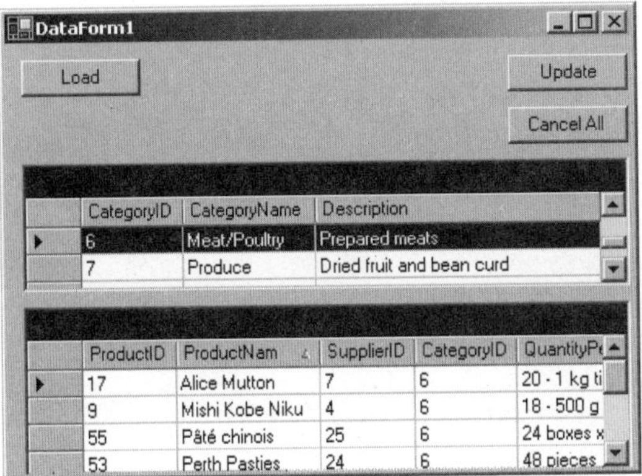

Figure A-9 The Data Form Wizard project in action.

Under the Hood

As I mentioned, one reason I wanted to describe the Data Form Wizard is to simply let you know that it exists. The other reason is to illustrate the code it generates. Build a few data applications, and then print and review the code. Looking over the code created by the wizard is a great way to become familiar with the Visual Basic .NET database access technology. For example, notice that the *Click* event handler of the Load button calls a routine to load the data set. This event handler is placed in a structured *Try…End Try* error handling block. The Data Form Wizard is an example of very good code and design. Here's some of the code created for our example:

```
Private Sub btnLoad_Click(ByVal sender As System.Object, _
    ByVal e As System.EventArgs) Handles btnLoad.Click

    Try
        Me.LoadDataSet()
    Catch eLoad As System.Exception
        System.Windows.Forms.MessageBox.Show(eLoad.Message)
    End Try
End Sub
```

Examine the *LoadDataSet* routine that the Load button calls. All the moving parts that could generate an error are encased in *Try* blocks. As I mentioned, this practice is the hallmark of good production code. The important lines are also commented. Spend a few minutes examining the code.

```
Public Sub LoadDataSet()
    Dim objDataSetTemp As DataFormWiz.dsDataWizard
    objDataSetTemp = New DataFormWiz.dsDataWizard()
    Try
        'Execute the SelectCommand on the DatasetCommmand
        ' and fill the dataset
        Me.FillDataSet(objDataSetTemp)
    Catch eFillDataSet As System.Exception
        'Add exception handling code here
        Throw eFillDataSet
    End Try
    Try
        'Merge the records that were just pulled from the data
        ' store into the main dataset
        objdsDataWizard.Merge(objDataSetTemp)
    Catch eLoadMerge As System.Exception
        'Add exception handling code here
        Throw eLoadMerge
    End Try
End Sub
```

When you examine the code that the wizard inserted to load the data set, you will be surprised at the amount of code required. Several *OleDB* commands were added to the code for us. Each of the update commands were added for us as well as all the other commands to load and update. If you are not a database expert, the Data Form Wizard can really make your life more productive. And it's a good instructor of how to write complex code to connect to a data store.

The Properties box of the first *OleDbDataAdapter*, shown in Figure A-10, shows just a few of the commands that were added for us. Of course, each of these commands is expanded to many lines within the program.

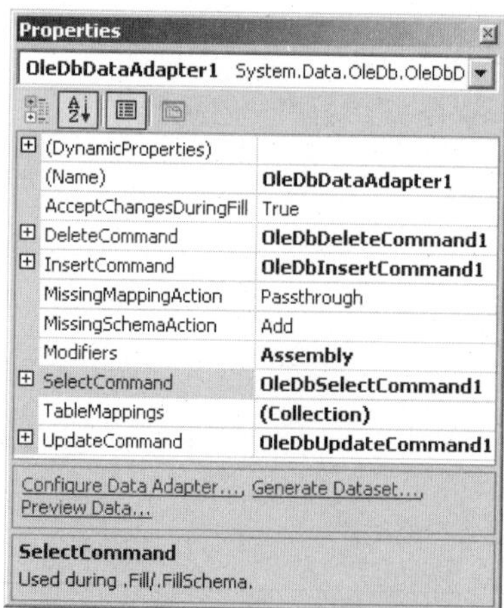

Figure A-10 The *OleDbDataAdapter* properties.

We can see that the wizard uses the OleDB provider. Although it is possible to modify the provider in the wizard-generated code to use the SqlClient provider, this change can be difficult. You must first modify references to any elements in the *System.Data.OleDb* namespace to *System.Data.Sql*. Next you must change the way parameters are handled. The SQL provider requires named parameters, which would require changes both in the SQL statements in the adapter's commands and in the commands' *Parameters* collection. If you want to switch to the SQL provider, you might find it easier to manually add *SqlConnection* and *SqlDataAdapter* objects and configure them, allowing Visual Studio .NET to configure their parameters. But unless the database is large and you are generating many round-trips, it's just as easy to leave the default OleDB provider.

Generating a Crystal Report from a Data Source

Another goody that's packed away in Visual Studio .NET is the Crystal Report viewer. Crystal Reports for Visual Studio .NET is the standard reporting tool for Visual Studio .NET. You can host reports on Web and Windows platforms and publish these reports as Web services on a server.

Building a Crystal Report

Let's step through how to generate a report from any data source. (This example assumes that you have Microsoft Access 2002 installed on your computer.) Start a new Windows application project, and give it the name CrystalExample. The default form will be added to the project. Two steps are required to display a Crystal Report in your Visual Basic .NET program. First you must build a report, and then you add a Crystal Viewer object to show the report. Let's start by adding a report control.

1. From the main IDE menu, select Project | Add New Item and select Crystal Report, as shown in Figure A-11. Click Open.

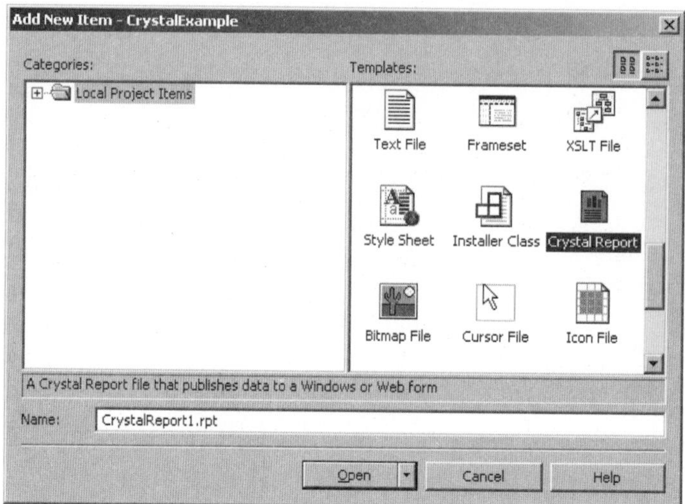

Figure A-11 Add a report control to the project.

2. The Crystal Report Wizard will then prompt us for the type of report we want to build, as shown in Figure A-12. Keep the default standard report, and then click OK.

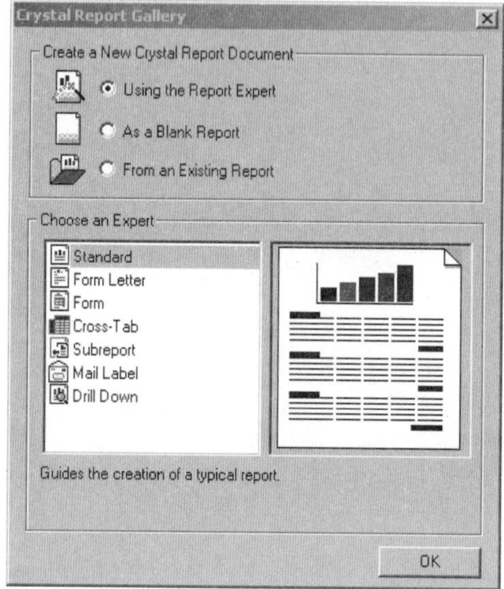

Figure A-12 Keep the default standard report.

3. The Crystal Report Wizard now displays the Standard Report Expert dialog box, as shown in Figure A-13. For this project, click the plus sign next to the OLE DB (ADO) folder in the Available Data Sources list box.

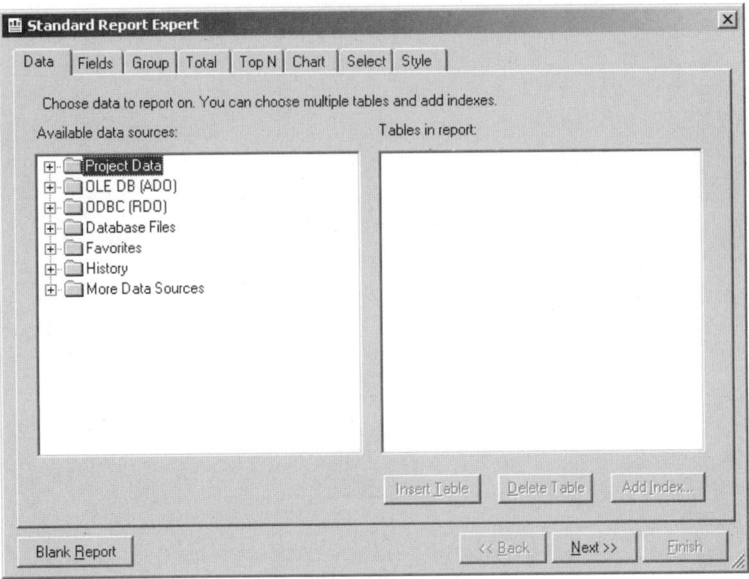

Figure A-13 The Standard Report Expert dialog box.

4. You'll next see the OLE DB (ADO) dialog box, as shown in Figure A-14. This time we will select an Access database to show the diversity of these tools. Select Microsoft Jet 4.0 OLE DB Provider, and then click Next.

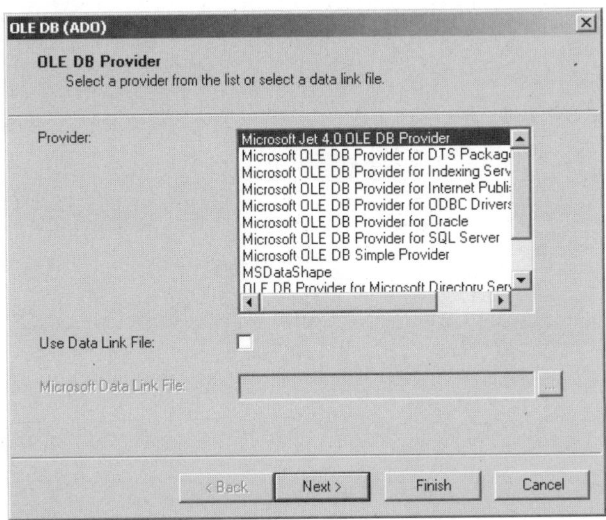

Figure A-14 The OLE DB (ADO) dialog box.

5. We next need to tell the wizard which database we want to connect to. If you have Access installed on your machine, click the button after the Database Name text box (shown in Figure A-15) and select the Access Northwind.MDB database. Click Next.

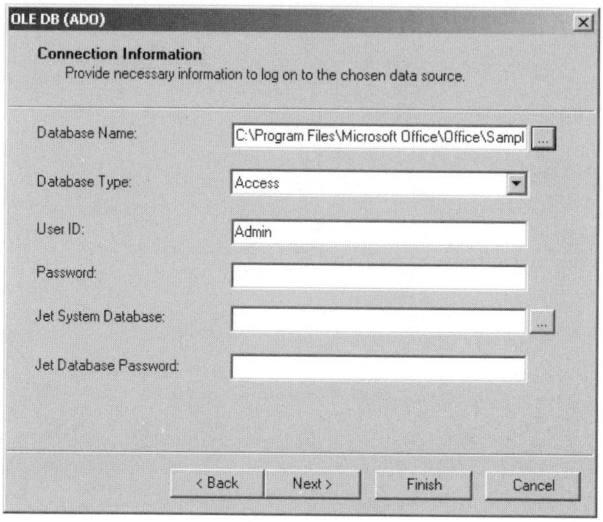

OLE DB (ADO)
Connection Information
Provide necessary information to log on to the chosen data source.
Database Name: C:\Program Files\Microsoft Office\Office\Sampl
Database Type: Access
User ID: Admin
Password:
Jet System Database:
Jet Database Password:
< Back | Next > | Finish | Cancel

Figure A-15 Select the Northwind database.

6. The Crystal Report Wizard now displays the Advanced Information dialog box. We don't need to change any information for this example, so click Finish. In the Standard Report Expert window, select the Categories and Products tables for our report, as shown in Figure A-16. Click Next.

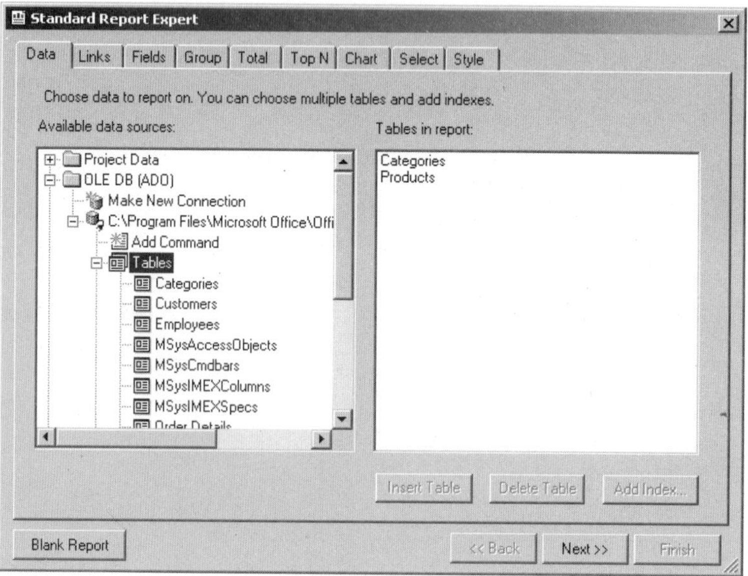

Figure A-16 Select the Categories and Products tables.

7. On the Links tab in the Standard Report Expert dialog box, keep the defaults, as shown in Figure A-17. You can see that the wizard mapped the primary key in Categories to the foreign key in Products. Click Next to display the Fields tab.

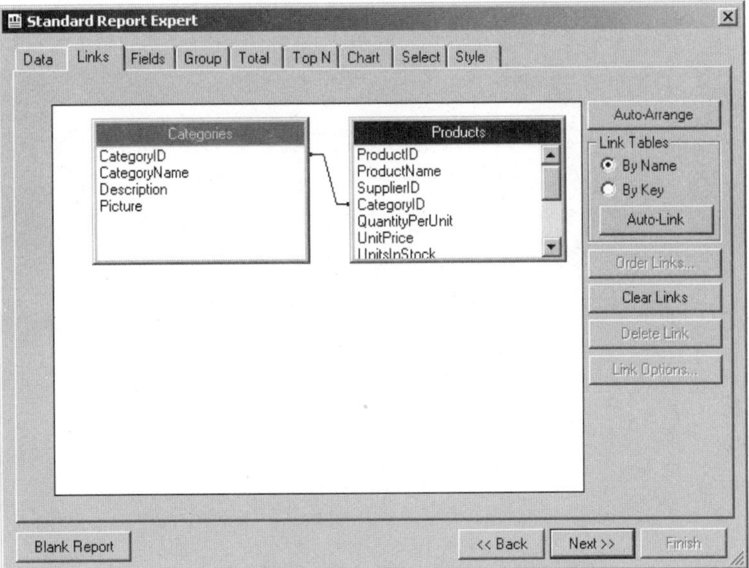

Figure A-17 The primary key in Categories is mapped to the foreign key in Products.

8. From the Categories table, select CategoryName and Description. From the Products table, select the ProductName, QuantityPerUnit, UnitPrice, and UnitsInStock fields, as shown in Figure A-18. Click Next to display the Group tab.

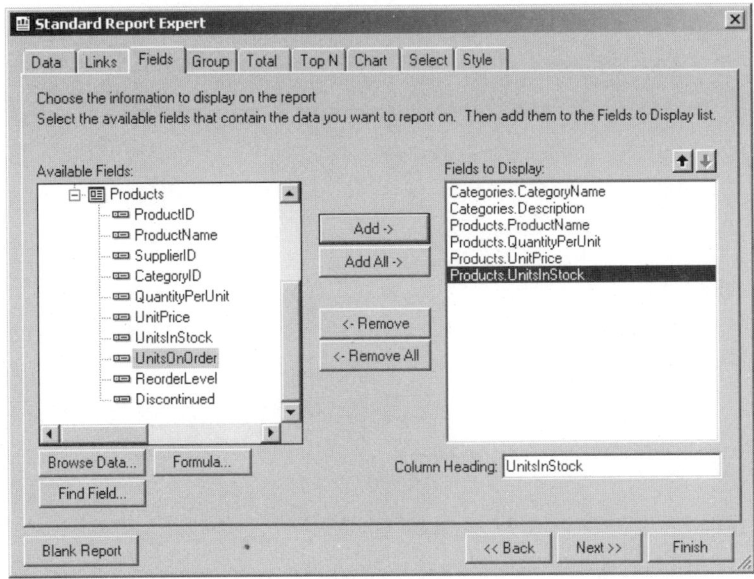

Figure A-18 Select the fields shown here.

9. We want to group the report by Categories and Products within each Category. Go ahead and select CategoryName and ProductName to group on, as shown in Figure A-19.

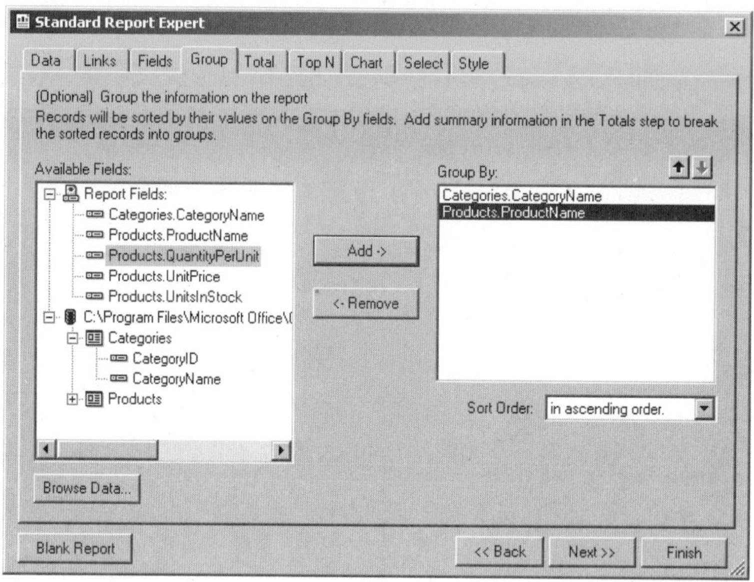

Figure A-19 Select CategoryName and ProductName to group on.

10. Click Next several times to accept the default settings for the Total, Top N, Chart, and Select tabs. When you get to the final tab, titled Style, add the title Category - Product Report, as shown in Figure A-20.

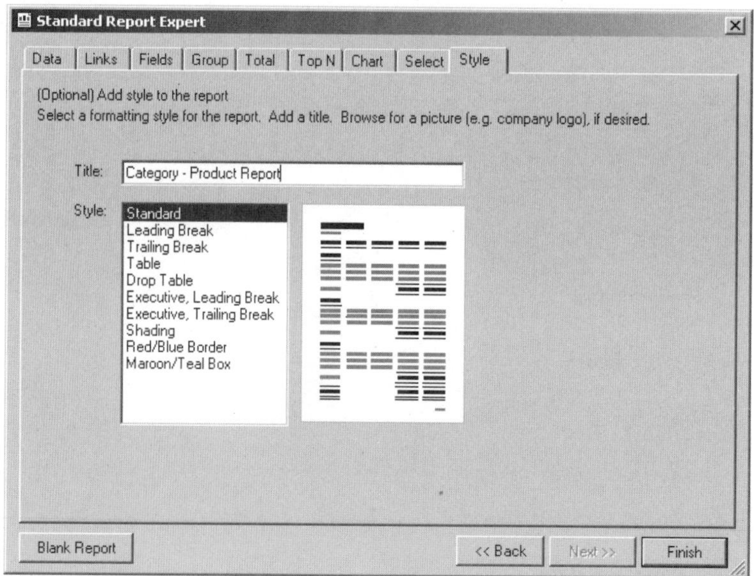

Figure A-20 Add the title Category - Product Report.

11. Click Finish. That's all there is to building a report. The new CrystalReport1.rpt, shown in Figure A-21, will be added to your project. Be sure to right-click the CrystalReport1 tab and click Save CrystalReport1.

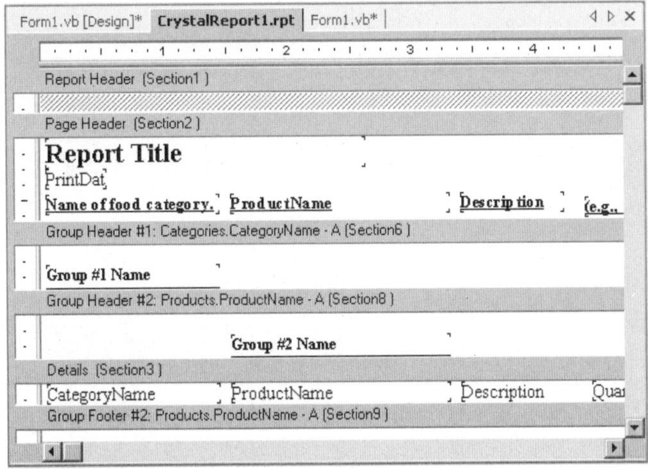

Figure A-21 The report is designed.

Getting Ready to View Our Report

We now have our report built, so it's time to set up the mechanism to view it. Luckily this is pretty easy. Just like we built the report without writing any code, we can do the exact same thing when we set up the viewer. Drag the CrystalReportViewer control from the Windows toolbox to the default form.

Right-click the CrystalReportViewer, and select Properties. Select the *Dock* property and select Fill, as shown in Figure A-22. This option will cause the viewer to fill the entire client area of the form.

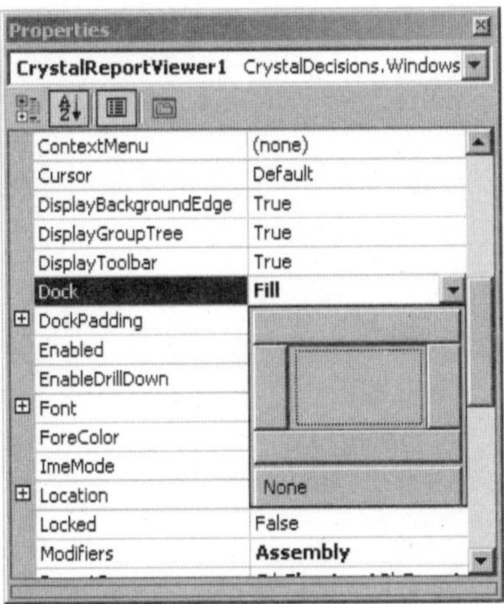

Figure A-22 Select the *Dock* property and select Fill.

The completed report is shown in Figure A-23. As you can see, the CrystalReportViewer control is pretty sophisticated. You can use the built-in functionality to page and print the report. When the application is running you can click the Export Report button (the envelope with the red arrow) to export the report to an Adobe Acrobat .pdf, a Microsoft Excel .xls, a Microsoft Word .doc, or a Rich Text Document .rtf file. You can also magnify areas or even find specific text within the report. All of this power is built into the viewer.

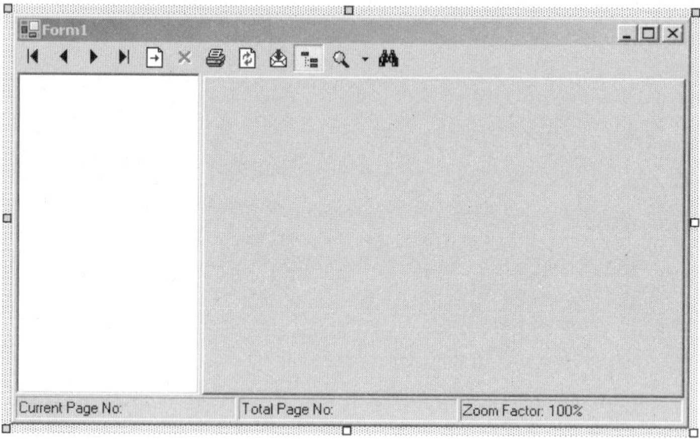

Figure A-23 The completed report.

All that's left is for us to tell the viewer which report we want displayed. Right-click the viewer once more, and select Properties. Select the *ReportSource* property, and click Browse. Find the CrystalReport1.rpt file we just built and select it. Now run the program. The program should look like Figure A-24.

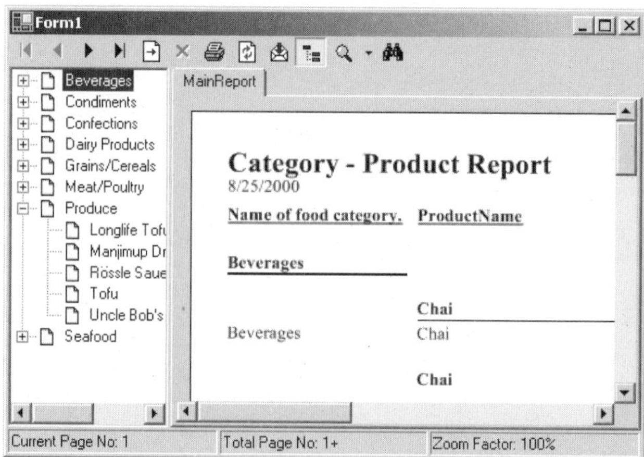

Figure A-24 The Crystal Report program in action.

Pretty powerful for not even having to write a single line of code. Explore the Crystal Reports help files to see how you can easily modify the default report to look like just about anything you want. As you might guess, a report added to a project is a strongly typed report. A report source file, containing a report class specific to this report, is automatically created for it. This report class has *ReportClass* as its base class.

Index

Send feedback about this index to *mspindex@microsoft.com*

Symbols and Numbers

& (ampersand), 52
{} (curly brackets), 187–88
&= operator, 74
*= operator, 74
+= operator, 74
–= operator, 74
/= operator, 74
\= operator, 75
^= operator, 75
[] (square brackets), 320
_ (underscore), 80

A

abstraction layers, 15
accelerator key (&), 52
access modifiers, 67, 77, 78–79
Active Server Pages (ASP), 497–98. *See also* ASP.NET
ActiveX controls, 64, 349
ActiveX Data Objects (ADO) vs. ADO.NET, 393–94, 395, 397, 495
Add New Item dialog box, 552
Add Reference dialog box, 115
Add Web Reference dialog box, 546, 547
AddressOf operator, 357, 358, 575
ADO (ActiveX Data Objects) vs. ADO.NET, 393–94, 395, 397–99, 495
ADO.NET
  vs. ADO, 393–94, 395, 397–99, 495
  basic objects, 399–402
  basic operations, 405–9
  commands for handling data source data, 405, 406–7

ADO.NET, *continued*
  connecting to data sources, 405, 406
  creating DataReader object, 405, 407–8
  data binding, 477–87
  helpful wizards, 595–603
  object model, 431–34
  role of data providers, 402–5
  role of XML, 395, 396, 399, 400, 443
ADTG (Advanced Data Table Gram) format, 394
Advanced Data Table Gram (ADTG) format, 394
AllowSorting property, 423
AlternatingBackColor property, 423
ampersand (&), 52
Apache, 537
API, 2. *See also* Win32 API
AppendText method, 173, 175, 177
application domains, defined, 184
Application log, 295, 379, 380
Application object, 84–86
application programming interface (API), 2
applications, 9. *See also* projects; Web Forms; Web services
Array data type, 59
ArrayList collection, 213–15, 575, 577, 581, 582, 583, 587
arrays
  binary searches, 200–202
  boundaries, 192, 193, 194–98
  vs. collections, 192, 213, 235–36
  creating, 192–94
  dimensionality, 192, 193
  dynamic, 203–4

arrays, *continued*
  initializing during declaration, 204–5
  limitations, 207
  list of methods, 201–2
  list of properties, 202
  locating elements, 200
  overview, 191
  properties, 192
  as reference types, 205–7
  reversing contents, 199
  role of With...End With construct, 193–94
  Roman numeral calculator example, 207–12
  sorting, 199
  in Throwback project, 207–12
  viewing in Locals window, 269
  in Visual Basic .NET, 192–94
  zero-based, 204
artificial intelligence. *See* Eliza program
ASP (Active Server Pages), 497–98. *See also* ASP.NET
ASP.NET. *See also* Web Forms
  overview, 498–500
  Page class, 506
  reasons for using, 498–500
  server controls, 503–5, 508
  starting simple Web application project, 500–501
.aspx files
  as code-behind files, 508–9, 519
  in Loan Application project, 519–20, 524–26
  overview, 507–8
  setting Web page properties, 509–10
  in simple Web Forms example, 503, 507–8
  viewing, 508–9
assemblies
  code signing, 330
  and common language runtime, 308
  creating Assembly Spy program, 310–15
  DLLs in, 308–9
  examining, 309–10
  global cache, 306–7, 333–35
assemblies, *continued*
  importing, 116, 320
  and manifests, 23
  modules in, 304
  in .NET Framework, 23, 38
  private, 304
  and reflection, 303, 309–10
  shared, 305–8
  side-by-side execution, 305–6
  storing multiple versions, 305–6
  strong names, 307–8, 330–33
  and version numbers, 23
  versioning, 335–38
  viewing via IL disassembler, 39–40
assembly cache, 305
Assembly object, 308–9
Assembly Spy program
  adding main menu, 315
  building executable file, 329
  creating, 313–15
  lists of form control properties, 314
  overview, 310–12
  properties dialog box, 337–38
  source code, 315–19
  viewing code, 320–29
AssemblyInfo.vb file, 331, 334, 503
Assert method, 279–81
Attach To Process dialog box, 391
Attributes property, 180–82
AutoGenerateCommands program, 465–66
AutoLog property, 380
AutomaticDelay property, 366
AutoPopDelay property, 366
Autos window, 271
AutoScale property, 63
AxHost class, 349
Aximp.exe file, 64

B

B2B (business-to-business) e-commerce, 533. *See also* Web services
BackColor property, 92, 155, 156
base class library (BCL), 12

base classes
overview, 58
role of namespaces, 58
and Web forms, 507
Windows.Forms.Form example, 42
base forms
background, 549–50
building, 550–52
overview, 549–50
BCL (base class library), 12
BeginUpdate method, 323
binary data types, 144
BinaryReader class, 174
BinarySearch method, 200–202
BinaryWriter class, 174
binding. *See* data binding
BindingContext object, 477, 485, 486
BindingContext program
adding code, 481–84
adding objects, 480
creating project, 480
how it works, 484–87
list of properties, 481
overview, 479–81
BindingFlags method, 327
Boolean data type, 146, 439
BorderStyle property, 63, 92
breakpoints, 267–68, 272
business-to-business (B2B) e-commerce, 533. *See also* Web services
Button_Click event handler, 67, 69, 72, 76
buttons
adding to forms, 67
moving on forms, 68
Byte data type, 59, 146, 157

C

C# language
and ASP.NET, 499
viewing class information via WinCV, 172
C and C++ programming languages
and class libraries, 12
history, 2, 3–4
vs. Visual Basic, 4, 17
CAB projects, 588
Cache class, 523
calculator. *See* Loan Application program
calendar control
adding code, 510–11
adding to Web form, 504–5
converting to HTML, 514
formatting, 509–10
setting properties, 509–10
syntax for referencing, 508
Web page display, 511–12
call stack, 271, 276–78
CanRead property, 174
CanSeek property, 174
CanWrite property, 174
Capacity property, 214
CaptionText property, 440
Catch block, 259–65, 276, 277, 361, 367, 441, 579
Changed event, 343, 357–60
ChangeType property, 358
Char data type, 59, 144, 146, 157
Checked property, 586
child forms, 553–54
child records, in parent/child database relationships, 455–62
ChildRelations collection, 473
Choose Assembly From Assembly Cache dialog box, 337
class libraries. *See* base class library
class modules vs. code modules, 226
Class view
Employee class example, 134–36
overview, 76
synchronizing, 134–36
viewing class hierarchies, 76–78, 134
viewing WindowsApplication1 program in, 77–78
classes. *See also* base class library
adding modules to projects, 110–11
creating, 109–40, 564–68
creating Employee class, 110–13, 118
creating instances, 118–19, 121
declaring, 118–20
defining at namespace level, 59–60

classes, *continued*
derived, 45, 122, 124
forms as, 41, 62
and inheritance, 56–57, 130–33
vs. objects, 50–51
overview, 50–51
protected members, 77
renaming, 88
role in Visual Basic .NET, 17–18
sealed, 171, 184
shared members, 72
static, 171, 172–73
vs. structures, 147
System namespace, 59–60
viewing hierarchy, 76–78, 134
writing, 109–40
Clear method, 201, 214, 583
Click event, 67, 69, 72, 76, 408, 422, 439, 440, 446, 460, 485, 511, 521, 551, 557, 560
client-side cursors, 398–99
clock program, 86–105
Clone method, 187, 201
Close method, 406
Closing event, 572–73
CLR. *See* common language runtime (CLR)
code
commented, 32
managed, 14, 20, 22
setting breakpoints, 267–68, 272
stepping through, 270–71
code modules
vs. class modules, 226
Dialog.vb file, 224–33
code signing, 330
code-behind files, 508–9, 519
collections. *See also* System.Collections namespace
vs. arrays, 192, 213, 235–36
in DataSet object model, 455, 473
overview, 191–92, 212, 213
COM (Component Object Model)
and ActiveX controls, 64, 349
overview, 5
referencing controls in Visual Basic .NET, 64
as unmanaged code, 349
COM interoperability, 5
COM controls. *See* ActiveX controls
Command object, 393, 403, 406–7, 429, 432, 433
commented code, 32
common language runtime (CLR)
and assemblies, 308
and exception handling, 261
and garbage collection, 13
illustrated, 15
overview, 7, 10, 13–14
role in .NET Framework, 10
vs. Visual Basic runtime, 13
common language specification (CLS), 10
communication standards, 534–35
CompanyBase program
adding inherited form, 552–54
building, 550–52
creating project, 550
list of form and control properties, 550
naming, 550
output type, 551
compilers
and just-in-time (JIT) compilation, 20, 21
role in .NET Framework, 9–10
complex types, 444–46
Component model namespace category, 59
Component Object Model. *See* COM
components. *See* COM
computers, history, 1
concatenating strings, 186, 188
Configuration namespace category, 59
Configure An Assembly dialog box, 336
Connection object, 393, 398, 403, 429, 432, 433

ConnectionString property, 406, 438
constraints, 472
ConstructorInfo object, 326–27, 328
constructors, defined, 140–41
ConsumeEightBall program
  adding code to get answers, 547–48
  building client program, 545–46
  creating project, 543–45
  list of controls and properties, 546
Contains method, 217
context menus, in Custom Text Control project, 557, 559–61
ContextMenu property, 560
ControlBox property, 63
controls, form. *See also* ActiveX controls; custom controls; server controls
  adding code, 98
  adding to forms, 51, 62, 90–91
  adding to toolbox, 346–47
  lightweight, 76
  naming, 87
  overview, 62, 63–65
  renaming, 87
cooperative multitasking, 2
Copy method, 177, 187, 201
copying Form1 class, 70–71
CopyTo method, 201
CORBA, 5
Count property, 214, 218, 248, 581
CreateCommand method, 406
Created event, 343, 356–60
CreateInstance method, 201
CreationTime property, 179
Crystal Report viewer, 603–11
curly brackets ({}), 187–88
currency conversion example, 6–7
Currency data type, 147
CurrencyManager object, 479
CursorLocation property, 398
custom controls
  adding code, 556–58
  adding to host forms, 558–59
custom controls, *continued*
  building, 556–58
  changing text box backgound color, 555
  creating, 555–61
  how the code works, 559–61
  overview, 555
Custom Text Control program
  adding code, 556–58
  adding to host forms, 558–59
  building, 556–58
  creating project, 555
  how program works, 559–61
  overview, 555
Customize Toolbox dialog box, 346–47, 367

D

DAO (Data Access Objects), 393
Data Access Objects (DAO), 393
Data Adapter Configuration Wizard, 414–18, 438
Data Adapter Preview dialog box, 419–20
data binding
  creating program example, 467–70
  record navigation example, 477–87
  running program example, 470–71
Data Form Wizard, 595–603
data grids, populating from persisted XML fles, 462–65
Data Link Properties dialog box, 412–13
Data namespace category, 59
data providers
  list in Data Link Properties dialog box, 412–13
  OLE DB .NET, 402, 403, 404, 405
  overview, 393, 402
  SQL Server .NET, 402, 403, 404, 405
data types
  arrays, 144
  binary, 144
  as classes, 59
  complex, 444–46
  features, 148–60

data types, *continued*
  Integer data type, 19
  Long data type, 19
  numeric, 144
  overview, 143–45
  reference, 144, 147–48, 160, 162, 205, 206
  safety issue, 13, 21, 152–57
  Short data type, 19
  strings, 144
  strong typing, 152
  value, 144, 145–47, 155, 162
  in Visual Basic .NET, 19, 144–45
  widening, 157–60
data widening, 157–60
DataAdapter object, 393, 403, 414–18, 425, 429, 432, 471
database relationships, 455–62
DataBinding program
  adding code, 468–70
  creating project, 467–69
  default form, 468
  how it works, 471–75
  list of properties, 468
  running program, 470–71
  updating data grid, 476
DataColumn object, 471, 472, 488, 577, 579
DataReader object, 393, 398–99, 403, 405, 407–8, 429, 432–33
DataRelation object, 397, 471, 472
DataRelations collection, 455
DataRow object, 400, 488, 489, 530, 579
DataSet object
  in BindingContext project, 484
  vs. DataReader object, 405
  list of XML methods, 401
  in Loan Application project, 529
  object model, 455
  overview, 393, 394–95, 399–400, 429
  role of data providers, 402
  role of tables, 395–97
  in SQLDataGrid project, 410, 414, 420–21, 425
  in System.Data namespace, 400
DataSet object, *continued*
  viewing properties, 461–62
  and XML, 401, 443
Dataset Properties dialog box, 461, 462
DataSetCommand object, 395, 398, 403–4
DataSource property, 426, 531
DataTable object
  in DataBinding project, 471, 472, 474
  list of properties, 401
  overview, 400–401, 472
  and relationship between multiple tables, 397
  role in ADO.NET library, 488–90
  in SQLDataGrid project, 425, 426
  in Sticky project, 577, 579
  in System.Data namespace, 400
DataTables collection, 455
DataView object, 402, 433, 467, 471, 474
date, formatting, 101–3
date arithmetic, 99–101
Date data type, 144, 146
DateTime class, 100, 179
DateTime object, 99–100, 101
DCOM (Distributed COM), 5, 7, 533
Debug class, 278
Debug toolbar, 270–71
Debug.Assert statement, 279–81
debugging
  Autos window, 271
  call stack, 271, 276–78
  configuring debugger, 273–75
  Disassembly window, 271, 272
  Locals window, 269, 271, 276
  Memory window, 271
  Modules window, 271
  overview, 268–69
  QuickWatch window, 271, 275–76
  Register window, 271
  Running Documents window, 271
  stepping through code, 270–71, 272–73
  Threads window, 271
  Watch window, 271
  Windows services, 389–92

Debug.WriteLine statement, 278–79
Decimal data type, 146, 157
DefaultView property, 474
delegates
  multicast, 356
  overview, 356
  in Sticky project, 575–76
Deleted event, 343, 356–60
deployment, types of projects, 588
DeQueue method, 216
derived classes, 45, 122, 124
Description property, 454
DesktopLocation property, 68
Destruct keyword, 43, 121
deterministic finalization, 160
dialog boxes, modal vs. modeless, 57
Dialog.vb file
  topology, 224–26
  writing, 226–33
DiffGram object, 447, 449–51
digital certificates, 330
Dim statement, 18, 120, 153, 154
Directory class, 180
DirectoryInfo class, 180–83
DirListBox control, 346, 368, 372
disassembler, IL, 39–40
Disassembly window, 271, 272
Dispose method, 43, 45–46, 65, 76, 84, 361, 370, 576, 582
Distributed COM (DCOM), 5, 7, 533
Division class. *See* Employee class example
DLL Hell, 9
DLLs (dynamic-link libraries), role in .NET, 9, 116–17
DNS (Domain Name System), 535
Do While construct, 408
Domain Name System (DNS), 535
Doppelganger example, 70–71
Double data type, 146, 157
DriveListBox control, 346, 367, 368, 372
drop-down lists, 522, 523–24
dynamic arrays, 203–4
dynamic-link libraries (DLLs), role in .NET, 9, 116–17

E

early binding, 19
e-commerce, 533, 537. *See also* Web services
EDI (Electronic Data Interchange), 5, 395
Edit Relation dialog box, 459, 460
Eight Ball. *See* ConsumeEightBall program; MagicEightBall program
Electronic Data Interchange (EDI), 5, 395
Eliza program
  coding, 222–53
  entry point, 236–39
  how it works, 220–22
  list of properties, 223
  overview, 219–20
  topology of Dialog.vb code module, 224–26
  viewing code, 234–35
  writing Dialog.vb code module, 226–33
Employee class example
  adding code to module, 111–13
  adding new module to project, 110–11
  adding references to project, 114–16
  creating, 110–13, 128
  creating instances, 118–19, 121, 136–40
  namespace, 118
  private member variables, 119, 123–24, 141
  properties, 127–29
  viewing class hierarchy, 134–36
Enabled property, 92
EnableRaisingEvents property, 358, 361, 379, 381
encapsulation, 77, 83, 141
#End Region statement, 31
EndUpdate method, 323
EnQueue method, 216
enumerating files and directories, 180–83
environmental variables, 287–89

Equals method, 149, 201, 244
Err object, 259
Error event, 343, 357, 360–61
error handling. *See also* debugging
  adding structured exception handling to programs, 261–67
  setting breakpoints, 267–68, 272
  types of errors, 258–59
ErrorFile.txt file, 288
errors
  logic, 258–59
  run-time, 258
  syntax, 258
  in Visual Basic .NET, 258–59
ErrorTrace class, 282–84, 289, 296
ErrorTrace.vb file, 284–88, 289, 296–300
event logging, 293–94, 295, 296, 300
Event Viewer, 294, 295–96, 378–81
event-driven model, 3
EventInfo property, 327
EventLog class, 380
EventLog object, 295, 296, 298, 378–79
events
  adding code, 99
  logging, 293–94, 295, 296, 300, 378–81
  overview, 48
  role in Windows, 3
exceptions, 256. *See also* structured exception handling
Exceptions dialog box, 274
exchange rate example, 6–7
EXE files. *See* executable files
executable files
  and assemblies, 23
  building, 32–33
  in .NET Framework, 23
  WindowsApplication1.exe file, 37
ExecuteReader method, 407, 433
Exists method, 177, 354

F

FieldInfo property, 327
File class. *See* System.IO.File class
file management. *See* Solution Explorer
File Sentinel program
  adding Sentinel class, 349–56
  building into Windows service, 373–74
  building user interface, 347–48
  creating project, 347
  Disable Sentinel button, 345, 367
  Enable Sentinel button, 365, 366, 367
  enhancing, 370–72
  how it works, 345–46
  overview, 344
  starting to write, 346–49
  writing user interface code, 362–70
File.Exists method, 177
FileInfo class, 177–80
FileListBox control, 346, 372
FileName property, 87–88
files
  copying, 177–78
  creating, 179–80
  enumerating, 180–83
  and FileInfo class, 177–80
  organizing, 26–27, 87
  reading and writing, 174, 175, 176–77
  vs. streams, 174
FileStream class, 173, 174, 464
FileSystemMonitor object, 381
FileSystemWatcher class
  in File Sentinel project, 344, 349, 350, 353–56
  overview, 343
  role of delegates, 356–58
Fill method, 425, 432, 460, 472
Filter property, 354, 355
Filterindex property, 321
Finalize method, 149, 150
Finally block, 260, 266–67
FindString method, 324

FindStringExact method, 324
firewalls, 12, 401
Flush method, 175, 361
focus, 3, 76, 91, 93
For Each construct, 215, 217
ForeColor property, 92
foreign-key restraints, 472
Form class, 62
Forms designer, 27, 29, 46, 62–63, 91
Form1 class
  cloning, 70–71
  creating copies, 70–71
  defined methods, 76
  source code, 65–67
Form1.vb file
  in first Visual Basic .NET program, 25, 27–33, 34
  renaming, 87–88
  source code, 27–29
Format method, 19, 101–3
FormatDateTime method, 100
Form_Initialize event handler, 43
Form_Load event handler, 27, 43, 76
forms
  adding buttons, 67
  adding controls, 51, 62, 90–91
  changing properties, 29, 62–63, 91, 92
  as classes, 41, 62
  inherited, adding to projects, 42, 552–54
  modal vs. modeless, 57
  moving buttons, 68
  naming, 87
  objects as, 52–54
  renaming, 87
  role of classes, 17–18
  role of inheritance, 41–42
  role of properties, 52
  stopping users from closing, 572–73
  user options, 91, 93
  Visual Basic .NET changes, 27–33
  Visual Basic .NET example, 27–33
Forms class, 62, 63
FormStartPosition property, 31
Framework services namespace category, 59
Friend access modifier, 67, 77, 78, 79
.frm files, 47
frmTimeClass form, 88, 89, 92, 94–96
FromOADate method, 100
.frx files, 47
FullPath property, 360

G

garbage collection
  described, 160–61
  role of CLR, 13
Generate Dataset dialog box, 420, 438, 458
Get property, 127
getAnswer method, 539, 540, 541
GetChanges method, 427, 433
GetConstructors method, 327
GetDateTime method, 407
GetDouble method, 407
GetFiles method, 182
getFuture method, 539, 540, 541
GetGuid method, 407
GetHashCode method, 149, 151
GetInt32 method, 407
GetLength method, 201
GetLowerBound method, 195, 197, 198, 202, 204
getProductDescription method, 536
GetString method, 407
GetType method, 149, 151, 325, 370
GetTypes method, 323
GetUpperBound method, 197, 198, 202, 204
GetValue method, 202
global assembly cache, 306–7, 333–35
Global.asax file, 503
Globalization namespace category, 59, 98–99
GoTo statement, 198
Grove, Andy, 4

H

hand coding, 465–66
handles, 76, 106
handling events, 48
Hardware Abstraction Layer (HAL), 15
heap, 160–61
Height property, 54
help files, 189
Hide method, 582
hideAll method, 576, 582
Host project, 558–59
HTML (Hypertext Markup Language)
  viewing source code, 512–15
  vs. XML, 442
HTML server controls, 504
HTTP (Hypertext Transfer Protocol), 534
HTTP Port 80, 12, 434

I

IBM, 537
IDE (integrated development environment)
  Class view, 76–78
  configuring, 23–25
  defined, 23
  Form1.vb tab, 25, 362
  frmTimeClass code, 94–96
  optimizing for Visual Basic, 23–25
  user control designer window, 556
  viewing lists of project files, 33–37
  Visual Basic .NET overview, 25–40
  Visual Studio, 10, 23.26
IETF (Internet Engineering Task Force), 535
If...Else construct, 250
iFormCounter object, 71, 72, 73
iInteger object, 18, 19
IIOP (Internet Inter-Orb Protocol), 533
IL (intermediate language) disassembler, 39–40
importing
  assemblies, 116, 320
  namespaces, 16, 113, 353
  overview, 41
Imports keyword, 16, 41, 251, 320
IncludeSubdirectories property, 354, 355
IndexOf method, 186, 200, 201
IndexOf property, 375
inflection point, 4
inheritance
  adding forms to projects, 552–54
  Doppelganger example, 70–76
  in Employee class example, 130–33
  and forms package, 40–41
  and Imports keyword, 41–42
  in .NET Framework, 41–42
  overview, 56–57, 83, 141
  visual, 549–54
Inheritance Picker dialog box, 552–53
inherited forms, adding to projects, 552–54
INI files, 35
InitialDelay property, 366
initialization, in Visual Basic .NET, 43–44
Initialize method, 202
InitializeComponent built-in procedure, 32, 46–47, 65, 72, 365, 381, 471
InitializeComponent function, 43, 44
Insert method, 246
installer
  adding to Windows services, 381–84
  how it works, 385
  installing specific services with, 385–86
  running to install services, 385–86
Integer data type, 144, 146, 157, 158–59
Integer keyword, 19
integers, 19, 71
integrated development environment. *See* IDE
IntelliSense, 18–19, 53, 85, 101
interfaces, role in COM and DCOM, 5. *See also* user interfaces
intermediate language. *See* IL (intermediate language) disassembler; MSIL
Internet Engineering Task Force (IETF), 535
Internet Inter-Orb Protocol (IIOP), 533
Interval property, 92

IsReadOnly property, 202
IsSynchronized property, 202
Item property, 489

J

Java, 7, 12, 537
JIT. *See* just-in-time (JIT) compilation
Join method, 186
JOIN queries, 395, 397
just-in-time (JIT) compilation, 20, 21

K

KeyDown event, 251–52
KeyOutput node, 590

L

label controls, 76
LastIndexOf method, 201
LBound method, 198
legacy ActiveX controls, 349
Length property, 202
lightweight controls, 76
line controls, 76
Load event, 48, 54, 292. *See also* Form_Load event handler
LoadFrom method, 322
Loan Application program
  adding code to the code-behind form, 519–20
  adding Payment Schedule page, 524–28
  adding second Web Form, 524–28
  background, 514–15
  creating project, 517–19
  enabling tracing, 532
  how calculator works, 529–32
  how program works, 521–23
  list of controls and properties, 517–18
  naming project, 517
  viewing finished product, 515, 516
  viewing HTML source code, 523–24
Locals window, 269, 271, 276
Location property, 68, 579, 580, 581, 585
logging events, 293–94, 295, 296, 300, 378–81
logic errors, 258–59
Long data type, 146, 157, 158–59
Long keyword, 19

M

Magic8.asmx file, 539
MagicEightBall program
  adding proxy class, 546–47
  creating project, 538
  naming, 538
  running program, 540–43
  viewing code, 539–40
managed code, 14, 20, 22, 349
managed heap, 160–61
managed providers, 402. *See also* data providers
manifests
  defined, 20
  viewing contents, 40
  what's in them, 23
Math library, 522
MaximizeBox property, 63, 92
Me keyword, 47
member variables, 119, 123–24, 141
MemberInfo object, 328
MemberwiseClone method, 149, 150
memory maps, 160–61
Memory window, 271
MenuItems collection, 574
MenuItems property, 574
merge module projects, 588
MessageBox class, 54–55, 57, 79, 80, 81, 82
MessageBox.Show example, 79–80
metadata, 20–21
MethodInfo property, 327
methods
  invoking, 54–56
  overloading, 79–82
  overridable, 124–25

methods, *continued*
overview, 52
vs. properties, 52–54
viewing in IDE, 53
virtual, 134, 141
Visual Basic .NET syntax, 53
MFC (Microsoft Foundation Classes), 12
Microsoft Intermediate Language, 20, 308
Microsoft .NET. *See also* .NET Framework
currency conversion example, 6–7
help files, 189
overview, 6–7
role of DLLs, 116–17
Microsoft Windows services. *See* Windows services
MinimizeBox property, 63, 92
Mod operator, 240, 242
modules
in assemblies, 304
code vs. class, 226
in .NET Framework, 23, 40
Modules window, 271
Mouse_Move event, 345
MoveNext method, 216, 407
MS-DOS
bringing up Command Prompt window, 385
history, 2
MsgBox function, 57
MsgBox method, 57
MSIL (Microsoft Intermediate Language), 20, 308
MSVCRT file, 13
multicast delegates, 356
multitasking, 2
MyBase keyword, 44, 45, 122–23

N

Name property, 92, 354, 465
namespace scoping, 340
namespaces
Employee class example, 118
importing, 16, 113, 353
naming syntax, 58–60
overview, 15–16, 58–61
second-level, 59–60
System.IO namespace, 59–60
System.Windows.Forms namespace, 41–42
viewing in Solution Explorer, 60–61
naming conventions for forms and controls, 87, 91
NASSL (Network Accessible Service Specification Language), 534
NavigateURL property, 524
.NET. *See* Microsoft .NET; .NET Framework; Visual Basic .NET
.NET Framework
help files, 189
illustrated, 11
international aspects, 98–99
navigating, 169
overview, 9–11, 164–65
role of DLLs, 116–17
role of Visual Basic .NET compiler, 9–10
Visual Basic .NET as .NET language, 164
and XML, 442
Network Accessible Service Specification Language (NASSL), 534
Network programming namespace category, 59
NetworkStream class, 174
New keyword, 72, 76, 84, 118, 120–21, 128, 140. *See also* Sub New construct
New Project dialog box, 25, 27, 501
NewArray function, 204
Nodes collection, 320, 327, 328
nondeterministic finalization, 161
Nothing keyword, 43, 362
NotifyFilters property, 355–56, 370–71
NotifyIcon control, 90, 564
NotOverridable keyword, 124
numeric data types, 144

O

Object Browser, 135, 136
Object data type, 59, 147, 148
object-oriented programming, 4, 16–18
objects
 vs. classes, 49–50
 creating, 118–19
 current instance, 47
 destroying, 43
 encapsulating, 77
 forms as, 52–54
 overview, 50–56
 role of methods, 52–54
 role of properties, 52–54
 vs. variants, 19, 151
 in Visual Basic .NET, 12
.ocx files, 349
OldFullPath property, 360
OldName property, 360
OLE DB .NET data provider, 402, 403, 404, 405, 406, 410, 603
OleDbCommand object, 403, 432
OleDbConnection object, 403, 406, 432
OleDbDataAdapter object, 403, 415, 602–3
OleDbDataReader object, 403
OleDbParameter object, 403
On Error Goto statement, 259
online calculator. *See* Loan Application program
OnPageLoad event, 506
OnStart method, 390
OnStop method, 380
Opacity property, 561
Open File dialog box, 311
Open method, 406
OpenFileDialog control, 321
OpenText method, 176
operators
 AddressOf operator, 357, 358, 575
 Mod operator, 240, 242
 new in Visual Basic .NET, 73, 74–75
Option Base statement, 204
Option Explicit option, 113, 153, 154, 155, 159
Option Strict option, 113, 153–54, 155, 157, 158, 159, 248
Optional keyword, 122
overloading
 constructors, 121–22, 123
 defined, 141
 methods, 79–82
Overrides keyword, 45
overriding, 124–26, 141

P

Page class, 506, 507
@Page directive, 506
Page_Load event, 520, 521
Page_Load event handler, 506
Page_Unload event, 521
parent/child database relationships, 455–62
parentheses, in function calling, 125–26
ParentRelations collection, 473
Parse method, 211
Path property, 353, 354, 355, 358
PCs, history, 1
Peek method, 217
persisting XML information, 446–51
Pmt function, 522
Point data type, 579, 580, 581, 584
polymorphism, 83
Port 80, 12, 434
portable executable (PE) files, 21, 97, 304
Position property, 479
preemptive multitasking, 2
Preserve keyword, 203, 213
Private access modifier, 77, 78, 79, 153
private assemblies, 304
private member variables, 119, 123–24, 141
probing, 308
profiles, creating in Visual Studio, 23–25
Programming basics namespace category, 59
programming languages, 2–4

programs. *See* projects
Project Explorer. *See* Solution Explorer
projects
  adding class modules, 110–11
  Assembly Spy project, 310–29
  BindingContext project, 479–87
  CompanyBase project, 550–54
  ConsumeEightBall project, 543–48
  creating in Visual Basic .NET, 25–26, 86, 110
  Custom Text Control project, 555–61
  DataBinding project, 467–76
  Eliza, 219–53
  File Sentinel project, 347–74
  Loan Application project, 517–32
  MagicEightBall project, 538–43
  multiple, 26–27
  naming, 86, 87, 91
  organizing files, 26–27, 87
  property pages, 88–89
  ReadFromXML project, 462–65
  role of project files, 88–89
  SQLDataGrid project, 410–28
  SqlXMLExample project, 436–42
  Sticky project, 564–94
  Throwback project, 207–12
  VB.NET Clock project, 86–105
  viewing lists of files, 33–37
properties
  changing, 29, 31–32, 46, 47, 55, 91–92
  default values, 31, 62, 63
  in Employee class example, 127–29
  Forms class, 62, 63
  vs. methods, 52–54
  overview, 52, 53, 141
  persisting values, 65
  reading, 54–56
  viewing in IDE, 53
  Visual Basic .NET syntax, 53
  writing, 54–56
property pages, 88–89, 502
PropertyInfo property, 327
Protected access modifier, 77, 78, 79, 150
Protected Friend access modifier, 77, 78, 79
providers. *See* data providers
Public access modifier, 78, 79, 118, 150, 153

Q

Query Builder, 417
Queue class, 216
queues, 216–18
QuickWatch window, 271, 275–76

R

RaiseEvent command, 560
Random class, 219, 247–48
Rank property, 202
RDO (Remote Data Objects), 393
Read method, 408
reader classes, 174
ReadFromXML program
  adding code, 462–63
  creating project, 462
  expanding records, 464
  how it works, 464–65
  running program, 463–64
reading files, 174, 175, 176–77
ReadToEnd method, 177
ReadXmlSchema method, 464, 579
record navigation
  BindingContext example, 480–87
  overview, 479
Recordset object
  vs. DataSet object, 395, 397
  role in ADO, 393–94
ReDim statement, 153, 203, 213, 238
reference types, 144, 147–48, 160, 162, 205, 206
reflection, 303, 309–10, 320
Reflection namespace category, 60, 310
#Region keyword, 31, 126

regions, 31, 46, 126
Register window, 271
registry, and DLL Hell, 9
relationships, database, 455–62
Remote Data Objects (RDO), 393
Remove method, 246
Renamed event, 343, 356, 357, 360–61
ReshowDelay property, 366
ResourceManager class, 97
RestoreDirectory property, 321
Return keyword, 237, 250
Reverse method, 199, 201
Rich, client-side GUI namespace category, 60
Roman numeral calculator example, 207–12
Round method, 522
RowChanged event, 472
RowChanging event, 472
RowDeleted event, 472
RowDeleting event, 472
RowFilter property, 474, 475
RowState property, 426
Run method, 84, 85
Running Documents window, 271
run-time errors, 258
Run-time infrastructure services namespace category, 60
runtimes, 4. *See also* common language runtime (CLR)

S

schema files. *See* XML schema
SCL (SOAP Contract Language), 534
SCM (Service Control Manager), 373, 380, 390
scope
  block-level, 338, 339, 340
  determining, 340–41
  module-level, 339
  namespace, 340
scope, *continued*
  procedure-level, 339
  project-level, 338, 339
  for variables, 338–41
SDL (Service Description Language), 534
sealed classes, 171, 184
Security log, 295
seeking, 174
SelectCommand property, 427
SelectionChanged event handler, 510
Sentinel class
  adding to Windows service project, 374–75
  creating for File Sentinel project, 349–56
Serialize method, 125, 134, 568
server controls, 503–5, 508
server-side cursors, 399
Service Control Manager (SCM), 373, 380, 390
Service Description Language (SDL), 534
Service1.asmx file. *See* Magic8.asmx file
Service1.vb file, 375–77
ServiceInstaller object, 381–82, 383
ServiceProcessInstaller object, 382, 383, 385
services. *See* Windows services
Services security namespace category, 60
Set command, 20
SetDataBinding method, 426
setup projects, 588
Setup Wizard, 588–90
SetValue method, 202
shared assemblies, 305–8
Shared keyword, 71–72, 120
shared members, 72
Short data type, 157
Short keyword, 19
Show method, 54–55, 79, 80, 81–82, 582
showAll method, 582
ShowDialog method, 57, 321, 560
side-by-side execution, 305–6
signcode, 330

Simple Object Access Protocol (SOAP), 7, 12, 401, 514, 534, 537
Single data type, 146, 157
Size property, 68, 579
.sln files, 27, 34
SOAP Contract Language (SCL), 534
SOAP (Simple Object Access Protocol), 7, 12, 401, 514, 534, 537
Solution Builder, 33, 103
Solution Explorer
  customizing installation process, 591
  list of files in WebForms project, 502–3
  overview, 26–27
  viewing namespaces, 60–61
  and Web Forms, 502
Sort method, 199, 201
Sort property, 475
sorting arrays, 199
source code. *See* code
Split method, 186, 219, 234, 584
Splitter control, 314
SQL Server .NET data provider, 402, 403, 404, 405, 406, 410
SqlClient class, 410, 440
SqlCommand object, 403, 407, 408, 432, 440
SqlCommandBuilder object, 427
SqlConnection object, 403, 406, 408, 413, 422, 432, 438, 603
SqlDataAdapter object, 403, 414–18, 422, 425–26, 438, 440–41, 457, 488, 603
  SQLDataGrid program
  adding code, 422–23
  adding connection to Northwind database, 410–12
  adding DataAdapter object, 414–18
  adding SqlConnection object, 413–14
  adding user interface controls, 418–19
  creating project, 410
  editing data, 424
  overview, 410
  previewing data, 419–21
SqlDataAdapter object, *continued*
  Retrieve Data button, 419, 423, 424
  running program, 423–24
  Update Database button, 419, 426
  updating data source, 426–28
  user interface, 418–19
  XML schema, 421–22
SqlDataReader object, 403, 408
SqlDataset object, 422
SqlParameter object, 403
SqlXMLExample program
  adding code, 439–40
  adding data adapters, 438, 457–58
  adding objects, 438
  creating project, 436–37
  generating XML from data set, 441
  how it works, 440
  list of properties, 437
  updating data source, 441–42
  viewing XML output, 443–44
  viewing XML schema, 444–46
square brackets ([]), 320
stacks
  and garbage collection, 160–61
  vs. queues, 218–19
StartLogging method, 381
StartPosition property, 29, 68, 92
static classes, 171, 172–73
Sticky program
  adding code to BaseNote form, 571–73
  adding deployment program, 588–92
  adding event handler delegates, 575–76
  building, 591–92
  constructing notes, 570–71
  creating BaseNote form, 570–71
  creating project, 564
  creating Serialize class, 564–70
  deploying program, 588–92
  how BaseNote form works, 585–87
  how it works, 574–82
  installing program on client machines, 592–94

Sticky program, *continued*
  properties for BaseNote form and controls, 570–71
  quitting program, 582–85
  storing notes in XML files, 562–63, 578–79
StopLogging method, 381
Stream class, 173
StreamReader class, 174, 176
streams
  vs. files, 174
  overview, 173
StreamWriter class, 174, 175, 358, 361
String class, 219, 234
String data type, 147, 148, 184
StringBuilder class, 186, 219, 243–47, 249, 320, 325
StringCollection class, 219, 234, 235, 248
strings
  cloning, 187–88
  concatenating, 186, 188
  copying, 187–88
  formatting, 187–88
  as immutable, 184
  as objects, 184, 185–86
  overview, 183–84
  splitting, 186
  uninitialized, 184–85
  and Visual Basic, 183–84
Strings class, 100
strong names
  vs. code signing, 330
  creating assemblies with, 330–33
  overview, 307–8
strong typing, 152, 161–62, 397
StrongName class, 330
Stroustrup, Bjorne, 3
Structure data type, 146, 147
structured exception handling
  adding to programs, 261–67
  overview, 260–61
  Try...Catch...Finally syntax, 261–67
structures vs. classes, 147
Sub Main procedure, 84, 106
Sub New construct, 42–43, 65, 72. *See also* New keyword
Substring method, 186
Sun Microsystems, 537
.suo files, 27, 35
synchronizing Class view, 134–36
syntax errors, 258
System class, 12
System log, 295
System namespace
  list of secondary namespaces, 166–68
  overview, 12, 59–60, 113, 165
System.Array class, 192, 198–202
System.CodeDom namespace, 59, 166
System.Collections namespace, 59, 166
System.Collections.ArrayList collection, 213–15
System.Configuration namespace, 59, 166
System.Data namespace, 59, 166, 400, 431
System.Data.OleDb namespace, 603
System.Data.SQL namespace, 603
System.Data.SQLClient namespace, 410
System.Diagnostics namespace, 59, 166, 278, 284
System.DirectoryServices namespace, 59, 166
System.Drawing namespace, 60, 166
System.Drawing.Color class, 155–56
System.EnterpriseServices namespace, 166
System.Exception class, 256, 262
System.FormatException errors, 255, 256
System.Globalization namespace, 59, 98–99, 166
System.IO namespace, 59, 166, 168, 171
System.IO.Directory class, 180
System.IO.File class, 171–73, 174, 175, 176–77, 180
System.IO.FileInfo class, 177–80
System.IO.FileSystemWatcher class, 343, 344, 353–56
  role of delegates, 356–58
  as toolbox component, 349, 350
System.Management namespace, 59, 166

System.Messaging namespace, 59, 166
System.Net namespace, 59, 167
System.Object class. *See also* Object data type
  and chain of inheritance, 172
  code example, 150–51
  Equals method, 149, 151
  Finalize method, 149, 150
  GetHashCode method, 149, 151
  GetType method, 149, 151
  list of methods, 149
  MemberwiseClone method, 149, 150
  overview, 147, 148–49
  ToString method, 149
SystemObserver class, 365
System.Resources namespace, 59, 167
System.Runtime namespace, 167
System.Runtime.CompilerServices namespace, 60
System.Runtime.InteropServices namespace, 60
System.Runtime.Remoting namespace, 60
System.Runtime.Serialization namespace, 60
System.Security namespace, 60, 167
System.ServiceProcess namespace, 167
System.ServicesProcess namespace, 59
System.String class, 147, 184. *See also* String data type
System.Text namespace, 59, 167, 234, 320
System.Text.RegularExpressions namespace, 59
System.Threading namespace, 59, 167
System.Timers namespace, 59, 167
System.Type class, 325
System.Web namespace, 60, 167
System.Web.Services namespace, 60
System.Windows.Forms namespace, 41–42, 60, 62, 167, 324
System.Windows.Forms.AxHost class, 349
System.Windows.Forms.Control class, 349
System.Windows.Forms.DLL class, 117
System.Windows.Forms.Form class, 41–42, 58, 62–63, 549
System.Xml namespace, 59, 167
System.Xml.Serialization namespace, 59

T

tables
  adding data, 492–93
  adding rows and columns, 492
  building programmatically, 490–92
  finding records, 493–94
  in Sticky program, 577
Tag property, 345
text boxes, changing background color, 555
Text property, 29, 31, 51, 55, 69, 71, 92, 322, 326, 465, 574
TextChanged event, 369
TextReader class, 174
TextWriter class, 174
Threads window, 271
Throwback program
  adding structured exception handling, 261–67
  creating project, 207–8
  debugging, 268–69
  and Try...Catch...Finally syntax, 261–67
  what can go wrong, 255–58
  writing code, 207–12
Tick event, 99
Ticks property, 99
time, formatting, 101–3
time arithmetic, 99–101
Time program, building, 103–5
Timer control, 90, 99
ToOADate method, 100
toolbox
  adding controls, 346–47
  HTML tab, 504
  viewing/hiding, 63, 90
  Web Forms tab, 503
ToolTip control, 366–70
tooltips, 345, 346
ToString method, 19, 71, 202
Trace class, 278. *See also* ErrorTrace class

trace level, setting, 288–89
Trace statement, 281–82
TraceSwitch object, 285, 298
tracing programs, 532
TreeNode class, 320, 326, 327, 328
TreeView control, 312, 314
Trim method, 585
TrimStart method, 584
TrimToSize method, 214
Try block, 259, 260, 262–64, 276, 277, 361, 367, 440, 579, 601
type libraries, 19, 20, 304
Type object, 325
type-safe code, 13, 21, 152–57

U

UBound method, 198
UDDI (Universal Discovery, Description, and Integration) specification, 535–36, 537
underscore (_), 80
uninstalling Windows services, 386
unique restraints, 472
Universal Discovery, Description, and Integration (UDDI) specification, 535–36, 537
UNIX, 5
unmanaged code, 349
Update method, 426, 441
user control designer window, 556
user controls. *See* custom controls
User Interface Editor, 591
user interfaces
- adding code to Form1.vb, 362–70
- adding controls, 347–48
- building, 347–48
- as first step in code writing, 346
- how code works, 365–66
- overview, 11, 94
- setting properties, 347–48
- for SQLDataGrid project, 418–19

users, form property options, 91, 93

V

validation controls, 504
value types, 144, 145–47, 155, 160, 162
variables
- changing dynamically in Locals window, 269
- member, 119, 123–24, 141
- private, 119–20
- reference type, 144, 147–48, 160, 162, 205, 206
- scoping rules, 338–41
- shared, 120
- value type, 144, 145–47, 155, 160, 162

variants vs. objects, 19, 151
vbFileMonitorService
- creating, 385–86
- debugging, 391–92
- viewing in Services window, 387–89

VB.NET clock program, 86–105
VBRUN file, 13
versioning, 335–38
_VIEWSTATE string, 513
virtual methods, 134, 141
Visible property, 92
Visual Basic. *See also* Visual Basic .NET
- vs. C++, 4, 17
- history, 4, 163, 164–65
- and .NET Framework, 164–65
- vs. Visual Basic .NET, 8–9, 43, 121

Visual Basic .NET
- code execution, 22
- configuring IDE, 23–25
- data types, 19, 144–45
- file organization, 26–27, 87
- help files, 189
- how it works, 18–20
- IDE overview, 25–40
- and managed code, 20
- as .NET language, 164
- as object-oriented, 16–18
- and record navigation, 479
- role of compiler, 9–10
- role of DLLs, 116–17

Visual Basic .NET, *continued*
steps in building programs, 20, 103–5, 346
syntax, 18–20
viewing lists of project files, 33–37
viewing/hiding toolbox, 63
vs. Visual Basic, 8–9, 43, 121
Web Form structure, 506–8
Windows Forms designer, 27, 29, 46, 62–63, 91
Visual Basic Projects folder, 25
Visual Basic Scripting Edition, 514
visual inheritance, 549–54
Visual Studio
creating profiles, 23–25
Crystal Report viewer, 603–11
IDE, 10, 23, 26
.sln files, 27, 34

W

W3C (World Wide Web Consortium), 535
Watch window, 271
Web applications. *See* ASP.NET; Web Forms; Web services
Web Forms
cleanup state, 520, 521
code module, 505
vs. code-behind forms, 519
designer window, 505
event handling state, 520, 521
HTML code, 505–6
HTML-based template, 505
list of project files, 502–3
loading pages state, 520, 521
Loan Application project, 514–32
overview, 17, 497
page initialization state, 520, 521
states in life cycle, 520–21
structure, 506–8
vs. Web services, 497
WebForms project, 500–14
Web methods, 539–40, 544
Web Service Description Language (WSDL), 534
Web services
building, 538–40
finding, 535–36
future, 537–38
overview, 11, 533–38
role in .NET, 6, 7, 11
role of communication standards, 534–35
running programs, 540–42
vs. Web Forms, 497
Web services namespace category, 60
Web setup projects, 588
Web.config file, 503
WebForm1.aspx file
as code-behind form, 508–9, 519
in Loan Application project, 519–20
setting Web Page properties, 509–10
in simple Web Forms example, 503, 507–8
viewing, 508–9
WebForm2.aspx file, 524–26
WebForms ASP.NET project
adding calendar control code, 510–11
creating project, 500–501
default workspace, 501–2
HTML presentation template, 505–8
list of files, 502–3
running Web Form, 511–12
server controls, 503–5, 508
setting Web page properties, 509–10
viewing code-behind file, 508–9
viewing HTML source code, 512–14
viewing WebForm1.aspx file, 508–9
Web Form structure overview, 506–8
WebForms.vsdisco file, 503
Weizenbaum, Joseph, 219, 220
Win32 API, 343, 349
WinCV tool
overview, 169, 183
searching in, 170, 171
starting, 169
viewing File class in, 171–73
Windows, history, 2–3
Windows API, 164, 165, 168
Windows Class Viewer. *See* WinCV tool

Windows Control Library projects, 556
Windows Explorer, viewing list of Visual Basic .NET project files, 33–37
Windows Forms, 17, 41–42, 499, 507
Windows Forms ColorDialog control, 555
Windows registry. *See* registry, and DLL Hell
Windows services
  adding installer, 381–84
  building File Sentinel project into, 373–74
  debugging specific services, 389–92
  how applications work, 377–86
  installing services, 385–86
  overview, 372–73
  running installer, 385–86
  running specific services, 388–89
  Service1.vb file, 375–77
  uninstalling, 386
  viewing specific services, 387–88
WindowsApplication1.exe file
  viewing assembly, 39–40
  viewing properties, 37, 38
WindowsApplication1.sln file, 34
WindowsApplication1.vbproj file, 35–37
Windows.Forms namespace, 62–63
WindowsState property, 63
WinForms.Form.ShownInTaskBar property, 63
With...End With construct, 193–94
wizards
  Data Adapter Configuration Wizard, 414–18, 438
  Data Form Wizard, 595–603
  Setup Wizard, 588–90
World Wide Web Consortium (W3C), 535
wrapper classes, 349
wrapper controls, 64
WriteEntry method, 379, 381
writeError method, 290, 300
WriteLine method, 175, 278–79, 361
WriteOnly property, 370, 371
writer classes, 174
WriteSchema method, 448
writeText method, 291
WriteXML method, 583
writing to files, 174, 175, 176–77

X

XCOPY command, 9, 306, 592
XML (Extensible Markup Language). *See also* SqlXMLExample program
  background, 442
  and data sets, 395, 396, 398, 434–35
  and DataSet object, 401, 443
  generating from SqlXMLExample data set, 441
  vs. HTML, 442
  as industry standard, 12
  and .NET Framework, 442
  overview, 12, 401, 434, 442
  persisting files, 446–51
  populating data grids from persisted files, 462–65
  role in ADO.NET data flow, 395, 396, 399, 400, 443
  in SqlXMLExample project, 443–44
  storing sticky notes, 562–63, 578–79
  Visual Basic .NET project files, 35–37
  writing to disk, 446–51
XML schema
  building blocks, 444–45
  elements and attributes, 444–45
  overview, 435
  and SQLDataGrid project, 421–22
  and SqlXMLExample project, 444–46
  Xsd.exe definition tool, 452–55
XmlTextReader class, 464, 465, 579
XSD. *See* XML schema
Xsd.exe program, 452–55

Z

zero-impact installation, 9

John Connell

John Connell is senior vice president and chief information officer at BankFinancial in Chicago, Illinois. John has a master's degree in business administration and a master's in computer science, specializing in artificial intelligence and telecommunications. His previous book, *Beginning Visual Basic 6 Database Programming* (Wrox Press, 1998) won the Amazon.com category best-seller award.

John teaches computer-programming classes at DePaul University in Chicago, where he is on the alumni board of directors. When not writing and thinking about Visual Basic .NET programs, John spends his time flying single-engine aircraft with his two sons.

John Connell and his son Garrett

The manuscript for this book was prepared and galleyed using Microsoft Word. Pages were composed by Microsoft Press using Adobe FrameMaker+SGML for Windows, with text in Garamond and display type in Helvetica Condensed. Composed pages were delivered to the printer as electronic prepress files.

Cover Designer:	Methodologie, Inc.
Interior Graphic Designer:	James D. Kramer
Principal Compositor:	Daniel W. Latimer
Interior Artist:	Rob Nance
Principal Copy Editor:	Lisa Pawlewicz
Indexer:	Julie Kawabata

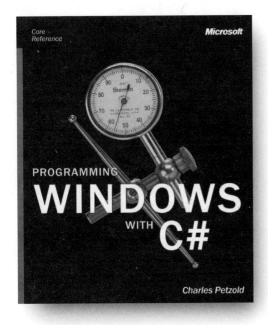

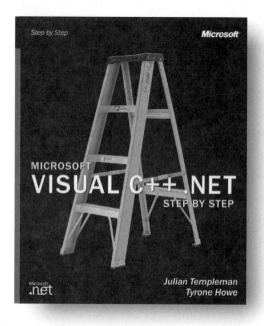

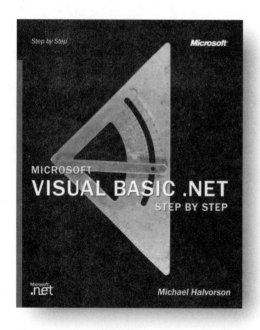

Get a **Free**
e-mail newsletter, updates, special offers, links to related books, and more when you
register on line!

Register your Microsoft Press® title on our Web site and you'll get a FREE subscription to our e-mail newsletter, *Microsoft Press Book Connections.* You'll find out about newly released and upcoming books and learning tools, online events, software downloads, special offers and coupons for Microsoft Press customers, and information about major Microsoft® product releases. You can also read useful additional information about all the titles we publish, such as detailed book descriptions, tables of contents and indexes, sample chapters, links to related books and book series, author biographies, and reviews by other customers.

Registration is easy. Just visit this Web page and fill in your information:

http://www.microsoft.com/mspress/register

Microsoft®

Proof of Purchase

Use this page as proof of purchase if participating in a promotion or rebate offer on this title. Proof of purchase must be used in conjunction with other proof(s) of payment such as your dated sales receipt—see offer details.

Coding Techniques for Microsoft® Visual Basic® .NET

0-7356-1254-4

____

CUSTOMER NAME

Microsoft Press, PO Box 97017, Redmond, WA 98073-9830

MICROSOFT LICENSE AGREEMENT

Book Companion CD

IMPORTANT—READ CAREFULLY: This Microsoft End-User License Agreement ("EULA") is a legal agreement between you (either an individual or an entity) and Microsoft Corporation for the Microsoft product identified above, which includes computer software and may include associated media, printed materials, and "online" or electronic documentation ("SOFTWARE PRODUCT"). Any component included within the SOFTWARE PRODUCT that is accompanied by a separate End-User License Agreement shall be governed by such agreement and not the terms set forth below. By installing, copying, or otherwise using the SOFTWARE PRODUCT, you agree to be bound by the terms of this EULA. If you do not agree to the terms of this EULA, you are not authorized to install, copy, or otherwise use the SOFTWARE PRODUCT; you may, however, return the SOFTWARE PRODUCT, along with all printed materials and other items that form a part of the Microsoft product that includes the SOFTWARE PRODUCT, to the place you obtained them for a full refund.

SOFTWARE PRODUCT LICENSE

The SOFTWARE PRODUCT is protected by United States copyright laws and international copyright treaties, as well as other intellectual property laws and treaties. The SOFTWARE PRODUCT is licensed, not sold.

1. **GRANT OF LICENSE.** This EULA grants you the following rights:
   a. **Software Product.** You may install and use one copy of the SOFTWARE PRODUCT on a single computer. The primary user of the computer on which the SOFTWARE PRODUCT is installed may make a second copy for his or her exclusive use on a portable computer.
   b. **Storage/Network Use.** You may also store or install a copy of the SOFTWARE PRODUCT on a storage device, such as a network server, used only to install or run the SOFTWARE PRODUCT on your other computers over an internal network; however, you must acquire and dedicate a license for each separate computer on which the SOFTWARE PRODUCT is installed or run from the storage device. A license for the SOFTWARE PRODUCT may not be shared or used concurrently on different computers.
   c. **License Pak.** If you have acquired this EULA in a Microsoft License Pak, you may make the number of additional copies of the computer software portion of the SOFTWARE PRODUCT authorized on the printed copy of this EULA, and you may use each copy in the manner specified above. You are also entitled to make a corresponding number of secondary copies for portable computer use as specified above.
   d. **Sample Code.** Solely with respect to portions, if any, of the SOFTWARE PRODUCT that are identified within the SOFTWARE PRODUCT as sample code (the "SAMPLE CODE"):
      i. **Use and Modification.** Microsoft grants you the right to use and modify the source code version of the SAMPLE CODE, *provided* you comply with subsection (d)(iii) below. You may not distribute the SAMPLE CODE, or any modified version of the SAMPLE CODE, in source code form.
      ii. **Redistributable Files.** Provided you comply with subsection (d)(iii) below, Microsoft grants you a nonexclusive, royalty-free right to reproduce and distribute the object code version of the SAMPLE CODE and of any modified SAMPLE CODE, other than SAMPLE CODE, or any modified version thereof, designated as not redistributable in the Readme file that forms a part of the SOFTWARE PRODUCT (the "Non-Redistributable Sample Code"). All SAMPLE CODE other than the Non-Redistributable Sample Code is collectively referred to as the "REDISTRIBUTABLES."
      iii. **Redistribution Requirements.** If you redistribute the REDISTRIBUTABLES, you agree to: (i) distribute the REDISTRIBUTABLES in object code form only in conjunction with and as a part of your software application product; (ii) not use Microsoft's name, logo, or trademarks to market your software application product; (iii) include a valid copyright notice on your software application product; (iv) indemnify, hold harmless, and defend Microsoft from and against any claims or lawsuits, including attorney's fees, that arise or result from the use or distribution of your software application product; and (v) not permit further distribution of the REDISTRIBUTABLES by your end user. Contact Microsoft for the applicable royalties due and other licensing terms for all other uses and/or distribution of the REDISTRIBUTABLES.

2. **DESCRIPTION OF OTHER RIGHTS AND LIMITATIONS.**
   - **Limitations on Reverse Engineering, Decompilation, and Disassembly.** You may not reverse engineer, decompile, or disassemble the SOFTWARE PRODUCT, except and only to the extent that such activity is expressly permitted by applicable law notwithstanding this limitation.
   - **Separation of Components.** The SOFTWARE PRODUCT is licensed as a single product. Its component parts may not be separated for use on more than one computer.
   - **Rental.** You may not rent, lease, or lend the SOFTWARE PRODUCT.
   - **Support Services.** Microsoft may, but is not obligated to, provide you with support services related to the SOFTWARE PRODUCT ("Support Services"). Use of Support Services is governed by the Microsoft policies and programs described in the

user manual, in "online" documentation, and/or in other Microsoft-provided materials. Any supplemental software code provided to you as part of the Support Services shall be considered part of the SOFTWARE PRODUCT and subject to the terms and conditions of this EULA. With respect to technical information you provide to Microsoft as part of the Support Services, Microsoft may use such information for its business purposes, including for product support and development. Microsoft will not utilize such technical information in a form that personally identifies you.

- **Software Transfer.** You may permanently transfer all of your rights under this EULA, provided you retain no copies, you transfer all of the SOFTWARE PRODUCT (including all component parts, the media and printed materials, any upgrades, this EULA, and, if applicable, the Certificate of Authenticity), **and** the recipient agrees to the terms of this EULA.
- **Termination.** Without prejudice to any other rights, Microsoft may terminate this EULA if you fail to comply with the terms and conditions of this EULA. In such event, you must destroy all copies of the SOFTWARE PRODUCT and all of its component parts.

3. **COPYRIGHT.** All title and copyrights in and to the SOFTWARE PRODUCT (including but not limited to any images, photographs, animations, video, audio, music, text, SAMPLE CODE, REDISTRIBUTABLES, and "applets" incorporated into the SOFTWARE PRODUCT) and any copies of the SOFTWARE PRODUCT are owned by Microsoft or its suppliers. The SOFTWARE PRODUCT is protected by copyright laws and international treaty provisions. Therefore, you must treat the SOFTWARE PRODUCT like any other copyrighted material **except** that you may install the SOFTWARE PRODUCT on a single computer provided you keep the original solely for backup or archival purposes. You may not copy the printed materials accompanying the SOFTWARE PRODUCT.

4. **U.S. GOVERNMENT RESTRICTED RIGHTS.** The SOFTWARE PRODUCT and documentation are provided with RESTRICTED RIGHTS. Use, duplication, or disclosure by the Government is subject to restrictions as set forth in subparagraph (c)(1)(ii) of the Rights in Technical Data and Computer Software clause at DFARS 252.227-7013 or subparagraphs (c)(1) and (2) of the Commercial Computer Software—Restricted Rights at 48 CFR 52.227-19, as applicable. Manufacturer is Microsoft Corporation/One Microsoft Way/Redmond, WA 98052-6399.

5. **EXPORT RESTRICTIONS.** You agree that you will not export or re-export the SOFTWARE PRODUCT, any part thereof, or any process or service that is the direct product of the SOFTWARE PRODUCT (the foregoing collectively referred to as the "Restricted Components"), to any country, person, entity, or end user subject to U.S. export restrictions. You specifically agree not to export or re-export any of the Restricted Components (i) to any country to which the U.S. has embargoed or restricted the export of goods or services, which currently include, but are not necessarily limited to, Cuba, Iran, Iraq, Libya, North Korea, Sudan, and Syria, or to any national of any such country, wherever located, who intends to transmit or transport the Restricted Components back to such country; (ii) to any end user who you know or have reason to know will utilize the Restricted Components in the design, development, or production of nuclear, chemical, or biological weapons; or (iii) to any end user who has been prohibited from participating in U.S. export transactions by any federal agency of the U.S. government. You warrant and represent that neither the BXA nor any other U.S. federal agency has suspended, revoked, or denied your export privileges.

DISCLAIMER OF WARRANTY

NO WARRANTIES OR CONDITIONS. MICROSOFT EXPRESSLY DISCLAIMS ANY WARRANTY OR CONDITION FOR THE SOFTWARE PRODUCT. THE SOFTWARE PRODUCT AND ANY RELATED DOCUMENTATION ARE PROVIDED "AS IS" WITHOUT WARRANTY OR CONDITION OF ANY KIND, EITHER EXPRESS OR IMPLIED, INCLUDING, WITHOUT LIMITATION, THE IMPLIED WARRANTIES OF MERCHANTABILITY, FITNESS FOR A PARTICULAR PURPOSE, OR NONINFRINGEMENT. THE ENTIRE RISK ARISING OUT OF USE OR PERFORMANCE OF THE SOFTWARE PRODUCT REMAINS WITH YOU.

LIMITATION OF LIABILITY. TO THE MAXIMUM EXTENT PERMITTED BY APPLICABLE LAW, IN NO EVENT SHALL MICROSOFT OR ITS SUPPLIERS BE LIABLE FOR ANY SPECIAL, INCIDENTAL, INDIRECT, OR CONSEQUENTIAL DAMAGES WHATSOEVER (INCLUDING, WITHOUT LIMITATION, DAMAGES FOR LOSS OF BUSINESS PROFITS, BUSINESS INTERRUPTION, LOSS OF BUSINESS INFORMATION, OR ANY OTHER PECUNIARY LOSS) ARISING OUT OF THE USE OF OR INABILITY TO USE THE SOFTWARE PRODUCT OR THE PROVISION OF OR FAILURE TO PROVIDE SUPPORT SERVICES, EVEN IF MICROSOFT HAS BEEN ADVISED OF THE POSSIBILITY OF SUCH DAMAGES. IN ANY CASE, MICROSOFT'S ENTIRE LIABILITY UNDER ANY PROVISION OF THIS EULA SHALL BE LIMITED TO THE GREATER OF THE AMOUNT ACTUALLY PAID BY YOU FOR THE SOFTWARE PRODUCT OR US$5.00; PROVIDED, HOWEVER, IF YOU HAVE ENTERED INTO A MICROSOFT SUPPORT SERVICES AGREEMENT, MICROSOFT'S ENTIRE LIABILITY REGARDING SUPPORT SERVICES SHALL BE GOVERNED BY THE TERMS OF THAT AGREEMENT. BECAUSE SOME STATES AND JURISDICTIONS DO NOT ALLOW THE EXCLUSION OR LIMITATION OF LIABILITY, THE ABOVE LIMITATION MAY NOT APPLY TO YOU.

MISCELLANEOUS

This EULA is governed by the laws of the State of Washington USA, except and only to the extent that applicable law mandates governing law of a different jurisdiction.

Should you have any questions concerning this EULA, or if you desire to contact Microsoft for any reason, please contact the Microsoft subsidiary serving your country, or write: Microsoft Sales Information Center/One Microsoft Way/Redmond, WA 98052-6399.

PN 097-0002296